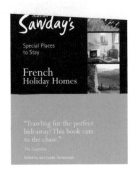

French Hotels & Châteaux

"Sawday, the expert on characterful hotels."
The Sunday Times

Edited by Susan Herrick Luraschi

French Holiday Homes

"Trawling for the perfect hideaway? This book cuts to the chase."
The Guardian

Edited by Ann Cooke-Yarborough

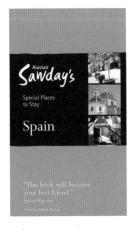

Italy

"They only endorse the very best."
The Italian

Edited by Kate Shepherd

Spain

"This book will become your best friend."
Spanish Magazine

Edited by Kathie Burton

Special Places to Stay

Eleventh edition
Copyright © 2009 Alastair Sawday
Publishing Co. Ltd
Published in 2009
ISBN-13: 978-1-906136-07-9

Alastair Sawday Publishing Co. Ltd,
The Old Farmyard, Yanley Lane,
Long Ashton, Bristol BS41 9LR, UK
Tel: +44 (0)1275 395430
Email: info@sawdays.co.uk
Web: www.sawdays.co.uk

The Globe Pequot Press,
P. O. Box 480, Guilford,
Connecticut 06437, USA
Tel: +1 203 458 4500
Email: info@globepequot.com
Web: www.globepequot.com

Printing: Butler, Tanner & Dennis, Frome
Maps: Maidenhead Cartographic Services
UK distribution: Penguin UK, London

Series Editor Alastair Sawday
Editors Emma Carey & Florence Oldfield
Assistant to Editors
Cristina Sanchez Gonzalez
Editorial Director Annie Shillito
Writing Jo Boissevain,
Ann Cooke-Yarborough, Viv Cripps,
Nicola Crosse, Janet Edsforth-Stone,
Monica Guy, Susan Herrick Luraschi,
Florence Oldfield, Helen Pickles
Inspections Katie Anderson,
Richard & Linda Armspach, Helen Barr,
Miranda Bell, Ann Cooke-Yarborough,
Jill Coyle, Meredith Dickinson,
Penny Dinwiddie, Janet Edsforth-Stone,
John & Jane Edwards, Valerie Foix,
Georgina Gabriel, Monica Guy,
Ann Haine, Diana Sawday Harris,
Suzanne & Barney Lenheim, Judith Lott,
Susan Herrick Luraschi,
Christine Matheson, Victoria Thomas,
Elizabeth Yates
Accounts Bridget Bishop, Amy Lancastle
Editorial Sue Bourner,
Jo Boissevain, Roxy Dumble
Production Julia Richardson,
Rachel Coe, Tom Germain,
Anny Mortada
Sales & Marketing & PR
Rob Richardson,
Sarah Bolton, Thomas Caldwell
Web & IT Joe Green,
Chris Banks, Phil Clarke, Mike Peake,
Russell Wilkinson

*We have made every effort to ensure the accuracy
of the information in this book at the time of
going to press. However, we cannot accept any
responsibility for any loss, injury or
inconvenience resulting from the use of
information contained therein.*

Alastair
Sawday's

Special Places
to Stay

French
Bed & Breakfast

4 Contents

The buildings

Beautiful as they were, our old offices leaked heat, used electricity to heat water and rooms, flooded spaces with light to illuminate one person, and were not ours to alter.

So in 2005 we created our own eco-offices by converting some old barns to create a low-emissions building. Heating and lighting the building, which houses over 30 employees, now produces only 0.28 tonnes of carbon dioxide per year. Not bad when you compare this with the 6 tonnes emitted by the average UK household. We achieved this through a variety of innovative and energy-saving building techniques, described below.

Insulation   We went to great lengths to ensure that very little heat will escape, by:
- laying insulating board 90mm thick immediately under the roof tiles and on the floor
- lining the whole of the inside of the building with plastic sheeting to ensure air-tightness
- fixing further insulation underneath the roof and between the rafters
- fixing insulated plaster-board to add another layer of insulation.

All this means we are insulated for the Arctic, and almost totally air-tight.

Heating   We installed a wood-pellet boiler from Austria, in order to be largely fossil-fuel free. The pellets are made from compressed sawdust, a waste product from timber mills that work only with sustainably managed forests. The heat is conveyed by water to all corners of the building via an under-floor system.

Water   We installed a 6000-litre tank to collect rainwater from the roofs. This is pumped back, via an ultra-violet filter, to the lavatories, showers and basins. There are two solar thermal panels on the roof providing heat to the one (massively insulated) hot-water cylinder.

Lighting   We have a carefully planned mix of low-energy lighting: task lighting and up-lighting. We also installed three sun-pipes – polished aluminium tubes that reflect the outside light down to chosen areas of the building.

Electricity   All our electricity has long come from the Good Energy Company and is 100% renewable.

Materials   Virtually all materials are non-toxic or natural. Our carpets, for example, are made from (80%) Herdwick sheep-wool from National Trust farms in the Lake District.

Doors and windows   Outside doors and new windows are wooden, double-glazed, beautifully constructed in Norway. Old windows have been double-glazed.

We have a building we are proud of, and architects and designers are fascinated by. But best of all, we are now in a better position to encourage our owners and readers to take sustainability more seriously.

Photo: Tom Germain

What we do

Besides moving the business to a low-carbon building, the company works in a number of ways to reduce its overall environmental footprint:

- all office travel is logged as part of a carbon sequestration programme, and money for compensatory tree-planting is dispatched to SCAD in India for a tree-planting and development project
- we avoid flying and take the train for business trips wherever possible; when we have to fly, we 'double offset'
- car-sharing and the use of a company pool car are part of company policy; recycled cooking oil is used in one car and LPG in the other
- organic and Fair Trade basic provisions are used in the staff kitchen and organic food is provided by the company at all in-house events
- green cleaning products are used throughout the office
- all kitchen waste is composted and used on the office organic allotment.

Our total 'operational' carbon footprint (including travel to and from work, plus all our trips to visit our Special Places to Stay) is just over 17 tonnes per year. We have come a long way, but we would like to get this figure as close to zero as possible.

For many years Alastair Sawday Publishing has been 'greening' the business in different ways. Our aim is to reduce our environmental footprint as far as possible – with almost everything we do we have the environmental implications in mind. (We once claimed to be the world's first carbon-neutral publishing company, but are now wary of such claims.) In recognition of our efforts we won a Business Commitment to the Environment Award in 2005, and in 2006 a Queen's Award for Enterprise in the Sustainable Development category. In that year Alastair was voted ITN's 'Eco Hero'.

We have created our own eco-offices by converting former barns to create a low-emissions building. Through a variety of innovative and energy-saving techniques this has reduced our carbon emissions by 35%.

Photo: Tom Germain

But becoming 'green' is a journey and, although we began long before most companies, we still have a long way to go.

In 2008 we won the Independent Publishers Guild Environmental Award. The judging panel were effusive in their praise, stating: "With green issues currently at the forefront of publishers' minds, Alastair Sawday Publishing was singled out in this category as a model for all independents to follow. Its efforts to reduce waste in its office and supply chain have reduced the company's environmental impact, and it works closely with staff to identify more areas of improvement. Here is a publisher who lives and breathes green. Alastair Sawday has all the right principles and is clearly committed to improving its practice further."

Our Fragile Earth series is a growing collection of campaigning books about the environment. Highlighting the perilous state of the world yet offering imaginative and radical solutions and some intriguing facts, these books will make you weep and smile. They will keep you up to date and well armed for the battle with apathy.

THE QUEEN'S AWARDS
FOR ENTERPRISE:
SUSTAINABLE DEVELOPMENT
2006

The pull of France is as powerful as ever. I went back and forth as a child, trailing an enthusiastic mother who couldn't get enough of it all, and am still excited by that moment of arrival – when the smells are different and the first sounds linger in the ear like so many incantations.

We have always been proud of our French B&Bs. We began with them and they have been an inspiration ever since, open-hearted, filled with panache and imagination, tireless in their devotion to making visitors feel special. I can hardly step outside my house without bumping into people who have stayed in these B&Bs, and they never fail to sing their praises.

You will find places of ravishing beauty, of vast age and where you eat like emperors. There will be wine from their own vineyards, vegetables from their own potagers, bread and pâtisseries from their own kitchens, soup from their own tureens. Buying food locally rather than from supermarkets is natural to the French – still. They wonder what has happened that we should be so different. (One reason is that local councils can make the key planning decisions in France, without fear of appeal.) There you can still wander down to the boulangerie in the morning and chat with the locals. Small towns still differ from each other, with shops carrying different names. Our B&Bs reflect this astonishing and delightful variety.

The last few years have been tough for French B&Bs, so they need your support. This year the weather was awful and travelers spread further afield. But I am sure that they will return, as I do, for France remains perhaps the most richly varied and rewarding of all European countries. New B&Bs are opening up, glitteringly up-to-date in ancient houses. There is renewed emphasis on good food and a focus on green ways of doing things, with turbines and solar panels popping up in surprising places. There are new ideas, new energy, new panache in France. These wonderful houses reflect it all.

Alastair Sawday

Photo: Tom Germain

On leafing through a rather dog-eared first edition of *French Bed & Breakfast*, we were struck by the number of names we recognised – Monsieur and Madame Lunes, the chestnut growers; the Maréchal-Petit family, whose organic farm is gradually making its way down the generations; and Madeleine Cabanes and her *menu curieux* of forgotten vegetables. Fifteen years on and you'll find all their places among the pages of this eleventh edition, the owners still indulging their guests with the same warmth and hospitality that has compelled so many of you to write to us over the years.

Rubbing shoulders with our old-timers are, of course, our new places. In this edition they number nearly two hundred – from the old, endearingly wonky farmhouse to the opulent château complete with immaculate châtelaine, and the city bolthole dotted with *objets d'art* and glitzy bathrooms. Whatever you're after, we're sure you'll find it here.

In this edition we have made a special effort to unearth those places that are positively trying to lighten their burden on the planet while maintaining the identity of true chambres d'hôtes. They include a solar-powered treehouse in the Dordogne where breakfast is winched up to you in a basket, a hemp-insulated gypsy caravan in Normandy, and an eco-lodge in the Gironde.

We've stood under spinning wind turbines, had a peek at composting loos and felt the sun's afternoon rays on our skin one minute and their transformation into piping hot water the next. We've followed proud owners around perfect organic vegetable gardens, marvelled at stunning eco restorations and listened intently to stories of eco heroism in a country which, like others in Europe, is waking up to a newer, greener age. We feel privileged to have met the owners who are making it happen and have loved sharing their enthusiasm for new ideas and green initiatives coming to life throughout their country.

All these places are found in our Ethical Collection, an award-based scheme designed to highlight our greenest places. We asked our owners to tell us why they thought they should to be part of this special collection, and were flooded with applications – from a couple who hold events at their farm to raise money for a village wind turbine, from (several) farms whose produce is

Photo right: Villa de Lorgues, entry 712
Photo left: Mas Pichony, entry 682

100% organic, and from residents battling against local bureaucracy to win the right to install discreet solar panels on their medieval roofs. We've tinted their pages to help you find them. They richly deserve this extra recognition and we hope you will seek them out.

Don't forget that you can play your part, too. Consider travelling by train to and in France; French trains are fast, efficient and cheap and, with the new London–Paris journey time of just over two hours, you could be leaving St Pancras in the morning and breakfasting in Paris, whooshing down Alpine pistes by lunchtime, or catching the late afternoon sun on the French Riviera. Many of our owners will happily pick you up from the nearest train or bus station and will lend bikes to help you get around without the need for a car.

A good chunk of our owners, of course, were 'green' long before the term existed; following in their ancestors' footsteps, they were growing their own vegetables, getting around by bicycle and nurturing their precious land. We salute them for not being 'green', or rather, for not trying to be; long may they continue to follow the slower path through life.

Emma Carey & Florence Oldfield

Photo: Maison Numéro Neuf, entry 495

It's simple. There are no rules, no boxes to tick. We choose places that we like and are fiercely subjective in our choices. We also recognise that one person's idea of special is not necessarily someone else's so there is a huge variety of places, and prices, in the book. Those who are familiar with our Special Places series know that we look for comfort, originality, authenticity, and reject the insincere, the anonymous and the banal. The way guests are treated comes as high on our list as the setting, the architecture, the atmosphere and the food.

Inspections

We visit every place in the guide to get a feel for how both house and owner tick. We don't take a clipboard and we don't have a list of what is acceptable and what is not. Instead, we chat for an hour or so with the owner and look round. It's all very informal, but it gives us an excellent idea of who would enjoy staying there. If the visit happens to be the last of the day, we sometimes stay the night. Once in the book, properties are re-inspected every three to four years so that we can keep things fresh and accurate.

Feedback

In between inspections we rely on feedback from our army of readers, as well as from staff members who are encouraged to visit properties across the series. This feedback is invaluable to us and we always follow up on comments. So do tell us whether your stay has been a joy or not, if the atmosphere was great

or stuffy, the owners cheery or bored. The accuracy of the book depends on what you, and our inspectors, tell us. A lot of the new entries in each edition are recommended by our readers, so keep telling us about new places you've discovered too. Please use the forms on our website at www.sawdays.co.uk, or later in this book (p. 438).

However, please do not tell us if the bedside light was broken, or the shower head was scummy. Tell the owner, immediately, and get them to do something about it. Most owners are

Photo: Château Bavolier, entry 425

more than happy to correct problems and will bend over backwards to help. Far better than bottling it up and then writing to us a week later!

Subscriptions

Owners pay to appear in this guide. Their fee goes towards the high costs of inspecting, of producing an all-colour book and of maintaining our website. We only include places that we like and find special for one reason or another, so it is not possible for anyone to buy their way onto these pages. Nor is it possible for the owner to write their own description. We will say if the bedrooms are small, or if a main road is near. We do our best to avoid misleading people.

Disclaimer

We make no claims to pure objectivity in choosing these places. They are here simply because we like them. Our opinions and tastes are ours alone and this book is a statement of them; we hope you will share them. We have done our utmost to get our facts right but apologise unreservedly for any mistakes that may have crept in.

You should know that we don't check such things as fire regulations, swimming pool security or any other laws with which owners of properties receiving paying guests should comply. This is the responsibility of the owners.

Photo right: Bruce Castle, entry 206
Photo left: Las Bourdolles, entry 538

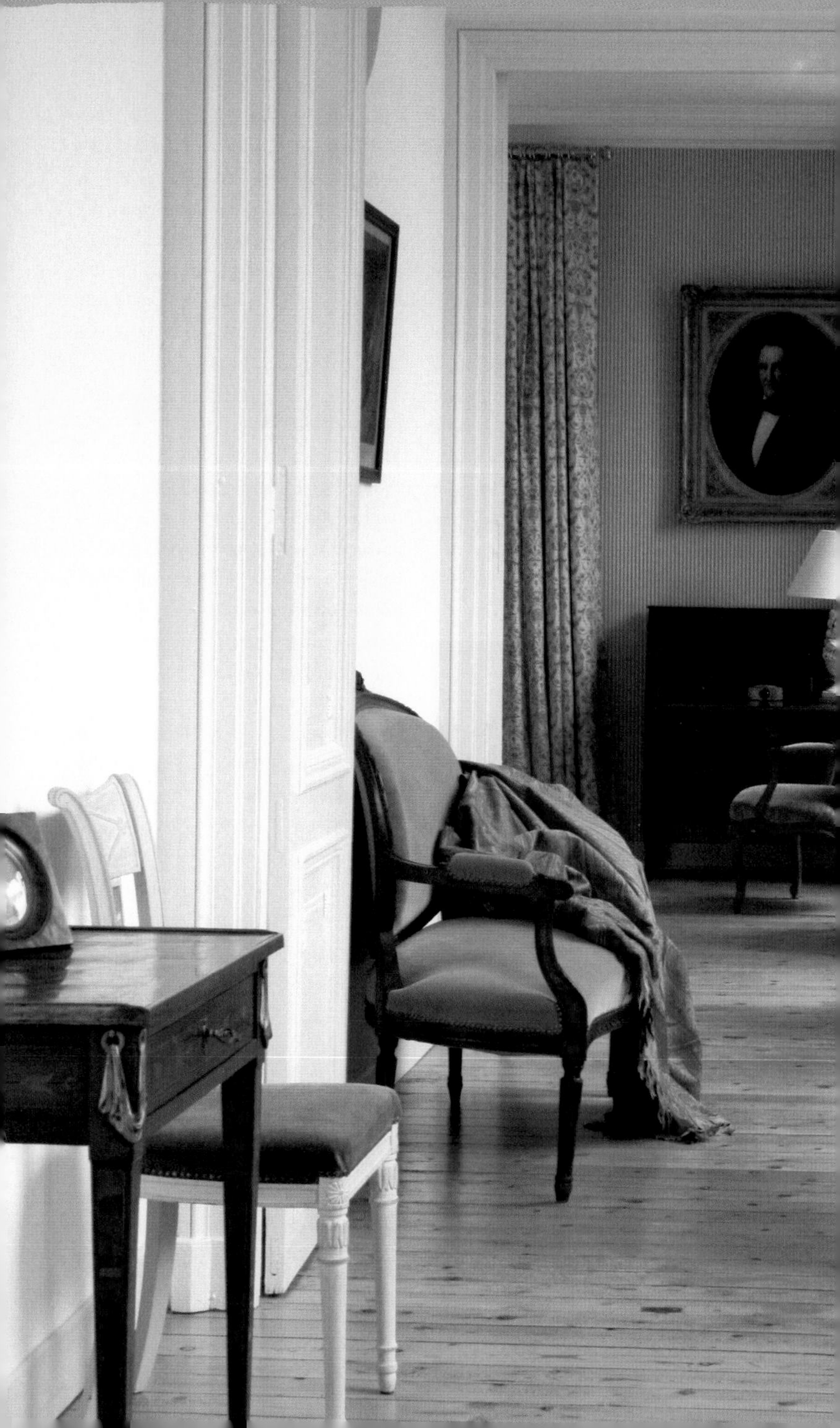

Finding the right place for you

All these places are special in one way or another. All have been visited and then written about honestly so that you can decide for yourselves which will suit you. Those of you who swear by Sawday's books trust our write-ups precisely because we don't have a blanket standard; we include places simply because we like them. But we all have different priorities, so do read the descriptions carefully and pick out the places where you will be comfortable. If something is particularly important to you then check when you book: a simple question or two can avoid misunderstandings.

Photo: Le Moulin de Varax, entry 650

Maps

Each property is flagged with its entry number on the maps at the front. These maps are a great starting point for planning your trip, but please don't use them as anything other than a general guide – use a decent road map for real navigation. Most places will send you detailed instructions once you have booked your stay.

Ethical Collection

We're always keen to draw attention to owners who are striving to have a positive impact on the world, so you'll notice that some entries are flagged as being part of our "Ethical Collection". These places are working hard to reduce their environmental footprint, making significant contributions to their local community, or are passionate about serving local or organic food. Owners have had to fill in a very detailed questionnaire before becoming part of this Collection – read more on page 434. This doesn't mean that other places in the guide are not taking similar initiatives – many are – but we may not yet know about them.

Symbols

Below each entry you will see some symbols, which are explained at the very back of the book. They are based on the information given to us by the owners. However, things do change: bikes may be under repair or a new pool may have been put in. Please use the symbols as a guide rather than an

absolute statement of fact and double-check anything that is important to you – owners occasionally bend their own rules, so it's worth asking if you may take your child or dog even if they don't have the symbol.

Children – The symbol 🚼 shows places which are happy to accept children of all ages. This does not mean that they will necessarily have cots, high chairs, etc. If an owner welcomes children but only those above a certain age, we have put these details at the end of their write-up. These houses do not have the child symbol, but even these folk may accept your younger child if you are the only guests. Many who say no to children do so not because they don't like them but because they may have a steep stair, an unfenced pond or they find balancing the needs of mixed age groups too challenging.

Pets – Our 🐕 symbol shows places which are happy to accept pets. It means they can sleep in the bedroom with you, but not on the bed. Be realistic about your pet – if it is nervous or excitable or doesn't like the company of other dogs, people, chickens, or children, then say so.

Owners' pets – The 🐈 symbol is given when the owners have their own pet on the premises. It may not be a cat! But it is there to warn you that you may be greeted by a dog, serenaded by a parrot, or indeed sat upon by a cat.

Quick reference indices

Throughout the book you'll find a number of quick-reference indices showing those places that offer a particular service, perhaps visits to local vineyards, or cookery or language courses. They are worth flicking through if you are looking for something specific.

Photo: Le Clos Saint Saourde, entry 677

Types of places

Some places have rooms in annexes or stables, barns or garden 'wings', some of which feel part of the house, some of which don't. If you have a strong preference for being in the throng or for being apart, check those details. Consider your surroundings, too: rambling châteaux may be cooler than you are used to; city places and working farms may be noisy at times; and that peacock or cockerel we mention may disturb you. Some owners give you a front door key so you may come and go as you please; others like to have the house empty between, say, 10am and 4pm. Remember that B&Bs are not hotels – don't expect room service, or your beds to be made, do go for a fascinating glimpse of a French way of life.

Rooms

Bedrooms – We tell you if a room is a double, twin/double (ie with zip and link beds), suite, family (any mix of beds for 3 or more people) or single. If 'antique beds' sound seductively authentic, remember they are liable to be antique sizes too (190cm long, doubles 140cm wide); if in doubt, ask, or book a twin room (usually larger). Owners can often juggle beds or bedrooms, so talk to them about what you need before you book. It is rare to be given your own room key in a B&B.

Bathrooms – Most bedrooms in this book have an en suite bath or shower room; we only mention bathroom details when they do not. So, you may get a 'separate' bathroom (yours alone but not in your room) or a shared bathroom. Under certain entries we mention that two rooms share a bathroom and are 'let to same party only'. Please do not assume this means you must be a group of friends to apply; it simply means that if you book one of these rooms you will not be sharing a bathroom with strangers. For simplicity we generally refer to 'bath'. This doesn't necessarily mean it has no shower; it could mean a shower only. If these things are important to you, please check when booking.

Sitting rooms – Most B&B owners offer guests the family sitting room to share, or they provide a sitting room specially for guests. If neither option is available we generally say so, but do check. And

Photo right: La Ferme de l'Oudon, entry 185
Photo left: Domaine de Moulin Mer, entry 259

do not assume that every bedroom or sitting room has a TV.

Meals

Unless we say otherwise, breakfast is included. This will usually be a good continental breakfast – traditionally pain de campagne with apricot jam and a bowl of coffee, but brioche, crêpes, croissants, and homemade cake are all on offer too. Some owners are fairly unbending about breakfast times, others are happy to just wait until you want it, or even bring it to you in bed.

Apart from breakfast, no meals should be expected unless you have arranged them in advance. Many places offer a table d'hôtes dinner to overnight guests. This means the same food for all **and absolutely must be booked ahead**, but will not be available every night. (We have indicated the distance to the nearest restaurant when dinner isn't offered; but be aware that rural restaurants stop taking orders at 9pm and often close at least one day a week.) Often the meal is shared with other guests at a communal table. These are sometimes hosted by Monsieur or Madame (or both) and are usually a wonderful opportunity to get to know your hosts and to make new friends among the other guests. Meal prices are quoted per person, although children will usually eat for less. Ask your hosts about reduced meal rates if you're travelling with little ones.

When wine is included this can mean a range of things, from a standard quarter-litre carafe per person to a barrel of table wine; from a decent bottle of local wine to an excellent estate wine.

Prices and minimum stays

Each entry gives a price PER ROOM for two people.

The price range covers a one-night stay in the cheapest room in low season to the most expensive in high season. Some owners charge more at certain times (during festivals, for example) and some charge less for stays of more than one night. Some owners ask for a two-night minimum stay and we mention this where possible.

Prices quoted are those given to us for 2009–2011 but are not guaranteed, so do double-check when booking.

Taxe de séjour is a small tax that local councils can levy on all visitors; you may find your bill increased by €0.50–€2 per person per day to cover this.

Booking and cancellation

Do be clear about the room booked and the price for B&B and for meals. It is essential to book well ahead for July and August, and wise for other months. Owners may send you a booking form or *contrat de location* (tenancy contract) which must be filled in and returned, and commits both sides. Requests for deposits vary; some are non-refundable, and some owners may charge you for the whole of the booked stay in advance.

Some cancellation policies are more stringent than others. It is also worth noting that some owners will take this deposit directly from your credit/debit card without contacting you to discuss it. So ask them to explain their cancellation policy clearly before booking so you understand exactly where you stand; it may well avoid a nasty surprise.

Remember that the UK is one hour behind France and people can be upset by telephone enquiries coming through late in their evening.

Payment

Few owners take credit cards but if they do, we have given them the appropriate symbol. (Check that your particular credit card is acceptable.) Euro travellers' cheques will usually be accepted; other currency cheques are unpopular because of commission charges. Virtually all ATMs in France take Visa and MasterCard.

Tipping

Owners do not expect tips. If you have been treated with extraordinary kindness, write to them, or leave a small gift. Please tell us, too – we love to hear, and we do note, all feedback.

Arrivals and departures

Say roughly what time you will arrive (normally after 4pm), as most hosts like to welcome you personally. Be on time if you have booked dinner; if, despite best efforts, you are delayed, phone to give warning.

Closed

When given in months this means the whole of the month(s) stated. So, 'Closed: November–March' means closed from 1 November to 31 March.

Photo: Domaine de Bourgville, entry 389

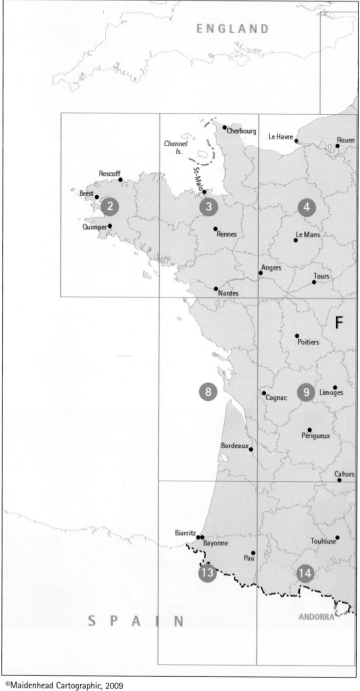

©Maidenhead Cartographic, 2009

Medical & emergency procedures

If you are an EC citizen, it's a good idea to have a European Health Insurance Card with you in case you need any medical treatment. It may not cover all the costs so you may want to take out private insurance as well.

To contact the emergency services dial 112: this is an EU-wide number and you can be confident that the person who answers the phone will speak English as well as French, and can connect you to the police, ambulance and fire/rescue services.

Other insurance

If you are driving, it is probably wise to insure the contents of your car.

Roads & driving

Current speed limits are: motorways 130 kph (80 mph), RN national trunk roads 110 kph (68 mph), other open roads 90 kph (56 mph), in towns 50 kph (30 mph). The road police are very active and can demand on-the-spot payment of fines.

Directions in towns

The French drive towards a destination and use road numbers far less than we do. Thus, to find your way à la française, know the general direction you want to go, ie the towns your route goes through, and when you see *Autres Directions* or *Toutes Directions* in a town, forget road numbers, just continue towards the place name you're heading for or through.

Photo: istock.com

Map 1   25

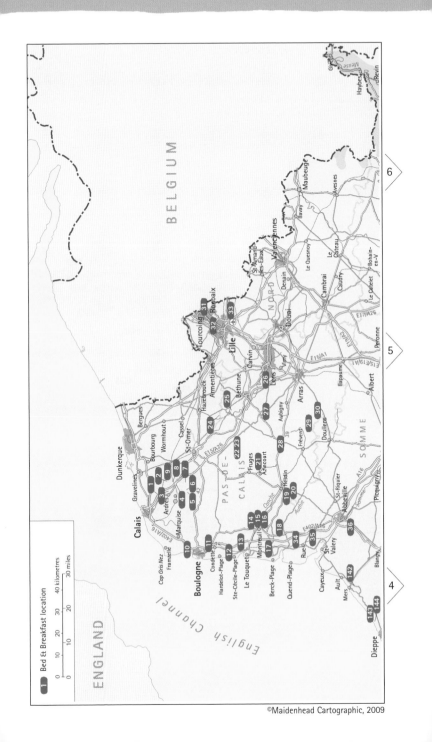

©Maidenhead Cartographic, 2009

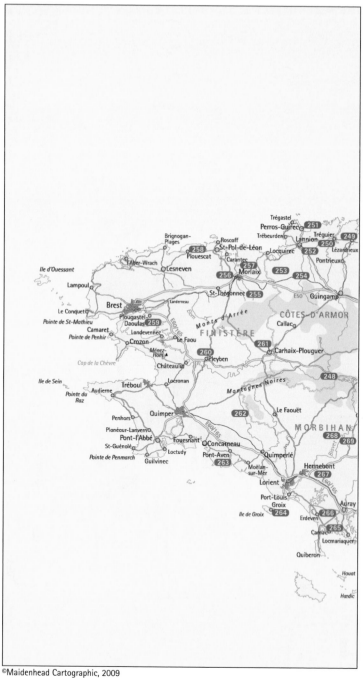

Map 3   27

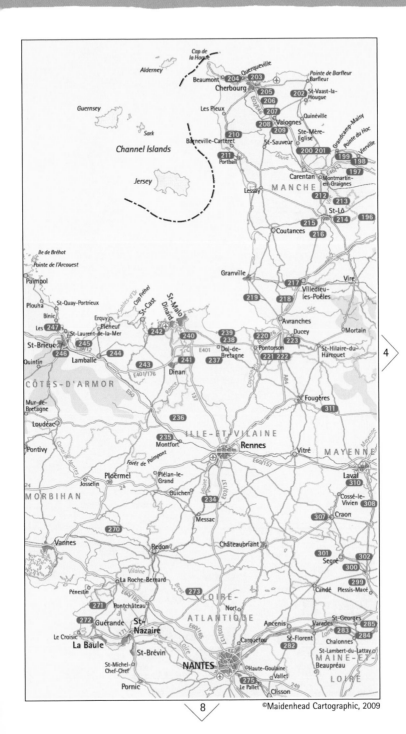

©Maidenhead Cartographic, 2009

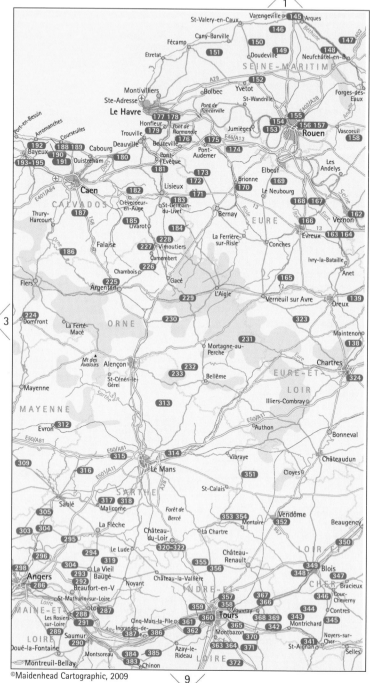

Map 5　　29

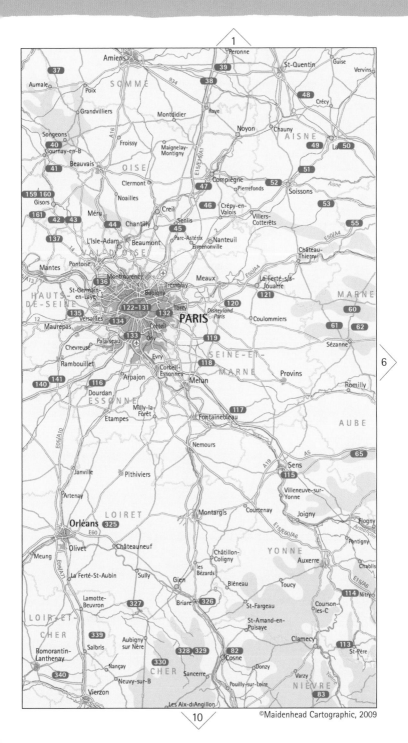

©Maidenhead Cartographic, 2009

©Maidenhead Cartographic, 2009

Map 7   31

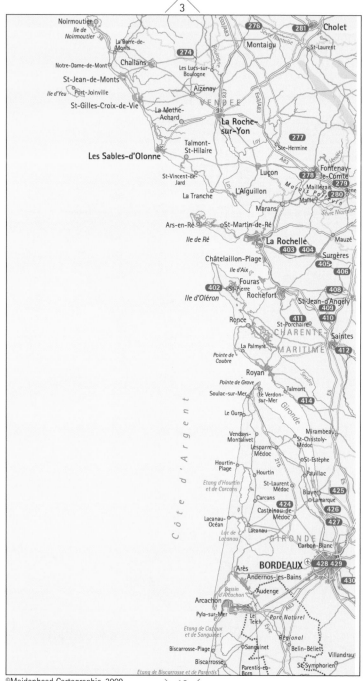

Map 9   33

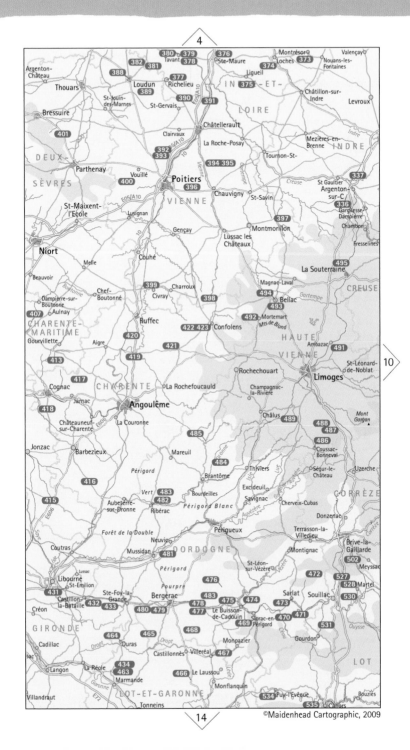

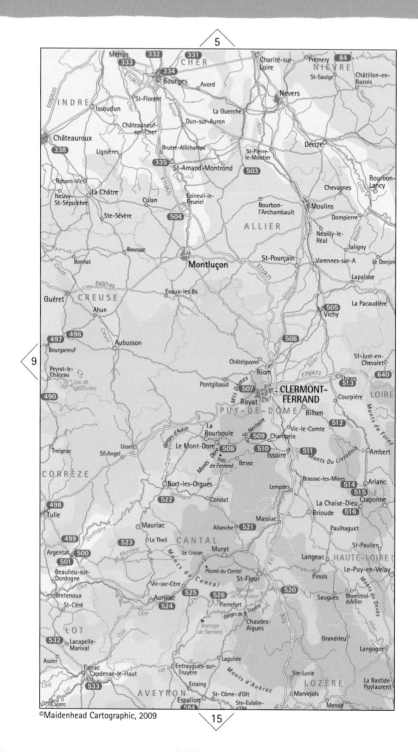

©Maidenhead Cartographic, 2009

Map 11

35

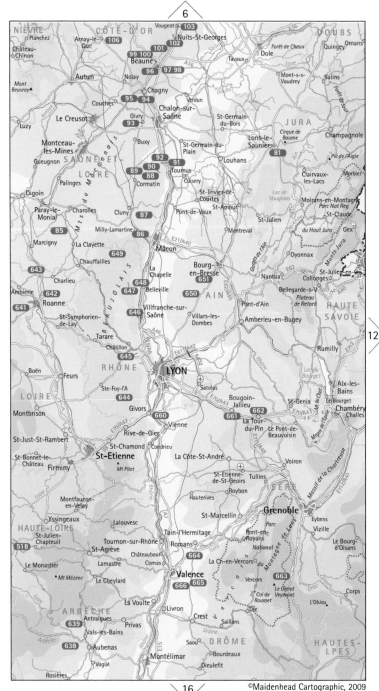

Map 13   37

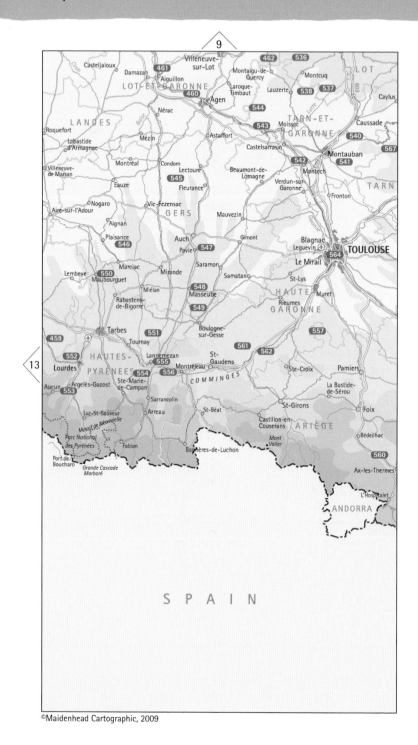

Map 15

39

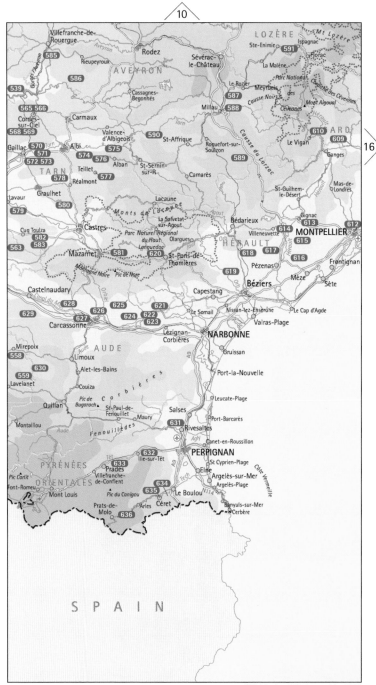

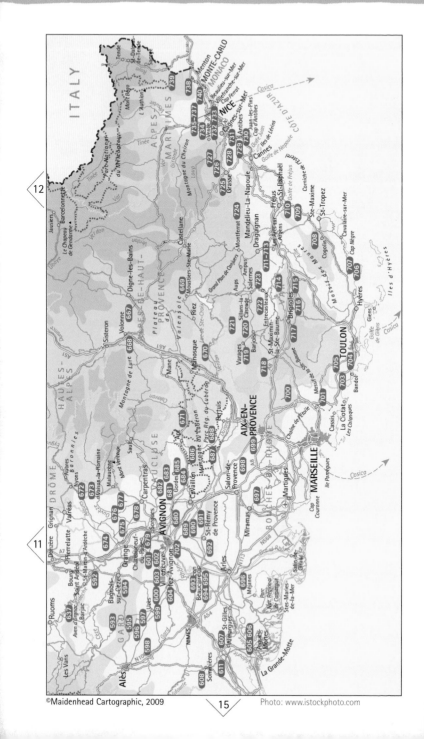

©Maidenhead Cartographic, 2009   15   Photo: www.istockphoto.com

The North • Picardy

The North

Ardres Bridge Cottage

A canal-side setting among rolling agricultural plains, usefully close to Calais. The gardens are peaceful, the owners offer friendly table d'hôtes. One bedroom on the ground floor looks over the flowery borders, the other has its own little balcony overlooking the pond – where farmyard fowl frolic – and a shower room downstairs. Both are country cosy and comfortable with floral bed linen and wooden furniture; bathrooms are more contemporary. You share the young and charming owners' sitting room: long and spacious with a big fire and plenty of squishy sofas. Breakfast is a feast and you can have it in bed!

Price	€50.
Rooms	2: 1 double; 1 double with separate shower. Cot available.
Meals	Dinner with wine, €15.
Closed	Never.
Directions	From Calais A16 exit 46; N43 to Pont d'Ardres; left before bridge on D228 for Guemps; immed. right at fork Rue du Fort Bâtard along canal for 2km; entrance on left.

Laurent Blanquart
Ardres Bridge Cottage,
678 rue du Fort Bâtard,
62610 Pont d'Ardres, Pas-de-Calais
Tel   +33 (0)3 21 96 63 92
Email   blanquart.laurent@wanadoo.fr
Web   www.ardres-bridge-cottage.com

Entry 1   Map 1

The North

La Motte Obin

Madame Breton is irreplaceable: a lovely old lady in a deep-country farmhouse, she talks lots, in French, and otherwise relies on radio and telly for company. Hers is an endearing, piecemeal family house with old-fashioned furniture, masses of photographs (19 grandchildren), lots of crochet and very steep stairs. Simple rooms have good beds and windows to fields of peace. Madame loves cooking country dishes for visitors and readers have praised her hospitality (and her breakfasts). Ask to see the exquisite vaulted stables – built for cows and carthorses, fit for thoroughbreds and prize-winners.

Price	€45.
Rooms	2: 1 double, 1 family room.
Meals	Dinner with wine, €20.
Closed	November-March.
Directions	A26 exit 2 for Tournehem; over N43, to Muncq Nieurlet, on for Ruminghem. House on left approx. 1.5km after leaving Muncq Nieurlet, at sign.

Françoise Breton
La Motte Obin,
62890 Muncq Nieurlet,
Pas-de-Calais
Tel   +33 (0)3 21 82 79 63

Entry 2   Map 1

Les Draps d'Or

It's been an inn since 1640 and Hilary, well integrated here, fits the tradition: vivacious, elegant and English, she enjoys receiving guests. The guest wing has its own (digicode) entrance straight off the street – you are as independent as you like. Up the narrow staircase to tidy, wood-floored rooms above: blue, yellow, green – fresh, spotless and bright. The child's room sports red ethnic weave curtains and a powder-blue frieze. All give onto the cobbled street but few cars pass at night. Ardres is a delightful little town; the 'Cloths of Gold' is a handy stopover on the way to Calais.

Le Manoir de Bois en Ardres

After 200 years of conversions, this house of history and unusual character stands, connected by glazed arches, cloister-like round its sheltered garden and old stone pond. Beyond, ponies graze beneath the mature trees of the ten-acre park: come to commune with nature. In the house and the outbuildings, striking rooms with floral furnishings are a hymn to Françoise's stencil and furniture-painting skills and the fruit of Thierry's collecting flair (his bric-a-brac shop occupies an old stable), the whole atmosphere an echo of this warm couple's joie de vivre. Just one dayroom: for convivial breakfasts.

Price	€54–€62.
Rooms	3: 2 doubles; 1 twin with separate shower, sharing 2 wcs. Extra twin for children.
Meals	Restaurants within walking distance.
Closed	Rarely.
Directions	From Calais A16, exit 46; N43 to Ardres; on right-hand side after church, house on corner.

Price	€65–€70.
Rooms	5: 1 double, 2 twins, 1 triple, 1 suite for 4.
Meals	Restaurant 1km.
Closed	Rarely.
Directions	From Calais A16, exit 46 for St Omer N43. Pass Les Attaques, Pont d'Ardres, 1st r'bout at Bois en Ardres; before 2nd r'bout left Rue de St Quentin for 1km; green gate.

Hilary Mackay
Les Draps d'Or,
152 rue Lambert d'Ardres,
62610 Ardres,
Pas-de-Calais
Tel   +33 (0)3 21 82 20 44
Email   hilary@drapsdor.com
Web   www.drapsdor.com

Françoise & Thierry Roger
Le Manoir de Bois en Ardres,
1530 rue de St Quentin,
62610 Ardres,
Pas-de-Calais
Tel   +33 (0)3 21 85 97 78
Email   roger@aumanoir.com
Web   www.aumanoir.com

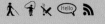

Entry 3   Map 1

Entry 4   Map 1

La Ferme de Beaupré

These lovely gentle people will take you happily into their gorgeous old house at the end of the tree-lined drive and ply you with fine home-grown organic food (ah, those breakfast jams). Lut, from Belgium, is a gracious and unpretentiously warm music teacher and mother of two boys – her welcome will touch you. Perfect, peaceful bedrooms (taupes, off-whites, toile de Jouy and a tiny room off with a bed for a child and a useful fridge; or modern red, white, rattan and wood). You have sole use of the living room; the garden bursts with peonies, lupins, roses and cherries. An adorable, very special place.

Price	€57.
Rooms	2 doubles.
Meals	Dinner with wine, €20.
Closed	Rarely.
Directions	From A26 exit 2 for Licques; through Tournehem & Bonningues lès Ardres; left after village to farm.

Lut & Jean-Michel Louf-Degrauwe
La Ferme de Beaupré,
129 rue de Licques,
62890 Bonningues lès Ardres,
Pas-de-Calais

Tel	+33 (0)3 21 35 14 44
Fax	+33 (0)3 21 35 57 35
Email	lut.degrauwe@nordnet.fr

Entry 5   Map 1

Le Manoir

The trompe l'oeil and frescoed friezes are lavish, from the panelling in the dining room to the 'marble' up the stairs. Sylvie and Pierre are restoring the old house with artistry and flair. Known in the village as Le Château, it's not really big but, with so many original details intact, it's a historian's delight. The attic rooms are romantic country-modern, those on the first floor elegantly French – deep mauve and moss green fabrics and papers and some spectacular carved wardrobes and beds. Excellent dinner, gardens with box parterre and trees, and a dayroom for guests.

Price	€70. Triple €90. €110 for 4.
Rooms	5: 3 doubles, 1 triple, 1 suite for 4.
Meals	Dinner with wine, €25–€40.
Closed	Rarely.
Directions	From A26 exit 2; left D217 for Zouafques, Tournehem; then Bonningues; house on right just after entering village.

Sylvie & Pierre Breemersch
Le Manoir,
40 route de Licques,
62890 Bonningues lès Ardres,
Pas-de-Calais

Tel	+33 (0)3 21 82 69 05
Email	pierre.breemersch@wanadoo.fr
Web	www.lemanoirdebonningues.com

Entry 6   Map 1

La Ferme de Wolphus

The family, who speak excellent English, do wine-tastings and will sell you wine and honey, are delightful but this is more gîte (three so far) than homely B&B. All is straightforward and simple, breakfast is in your own quarters (or the family kitchen for very early starts), where basic pine furniture and slatting grace the smallish, under-the-eaves rooms and some windows give onto the garden. The closeness to ferry ports is seductive, though the nearby main road may disturb some. Lake, old trees, sheep and peacocks hug both farmhouse and outbuildings. Basic, busy, friendly – and great value.

La Bohême

Extrovert Sonia loves music, painting, cooking and spoiling her guests. White walls, dark wooden doors, floors and beams, solid, good-looking furniture – it's 'French rustique'. The bedroom under the eaves is prettily decorated in red toile de Jouy and looks onto the garden; the suite, in stylish white and grey with a good big bathroom, is in a separate building and perfect for a family (but watch the stairs). You'll adore the garden, bursting with life, full of secret corners. This is walking and pony-trekking country and if you'd like to trade car for horse, Sonia's daughter will happily organise rides. *Pets extra €5 per night.*

Price	€44–€48. Triple €58–€62. Quadruple €75.
Rooms	3: 1 quadruple; 2 triples, each with shower, sharing wc on floor below.
Meals	Restaurants nearby.
Closed	Rarely.
Directions	From A26 exit 2 onto D943 for Calais. Wolphus on left 1km after junction, with woods beside road. Be careful turning in.

Price	€55–€58.
Rooms	3: 2 doubles, 1 family suite.
Meals	Dinner with wine, €23.
Closed	Rarely.
Directions	From A26 exit 2; cross N43; 1st left D226 for Zutkerque; past Chatêau de Cocove; house 4th on right.

Jean-Jacques Behaghel
La Ferme de Wolphus,
62890 Zouafques,
Pas-de-Calais
Tel   +33 (0)3 21 35 61 61
Email   info@wolphus.com
Web   www.wolphus.com

Sonia Benoît
La Bohême,
1947 rue de la Grasse Payelle,
62370 Zutkerque, Pas-de-Calais
Tel   +33 (0)3 21 35 70 25
Email   sonia-benoit-la-boheme@wanadoo.fr
Web   perso.wanadoo.fr/sonia-la-boheme

Les Fuchsias

There is something touchingly mixed-up-Victorian about this unusual house with its gingerbread cutouts, variegated roofs and copsy garden of woodland thrown against lawns and fields with quantities of migrating birds flying past. Monsieur is chatty (in English), charming and informative; Madame is quieter but very attentive and tends her house, cats and guests with loving care. Guests have their own cosy colourful sitting and breakfast rooms. Bedrooms have fresh modern furnishings – pretty duvets, wicker armchairs, antique samplers; the family room and the attic suite are particularly inviting.

Price	€50-€55.
Rooms	3: 1 suite for 4; 1 twin, 1 family room, sharing separate wc.
Meals	Brasserie 50m; restaurants 2km.
Closed	Rarely.
Directions	A16 exit 46; N43 for Ardres & St Omer. In Bois en Ardres, 2nd left after r'bout; house on this road.

	Bernadette Balloy
	Les Fuchsias,
	292 rue du Général de St Just,
	62610 Bois en Ardres, Pas-de-Calais
Tel	+33 (0)3 21 82 05 25
Fax	+33 (0)3 21 82 05 25
Email	lesfuchsias@aol.com
Web	www.lesfuchsias-ardres.fr.fm

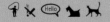

Entry 9   Map 1

The North

La Goélette

A great place from which to explore the 'Opal Coast', made fashionable by the British in the Thirties. *Monsieur Hulot's Holiday* is a perfect image of the little seaside town and this exuberant house on the front. Mary's décor is soberly luxurious, in keeping with the period: white linen, wooden floors, carefully chosen fabrics and furniture, lots of books. She and Franck are charming and Mary, who used to work for Eurostar, speaks excellent English. One room is snug; two, both huge, share the breakfast room's sea views; wake to the sound of the sea.

Price	€90-€150.
Rooms	4: 2 doubles, 2 twins.
Meals	Dinner with wine, €45.
Closed	Rarely.
Directions	A16 exit 3 to Wimereux; to sea front. House approx. halfway along promenade, 100m left of Hôtel Atlantic (with back to sea). Private covered parking available.

	Mary Avot
	La Goélette,
	13 Digue de Mer,
	62930 Wimereux, Pas-de-Calais
Tel	+33 (0)3 21 32 62 44
Fax	+33 (0)3 21 33 77 54
Email	mary@lagoelette.com
Web	www.lagoelette.com

Entry 10   Map 1

Le Clos d'Esch

The golden stone of the oldest farmhouse in the village is easy on the eye. Flowers flourish to the front, the garden and orchard run down to the stream, the retired horses are happy in their stables (the stud farm is further away). Your hosts, aided by daughter Véronique, are discreetly friendly and obliging, and give you delicious breakfasts at marble-topped tables. The bedrooms, one in an outbuilding overlooking courtyard and wooded hills, have a traditional décor; the triple sports a wrought-iron bed with a leopard-skin cover, and a new terrace; the sitting room, too, is spotless and cosy. Good value.

Price	€43-€55.
Rooms	5: 2 doubles, 2 twins, 1 triple.
Meals	Auberge in village.
Closed	Never.
Directions	From Boulogne D940 to St Léonard; at 2nd lights, left on small road to Echinghen (no sign); in village, left in tiny street immed. after sharp bend; left 1st gateway.

Jacqueline & Jean-Pierre
Boussemaere
Le Clos d'Esch,
62360 Echinghen, Pas-de-Calais

Tel	+33 (0)3 21 91 14 34
Fax	+33 (0)3 21 91 06 41
Email	jp-boussemaere@wanadoo.fr
Web	le-clos-d-esch.com

Entry 11   Map 1

Le Moulin

No more milling at the moulin, but the lake is there and it's good to throw open a window and watch the ducks. This is a classically French B&B with black leather easy chairs in the living/dining/sitting room, an enticing velvet chair or two in the bedrooms, and painted white tables against candy-stripe walls. Delicious breakfasts are shared with guests from the sprinkling of gîtes in the grounds. All is warm and inviting in this big, reassuring, lakeside mill house, built in 1855. Christine is reserved but very welcoming – and you are a spade's throw from the local sandy beach.

Price	€55-€60.
Rooms	3 doubles.
Meals	Restaurants 5km.
Closed	Rarely.
Directions	A16 exit 27 Neufchâtel Hardelot & Ste Cécile; D940 for Boulogne & Le Touquet; house near church on entering Dannes.

Christine Lécaille
Le Moulin,
40 rue du Centre, 62187 Dannes,
Pas-de-Calais

Tel	+33 (0)3 21 33 74 74
Fax	+33 (0)3 21 33 74 74
Email	christine.lecaille@free.fr
Web	www.au-moulin.com

Entry 12   Map 1

La Longue Roye

This remote but fabulous set of buildings was a Cistercian farm and the 13th-century barn – a 'harvest cathedral' – is worth the detour alone. Old arches spring, the brickwork dazzles, the courtyard focuses properly on its duckpond, the guest quarters – country-cottage bedrooms (most with space for a sofabed), big breakfast room with stone country fireplace and little tables – are in a beamy outbuilding and the place still breathes monastic peace. Your farming hosts work hard to maintain their precious legacy, work the land and breed pheasants as well as take in guests. Breakfasts are modest.

Le Vert Bois

Ancient peace, delightful people, fields as far as the eye can see. And it's majestic for a farm – the house, outbuildings and courtyard are immaculately preserved. Young Étienne, Véronique and their family grow cereals, keep cows and look after guests – charmingly – in a converted cowshed. Upstairs are a cosy double and a pretty twin; ceilings slope, walls are spotless, bedcovers quilted, bathrooms pristine. A log-fired dayroom with a kitchen and sofas is in the offing; breakfasts are good. The rampart town of Montreuil is minutes away for shops, restaurants and "astonishing points of view".

Price	€60.
Rooms	5: 4 doubles, 1 family suite for 4.
Meals	Restaurants nearby.
Closed	Rarely.
Directions	From Calais A16 for Amiens; exit 25, N1 for Montreuil; left for Longvilliers; signed.

Price	€55.
Rooms	2: 1 double, 1 twin.
Meals	Restaurants nearby.
Closed	Rarely.
Directions	From Montreuil, arriving in Neuville, right opp. antique shop; after 0.5km left at fork; signed.

Anne & Jean-Philippe Delaporte
La Longue Roye,
62630 Longvilliers,
Pas-de-Calais

Tel	+33 (0)3 21 86 70 65
Fax	+33 (0)3 21 86 71 32
Email	delaporte@la-longue-roye.com
Web	www.la-longue-roye.com

Étienne & Véronique Bernard
Le Vert Bois,
62170 Neuville sous Montreuil,
Pas-de-Calais

Tel	+33 (0)3 21 06 09 41
Fax	+33 (0)3 21 06 09 41
Email	etienne.bernard6@wanadoo.fr
Web	gite.montreuil.online.fr

Entry 13   Map 1

Entry 14   Map 1

La Rodière

Behind a grand old façade in lovely Montreuil hides the wonder of an free-standing wooden staircase, a local speciality in the 17th century. Two spacious, old-fashioned rooms up here with high ceilings, parquet floors: the twin over the street has original cupboards; the double over the back is cosily alcoved. Families may prefer the privacy of the snugger room across the yard: pretty blue head cushions and duvet-clothed bunks. There's a softly lit guest sitting room, too. The baths could fill more speedily but the buffet breakfasts are plenteous and Madame is the calmest, smiliest, most unobtrusive hostess.

L'Overgne

A calm genuine welcome and not even a cockerel to disturb the peace. Elderly Madame is as self-assured and pragmatic as you would expect of someone who brought up nine children. The farm buildings lie empty and silent around the 18th-century farmhouse on the hill, and the bedrooms are simple and dated. Good breakfasts (cheese, homemade jam, fresh baguettes and croissants) are served in a fine old-fashioned 'front room' with a velvet three-piece suite and a carved polished table. Madame is a fount of local knowledge and loves getting to know her guests properly. Bring woollies in winter!

Price	€55-€60.
Rooms	4: 2 doubles, 1 twin, 1 family room.
Meals	Restaurant 50m.
Closed	Rarely.
Directions	In Montreuil, drive to top, Place Darnétal; house on right facing square. Ask about parking.

Price	€45-€50.
Rooms	2: 1 double, 1 twin.
Meals	Restaurants 3km.
Closed	December-February.
Directions	From A16 exit 26 to Montreuil; D349 for Hesdin; through Beaumerie St Martin; 1st right at sign.

Mme Louchez
La Rodière,
77 rue Pierre Ledent,
62170 Montreuil sur Mer,
Pas-de-Calais
Tel   +33 (0)3 21 81 54 68
Email   louchez.anne@wanadoo.fr
Web   www.larodiere.com

Francis & Jeanne-Marie Locqueville
L'Overgne,
62170 Beaumerie St Martin,
Pas-de-Calais
Tel   +33 (0)3 21 81 81 87
Email   jmarie.locqueville@wanadoo.fr

Entry 15   Map 1

Entry 16   Map 1

The North

Villa Marie

You can smell the sea air from the garden of this 1903 urban villa, built as a holiday home for a retired colonel. Viviane is vivacious and gives you delicious flexibly timed breakfasts with homemade pancakes and waffles. Choose between the rooms in the main house – floral-printed bedspreads, antiques, crochet, sloping ceilings – or independence in the garden lodge: fresh, clean, pretty, with a charming terrace. The garden is a good size, and totally walled, with fruit trees, shrubs and conifers; find a shady spot here, or head for the coast and some great seafood restaurants. *Ask about watercolour / oil painting classes.*

Price	€60 (€65 Sat). Suite €110.
Rooms	4: 1 family suite for 4. Lodge: 1 double, 1 twin/double, 1 family suite for 3 & kitchenette.
Meals	Restaurant 2.5km; choice 15 minutes. Kitchenette available.
Closed	Rarely.
Directions	Calais A16 exit 25 onto D303 for Berck, 2.5km; left to Verton. Through village; left at church to junction; entrance on right hand corner opp. school.

Viviane Brocard
Villa Marie,
12 rue des Écoles,
62180 Verton, Pas-de-Calais

Tel	+33 (0)3 21 94 05 49
Email	phbrocar@wanadoo.fr
Web	monsite.wanadoo.fr/villamarie

Entry 17   Map 1

The North

Ferme du Saule

Readers have called Le Saule "a little treasure". And we know that the Trunnets' smiles are genuine, their converted outbuilding handsome and perfectly finished (down to mosquito nets on windows), the ground-floor rooms solidly traditional, the beds excellent, the dayroom proud of its beautiful armoire, and you get your own little table for breakfast. Monsieur and his son are only too happy to show you the flax production process (it's fascinating); young Madame looks after her little one and cares beautifully for guests. Proclaimed "the best cowshed I've ever stayed in" by one happy guest.

Price	€55.
Rooms	5: 1 double, 3 family rooms for 3, 1 suite for 4.
Meals	Restaurants 6km.
Closed	Rarely.
Directions	From A16 exit Montreuil; just before town right at lights; left D349 to Brimeux; left at junc., pass church, house on right, signed. From N39 exit Campagne les Hesdin.

Trunnet Family
Ferme du Saule,
20 rue de l'Église,
62170 Brimeux, Pas-de-Calais

Tel	+33 (0)3 21 06 01 28
Fax	+33 (0)3 21 81 40 14
Email	fotrunnet@wanadoo.fr
Web	perso.wanadoo.fr/fermedusaule

Entry 18   Map 1

La Hotoire

New owners have arrived at the farmhouse by the village church – along with two donkeys, one cockerel, a clutch of hens, a cat and a dog. The farmhouse was built in Picardian style around a central courtyard and now the outbuildings house the guests. Ground-floor rooms have wonky timbers, cream tiled floors, pastel colours, modern bathrooms, private entrances and are decently spacious. There's also a light-filled dayroom for breakfast. Walk in the hills and woods behind and spot the wild deer – maybe one of the sweet donkeys will accompany you – or rent bikes in Hesdin. Ideal for young families.

Price	€55-€75.
Rooms	2: 1 double; 1 quadruple & kitchenette, shower & separate wc.
Meals	Restaurants 3-4km.
Closed	Rarely.
Directions	From Hesdin D928 for St Omer; 1st left D913 through Huby St Leu to Guisy; farm between Mairie & church.

Christophe & Emmanuelle Buisine
La Hotoire,
2 place de la Mairie, 62140 Guisy,
Pas-de-Calais

Tel	+33 (0)3 21 81 00 31
Fax	+33 (0)3 21 81 00 31
Email	a.la.hotoire@wanadoo.fr
Web	www.lahotoire.com

Entry 19   Map 1

Ferme Prévost de Courmière

In the old farmhouse – 1680 is depicted in black flint on the façade – are comfort and peace in great measure: fine white and floral bed linen, freshly draped bedheads, oriental rugs. With the house restoration behind them, your hospitable ex-Parisian hosts are turning their stylish attention to the central courtyard, reviving the old orchard and calmly embarking on B&B. Bedrooms (one on the ground floor, the suite spread over two) are pure, fresh, new and extremely charming. Breakfast is a moveable feast; dinner celebrates the most delicious Flemish dishes, served at a large table in a light, lofty room.

Price	€55-€70.
Rooms	4: 3 doubles, 1 suite for 4, each with sitting room.
Meals	Dinner with wine, €25.
Closed	Rarely.
Directions	From Calais A16 to Paris exit 25; N1 for 600m; D939, 17km; D138 at r'bout D134 to Capelle. In village 2nd right & right again.

Annie Lombardet
Ferme Prévost de Courmière,
510 rue de Crécy,
62140 Capelle lès Hesdin,
Pas-de-Calais

Tel/Fax	+33 (0)3 21 81 16 04
Email	ferme-prevost-de-courmiere@wanadoo.fr
Web	prevostdecourmiere.monsite.wanadoo.fr

Entry 20   Map 1

La Gacogne

Enter a 1750 arched orangery (the tower) filled with a very long table, an open fire and 101 curiosities. Alongside teddies… chain-mail bodices, longbows, crossbows and similar armoured reminders of nearby Agincourt greet the eye. It is a treat to be received in this most colourful and eccentric of parlours for hearty continental breakfasts and hostly diligence. Motherly Marie-José and knightly Patrick have lived here for years. Small bedrooms in the outbuilding are farmhouse simple with heavy-draped medieval touches, a lush garden melts into a conifer copse and your hosts are charmingly eccentric.

Ferme de la Vallée

This is a real farm, so don't expect pretty-pretty – but Madame is a character and her welcome's top class. Readers return, for the atmosphere and the food. Amazing how much space lies behind the simple frontage of this street-side farmhouse, and every little corner is crammed with 40 years' worth of collecting: porcelain, plates, jugs, baskets of crystal decanter stoppers, collectable plastics – the list is long. Come for comfy beds, spacious dayroom areas, billiards, table football (a vintage table) and games. It's intrinsically French despite the eccentricities – and Madame is huge fun.

Price	€60. Triple €70.
Rooms	4: 3 doubles, 1 triple.
Meals	Restaurant 1km; choice 6-15km.
Closed	Rarely.
Directions	From St Omer D928 for Abbeville. At Ruisseauville left for Blangy Tramecourt; at next x-roads, left for Tramecourt; house after 100m.

Price	€46.
Rooms	3: 1 twin, 1 triple, 1 suite.
Meals	Dinner with wine, €20.
Closed	Rarely.
Directions	A26 exit Thérouanne; then D341 for Arras; after Le Vert Dragon restaurant, 1st right at r'bout.

Patrick & Marie-José Fenet
La Gacogne,
62310 Azincourt,
Pas-de-Calais

Tel	+33 (0)3 21 04 45 61
Fax	+33 (0)3 21 04 45 61
Email	fenetgeoffroy@aol.com
Web	www.gacogne.com

Brigitte de Saint Laurent
Ferme de la Vallée,
13 rue Neuve, 62190 Auchy au Bois,
Pas-de-Calais

Tel	+33 (0)3 21 25 80 09
Fax	+33 (0)3 21 25 80 09
Email	brigitte.de-saint-laurent@wanadoo.fr
Web	fermedelavallee.free.fr

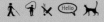

Entry 21   Map 1

Entry 22   Map 1

Les Cohettes

Elegant and vivacious Gina cares deeply that everyone be happy, adores her guests and does brilliant table d'hôtes. A full house makes quite a crowd and when B&B and gîte guests come together there can be over a dozen at table. But the spacious garden opens its arms to all and has some comforting mature trees under which guests may link up for summer *pétanque*. Pretty and cosy bedrooms in the attic of the long low farmhouse are colour coded, while the garden suite is snug with its own little patio. No cockerels, no barking dogs, just an affectionate tabby cat basking in the sun. Readers love it all.

Price	€53–€58.
Rooms	4: 2 doubles, 1 twin, 1 family suite for 4.
Meals	Dinner with wine, €23.
Closed	Rarely.
Directions	From Calais A26 exit 4 to Thérouanne; D341 to Auchy au Bois, 12km. Right at Le Vert Dragon restaurant. 1st left; 2nd house on right after church.

Gina Bulot
Les Cohettes,
28 rue de Pernes,
62190 Auchy au Bois,
Pas-de-Calais
Tel +33 (0)3 21 02 09 47
Email temps-libre-evasion@wanadoo.fr
Web www.chambresdhotes-chezgina.com

Entry 23 Map 1

The North

La Peylouse Manoir

Such an entertaining place to stay: a tall, grey and red mansion furnished in a madly eclectic mix of styles, and landscaped gardens full of ancient exotic trees. Intriguing military associations, too, from arms manufacture for the Sun King (the bullet workshop is still in the grounds) to barracks for the Royal Welch Fusiliers. Best of all, fun, knowledgeable and immensely hospitable hosts. Bedrooms range from cosy 19th-century boudoir to New York studio-style but all are good and very comfortable, with views over the spectacular grounds. The canal marina is just a stroll away: you could even arrive by boat.

Price	€80–€160.
Rooms	4: 2 doubles, 2 suites: 1 for 2, 1 for 4.
Meals	Restaurants within walking distance.
Closed	Rarely.
Directions	Calais A26 exit 5; D916 for Hazebrouck, 12km to St Venant; left to town centre, right after church between Mairie & Poste to Rue du 8 mai for 50m; entrance on left.

Luce Rousseau
La Peylouse Manoir,
Parc & Jardins de la Peylouse
23 rue du 8 mai 1945,
62350 Saint Venant, Pas-de-Calais
Tel +33 (0)3 21 26 92 02
Email contact@lapeylouse.fr
Web www.lapeylouse.fr

Entry 24 Map 1

Le Château de Philiomel

Overlooking a lake and leafy parkland, this commanding, Italianate mansion has the right ingredients – pillars, portico, marble fireplaces – to give you grand ideas, yet is designed with a light touch. Vast bedrooms are hotel-perfect in muted colours with a cool mix of contemporary furniture and antiques; bathrooms are bold and modern. Elegant buffet breakfasts are taken at separate tables in an uncluttered white space of panelling, parquet and shining silver. Unwind on this private estate (the owners live next door) in immaculate solitude. There are two Michelin stars within a ten-minute drive.

Ferme du Moulin

Terraced houses in front, a perfect little farmyard behind, the kindest of hosts within – it's a privilege to meet such splendid human beings, retired farmers of old-fashioned simple good manners, he silently earthy, tending his garden, she comfortably maternal, delighting in her freedom to indulge her wanderlust at last. Their modest, old-fashioned French farmers' house is stuffed with collections of bric-a-brac; their genuine chambres d'hôtes are family-furnished, floral-papered, draped with all sorts and conditions of crochet. Breakfasts are good and you are perfectly placed for those battlefields.

Price	€80-€120.
Rooms	4 doubles.
Meals	Restaurants 2km.
Closed	Never.
Directions	From Calais A26 exit 5; right at r'bout for Lillers on Rue du Général de Gaulle; 1st right Rue Philiomel; square-pillared gateway with high gate.

Price	€38.
Rooms	2: 1 double, 1 triple, each with shower or separate bath, sharing wc.
Meals	Restaurants 500m.
Closed	Rarely.
Directions	A26 from Calais, exit Aix-Noulette for Liévin; 2nd r'bout for Givency. House 300m; public car park.

Frédéric Devys
Le Château de Philiomel,
Rue Philiomel, 62190 Lillers,
Pas-de-Calais
Tel   +33 (0)3 21 61 76 76
Fax   +33 (0)3 21 61 76 76
Email   contact@philiomel.com
Web   www.lechateaudephiliomel.com

M & Mme Dupont
Ferme du Moulin,
58 rue du Quatre Septembre,
62800 Liévin,
Pas-de-Calais
Tel   +33 (0)3 21 44 65 91

Entry 25   Map 1

Entry 26   Map 1

La Maison de Campagne

Perched on a hill with delightful views over garden and meadow to valley beyond, a newish house and super B&B. Many people drive straight through this area so take the chance to get to know it with people who belong; after years as a librarian, Madame has thrown herself into local tourism and loves taking guests on visits – particularly horticultural ones. You enter through the conservatory, every window has the view and bedrooms, one up, one down, are simple but welcoming. Children love it here, farm trips are possible, and you might be treated to homemade brioche, walnut wine and genuine French cooking.

Le Loubarré

The period of each piece shows on its face, so you expect the elegantly coffered ceilings, the deeply carved woodwork, the vast Louis XIII dresser... though nothing prepares you for the neo-gothic stone fireplace! No sitting room but the bedrooms in the stables are pretty and spotless, some up, some down, each with good fabrics, some antiques, a neat shower room. Madame loves telling tales of the house and its contents, and keeps a few goats, and two donkeys, in the quiet garden (a weekend racetrack in the valley, though). Both your hosts work constantly on their beloved house.

Price	€45. Family suite €80.
Rooms	2: 1 family suite; 1 double with separate wc.
Meals	Dinner with wine, €25.
Closed	Rarely.
Directions	From Calais, exit 5, D916 for St Pol/Ternoise. In Cauchy à la Tour, D341 left to Arras, Division, Houdain. At 'STOP' in Houdain; D86 right to Magnicourt en Comté. In village, follow signs 'Mairie, École, Église'.

Price	€48.
Rooms	5: 2 doubles, 3 twins.
Meals	Restaurants within walking distance. Guest kitchen.
Closed	Rarely.
Directions	From St Pol sur Ternoise D343 NW for Fruges. Just after entering Gauchin Verloingt, right Rue de Troisvaux; right Rue des Montifaux. House on right.

	Jacqueline Guillemant
	La Maison de Campagne,
	6 rue de l'Europe,
	62127 Magnicourt en Comté,
	Pas-de-Calais
Tel	+33 (0)3 21 41 51 00
Email	jguillemant@gmail.com
Web	www.lamaisondecampagne.com

	Marie-Christine & Philippe Vion
	Le Loubarré,
	550 rue des Montifaux,
	62130 Gauchin Verloingt,
	Pas-de-Calais
Tel	+33 (0)3 21 03 05 05
Email	mcvion.loubarre@wanadoo.fr
Web	www.loubarre.com

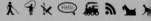

Château de Grand Rullecourt

A remarkable mix of place and people. This dynamic family, all eight of them, have almost finished rebuilding their monumental château and brightening their escutcheon while being publishers in Paris and brilliant socialites: fascinating people, phenomenal energy, natural hospitality that makes up for any residual damp or winter chill. Built in 1745, the château has many rooms and striking grandeur: come play lord and lady in chandeliered, ancestored salons, discover an aristocratic bedroom with big windows, walk the rolling green parkland as if it were your own. It's another world.

Château de Saulty

The re-lifted stately face looks finer than ever in its great park and apple orchards. Inside, it's a warm, embracing country house with a panelled breakfast room, an amazing, museum-worthy, multi-tiled gents cloakroom and, up the wide old stairs, quietly luxurious bedrooms, some very big, furnished with printed fabrics and period pieces. Be charmed by wooden floors and plain walls in sunny tones, perhaps an old fireplace or a mirrored armoire. Quiet and intelligent, Sylvie will make you feel welcome while serenely concocting delicious jams and managing her young family.

Price	€95. Extra person €20.
Rooms	5: 4 doubles, 1 suite for 2-5.
Meals	Restaurants within 4km.
Closed	Rarely.
Directions	From Arras N39 for St Pol & Le Touquet 5km; left D339 to Avesnes le Comte; D75 for Doullens & Grand Rullecourt 4km. Château in village square; signed.

Price	€60. Suites €85.
Rooms	4: 1 double, 1 triple, 2 family rooms.
Meals	Restaurants 1-9km.
Closed	January.
Directions	From Arras N25 towards Amiens 17km. In L'Arbret, 3rd right to Saulty; follow signs.

Patrice & Chantal de Saulieu
Château de Grand Rullecourt,
62810 Grand Rullecourt,
Pas-de-Calais

Tel +33 (0)3 21 58 06 37
Fax +33 (0)3 21 58 06 37
Email psaulieu@routiers.com
Web www.chateaux-chambres-hotes.com

Emmanuel & Sylvie Dalle
Château de Saulty,
82 rue de la Gare,
62158 Saulty, Pas-de-Calais

Tel +33 (0)3 21 48 24 76
Fax +33 (0)3 21 48 18 32
Email chateaudesaulty@nordnet.fr

Entry 29   Map 1

Entry 30   Map 1

Le Jardin d'Alix

A quiet, elegant residential quarter – but hop on the tram and in 20 minutes you're in the historic, fascinating centre of Lille. Alexandra's light, airy house, tucked away from the road, was built a mere half century ago by a well-known local church architect. Though there's no guest sitting room, the grey-carpeted passage leading to the bedrooms has an internet post and books galore. Bedrooms are small and attractive, give onto the gorgeous garden – Alexandra's passion – and are hung with her bright paintings. Breakfast on homemade bread and jams served on fine porcelain in a spotless high-tech kitchen. *Minimum stay 2 nights. Trams from Lille train stations stop near house.*

Price	€50–€65.
Rooms	2: 1 double, 1 suite.
Meals	Restaurants 3 minutes by tram.
Closed	Rarely.
Directions	From Dunkerque A25 to Lille; N356 for Tourcoing exit 12 Marcq en Barœul Chât. Rouge; right Ave. de la Marne; straight on; gate 2m after entering Tourcoing. Tram stop: Ma Campagne.

Alexandra Hudson
Le Jardin d'Alix,
45 bis avenue de la Marne,
59200 Tourcoing, Nord
Tel +33 (0)3 20 36 72 08
Email alexandra.hudson@hotmail.fr
Web www.lejardindalix.com

Entry 31   Map 1

Château de Courcelette

From the small-town back street, enter unexpected 18th-century elegance – pilasters, panelling, marble, medallions – then a beautiful brick and cobble terrace to an acre of superb walled garden: bliss so near Lille, and the oldest château left standing in the area. Your hosts will enchant you with their courtesy and deep love for Courcelette, their energy in preserving its classical forms, their care for your comfort; Madame bubbles and chats, Monsieur charms quietly. Pale bedrooms with original doors and handsome antiques set the tone for this quietly luxurious and civilised house. One of the best.

Price	€95. €140 for 4.
Rooms	4: 2 doubles, 1 twin/double, 1 suite for 4.
Meals	Dinner with wine, €35.
Closed	Never.
Directions	On Villeneuve d'Ascq road; exit 7 Roubaix Est. for Wattrelos (D700); left at 2nd r'bout to Lys Lez Lannoy; after 100m left to Lannoy; at x-roads follow 'les orchidées', right at Rue St Jacques, 1st right, right into blind alley.

Brame Family
Château de Courcelette,
17 rue César Parent,
59390 Lannoy, Nord
Tel +33 (0)3 20 75 45 67
Fax +33 (0)3 20 75 45 67
Email contact@chateau-de-courcelette.com
Web chateau-de-courcelette.com

Entry 32   Map 1

The North

Ferme de la Noyelle

The 17th-century archway leads into a typical enclosed farmyard where you feel sheltered and welcomed: these attentive dairy farmers and their young family love having guests. Once installed, you can hardly believe that this patch of countryside is surrounded by shopping outlets and transport links. Guest rooms in the old stables – the standard conversion job includes a kitchen – are in simple cottagey style with careful colour matches and wide showers. Another wing houses a modest restaurant open at weekends. Good value, lovely people – and Belgium five minutes away. *Direct metro to Lille.*

Price	€44.
Rooms	4: 1 double, 1 twin, 1 triple, 1 family room.
Meals	Dinner with wine, €16. Guest kitchen.
Closed	Rarely.
Directions	A16 from Calais to Dunkerque; A25 to Lille; A1 to Paris, after 1km follow A22 Bruxelles for 1km; exit 2 Cysoing/cité scientifique. At Sainghin follow Chambres d'Hôtes signs.

	Dominique & Nelly Pollet
	Ferme de la Noyelle,
	832 rue Pasteur, 59262
	Sainghin en Mélantois, Nord
Tel	+33 (0)3 20 41 29 82
Email	dominique-nelly.pollet@wanadoo.fr
Web	perso.wanadoo.fr/dpollet

Entry 33   Map 1

Picardy

La Bergerie

That simple face hides character and riches: a beamed living room, marble floor, old fireplace and good antiques; an overwhelmingly pretty breakfast room full of plants and brocante; two French-formal, mostly pink bedrooms, one reached by a steep spiral outside stair, which can also be a suite: fine linen, good bathrooms, beams and views over the 12th-century church of the sweet village, and the large lush garden. Your hosts are absolutely charming – Madame may make you fresh fruit brioche for breakfast. Outside, a summer kitchen, an avenue of swishing poplars, a pony grazing, bantams scuttling – what a picture!

Price	€65–€75.
Rooms	2 doubles, one with extra single bed & kitchenette.
Meals	Restaurant 5km.
Closed	Rarely.
Directions	From Paris A16 exit 24 (25 from Calais); N1 for Montreuil 25km; in Vron left to Villers; right Rue de l'Église; at end of road, left unpaved lane; house left up poplar tree-lined ave.

	Pierre & Sabine Singer de Wazières
	La Bergerie,
	80120 Villers sur Authie, Somme
Tel	+33 (0)3 22 29 21 74
Email	alabergerie@wanadoo.fr
Web	www.alabergerie.canalblog.com

Entry 34   Map 1

Picardy

La Tour Blanche

In grand French style, stable your steed in fine boxes beneath the immensely tall sheltering trees, swirl up the staircase to superb rooms, each a symphony in fabric and colour – red or blue, green or white – with good beds on polished floors and a gentle view of the little church: all is handsome, sober and serene. And bathrooms are brand new. Your active, intelligent young hosts happily share their generous family house and big garden with guests, two children and half a dozen horses. There are games to play, bikes to hire, Amiens to visit and the shimmering Somme estuary to walk you into bird heaven.

Price	€90-€170.
Rooms	4: 3 doubles, 1 twin.
Meals	Dinner with wine, €40. Guest kitchen.
Closed	Rarely.
Directions	Calais A16 exit 24 onto D32; at 1st r'bout left onto D632 to Forest Montiers, 500m to house, entrance on left.

Hélène & Benoît Legru
La Tour Blanche,
10 rue de la Ville,
80120 Forest Montiers, Somme

Tel	+33 (0)3 22 23 69 13
Email	info@latourblanche.net
Web	www.latourblanche.net

Entry 35   Map 1

Picardy

Château des Alleux

The potager gives artichokes, asparagus, peaches and pears, the farmyard chickens, the fields lamb, the woods game… and they make their own cider. The château has been in the family since the Revolution; its pretty blue and yellow guest room has a four-poster and overlooks that munificent garden. Rooms in the cottage are modern, low-ceilinged and softly lit; both have kitchenettes, ideal for families, and the mezzanine suite has a log fire. Dense trees protect from distant motorway hum; home-produced dinners and local wines, shared in the château with your engaging hosts, are a treat.

Price	€60-€70. Suite €80-€100
Rooms	3: 2 doubles, 1 family suite, 2 with kitchenette.
Meals	Dinner with wine, €20.
Closed	Rarely.
Directions	From Calais A16 for Abbeville onto A28 for Rouen 4km; exit Monts Caubert 3; right at stop sign; D928 to Croisettes; right for Les Alleux not Béhen.

René-François & Élisabeth
de Fontanges
Château des Alleux,
Les Alleux, 80870 Béhen, Somme

Tel	+33 (0)3 22 31 64 88
Fax	+33 (0)3 22 31 64 88
Email	chateaudesalleux@wanadoo.fr

Entry 36   Map 1

Picardy

3 rue d'Inval

Imposing and old-fashioned – in the best possible sense. You soon relax into the homely atmosphere created by your calm, hospitable, country hosts – the first in the Somme to open their house for B&B. Aart keeps honey, cider and calvados in the vaulted cellars and tends the serried tulips and dahlias and the gloriously billowing shrubs; Dorette was mayor for 24 years. Her big uncluttered bedrooms (smaller on the second floor) are comfortable, modern shower rooms are big enough for a third bed, and the panelled dining room is a proper setting for a good breakfast. A great place to stay, with fishing on the lake.

Price	€45-€50. Triples €65.
Rooms	4: 1 double, 3 triples, all with shower & basin, sharing wc.
Meals	Restaurants 12km. Kitchen available.
Closed	Rarely.
Directions	From Abbeville A28 for Rouen, 28km, exit 5; left at Bouttencourt D1015 to Sénarpont; D211 for Le Mazis, 4.5km; follow Chambres d'Hôtes signs.

Dorette & Aart Onder de Linden
3 rue d'Inval,
80430 Le Mazis, Somme

Tel	+33 (0)3 22 25 90 88
Fax	+33 (0)3 22 25 76 04
Email	onderdelinden@wanadoo.fr
Web	www.lemazis.com

Entry 37   Map 5

Picardy

Château d'Omiécourt

On a working estate, Omiécourt is a proudly grand 19th-century château and elegant family house (the Thézys have four teenage children), with tall slender windows and some really old trees. Friendly if formal, communicative and smiling, your hosts have worked hugely to restore their inheritance and create gracious French château guest rooms, each with an ornate fireplace, each named for a different period. In an outbuilding near the two pools is a neat and cosy apartment with sloping ceilings; there's a 'boutique', too, of pretty things. A house of goodwill where you will be very comfortable. *Min. stay 2 nights July/August.*

Price	€95.
Rooms	5 + 1: 2 doubles, 2 family rooms, 1 suite for 3. Apartment for 4.
Meals	Light supper in rooms, €10-€15. Restaurants 12km.
Closed	Rarely.
Directions	From A1 south for Paris; exit 13 onto N29 for St Quentin; in Villers Carbonnel right at lights onto N17 for 9km to Omiécourt; right in village, château on right.

Dominique & Véronique de Thézy
Château d'Omiécourt,
80320 Omiécourt, Somme

Tel	+33 (0)3 22 83 01 75
Fax	+33 (0)3 22 83 09 56
Email	thezy@terre-net.fr
Web	www.chateau-omiecourt.com

Entry 38   Map 5

Picardy

1 rue Génermont

In serene country, a dazzling house whose hill-shaped roof becomes a timbered vault way above swathes of natural stone floor. The Picardy sky pours in and fills the vast minimally furnished living space and your hostess shows pleasure at your amazement… then serves you superb food and intelligent conversation. Bedrooms are pure and peaceful: white walls, patches of colour, crazy-paved floors, excellent beds and design-conscious bathrooms, 1930s antiques and touches of fun. Civilised seclusion… and modern European history and the First World War battlefields at your door. *Ask about gourmet weekends.*

Price	€60-€64.
Rooms	4: 2 twins, 1 family room, 1 suite for 4.
Meals	Dinner with wine, €25-€28.
Closed	Rarely.
Directions	From A1 exit 13 on D1029 for St Quentin; in Villers Carbonnel, right at r'bout onto D1017 for 5km to Fresnes Mazancourt; house next to church.

Martine Warlop
1 rue Génermont,
80320 Fresnes Mazancourt, Somme
Tel   +33 (0)3 22 85 49 49
Fax   +33 (0)3 22 85 49 49
Email martine.warlop@wanadoo.fr
Web   www.maison-warlop.com

Entry 39   Map 5

Picardy

Les Jardins du Vidamé

In beautiful 17th-century Gerberoy (records go back to 923 AD), this venerable place, Ben's family home, has real age and oodles of ancient charm in a multitude of timbers, cobbles and bricks where untamed roses ramble and wisteria wends its way. Bedroom walls are intensely, Frenchly floral; photographs, prints and mellow watercolours talk from the past; add a heavy carved bedstead, the odd bit of mahogany, and the atmosphere is of another period. Even the bathroom looks 1920s. Your delightful young hosts, busy with small children and tea room, will happily chat and may share their family-cluttered living room.

Price	€70.
Rooms	1 family suite.
Meals	Dinner €20. Wine by the glass €3-€7. Tea room/restaurant in outbuilding.
Closed	December-January.
Directions	From Beauvais D901 & D133 to Gerberoy. In village square, left of arched building Rue Henri Le Sidaner, up hill, 1st left Impasse du Vidamé; entrance on right.

Céline & Ben Guilloux
Les Jardins du Vidamé,
4 impasse du Vidamé,
60380 Gerberoy, Oise
Tel   +33 (0)3 44 82 45 32
Email infolesjardinsduvidame@orange.fr
Web   les-jardins-du-vidame.com

Entry 40   Map 5

Picardy

Les Chambres de l'Abbaye

Chloé and her artist husband have the most unusual, delightful house in a village with a fine Cistercian abbey. You are free to roam a series of beautiful rooms downstairs, read a book in the pale blue formal salon, visit Jean-François' studio whose striking exciting pictures decorate the rooms, too. The suite is on the first floor, the two others higher up; all are fresh, immaculate, groomed like a French lady. You eat well and much is homemade, including walnut liqueur and wine from their own trees; walk it off round the partly unmanicured garden with its summerhouse and pond. It's a pleasure to stay here.

Ethical Collection: Food.
See page 432.

Price	€85. €105 for 3.
Rooms	3: 2 doubles, 1 family suite for 3.
Meals	Dinner with wine, €23.
Closed	Christmas.
Directions	From A16 exit 15 to Beauvais; N31 for Rouen, 25km; left to St Germer de Fly centre; entrance on left down hill just before church.

Chloé Comte
Les Chambres de l'Abbaye,
2 rue Michel Greuet,
60850 St Germer de Fly, Oise

Tel	+33 (0)3 44 81 98 38
Fax	+33 (0)3 44 81 98 38
Email	comte.resa@free.fr
Web	www.chambres-abbaye.com

Entry 41   Map 5

Picardy

La Maison Nature

Doze under the lilacs, gaze over plains, take an aperitif to the terrace. This is lazy, languorous living. Guests stay in two granite cottages but share the lovely rambling garden of this elegant, shuttered, 19th-century house. Charming with whitewash and open-stone walls, wooden and iron bedsteads, floral quilts and snug seats, bedrooms are touched with candles and treats. One bathroom (minimalist-pretty) is perched among the rafters. Breakfast beautifully at the long dining table – or in the view-filled garden where ladders and swings hang from ancient trees. Spirited Claudine, ex-media, is mother of three. *Pets extra €5 per night. Massage.*

Price	€95–€105.
Rooms	2 doubles.
Meals	Dinner with wine, €25.
Closed	Never.
Directions	From Gisors D15 to Paris for 4km; right after leisure park to Montjavoult; over x-roads to Le Vouast; 1st right onto Chemin Vert; after small car park house on left, big wooden gates.

Claudine & Patrik Coze
La Maison Nature,
17 rue du Chemin Vert,
Le Vouast,
60240 Montjavoult, Oise

Mobile	+33 (0)6 60 75 45 56
Email	lamaisonnature@orange.fr
Web	www.lamaisonnature.com

Entry 42   Map 5

Picardy

Le Clos

The sprucest of farmhouses, whitewashed and Normandy-beamed, sits in the lushest, most secret of gardens, reached via a door in the wall. Inside, a remarkably fresh, open-plan and modernised interior, with a comfortable sitting room to share. Your bedroom, spacious, neat, uncluttered and warm, is above the garage; the bedding is the best, the shower room spotless and modern with coloured towels. Dine with your informative hosts by the old farm fireplace on tarte aux pommes du jardin – Monsieur is chef, Madame, a retired teacher, keeps you gentle company. A peaceful spot, close to Paris.

Ethical Collection: Food.
See page 432.

Price	€56. €68 for 3.
Rooms	2 family rooms for 3.
Meals	Dinner with wine, €25.
Closed	Rarely.
Directions	From A16 exit 13 for Gisors & Chaumont en Vexin approx. 20km; after Fleury left to Fay les Étangs; 2nd left; house on left.

Philippe & Chantal Vermeire
Le Clos,
3 rue du Chêne Noir, 60240
Fay les Étangs, Oise

Tel	+33 (0)3 44 49 92 38
Fax	+33 (0)3 44 49 92 38
Email	philippe.vermeire@wanadoo.fr
Web	www.leclosdefay.com

Entry 43   Map 5

Picardy

Le Château de Fosseuse

Your tall windows look over the great park fading away to wooded hillside (with railway); beneath your feet are 16th-century bricks. A monumental staircase ushers you up to big, canopied, glorious-viewed bedrooms that are château-worthy but not posh; behind the panelling of one is a secret staircase. Your hosts are a fascinating, cultured marriage of exquisite French manners and Irish warmth who labour on to save their family home and genuinely enjoy sharing it. Antique rugs line the hall's walls; gumboots for guests (all sizes) wait by the door; Michelin stars are a very short drive. *Children over 4 welcome.*

Price	€80. Suite €100-€156.
Rooms	3: 2 doubles, 1 suite for 2-4.
Meals	Restaurant 2km.
Closed	Rarely.
Directions	From A16 exit 13 for Esches D923; in Fosseuse, château gate on right at traffic lights.

Shirley & Jean-Louis Marro
Le Château de Fosseuse,
60540 Fosseuse, Oise

Tel	+33 (0)3 44 08 47 66
Fax	+33 (0)3 44 08 47 66
Email	chateau.fosseuse@wanadoo.fr
Web	www.chateau-de-fosseuse.com

Entry 44   Map 5

Picardy

Château de Saint Vincent

An enchantment for garden lovers who want real, old château style but not plush bathrooms. Madame is still repairing her 200-year-old family home and garden, her great love – complete with stream and island – and a work of art. The house is elegantly well-worn, you breakfast in a darkly handsome room, sit in a totally French oak-panelled salon, sleep in 210cm-long antique sleigh beds. The second bedroom is simpler, and the washing arrangements, with continental bath, not American standard. But Madame's passion for house and garden will convince you. *Children over 10 welcome.*

Price	€110.
Rooms	2 twins. Children's room available.
Meals	Auberge 3km.
Closed	Mid-October to mid-May.
Directions	From Senlis D330 for Borest & Nanteuil for 8km; right at cemetery; 1st right; across Place du Tissard towards big farm; left Rue de la Ferme; gates at bottom, No. 1.

Hélène Merlotti
Château de Saint Vincent,
1 rue Élisabeth Roussel,
60300 Borest, Oise

Tel	+33 (0)3 44 54 21 52
Fax	+33 (0)3 44 54 21 52

Picardy

Le Prieuré

The stones date from the 14th century and one gothic wall still has its vast window. Inside, rooms are airy, sophisticated and gracious, as is your hostess, a welcoming, vivacious mother of two. Pretty bedrooms are in their own little wing, very cosy and dressed in fashionable colours; two have views of the neighbouring church spire. No salon for guests, but a convivial table for breakfast served off elegant china, and a big walled and manicured garden with tennis court and pool. Paris is 40 minutes away, the airport is even closer – and you can hike in the forest of Compiègne.

Price	€80-€100.
Rooms	3: 2 doubles; 1 twin with separate shower.
Meals	Restaurant in village.
Closed	Rarely.
Directions	A1 for Lille, exit 8 Senlis for Chamant & Compiègne; after Villeneuve sur Verberie right onto D554 to Nery. High walled property next to village church, tall double doors.

Caroline Benqué
Le Prieuré,
1 place de l'Église, 60320 Nery, Oise

Tel	+33 (0)3 44 88 20 17
Fax	+33 (0)3 44 88 20 17
Email	c-benque@hotmail.fr
Web	prieure.nery.free.fr

La Gaxottière

The high walls guard a secret garden, a goldfish pond, lots of intriguing mementos and a blithe, animated hostess – a retired chemist who loves her dogs, travelling and contact with visitors. In the old house, the two mellow, beamed, fireplace'd rooms for breakfasts are brimful of old pieces and personal collections; two bedrooms have log fires and bathrooms are old-fashioned. Madame lives in the brilliantly converted barn; all is harmony and warmth among the antiques. Drink it all in with this great soul's talk of France and the world. Sleep in peace, wake to the dawn chorus and breakfast in the sunshine.

La Commanderie

Up here on the hill, not easy to find, is a Templar hamlet and a millennium of history: an enclosed farmyard, a ruined medieval chapel framing the sunrise, a tithe barn with leaping oak timbers – and this modern house. Marie-José, an unhurried grandmother of generous spirit, welcomes genuinely, loves the history, harvests her orchards and vegetables, and cooks her produce deliciously. Bedrooms are in plain, dated farm style but open the window and you fall into heaven, the view soars away on all sides of the hill, even to Laon cathedral. Homely, authentic – most readers love it. *Sawday self-catering also.*

Price	€50–€60.
Rooms	3: 1 double, 1 twin, 1 single.
Meals	Dinner with wine, €20.
Closed	Rarely. Book ahead.
Directions	A1 exit 10; N31 for Compiègne for 4km, 1st right after 1st r'bout onto to small lane for Jaux. 1st right to Varanval, over hill. House on right opp. château gates.

Price	€41–€46.
Rooms	3: 1 double, 2 family suites: 1 for 3, 1 for 4.
Meals	Dinner with wine, €15.
Closed	Rarely.
Directions	From Calais A26 for Reims, exit 12 to Crécy sur Serre; D35 to Pont à Bucy; 1st left to Nouvion et Catillon; D26 right for La Ferté Chevresis, 4km; small lane left up hill to Catillon. Drive through farm on left. Signs.

Françoise Gaxotte
La Gaxottière,
363 rue du Champ du Mont,
Hameau de Varanval,
60880 Jaux, Oise
Tel +33 (0)3 44 83 22 41
Email lagaxottiere@tele2.fr

José-Marie Carette
La Commanderie,
Catillon du Temple,
02270 Nouvion et Catillon, Aisne
Tel +33 (0)3 23 56 51 28
Fax +33 (0)3 23 56 50 14
Email carette.jm@wanadoo.fr

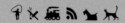

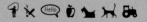

Entry 47   Map 5

Entry 48   Map 5

Picardy

Domaine de l'Étang

The village on one side, the expansive estate on the other, the 18th-century wine-grower's house in between. There's a civilised mood: Monsieur so well-mannered and breakfast served with silver and choice china. A dayroom for guests, too. Wake to church-spire and rooftop views in rooms with soft comfort where, under sloping ceilings, French toile de Jouy is as inviting as English chintz (your hosts spent two years in England). Bathrooms are frilled and pretty. Shrubs hug the hem of the house, a pool is sunk into the lawn behind and Laon trumpets the first gothic cathedral of France.

Picardy

Le Clos

Authentic country hospitality and family cooking are yours in the big old house. Madame is kindly and direct; Monsieur is the communicator (mainly in French), knows his local history and loves the hunting horn. It's cosily unposh: matched floral curtains, Frenchly-papered walls, original wainscotting throughout, funny old prints in bedrooms, comforting clutter in the vast living room, tourist posters in the corridors. The master bedroom is superb, others are simple but fine; one has a ship's shower room, all look onto green pastures. And there's a pretty lake for picnics across the narrow road. *Sawday self-catering also.*

Price	€60–€65.		Price	€50–€55.
Rooms	3: 1 double, 1 twin; 1 double with separate bath.		Rooms	4 : 2 doubles, 1 twin, 1 suite for 5 (1 triple, 1 twin).
Meals	Restaurants nearby.		Meals	Dinner with wine, €22.50, not school holidays. Restaurant in village.
Closed	Never.		Closed	20 October to mid-March, except by arrangement.
Directions	A26 for Soissons exit 13; after r'bout right to Mons en Laonnois, Clacy & Thierret; from centre of Mons cross flyover; right after 30m.		Directions	From A26 E17 exit 13 on N2 for Laon; 2nd left to Athies sur Laon; D516 to Bruyères & M. 7km; left D967 for Fismes; Chérêt sign leaving Bruyères; house on left on entering Chérêt.

Mme Woillez
Domaine de l'Étang,
2 rue St Martin,
02000 Mons en Laonnois, Aisne
Tel   +33 (0)3 23 24 44 52
Email   gitemons@aol.com
Web   www.domainedeletang.fr

Michel & Monique Simonnot
Le Clos,
02860 Chérêt, Aisne
Tel   +33 (0)3 23 24 80 64
Email   leclos.cheret@club-internet.fr
Web   www.lecloscheret.com

Entry 49   Map 5

Entry 50   Map 5

Picardy

La Quincy

The old family home, faded and weary, timeless and romantic, is well loved and lived in by this charming, natural and quietly elegant couple. Corridors cluttered with books, magazines and traces of family life lead to an octagonal tower, its great double room and child's room across the landing imaginatively set in the space. A fine antique bed on a fine polished floor, charming chintz, erratic plumbing and two parkland views will enchant you. Shrubs hug the feet of the delicious 'troubadour' château, the garden slips into meadow, summer breakfast and dinner (good wine, book ahead) are in the orangery. Special.

Price	€60.
Rooms	1 family suite for 3.
Meals	Dinner with wine, €20.
Closed	Rarely.
Directions	From A26 exit 13 for Laon; Laon bypass for Soissons; N2 approx. 18km; right D536; through Nanteuil for La Quincy; château on right outside village.

	Jacques & Marie-Catherine Cornu-Langy
	La Quincy,
	02880 Nanteuil la Fosse, Aisne
Tel	+33 (0)3 23 54 67 76
Fax	+33 (0)3 23 54 72 63
Email	la.quincy@yahoo.fr

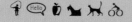

Entry 51   Map 5

Picardy

Domaine de Montaigu

This inviting 18th-century house is run with aplomb by two delightful, gentlemanly hosts. It feels like a small hotel, is welcoming, comfortable, has a small sauna and an outdoor pool. Montaigu's history is reflected in five antique-furnished, frilled and furbelowed rooms in pure French style, while 'Colette' flaunts an extraordinary 1950s collector's set of mirror-fronted furniture. In the dining room, where breakfast and dinner are served at sensible prices, a long table is set about with Louis XVI chairs, sideboards heave with glassware and tassels drip from a satin-velvet sofa. Shamelessly flamboyant!

Price	€80–€100.
Rooms	5: 4 doubles, 1 suite for 4.
Meals	Dinner with wine, €30.
Closed	Rarely.
Directions	From Paris north on A1; exit 9 to Compiègne; N31 for Soissons. 5km after Jauzy right onto D943 to Le Soulier (don't take 1st turning to Ambleny). Signed to Domaine.

	Philippe de Reyer
	Domaine de Montaigu,
	16 rue de Montaigu,
	02290 Ambleny, Aisne
Tel	+33 (0)3 23 74 06 62
Fax	+33 (0)3 23 74 06 62
Email	info@domainedemontaigu.com
Web	www.domainedemontaigu.com

Entry 52   Map 5

Picardy

Ferme de Ressons

Ressons is home to a dynamic, intelligent, well-travelled couple who, after a hard day's work running this big farm (Jean-Paul) or being an architect (Valérie) and tending three children, will ply you in apparently leisurely fashion with champagne, excellent dinner and conversation; they also hunt. The deeply carved Henri III furniture is an admirable family heirloom; rooms are airy and colour-coordinated, beds are beautiful, views roll for miles and sharing facilities seems easy. An elegant, sophisticated house of comfort and relaxed good manners, bordering the Champagne region. *Fishing in small lake. Sawday self-catering also.*

Price	€48–€50.
Rooms	5: 1 double, 1 twin, each with bath, sharing wc; 2 doubles, 1 twin, sharing bath & 2 wcs.
Meals	Dinner €19. Wine €14; champagne €18.
Closed	Rarely.
Directions	From Fismes D967 for Fère en Tardenois & Château Thierry 4km. Don't go to Mont St Martin, on 800m beyond turning; white house on left.

Valérie & Jean-Paul Ferry
Ferme de Ressons,
02220 Mont St Martin, Aisne
Tel +33 (0)3 23 74 71 00
Fax +33 (0)3 23 74 28 88
Email ferryressons@orange.fr

Entry 53 Map 5

Champagne – Ardenne

Champagne – Ardenne

5 rue du Paradis

The Harlauts love entertaining and are keen to provide good value and, even though they produce their own champagne and bottles are for sale, it is for the authentic country cooking and the atmosphere that guests return. Barbecue dinners are regularly served on the terrace overlooking a vast and lovely garden. There are steep narrow stairs up to the warm, wood-floored, uncluttered guest rooms, two of which share a loo – a minor concern as everything is fresh and spotless and they make an excellent family suite. The village is pretty, typical of the delightful Champagne region.

Price	€49-€54.
Rooms	2 + 1: 1 double, 1 family suite for 2-4. 1 apartment for 2.
Meals	Dinner with wine, €27.
Closed	December, January & Easter.
Directions	From A26 exit 15 (Reims La Neuvillette) onto N44 for Laon 2km; left to St Thierry; house in village.

Évelyne & Remi Harlaut
5 rue du Paradis,
51220 St Thierry, Marne
Tel   +33 (0)3 26 03 13 75
Fax   +33 (0)3 26 03 03 65
Email contact@champagne-harlaut.fr
Web   www.champagne-harlaut.fr

Entry 54   Map 6

Champagne – Ardenne

La Brouilletière

Independent champagne growers, the Aristons delight in showing guests round vineyards and cellars (tastings included). Indeed Madame, a wonderful person, started doing B&B for champagne buyers who did not want to leave after tasting! Through the flower-filled courtyard and up a private staircase to lovely, light, airy, attic bedrooms with fresh white walls, beams, matching curtains and covers; one has its own kitchenette and the showers are excellent. Breakfast is served in the characterful old family house. A treat to be so near Reims. *Latest bookings 7pm. Minimum stay 2 nights in family room.*

Price	€55-€60. Family room €75 (min. 2 nights).
Rooms	4: 3 doubles, 1 family room for 3 & kitchenette.
Meals	Restaurants 11km.
Closed	Christmas-January.
Directions	From A4 exit 22 on N31 Fismes to Jonchery sur Vesle; left D28 to Savigny sur Ardres; right D386 to Crugny 3km; left D23 to Brouillet; house on right, sign.

Remi & Marie Ariston
La Brouilletière,
4 & 8 Grande Rue, 51170 Brouillet, Marne
Tel   +33 (0)3 26 97 43 46
Fax   +33 (0)3 26 97 49 34
Email contact@champagneaspasie.com
Web   www.champagneaspasie.com

Entry 55   Map 5

Champagne – Ardenne

Château de Juvigny

Oozing old-world charm, this handsome 1705 château wraps you in its warmth. The family have occupied one wing for 200 years and it exudes a wonderfully easy-going elegance, thanks to Grandmama Brigitte. There are chandeliers, polished floorboards, wainscotting and antiques, old-fashioned bathrooms, cracked floor tiles, rustic outbuildings. Bedrooms, in the old servants' quarters, are informally stylish with marble fireplaces, pretty bedcovers and views over parkland, formal gardens and the lake… You breakfast beneath a vast (but deteriorated!) portrait of an ancestor. Charming, unfussy country comfort.

Price	€90–€130.
Rooms	5: 3 doubles, 1 twin, 1 suite for 2-4.
Meals	Restaurant 5km.
Closed	Mid-December to mid-March, except by arrangement.
Directions	A26 exit 17, St Gibrien for Épernay; in Matougues 1st right to château.

Brigitte & Alain Caubère d'Alinval
Château de Juvigny,
8 avenue du Château, 51150 Juvigny,
Marne
Tel   +33 (0)6 78 99 69 40
Fax   +33 (0)3 26 64 86 24
Email   information@chateaudejuvigny.com
Web   www.chateaudejuvigny.com

Entry 56   Map 6

Champagne – Ardenne

189 rue Ferdinand Moret

This couple have flung their rich welcome out into the woods with four cottage-cosy bedrooms on top of the lovely big room in their own house 2km away. Éric is a creative handyman, both are ardent trawlers of brocante stalls, the results are a personal mix of antique styles against pastel paints, polished floorboards and gorgeously dressed beds. There are four pretty bedrooms and a handsome old-fitted kitchen/diner in the big house in the woods, and a piano, bar billiards, a private lake. Sylvie and Éric bend over backwards to bring you delicious meals, outstanding breakfasts, champagne receptions – and their sparkling presence. *Sawday self-catering also.*

Price	€60–€75. Suites €90–€95.
Rooms	5 + 1: 1 family room for 3-4; 4 suites for 2 with separate bath. House in woods for 10.
Meals	Restaurants nearby.
Closed	Rarely.
Directions	From Épernay, Place de la République, D3 for Châlons; right at 1st r'bout, right at 2nd r'bout for Avize; 1st right for Cramant.

Sylvie & Éric Charbonnier
189 rue Ferdinand Moret,
51530 Cramant, Marne
Tel   +33 (0)3 26 57 95 34
Email   eric-sylvie@wanadoo.fr
Web   www.ericsylvie.com

Entry 57   Map 6

Champagne – Ardenne

Le Vieux Cèdre

The façade and trees are grand, the interior is gorgeous. The huge, original-panelled dining room looks straight through to a grassy slope and the atmosphere is hospitably informal, a mix of elegant old and brilliant new, French and English, champagne and motor-biking. A spectacular 19th-century staircase leads to temptingly pretty, artistic bedrooms: two have space, light and luxurious sitting/bathrooms; the smaller has a richly canopied bed and a great claw-footed bath within. She is a lively, lovely mother of two; Didier makes the champagne and continues his fine restoration work.

Price	€65.
Rooms	3: 2 doubles, 1 twin.
Meals	Restaurants in Épernay, 8km.
Closed	2 weeks in August, 2 weeks in September & Christmas.
Directions	From Calais A26 to Reims; N51 to Épernay; follow for Châlons en Champagne then to Avize; head for Lycée Viticole, house opp. lycée.

Imogen & Didier Pierson Whitaker
Le Vieux Cèdre,
14 route d'Oger,
51190 Avize, Marne
Tel   +33 (0)3 26 57 77 04
Fax   +33 (0)3 26 57 97 97
Email   champagnepiersonwhitaker@club-internet.fr

Entry 58   Map 6

Champagne – Ardenne

La Madeleine

The quiet is so deep that the grandfather clock ticking inside – and the doves cooing in the trees outside – can seem deafening. A timeless feel wafts through the new house from that clock, the pretty, traditionally decorated bedrooms (sleigh beds and Louis Philippe furniture), the piano and a lovely old sideboard. Huguette and her husband, who runs the dairy farm, are generous hosts offering traditional unpretentious farmhouse hospitality; they take gîte guests, too. You can opt for champagne from their son-in-law's nearby vineyard, with a meal to match the quality of the wine and Huguette's welcome.

Price	€50.
Rooms	3: 2 doubles, 1 triple.
Meals	Dinner with wine, €23; with champagne €32.
Closed	Rarely.
Directions	From Châlons en Champagne D933 to Bergères (29km); right D9 through Vertus; left, follow signs to La Madeleine 3km (between Vertus & Sellieres).

Huguette Charageat
La Madeleine,
51130 Vertus, Marne
Tel   +33 (0)3 26 52 11 29
Fax   +33 (0)3 26 59 22 09
Email   charageat.la.madeleine@wanadoo.fr

Entry 59   Map 6

Champagne – Ardenne

Ferme de Bannay

Bannay bustles with hens, ducks, guinea fowl, turkeys, donkey, sheep, cows, goats… the chatter starts at 6am. Children love this once-dairy farm, and its higgledy-piggledy buildings; school groups come to visit. The deep-country house brims with beams, bedrooms are dressed in white and ivory tones, with quilted bedcovers and scatter cushions, artificial flowers fill many a nook and cranny and one bathroom is behind a curtain. Little English is spoken but the welcome is so endearing, the generosity so genuine, the food so delicious, that communication is easy. Superb outings in the area for all.

Price	€52–€64.
Rooms	3: 1 triple, 1 quadruple, 1 suite for 2-3 & kitchen.
Meals	Dinner with wine, €30; with champagne €38.
Closed	Rarely.
Directions	From Épernay D51 for Sézanne; at Baye, just before church, right D343; at Bannay right; farm before small bridge (30 mins from Épernay).

Muguette & Jean-Pierre Curfs
Ferme de Bannay,
1 rue du Petit Moulin,
51270 Bannay, Marne

Tel	+33 (0)3 26 52 80 49
Fax	+33 (0)3 26 59 47 78
Email	mjpcurfs@aliceadsl.fr

🚶 🐓 (Hello) 🐕 🐎 🚜

Entry 60 Map 5

Champagne – Ardenne

Ferme de Désiré

A quietly talkative, personable couple with baby and big gentle dog welcome you to this majestic 17th-century farm. Through the huge arch is a gravelled courtyard enclosed by immaculate outbuildings and farmhouse; potted palms add an exotic touch. In the converted stables, guests have a living room with original mangers, log fire and kitchenette, then steep stairs up to two simply decorated, carpeted, roof-lit rooms. Dine round the convivial table flanked by carved armoires on free-range chicken in champagne and home-grown vegetables. Farmland reaches as far as the eye can see. *Minimum stay 2 nights bank holiday weekends.*

Price	€55–€65.
Rooms	3: 2 doubles, 1 twin.
Meals	Dinner with wine, €30.
Closed	Rarely.
Directions	From Calais A26 to St Quentin; D1 to Montmirail; D373 for Sézanne, 7km. On leaving Le Gault left at silo; sign.

Anne & David Chéré-Boutour
Ferme de Désiré,
51210 Le Gault Soigny, Marne

Tel	+33 (0)3 26 81 60 09
Fax	+33 (0)3 26 81 60 09
Email	domaine_de_desire@yahoo.fr
Web	www.ferme-desire.com

🚶 🐓 ✗ (Hello) 🐕 🐎 🚜 ♻

Entry 61 Map 5

Auprès de l'Église

New Zealanders Michael and Glenis do excellent table d'hôtes and delight in sharing their restored 19th-century house full of surprises: some walls are unadorned but for the mason's scribbles. The upstairs suite is separated by a fabulous wall of bookcases and an attic stair, the ground floor has a French country feel, one more suite leads off the hall, and communal areas all merge into one airy space overlooking the courtyard and Oyes church. Quirky brocante abounds yet the comforts are resolutely modern. Charming Sézanne is a 20-minute drive and the marshlands are rich with birds. *Sawday self-catering also.*

Price	€70–€100.
Rooms	2 suites for 2-4.
Meals	Dinner with champagne, €25–€30.
Closed	Rarely.
Directions	From A26 exit 26 Reims; D951 through Épernay for Sézanne; 10km after Champaubert left at Soizy aux Bois to Oyes; house next to church, big double gates.

Glenis Foster
Auprès de l'Église,
2 rue de l'Église,
51120 Oyes, Marne

Tel	+44 (0)7808 905 233
Email	enquiries@aupresdeleglise.com
Web	www.champagnevilla.com

Entry 62   Map 5

5 rue St Bernard

Natural, unsophisticated country folk in the back of beyond. Madame fun and an excellent cook (lots of organic and farm-grown ingredients), Monsieur a whizz on local history, both proud of their country heritage, deeply committed to 'real B&B'. In a sleepy village, they chose this roadside house to retire to, did the guest rooms in happy colours that perfectly set off the mix of old and new furniture on lino floors, fitted lovely linen, good mattresses, clean-cut bathrooms. Two rooms have their own entrance, the third is upstairs in their 'wing'; the garden is a perfect place for boisterous children.

Price	€40–€44.
Rooms	3: 1 double, 1 quadruple, 1 suite for 4.
Meals	Dinner with wine, €17, November–March only. Restaurant 9km.
Closed	Christmas & 1 January.
Directions	From A4 exit Ste Menehould D982 (382 on some maps) to Givry en Argonne; left D54 to Les Charmontois (9km).

M & Mme Patizel
5 rue St Bernard,
51330 Les Charmontois, Marne

Tel	+33 (0)3 26 60 39 53
Fax	+33 (0)3 26 60 39 53
Email	nicole.patizel@wanadoo.fr
Web	www.chez.com/patizel

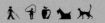

Entry 63   Map 6

Champagne – Ardenne

Les Épeires

This was the family's summer house for two centuries and has been their main house for one: Madame will show you the family books, lovely old furniture and mementos and tell you the stories (of Louis XIV's envoy to Peter the Great who was an ancestor…) in incredibly fast French. She does her own bookbinding, adores her rose garden, a jungle of perfume and petals, and has a couple of horses in the paddock; there are racehorses elsewhere. A blithe and extrovert soul, she serves memorable French dinners before a log fire and offers you a simple bedroom as country-cosy as the old house.

Price	€50. €65 for 3.
Rooms	1 triple.
Meals	Dinner with wine, €25; with champagne €37.
Closed	Rarely.
Directions	From Calais A26 dir. Reins exit 21 Brienne le Château for Soulaines, through La Chaise; right dir. Fuligny.

Nicole Georges-Fougerolle
Les Épeires,
17 rue des Écuyers,
10200 Fuligny, Aube
Tel   +33 (0)3 25 92 77 11
Fax   +33 (0)3 25 92 77 11

Entry 64   Map 6

Champagne – Ardenne

Domaine du Moulin d'Eguebaude

A delightful mill – and trout farm. The secluded old buildings in the lush riverside setting are home to a fish restaurant, several guest rooms and 50 tons of live fish. Delicious breakfast and dinner are shared with your enthusiastic hosts, who started the business 40 years ago; groups come for speciality lunches, anglers come to fish. Bedrooms under the eaves are compact, small-windowed, simply furnished, decorated in rustic or granny style, the larger annexe rooms are more motel-ish. Lots of space for children, and good English spoken. More guest house than B&B.

Price	€60-€73.
Rooms	6: 2 doubles, 1 twin, 1 triple, 2 family rooms.
Meals	Dinner with wine, €23.
Closed	Christmas, New Year & occasionally.
Directions	From Paris A5 exit 19 on N60 to Estissac; right on to Rue Pierre Brossolette; mill at end of lane, 1km.

Alexandre & Sandrine Mesley
Domaine du Moulin d'Eguebaude,
36 rue Pierre Brossdette,
10190 Estissac, Aube
Tel   +33 (0)3 25 40 42 18
Fax   +33 (0)3 25 40 40 92
Email   eguebaude@aol.com

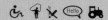

Entry 65   Map 5

Champagne – Ardenne

Domaine de Boulancourt

This large and splendid farmhouse is irresistible. For fishermen there's a river, for birdwatchers a fine park full of wildlife (come for the cranes in spring or autumn); for architecture buffs, the half-timbered churches are among the "100 most beautiful attractions in France". Bedrooms are comfortable and attractive; afternoon tea is served by the piano in the elegant panelled salon; dinner, possibly home-raised boar, duck or carp, is eaten at one or several tables but not with your delightful hosts who live in another wing and prefer to concentrate on their good home cooking.

Price	€65-€75. Suite €75. Singles €60-€70.
Rooms	5: 2 doubles, 2 twins, 1 suite.
Meals	Dinner with wine, €25.
Closed	December to mid-March.
Directions	Troyes D960 to Brienne; D400 for St Dizier; at Louze D182 left to Longeville; D174 for Boulancourt; house on left at 1st x-roads, sign 'Le Désert' just before Boulancourt.

Philippe & Christine Viel-Cazal
Domaine de Boulancourt,
Le Désert,
52220 Longeville sur la Laines,
Haute-Marne

Tel	+33 (0)3 25 04 60 18
Fax	+33 (0)3 25 04 60 18
Email	dom.boulancourt@wanadoo.fr

Entry 66   Map 6

Champagne – Ardenne

Massin Perrette

While restoring the old house, the Poopes were enchanted to 'meet' the former owners in the shape of old photographs in the attic: they inspired the décor of the classically ruffled, satiny French bedrooms. Évelyne and Michel adore doing B&B, are lovely, natural hosts and do all they can to make you feel at home. Breakfast, at separate tables, is deeply local: yogurt from the farm, honey from the village and Évelyne's jam; dinner, always an unusual menu, in the pastel-panelled dining room is superb value. Michel is chief cook, lawn-mower and hedge-cutter; the garden, too, is impeccably tended.

Price	€53-€68.
Rooms	5: 1 double, 1 twin, 2 triples, 1 suite for 4.
Meals	Dinner with wine, €18. Light supper with wine, €6.
Closed	Rarely.
Directions	From A31 exit 7 to north Langres; N19 for Vesoul for 40km. Right at Chambres d'Hôtes sign to Pressigny; just after pond on left.

Évelyne & Michel Poope
Massin Perrette,
24 rue Augustin Massin,
52500 Pressigny, Haute-Marne

Tel	+33 (0)3 25 88 80 50
Fax	+33 (0)3 25 88 80 49
Email	e.m.poope@wanadoo.fr
Web	www.massin-perrette.com

Entry 67   Map 6

Champagne – Ardenne

La Montgonière

Knee-high wainscotting, opulent fabric, hand-painted wallpaper discovered in the attic: some of the treats in store at this village mansion built in 1673. The first owner was seen off during the Revolution and the house was later sold to the family of the current one: smiling, self-assured Madame who swapped law for B&B and has no regrets. Book-lined walls and elegant fauteuils encourage cogitation under the eaves, French windows open to a delightful walled garden and the passageways are lined with oriental rugs. Refined living with a relaxed mood and Élisabeth an accomplished cook. Readers love this place.

Price	€90-€130.
Rooms	3: 2 doubles, 1 suite for 3-4.
Meals	Dinner with wine, €25.
Closed	Never.
Directions	From Reims D980; D947 for Luxembourg; Harricourt is 18km after Vouziers, 2km before Buzancy.

Élisabeth Regnault de Montgon
La Montgonière,
1 rue St Georges,
08240 Harricourt, Ardennes

Tel	+33 (0)3 24 71 66 50
Fax	+33 (0)3 24 71 66 50
Email	regnault.montgon@wanadoo.fr
Web	www.lamontgoniere.net

Entry 68   Map 6

Art

Courses in art, pottery and sculpture available.

Lorraine • Alsase • Franche Comté

Lorraine

Villa Les Roses

Monsieur's seemingly endless restoration of these venerable buildings – one house is 400, the other 300 years old – is finished, and very nicely too: fine woodwork, stylish furniture, an intriguing gas chandelier in the dining room, elegant terraces and superb grounds with a children's play area. Madame is charmingly lively; her attractive rooms (dark and cool after a long hot day in the car) have goodnight chocolates, kettle kits, smallish shower rooms and lots of religion on view – bedside Bibles are French Catholic, not American Gideon. Breakfasts are excellent.

Price	€55-€80.
Rooms	4: 2 doubles, 1 twin, 1 family room.
Meals	Restaurants 300m.
Closed	Never.
Directions	From A4 exit Ste Menehould; N3 for Verdun-Chalons; sign in La Vignette, hamlet before Les Islettes; 1st building on left.

Mme Christiaens
Villa Les Roses,
La Vignette, Les Islettes,
55120 Clermont en Argonne, Meuse
Tel   +33 (0)3 26 60 81 91
Fax   +33 (0)3 26 60 23 09
Email   gites-christiaens@wanadoo.fr

Entry 69   Map 6

Lorraine

Château de Jaulny

Great for young knights and ladies – the fortified castle on its rocky hilltop comes with dungeon and keep. Anna was brought up here and knows all the history, Hugues helps restore, and invites schools for archery and courses in medieval life. Portraits of Joan of Arc were discovered beneath wattle and whitewash during the French Revolution…Today the noble swathe of stone stair is embellished with a wrought-iron banister, spacious bedrooms are decorated in 19th-century style (including a new room for families) and generous meals are served before a great fireplace. Bring jumpers in winter!

Price	€60-€105.
Rooms	4: 3 doubles, 1 family room for 4.
Meals	Dinner with wine, €32.
Closed	Never.
Directions	A4 exit 32 Fresne en Woëvre for Pont à Mousson; Thiaucourt; Jaulny.

Anna Collignon & Hugues Drion
Château de Jaulny,
4 rue du Château, 54470 Jaulny,
Meurthe-et-Moselle
Tel   +33 (0)3 83 81 93 04
Email   jaulnychateau@free.fr
Web   chateaudejaulny.free.fr

Entry 70   Map 6

Lorraine

51 rue Lorraine

Alina came from Poland with a bundle of talents; a professional gardener, she paints, embroiders, decorates. Gérard, a retired French architect, has won a prize for his brilliant conversion of this dear little 200-year-old house. Their skills and taste for contemporary and ethnic styles shine through the house, their thoughtful, artistic personalities enliven the dinner table, their environmentalist passion informs their lives. Expect gorgeous vegetarian food if you ask for it; delicious meaty things too. No sitting room but comfortable, simple, spotless bedrooms, and a lovely garden and patio for summer.

Ethical Collection: Food.
See page 432.

Price	€57-€60.
Rooms	2: 1 double, 1 triple.
Meals	Dinner with wine, €19-€23.
Closed	Rarely.
Directions	From Metz D3 NE for Bouzonville approx. 21km; right on D53a to Burtoncourt; On left in main street.

Alina & Gérard Cahen
51 rue Lorraine,
57220 Burtoncourt, Moselle
Tel   +33 (0)3 87 35 72 65
Fax   +33 (0)3 87 35 72 65
Email   ag.cahen@wanadoo.fr
Web   www.maisonlorraine.com

Entry 71   Map 7

Lorraine

Château d'Alteville

A solidly reassuring family château in a peaceful, privileged setting: wake to a chorus of birds. Bedrooms are *vieille France*; not large (bar one, special for its view onto fantastic old trees) but with the patina of long history. Bathrooms are functional but adequate. The real style is in the utterly French, many-chaired salon and the dining room — reached through halls and hunting trophies, past library and billiards — with a huge table where dinners are enjoyed by candlelight in the company of your charming hosts. Madame, the soul of the house, cooks with skill and fills the place with flowers.

Price	€68-€91.
Rooms	5: 4 doubles, 1 twin.
Meals	Dinner €31-€38.50. Wine €10.
Closed	Mid-October to mid-April.
Directions	From Nancy N74 for Sarreguemines & Château Salins. At Burthecourt x-roads D38 to Dieuze; D999 south 5km; left on D199F; right D199G to château.

David & Agnieszka Barthélémy
Château d'Alteville,
Tarquimpol,
57260 Dieuze, Moselle
Tel   +33 (0)3 87 05 46 63
Fax   +33 (0)3 87 05 46 64
Email   chateau.alteville@caramail.com

Entry 72   Map 7

Alsace

86 rue du Général de Gaulle

A real old Alsatian farmhouse in the wine-growing area where you can be in a bustling village street one minute and your own peaceful little world the next. It is on a busy main road but the bedrooms, in the separate guest wing, are at the back. Their simplicity is reflected in the price. Your hosts retired from milk and wine production in order to have more time for guests; Marie-Claire still teaches German, Paul serves breakfast in the garden or in the dining room — and makes eau de vie. A useful place to know at the start of the Route des Vins, and very close to gorgeous, glamorous Strasbourg.

Price	€36-€39.
Rooms	3 doubles.
Meals	Restaurant 200m.
Closed	Rarely.
Directions	From Saverne A4 exit 45 onto N404 & D1004 for Strasbourg, 16km. In middle of Marlenheim on right, before post office.

Paul & Marie-Claire Goetz
86 rue du Général de Gaulle,
67520 Marlenheim, Bas-Rhin

Tel	+33 (0)3 88 87 52 94
Email	goetz.paul@wanadoo.fr

Entry 73   Map 7

Alsace

Maison Fleurie

Bubbling, friendly and generous, Doris has been receiving guests for years: she learnt the art at her mother's knee and will greet you with the warmest welcome. Her peaceful chalet in a residential neighbourhood is a real home, surrounded by breathtaking mountain views. Both she and her husband are upholsterers so furnishings in the neat, traditional bedrooms are perfect, strong colours giving depth to modernity. Guests have their own quarters, with a log fire in the breakfast room, tables laden with goodies in the morning — try the homemade organic fruit jams and Alsace cake — and geraniums cascading. Great value.

Price	€56-€63.
Rooms	3: 2 doubles, 1 twin.
Meals	Restaurants nearby.
Closed	Rarely.
Directions	From Colmar A35 & N83 Sélestat (exit 17); N59 & D424 to Villé; D697 to Dieffenbach au Val. Careful: ask for exact address as two other Engels do B&B!

Doris Engel-Geiger
Maison Fleurie,
19 route de Neuve Église,
Dieffenbach au Val,
67220 Villé, Bas-Rhin

Tel/Fax	+33 (0)3 88 85 60 48
Email	engel-thierry@wanadoo.fr
Web	www.lamaisonfleurie.com

Entry 74   Map 7

Alsace

34 rue Maréchal Foch

At the centre of a working vineyard in gorgeous old Dambach is a typical, geranium-hung Alsatian house built by the first Ruhlmann wine-grower in 1688. Wine buffs enjoy seeing the cellars and non-drinkers can taste the sweet water springing from the Vosges hills. The bedrooms, in the guest wing under the sloping roof, have new carpets and old family furniture, a couple of them with rather gloomy outlooks. There's no sitting room but a huge relic-filled guest dayroom: a wine press, a grape basket, a ceramic stove; no garden but a yard for watching the winery at work. Laurence speaks excellent English.

Price	€52.
Rooms	4 doubles.
Meals	Restaurants within walking distance.
Closed	Mid-September to mid-March.
Directions	From Sélestat north on D35, 8km. House in village centre, approx. equidistant between town gates on main road.

Jean-Charles & Laurence Ruhlmann
34 rue Maréchal Foch,
67650 Dambach la Ville,
Bas-Rhin
Tel +33 (0)3 88 92 41 86
Fax +33 (0)3 88 92 61 81
Email vins@ruhlmann-schutz.fr
Web www.ruhlmann-schutz.fr

Entry 75 Map 7

Alsace

La Haute Grange

On the side of a hill with views down the valley, this 19th-century farmhouse is surrounded by forests and wildflower meadows. Rural and spoiling all at once, it is a place for de-stressing… deeply comforting bedrooms and suites, subtle and spicy colours, spoiling bathrooms. A large sitting room with open fireplace has an honesty bar and hundreds of books; step onto the patio and enjoy the views. Margaret and Philippe will greet you warmly and can help plan your days: it is possible to walk to the village for plenty of restaurants but dinner here is good too – a taste of Alsace with local wines. *Sawday self-catering also.*

Price	€80–€110.
Rooms	4: 2 doubles, 2 suites.
Meals	Dinner with wine, €45.
Closed	Never.
Directions	From Colmar CD415 to St Dié; right after Kaysersberg to Fréland. Thro' village, right after garage to La Chaude Côte; cont. 1km; right for La Haute Grange.

Margaret & Philippe Kalk
La Haute Grange,
La Chaude Côte,
68240 Fréland, Haut-Rhin
Tel +33 (0)3 89 71 90 06
Email lahautegrange@aol.com
Web www.lahautegrange.fr

Entry 76 Map 7

Alsace

Domaine Thierhurst

Bénédicte and Jean-Jacques are so welcoming in their sturdily luxurious modern house: he, quiet and courteous, runs the farm; she, dynamic and initially a touch formidable, opens her soul — and all the doors of her house — to make you feel at home. She knows the delights of Alsace and nearby Germany intimately, concocts scrumptious authentic Alsatian food in the octagonal kitchen-diner and loves your amazement at the upstairs 'bathroom-extraordinaire' with its vast Italianate rain shower. Pale, Turkish-rugged suites have all contemporary comforts and the large young garden matures a little every day.

Price	€100.
Rooms	2: 1 double, 1 suite.
Meals	Dinner with wine, €45.
Closed	Never.
Directions	From A36 for Colmar, exit Neuf-Brisach. Through Hirtzfelden-Fessenheim; between Balgau & Heiteren, turn right. Follow Pèlerinage Notre-Dame de la Thierhurst.

Bénédicte & Jean-Jacques Kinny
Domaine Thierhurst,
68740 Nambsheim, Haut-Rhin
Tel   +33 (0)3 89 72 56 94
Fax   +33 (0)3 89 72 90 78
Email jean-jacques.kinny@wanadoo.fr
Web   www.kinny.fr

Entry 77   Map 7

Franche Comté

Champs Bayeux

Enter the cluttered, colourful conservatory, then the flamboyant dining room with warm ceramic stove and basking cat. Dressers heave with porcelain and silver, rustic walls with artwork — much of it Daniel's. He is enthusiastic, artistic, loquacious, Astride is gentle, ever on the go; both are endearing and kind. They lend you compasses, maps, bikes for trekking the foothills, even skis should snow abound; their new house is on the edge of the forest. Spacious bedrooms are attic-cosy and full of French flourishes, dinners are wonderfully convivial, and the garden leads out to deer and red squirrels.

Price	€69.
Rooms	3: 2 doubles, 1 family room for 4.
Meals	Dinner with wine, €25.
Closed	November, except weekends; 2 weeks in May.
Directions	From A36 exit 14 N83 for Mulhouse; in Les Errues left for Anjoutey & Étueffont; at r'bout right for Rougemont; left at 1st bend; house at end.

Astride & Daniel Elbert
Champs Bayeux,
10 rue de la Chapelle,
90170 Étueffont, Territoire de Belfort
Tel   +33 (0)3 84 54 68 63
Email champsbayeux@orange.fr
Web   pagesperso-orange.fr/chambres-tourisme

Entry 78   Map 7

Franche Comté

Le Château

As part of its vast 100m2 suite, this château has one of the most extra-ordinary bathrooms this side of the Saône: panels hung with old engravings, a (small) sunken bath and an Italian chandelier making an atmosphere of madly elegant luxury; bedroom and salon are just as amazing. All this and a family feel. Antiques, attention to detail, a charming hostess with an easy laugh, make it a very special place. Dinner, carefully chosen to suit guests' tastes (if you want snails, you'll have to ask), is exquisitely presented on Gien porcelain, on the terrace in summer. Untouched 18th-century living.

Price	€70.
Rooms	1 suite for 3.
Meals	Dinner with wine, €20.
Closed	September to mid-May.
Directions	From A36 exit 3 D67 to Gray 35km; entering Gray right D474; fork left D13 to Beaujeu & Motey sur Saône; left to Mercey; signed in village.

	Bernadette Jantet
	Le Château,
	70130 Mercey sur Saône,
	Haute-Saône
Tel	+33 (0)3 84 67 07 84

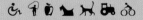

Entry 79   Map 6

Franche Comté

Les Egrignes

Refinement, loving care and high craftsmanship: you are welcomed to this exquisite house by a couple who have breathed new life into the lovely old stones and mouldings. Quiet Roland combs auctions for fine rugs, old mirrors, modern paintings, piano; bubbly Fabienne puts thick curtains, pretty desks, carved armoires and soft sofas in vast pale-walled bedrooms and deluxe bathrooms. He gardens passionately (the half-wheel potager is breathtaking), she cooks brilliantly. Remarkable hosts, interior designers of much flair, they are fun and excellent company. Elegant perfection. *Minimum stay 2 nights June-September.*

Price	€85.
Rooms	3: 1 twin/double, 2 suites for 2-4.
Meals	Dinner with wine, €27.50.
Closed	Rarely.
Directions	From Troyes A31 exit 6 Langres-Sud through Longeau; D67 through Gray for Besançon. Cult on right 21km after Gray; signed in village.

	Fabienne Lego-Deiber
	Les Egrignes,
	70150 Cult, Haute-Saône
Tel	+33 (0)3 84 31 92 06
Fax	+33 (0)3 84 31 92 06
Email	lesegrignes@wanadoo.fr
Web	les-egrignes.com

Entry 80   Map 6

Franche Comté

Rose Art

An endearingly courteous and generous couple live here with all the time in the world for you and a delightful art gallery in their vaulted basement: Madame embroiders but shows other artists' work and their son produces good organic wines and eaux de vie. It's a fairly average old wine merchant's house but the picturesque village, the rooms under the roof, the lovely view of orchards and meadows and the brook to sing you to sleep, after a fine meal with your adorable hosts, make it special. And there's a tempting garden with a playhouse for children, and a piano anyone may play – or golf down the road.

Ethical Collection: Environment; Food.
See page 432.

Price	From €50.
Rooms	2: 1 twin, 1 suite for 4-5.
Meals	Dinner €15. Wine €10-€12.
Closed	Rarely.
Directions	In Lons le Saunier for Chalon; right before SNCF station D117 for Macornay; D41 to Vernantois; left before houses & follow signs.

	Monique & Michel Ryon Rose Art, 8 rue Lacuzon, 39570 Vernantois, Jura
Tel	+33 (0)3 84 47 17 28
Fax	+33 (0)3 84 47 17 28
Email	rose.art@wanadoo.fr

Entry 81   Map 11

Burgundy

Burgundy

Le Prieuré Saint Agnan

The sunsets are special, the breakfasts are glorious with a choice of 15 teas and homemade compotes and jams. After a day scouting the best wineries, bets are on that you'll return to tea or apéritif on the garden terrace that looks over the Loire to the hills of Sancerre. This lovely 19th-century Benedictine priory is attached to the church (bells stop at 10pm) Run by sincerely friendly, unpretentious owners, it is a perfect place for those who like to wander into town and stroll home after dinner. Bedrooms are warmly immaculate, some overlooking the river; the luscious honeymoon quarters have their own terrace.

Price	€80–€120.
Rooms	5: 4 doubles, 1 twin/double.
Meals	Restaurants within walking distance.
Closed	Rarely.
Directions	From Sancerre D955. Gate next to St Agnan church.

Christine Grillères
Le Prieuré Saint Agnan,
Impasse du Prieuré,
Place Saint Agnan,
58200 Cosne sur Loire, Nièvre
Tel   +33 (0)6 99 03 07 75
Email   prieure.saint.agnan@orange.fr
Web   prieuresaintagnan.blogspot.com

Entry 82   Map 5

Burgundy

La Villa des Prés

Deep in real peace-wrapped country, this place of secluded old-style comfort and breathtaking views of the Morvan has new and rightly enthusiastic Dutch owners: it's gorgeous. Inside are open fires, antique beds, sympathetic period decorations, antique linen and super modern showers. Rooms are vast and there are two salons, one gloriously golden green, for lazing about. A baronial double stair leads down to the fine garden and the ha-ha where, rather endearingly, chickens may be roaming and Cannelle, the lab, keeps guard. A base for church, château and vineyard visits, and a child's paradise. *Minimum stay 3 nights.*

Price	€85–€105.
Rooms	5 twins/doubles.
Meals	Complimentary dinner for 7-night stays (Sat only). Restaurant in village, 300m. Guest kitchen.
Closed	October–March.
Directions	From Nevers, D977 to Prémery. D977 bis for Corbigny; St Reverien 15km; signed.

Kees & Inge Stapel
La Villa des Prés,
Route de Corbigny,
58420 St Reverien, Nièvre
Tel   +33 (0)3 86 29 03 81
Email   villa-des-pres@orange.fr
Web   www.villa-des-pres.com

Entry 83   Map 5

Burgundy

Domaine des Perrières

Make the most of seasonal farm produce and traditional French food: the visitors' book is plump with praise. Madame the farmer's wife loves cooking (delectable pastries and jams) and making you feel at home. Wheat fields wave to the horizon, farm and cows are next door, this is 360 hectares of deepest France. Inside, simple, straightforward rooms, green friezed walls, a bathroom in blue; all is airy and light, cheerful and double-glazed. No sitting room to share but after a day on horses or bikes (the cross-country trails are inspiring) and a long, leisurely supper, most guests retire gratefully to bed.

Ethical Collection: Environment; Food.
See page 432.

Price	€40–€75.
Rooms	2: 1 twin, 1 family room.
Meals	Dinner with wine, €25.
Closed	Rarely.
Directions	From Brinon/Beuvron D34 or Premery D977b. Between Crux la Ville and St Reverien, follow D34. Signed.

Pascale Cointe
Domaine des Perrières,
58330 Crux-La-Ville, Nièvre
Tel   +33 (0)3 86 58 34 93
Fax   +33 (0)3 86 58 26 00
Email pbcointe58@orange.fr
Web   perso.wanadoo.fr/domainedesperrieres

Entry 84   Map 10

Burgundy

Château de Vaulx

Vaulx was described in 1886 as "well-proportioned and elegant in its simplicity". It is as lovely now and in the most beautiful position, high on a hill, with views that stretch to distant mountains. Delightful Marty will escort you to the west wing then create a delicious dinner. Expect a fully panelled drawing room with chandeliers, a huge dining room with fresh flowers, and manicured lawns and box balls tightly topiaried — stroll down the romantic avenues in dappled sunlight. In the village, a 13th-century bell tower; nearby, one of the best chocolate makers in France (monthly tastings and lessons).

Price	€100–€115. Suites €139. Apt €190.
Rooms	4 + 1: 2 doubles, 2 family suites for 4. 1 apartment for 5.
Meals	Dinner €30. Wine €17. Restaurant 3km.
Closed	Rarely.
Directions	From Charolles, D985 for Clayette 8km. 1km after crossing railway, 2nd road signed Vaulx. Up to top of hill, right at junc. Bell on iron gate.

Marty Freriksen
Château de Vaulx,
71800 Saint Julien de Civry,
Saône-et-Loire
Tel   +33 (0)3 85 70 64 03
Fax   +33 (0)3 85 70 64 03
Email marty@chateaudevaulx.com
Web   www.chateaudevaulx.com

Entry 85   Map 11

Burgundy

Le Tinailler d'Aléane

The lovely stones and cascading geraniums outside, the silk flowers, frilly lampshades and polished furniture inside have an old-world charm. The breakfast room is cosily stuffed with bric-a-brac, bedrooms are family-simple. Madame was a florist: she arranges her rooms as if they were bouquets, is always refreshing them and might put a paper heart on your pillow wishing you *bonne nuit*. She doesn't refuse children but may well be happier if you arrive with a little dog under your arm. She or her husband can do winery visits for non-French speakers. Ask for the larger room; the smaller feels cramped.

Price	€50.
Rooms	2 doubles.
Meals	Restaurants 3–5km.
Closed	Sundays in winter.
Directions	A6-N79 Cluny Charolles exit La Roche Vineuse. At junc. right to Charnay D17; on for 500m; left at r'bout for Sommeré; at village square, up hill follow EH signs, house at top on left, bell by gate.

Éliane Heinen
Le Tinailler d'Aléane,
Sommeré,
71960 La Roche Vineuse,
Saône-et-Loire
Tel +33 (0)3 85 37 80 68
Fax +33 (0)3 85 37 80 68

Entry 86   Map 11

Burgundy

Château des Pommiers

You don't often trek into deepest Burgundy and wash up at a groovy restaurant run by a couple of Brits. Steve and Vivienne have had many lives and are now a pair of imaginative cooks. He is a musician (a piano sits in the salon) and a biker, she dabbles in homeopathy and knows a thing or two about good bedding and a warm welcome; Vivienne can 'work a room', making sure they have all chosen their activities for the day – walking trails are her speciality. You can of course hunker down with a good book in the Wendy House and gaze over the rolling hills in the distance. Bedrooms are fresh, comfortable and big.

Price	From €95.
Rooms	6: 5 doubles, 1 suite for 3.
Meals	Dinner, 2 courses, from €29.50. Wine from €19.
Closed	October-March.
Directions	A6 exit 28 for Charbonnières 0.5km; left to Blany 2km; at next T-junc. right thro' Laizé, St Maurice de S. to Azé. Left D85 for Igé; thro' Chussin; cont. 1km; 1st house in Martoret on left, after sign.

Steve & Vivienne Taylor
Château des Pommiers,
Le Martoret, 71960 Igé,
Saône-et-Loire
Tel +33 (0)3 85 33 41 46
Fax +33 (0)3 85 33 35 18
Email burgundyxp@wanadoo.fr
Web www.burgundyxp.com

Entry 87   Map 11

Burgundy

Château de Nobles

Oceans of history behind it (a prehistoric *menhir* stands in the grounds) and owners bursting with more restoration ideas and passionate about it. Monsieur cultivates the vines and the wine: wine production started here in the 10th century. The bedrooms, in a renovated building near the main, dreamlike, 13th-15th-century château, are fresh and unfussy in the stylish way so many are in France – the bigger one is a gem, with its superb beams, vast mezzanine, little veranda, huge new bath. Breakfast is in the château, a delightfully lived-in listed monument. Irresistible.

Price	€85.
Rooms	3: 1 double, 1 triple, 1 family room.
Meals	Restaurants within 7km.
Closed	November-March.
Directions	From Tournus D14 for Cormatin. Passing Brancion on right continue on main road for 1.5km. Towers opposite on bend.

Bertrand & Françoise de Cherisey
Château de Nobles,
71700 La Chapelle sous Brancion,
Saône-et-Loire

Tel	+33 (0)3 85 51 00 55
Email	b.de.cherisey@orange.fr

Entry 88   Map 11

Burgundy

La Ferme

Children may be able to watch the goats being milked in the clean, enclosed farmyard, and help if they (and the nannies) like. There are horses too. Your hard-working hosts, with three children of their own and sensitive to the needs of families, have made a two-bedroomed family suite at the top of the old stone farmhouse. Bathrobes are provided for grown-ups, so everyone feels cared for. All is sparkling and charmingly simple. People return, not only for the relaxing experience but also to stock up on the homemade cheeses, mouthwatering jams and local wines that the family make and sell.

Price	€63-€72.
Rooms	4: 2 twins, 2 family suites & kitchen.
Meals	Restaurant nearby.
Closed	Rarely.
Directions	From Tournus D14 for Cluny. At Chapaize, D314 to Bissy sous Uxelles; house next to church.

Pascale & Dominique de La Bussière
La Ferme,
71460 Bissy sous Uxelles,
Saône-et-Loire

Tel	+33 (0)3 85 50 15 03
Fax	+33 (0)3 85 50 15 03
Email	dominique.de-la-bussiere@wanadoo.fr
Web	www.bourgogne-chambres-hotes.fr

Entry 89   Map 11

Burgundy

Château de Messey

An impressive bull shares the buttercup meadows with this 16th-century wine château on the *Route des Vins*. Wandering woodland paths, ducks on the river... it has the dreamiest setting. Most of the bedrooms are in the rambling rustic vine-workers' cottages built around a grassed courtyard. The pricier ones, graced with high ceilings, are in the serene château – and a superior elegance reigns in the salon. Young Delphine and Markus, who have taken over from her parents, live in one of the cottages and manage rooms at both venues with charming efficiency. A most welcoming, if sometimes busy, place.

Burgundy

Le Crot Foulot

Gutsy Jan and Annie sold their prize-winning restaurant in Brussels and filled their cellar while putting the finishing touches to this handsome wine-grower's house. Golden stones outside, a clean minimalism inside: Belgians always pull this off with flair. An elegant glass and wood staircase leads to muted bedrooms with delicate pale timbers revealed and glorified. In the open kitchen you can watch Jan whip up his mussel mousse while a farmyard chicken sizzles with citrus fruits in the oven. Annie will have brought up the perfect nectar for the menu. All is well in Burgundy tonight! *Children over 8 welcome.*

Price	Château €115–€120. Vine workers' rooms €90–€130. Cottages €250–€660 per week.
Rooms	7 + 4: 2 doubles, 2 twins, 2 twin/doubles, 1 triple. 4 cottages for 2-6.
Meals	Dinner €30. Wine €7–€10. Restaurant 2km.
Closed	Occasionally.
Directions	A6 exit Tournus; in centre right on D14. Château on left of D14 between Ozenay & Martailly, 9km from Tournus.

	Delphine & Markus Schaefer
	Château de Messey,
	71700 Ozenay,
	Saône-et-Loire
Tel	+33 (0)3 85 51 16 11
Fax	+33 (0)3 85 51 33 82
Email	chateau@demessey.com
Web	www.demessey.com

Price	€89–€108. Apartment €180.
Rooms	5 + 1: 1 twin, 3 twins/doubles, 1 family room for 3. Apartment for 2-4 with kichenette.
Meals	Dinner €33. Wine from €15.
Closed	Never.
Directions	A6 exit 27 Tournus, N6 for Sennecey & Chalon for 4km, left for Jugy D182. Thro' village, house on right. Look for big roofs with roof windows.

	Annie Coeckelberghs & Jan Hostens
	Le Crot Foulot,
	71240 Jugy,
	Saône-et-Loire
Tel	+33 (0)3 85 94 81 07
Email	crotfoulot@orange.fr
Web	crotfoulot.com

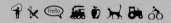

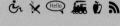

Burgundy

Abbaye de la Ferté

A privileged spot within a handsome estate. The abbot's palace is all that's left of the former abbey – glimpse the oversized staircase on your way to convivial breakfasts in the intimate, very fine dining room. Guests stay in the peaceful, spacious dovecot by the road, its stunning pigeon-nest bathroom in the loft, or in the equally immaculate gatehouse, its inner stone walls impeccably restored, its tub armchairs dressed in deep pink. There are log fires and and tea trays, art books and a bottle of local wine. It's a five-minute walk to breakfast where your young hosts make it all pleasingly eccentric and fun. *Sawday self-catering also.*

Burgundy

Manoir du Clos de Vauvry

A ceramic stove as big as two men dominates the breakfast room of this charming 17th-century royal hunting lodge. Summer breakfasts are on the terrace. The whole place has an air of exaggeration: over-generous stairs, ingenious double windows, voluptuous ceilings, all totally French with floral wallpapers and embroidered bedcovers in magnificent bedrooms, 1930s tiled bathrooms (one whirlpool) and immaculate linen. This adorable couple knows everyone in wine growing and Marie helps you all she can over another cigarette. Burgundy has so much to offer, as well as superb wines… wonderful.

Price	€70-€110.
Rooms	2 suites: 1 for 2-4, 1 for 4.
Meals	Dinner with wine, €25.
Closed	Rarely.
Directions	From A6 exit Chalon south, N6 for Varrennes le Grand; D6 for Le Lac de Laives to La Ferté; at x-roads signed La Ferté, press intercom at large iron gates.

Price	€70-€76. Suites €130-€140.
Rooms	3: 1 twin, 2 suites: 1 for 4, 1 for 5.
Meals	Dinner with wine, €26.
Closed	Rarely.
Directions	From Chalon Sud, N80 for Montceau les Mines 9km; D981 exit Givry; follow Complexe Sportif signs, Rue de Sauges; 2nd on left.

Jacques & Virginie Thenard
Abbaye de la Ferté,
71240 St Ambreuil,
Saône-et-Loire
Mobile +33 (0)6 22 91 40 11
Email abbayedelaferte@aol.com
Web www.abbayeferte.com

Marie & Daniel Lacroix-Mollaret
Manoir du Clos de Vauvry,
3 rue des Faussillons, 71640
Givry Sauges, Saône-et-Loire
Tel +33 (0)3 85 44 40 83
Fax +33 (0)3 85 44 40 83
Email daniel.mollaret@wanadoo.fr
Web www.clos-de-vauvry.com

Entry 92 Map 11

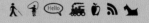

Entry 93 Map 11

Burgundy

Clos Belloy

The two Dominques love their manor and nothing is too much trouble for them. A timeless charm breathes from the stone of the enclosed courtyard and house with its delicate Burgundian double staircase. Count them: seven shades of pale green dress the walls in the salon, while hand-painted doors and ceilings delight in curlicues of sky blue and rose-bud. Meticulous bedrooms, a scattering of antiques, French windows, gourmet breakfasts, lavender, roses and hydrangea in the garden... it's all very 18th century, airy, refined and light. Don't miss the local Rully wine, be it white chardonnay or red pinot noir.

Price	€100-€115.
Rooms	4: 1 double, 1 family room for 3, 2 suites for 2-4.
Meals	Restaurant 300m.
Closed	Rarely.
Directions	From A6 exit 24.1 Beaune & Chagny for Chagny then Rully on D981; signed.

Dominique & Dominique Belloy
Clos Belloy,
12 Grand Rue, 71150 Rully,
Saône-et-Loire

Tel	+33 (0)3 85 87 11 38
Email	closbelloy@yahoo.fr
Web	www.closbelloy.fr

Entry 94   Map 11

Burgundy

La Messalière

Done a while ago with passion and panache, the variegated, old-fashioned bedrooms – mock medieval, Provençal, Jouy-romantic – in the venerable and slightly crumbling wine-grower's house are part of a full French experience. Your hostess, a friendly outgoing person who loves to chat with guests, used to have a dress shop and looks the part. The old wedding-gowned models in some bedrooms and changing-room doors in the smallish worn bathrooms (one is low if you're tall) were part of this past life. She does it all herself and you will be intrigued by curios in the heavily-draped salon. *Minimum stay 2 nights.*

Price	€65-€110. Extra person €20.
Rooms	4: 3 doubles, 1 suite for 2.
Meals	Dinner with wine, €30. Restaurants in village.
Closed	November-March.
Directions	From A6 for Autun exit Chalon N; at St Léger sur Dheune; 1st right in centre of village for Santenay & Chagny.

Mireille Marquet
La Messalière,
29 rue du 8 mai 1945, 71510
St Léger sur Dheune, Saône-et-Loire

Tel	+33 (0)3 85 45 35 75
Fax	+33 (0)3 85 45 40 96
Email	reservations@saintlegersurdheune.com
Web	www.lamessaliere.com

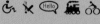

Entry 95   Map 11

Burgundy

Le Clos des Saunières

A mile from the road to beautiful Beaune is this handsome old wine-grower's house and upmarket B&B. Five guest rooms have been installed in the sturdy towered wing, with modern tiled floors and immaculate walls, decorative beds and perfect linen. Bathrooms are irreproachable. Your extremely well-travelled hosts give a professional welcome and love dining with guests; Bruno, recently retired from the hotel world, is a terrific chef. And there's a guest sitting room with two black leather armchairs to retire to. Wine-tasting jaunts by horse-drawn carriage across the vineyards are planned – great fun.

Price	€120-€180.
Rooms	5: 1 twin, 2 family rooms for 3, 2 suites for 4.
Meals	Dinner with wine, €35.
Closed	December-February.
Directions	A6 exit 24-1 Hospices de Beaune; left 1st r'bout for Chalon, Autin; over 2nd r'bout, left at 3rd for Bligny les B; before r'way bridge, small road on right; right at end. After 50m, left at x-roads; 1st house on right.

Fabienne & Bruno Guillemin
Le Clos des Saunières,
Hameau de Curtil, 2 rue de la Cardine,
21200 Bligny les Beaune, Côte-d'Or
Tel   +33 (0)3 80 22 38 89
Fax   +33 (0)3 80 24 79 37
Email   bruno@bed-and-breakfast-beaune.com
Web   www.bed-and-breakfast-beaune.com

Entry 96   Map 11

Burgundy

14 avenue Charles Jaffelin

If your French is imperfect but you fancy becoming fluent in the lore of Burgundy – the region and its wine – this is the place for you. Indeed, Jonathan and Susie have worked in practically every wine-growing region of France over the past 20 years. Just outside the ramparts of the old town, peeping over high walls, the house has two creeper-clad wings joined by a tower. Once inside, guests have their own door up to super bedrooms on two floors and wcs in a tower. The walled garden behind has a child-safe pool, and you will be welcomed on arrival with a glass (or two) of something local. Cosy, friendly, relaxing.

Price	€120.
Rooms	2: 1 double, 1 suite for 2-4.
Meals	Restaurants within walking distance.
Closed	Rarely.
Directions	On one-way road round ramparts of Beaune, exit for Auxerre (RN, not m'way); house on right after 200m, big white gates.

Susie Lyddon
14 avenue Charles Jaffelin,
Route de Bouze,
21200 Beaune, Côte-d'Or
Tel   +32 (0)2 647 38 93 (Belgium)
Email   lyddon@skynet.be
Web   www.routedebouze.com

Entry 97   Map 11

Burgundy

Les Planchottes

If you find yourself in the Mecca of Wine, surely you should stay with a family of winegrowers like the Bouchards? – and sip your aperitif in the courtyard looking out over their organic vineyards. They are charming people, passionate about food, wine and matters 'green'; Cécile's breakfasts linger long in the memory. The townhouse – once three cottages – is immaculate inside. The craftsmanship of new oak and stone, the quiet good taste of the colours, the space in the comfortable bedrooms, the sparkling lights in the bathrooms – they beat most three-star hotels into a cocked hat. The garden is a hidden gem.

Burgundy

Sous le Baldaquin

Once Yves, the perfect host, swings open the huge doors of his townhouse in the heart of buzzing Beaune, the 21st century disappears, the serene garden tugs at your soul and peace descends. Play the count, countess or courtesan as you mount the stone staircase to your small, perfect cocoon, past walls and ceiling painted in a pale trompe l'œil allegory. Gracious and elegant are the aubergine and willow-green taffeta drapes and beribboned baldaquin, thoughtful is the violet cordial in an antique flask, seductive are the bathroom's crystal and seashell chandeliers. To call this romantic is an understatement.

Price	€95–€100.
Rooms	2: 1 double, 1 twin.
Meals	Restaurants 100m.
Closed	January–February.
Directions	On one-way road round ramparts of Beaune, 200m after War Memorial, right at 2nd traffic light; Rue Sylvestre Chauvelot starts at Peugeot garage.

Price	€100–€110.
Rooms	1 double.
Meals	Restaurants within walking distance.
Closed	Rarely.
Directions	From A6 exit 24 Beaune St Nicolas; left after 4th light on circular bd. Private garage available.

Christophe & Cécile Bouchard
Les Planchottes,
6 rue Sylvestre Chauvelot,
21200 Beaune, Côte-d'Or

Tel	+33 (0)3 80 22 83 67
Fax	+33 (0)3 80 22 83 67
Email	lesplanchottes@voila.fr
Web	lesplanchottes.free.fr

Entry 98   Map 11

Yves Cantenot
Sous le Baldaquin,
39 rue Maufoux, 21200 Beaune,
Côte-d'Or

Tel	+33 (0)3 80 24 79 30
Fax	+33 (0)3 80 24 79 30
Email	yves.cantenot@laposte.net
Web	www.souslebaldaquin.fr

Entry 99   Map 11

Burgundy

Le Clos Champagne Saint Nicolas

Le Clos is nicely set back from the main road and Beaune is a ten-minute stroll. Built to take guests, the spanking new extension wing has spanking new bedrooms, modern bits in the bathrooms and a salon overlooking the garden. Fabrics, bedding and antiques reveal Anne as a woman of taste who has thought of everything, even a guest kitchen for your morning spread of homemade jams, cake, croissants, bread, yogurt and fresh fruit. Knowledgeable natives, hospitable hosts, she and Bruno fill you in on the sights, the restaurants and the vineyards over a welcoming glass of wine. *Easy access from A6.*

Price	€95.
Rooms	3 doubles.
Meals	Restaurants within walking distance. Guest kitchen.
Closed	Rarely.
Directions	A6 exit 24 Beaune St Nicolas; 3rd exit at r'bout for Beaune; straight on & over bridge, after 1st lights on for 300m; house on left.

Bruno & Anne Durand de Gevigney
Le Clos Champagne Saint Nicolas,
114 ter route de Dijon,
21200 Beaune, Côte-d'Or
Tel +33 (0)3 80 61 24 92
Email closchamp.stnicolas@free.fr
Web closchamp.stnicolas.free.fr

Entry 100 Map 11

Burgundy

Maison des Abeilles

Madame, a genuine Burgundian with family in all the surrounding villages, believes in simplicity, quality and conviviality, and has now renovated all her rooms in the converted barn and adjacent workers' cottages. Each has an outside door, two are up an outside stair, bathrooms are snug, some with half baths, and the décor is newly whitewashed stone walls, fresh fabrics, wooden ceilings and floors, some bits of rustic rough plaster. Although there's no sitting room, breakfast in the darkly atmospheric dining room looking onto hollyhocks and a fig tree is communal, round one big table.

Price	€58–€90.
Rooms	3: 2 doubles, 1 family suite for 4.
Meals	Dinner with wine, €26.
Closed	Rarely.
Directions	A6 exit Beaune St Nicolas; D974 for Dijon. In Ladoix Serrigny, left at chemist for Magny les Viliers; in village, 1st left onto Rue du Lavoir; tree-lined square, left to Pernand for 2-3m, park alongside trees.

Jocelyne Gaugey
Maison des Abeilles,
Route de Pernand Vergelesses,
21700 Magny les Villers, Côte-d'Or
Tel +33 (0)3 80 62 95 42
Email joel.gaugey@wanadoo.fr
Web perso.wanadoo.fr/maison-des-abeilles

Entry 101 Map 11

Burgundy

Les Hêtres Rouges

A pretty old Burgundian hunting lodge, 'Copper Beeches' stands in a walled garden full of ancient trees and has an unexpected air of Provence inside: beautifully judged colour schemes (Madame paints), fine furniture, numerous *objets*, a tomcat or two, burning incense and the odd sprig of flowers. Your hosts extend a warm, genuine yet ungushing welcome to the weary traveller – up a steep stair are low rooms with dark character and fine linen. The absolutely charming guest cottage is cat free and nicely independent. Breakfast has the savour of yesteryear: yogurt, fresh bread and homemade jam. *Sawday self-catering also.*

Price	€88. Cottage €115 (€600 per week).
Rooms	2: 1 twin, 1 twin/double.
Meals	Restaurants 8km.
Closed	Rarely.
Directions	From A31 exit 1 on D35 for Seurre 3km; right to Quincey then Antilly, 4km. House on right.

Jean-François & Christiane Bugnet
Les Hêtres Rouges,
Antilly,
21700 Argilly, Côte-d'Or
Tel +33 (0)3 80 62 53 98
Email leshetresrouges@free.fr
Web www.leshetresrouges.com

Entry 102 Map 11

Burgundy

La Closerie de Gilly

The generous warmth of the green-shuttered façade reaches indoors, too, where a beautiful Alsatian ceramic stove stands beside huge plants in the sunny breakfast salon and the guest rooms are airy and florally friezed. Interesting prints on the walls too. Your hosts are chatty and friendly. Monsieur teaches economics, they both conduct sessions in English on the geographical diversity of the wine areas along with samplings and suggestions of vineyards to visit. The entrance to the gardens and house may seem narrow but don't get it wrong: you are very welcome and can always leave the car outside.

Price	€75-€85.
Rooms	2: 1 double, 1 family room.
Meals	Restaurant 200m-1km.
Closed	Christmas.
Directions	From A31 exit Nuits St Georges; N74 for Dijon; at Vougeot r'bout head for Gilly centre; 1st right after bridge.

André & Sandrine Lanaud
La Closerie de Gilly,
16 avenue du Recteur Bouchard,
Gilly lès Cîteaux,
21640 Vougeot, Côte-d'Or
Tel/Fax +33 (0)3 80 62 87 74
Email info@closerie-gilly.com
Web www.closerie-gilly.com

Entry 103 Map 11

Burgundy

34 rue de Mazy

You cannot forget the lifeblood of Burgundy: wine buffs will love the twisting drive along the *Route des Vins* into the gravelled courtyard of this fine old wine-grower's house. Your courteous host knows a lot about wine and loves to practise his English, so sample an aperitif in his atmospheric stone-arched cellar; there are locally-pressed fruit juices too. The house has a classic stone staircase and generous windows, the comfortable and homely bedrooms are reached by outside steps, the breakfast room has flagstones and ochre-coloured walls. In summer, breakfast is in the well-kept, willow-draped garden.

Burgundy

Domaine de Serrigny

Just yards from a pretty stretch of the Burgundy Canal, a townhouse with high walls and magnificent views to perfect little Châteauneuf en Auxois. Charles and Marie-Pascale are stylish, informal and huge fun; so is their home. Fabulous antiques, interesting art and textiles, space for children to roam and bedrooms that are a beautiful mix of styles. Something for everyone here from grand salon to zen attic; all are delightful and bathrooms are bliss. Frolic in the garden with its large lawn, colourful pots, decked pool and tennis court; have breakfast here or in the large open-plan sitting/dining room. Heaps of charm.

Price	€60.
Rooms	2: 1 double, 1 family room for 4-5.
Meals	Restaurant 300m.
Closed	Rarely.
Directions	From Lyon N on A6, A31 exit Nuits St Georges; N74 for Dijon. After approx. 13km left to Marsannay. From the North on A5, A38 exit Dijon South.

Price	€88–€97. Suite €112.
Rooms	4: 2 doubles, 1 family room, 1 suite for 2.
Meals	Auberge opposite.
Closed	Rarely.
Directions	A6 Paris-Lyon exit Pouilly en Auxois; follow Pouilly en Auxois, then Créancey (2km). In Créancy for Vandenesse en Auxois 7km. In village, 1st left, 50m on right.

Jean-Charles & Brigitte Viennet
34 rue de Mazy,
21160 Marsannay la Côte,
Côte-d'Or
Tel +33 (0)3 80 59 83 63
Email viennet.jean-charles@wanadoo.fr
Web perso.wanadoo.fr/gite.marsannay

Charles & Marie-Pascale Chaillot
Domaine de Serrigny, Lieu dit "le Village",
Route Départementale,
21320 Vandenesse en Auxois,
Côte-d'Or
Tel/Fax +33 (0)3 80 49 28 13
Email chaillot.mp@wanadoo.fr
Web www.domaine-de-serrigny.com

Entry 104   Map 6

Entry 105   Map 6

Burgundy

La Monastille

Stunning flagstones in the breakfast room (where pancakes and homemade jams are served) and wooden doors that creak open to cosy rooms. In a village of 49 souls (and 2,000 cows!) is La Monastille, built in 1750 as a wealthy farmhouse. Generous Madame is passionate about history, antiques, food and loves her English guests. Supper at the big table might be pot-au-feu with chicken from the farm next door. Wines flow. Bedrooms are a soothing mix of muted walls, dark old furniture and flowery bed covers, the dear little room in the tower is reached via many steps and outside is a lovely garden.

Price	€70.
Rooms	4 doubles.
Meals	Dinner with wine, €25.
Closed	Rarely.
Directions	From Beaune D970 to Bligny sur Ouche; after village left to Êcutigny; right to Thomirey; house with terracotta flower pots by church.

	Françoise Moine
	La Monastille,
	21360 Thomirey, Côte-d'Or
Tel	+33 (0)3 80 20 00 80
Fax	+33 (0)3 80 20 00 80
Email	moine.francoise@wanadoo.fr
Web	www.monastille.com

Entry 106   Map 11

Burgundy

Château les Roches

Way off any beaten track, at almost 500m altitude, with an unobscured view over the Serein valley and the lush forests of the Morvan, the bourgeois mansion sits quietly behind tall gates. A judge's passion for his mistress inspired this 1900s jewel, a haven of peace in a medieval village of 300 souls. Young Tobias, who's American, and German Marco fell just as hard – and have restored it remarkably. The bones were good so they added perfect furnishings to the light and spacious rooms and made the bathrooms sinful. Full of promise, it is already a perfect getaway. Don't miss the twice-weekly dinners.

Price	€140–€165. Cottage €950 per week.
Rooms	6 + 1: 4 doubles, 2 family rooms for 3. Cottage for 4.
Meals	Dinner €29. Picnic lunch €15. Wine €16.
Closed	January-February.
Directions	A6 exit 24 Pouilly en Auxois for Saulieu, D977 for 25 mins; right D36 Mont St Jean for 2km; 2nd sign for Mont St Jean up hill; right at restaurant Le Medieval; Château left, tall gates; signed.

	Tobias Yang & Marco Stockmeyer
	Château les Roches,
	Rue de Glanot,
	21320 Mont Saint Jean, Côte-d'Or
Tel	+33 (0)3 80 84 32 71
Email	info@lesroches-burgundy.com
Web	www.lesroches-burgundy.com

Entry 107   Map 6

Burgundy

Burgundy

Villa le Clos

French country hospitality at its finest, meals you will remember for ever (people copy Madame's recipes), a sun trap by the summer house for your own barbecue, stupendous valley views over historic Alésia where Caesar fought Vercingétorix in 52BC (brush up your Asterix), great walks, medieval villages and a modern house set among bright tulips, terraced features and birdsong. Inside, beyond the Alpine mural, you find spotless rooms, good mattresses and bathrooms, a colourful chintzy décor – all endearingly French. Above all, you will remember these wonderfully warm, kind and thoughtful people.

Manoir de Tarperon

Tarperon is uniquely French. An ageless charm breathes from the ancient turrets, the fine antiques, the paintings and the prints, while Soisick is young and good fun, with an unstuffy formality – if you can't find her, walk in and make yourself at home, she's not far. The rooms are full of family furniture in an uncontrived, fadedly elegant, lived-in décor; the bathrooms are family style, with lots of unusual bits. Dinner, superbly cooked by Claudine and Soisick, is a treat. All this and lovely gardens with a donkey, fly-fishing at €25 a day. and painting courses. *Minimum stay 2 nights. Whole house available for rent.*

Price	€50.		Price	€70–€75. Triple €90–€95.
Rooms	2: 1 double, 1 twin, each with curtained shower, sharing wc.		Rooms	5: 3 doubles, 1 twin, 1 triple.
Meals	Dinner with wine, €20.		Meals	Dinner with wine, €28–€30, at husband's restaurant next door.
Closed	October–March.		Closed	2 November–March.
Directions	From Dijon N71 for Châtillon sur Seine; after Courceau D6 left & follow signs; house on D19A near junc. with D6 (50km from Dijon).		Directions	From Dijon N71 for Châtillon sur Seine, 62km; D901 right for Aignay le Duc. Tarperon sign on D901.

	Claude & Huguette Gounand			**Soisick de Champsavin**
	Villa le Clos,			Manoir de Tarperon,
	Route de la Villeneuve,			21510 Aignay le Duc, Côte-d'Or
	21150 Darcey, Côte-d'Or		Tel	+33 (0)3 80 93 83 74
Tel	+33 (0)3 80 96 23 20		Fax	+33 (0)3 80 93 83 74
Fax	+33 (0)3 80 96 23 20		Email	manoir.de.tarperon@wanadoo.fr
Email	claude.gounand@orange.fr		Web	www.tarperon.fr

Entry 108   Map 6

Entry 109   Map 6

Burgundy

Rue Hoteaux

A master stone mason built this house in the 19th century and left many marks of his consummate skill in stairs and fireplaces as well as his quarry at the back where the Escots have made a spectacular flower-filled rock garden – Madame's passion. They are a relaxed, generous couple, she bubbly and proud of her many grandchildren, he shyer but a mine of information; both love having people to stay. In the converted barn, the big ground-floor stable room has a finely clothed bed, white slatted walls and good yellow wallpaper… or climb the lovely winding stairs to the pretty attic room. Both have views on the garden.

Price	€80-€95.
Rooms	2: 1 triple, 1 family room for 3.
Meals	Restaurants 3-7km.
Closed	November to mid-April.
Directions	From Montbard D980 for Châtillon; right in village of Puits. House on right next to large tree.

Gilberte & Jean Escot
Rue Hoteaux,
Rue Hoteaux,
21400 Puits, Côte-d'Or

Tel   +33 (0)3 80 93 14 83
Email   gilbertemichel@free.fr
Web   chambrepuits.free.fr

Entry 110   Map 6

Burgundy

La Cimentelle

After an astoundingly beautiful drive you reach this handsome family house built by titans of the cement industry at the turn of the last century: the pool sits on top of the old factory. Come for extraordinary food (both hosts are gourmet cooks), thoughtfulness, friendly chat and the loveliest rooms. Three are works of art and a touch of fun: a Murano mirror, an antique desk, pink faux-baroque wallpaper and stunning white linen curtains. Swish bathrooms glow with monogrammed towels and showers in Italian mosaic. Family suites at the top of the house are huge. Don't miss it, you'll need at least two nights.

Price	€70-€95. Suites €100-€170.
Rooms	5: 3 doubles, 2 family suites.
Meals	Dinner with wine, €32. Pool lunches.
Closed	Never.
Directions	A6 exit 21 Nitry for Avallon D944 12km; D105 left to Vassy. House in village, 3rd gate after church. Signed. Do not confuse with Vassy sous Pisy.

Nathalie & Stéphane Oudot
La Cimentelle,
4 rue de la Cimentelle,
89200 Vassy-lès-Avallon, Yonne

Tel   +33 (0)3 86 31 04 85
Email   lacimentelle@orange.fr
Web   www.lacimentelle.com

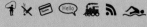

Entry 111   Map 6

Burgundy

Maison Crème Anglaise

They named the gracious old house after their desserts, served with *crème anglaise*. From a Tintin collection to Custard the dog, this mellow old place is full of surprises. Swallows nest in a medieval archway, a staircase winds up a tower and the garden falls steeply away giving unforgettable views. Meals are accompanied by candles and flowers, bedrooms are airy and appealing and the charming bathroom is shared. Graham and Christine, open and friendly, hold recitals, art exhibitions and summer *salons de thé* in the courtyard. The hilltop village is historic, the peace is a balm.

Price	€60.
Rooms	3: 2 doubles, 1 twin, sharing bathroom.
Meals	Dinner with wine, €25. Special events catered for.
Closed	Rarely.
Directions	A6 exit 22; follow sign on left "Montreal 9kms" ; in village centre through medieval arch & up hill; 80 yds before town hall on right.

Graham & Christine Battye
Maison Crème Anglaise,
22 Grande Rue,
89420 Montréal, Yonne
Tel   +33 (0)3 86 32 07 73
Fax   +33 (0)3 86 32 07 73
Email   grahambattye@maisoncremeanglaise.com
Web   www.maisoncremeanglaise.com

Entry 112   Map 6

Burgundy

Cabalus

Inimitable. You are on the top of the 'eternal hill' at the centre of one of the most revered historic sites in France; ancient and atmospheric, the old pilgrims' hospice stands in the shadow of the Basilica. A gallery of quietly intriguing, tempting objects and a much-loved coffee shop occupy the 12th-century vaulted hall but guests have that vast fireplace to themselves for organic breakfasts. Rooms are simple, artistic, authentic. Eccentric Monsieur Cabalus is the perfect gentleman with a fine sense of humour, younger Madame is a most welcoming artist. And the morning mists hang in the valley.

Price	€58-€75.
Rooms	4: 2 doubles; 2 doubles, each with shower, sharing wcs.
Meals	Dinner €20. Wine €15.
Closed	Rarely.
Directions	In Vézelay centre take main street up to Basilica. Park, walk down main street, ring at 2nd door on right.

M Cabalus
Cabalus,
Rue Saint Pierre,
89450 Vézelay, Yonne
Tel   +33 (0)3 86 33 20 66
Email   contact@cabalus.com
Web   www.cabalus.com

Entry 113   Map 5

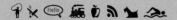

Burgundy

Le Moulinot

The handsome millhouse, surrounded by herons, kingfishers and a rushing river, is reached via a narrow, private bridge. Wander the beautiful grounds or settle yourself in the most inviting sitting room, complete with roaring log fire when it's cold. Leigh and Cinda are charming hosts who delight in sharing their watery world. There's a canoe and a lake where Leigh has sunk a brilliant natural-looking swimming pool; and balloon flights can be arranged. The big, light bedrooms are freshly decorated with good bathrooms and the mill race is generally noisier than the road. Wonderful. *Children over 8 welcome.*

Price	€65–€90.
Rooms	6: 5 doubles, 1 twin.
Meals	Restaurants nearby.
Closed	Rarely.
Directions	From Auxerre N6 for Avallon, 22km; just before Vermenton village sign, sharp right, double back & over bridge.

Leigh & Cinda Wootton
Le Moulinot,
89270 Vermenton, Yonne
Tel +33 (0)3 86 81 60 42
Email info@moulinot.com
Web www.moulinot.com

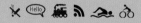

Entry 114 Map 5

Burgundy

La Maison d'Aviler

On each floor, eight tall windows look down on the resplendent garden that shelters Aviler from noise. At the back is the Yonne where barges peacefully ply: what a setting. The house was originally a workhouse – destitution in 18th-century France had its compensations. Your hosts were interior decorators by trade and collectors by instinct, so expect subtle but sumptuous detail in elegantly French bedrooms and advice on the best local auctions. Monsieur will even help you bid! Sens has a memorable cathedral, a tempting market, and the shops and restaurants of this lovely town simply yell 'quality'.

Price	€77.
Rooms	3: 1 double, 1 suite for 3; 1 twin with separate shower.
Meals	Restaurants in Sens.
Closed	Mid-January to mid-February.
Directions	From A19 exit Sens, St Denis les Sens towards Sens centre ville. Right between Mercedes garage and restaurant. Left at river, follow road on right bank to No. 43. Green iron gates.

Christiane & Bernard Barré
La Maison d'Aviler,
43 quai du Petit Hameau,
89100 Sens, Yonne
Tel +33 (0)3 86 95 49 25
Email daviler@online.fr
Web www.daviler.online.fr

Entry 115 Map 5

Paris – Île de France

Le Logis d'Arnières

Several centuries shaped this old hunting lodge, then it was determinedly 'modernised' in the 1920s Art Deco style: high-windowed, fully-panelled dining room with extraordinary dressers, fabulous bathroom fittings. It is exuberantly sober and shapely with Versailles parquet and fine fireplaces as well. Tae, from Chile, uses her perfect sense of style and colour to include these respected elements in her décor alongside richly baroque Chinese chairs and lots of South American pieces and paintings. Quiet spot, vast natural garden, joyous hosts, perfect for Chartres, Paris, Versailles.

L'Atalante

Cocooned behind the garden walls, one of two hideaways leads straight off the garden. The uncluttered, open-plan space is fresh and bright with its cool cream floors, nautical stripes and pale walls, and, with its curtained-off sitting area and fire, most inviting. Up under the eaves is a fresh two-bedroomed suite overlooking the beautiful peonies and pathways. Tinkle the ivories in the *salon de musique*, stretch out on the flower-freckled lawn. You can use the kitchenette if you want to be independent or join your charming, interested and interesting hosts for dinner. One of our favourites.

Price	€80 for 2. €120 for 4.
Rooms	2 suites for 5.
Meals	Restaurant 200m.
Closed	Rarely.
Directions	From Paris A10 exit 10 to toll gate, right after toll; right again on D27 to St Cyr; continue for Arpajon; 1st house on left.

Price	€58.
Rooms	2 suites: 1 for 2-4, 1 for 2-5.
Meals	Dinner with wine, €22. Guest kitchen.
Closed	Rarely.
Directions	From A5 exit 17 on D210 for Provins 2km; right D133 1km; left for Gardeloup. Left to Grand Buisson.

Claude & Tae Dabasse
Le Logis d'Arnières,
1 rue du Pont-Rué,
91410 St Cyr sous Dourdan, Essonne
Tel   +33 (0)1 64 59 14 89
Fax   +33 (0)1 64 59 07 46
Email   taedabasse@free.fr
Web   www.dabasse.com/arniere

Florence & Georges Manulelis
L'Atalante,
8 rue Grande du Buisson,
77148 Laval en Brie, Seine-et-Marne
Mobile +33 (0)6 86 18 54 98
Email   latalante@free.fr
Web   latalante.free.fr

Entry 116   Map 5

Entry 117   Map 5

Paris – Île de France

Ferme de Vert St Père

Cereals and beets grow in wide fields and show-jumpers add elegance to the fine landscape. A generous farmyard surrounded by very lovely warm stone buildings encloses utter quiet and a genuine welcome from young hosts and labradors alike, out here where Monsieur's family has come hunting for 200 years. Family furniture (the 1900s ensemble is most intriguing) and planked floors in beautiful bedrooms, immaculate mod cons and a super living area for guests in a beamy outbuilding with open fire, sofa, kitchen and TV. Exceptional house and setting, and a Michelin-starred auberge in the village.

Manoir de Beaumarchais

It's charmingly bourgeois, and the welcome is warmly French. The house is a fascinating architectural cuckoo, an 'Anglo-Norman' face concealing an unspoilt 1920s interior with great arched windows and crested tiles. All is elegant, comfortable, beautifully furnished. Views are of stretching pastures. Your suite, as untouched as the aqua-panelled salon, is pretty, intimate and stylish, with a boudoir sitting room in the tower. Big breakfasts appear at the long dining table where, in good English, your retired hosts enjoy telling the history of grandfather's hunting lodge (they still organise shoots).

Price	€62. Apartments €96.
Rooms	1 + 2: 1 family room for 3. 2 apartments for 4.
Meals	Restaurant in village (check opening times).
Closed	Christmas.
Directions	From A5 exit 15 on N36 towards Meaux, 200m; 2nd right to Crisenoy after TGV bridge, through village for Tennis/Salle des Fêtes; 1.5km to farm.

Price	Suite €150.
Rooms	1 suite.
Meals	Restaurants nearby.
Closed	Rarely.
Directions	A4 to Metz exit 13 to Villeneuve le Comte; right opp. church D96 for Tournan; thro' Neufmoutiers, right opp. church, cont. 250m on D96; 1st left small road for Beaumarchais 1.5km; gates on left.

Philippe & Jeanne Mauban
Ferme de Vert St Père,
77390 Crisenoy, Seine-et-Marne
Tel +33 (0)1 64 38 83 51
Fax +33 (0)1 64 38 83 52
Email mauban.vert@wanadoo.fr
Web vert.saint.pere.free.fr

Nathalie & Michael Mavrinac
Manoir de Beaumarchais,
77610 Les Chapelles Bourbon,
Seine-et-Marne
Tel +33 (0)1 64 07 11 08
Email info@beaumarchais.eu
Web www.beaumarchais.eu

Entry 118   Map 5

Entry 119   Map 5

Le Moulin de Saint Martin

Agnès, gentle, with artistic flair, and Bernard, gregarious, charming, convivial… together they have created a delectable B&B. The old mill is on an island encircled by Corot's Grand Morin river; lovely old willows lap the water, the pretty villages of Le Voulangis and Crécy lie beyond. A warm sober elegance prevails: there are 17th-century floorboards topped by oriental rugs; Asian antiques and art in gilt frames; cherry-red toile and snowy bed linen; terraces for summer views; log fires for nights in. Disneyland Paris, a world away, is a short drive; fine châteaux beckon. *Minimum stay 2 nights.*

Price	€65–€70.
Rooms	2: 1 double, 1 twin/double.
Meals	Dinner €20. Wine €15.
Closed	Rarely.
Directions	From Paris A4 for Metz, exit 16 for Crécy; 3rd lights right; through Crécy for Voulangis & Tigeaux. Leaving Crécy left, Le Moulin 200m, signed. Ring bell.

	Bernard & Agnès Gourbaud
	Le Moulin de Saint Martin,
	7 rue de Saint Martin,
	Voulangis,
	77580 Crécy la Chapelle,
	Seine-et-Marne
Tel	+33 (0)1 64 63 69 90
Email	moulindesaintmartin@orange.fr

Entry 120 Map 5

Le Clos de la Rose

For birdwatchers and garden lovers (masses of roses, age-old trees), champagne buffs and cheese tasters (Brie on the doorstep, historic Provins nearby), this gorgeous green retreat from crazed Paris – cool, quiet, elegantly homely – has been restored with fine respect for an old flint house: limewash, wood, terracotta, a great gathering of books, paintings, prints. Both your hosts work from home and look after guests with care and intelligence. Bedrooms have pretty colours and mixed-style furniture, the adorable cottage (with kitchen) is ideal for a longer stay. *Minimum stay 2 nights. Ask about local wine tours.*

Price	€64–€138.
Rooms	3: 2 doubles.
	1 cottage for 2 & kitchen.
Meals	Restaurant 5-minute drive.
Closed	Rarely.
Directions	From Paris A4 for Reims; exit 18 to La Ferté sous Jouarre; D407 for Montmirail; through woodland to Montapeine (6km from r'bout in La Ferté); D68 for St Ouen; 1.8 km right; 400m to black gate.

	Martine & Jean-Paul Krebs
	Le Clos de la Rose, 11 rue de la Source
	L'Hermitière, 77750 St Cyr sur Morin,
	Seine-et-Marne
Tel	+33 (0)1 60 44 81 04
Fax	+33 (0)1 60 24 40 84
Email	infos@rosa-gallica.fr
Web	www.clos-de-la-rose.com

Entry 121 Map 5

Paris – Île de France

Châtelet district

You will meet a most civilised couple – she bubbly and interested, he quietly studious, a university professor – in their very personal, gently refined apartment where original timbers, saved from the renovator's axe, divide the living room and two friendly cats proclaim the cosiness. It is beautifully done and eminently French, like a warm soft nest, antique-furnished, lots of greenery, interesting art. Mona greatly enjoys her guests and is full of tips on Paris. The attractive, compact guest quarters down the corridor are nicely private with good storage space, pretty quilts and lots of light. *Minimum stay 2 nights.*

Price	€90.
Rooms	1 twin.
Meals	Restaurants nearby.
Closed	Summer holidays.
Directions	Metro: Châtelet (1, 4, 7, 11, 14) or Pont Neuf (7) (between Louvre & Notre Dame). Parking: Conforama car park, via Rue du Pont Neuf then Rue Boucher. Lift to 3rd floor.

	Mona Pierrot
	Châtelet district,
	75001 Paris
Tel	+33 (0)1 42 36 50 65

Entry 122   Map 5

Paris – Île de France

Bonne Nuit Paris

Absolute Paris, 300 years old but not grand, beams galore and modern comforts, independent rooms and a warm family welcome, little streets, friendly markets: this is real privilege. Charming, intelligent Jean-Luc serves his own honey, Denise's jams and fresh baguette in their generous, rambling living room. Guest rooms are on the floor below. Each has a fun-lovingly colourful shower room, a lot of quirk (the last word in creative basins) and an appealing mix of old woodwork and contemporary prints. Simplicity, panache and personality, real attention and service are the hallmarks: you will feel well cared for.

Price	€150. Extra person €75.
Rooms	3: 2 doubles, 1 triple.
Meals	Restaurants within walking distance.
Closed	Rarely.
Directions	Metro: République (2, 3, 5, 8, 11); Bus: 20, 46, 56, 65, 75; 3 car parks €50 for 3 days.

	Denise & Jean-Luc Marchand
	Bonne Nuit Paris,
	63 rue Charlot, 75003 Paris
Tel	+33 (0)1 42 71 83 56
Email	jean.luc@bonne-nuit-paris.com
Web	www.bonne-nuit-paris.com

Entry 123   Map 5

Paris – Île de France

Notre Dame district

At the end of the street are the Seine and the glory of Notre Dame. In a grand old building, up a 17th-century staircase, the unaffected tall-windowed rooms look down to peace in a little garden. The low-mezzanined family room has a bathroom off the internal landing where a simple breakfast is laid beside the spiral stair. Upstairs, the second, smaller, room has the bed in the corner and a fresh décor. Madame is polyglot, active and eager to help when she is available, and leaves breakfast ready if she has to go out. She and her daughter appreciate the variety of contact guests bring.

Price	€85–€150.
Rooms	2: 1 double; 1 quadruple with separate bathroom.
Meals	Continental breakfast left ready if owner has to go out.
Closed	Rarely.
Directions	From street, enter 2407. In courtyard, ring house bell on left. Metro: Maubert-Mutualité (10). RER/Metro: St Michel. Book parking ahead.

	Brigitte Chatignoux
	Notre Dame district,
	75005 Paris
Tel	+33 (0)1 43 25 27 20
Email	brichati@hotmail.com

Entry 124   Map 5

Paris – Île de France

National Assembly/Invalides district

In a provincial-quiet city street, classy dressed stone outside, intelligence, sobriety and style inside. Madame takes you into her vast, serene apartment: no modern gadgets or curly antiques, just a few good pieces, much space and light-flooded parquet floors. Beyond the dining room, your cosy buff bedroom gives onto a big, silent, arcaded courtyard. Your hosts have lived all over the world, and Madame, as quiet and genuine as her surroundings, now enjoys her country garden near Chartres and the company of like-minded visitors – she is worth getting to know. *Stays of 2+ nights preferred.*

Price	€85.
Rooms	1 twin/double.
Meals	Restaurants within walking distance.
Closed	Rarely.
Directions	Metro: Solférino (12), Assemblée Nationale (12) or Invalides (8). Parking: Invalides. Lift to 2nd floor.

	Élisabeth Marchal
	National Assembly/Invalides district,
	10 rue Las Cases,
	75007 Paris
Tel	+33 (0)1 47 05 70 21

Entry 125   Map 5

Paris – Île de France

Étoile-Champs Elysées

Even the air feels quietly elegant. Soisick uses no frills, just good things old and new: the sense of peace is palpable (nothing to do with double glazing). Her flat turns away from the rowdy Champs Élysées towards classy St Honoré: ask this gentle Parisian for advice about great little restaurants – or anything Parisian. The simple generous bedroom has size and interest – an unusual inlaid table is set off by white bedcovers – and leads to a dressing room fit for a star and your tasteful white and grey bathroom. With three windows, parquet floor and its mix of antique and modern, the living room is another charmer.

Price	€90.
Rooms	1 twin/double.
Meals	Restaurants nearby.
Closed	Rarely.
Directions	Metro: George V (1), Charles de Gaulle Étoile (1, 2, 6, RER). Parking: Étoile. Bus: Air France airport bus Étoile; 22, 30, 31, 52, 73, 92, 93, Balabus.

Soisick Guérineau
Étoile-Champs Elysées,
1 rue Lamennais, 75008 Paris
Tel   +33 (0)1 40 39 04 38
Email soisick.guerineau@wanadoo.fr

Entry 126   Map 5

Paris – Île de France

Montparnasse district

A little white blue-shuttered house in a cobbled alley, just behind Montparnasse? It's not a dream and Janine, a live-wire cinema journalist who has lived in Canada, will, when available, welcome you to her pretty wood-ceilinged kitchen/diner; she's a night bird so breakfast will be laid for you to do your own. The bedroom across the book-lined hall is a good, square room with a highly pleasing mix of warm fabrics, honeycomb tiles, white walls, old chest and contemporary paintings. The new white and pine bathroom has space, all mod cons and good cupboards. So peaceful. *Minimum stay 2 nights. Sawday self-catering also.*

Price	€70. Single €60.
Rooms	1 double.
Meals	Restaurants nearby.
Closed	July-September.
Directions	Metro: Gaîté (13). RER: Denfert-Rochereau; airport buses nearby. Bus: 28 58.

Janine Euvrard
Montparnasse district,
75014 Paris
Tel   +33 (0)1 43 27 19 43
Fax   +33 (0)1 43 27 19 43
Email janine.euvrard@orange.fr

Entry 127   Map 5

Montparnasse district

Filled with books, paintings and objects from around the world, the Monbrisons' intimate little flat is old and fascinating. Lively American Cynthia, an art-lover, and quintessentially French Christian, knowledgeable about history, wine and cattle-breeding, offer great hospitality, thoughtful conversation, and may take you to historical landmarks. Their guest room, quiet and snug, has a king-size bed and a good bathroom with views of trees. Twice a week, the open market brings the real food of France to your street; shops, cafés and restaurants abound; you can walk to the Luxembourg Gardens. *Enquire about their B&B in south-west France.*

Montmartre

In Montmartre village, between busty boulevard and pure-white Sacré Cœur, barrister Valérie and her architect husband offer a super-chic and ideally autonomous studio off their charming, pot-planted and cobbled courtyard with your bistro table and chairs. A bed dressed in dramatic red against white walls, an antique oval dining table, a pine-and-steel gem of a corner kitchen, a generous shower, a mirror framed in red. Valérie's discreet decorative flourishes speak for her calm, positive personality and her interest in other lands. A delicious Paris hideaway you can call your own. *Minimum stay 3 nights.*

Price	€85.
Rooms	1 twin/double.
Meals	Occasional dinner with wine, €20.
Closed	August.
Directions	Metro: Edgar Quinet (6) or Montparnasse (4, 6, 12, 13). Airport buses from Orly & Charles de Gaulle to Montparnasse (5-minute walk).

Price	€100 (€650 per week).
Rooms	1 studio for 2 & kitchenette.
Meals	Breakfast not included. Restaurants nearby.
Closed	Rarely.
Directions	Metro: Anvers Sacre Coeur (2). Metro/ RER: Gare du Nord. Bus: 30, 31, 54, 85. Car park: Rue Fentrier.

	Christian & Cynthia de Monbrison
	Montparnasse district,
	75014 Paris
Tel	+33 (0)1 43 35 20 87
Fax	+33 (0)1 43 35 20 87

	Valérie Zuber
	Montmartre,
	75018 Paris
Mobile	+33 (0)6 30 93 81 35
Fax	+33 (0)1 42 58 47 40
Email	studiodamelie@wanadoo.fr
Web	www.paris-oasis.com

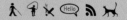

Paris – Île de France

Belleville district

The street throbs with multicultural motley but from the top of this clean modern block you can stretch your eyes across Paris to the scintillating towers of La Défense or round to the Parc de Belleville, a surprising green hillside above the city. Your pretty room lets in fabulous sunsets over the Eiffel Tower and no noise. The flat is all white walls, modern parquet floors and fine old family furniture, lots from Provence where your very proper, elderly hostess used to live. Madame serves fresh pastries at breakfast and tells you all about everything with great verve. *Minimum stay 2 nights. Spanish spoken.*

Price	€73.
Rooms	1 double.
Meals	Restaurants within walking distance.
Closed	Rarely.
Directions	Metro: Belleville (2, 11) 200m: 15 mins to centre. Parking & directions: ask owners. Lift to 9th floor.

Danièle de la Brosse
Belleville district,
29 rue Belleville,
75019 Paris
Tel +33 (0)1 42 41 99 59
Fax +33 (0)1 42 41 99 59
Email dan.delabrosse@wanadoo.fr
Web www.fleursdesoleil.fr/crans-maisons/75-delabrosse.htm

Entry 130   Map 5

Paris – Île de France

Belleville district

Sabine, artist and art therapist, "feeds people with colours". Jules makes the organic bread with a dazzling smile, and big, beautiful Taquin, his guide dog, loves people. Kindly and artistic, they live calmly in this bit of genuine old Paris between two tiny gardens and a tall house. The simple guest room, with good double bed and flame-covered sleigh-bed divan, a welcome tea-maker and an old-fashioned bathroom, shares a building with Sabine's studio. Healthfoody continental breakfast is in the cosy family room in the main house or outside under the birdsung tree. Such peace in Paris is rare. *Minimum stay 2 nights.*

Price	€70.
Rooms	1 family room for 3.
Meals	Restaurants within walking distance.
Closed	July-August.
Directions	Metro: Jourdain (11) or Place des Fêtes (11). Parking: Place des Fêtes. Bus: 26, 48, 60.

Sabine & Jules Aïm
Belleville district,
75019 Paris
Tel +33 (0)1 42 08 23 71
Fax +33 (0)1 42 40 56 04
Email jules.aim@free.fr

Entry 131   Map 5

Villa Mansart

Wind your way up the handsome staircase and nudge open the attic door. The guest sitting room has sunny walls and ethnic rugs on pristine floors. Slim, arched bedrooms are blue or vanilla-and-orange with family furniture and windows that peep over the rooftops. Breakfast on fresh fruit and mini-pastries in an elegant dining room or on the terrace. Marble steps, rescued from a local demolition, sweep down to a huge, immaculate lawn; a curtain of trees shields you from the suburbs. All is peace and calm yet only 20 minutes from the centre of Paris. *Garage available. Minimum stay 2 nights.*

Le Clos des Princes

Twenty minutes on the train and you're in Paris. Here, behind wrought-iron gates in an elegant suburb, the French mansion sits in an exuberant town garden of pergolas, box bushes and mature trees. Your kind, attentive hosts — she an ex-English teacher, he with a passion for Prudhomme — give you the poet/philosopher's two-room first-floor suite; he lived here in 1902. Polished floorboards, pretty prints, choice antiques, decorative perfume bottles by a claw-footed tub — all dance to the 19th-century theme. Breakfast unveils gorgeous porcelain and delicious homemade muffins and jams.

Price	€84. Triple €114. Singles €70.
Rooms	2: 1 double, 1 triple. Extra single bed in sitting room.
Meals	Restaurants nearby.
Closed	Rarely.
Directions	From Paris A4 exit 5 for Pont de Nogent; at exit keep left, don't take tunnel; along viaduct; at 2nd lights under bridge; Ave. L. Rollin for Le Perreux centre; next lights straight on; 2nd left 200m.

Price	€95-€110.
Rooms	1 suite for 2 with separate bath. Sofabed available for children.
Meals	Restaurant 400m.
Closed	Mid-July to August.
Directions	From Paris Périphérique, exit Porte d'Orléans onto N20; A86 after Bourg la Reine to Versailles; exit 28 for Châtenay Malabry; over at Salvador Allende r'bout; right at 2nd r'bout; house on left.

Françoise Marcoz
Villa Mansart,
9 allée Victor Basch,
94170 Le Perreux sur Marne,
Val-de-Marne

Tel/Fax +33 (0)1 48 72 91 88
Email villamansart@yahoo.fr
Web www.villamansart.com

Christine & Eric Duprez
Le Clos des Princes,
60 avenue Jean Jaurès,
92290 Châtenay Malabry,
Hauts-de-Seine

Tel +33 (0)1 46 61 94 49
Email ce.duprez@yahoo.com

Entry 132   Map 5

Entry 133   Map 5

Paris – Île de France

L'Orangerie

In a garden full of roses, behind the busy avenue that leads straight to the château, a mini Marie-Antoinette Trianon houses two little luxury flats. Arched windows light a pale living area where a modern plush sofa stands on new parquet flanked by Louis XV chairs. The bathroom is marble, the mezzanine bedroom generously comfortable and everything is brand new – except the antiques. One flat has a fuchsia-flashed colour scheme, the other is a more sober taupe. Two couples can easily share the terrace, and breakfast awaits you at the friendly café over the road. Extraordinarily civilised. *Minimum stay 2 nights. Sawday self-catering also.*

Paris – Île de France

7 rue Gustave Courbet

Behind the modest façade, on an upmarket housing estate, is a generous interior where Madame's paintings stand in pleasing contrast to elegant antiques and feminine furnishings. Picture windows let the garden in and the woods rise beyond. The larger guest room is soberly classic in blue, with a fur throw and big bathroom; the smaller one with skylight, books and bath across the landing is excellent value. Madame, charming and gracious, sings as well as she paints and enjoys cooking elegant regional dinners for attentive guests; she is very good company. Small, intimate, privileged, and so near Versailles.

Price	From €135.
Rooms	1 + 2: 1 double. 2 apartments for 2.
Meals	Breakfast in café (included in price). Restaurants 300m. Light supper available.
Closed	Rarely.
Directions	Paris A13 to Rouen; after 7km exit 5 for Versailles-Centre/Château. Left, then Bd Jardy; Bd du Général Pershing & Ave. des États-Unis. Ave. de St Cloud until Château. Left on Ave. Rockefeller, 1st left Ave. de Paris. No. 37 6th lights on left.

Price	€55–€70.
Rooms	2: 1 double; 1 double with separate bath.
Meals	Dinner with wine, €18.
Closed	Rarely.
Directions	Paris A13 on A12 for St Quentin en Yvelines; exit N12 for Dreux; exit to Plaisir Centre; 1st exit off r'bout for Plaisir Les Gâtines, 1st left for 400m; right into Domaine des Gâtines; consult roadside plan.

Patricia White-Palacio
L'Orangerie,
37 avenue de Paris,
78000 Versailles, Yvelines
Tel +33 (0)9 53 61 07 57
Email mp.white@free.fr

Hélène Castelnau
7 rue Gustave Courbet,
Domaine des Gâtines,
78370 Plaisir, Yvelines
Tel +33 (0)1 30 54 05 15
Fax +33 (0)1 30 54 05 15
Email hcastelnau@club-internet.fr

Entry 134 Map 5

Entry 135 Map 5

Paris – Île de France

Les Colombes

On the doorstep of Paris, in the grounds of a royal château, surrounded by quiet tree-lined residential avenues, it's a trot from an atmospheric racecourse, almost on the banks of the Seine, with forest walks, good restaurants, efficient trains to and from Paris, impeccable, harmonious rooms, table d'hôtes and a deeply pretty garden to relax in. What Les Colombes lacks in old stones it makes up for in a welcome steeped in traditional hospitality – and that includes generous breakfasts, home-grown fruit and veg at dinner – and glowing antiques. Courteous, caring French hosts and great value. *15 mins by train to Paris.*

Price	€75-€82.
Rooms	3: 2 doubles, 1 twin.
Meals	Dinner with wine, €35.
Closed	Rarely.
Directions	A15 exit 5 D392 thro' Cormeilles en P; right D121 to Sartrouville; right D308/Ave. Maurice Berteaux to Maisons-Laffitte; at château r'bout, 2nd right Ave. Carnot; over 3 x-roads to Ave. Béranger.

Irène & Jacques James
Les Colombes,
21 avenue Béranger,
78600 Maisons Laffitte, Yvelines
Tel   +33 (0)1 39 62 82 48
Email   jacques.james@orange.fr
Web   perso.orange.fr/les-colombes

Entry 136   Map 5

Paris – Île de France

Château d'Hazeville

Utterly original, a meld of brimming creativity and scholarship, Hazeville dazzles. Your artist host uses his fine château-farm, dated 1400s to 1600s, as a living show of his talents: huge abstract paintings, hand-painted plates and tiles, a stunning 'Egyptian' reception room (and loos), and now photography. The old stables house hi-tech artisans. Beautifully finished guest rooms in the *pigeonnier* are deeply luxurious; generous breakfasts come on china hand-painted by Monsieur to match the wall covering; he also knows the secret treasures of the Vexin. *Children over 7 welcome. Hot-air ballooning possible.*

Price	€135.
Rooms	2: 1 double, 1 twin.
Meals	Restaurants within 5-10km.
Closed	Weekdays & school term time.
Directions	From Rouen N14 for Paris; 20km before Pontoise, at Magny en Vexin, right D983 to Arthies; left D81 through Enfer; château on left.

Guy & Monique Deneck
Château d'Hazeville,
95420 Wy dit Joli Village,
Val-d'Oise
Tel   +33 (0)1 34 67 06 17
Fax   +33 (0)1 34 67 17 82

Entry 137   Map 5

Paris – Île de France

Les Chandelles

At the end of a pretty village, a converted farmhouse behind high gates. Jean-Marc teaches golf to all ages and levels, Catherine is full of enthusiasm and advice for visitors. They, their son and two big sloppy dogs receive you with alacrity in the old beamed kitchen then send you up steep barn stairs to simple white rooms where patches of bright colour punctuate the space. The two lovely new rooms, bigger, higher (more steep stairs) and more luxurious in fabric and fitting, are good for families, and there's a wood-clad sitting room for guests, its sofa spread with an African throw. *Self-catering possible.*

Price	€60–€80. Family room €115–€150.
Rooms	5: 1 double, 2 twins, 2 family rooms.
Meals	Restaurants in Nogent le Roi & Maintenon. Kitchen available on request.
Closed	Rarely.
Directions	From Paris A13, A12, N12, exit Gambais for Nogent le Roi. Entering Coulombs, left at lights for Chandelles; left at x-roads 1.5km; house on right.

Catherine & Jean-Marc Simon
Les Chandelles,
19 rue des Sablons, Chandelles,
28130 Villiers le Morhier, Eure-et-Loir

Tel	+33 (0)2 37 82 71 59
Fax	+33 (0)2 37 82 71 59
Email	info@chandelles-golf.com
Web	www.chandelles-golf.com

Entry 138 Map 4

Paris – Île de France

La Ferme des Tourelles

A straightforward welcome, an unpretentious house with that friendly, lived-in air – what matter if sometimes it's the oilcloth on the table. This extended family of amiable, down-to-earth farmers love having children and guests around and lead a sociable life. Low-beamed bedrooms are modest but immaculate with imitation parquet and very good mattresses. In summer, meals can be taken under canvas in the flower-filled courtyard. Readers have told of hilarious evenings in approximate French and English over honest, family meals, often made with home-grown vegetables. Usefully near Paris.

Price	€53.
Rooms	2 family rooms: 1 for 3, 1 for 4.
Meals	Dinner with wine, €19.
Closed	Rarely.
Directions	From Dreux N12 to Broué; D305 to La Musse (La Musse between Boutigny & Prouais); Chambres d'Hôtes signs.

Maréchal-Petit Family
La Ferme des Tourelles,
11 rue des Tourelles, La Musse,
28410 Boutigny Prouais, Eure-et-Loir

Tel	+33 (0)2 37 65 10 29
Fax	+33 (0)2 37 65 10 29
Email	la-ferme.des-tourelles@orange.fr
Web	www.lafermedestourelles.com

Entry 139 Map 4

Paris – Île de France

Château de Jonvilliers

Delightful hosts: Virginie beautifully French, Richard a gentle Europeanised American, and their two sons. Down a wooded drive and set in a big leafy garden, the family house has tall windows, fine proportions and the air of a properly lived-in château: elegance and deep armchairs by the marble fireplace under crystal chandeliers. The top floor has been converted into five good rooms with sound-proofing, big beds, masses of hot water, rich, bright colour schemes... and just the right amount of family memorabilia: oils, engravings, lamps, old dishes. It feels easy, intelligent and fun.

Paris – Île de France

La Ferme de Bouchemont

Renovated with boldness, style and plenty of charm, this lofty farmhouse reflects the creative talents of its French/Spanish jewellery designer owners. Rooms blend traditional features – tiled floors, aged beams, brick alcoves – with neo-classical and contemporary furnishings. The guest entrance leads to an airy breakfast room – off which a pretty terraced garden – and stairs to a bedroom of soft, country-house elegance. Up again – wow! A dramatic bedroom in coffee and cream: très chic. Gorgeous bathrooms, generous breakfasts, discreet hosts: a stylish gem deep in the country. *Minimum stay 2 nights July/August.*

Price	€70–€90.
Rooms	5: 4 doubles, 1 triple.
Meals	Restaurants 5km.
Closed	Rarely. Book ahead.
Directions	A11 exit Ablis on N10 for Chartres. At Essars, right to St Symphorien, Bleury & Ecrosnes; right & immed. left to Jonvilliers, 2.5km. White château gates straight ahead.

Price	€100.
Rooms	2 suites.
Meals	Dinner €35. Wine €10.
Closed	Never.
Directions	Chartres N10 to Rambouillet 24km; left to St Symphorien le Château then for Château d'Esclimont; pass château gate; immed. left for 400m to Bouchemont; on left opp. pond.

Virginie & Richard Thompson
Château de Jonvilliers,
17 rue Lucien Petit-Jonvilliers,
28320 Ecrosnes, Eure-et-Loir

Tel	+33 (0)2 37 31 41 26
Fax	+33 (0)2 37 31 56 74
Email	information@chateaudejonvilliers.com
Web	www.chateaudejonvilliers.com

Maria Calderon & Didier Thébaud
La Ferme de Bouchemont,
11 rue de la Remarde, 28700
St Symphorien le Château, Eure-et-Loir

Tel	+33 (0)2 37 90 97 18
Fax	+33 (0)2 37 90 99 90
Email	il.etait.une.fois@wanadoo.fr
Web	www.la-ferme-de-bouchemont.com

Entry 140   Map 5

Entry 141   Map 5

Normandy

Normandy

Manoir de Beaumont

In the old hunting lodge for guests, a vast, boar- and stag's-headed dayroom with log fire, chandelier and bedrooms above – ideal for parties. In the main house (charming, heavily wallpapered, colourful) is the handsome Jouy'd room for four. From the very lovely garden are hilltop views. Monsieur manages the Port and is a mine of local knowledge; Madame tends house, garden and guests, masterfully. Proud of their region, naturally generous, elegant, poised, they are keen to advise on explorations: nature, hiking, historical visits… Legend has it that Queen Victoria 'stopped' at this very gracious house.

Price	€48–€56. Extra person €12.
Rooms	3: 1 double, 1 quadruple, 1 suite.
Meals	Restaurants 2-5km.
Closed	Rarely.
Directions	D49 to Eu; before Eu left for Forest of Eu & Route de Beaumont; house 3km on right.

Catherine & Jean-Marie Demarquet
Manoir de Beaumont,
76260 Eu, Seine-Maritime

Tel	+33 (0)2 35 50 91 91
Fax	+33 (0)2 35 50 19 45
Email	catherine@demarquet.eu
Web	www.demarquet.eu

Entry 142   Map 1

Normandy

Le Clos Mélise

In a charming village on the edge of a green, a dear little cottage in a big sloping garden. Madame is a quietly-spoken, welcoming and attentive hostess, keeps a spotless and pretty house, and joyfully paints with oils; her love of colour is reflected inside and out. The attic bedroom, up a steep staircase, may be small but is delightfully cosy; the other two, one large, one small, are on the ground floor of an adjacent wing, each with a door to the garden. Walls are toile de Jouy'd, floorboards are polished, fluffy towels are tied with bright bows, and breakfasts are delicious.

Ethical Collection: Environment.
See page 432.

Price	€45.
Rooms	3 doubles.
Meals	Restaurant in village.
Closed	Rarely.
Directions	From Le Tréport D925 for Dieppe 15km; in Biville sur Mer right Rue de l'Église; No. 14 faces you in middle of fork in road.

Marie-José Klaes
Le Clos Mélise,
14 rue de l'Église,
76630 Biville sur Mer,
Seine-Maritime

Tel	+33 (0)2 35 83 14 71
Email	closmelise@wanadoo.fr

Entry 143   Map 1

Normandy

Manoir de Graincourt

A large and rather grand Anglo-Norman-style villa bang next to an impressive 11th-century church in a small village. You are surrounded by wide lush gardens with neat hedges and mature trees. Bedrooms, four in the main house, are a flurry of colour, polished floorboards and some fine rural antiques; the fifth is in the converted stables where a games room lies. Your very professional hosts give you a vibrant red guest sitting room and dinner in the Aga-warm kitchen at a communal table – maybe scallop flan, beef stew, Norman cheeses. You are close to the seaside, golf courses and beautiful gardens.

Ethical Collection: Environment.
See page 432.

Price	€90-€130. €150 for 4.
Rooms	5: 1 twin, 4 family rooms: 3 for 2-3, 1 for 2-4.
Meals	Dinner with wine, €37.
Closed	Rarely.
Directions	From Dieppe ferry D925 5km to Derchigny village; take road opp. petrol station & follow signs to Église; house next to church.

Philippe & Anne-Lise Baron
Manoir de Graincourt,
10 place Ludovic Panel,
76370 Derchigny Graincourt,
Seine-Maritime
Tel/Fax +33 (0)2 35 84 12 88
Email contact@manoir-de-graincourt.fr
Web www.manoir-de-graincourt.fr

Entry 144   Map 1

Normandy

Saint Mare

A fresh modern house under a steep slate roof in a lush green sanctuary; it could not be more tranquil. The garden really is lovely and worth a wander – a tailored lawn, a mass of colour, huge banks of rhododendrons for which the village is renowned (three of its gardens are open to the public). Claudine runs home and B&B with effortless efficiency and gives you homemade brioches for breakfast; smiling Remi leads you to guest quarters in a freshly wood-clad house reached via stepping stones through the laurels. Bedrooms are comfortable, sunny, spotless, shining and utterly peaceful – two are big enough to lounge in.

Price	€65-€80. €105-€120 for 4.
Rooms	3: 1 suite for 2, 1 suite for 2 & kitchenette, 1 suite for 4.
Meals	Restaurants 20-minute walk.
Closed	Rarely.
Directions	From Dieppe D75 to Varengeville sur Mer, 8kms; 1st left after entering village onto Chemin des Petites Bruyères; house on left.

Claudine Goubet
Saint Mare, Le Quesnot,
Chemin de Petites Bruyères,
76119 Varengeville sur Mer,
Seine-Maritime
Tel +33 (0)2 35 85 99 28
Email claudine.goubet@chsaintmare.com
Web www.chsaintmare.com

Entry 145   Map 4

Normandy

Chalet du Bel Event

Informal elegance, French charm from 1864, a dose of American antiques and masses of warmly impressionistic paintings. Boston-born Daniel adopted France, married chiropractor Virginie, had three children and chose these two houses, one for B&B, one for the family, in an area they both love; then his mother, a prolific painter, joined them. They put books everywhere and create a youthful, unsmart, very laid-back atmosphere. The guest-house dining, sitting and music rooms have a period feel: old floors, high ceilings, views to the delicious garden, lots of stairs to the top rooms.

Normandy

Château Le Bourg

Silk bedspreads and scatter cushions, soaps, colognes and fresh roses… and Leonora's mix of English mahogany and French fabrics is as refined as her dinners. Having finished the soberly elegant bedrooms of her grand 19th-century mansion (the creamy room with the boudoir touches is en suite) she is turning her attention to the garden: it will undoubtedly delight. An intelligent hostess and fine cook, she is both entertaining and generous, handles house parties for celebrations and has a mass of books for you to browse on your return from walking the old railway line or exploring the cliffs. *Sawday self-catering also.*

Price	€49-€60.		Price	€85-€100.
Rooms	4 doubles. Extra beds for children.		Rooms	2 doubles.
Meals	Bistro-épicerie in village.		Meals	Dinner with wine, €30-€65.
Closed	Rarely.		Closed	Rarely.
Directions	From Dieppe D925 for St Valéry en Caux; 3.5km after Le Bourg Dun, left for La Chapelle sur Dun; opp. church, left at café go to end; on left.		Directions	A16 from Calais; exit 23 to A28, exit 6 for Londinières. D12 for 8km to Bures en Bray. House opposite church, with high iron gates between red & white brick pillars.

	Daniel Westhead			Leonora Macleod
	Chalet du Bel Event,			Château Le Bourg,
	76740 La Chapelle sur Dun,			27 Grande Rue, 76660 Bures en Bray,
	Seine-Maritime			Seine-Maritime
Tel	+33 (0)2 35 57 08 44		Tel	+33 (0)2 35 94 09 35
Email	info@chaletdubelevent.com		Fax	+33 (0)2 35 94 09 35
Web	www.chaletdubelevent.com		Email	leonora.macleod@wanadoo.fr

Entry 146   Map 4

Entry 147   Map 4

Normandy

23 Grand Rue

Peter loves his wines (he was in the trade), Madeleine is energetic and vivacious, both welcome you generously at their 'maison bourgeoise' on the edge of a château village. Set back from the road behind fence and clipped hedge are four cosy classically furnished bedrooms: books and fresh flowers, immaculate duvets, smart French furniture, a calvados nightcap on the landing. Shower rooms are small and beautifully tiled. There's a conservatory for breakfast, a front room for relaxing and, at a table dressed with silver, French dinners are served. Dieppe, Rouen, Honfleur: all are wonderfully close.

Price	€45–€70.
Rooms	4: 2 doubles, 1 twin; 1 triple with separate bath.
Meals	Dinner with wine, €25.
Closed	Rarely.
Directions	A28 exit 9 to Neufchâtel en Bray; D1 Dieppe to Mesnières en Bray. Through village, tall cream house on left after village centre, 150m after café.

Peter & Madeleine Mitchell
23 Grand Rue,
76270 Mesnières en Bray,
Seine-Maritime

Tel	+33 (0)2 32 97 06 31
Email	info@23grandrue.com
Web	www.23grandrue.com

Entry 148   Map 4

Normandy

La Charretterie

A delicious 18th-century working farmhouse, in the family for three generations. Views sail over pastures, cows and gorgeous garden: clumps of lavender, exuberant roses, weathered teak, hazes of flowers. The Prévosts are a courteously friendly pair whose efficiency shines. Expect fresh, harmonious and beamy bedrooms, one under the eaves, the other down, and two shower rooms immaculately dotted with mosaics and fresh flowers. No sitting room but a big breakfast room warm, woody and inviting, its long table spread with homemade breads, brioche, yogurts and jams. A super stopover on the way to the coast.

Price	€60.
Rooms	2: 1 double, 1 quadruple.
Meals	Restaurants 3km.
Closed	Never.
Directions	From Dieppe D927 for Rouen; exit Bacqueville en Caux onto D149 for Bacqueville, 2km; right, then immed. left into Rue du Pavé; over 3 x-roads, on for 800m. House behind farmyard entrance.

Corinne & Arnaud Prévost
La Charretterie,
4 rue du Tilleul, 76730 Pierreville,
Seine-Maritime

Tel	+33 (0)2 35 04 26 45
Email	arnaud.prevost@cegetel.net
Web	charretterie.perso.cegetel.net

Entry 149   Map 4

Normandy

Le Clos du Gui Nel

Brace yourself for the last lap home or, better still, unwind in this leafy Norman oasis, neatly set between Dieppe and Le Havre. Welsh cob ponies graze in the lee of a little Norman church and bantams strut by this beautifully restored farmhouse. A deep pitched roof caps the attractive timbered façade, the stout oak doors and the high windows. Comfortable, immaculate ground-floor rooms have their own entrance. If up and about early you may meet Etienne, a doctor, as he dashes off to work, or chat to Catherine about her beloved cobs as you breakfast on French pastries in the handsome dining room.

Price	€75.
Rooms	2 doubles.
Meals	Restaurant 2km.
Closed	Never.
Directions	From Dieppe D925 to Veules les Roses; D142 to Fontaine le Dun; D89 Bourville to Canville les Deux Églises. Do not go into Bourville; entrance on right next to small church set back from road.

Catherine & Etienne Stevens
Le Clos du Gui Nel,
4 rue de Canville,
76740 Bourville,
Seine-Maritime
Tel   +33 (0)2 35 57 02 31
Email contact@gui-nel.com
Web   www.gui-nel.com

Entry 150   Map 4

Normandy

Le Clos du Vivier

The lush garden shelters fantails, ducks, bantams, sleek cats and a phenomenal variety of shrubs and flowering plants. While Monsieur works in town, Madame tends all this, and her guests, with respect for everyone's privacy; she also offers guidance on hiking, and there's tennis and fishing nearby. She's an intelligent, active and graceful person, her bedrooms, some under sloping ceilings, are snugly, cosily colourful, her bathrooms big and luxurious, her breakfast richly varied. After a jaunt, you can read their books, relax among their lovely antiques or make tea in their breakfast room. And the cliffs at Étretat are 20 minutes away.

Price	€90–€100.
Rooms	3: 1 twin/double, 1 triple, 1 suite for 5 (1 double, 1 triple).
Meals	Restaurants in Valmont, 1km.
Closed	Rarely.
Directions	From Dieppe D925 W for Fécamp 60km; left D17 to Valmont centre; left D150 for Ourville 1.2km; right Chemin du Vivier; house 2nd entrance on right (No. 4), signed 'Fleur de Soleil'.

Dominique Cachera & François Grev
Le Clos du Vivier,
4-6 chemin du Vivier,
76540 Valmont, Seine-Maritime
Tel   +33 (0)2 35 29 90 95
Fax   +33 (0)2 35 27 44 49
Email le.clos.du.vivier@wanadoo.fr
Web   www.leclosduvivier.com

Entry 151   Map 4

Normandy

Manoir de la Rue Verte

The 300-year-old house stands in a classic, poplar-sheltered Seine-Maritime farmyard, its worn old stones and bricks and the less worn flints bearing witness to its age, as does the fine timberwork inside. Otherwise it has been fairly deeply modernised, but your retired farmer hosts and the long lace-clothed breakfast table before the winter log fire are most welcoming. Madame was born here, has a winning smile and loves to talk – in French. Her pleasant rooms are in good, rural French style and the only sounds are the occasional lowing of the herd and the shushing of the poplars.

Price	€48-€50.
Rooms	4: 1 double, 1 triple; 2 doubles sharing shower & wc.
Meals	Auberge 1km; restaurant 4km.
Closed	Rarely.
Directions	From Dieppe N27 for Rouen 29km; right N29 through Yerville, cont. 4.5km; left D20 to Motteville; right to Flamanville. 21 rue Verte behind church. Farm 300m on left; signed.

Yves & Béatrice Quevilly Baret
Manoir de la Rue Verte,
21 rue Verte,
76970 Flamanville,
Seine-Maritime
Tel   +33 (0)2 35 96 81 27

Entry 152   Map 4

Normandy

Manoir Le Brécy

Jérôme has happy childhood holiday memories of this large 17th-century manor house; he and Patricia moved in some years ago to join his *grand-mère*, who had been living alone in a few rooms for years. A long path flanked by willows leads down to the Seine: perfect (when not mud-bound!) for an evening stroll. Your suite (twin room, small sitting room) is on the ground floor, in classically French coral and cream, its windows opening to a walled garden. Breakfast is when you fancy: brioches, walnuts, fresh fruit in a pretty green-panelled room. Ask Patricia about the Abbey and walks to its gardens.

Ethical Collection: Environment.
See page 432.

Price	€78-€83.
Rooms	1 suite & kitchenette.
Meals	Restaurant in village.
Closed	Rarely.
Directions	From Paris A13 exit 24 'Maison Brulée'; ferry from La Bouille-Bac to Sahurs; left for St Martin de Boscherville; after Quevillon, 2nd left for Le Brécy; signed.

Jérôme & Patricia Lanquest
Manoir Le Brécy, 72 route du Brécy,
76840 St Martin de Boscherville,
Seine-Maritime
Tel   +33 (0)2 35 32 69 92
Fax   +33 (0)2 35 32 00 30
Email   jlanquest@tele2.fr
Web   home.tele2.fr/lebrecy

Entry 153   Map 4

Normandy

Manoir de Captot

Gracious living is declared at the pillared gates, the drive curves through horse pastures to a serene 18th-century mansion, the forest behind may ring with the stag's call, the heads of his kin abound. Peacefully formal, it is a fine classic French interior: gorgeous primrose-yellow dining room with an oval mahogany table for breakfast, collection-filled drawing room, one beautiful high first-floor bedroom with the right curly antiques and pink Jouy draperies (the attic suite is a touch plainer). Madame cherishes her mansion and resembles it: gently friendly with impeccable manners.

Price	€85–€95. Child's twin €40.
Rooms	3: 1 double, 1 family suite, 1 child's twin.
Meals	Restaurants nearby.
Closed	Rarely.
Directions	From Rouen D982; north side of river Seine going west 3km to Canteleu on left; D351 for Sahurs; entrance on right 900m after church, big iron gates.

Michèle Desrez
Manoir de Captot,
42 route de Sahurs,
76380 Canteleu, Seine-Maritime
Tel   +33 (0)2 35 36 00 04
Email   captot76@yahoo.fr
Web   www.captot.com

Normandy

22 rue Hénault

The elegant black door hides a light, stylish interior with soul-lifting views across old Rouen to the spires of the cathedral. Dominique, a cultured hostess full of energy and enthusiasm, has a flair for decoration – as her paintings, coverings and contemporary and country furniture declare. Oriental rugs on parquet floors, French windows to balcony and garden, bedrooms brimful of interest. Nothing standard, nothing too studied, a very personal home and leisurely breakfasts promising delicious surprises. The house's hillside position in this attractive suburb is equally special. Such value! *Covered garage space for one car.*

Price	€58.
Rooms	3 doubles.
Meals	Restaurant 1km.
Closed	October-November.
Directions	In Rouen follow Gare SNCF signs; Rue Rochefoucault right of station; left Rue des Champs des Oiseaux; over 2 traffic lights into Rue Vigné; fork left Rue Hénault; black door on left.

Dominique Gogny
22 rue Hénault,
76130 Mont St Aignan,
Seine-Maritime
Tel   +33 (0)2 35 70 26 95
Email   chambreavecvue@online.fr
Web   chambreavecvue.online.fr

Normandy

45 rue aux Ours

You are in a privileged position in the heart of old Rouen, 100m from the cathedral. This beamed and passaged building of character, built around a cobbled courtyard, is, inside, a gothic cubby hole full of charm and peculiarity: a treasure trove of religious curios and ethnic pieces, bric a brac and family memorabilia. Once he has warmed to you, dry-humoured Monsieur enjoys sharing – in English, German or Norman – the history of Rouen. Bedrooms are unmodernised and simple, bathrooms just adequate, breakfast generous and good, and Madame kindly attentive. Authentic – and fun. *Car park a short walk.*

Price	€62. Apartment €70.
Rooms	1 + 1: 1 double. 1 apartment for 5.
Meals	Restaurants within walking distance.
Closed	Rarely.
Directions	On cathedral-side embankment: at Théâtre des Arts, Rue Jeanne d'Arc; Rue aux Ours 2nd on right but NO parking: leave car in Bourse or Pucelle car park & walk.

Philippe & Annick
Aunay-Stanguennec
45 rue aux Ours,
76000 Rouen,
Seine-Maritime
Tel   +33 (0)2 35 70 99 68

Normandy

Le Clos Jouvenet

From your bath you gaze upon the cathedral spire. It is a privilege to stay in these refined city surroundings, safely inside a serene walled garden above the towers of Rouen. The garden is as elegantly uncomplicated as the house and its Belgian owners, the décor classic sophisticated French to suit the gentle proportions: there are pretty pictures and prints, lots of books, handsome antique furniture and breakfast is served in the kitchen, warmed by slate and oak. Madame is charming, Monsieur enjoys guests too, and you wake to birdsong and church bells. *Priority to 2 nights at weekends & high season.*

Price	€85–€110.
Rooms	4: 2 doubles, 2 twins/doubles.
Meals	Restaurants within walking distance.
Closed	Mid-December to mid-January.
Directions	From train station for Bd de L'Yser for Boulogne-Amiens; take Neufchatel road in same direction, 1st right Rue du Champ du Pardon; Rue Jouvenet; left at lights; 2nd right.

Catherine de Witte
Le Clos Jouvenet,
42 rue Hyacinthe Langlois,
76000 Rouen, Seine-Maritime
Tel   +33 (0)2 35 89 80 66
Fax   +33 (0)2 35 98 37 65
Email   cdewitte@club-internet.fr
Web   www.leclosjouvenet.com

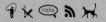

Normandy

Château de Fleury la Forêt

A huge place that breathes comfort – and a challenge for the young Caffins: half the château's 65 rooms have yet to be restored. They live in one wing, you in another; a museum sits in between. The handsome guest suite is pale-panelled and red-brocaded, with a separate room for children; the double elegantly and creamily draped. The immense entrance hall has a giant dolls house and a multitude of antlers; there are stylish lawns to the front and majestic trees, stables for the show-jumpers, a maize-maze for you. Breakfast is at a vast table in a kitchen lined with blue porcelain. *Giverny a 40-minute drive.*

Price	€78. Suite €120.
Rooms	2: 1 double, 1 family suite for 4.
Meals	Restaurants 6km.
Closed	Rarely.
Directions	From Gournay en Bray N31 for Rouen 17km; left D921 to Lyons la Forêt; D6 for Étrépagny; 1st left for Château de Fleury; left at fork; 5km, house on right, signed.

	Kristina Caffin
	Château de Fleury la Forêt,
	27480 Lyons la Forêt, Eure
Tel	+33 (0)2 32 49 63 91
Fax	+33 (0)2 32 49 71 67
Email	info@chateau-fleury-la-foret.com
Web	www.chateau-fleury-la-foret.com

Entry 158   Map 4

Normandy

Le Moulin Auguérard

The bedrooms are pretty, the building is lofty and the owners are charming and attentive. Nadine works in marketing, Guy works in Paris. You have a ground-floor sitting room with an open fire, a cosy feel and a stair curving up to one of the family's bedrooms above – and the guest double, which has a seagrass floor and a pretty antique bed. On the second floor is the much bigger triple: stripped boards, elegant fireplace, soaring views. (Note: between the floors is an independent flat that the owners plan to buy.) The garden is whimsical, the village is delightful and the mill race flows by. *Open weekends only.*

Price	€60–€70.
Rooms	2: 1 double, 1 triple.
Meals	Restaurant 600m.
Closed	Closed weekdays (July to mid-August open 7 days a week).
Directions	Beauvais D981 to Gisors; right by château for St Denis; at St Paër right D17 into St Denis. Thro' village, house at far end; entrance on right after public gardens.

	Nadine & Guy Masurier
	Le Moulin Auguérard,
	46 rue Guérard,
	27140 St Denis le Ferment, Eure
Tel	+33 (0)2 32 27 09 62
Email	lemoulinauguerard@orange.fr
Web	www.lemoulinauguerard.com

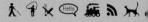

Entry 159   Map 5

Normandy

La Lévrière

It's aptly named: the garden laps at the river bank where ducks and moorhens nest. Trout swim, birds chirrup, deer pop by – a dreamy village setting. Madame is charming and takes everything (including escaped horses in the garden!) in her stride and her entire young family love it when guests come to stay. Breakfast is at an oak table with blue-painted chairs; garden loungers tempt you to stay all day. Two bedrooms are in the granary, one up, one down, the third in the attic of the coach house. Creamy walls, sweeping floors, rafters, toile de Jouy, fresh flowers. Stay for a long while.

Price	€65-€70.
Rooms	3: 1 triple, 2 suites: 1 for 3, 1 for 4.
Meals	Restaurant opposite.
Closed	Never.
Directions	From Gisors; right by château for St Denis; at St Paër right onto D17 into St Denis; house on right, signed.

Sandrine & Pascal Gravier
La Lévrière,
24 rue Guérard,
27140 St Denis le Ferment, Eure
Tel   +33 (0)2 32 27 04 78
Email   sandrinegravier@wanadoo.fr
Web   www.normandyrooms.com

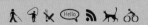

Entry 160   Map 5

Normandy

Les Ombelles

Madame's home is old-fashioned cosy. To one side are pretty old houses and church; behind, a cottagey garden that runs down to the Epte – the river that Monet diverted at Giverny (35km) for his famous ponds. Madame, poised and intelligent, shares her great knowledge of all things Norman, including food, and has devised her own detailed tourist circuits. Smallish roadside bedrooms have antiques and traditional wallpaper, a pretty hand-painted wardrobe from Lorraine and an Art Deco brass bed. No dayroom for guests, but you may share the owner's sitting room.

Price	€55-€60.
Rooms	3: 1 double, 1 suite; 1 double with separate bath & wc.
Meals	Dinner with wine, €20.
Closed	Mid-November to mid-March.
Directions	From Dieppe D915 to Gisors. Cross Gisors; D10 for Vernon. In Dangu, Rue du Gué is beside River Epte.

Nicole de Saint Père
Les Ombelles,
4 rue du Gué,
27720 Dangu, Eure
Tel   +33 (0)2 32 55 04 95
Email   vextour@aol.com
Web   www.lesombelles.fr

Entry 161   Map 5

Normandy

La Réserve

Big and beautiful, old and new, refined, relaxed and unpretentious. The Brunets, as delightful as their house, have the lightness of touch to combine the best of modern French taste with an eye for authenticity in a brand new house. Light floods in through recycled château windows on both sides of the classically narrow *maison de campagne*. Outside: soft limewash walls hemmed by lavender fields; inside: matt grey woodwork, handsome rugs on polished floors, gorgeous fabrics and fine antiques. Deep woodland on three sides... in summer take a deckchair to the orchards and sit under the apple trees. Wonderful.

Ethical Collection: Environment.
See page 432.

Price	€100-€160.
Rooms	5: 2 doubles, 3 twins.
Meals	Restaurants 1.5-4km.
Closed	December-March, except by arrangement.
Directions	From A13 exit 16 to Giverny; left Rue Claude Monet; after church & Hotel Baudy, 1st left Rue Blanche Hoschedé Monet; Chemin du Grand Val, 1.2km; left on white arrow, immed. right on track 800m, left to house.

	Didier & Marie Lorraine Brunet
	La Réserve,
	27620 Giverny, Eure
Tel	+33 (0)2 32 56 99 09
Fax	+33 (0)2 32 56 99 09
Email	mlreserve@gmail.com
Web	www.giverny-lareserve.com

Normandy

Clos de Mondétour

Tiny church to one side, lazy river behind, views to weeping willows and majestic limes – the house oozes grace and tranquillity. Grégoire and Aude have created a calm, charming atmosphere inside: this is a family home. Lofty, light-drenched bedrooms with polished floorboards, antiques and monogrammed bed linen are beautifully refined; bathrooms are light and luxurious. The living area, with a striking tiled floor and bold colours, is a restful space in which to settle in front of a log fire – or enjoy a special breakfast among fresh flowers and family silver. Aude's horses graze in the meadow behind.

Price	€90-€120.
Rooms	2: 1 double, 1 twin.
Meals	Restaurants nearby.
Closed	Rarely.
Directions	A13 to Paris, exit 17 for Gaillon; D31 to Auteuil Authouíllet; main street in village left to Chambray D836; D63 for 2km to Fontaine. Entrance next to phone box.

	Aude Jeanson
	Clos de Mondétour,
	17 rue de la Poste,
	27120 Fontaine sous Jouy, Eure
Tel	+33 (0)2 32 36 68 79
Email	aude.2bjeanson@wanadoo.fr
Web	www.closdemondetour.hbg.fr

Normandy

L'Aulnaie

Michel and Éliane have invested natural good taste in their restoration of this lovely 19th-century farmhouse in a particularly pretty village. Guests share a self-contained part of the house with its own dayroom and breakfast area, and there's lots of space to settle in, with books, music and open fire. Bedrooms are gentle, beautiful, fresh, with toile de Jouy fabrics, plain walls and honey-coloured floors. Enthusiastic, charming Éliane is an amateur painter and inspired gardener, pointing out the rich and the rare; lawns sweep down to a stream that meanders beneath high wooded cliffs. Such value!

Price	€75.
Rooms	2: 1 double, 1 twin.
Meals	Restaurants nearby.
Closed	Rarely.
Directions	A13 exit 16 for Cocherel; after 10km to Chambray; left at monument; left after 100m to Fontaine sous Jouy. In centre right Rue de l'Ancienne Forge for 800m; Rue de l'Aulnaie on right.

Éliane & Michel Philippe
L'Aulnaie,
29 rue de l'Aulnaie,
27120 Fontaine sous Jouy, Eure

Tel   +33 (0)2 32 36 89 05
Fax   +33 (0)2 32 36 89 05
Email   emi.philippe@worldonline.fr
Web   chambre-fontaine.chez-alice.fr

Entry 164   Map 4

Normandy

Manoir Les Perdrix

The young, hands-on owners of Les Perdrix are full of infectious enthusiasm for their new enterprise: running a themed, welcoming, upmarket B&B. Food tastings, painting courses, walking weekends – they can do it all! In the throes of serious restoration, the old house has an intimate dining room for tasty breakfasts and jolly dinners, a cavernous reception room and comfortable bedrooms off a winding second-floor corridor: thick duvets and pretty linen, coordinated fabrics and polished floors, shower gels and plush bathrooms. The run-around garden – great for kids – is within earshot of the road to Verneuil.

Price	€75–€95. Extra person €15.
Rooms	3: 2 twins/doubles, 1 family suite for 4.
Meals	Dinner with wine, €15–€22.
Closed	Rarely.
Directions	From Paris A13 for Versailles & Rouen to A12; N12 to Dreux; approx. 25km after Dreux do not take 1st or 2nd exits for Tillières, but next right, signed. Left at fork for entrance.

Christine Vandemoortele
Manoir Les Perdrix,
Les Marnières,
27570 Tillières sur Avre, Eure

Tel   +33 (0)6 21 21 08 52
Email   postmaster@manoirlesperdrix.fr
Web   www.manoirlesperdrix.fr

Entry 165   Map 4

Normandy

Clair Matin

Handsomely carved Colombian furniture, strong colours, interesting prints – not what you expect to find inside an 18th-century manor with a Norman cottage face and a surprising turret. Your charming Franco-Spanish hosts raised five children in South America before renovating their French home – it joyfully vibrates with echoes of faraway places. Bedrooms, not huge, are solidly comfortable; bathrooms are immaculate. There are fresh breads and homemade jams at the huge Andean cedar breakfast table, and good conversation. Jean-Pierre is a passionate gardener and his plantations are maturing beautifully.

Price	€60–€75. €90–€100 for 4.
Rooms	3: 1 double, 1 family room, 1 suite.
Meals	Auberges 6km.
Closed	Rarely.
Directions	From A13 exit 17 for Gaillon D316 for Évreux through Autheuil, St Vigor & up hill 11km; right to Reuilly; house on road, 200m past Mairie on right.

Jean-Pierre & Amaia Trevisani
Clair Matin,
19 rue de l'Église,
27930 Reuilly, Eure
Tel   +33 (0)2 32 34 71 47
Fax   +33 (0)2 32 34 97 64
Email   bienvenue@clair-matin.com

Entry 166   Map 4

Normandy

Manoir de la Boissière

Madame cooks great Norman dishes with home-grown ingredients served on good china. She has been doing B&B for years, is well organised and still enjoys meeting new people when she's not too busy. Guest quarters, independent of the house, have pretty French-style rooms, good bedding and excellent tiled shower rooms while the caringly restored 15th-century farm buildings, the animated farmyard (peacocks, ducks, black swans) and the furniture – each item carefully chosen, some tenderly hand-painted – all give it character. Near the motorway yet utterly peaceful: an exceptional situation.

Price	€50–€52. Triple €70.
Rooms	5: 2 doubles (one with kitchenette), 2 twins, 1 triple.
Meals	Dinner with cider, €24. Guest kitchen.
Closed	Rarely.
Directions	From Rouen N15 for Paris 40km; at Gaillon right D10 for La Croix St Leufroy approx. 7km; in La Boissaye, Chambres d'Hôtes signs.

Clotilde & Gérard Sénécal
Manoir de la Boissière,
Hameau la Boissaye,
27490 La Croix St Leufroy, Eure
Tel   +33 (0)2 32 67 70 85
Fax   +33 (0)2 32 67 03 18
Email   chambreslaboissiere@wanadoo.fr
Web   www.chambres-la-boissiere.com

Entry 167   Map 4

Normandy

La Londe

The big flowery garden flows down to the river and the old farmhouse and yesteryear buildings are as neat as new pins. Sweet Madeleine devotes herself to home and guests. Bedrooms are neat, clean, pretty, sober and relaxing; the double's French windows open to the garden, the perfect small suite sits under the eaves. Expect antique lace, silver snuff boxes (Madame dealt in antiques), a kitchen/salon for guests and fine breakfasts with garden views. A form of perfection in a privileged and peaceful spot: woods and water for walking, canoeing, fishing; Giverny – or Rouen – a half-hour drive.

Price	€56-€60.
Rooms	2: 1 double, 1 suite for 3.
Meals	Restaurants 5km. Guest kitchen.
Closed	Rarely.
Directions	A13 exit 19 for Louviers & Évreux; 2nd exit N154 to Acquigny; D71 through Heudreville for Cailly to La Londe; left; house on right.

Madeleine & Bernard Gossent
La Londe,
4 sente de l'Abreuvoir,
27400 Heudreville sur Eure, Eure
Tel +33 (0)2 32 40 36 89
Fax +33 (0)2 32 50 25 34
Email madeleine.gossent@online.fr
Web www.lalonde.online.fr

Entry 168 Map 4

Normandy

Au Vieux Logis

They are full of character and terribly French, this artist owner and her crooked house marked by the slings and arrows of 500 years: wonky floorboards, bathrooms among the beams, old-fashioned floral bedrooms and a sensuous garden full of old favourites: lilac and honeysuckle, luscious shrubs and fruit trees. Set in the middle of the village, the quiet old house has an atmosphere that inspires ease and rest. (Saint-Exupéry, author of the *Le Petit Prince* and a friend of Madame's father, stayed here.) Madame, a good, generous soul, was once an antique dealer so breakfast is served on old silver.

Price	€48-€96.
Rooms	4: 2 doubles, 1 triple, 1 quadruple.
Meals	Dinner €17. Wine €15.
Closed	Rarely.
Directions	A13 exit 19 to Louviers; D313 for Elbeuf 11km; left on D60 to St Didier des Bois. House with white iron gate opp. church.

Annick Auzoux
Au Vieux Logis,
27370 St Didier des Bois, Eure
Tel +33 (0)2 32 50 60 93
Fax +33 (0)2 32 25 41 83
Email levieuxlogis5@orange.fr
Web www.levieuxlogis.fr

Entry 169 Map 4

Normandy

Manoir d'Hermos

The sedately old-French panelled rooms with good antiques and satin touches are up the grand old staircase of this 16th-century house where brick and sandstone sit in peace by birdy orchard, pastoral meadows and spreading lake. Madame is a most welcoming hostess, full of spontaneous smiles, who puts flowers everywhere and whose family has owned the house for 100 years. She also organises seminars (not when B&B guests are here), serves breakfasts and brunches at separate tables and gardens brilliantly: trees are being planted to Napoleonic plans discovered in the archives.

Normandy

Les Clématites

An enchanting *maison de maître*, one of several that housed the nimble-fingered ribbon weavers, with the bonus of fine table d'hôtes. Hidden amid the fields of the Normandy plains, it stands in a dream of a garden, overgrown here, brought to heel there, flanked by a majestic walnut and age-old pears, filled with shrub roses; the odd forgotten bench adds to the Flaubertian charm. Inside, Marie-Hélène, bright-eyed and eager, has used Jouy cloth and elegant colours to dress the country-French bedrooms that fill the first floor. These ex-Parisian hosts are courteous, considerate, truly endearing.

Price	€59-€75. Triple €78-€94. Quadruple €113.
Rooms	2: 1 triple, 1 quadruple.
Meals	Restaurants 2-8km.
Closed	Never.
Directions	From A13, A28 exit 13. D438 on left for 400m, right to D92; on for 1km, signed.

Price	€65.
Rooms	3: 1 double, 1 twin, 1 triple.
Meals	Dinner with wine, €25.
Closed	Rarely.
Directions	From Évreux D613 for Lisieux 50km; entering Duranville right D41 for St Aubin de Scellon 2.5km; drive on right.

Béatrice & Patrice Noël-Windsor
Manoir d'Hermos,
27800 St Éloi de Fourques, Eure
Tel   +33 (0)2 32 35 51 32
Fax   +33 (0)2 32 35 51 32
Email contact@hermos.fr
Web   www.hermos.fr

**Marie-Hélène François
& Hughes de Morchoven**
Les Clématites,
Hameau de la Charterie,
27230 St Aubin de Scellon, Eure
Tel   +33 (0)2 32 45 46 52
Email la.charterie@wanadoo.fr
Web   monsite.orange.fr/la.charterie

Entry 170   Map 4

Entry 171   Map 4

Normandy

Les Hauts Vents

Corine, a farmer's daughter, was born nearby and is cheerfully passionate about the area and its rural heritage. Her bewitching garden – where, Monet-style, a bridge spans the lily pond – is listed as a protected bird sanctuary. The house is long, low and typical Normandy. Two of the bedrooms are on the first floor of a converted outbuilding, all are painted in joyous colours and are freshly, modestly furnished. Breakfast is in the family's conservatory where musical instruments jostle with collections of plants, teapots and Russian dolls. Camargue horses and a donkey graze in the paddock. An enchanting place.

Ethical Collection: Food.
See page 432.

Price	€60. Extra person €13.
Rooms	3: 1 double, 1 triple, 1 family room for 5.
Meals	Dinner with wine, €22. Light supper €15.
Closed	Rarely.
Directions	From Rouen A13 for Caen exit 2; N175 to Pont-Audemer; D810 for Bernay; 1km before Lieurey, right to Les Hauts Vents, 1st right Chemin du Seureur, 1st entrance on left, No. 60.

	Corine Angevin
	Les Hauts Vents,
	27560 Lieurey, Eure
Tel	+33 (0)2 32 57 99 27
Email	corine.angevin@free.fr
Web	leshautsvents.free.fr

Entry 172   Map 4

Normandy

Le Coquerel

Jean-Marc brims with ideas for your stay and love for his garden, modern art and long divine dinners with guests. He has turned the old cottage, surrounded by soft pastures, into a country gem in a flower-exuberant garden. Inside, a mix of the sober, the frivolous, the cultured and the kitsch: old and modern pieces, rustic revival and leather, paintings and brocante. Bedrooms stand out in their uncomplicated good taste, bathrooms are irreproachable, but it's your host who makes the place: duck in cider, strawberry soup and laughter, butterflies alighting on the table at breakfast. *Unfenced water.*

Price	€54–€58. Triple €65. Family room €78.
Rooms	5: 1 double, 1 twin, 1 triple, 2 family rooms.
Meals	Dinner with wine, €24. Picnic available
Closed	Rarely.
Directions	From Pont Audemer D810 for Bernay 12km; right through St Siméon; up hill for Selles; house on left at top.

	Jean-Marc Drumel
	Le Coquerel,
	27560 St Siméon, Eure
Tel	+33 (0)2 32 56 56 08
Fax	+33 (0)2 32 56 56 08
Email	moreau-drumel@wanadoo.fr
Web	perso.wanadoo.fr/chambreshotes

Entry 173   Map 4

Normandy

Les Aubépines

That lovely timber frame embraces a heart-warming antique clutter spread over original bricks, beams, tiles and carved family furniture. Guests share this marvellous space as family; Madame welcomes and cooks with delight (maybe over an open fire) and tends the intimate paradise of her garden whence views glide over forested hills; Monsieur smiles, charms and mends everything. The delicious bedrooms are subtly lit by dormer windows, country-furnished, pastel-hued and comfortably bathroomed; the suite has steep rafters and a smart new shower room. Outstanding – they deserve a medal!
Minimum stay 2 nights.

Price	€65–€70.
Rooms	3: 2 twins/doubles, 1 suite for 4.
Meals	Dinner with wine, €25.
Closed	October–February, except by arrangement.
Directions	From Paris A13 exit 26 for Pont Audemer D89; at 'Médine' r'bout. on for Évreux & Appeville Annebault 4km; left immed. after Les Marettes sign, follow Chambres d'Hôtes signs.

Françoise & Yves Closson Maze
Les Aubépines,
Aux Chauffourniers,
27290 Appeville dit Annebault, Eure
Tel +33 (0)2 32 56 14 25
Fax +33 (0)2 32 56 14 25
Email clossonmaze@orange.fr
Web pagesperso-orange.fr/lesaubepines

Entry 174   Map 4

Normandy

Les Sources Bleues

A privileged setting on the banks of the Seine just below Rouen… once every four years the great armada comes sailing by. The garden (old trees, long grasses, the odd goat) is 50m from the water's edge; there are binoculars for birdwatching. This is a Panda (WWF) house and for guests only: the owners live next door. Bedrooms are in need of a lick of paint but are old-fashioned and charming, the family rooms are squeezed into the attic. You get beams and panelling and windows onto that stunning view, a kitchen/diner, a surprisingly fancy sitting room. Monsieur cooks and Madame has all the time in the world for you.

Price	€55–€68. €78 for 4. Singles €48.
Rooms	4: 2 quadruples, 2 suites for 3.
Meals	Dinner €20. Wine €12–€14; cider €5.
Closed	Rarely.
Directions	From Pont Audemer D139 NE for 10km to Bourneville & D139 to Aizier. There, left at Mairie for Vieux Port, D95; on right.

Yves & Marie-Thérèse Laurent
Les Sources Bleues,
Le Bourg,
27500 Aizier, Eure
Tel +33 (0)2 32 57 26 68
Fax +33 (0)2 32 57 42 25
Web www.les-sources-bleues.com

Entry 175   Map 4

Normandy

Le Moulin

You will warm to this couple who, whatever they turn their hand to – once farm and DIY store, now garden and chambres d'hôtes – turn it to perfection. The lovely half-timbered mill, operating from 1769 to 1965, is in working order still – ask Monsieur to give you a demo at breakfast. Two neat, comfortable and enticing bedrooms have bird's-eye garden views, polished floorboards, gentle hues and dormer windows that open to the sound of trickling waters. The N178 may be close by but the setting is bucolic. There's gourmet dining in Conteville, and a sweet, simple restaurant up the road.

Price	€60. Suite €65.
Rooms	2: 1 double, 1 family suite for 3.
Meals	Restaurants 2km.
Closed	Never.
Directions	From Le Havre exit Tancarville, N178, 10km; 1st right to Foulbec, signed.

Mme Derouet
Le Moulin,
27210 Foulbec, Eure

Tel +33 (0)2 32 56 55 25
Email raymond.derouet@free.fr
Web www.location-honfleur.com/
FR_detail_chambre.asp?numeroauto=37

Entry 176   Map 4

Normandy

La Petite Folie

Two townhouses doubling as havens from the artistic bustle of Honfleur. Built for a sea captain in the 1830s, one displays grand mansarde windows, its more modest 14th-century neighbour houses two self-catering apartments. American Penny married French Thierry, together they created lavish bedrooms, each an enchanting mix of handsome bedsteads, plump duvets, lacquered armchairs, mahogany chests. The garden is a compact, neatly planted square of charm, its focal point a summerhouse with a Byzantine flourish and belvedere views out to sea. All this, and a delightful hostess. *Minimum stay 2 nights weekends & holidays.*

Price	€135. Extra person €25.
Rooms	5: 4 doubles, 1 twin. Extra bed available.
Meals	Restaurants nearby.
Closed	January.
Directions	From Paris A13 exit A29 for Honfleur; follow signs for centre, then 'Naturospace'. Over bridge, cont. on to Rue Haute; keep right of pink house. On for 100m; cream house on right, green shutters.

Penny & Thierry Vincent
La Petite Folie,
44 rue Haute, 14600 Honfleur,
Calvados

Mobile +33 (0)6 74 39 46 46
Email info@lapetitefolie-honfleur.com
Web www.lapetitefolie-honfleur.com

Entry 177   Map 4

Normandy

Au Grey d'Honfleur

There's a secret, fairytale look to this pair of tall narrow houses in a quiet cobbled backstreet. You don't quite know what to expect but you'll be enchanted by the sense of being somewhere rare and special. Stairs and steps in all directions link the little rooms; age-old beams and sloping ceilings contrast with imaginative décor and perfect modern luxury. Josette, a globe-trotting lawyer, knows a thing or two about what's required of a guest bedroom... The formal, delightful miniature terraced garden and fountain, looking down over the haphazard roofs of medieval Honfleur, add to the delight. One of the loveliest. *Minimum stay 2 nights.*

Price	€110–€145.
Rooms	2 doubles.
Meals	Restaurants within walking distance.
Closed	Never.
Directions	From fountain r'bout at entrance to town, ahead to Bassin; left onto Rue de la République, 2nd right to Rue de Près, left to Rue de la Foulerie, left again to Rue de la Bavole. No. 11 on left; car park 50m.

	Josette Roudaut
	Au Grey d'Honfleur,
	11 rue de la Bavole,
	14600 Honfleur, Calvados
Mobile	+33 (0)6 85 07 50 45
Email	info@augrey-honfleur.com
Web	www.augrey-honfleur.com

Normandy

La Cour Sainte Catherine

Through the Norman gateway into the sun-drenched courtyard; Liliane and history embrace you. The building was first a convent, then fishermen's cottages, later a *ciderie*. Now this historic quarter is a conservation area and all has been properly restored. Breakfast viennoiseries are served in the huge beamed room where the apples were once pressed; in summer you relax in the courtyard with fellow guests. Bedrooms are sunny, airy, impeccable, contemporary, one in the hayloft with its own outside stair. There's a small sitting room for guests and Honfleur at your feet; charming Liliane knows the town intimately. *Sawday self-catering also.*

Ethical Collection: Environment. See page 432.

Price	€75–€95. Extra bed €25.
Rooms	6: 2 doubles, 2 twins/doubles, 2 family suites.
Meals	Restaurants nearby.
Closed	Never.
Directions	From St Cathérine Church for Hotel Maison de Lucie; after hotel 1st left; left again. Signed.

	Liliane & Antoine Giaglis
	La Cour Sainte Catherine,
	74 rue du Puits,
	14600 Honfleur, Calvados
Tel	+33 (0)2 31 89 42 40
Email	coursaintecatherine@orange.fr
Web	www.coursaintecatherine.com

Normandy

Manoir de la Marjolaine

The Parisian burgher who built Marjolaine in 1850 designed a toes-in-the-water holiday house – then the sea retreated 300 yards. So you are behind the dunes, on the edge of Cabourg, with beach and village an easy walk (mind the road). Your friendly host is genuinely interested in people, chatting easily in his antique-furnished, tapestry-curtained dining room. He has created five comfortable bedrooms with some exotic moods – African (with great balcony views), super-ornate rococo, black and white baroque, pre-Art Deco pitchpine. Jacuzzi bathrooms, and a good feel of bourgeois comfort all over.

Price	€80-€120. Suite €130.
Rooms	4: 2 doubles, 1 family room, 1 suite for 3.
Meals	Restaurants 200m.
Closed	Rarely.
Directions	From Caen D513 to Cabourg; after 1st Citroën garage on right, left into Chemin de Cailloue; 200m stop; left, house signed on left.

Éric Faye
Manoir de la Marjolaine,
5 avenue du Président Coty,
14390 Le Home Varaville, Calvados
Tel +33 (0)2 31 91 70 25
Fax +33 (0)2 31 91 77 10
Email eric.faye@orange.fr
Web manoirdelamarjolaine.free.fr

Entry 180 Map 4

Normandy

Clos St Hymer

The approach is down a leafy lane, dotted with primroses in spring. Françoise has been doing B&B for years, and is ever ready to welcome guests to her typically Norman house where space is well organised and you won't feel crowded in any way. In the sitting/dining room is a roaring, open-doored wood-burning stove, in the muted double bedroom a deep mauve cotton spread and Louis XIII wardrobe, in the triple an *armoire de mariage* and sliding glass windows. Both bedrooms look onto the pretty garden, complete with table tennis. Typically French, and friendly. Breakfasts are simple affairs.

Price	€65-€75.
Rooms	2: 1 double, 1 triple.
Meals	Dinner with wine, €25.
Closed	January.
Directions	From Pont l'Évêque D579 for Lisieux. At Le Breuil en Auge r'bout D264 to Le Torquesne. 1st right after church, Chemin des Toutains. House 500m on.

Françoise Valle
Clos St Hymer,
14130 Le Torquesne,
Calvados
Tel +33 (0)2 31 61 99 15
Email leclossthymer@wanadoo.fr
Web leclossainthymer.com

Entry 181 Map 4

Normandy

Manoir de Cantepie

It may have a make-believe face, among the smooth green curves of racehorse country, but it is genuine early 1600s and amazing from all sides. Inside, an astounding dining room, resplendently carved, panelled and painted, serves for tasty organic breakfasts. Bedrooms, all incredible value, have a sunny feel, and are delightful: one with white-painted beams and green toile de Jouy, another in yellows, a third with a glorious valley view. Madame, a beautiful Swedish lady, made the curtains and covers. She and her husband are well-travelled, polyglot and cultured: they make their B&B doubly special.

Price	€75.
Rooms	3: 2 doubles, 1 twin.
Meals	Restaurant 1km.
Closed	Mid-November to February.
Directions	From Caen N13 for Lisieux 25km; at Carrefour St Jean, D50 (virtually straight on) for Cambremer; 5km from junc., house on right; signed.

Christine & Arnauld Gherrak
Manoir de Cantepie,
Le Cadran,
14340 Cambremer,
Calvados
Tel   +33 (0)2 31 62 87 27
Fax   +33 (0)2 31 62 87 27

Entry 182   Map 4

Normandy

La Baronnière

The Baron moved on but left a half-timbered glory of a manor house, expanses of grass dotted with apple trees, a stream-fed lake, sheep in a nearby pasture – enchanting. Geese gabble, birds triumph, children rejoice (dens in trees, games on lawns, bikes). Christine, who is English, loves caring for the old house and chatting with her guests; her French husband cooks beautiful meals served in the pretty conservatory. One room is in the old pantry, with a Louis XIV bed on old honeycomb tiles, the other, up an outside staircase in the handsome timbered barn. *Unfenced water. Minimum stay 2 nights. Telephone bookings only. Sawday self-catering also.*

Price	€70–€90.
Rooms	2 doubles.
Meals	Dinner with wine, €40–€50.
Closed	Rarely.
Directions	From Liseux N13 for Evreux; D145 at Thiberville to la Chapelle Hareng. Follow signs; do not go into Cordebugle.

Christine Gilliatt-Fleury
La Baronnière,
14100 Cordebugle,
Calvados
Tel   +33 (0)2 32 46 41 74
Fax   +33 (0)2 32 44 26 09
Email   labaronniere@wanadoo.fr
Web   labaronniere.com

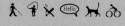

Entry 183   Map 4

Côté Jardin

Behind the urbanity of this fine house in the centre of old Orbec (timbers, thatch, cider orchards), you discover the stableyard with the guest rooms, a pretty garden and a lively little stream. Your hosts came back from African jobs in 2002 and the atmosphere over breakfast in the family kitchen is warm and friendly: they enjoy life and laugh a lot. The coachhouse room has an African theme, *naturellement*, and a splendid tiled shower; up a steep outside staircase, the coachman's room is pale green and floral; the other two are colourful and inviting, too. *Watch children near unfenced water.*

Ethical Collection: Community. See page 432.

La Ferme de l'Oudon

With infectious enjoyment, Madame has rescued this old house, blending designer modern with atmospheric ancient and creating an exciting yet serene haven of well-being. Monsieur is a great decorator. Come and chat in the kitchen conservatory, mingle with this lively couple, admire the potager. The honeymoon-perfect Lavoir suite over the lily pond has fireplace and flat screen, trendy shower and corkscrew stairs up to a sunken bed. The other two have just as much personality. Bathrooms are excellent with careful detail and colour splashes. Taste, panache, generosity. *Use of spa for 2+ night stays. Sawday self-catering also.*

Ethical Collection: Environment. See page 432.

Price	€70.
Rooms	5: 4 doubles, 1 family room for 3-4.
Meals	Occasional dinner €20. Restaurants in Orbec.
Closed	Rarely.
Directions	Orbec 19km south of Lisieux on D519. Turn into village; house on main street on left next to L'Orbecquoise restaurant.

Price	€110-€180.
Rooms	3: 2 doubles, 1 suite.
Meals	Dinner €40, weekdays only. Restaurants 2km.
Closed	December/January.
Directions	A13 exit 29a for La Haie Tondue; D16 to Carrefour St Jean; N13 for Crèvecoeur 3km; D16 to St Pierre sur Dives then D40 to Berville. La Ferme at last x-roads, on left.

Georges & Véronique Lorette
Côté Jardin,
62 rue Grande,
14290 Orbec, Calvados

Tel	+33 (0)2 31 32 77 99
Fax	+33 (0)2 31 32 77 99
Email	georges.lorette@wanadoo.fr
Web	www.cotejardin-france.be

Patrick & Dany Vesque
La Ferme de l'Oudon,
12 route d'Écots,
14170 Berville l'Oudon, Calvados

Tel	+33 (0)2 31 20 77 96
Fax	+33 (0)2 31 20 67 13
Email	contact@fermedeloudon.com
Web	www.fermedeloudon.com

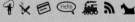

Entry 184 Map 4

Entry 185 Map 4

Normandy

Arclais

Such very special people, quietly, uncomplicatedly intelligent: what the house lacks in years is made up for tenfold by their timeless, down-to-earth Norman hospitality. Close to all things natural, they plough their big veg patch with a cob horse, provide breakfast on a long table in the family dining room, offer good rooms with walls covered in old-fashioned farming photos, where you wake to soul-lifting views over the hushed hills of La Suisse Normande. Nothing gushy; these are independent, strong, charming people who take you to their bosom and genuinely care for your well-being and that of the land.

Price	€44.
Rooms	1 double.
Meals	Occasional dinner with cider, €16.
Closed	Rarely.
Directions	From Caen D562 for Flers, 35km; at Le Fresne D1 for Falaise, 4km; house on right, signed.

	Roland & Claudine Lebatard
	Arclais,
	14690 Pont d'Ouilly, Calvados
Tel	+33 (0)2 31 69 81 65
Fax	+33 (0)2 31 69 81 65
Email	lebatardclaudine@orange.fr
Web	arclais.free.fr

Entry 186   Map 4

Normandy

Château des Riffets

The square-set château stands handsome still as the park recovers from the 1987 storm. Taste the wines and "world's best cider" (says Monsieur), admire yourself in myriad gilded mirrors, luxuriate in a jacuzzi, bare your chest to a rain shower, play the piano, appreciate Madame's superb cooking, and lie at last in an antique bed in one of the great, cherished bedrooms. Take a stroll in the 40-acre wooded park, hire a nearby horse or a canoe, hone your carriage-driving skills. Period ceilings, tapestries and furniture make Riffets a real château experience; the people make it very human. *Ask about wine-tastings.*

Price	€120–€170.
Rooms	4: 2 doubles, 2 suites.
Meals	Dinner with wine & calvados, €50.
Closed	Rarely.
Directions	From Caen N158 for Falaise; at La Jalousie, right D23; right D235 just before Bretteville; signed.

	Anne-Marie & Alain Cantel
	Château des Riffets,
	14680 Bretteville sur Laize, Calvados
Tel	+33 (0)2 31 23 53 21
Fax	+33 (0)2 31 23 75 14
Email	chateau.riffets@wanadoo.fr
Web	www.chateau-des-riffets.com

Entry 187   Map 4

Normandy

Le Clos St Bernard

It was the second farmhouse to be built in the village – and named, 400 years later, in honour of the family dog. Madame loves her house, its history, her family and her guests, and delights in concocting Breton breakfasts of *tergoule*, crêpes, fresh juices, rice pudding. Bedrooms have tiled floors, pretty bedcovers, interesting antiques, showers have embroidered towels and the two-bedroom suite under the eaves is worth the climb. There's a big guest dining salon (with kitchenette where the hens once lived) that opens to a garden terraced against salt breezes. Charming, and great value.
Minimum stay 2 nights. Sawday self-catering also.

Ethical Collection: Environment.
See page 432.

Price	€60.
Rooms	2: 1 double, 1 twin.
Meals	Restaurant in village.
Closed	Mid-December to mid-January.
Directions	From Caen take ring road N; exit 5 for Douvres la Délivrande; 8km, for Courseulles & Mer; at next r'bout D35 left to Reviers; straight at r'bout; 1st left into Rue de l'Église; house at top of road.

	Nicole Vandon
	Le Clos St Bernard,
	36 rue de l'Église, 14470 Reviers,
	Calvados
Tel	+33 (0)2 31 37 87 82
Fax	+33 (0)2 31 37 87 82
Email	leclosbernard@wanadoo.fr
Web	www.leclosbernard.com

Entry 188   Map 4

Normandy

La Malposte

It's just plain lovely, this little group of stone buildings with wooden footbridge over the rushing river, trees and flowers and hens. There's the age-old converted mill for the family and the hunting lodge for guests, where Madame's talented decoration marries nostalgic past (antiques, old prints, photographs) and designer-hued present. A spiral stair winds to a sitting/dining room with guest kitchen and homemade preserves (superb fig jam!); sun pours into the suite at the top. Woods for nut-gathering, beaches nearby, table tennis and that playful stream. Your hosts are sweet and love having families.

Price	€68.
Rooms	3: 1 double; 1 double, 1 twin, sharing shower & wc.
Meals	Restaurants 2-3km. Guest kitchen.
Closed	Rarely.
Directions	From Ouistreham D35 through Douvres & Tailleville; over D404; right at r'bout entering Reviers; 2nd Chambres d'Hôtes on left.

	Patricia & Jean-Michel Blanlot
	La Malposte,
	15 rue des Moulins,
	14470 Reviers, Calvados
Tel	+33 (0)2 31 37 51 29
Fax	+33 (0)2 31 37 51 29
Email	jean-michel.blanlot@wanadoo.fr
Web	www.lamalposte.com

Entry 189   Map 4

Le Mas Normand

A fun place, warm and colourful. Mylène is a live wire, Christian quieter, both are sociable, informal and attentive. They've done a great job on their lovely 18th-century house: old stonework and beams, modern showers, a modern-rustic style, Provençal fabrics and soaps from Mylène's native Drôme. Bedrooms are sheer delight: the sunny double on the ground floor, the charming suites across the yard, one with an *armoire de mariage*, the new family room a big cosy comfy eco caravan. Christian is a trained chef: good food is guaranteed. Ducks, geese and hens roam, the beach is at the end of the lane. Special.

Le Manoir de Basly

In the comfortingly walled luxury of an old stone manor and well-kept antiques, this is a place of classic French refinement where you are received by gracious, friendly hosts who enjoy sharing their lifelong knowledge of their region. In the main house: two faultlessly elegant bedrooms – original stones and timbers, draped beds, delicate muslin, stitched cotton, rich brocade in soft colours – and the guests' living room. On the ground floor of the tiny cottage, the cherry on the cake: a sweet pale bedroom, more lovely furniture, a welcoming sitting area and… a wee terrace of its own. A naturally sophisticated welcome.

Price	€65. Suite €80-€120. Gypsy caravan €80-€100.
Rooms	4: 1 double, 2 suites for 3-4. Gypsy caravan for 2-4.
Meals	Dinner with wine, €40-€44.
Closed	Rarely. Book ahead.
Directions	From Caen D7 for Douvres 8km; left D404 5.5km; D79 to Courseulles sur Mer; D514 to Ver sur Mer; at village entrance 1st left Ave. Provence; 1st right; 1st left cul-de-sac; at end on right.

Price	€90-€130.
Rooms	3: 2 doubles, 1 twin.
Meals	Restaurants nearby.
Closed	Rarely.
Directions	Caen ring road exit 5, D7 for Douvres la Délivrande 10km; at r'bout left D404 to Courseulles sur Mer; 2nd left to Basly. In village opp. Canadian memorial; tall blue gates.

Christian Mériel & Mylène Gilles
Le Mas Normand,
8 impasse de la Rivière,
14114 Ver sur Mer, Calvados

Tel	+33 (0)2 31 21 97 75
Fax	+33 (0)2 31 21 97 75
Email	lemasnormand@wanadoo.fr
Web	www.lemasnormand.com

Monique Casset
Le Manoir de Basly,
2 route de Courseulles,
14610 Basly, Calvados

Tel	+33 (0)2 31 80 12 08
Fax	+33 (0)2 31 80 12 08
Email	lemanoirdebasly@wanadoo.fr
Web	lemanoirdebasly.ifrance.com

Normandy

La Closerie

Dine in — the table d'hôtes makes this special. You'll feast on local dishes and fish caught and cooked by Laurent, a former chef. He and Sandrine are charming, kind, unassuming hosts who live with their family at one end of the 18th-century farmhouse; guests have a separate entrance to their wing. Bedrooms are big, comfortable, uninspiring, shower rooms are spotless, and a wide gravelled courtyard, open to the country road (not suitable for young children) serves as garden and terrace. You're surrounded by flat agriculture but there are beaches and cycling circuits close by, and châteaux and markets aplenty.

Price	€55-€60.
Rooms	2 family rooms for 2-5.
Meals	Dinner with wine, €28.
Closed	Rarely.
Directions	Caen D7 for Douvres 8km; left to D404 & D79 to Courseulles sur Mer, then D514 to Ver sur Mer; 2km, then left for Meuvaines. Left at x-roads onto D65; 20m, house on left with front courtyard.

Sandrine & Laurent Melet
La Closerie,
Route d'Arromanches,
14960 Meuvaines, Calvados
Tel   +33 (0)2 31 21 30 34
Email   sandrine.melet@wanadoo.fr
Web   www.chambres-hotes-ver-sur-mer.com

Entry 192   Map 4

Normandy

Manoir des Doyens

The lovely old house of golden stone is the warmly natural home of interesting people: an extrovert military historian who runs battlefield tours, and his gentle lady. Rosemary goes the extra mile for guests and serves her own jams for breakfast. Stone stairs lead to old-fashioned, comfortably casual guest rooms and good, clean bathrooms, the courtyard houses visiting grandchildren's swings, slide, rabbits and games room, the family sitting room is shared and there are always interesting people to chat to over breakfast or a calvados. A 15-minute walk from town but all you hear is the honk of the goose!

Price	€55.
Rooms	3 triples.
Meals	Restaurants 1km.
Closed	Rarely.
Directions	From N13 exit 37 for Bayeux & St Lô; for Bayeux; 2nd left. Signed St Loup Hors & Chambres d'Hôtes.

Lt Col & Mrs Chilcott
Manoir des Doyens,
Saint Loup Hors,
14400 Bayeux, Calvados
Tel   +33 (0)2 31 22 39 09
Fax   +33 (0)2 31 21 97 84
Email m-jp.chilcott@aliceadsl.fr

Entry 193   Map 4

13 rue aux Coqs

This delicious couple, she softly-spoken and twinkling, he jovial and talkative (French only!), have retired from farming and moved into the heart of Bayeux – you can glimpse the cathedral spires from their townhouse, once part of the old bishop's palace. Beyond the wisteria, the door opens onto a lofty beamed living room rejoicing in good antiques and a monumental fireplace – through another is the kitchen. Up the ancient stone stair to pretty guest rooms – excellent new bedding, pastel-tiled showers – that look quietly over the pocket-handkerchief back garden. History all around, and no need for a car.

Clos de Bellefontaine

Come to be pampered and effortlessly spoiled at this elegant townhouse, a ten-minute stroll from the famous Tapestry. Bedrooms are chic and gracious with choice antiques, colours are mocha and white, floors polished parquet or seagrass. Choose the top floor for snugness and charm, the first floor for grandeur and space. With a walled garden and two handsome ground-floor salons – antiques, family photographs, help-yourself refreshments – to lounge around in; you won't miss home. Carole's breakfasts, with homemade tarts, fruit compotes and cheeses, are the highlight of the stay.

Price	€59.
Rooms	3: 2 doubles, 1 twin.
Meals	Restaurant 50m.
Closed	Never.
Directions	From Caen N13 to Bayeux; for Gare SNCF; right after traffic lights; over 1st x-roads & traffic lights, park on left; house 50m on right, signed.

Price	€95-€130.
Rooms	2: 1 double, 1 twin.
Meals	Restaurants nearby.
Closed	Rarely.
Directions	Caen ring road N13 for Cherbourg, exit 36 to Bayeux. Left at 1st r'bout onto Bd Montgomery; 1st right at 200m; house on left behind tall black iron gates. Don't confuse with Château de Bellefontaine.

	Louis & Annick Fauvel
	13 rue aux Coqs,
	14400 Bayeux,
	Calvados
Tel	+33 (0)2 31 22 52 32
Fax	+33 (0)2 31 51 01 90

	Carole & Jérôme Mallet
	Clos de Bellefontaine,
	6 rue de Bellefontaine,
	14400 Bayeux, Calvados
Mobile	+33 (0)6 81 42 24 81
Email	clos.bellefontaine@wanadoo.fr
Web	clos.bellefontaine.monsite.wanadoo.fr

Normandy

La Suhardière

Up the drive, across the spotless (non-working!) farmyard to be met by your charmingly hospitable hostess who delights in gardening and cooking – dinner is a wonderful affair. Beyond the dinky little hall, the salon, with its high-backed chairs, beams and antimacassars, is a good place for a quiet read. The big sunny bedrooms are cosily frilly with quantities of lace, country furniture and gentle morning views over the garden dropping down to the pond (and you may fish). Special are the walks in the pretty rolling countryside, the homemade yogurt and cider, and pillows for the asking. *Small dogs welcome.*

Price	€50.
Rooms	3: 2 doubles, 1 suite.
Meals	Dinner with wine, €22.
Closed	Rarely.
Directions	From Caen A13 for Cherbourg, exit Carpiquet (airport) & Caumont l'Éventé D9; 500m before Caumont, house signed left.

Alain & Françoise Petiton
La Suhardière,
14240 Livry,
Calvados
Tel   +33 (0)2 31 77 51 02
Fax   +33 (0)2 31 77 51 02
Email   petiton.alain@wanadoo.fr

Entry 196   Map 3

Normandy

La Fresnée

A little bridge over a stream brings you to the impressive 19th-century house, owned by a lovely young farming family. One wing is the old bake house, and the hay barn and stables are for the guests. Rooms are sunny, contemporary and charming – original features, carefully chosen furnishings, pretty touches. Breakfasts are served beautifully in the family dining room where a wall hanging hides a fresco painted by an occupying German soldier. Outside, a garden to play in and an amazing 'Labyrinthe de Bayeux' for families: a five-hectare summertime maize-maze created by Pierre-Yves. A happy find.

Price	€65.
Rooms	4: 1 double, 1 twin, 2 family rooms: 1 for 3, 1 for 4.
Meals	Restaurant in village, 1km.
Closed	January.
Directions	From Bayeux N13 for Cherbourg exit 38; through Tour en Bessin for Mosles; D206 for Blay; over dual carriageway; house signed 1km on right.

Cathérine & Pierre-Yves Robidou
La Fresnée,
14400 Mosles,
Calvados
Tel   +33 (0)2 31 21 04 31
Email   catherine@lafresnee.com
Web   www.lafresnee.com

Entry 197   Map 3

Normandy

Le Mouchel

An interesting couple, she natural, s trong and brave, he softly-spoken and communicative, they have been busy doing B&B for 20 years now as well as running a large dairy herd. Their 300-year-old farmhouse contains two of the guest rooms; the family room is in the more recent extension with a somewhat café-like breakfast room that leads onto a pretty patio. There's also a largish grassy area for run-around children. Rooms are floral, shiny floorboarded and have excellent beds and shower rooms. D-Day Omaha Beach lies near the small village of St Laurent sur Mer.

Price	€52.
Rooms	3: 1 double, 1 triple, 1 family room for 4.
Meals	Restaurants in St Laurent sur Mer, 4km.
Closed	Rarely.
Directions	From Cherbourg N13 S 76km; exit Formigny for St Laurent sur Mer; after church right 800m: entrance on left.

	Odile & Jean-Claude Lenourichel
	Le Mouchel,
	14710 Formigny, Calvados
Tel	+33 (0)2 31 22 53 79
Fax	+33 (0)2 31 21 56 55
Email	odile.lenourichel@orange.fr

Entry 198   Map 3

Normandy

Le Château

The château dates proudly from 1580. In the yard behind it, now restored to tremendous shape and character as a garden area for guests, an ancient arched barn houses three beamy bedrooms (admire the astounding roof timbers through a trap window). Just beyond the flowering stone steps, the fourth room is in a tiny cottage. These country-elegant rooms are beautiful in Jouy and stripes, restful and private. Madame is a warm, well-read, eco-friendly person who speaks good English, loves having guests and can discourse at fascinating length about the Vikings, the Inuit, the Dukes of Normandy…

Price	€70–€85.
Rooms	4: 2 doubles, 1 twin, 1 suite for 5.
Meals	Restaurants within walking distance.
Closed	December to mid-January.
Directions	From Cherbourg N13; D514; exit for Grandcamp Maisy; at edge of village continue on D514 for Vierville sur Mer; just after water tower & football field, right (signed tennis club). House at end of lane, 400m.

	Dominique Bernières
	Le Château,
	Chemin du Château,
	14450 Grandcamp Maisy, Calvados
Tel	+33 (0)2 31 22 66 22
Email	marionbandb@wanadoo.fr
Web	perso.wanadoo.fr/alain.marion/gbindex.html

Entry 199   Map 3

Normandy

L'Hermerel

Some sort of perfection? A round pigeon tower and a private chapel complete the picture of this charming fortified working farm which is partly 15th-century. The lofty beamed rooms and vast fireplaces have been carefully restored and it all feels unpretentiously stylish with a friendly, relaxed atmosphere. Up the old worn stone stair of the interconnecting wing to green velvet armchairs, taffeta drapes and vases of wild flowers: these bedrooms have been decorated quite beautifully. Breakfasts of compotes, farm milk, special jams and breads, a walled garden to share and the sea a short walk away.

Price	€70.
Rooms	3: 1 twin/double, 1 family room, 1 suite.
Meals	Restaurants in Grandcamp Maisy.
Closed	November-March.
Directions	From Bayeux N13 30km west; exit D514 to Osmanville & on for Grandcamp 4km; left D199a for Géfosse Fontenay 400m; follow signs on right.

François & Agnès Lemarié
L'Hermerel,
14230 Géfosse Fontenay, Calvados
Tel +33 (0)2 31 22 64 12
Fax +33 (0)2 31 22 76 37
Email lemariehermerel@aol.com
Web www.manoir-hermerel.com

Entry 200 Map 3

Normandy

Ferme-Manoir de la Rivière

Breakfast by the massive fireplace may be candle- or oil-lamp-lit on dark mornings in this 13th-century fortress of a dairy farm, with its ancient tithe barn and little watchtower. Isabelle is proud of her family home, its flagstones worn smooth with age, its high vaulted stone living room ceiling with the second-floor rooms, one narrow with a shower in a tower, one with exposed beams, furnished with *ciel de lit* drapes. Her welcome is warm, her energy boundless; she is ever improving her rooms and cooking imaginative Norman cuisine — much supported by Gérard. A great team. *Out-of-season cookery weekends. Sawday self-catering also.*

Ethical Collection: Environment; Food.
See page 432.

Price	€60-€75.
Rooms	3: 1 double, 2 triples.
Meals	Dinner with cider or wine, €25, during low season.
Closed	Rarely.
Directions	From Bayeux N13 30km west; exit on D514 to Osmanville & on for Grandchamp, 5km; left for Géfosse Fontenay; house 800m on left before church.

Gérard & Isabelle Leharivel
Ferme-Manoir de la Rivière,
14230 Géfosse Fontenay, Calvados
Tel +33 (0)2 31 22 64 45
Fax +33 (0)2 31 22 01 18
Email leharivel@wanadoo.fr
Web www.chez.com/manoirdelariviere

Entry 201 Map 3

Normandy

La Fèvrerie

One of our very best. Your blithe, beautiful, energetic hostess is a delight. Her shyly chatty ex-farmer husband now breeds horses while she indulges her passion for interior decoration: her impeccable rooms are a festival of colours, textures, antiques, embroidered linen. It's a heart-warming experience to stay in this wonderful old building where they love having guests; the great granite hearth is always lit for the delicious breakfast which includes local specialities on elegant china; there is a richly-carved 'throne' at the head of the long table. A stupendous place, very special people. *Sawday self-catering also.*

Price	€67–€75.
Rooms	3: 2 doubles, 1 twin. Children's room available.
Meals	Restaurants 3km.
Closed	Rarely.
Directions	From Cherbourg D901; after Tocqueville right, D10; 1st left.

Marie-France & Maurice Caillet
La Fèvrerie,
50760 Ste Geneviève, Manche
Tel   +33 (0)2 33 54 33 53
Fax   +33 (0)2 33 22 12 50
Email   lafevrerie@wanadoo.fr

Entry 202   Map 3

Normandy

Maison Duchevreuil

Rejoice in this oasis (where nuns lived until 1914) on the built-up edge of bustling Cherbourg. Plants and flowers tumble prettily over the edges of the narrow canal that feeds the sloping horseshoe-shaped pond with rainwater collected from 18th-century roofs. A wide stone stair leads to the walled garden and a multitude of paths, trees, shrubs — and teak furniture to lounge on. Converted farm buildings house guest bedrooms full of light and attractively dressed with striking colours and rug-strewn parquet: not fussy but classy. Like her house and garden, Madame is charming and elegant.

Price	€100. Extra bed €20.
Rooms	2 suites for 2-4.
Meals	Restaurants nearby.
Closed	Rarely.
Directions	With Cherbourg railway station on right, straight to Équeurdreville for 2km; after tunnel left to Octeville; 200m lights; right to Val Abbé; 3rd right; archway end of road.

Sophie Draber
Maison Duchevreuil,
36 avenue Duchevreuil,
50120 Équeurdreville, Manche
Tel   +33 (0)2 33 01 33 10
Email   drabersophie@hotmail.com
Web   perso.wanadoo.fr/maison-duchevreuil

Entry 203   Map 3

Normandy

Eudal de Bas

Old-fashioned hospitality in a modern house. You are just a mile from the (often) glittering sea and Michel, who used to make submarines, has a passion for sailing. He and Éliane are hosts of the best sort; easy, friendly, helpful but not intrusive. His shipbuilding skill is evident: the attic space has been cleverly used to make two snug rooms with showers (one with a kitchenette); the landing is a pleasant sitting area. A brilliantly quiet position, simple décor, spotless rooms and Éliane will even rise early for dawn ferry-catchers. It's ideal for beach holidays and channel crossing alike.

Price	€49-€52.
Rooms	2: 1 double, 1 triple & kitchenette.
Meals	Restaurants within 2km.
Closed	Rarely.
Directions	From Cherbourg D901 then D45 W 13km to Urville Nacqueville; 1st left by Hôtel Le Beau Rivage; up hill D22 for 2km; 2nd left; sign.

Michel & Éliane Thomas
Eudal de Bas,
1 rue Escènes,
50460 Urville Nacqueville, Manche
Tel   +33 (0)2 33 03 58 16
Fax   +33 (0)2 33 03 58 16
Email   thomas.eudal@wanadoo.fr
Web   pagesperso-orange.fr/gitethomas

Entry 204   Map 3

Normandy

Hameau Saint Jean

Standing near the Normandy coastal hiking path, the old stone manor looks proudly across the town and out to sea. Retired from farming, the sociable Guérards welcome guests with courtesy and happily point them towards the (distant!) cliff walks, the nearby blue-green Château Ravalet and other hidden sights. This is living in French genteel style, everything in its beautiful place, spotless and well-loved, bedrooms spacious and bathrooms simple. You are in quiet country, just 6km from the ferries – the triple room with its outside entrance is ideal for early ferry-catchers and Madame leaves a breakfast tray.

Price	€56-€60.
Rooms	3: 1 double, 1 twin, 1 triple.
Meals	Restaurants 3km.
Closed	Rarely.
Directions	From Cherbourg D901 to Tourlaville & for St Pierre Église. Right at exit for Château Ravalet & St Jean; up hill to Centre Aéré, follow Chambres d'Hôtes signs.

Mme Guérard
Hameau Saint Jean,
50110 Tourlaville,
Manche
Tel   +33 (0)2 33 22 00 86

Entry 205   Map 3

Normandy

Bruce Castle

Live graciously – even if it's only for a stopover (Cherbourg is 15km away). The Fontanets are a charming and amusing couple and their 1914 neo-classical mansion is full of pretty antiques. From the restrained elegance of the hall a handsome white staircase sweeps up to big, serene bedrooms with garden and woodland views; oriental rugs and crystal chandeliers add another dash of luxury. Breakfast off white porcelain with antique silver cutlery in a charming dining room that doubles as a dayroom for guests. In the 20-acre grounds are the ruins of an 11th-century castle... to stay here is a huge treat.

Price	€100–€120.
Rooms	2 doubles.
Meals	Restaurant 8km.
Closed	Rarely.
Directions	From Cherbourg N13 for Valognes & Caen exit to D119, then D50 to Brix. Left just before church; entrance on left.

	Anna-Rose & Hugues Fontanet
	Bruce Castle,
	13 rue du Castel,
	50700 Brix, Manche
Tel	+33 (0)2 33 41 99 62
Email	bruce-castle@orange.fr
Web	www.bruce-castle.com

Normandy

Manoir de Bellaunay

Even the smallest bathroom oozes atmosphere through its *œil de bœuf*. The youngest piece of this fascinating and venerably ancient house is over 400 years old; its predecessor stood on the site of a monastery, the fireplace in the lovely 'Medieval' bedroom carries the coat of arms of the original owners. For the rooms, they have hunted carved *armoires de mariage*, lace canopies, footstools – and hung tapestry curtains at the windows. Your ex-farmer hosts share their energy enthusiastically between this wonderful house, its small dense garden, and their guests. Sheer comfort among warm old stones.

Price	€60–€90.
Rooms	3: 2 doubles, 1 suite for 3.
Meals	Restaurants 4km.
Closed	November-March.
Directions	On RN13 exit at Valognes; follow Route de Quettehou D902; house 3km after Valognes, No. 11.

	Christiane & Jacques Allix-Desfauteaux
	Manoir de Bellaunay,
	50700 Tamerville, Manche
Tel	+33 (0)2 33 40 10 62
Fax	+33 (0)2 33 40 10 62
Email	bellauney@wanadoo.fr
Web	www.bellauney.com

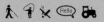

Normandy

Brown Owl House

Philomena and Pierre – she Irish, he French – are generous, hospitable and fun and you pretty much get the run of their big, solid, 400-year-old farmhouse. The style is contemporary-formal and the atmosphere chatty and laid back. Philomena is a professionally trained cook: book 24 hours ahead and you will be treated to a delectable Anglo-French dinner. The living room, vast and open-plan, is part clear up to the rafters, part overlooked by an attractive mezzanine. The peaceful and immaculate two-bedroom suites have honey-coloured floorboards and views over the immense garden and tree-lined fields.

Price	€45-€65.
Rooms	5: 1 family room; 3 doubles, 1 twin, sharing 2 baths.
Meals	Dinner with wine, €27.
Closed	Never.
Directions	N13 Cherbourg to Valognes then D2 for 8.5km; right onto D126 to Golleville. In village centre, right to Route du Château, entrance to No. 7 on left.

Philomena & Pierre Van der Linden
Brown Owl House,
7 route du Château,
Ferme de la Poissonnerie,
50390 Golleville, Manche
Tel +33 (0)2 33 01 20 45
Email contact@brown-owl-house.com
Web www.brown-owl-house.com

Entry 208   Map 3

Normandy

Le Château

Gravel crunches as you sweep up to the imposing granite château on the Cherbourg peninsula. The beguiling fairytale turrets and Françoise's welcome soon work their magic. External stone stairs lead to the red-velvet charm of the *Chambre Château* (with secret grille where maids peeped into the chapel below); ancient chestnut stairs in the converted farm building lead to simple family rooms. In the morning, as you breakfast generously in a light-flooded, pink-panelled family dining room and sip your café au lait, you might like to nod a grateful 'merci' to Bernard's obliging Normandy cows.

Price	€60-€80-€90.
Rooms	3: 2 doubles, 1 suite for 4.
Meals	Restaurant 500m.
Closed	Never.
Directions	From Valognes D2 for St Sauveur le Vicomte; left onto D24, 3km; auberge Pont Cochon left before bridge. Driveway on left opp. church.

Françoise Lucas de Vallavieille
Le Château,
50700 Flottemanville Bocage,
Manche
Tel +33 (0)2 33 40 29 02
Fax +33 (0)2 33 95 23 51
Email contact@chateau-flottemanville.com
Web www.chateau-flottemanville.com

Entry 209   Map 3

Normandy

Le Château

The wonderful granite château with towers, turrets and castellations gives entry to a big safe courtyard – sanctuary during times of invasion – and wild breakers crash on the endless beach 1km away. It is your hosts' mission in life to restore and revive! They and their home are irreproachably French and civilised – books, fine china, panelling, gilt mirrors, plush chairs, engravings. Your two-bedroom suite has ancient floor tiles, new bedding, a loo in a tower. Stay a while, make your own breakfast with homemade jam and fresh eggs – you may use the grand dining room – and get to know your remarkable hostess.

Price	€85–€130.
Rooms	1 family suite for 2-4.
Meals	Restaurants 2-3km.
Closed	Rarely.
Directions	From Cherbourg D650 for Carteret; 3km after Les Pieux, right D62 to Le Rozel; right D117 into village; house just beyond village.

Josiane & Jean-Claude Grandchamp
Le Château,
50340 Le Rozel,
Manche

Tel +33 (0)2 33 52 95 08
Fax +33 (0)2 33 02 00 35

Normandy

La Roque de Gouey

A fishing, sailing port and a bridge with 13 arches: a pretty place to stay. The enchanting *longère* is the home of two of our favourite owners: Madame, the same honest open character as ever and Monsieur, retired, who has time to spread his modest farmer's joviality. Your side of the house has its own entrance, dayroom and vast old fireplace where old beams and *tommettes* flourish. The bedrooms up the steepish outside stairs are small, with pretty bedcovers and antiques that are cherished, the ground-floor room is larger, and the breakfast tables sport flowery cloths. Brilliant value.

Price	€50. €65 for 3.
Rooms	4: 1 double, 1 twin, 1 family for 3, 1 family suite for 5.
Meals	Restaurants 500m. Guest kitchen.
Closed	Rarely.
Directions	From St Sauveur le Vicomte D15 to Portbail; right just before church Rue R. Asselin; over old railway; house 250m on right.

Bernadette Vasselin
La Roque de Gouey,
Rue Gilles Poërier,
50580 Portbail, Manche

Tel +33 (0)2 33 04 80 27
Fax +33 (0)2 33 04 80 27
Email vasselin.portbail@orange.fr

Normandy

La Vimonderie

Sigrid's big country kitchen and crackling fire are the heart of this fine 18th-century granite house and you know instantly you are sharing her home: the built-in dresser carries pretty china, her pictures and ornaments bring interest to the salon and its Normandy fireplace, and she proudly tells how she rescued the superb elm staircase. A fascinating person, for years a potter in England, she has retired to France and vegetarian happiness. Bedrooms have colour and lace, unusual antiques and original beams. Five acres of garden mean plenty of space for children and grown-ups alike. Great value. *Minimum stay 2 nights.*

Price	€45-€50.
Rooms	2 doubles.
Meals	Dinner with wine, from €22. Light supper from €12. Picnics from €5. Guest kitchen.
Closed	January-February.
Directions	From Carentan N174 to St Lô for 12-13km; before major r'bout D377 for Cavigny; 4th house on right.

Sigrid Hamilton
La Vimonderie,
50620 Cavigny, Manche
Tel   +33 (0)2 33 56 01 13
Fax   +33 (0)2 33 56 41 32
Email   sigrid.hamilton@googlemail.com
Web   www.lavimonderie.com

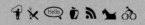

Entry 212   Map 3

Normandy

Le Suppey

The Franco-American Buissons fully redecorated their 18th-century farmhouse five years ago, with its old stables – horses and buggies live here – and outbuildings flanking a flowered yard. Rooms are sprigged in peach or green, beds have new mattresses, the marble-topped rustic furniture is locally made, the watercolours are done by an aunt. It is all simple, sunny and most welcoming. Jean works during the week; Nancy, perfectly bilingual and very present, loves having guests. There's a green and secluded garden for picnics, and a small spring that has great damming-up potential for little ones!

Price	€50. Extra bed €6.
Rooms	2 doubles.
Meals	Restaurants in St Lô, 5km.
Closed	Rarely.
Directions	From St Lô D6 for Isigny sur Mer to intersection Les Forges; C7 left for Villiers Fossard. House 1.2km on left.

Jean & Nancy Buisson
Le Suppey,
50680 Villiers Fossard,
Manche
Tel   +33 (0)2 33 57 30 23
Email   nancy.buisson@wanadoo.fr
Web   perso.wanadoo.fr/nancy.buisson

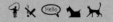

Entry 213   Map 3

Normandy

Le Cauchais

Just one bedroom in a farmhouse of elegance and calm: lovely to feel you're a privileged guest. And dinner every other night – Sally is a talented cook. Enter the sturdy Norman house to find a beamed sitting room with a fireplace and an enticing wall of books, and doors to a large terrace with views of pastures and cows. Super walks from the house – the banked lanes spill with primroses in spring – and the landing beaches are half an hour's drive. Your bedroom, quietly sophisticated and serene, has English touches of chintz and two velvet boudoir easy chairs with a garden view. Beautiful.

Normandy

1 Saint Léger

The totally French farmhouse, 19th-century without, rustic trad within, is colourful, neat, immaculate. One room is pink-flavoured, the other blue, each with bits of crochet, a carved armoire (one *cherbourgeoise*, the other from St Lô) and a clean, compact shower room; the gloriously ostentatious blue bathroom is also yours for the asking – giant tub and plants rampaging. But most special of all is the charming, elegant Madame Lepoittevin, full of smiles and laughter, actively involved in a walking group in summer – why not join in? You can picnic in the pretty garden or cook your own on the barbecue.

Price	€60.
Rooms	1 double.
Meals	Dinner with wine, €25.
Closed	Rarely.
Directions	From St Lô D6 for Isigny 3km; 3rd turning on right to Le Cauchais; entrance on right at end of lane at bottom of hill.

Price	€40.
Rooms	2: 1 double; 1 double with shower & separate wc.
Meals	Restaurants 2-10km.
Closed	1st two weeks in March.
Directions	From St Lô D972 for Coutances, through St Gilles; house sign on left, 4km after St Gilles, on D972.

	Sally Worthington
	Le Cauchais,
	Route d'Isigny,
	50000 Saint Lô, Manche
Tel	+33 (0)2 33 06 01 17
Email	sarahwor@hotmail.com

	Micheline Lepoittevin
	1 Saint Léger,
	50570 Quibou, Manche
Tel	+33 (0)2 33 57 18 41
Fax	+33 (0)2 33 57 18 41
Email	rico123@hotmail.com

Normandy

La Rhétorerie

Here is old-style, down-to-earth, French country hospitality. Madame, an elderly live wire, full of smiles, humorous chat and spontaneous welcome, plays the organ in the village church. Monsieur, a retired farmer, is quietly interested. Their bedrooms have old family furniture (admire *grand-mère's* elaborately crocheted bedcover), good mattresses, simple washing arrangements. It is all spotless and guests have a large, colourful dayroom, formerly the *pressoir*, with massive beams, lots of plants and a kitchen – the greatstone is now a flower feature outside. Kids can sit on the donkeys and collect the eggs.

Price	€42.
Rooms	2: 1 twin, 1 twin/double, each with shower, sharing wc.
Meals	Restaurant 1km; choice 4km. Kitchen available.
Closed	Rarely.
Directions	From St Lô D999 for Percy exit 5, 3km; right D38 for Canisy. House 1km on right.

Marie-Thérèse & Roger Osmond
La Rhétorerie,
Route de Canisy,
50750 St Ébremond de Bonfossé,
Manche
Tel +33 (0)2 33 56 62 98

Entry 216   Map 3

Normandy

Château des Boulais

There is space and grandeur in this mixed-period château and Madame and her Dutch professor partner have bravely taken up the challenge: the onetime *colonie de vacances* is being licked into stylish shape. The parquet-floored sitting room is vast; bedrooms have antique beds and strong plain colours alongside old wooden floors and fireplaces – it's great fun and the views sail out of those big windows across copses and woods for miles. Your colourful hostess enjoys meeting new people and hearing about their lives; the four teenagers – and the dogs – are a delight. Friendly, easy, comfortable.

Price	€55-€80.
Rooms	3: 2 doubles, 1 suite.
Meals	Dinner with wine, €25.
Closed	Christmas & New Year.
Directions	From Villedieu les P. N175 & D524 for Vire 1.5km; right D999 for Brécey. After Chérencé le H. left thro' St Martin B. to sawmill; follow signs to Loges sur Brécey; house 2km, 3rd left after wood.

Taco Vogelzang
Château des Boulais,
Loges sur Brécey,
50800 St Martin le Bouillant,
Manche
Tel +33 (0)2 33 60 32 20
Email chateau-des-boulais@orange.fr
Web www.chateau-des-boulais.com

Entry 217   Map 3

Normandy

Manoir de la Porte

A pepperpot turret to give a medieval flourish to the sturdy, creeper-dressed 16th-century manoir. There's a Japanese bridge to take you to the jungly island, a large and luscious garden, two bright, romantic top-floor bedrooms with old-fashioned bathrooms and a tempting sitting area; a fabulously ancient, tiled dining room with huge fireplace, a trio of tables and solid granite walls... the ingredients of rustic character are here. Add ethnic rugs dotted about, a pair of curly-toed Rajasthani slippers on the venerable stone stairs – and know that your friendly, chatty, ex-army hosts are great travellers.

Price	€62–€76.
Rooms	2 family rooms for 3.
Meals	Dinner with wine, €21.
Closed	Rarely.
Directions	Caen A84 for Rennes exit 37 to Villedieu les P.; thro' town; D975 for Avranches to Le Parc. Right at lights D39 to Ste Pience & D476 for Noirpalu 1.5km; at junc. D175 for Bourguenolles; house 400m on left.

Annick & Hervé Lagadec
Manoir de la Porte,
50870 Sainte Pience, Manche
Tel   +33 (0)2 33 68 13 61
Email   manoir.de.la.porte@wanadoo.fr
Web   www.manoir-de-la-porte.com

Entry 218   Map 3

Normandy

La Haute Gilberdière

Generous, artistic and young in spirit, the Champagnacs are a privilege to meet. Their 18th-century *longère* bathes in a floral wonderland: roses climb and tumble, narrow paths meander and a kitchen garden grows your breakfast – wander and revel or settle down in a shady spot. Inside, bedrooms are perfect with handsome antiques, pretty bed linen and polished floors, or modern with pale wood and bucolic views. The honey-coloured breakfast room is warmly contemporary – all timber and exposed stone; Monsieur's bread comes warm from the oven served with homemade jams. Wonderful. *Minimum stay 2 nights.*

Price	€60–€120.
Rooms	3 + 1: 2 doubles, 1 twin, sharing bath. Barn for 2-4.
Meals	Restaurants 5km.
Closed	November-March.
Directions	From Avranches D973 for Granville & Sartilly; left at end of village D61 for Carolles; after 800m house on left.

Édith & Pierre Champagnac
La Haute Gilberdière,
50530 Sartilly, Manche
Mobile   +33 (0)6 80 87 17 62
Email   champagnac@libertysurf.fr
Web   www.champagnac-farmhouse.com

Entry 219   Map 3

Normandy

Le Petit Manoir

That view is definitely worth the detour, and you can walk to Mont St Michel in two hours. The Gédouins keep cows and pigs; Annick, a reserved former teacher, makes jams, crêpes and occasionally breakfast rice pudding (a Breton speciality); Jean is mayor. The small rooms are French country style, without frills or soft touches, just a few little pictures on lightly patterned walls, and spotlessly clean. In the courtyard are passionfruit and figs; two large cider presses brim with geraniums and the old stone bakery will charm you. All is rural peace in this tiny village by the marshes.

Price	€38.
Rooms	2: 1 double, 1 twin.
Meals	Restaurants 500m-2km.
Closed	Never.
Directions	From A84 exit 34 for Pontorson; after Précey right to Servon, then right at church for 500m; farm on left.

Annick, Jean & Valérie Gédouin
Le Petit Manoir,
21 rue de la Pierre du Tertre,
50170 Servon, Manche
Tel   +33 (0)2 33 60 03 44
Email   agedouinmanoir@laposte.net
Web   chambresgedouin.com

Entry 220   Map 3

Normandy

La Ferme de l'Étang

Authentic farm B&B in a glorious setting. Ivy on walls, beamed attic bedrooms, fresh flowers, woodland walks, lake and château across the way – and a proper farming family. Jean-Paul and Brigitte, friendly, interested people, travel a lot and talk well. He is a dairy farmer; she collects copper and brass. Delicious country meals are shared at the big table in the dining room with its huge fireplace. A splendid staircase leads you up to the snug, cottagey yet unfussy bedrooms and their decidedly unposh bathrooms. Children love it – there are games galore, swings in the garden and cows all around.

Price	€47.
Rooms	4: 2 doubles, 2 family rooms.
Meals	Dinner with wine, €16.
Closed	Rarely.
Directions	Cherbourg A84 exit 34 for Mt St Michel & St Malo 600m; exit for Mt St Michel & Rennes D43 for Rennes. At r'bout D40 for Rennes, 5.5km; D308 left; signed.

Jean-Paul & Brigitte Gavard
La Ferme de l'Étang,
Boucéel, Vergoncey,
50240 St James, Manche
Tel   +33 (0)2 33 48 34 68
Email   jpgavard@club-internet.fr

Entry 221   Map 3

La Gautrais

Come for a slice of French farmhouse life. Madame is quietly friendly, "makes a superb soufflé" and mouthwatering Norman cuisine – she loves it. She and Monsieur cook, serve, clear, and always find time for a glass of calvados with their guests. The old granite stable block, built in 1622, was last modernised in the 1970s. Polished floors, spare furnishings, cots in the attic rooms, a couple of kitchenettes and a dining room with big table make this suitable for families on a budget. The poetically-named but perfectly ordinary Two Estuaries motorway now provides quick access one kilometre away.

Price	From €50.
Rooms	5: 2 doubles, 1 twin, 2 suites for 4–5, some with kitchenette.
Meals	Dinner with wine, €19.
Closed	Christmas.
Directions	From A84 exit 32 at St James then D12, following signs for Super U store for Antrain, 1km. On right.

François & Catherine Tiffaine
La Gautrais,
50240 St James, Manche
Tel +33 (0)2 33 48 31 86
Fax +33 (0)2 33 48 58 17
Email ctiffaine@hotmail.fr
Web tiffaine.perso.cegetel.net

Entry 222　Map 3

Les Blotteries

Monsieur, formerly a fire officer, is proud of his restoration of the old farm (the B&B is his project; Madame works in town). He is an attentive, positive host, full of smiles and jokes, and has done a good job. Old granite glints as you pass into the softly-curtained entrance; an original hay rack hangs above. One bedroom is on the first floor, another is in the former stable, a third in the old bakery: a ground-floor family room whose large windows overlook the courtyard. The cream breakfast room is simple and elegant and the fields around are open to all so no need to worry about the road at the front.

Price	€70–€75.
Rooms	3: 1 double, 2 family rooms.
Meals	Restaurants 1km.
Closed	Rarely.
Directions	From A84 exit 33; right at r'bout & uphill for approx. 300m to next r'bout; left then left again, D998 for St James; house on right after 5km.

Laurence & Jean-Malo Tizon
Les Blotteries,
50220 Juilley, Manche
Tel +33 (0)2 33 60 84 95
Fax +33 (0)2 33 60 84 95
Email bb@les-blotteries.com
Web www.les-blotteries.com

Entry 223　Map 3

Normandy

Château de La Maigraire

Built in 1860, it stands in pretty grounds with its own little carp-filled lake and friendly wildfowl. Monsieur, an interior designer, took it on with his organist cousin, and did a brilliant restoration. You find an elegant salon with a rosewood baby grand, a cosy sitting room filled with books and original wall covering, and three sunny bedrooms furnished with antiques, one with its own terrace. Bathrooms have oodles of towels; croissants and homemade jams are presented on antique Limoges: Monsieur loves to please. You are encouraged to enjoy it during the day, even picnic in the peaceful grounds.

Price	€100–€120.
Rooms	3: 1 double, 2 suites: 1 for 3, 1 for 4.
Meals	Restaurants nearby.
Closed	Rarely.
Directions	From D962, between Flers & Domfront, D260 for Forges de Varennes & Champsecret for 1.5km; left into La Maigraire hamlet.

Jean Fischer
Château de La Maigraire,
61700 St Bômer les Forges, Orne
Tel +33 (0)2 33 38 09 52
Fax +33 (0)2 33 38 09 52
Email la.maigraire@orange.fr
Web chateaudelamaigraire.monsite.orange.fr

Entry 224 Map 4

Normandy

Le Mesnil

There are fresh flowers everywhere and your hosts, retired farmers, offer true country hospitality. Peace is the norm, not the exception, in this deeply rural spot, racehorses graze in the pasture and you are unhesitatingly received into a warm and lively extended family. The rooms, in a converted outbuilding, have an appropriately rustic air with beams, old wardrobes and kitchenettes. The ground-floor room has a little private garden; up steepish stairs the bedroom is bigger. Breakfast is in the family dining room, with tiled floors and a large fireplace. Children are welcome to visit the family farm next door.

Price	€45.
Rooms	2 doubles & kitchenette.
Meals	Restaurant 5km.
Closed	Rarely.
Directions	From Argentan N158 for Caen; after Moulin sur Orne sign, left; house 800m on left; signed (3.5km from Argentan).

Janine & Rémy Laignel
Le Mesnil,
61200 Occagnes,
Orne
Tel +33 (0)2 33 67 11 12

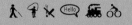

Entry 225 Map 4

Normandy

Les Gains

There's homemade elderflower cordial if you arrive on a hot day, or the smell of fresh bread may greet you: this converted manor farm with its pigeon tower and duck stream has a lived-in family feel. Your hosts – lovely country people – have 800 sheep and 300 apple trees, work hard and are thoroughly integrated, as are their daughters. Bedrooms in the old cheese dairy are painted in light colours with touches of *fantaisie* and Diana's decorative stencils. Breakfast is superb, dinner is for lingering over; both happen under the pergola in fine weather. Laid-back, rural and bucolic.

Price	€55–€60.
Rooms	3: 1 double, 1 twin, 1 triple.
Meals	Dinner with wine, €28.
Closed	November–March.
Directions	A28 exit 16; into Gacé; D13 to Chambois & Trun for 10km; at bar/restaurant right D26 to Vimoutiers; house signed at entry to Survie.

Diana & Christopher Wordsworth
Les Gains,
Survie, 61310 Exmes, Orne

Tel	+33 (0)2 33 36 05 56
Fax	+33 (0)2 33 35 03 65
Email	lesgains@aliceadsl.fr
Web	www.lesgains.co.uk

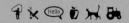

Normandy

Le Prieuré St Michel

An atmospheric time warp for the night on the St Michel pilgrim route: traditional décor in the timbered 14th-century monks' storeroom with tapestry wall covering and antiques, or the old dairy, or a converted stable; a huge 15th-century cider press for breakfast in the company of the Ulrichs' interesting choice of art; a chapel for yet more art, a tithe barn in magnificent condition for fabulous receptions, perfectly stupendous gardens, a sort of medieval revival. Your hosts are totally devoted to their fabulous domain and its listed buildings and happy to share it with guests who appreciate its historical value.

Price	€95–€135.
Rooms	4: 2 doubles, 2 suites for 3.
Meals	Restaurant 4km.
Closed	Rarely.
Directions	From Lisieux D579 for Livarot & Vimoutiers. D916 for Argentan. Right 3km after Vimoutiers D703 for Crouttes. Le Prieuré is 500m after village.

Jean-Pierre & Viviane Ulrich
Le Prieuré St Michel,
61120 Crouttes, Orne

Tel	+33 (0)2 33 39 15 15
Fax	+33 (0)2 33 36 15 16
Email	leprieuresaintmichel@wanadoo.fr
Web	www.prieure-saint-michel.com

Normandy

L'Orangerie

Madame Gran has a talent for enjoying things: painting, bridge, languages, music – and people. The faded blue signs lead to a feudal-feel hamlet (church, presbytery, mairie, house) where this very elegant orangery is the only trace of the old estate. Breakfast in the large, sunny, familial kitchen, enjoy opera and wine on the terrace, sink into a smart deep sofa; Madame loves you to feel at home. Bedrooms are simpler, with small mansard windows, rugs on parquet floors and old-style beds. The lovely grounds summon you out to Norman woods, walks, horses (yours too, if you wish) – and peace.

Price	€60-€80.
Rooms	4: 2 doubles; 1 double, 1 triple, sharing bath.
Meals	Restaurants 12km.
Closed	Never.
Directions	From Vimoutiers for Orbec; D248 for Pontchardon; follow signs for Avernes. House immed. on left after church.

Marie-Christine Gran
L'Orangerie,
61470 Avernes St Gourgon,
Orne
Tel   +33 (0)2 33 67 48 37
Email   marie-christine.gran@wanadoo.fr

Entry 228   Map 4

Normandy

La Bussière

It's angular inside too, the pitch-pine staircase elbowing its way right up to the guests' top floor where the sky rushes in. The house was built by Monsieur's parents in 1910 in open-plan American style. Sliding glass partitions give grandly generous dining and sitting rooms; bedrooms are excellent, much-windowed, soft-coloured and -bedded, marble-fireplaced, old-mirrored. Impeccable and full of personality, the house is the pride and joy of your intelligent hostess who laughs easily and manages her home, family and guests expertly. In the steeply sloped garden, a sandpit and trikes. *Arrivals after 6pm.*

Price	€64.
Rooms	2: 1 twin, 1 suite for 4.
Meals	Dinner with wine, €26.
Closed	December-February.
Directions	From Argentan N26 E for 37km. Entrance 4km after Planches on right by small crucifix; long lime-bordered drive.

Antoine & Nathalie Le Brethon
La Bussière,
61370 Ste Gauburge Ste Colombe,
Orne
Tel   +33 (0)2 33 34 05 23
Fax   +33 (0)2 33 34 71 47
Email   nlebrethon@orange.fr

Entry 229   Map 4

Le Marnis

This is Barbara's "corner of paradise" and her delight is contagious. In utter peace among the cattle-dotted Norman pastures, here is one brave, outspoken woman, her horses, dogs and cats in a low-lying farmhouse, beautifully rebuilt "from a pile of stones", where old and new mix easily and flowers rampage all around. The lovely sloping garden is all her own work too – she appears to have endless energy. The pastel guest rooms, one upstairs with orchard views, the other down, with doors to the garden, are pleasantly floral. The village provides everything, and Sées is nearby. *Babies & children over 10 welcome.*

Price	€60-€65.
Rooms	2: 1 double, 1 twin.
Meals	Restaurant in village, 1.5km.
Closed	Rarely.
Directions	From Courtomer, past Mairie right after last building for Tellières. Left at wayside cross for Le Marnis. 2nd lane on right.

Barbara Goff
Le Marnis,
Tellières le Plessis,
61390 Courtomer, Orne
Tel +33 (0)2 33 27 47 55
Email barbara.goff@wanadoo.fr

Entry 230   Map 4

Château de la Grande Noë

Trompe-l'œil marble and Wedgwood mouldings inherited from an Adam-inspired ancestor who escaped the French Revolution; chamber music in the log-fired drawing room; breakfast in the dining room wrapped in oak panelling inlaid with precious woods; elegant, alcoved bedrooms full of antiques, books, ancestral portraits, much soft comfort, a bathroom through a secret door, a loo in a tower: it's a fascinating, human place. And the delightful Longcamps are a civilised, friendly couple, she vivaciously cultured and musical, he a retired camembert-maker who enjoys his estate. Walks start 2km away.

Price	€100-€120.
Rooms	3: 2 doubles, 1 twin.
Meals	Restaurants 5km.
Closed	December-March, except by arrangement.
Directions	From Verneuil sur Avre, N12 SW 24km to Carrefour Ste Anne. Left D918 for Longny au Perche for 4.5km; left D289 for Moulicent. House 800m on right.

Jacques & Pascale de Longcamp
Château de la Grande Noë,
61290 Moulicent, Orne
Tel +33 (0)2 33 73 63 30
Email contact@chateaudelagrandenoe.com
Web www.chateaudelagrandenoe.com

Entry 231   Map 4

Normandy

La Simondrière – La Corbinière

Your English hosts take great care of you in the Percheron farmhouse they have rescued and restored – and enjoy sharing their enthusiasm for this beautiful, undiscovered, horse-breeding region. Feel free to potter on their land or to venture further afield, then come back to a friendly cup of tea and a truly delicious supper in the dining room. Bedrooms are beamy, cosy and uncomplicated, with good mattresses and warm duvets; in the big square sitting room are books, maps and voluminous easy chairs. A super country place in a forested region, and Rex and Helen are wonderful company. Readers are full of praise.

Price	€65.
Rooms	3: 1 double, 1 twin, 1 family room.
Meals	Dinner with wine, €25.
Closed	December.
Directions	From Mortagne au Perche D931 for Mamers for 8km; right on D650 for Coulimer at small x-roads. House 800m on left, last of small hamlet of houses.

Helen Barr
La Simondrière – La Corbinière,
61360 Coulimer, Orne

Tel	+33 (0)2 33 25 55 34
Fax	+33 (0)2 33 25 49 01
Email	helenbarr@wanadoo.fr

Entry 232   Map 4

Normandy

Le Tertre

Pilgrims have trudged by towards Mont St Michel since the 1500s and the search for inner peace continues: yoga and meditation groups come but never overlap with B&B. Anne talks brilliantly about her exotic travels, is active in the village and pours her creative energy into her house, with the help of an excellent restorer. Each elegantly simple room has a clear personality, good beds and sitting space, antiques, soft colours and privacy. One has a six-seater jacuzzi, another a fine set of ivory-backed brushes, the third an impressive bureau. Stunning views, super breakfast in the big kitchen, served with love.

Price	€72–€130.
Rooms	3: 2 doubles, 1 twin.
Meals	Restaurants 6km.
Closed	January.
Directions	From Alençon D311 for Mamers, left for Contilly & Montgaudry D113, 5km. Follow signs.

Anne Morgan
Le Tertre,
61360 Montgaudry, Orne

Tel	+33 (0)2 33 25 59 98
Fax	+33 (0)2 33 25 56 96
Email	annemorgan@wanadoo.fr
Web	www.french-country-retreat.com

Entry 233   Map 4

Brittany

Brittany

Épineu

Fear not, the farm mess is forgotten once you reach the cottage and the long, rural views beyond. Through that timbered porch, a sociable, sprightly and unpretentious lady will lead you into her big, wood-floored and -ceilinged country dining room – warmed in winter by the old stone fireplace. It is uncluttered and soberly French. Bedrooms are a good size, the most characterful one (by far) in the main house. The country garden is tended with love and pride and produces vegetables for dinner. You will be spoiled outrageously at dinner, and Madame will join you if you are just two. A joy.

Price	€55. €75 for 3. Extra bed €20.
Rooms	1 triple.
Meals	Dinner €22. Restaurant 3km.
Closed	Never.
Directions	From Rennes N137 S exit Poligné D47 for Bourg des Comptes for 4km; left & drive thro' L'Aubriais to next hamlet, Épineu; right into & across farmyard, down lane 20m, cottage on right.

Yvette Guillopé
Épineu,
35890 Bourg des Comptes,
Ille-et-Vilaine
Tel +33 (0)2 99 52 16 84

Entry 234   Map 3

Brittany

Château du Pin

Watercolourist and photographer, the brave, artistic Ruans have launched with passionate enthusiasm into renovating a small château with its ruined chapel, stables and thrilling atmosphere. For art and simplicity this is the place. The original staircase curves up to the 'literary' guest rooms: romantic *Proust*, light-flooded *George Sand*, immaculate *Victor Hugo*; each shower is behind a great rafter; the stunning drawing room with antique snooker table wears rich reds. It's brilliant, and great fun. Your gentle hosts will join you for an aperitif – then create dinner for you.

Price	€90-€180.
Rooms	6: 2 twins/doubles, 1 suite for 2, 2 family suites for 4. Cottage for 3-4.
Meals	Dinner €30. Wine €10-€30.
Closed	Rarely.
Directions	From Rennes N12 west to Bédée 23km; D72 to Montfort sur Meu; D125 for St Méen le Grand; château 3km on left.

Catherine & Luc Ruan
Château du Pin,
35370 Iffendic près de Montfort,
Ille-et-Vilaine
Tel   +33 (0)2 99 09 34 05
Fax   +33 (0)2 99 09 03 76
Email luc.ruan@wanadoo.fr
Web   www.chateaudupin-bretagne.com

Entry 235   Map 3

Brittany

Château du Quengo

Two fascinating generations of an ancient Breton family welcome you open-armed to their inimitable house where history, atmosphere and silence rule: private chapel, Bio-garden and rare trees outside, carved chestnut staircase, Italian mosaic floor, 1900s wallpaper, about 30 rooms inside. Anne plys you with homemade delights and knows the family history; Alfred builds organs and merrily serves breakfast. The bedrooms have antique radiators and are properly old-fashioned, our favourite the family room. No plastic coathangers, few mod cons – just humorous hosts and a beautiful place. *Sawday self-catering also.*

Ethical Collection: Environment; Food.
See page 432.

Price	€50–€75.
Rooms	5: 1 family room for 3; 2 doubles, 2 twins, sharing 2 baths.
Meals	Restaurants 1.5-5km. Kitchen available.
Closed	Rarely.
Directions	From N12 for St Brieuc exit at Bédée D72 to Irodouer; 1st right before church to Romillé; château entrance 600m on left, signed.

Anne & Alfred du Crest de Lorgerie
Château du Quengo,
35850 Irodouër,
Ille-et-Vilaine

Tel	+33 (0)2 99 39 81 47
Email	lequengo@hotmail.com
Web	www.chateauduquengo.com

Entry 236   Map 3

Brittany

Le Mesnil des Bois

Fringed by lawn in a forest clearing is a cluster of buildings, part of a 16th-century manor. The manor is awaiting renovation but the Villettes' own long, creeper-covered house has been transformed. They live at one end, guests at the other and the ample living space – rugs, books, rich warm colours – is generously shared. Bedrooms, understatedly luxurious, have paintings and books; a nearby cottage has become a family suite. Home-cooked food and a whole forest to wander in at will… the sense of space is exhilarating and the entire place captivating. *Minimum stay 2 nights holiday weekends & July/August.*

Price	€95–€150.
Rooms	5: 1 double, 1 twin, 3 family rooms for 2-3.
Meals	Restaurant 1km.
Closed	Mid-November to February.
Directions	From Rennes, exit Miniac Morvan; right to Tressé for Tronchet; at x-roads, right to Lanhélin, D73; forest on right, take forest road. Signed.

Martine Villette
Le Mesnil des Bois,
35540 Le Tronchet,
Ille-et-Vilaine

Tel	+33 (0)2 99 58 97 12
Email	villette@le-mesnil-des-bois.com
Web	www.le-mesnil-des-bois.com

Entry 237   Map 3

Brittany

Le Presbytère

Solid granite, earth energy: inside its walled garden, the vast old priest's house is warm, reassuring and superbly restored: fine old timbers, antiques, panelling, hangings. Some bathrooms are old-fashioned but each bedroom has character... a Breton bed or a canopy, a staircase straight or spiral, antique fabrics, white bedcovers, a garden view; our favourites are those with private entrances. There's a sense of its never ending, there's even a classy mobile home. Madame, a lovely energetic and warmly attentive person, loves cooking. You will leave with new friends in your address book.

Price	€49. €70 for 3.
Rooms	5: 1 double, 2 triples, 1 suite for 3; 1 twin sharing bath.
Meals	Dinner €18–€20. Wine list €8.50-€20.
Closed	Last two weeks in January.
Directions	From Pontorson D219 to Vieux-Viel; follow signs for 'Chambres d'Hôte Vieux-Viel'; next to church.

Madeleine Stracquadanio
Le Presbytère,
35610 Vieux-Viel, Ille-et-Vilaine
Tel   +33 (0)2 99 48 65 29
Fax   +33 (0)2 99 48 65 29
Email   madeleine.stracquadanio@voila.fr
Web   www.vieux-viel.com

Entry 238   Map 3

Brittany

La Hamelinais

The lovely farmhouse goes back to 1718 – Madame arrived here at the age of 15. Expect old beams, exposed stones, few mod cons and bags of rustic charm. But it's Marie-Madeleine who makes this place special: up before breakfast to prepare a roaring fire in the magnificent granite fireplace and, in summer, giving her all to garden and orchard. Gentle, bright-eyed Jean, just retired from the farm, says he "travels through his guests". Rooms are old-fashioned and homely (white bedspreads on comfy beds), your hosts know and love their region intimately and the sea is very close. *Stays of 2+ nights preferred.*

Price	€47–€50.
Rooms	2: 1 double, 1 triple.
Meals	Restaurants 4km.
Closed	Rarely.
Directions	From St Malo N137 for Rennes 15km; exit N176 for Mt St Michel 12km. At Dol de Bretagne D80 for St Brolâdre 3km; left D85 for Cherrueix; house sign on right before 3rd bridge.

Jean & Marie-Madeleine Glémot
La Hamelinais,
35120 Cherrueix,
Ille-et-Vilaine
Tel   +33 (0)2 99 48 95 26
Email   lahamelinais@orange.fr

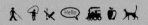

Entry 239   Map 3

Brittany

Les Mouettes

House and owner are imbued with the calm of a balmy summer's morning, whatever the weather. Isabelle's talent seems to touch the very air that fills her old family house (and smokers are not spurned!). Timeless simplicity reigns; there is nothing superfluous: simple carved pine furniture, an antique wrought-iron cot, dhurries on scrubbed plank floors, palest yellow or mauve walls to reflect the ocean-borne light, harmonious striped or gingham curtains. Starfish and many-splendoured pebbles keep the house sea-connected. The unspoilt seaside village, popular in season, is worth the trip alone.

Price	€50.
Rooms	5: 4 doubles, 1 twin.
Meals	Restaurants in village.
Closed	Rarely.
Directions	From St Malo, N137 for Rennes. 6km after St Malo, right on D117 to St Suliac (3km from N137 exit to village entrance). Road leads to Grande Rue down to port; house at top on right.

Isabelle Rouvrais
Les Mouettes,
17 Grande Rue,
35430 St Suliac,
Ille-et-Vilaine

Tel	+33 (0)2 99 58 30 41
Email	contact@les-mouettes-saint-suliac.com
Web	www.les-mouettes-saint-suliac.com

Entry 240   Map 3

Brittany

La Maison Neuve

Fabrice whips up wonderful aperitifs, Nicole spoils you with her cooking – home-baking at breakfast, a feast of surprises at dinner. Set in pretty Breton countryside, close to golf, riding and beaches, the 19th-century farmhouse combines original features with a light, modern style. Fresh, French bedrooms – one with hand-painted furniture, another with a wrought-iron four-poster – are dotted with objects from Japanese travels. On chilly evenings, cosy up to the fire in the grand granite fireplace; in the summer, wander meadow, garden and woodland. A sauna and spa are planned. *Minimum stay 2 nights weekends.*

Price	€78.
Rooms	5: 2 doubles, 1 twin, 2 family rooms for 3.
Meals	Dinner with wine, €28.
Closed	Rarely.
Directions	N137 from St Malo; exit Miniac Morvan; left onto Rue de la Blainerie, 400m after petrol station; on for 800m; left to Bas Gouillon. House 300m on right.

Nicole & Fabrice Barbot
La Maison Neuve,
35540 Miniac Morvan,
Ille-et-Vilaine

Tel	+33 (0)2 99 58 05 38
Fax	+33 (0)2 99 58 05 38
Email	fbarbot@wanadoo.fr
Web	www.la-maison-neuve.com

Entry 241   Map 3

Brittany

Le Clos Saint Cadreuc

Your warm hosts put good Breton dishes on your plate, and pour good organic wines – they create a welcoming atmosphere in their stone farmhouse. The very French rooms in the converted stables – two just finished: spacious, lovely, with huge walk-in showers – are enlivened by primitive West Indian paintings. More colour and space in the open-plan dining/sitting room: a good place to spend time in. Between house and stables is a pretty sheltered garden for picnics and DIY barbecues – great for families. Real peace in this quiet hamlet just 2km from the coast and a stone's throw from Mont St Michel.

Brittany

Malik

The everyday becomes remarkable in these people's hands: we seldom consider modern houses but sensitively-designed Malik sailed in. Clad in red cedar, and open-plan, its wood, metal and sliding glass doors are in harmony with the dense trees, and every detail is taken care of. Harmonious covers on good beds, oriental wall hangings on plain walls, private patios, monogrammed towels and lovely soaps. Breakfast, *un peu brunch*, is carefully attended to, and breads and jams homemade. Lovely people and an exquisitely serene house that seems to hug its garden to its heart. A haven on the edge of a small town.

Price	€67. Family room €72.
Rooms	5: 2 doubles, 2 family rooms, 1 suite.
Meals	Dinner with wine, €25.
Closed	Rarely.
Directions	From St Malo D168 for St Brieuc. At 1st r'bout after Ploubalay D26 for Plessix Balisson for 4km to hamlet; house on right, signed.

Price	€79. €122 for 4.
Rooms	2: 1 suite with sitting room, 1 suite for 4.
Meals	Restaurants within walking distance.
Closed	December-March.
Directions	From Dinan N176 W for St Brieuc for approx. 12km; right to Plélan le Petit. Follow signs to Centre & Mairie; at Mairie right for St Maudez, 2nd right.

Brigitte & Patrick Noël
Le Clos Saint Cadreuc,
22650 Ploubalay,
Côtes-d'Armor
Tel +33 (0)2 96 27 32 43
Email clos-saint-cadreuc@wanadoo.fr
Web www.clos-saint-cadreuc.com

Martine & Hubert Viannay
Malik,
Chemin de l'Étoupe,
22980 Plélan le Petit,
Côtes-d'Armor
Tel +33 (0)2 96 27 62 71
Email bienvenue@malik-bretagne.com
Web www.malik-bretagne.com

Entry 242   Map 3

Entry 243   Map 3

Brittany

Le Manoir de la Villeneuve

Wrapped in rolling lawns, wooded parkland and sweeping drive, this manor house seems untouched by the 21st century. Light, airy pools of calm – high ceilings, tall windows, polished floorboards – are furnished with a contemporary elegance while plain walls, beams and tomette floors have been allowed to glow. Bedrooms are comfortable spaces of gentle colours and well-chosen antiques, some with beams and sloping ceilings; the stunning suite with its own salon has a vast bathroom. Breakfast handsomely, then explore Dinan, St Brieuc, the coast… or relax in the garden. A gracious home run by well-organised hosts.

Price	€70-€130.
Rooms	4: 2 doubles, 1 twin/double, 1 suite for 3.
Meals	Restaurant 2km.
Closed	Rarely.
Directions	RN12 Rennes-St Brieuc; exit D768 for Plancoët & Dinard to Lamballe; 1st r'bout to Pleneuf Val Andre; 2nd r'bout to St Aaron; 300m left, follow signs.

	Nathalie Peres
	Le Manoir de la Villeneuve,
	22400 Lamballe,
	Côtes-d'Armor
Tel	+33 (0)2 96 50 86 32
Email	manoirdelavilleneuve@wanadoo.fr
Web	www.chambresaumanoir.com

Entry 244   Map 3

Brittany

Château de Bonabry

An extraordinary old château, built in 1373 by the Viscount's ancestor, with vastly wonderful bedrooms, a lively, lovable couple of aristocratic hosts bent on riding, hunting and entertaining you, fields all around and the sea at the end of the drive. Breakfast till ten on crêpes, croissants and quince jam. Madame is using her energy and taste in renovating some of the rooms; in one suite, a canopied bed, colourful rugs and a stag's head on a lustrous wall. Windows tall, portraits ancestral, chapel 18th century, roses myriad – and bathrooms with hand-embroidered towels. Incomparable. *Sawday self-catering also.*

Price	€100-€145.
Rooms	3: 2 suites; 1 double with separate bath.
Meals	Restaurants within 10km.
Closed	October-Easter.
Directions	From St Brieuc N12 for Lamballe exit Yffigniac Hillion; left D80 to Hillion; D34 for Morieux, 200m to roadside cross on left by château gates.

	Vicomtesse Louis du Fou de Kerdaniel
	Château de Bonabry,
	22120 Hillion, Côtes-d'Armor
Tel	+33 (0)2 96 32 21 06
Fax	+33 (0)2 96 32 21 06
Email	bonabry@wanadoo.fr
Web	www.bonabry.fr.st

Entry 245   Map 3

Brittany

14 rue des Capucins

Big, solid and well-loved, this place wraps you in comfortable, old-world charm. The Pontbriands and their friendly dog are on hand (to suggest restaurants, ferry you to the station...), yet leave you free to enjoy their home. Downstairs is warm with oak doors and panelling, family antiques, oriental rugs, deep sofas and old leather chairs. The two bedrooms and one bathroom are light and prettily old-fashioned with floral wallpapers and a melee of furnishings. St Brieuc is on the doorstep, beaches are 15 minutes away, St Malo and Dinan an hour. And there's a lovely walled garden for lazy breakfasts. La vraie France.

Price	€65–€80.
Rooms	2: 1 twin/double, 1 suite for 2-5, sharing bath.
Meals	Restaurant 5-minute walk. Guest kitchenette.
Closed	November-February.
Directions	N12 Rennes-Brest to St Brieuc. House in centre of town. Directions on booking.

Serge & Bénédicte de Pontbriand
14 rue des Capucins,
22000 St Brieuc,
Côtes-d'Armor
Tel   +33 (0)2 96 62 08 21
Fax   +33 (0)2 96 62 16 99
Email benedictedepontbriand@hotmail.fr

Entry 246   Map 3

Brittany

Manoir de la Ville Éveque

A wonder at every turn. The salon is light and luminous, touched with an eclectic collection of *objets*, much oriental, Monsieur's amazing Egyptian photographs, and the bronze and marble works of sculptor Pierre Roche whose summer retreat this was. Yours now, in all its Breton austerity, and its superb gardens falling away to the wildflower wood, with private footpath to the shore. Organic breakfasts are taken at separate tables; views stretch over the garden to the sea. Isabelle offers massage therapy with essential oils, serene bedrooms enjoy Egyptian names, and the children's room is up in the eaves.

Price	€75–€105.
Rooms	4: 2 doubles, 1 family suite, 1 suite.
Meals	Restaurants 2-4km.
Closed	November-March.
Directions	RN12 west of St Brieuc; D768, exit Les Rampes for Pordic; at 2nd r'bout for Pordic centre; right at church; left at r'bout past Mairie, 700m; 3rd right; 1st left.

Isabelle & Jean-Yves Le Fevre
Manoir de la Ville Éveque,
56 rue de la Ville Éveque,
22590 Pordic, Côtes-d'Armor
Tel   +33 (0)2 96 79 17 32
Email keryos@wanadoo.fr
Web   www.keryos.com

Entry 247   Map 3

Brittany

Toul Bleïz

Have breakfast in the courtyard of this traditional Breton cottage serenaded by birds. There may be standing stones, badgers and wild boar on the moors behind but civilisation is a five-minute drive – perfect. An art teacher in her other life, Julie takes people out painting while Jez runs vegetarian cookery courses. Inside: exposed stone walls, renovated wood, comfy white sofas, quiet good taste. The ground-floor bedroom has a patchwork quilt, lace pillows and doors onto the garden. You'll love this place. *Not suitable for children.*

Price	€55.
Rooms	1 double.
Meals	Dinner with wine, €22.
Closed	Rarely.
Directions	From N164 D44 for Gorges du Daoulas; left at junction for Allées Couvertes; continue through hamlet; past lay-by on right; Toul Bleïz next track on right.

Julie & Jez Rooke
Toul Bleïz,
22570 Laniscat,
Côtes-d'Armor

Tel	+33 (0)2 96 36 98 34
Email	jezrooke@hotmail.com
Web	www.phoneinsick.co.uk

Entry 248 Map 2

Brittany

Manoir de Coat Gueno

The 15th-century manor house, only a few minutes' drive from the fishing ports, headlands and long sandy beaches, is cocooned in countryside. Wrapped in a rich fluffy towel, gaze out of your lavishly furnished bedroom onto the lawns below. You may hear the crackling of the log fire in the vast stone hearth downstairs, lit by your perfectionist host, the splash and laughter of guests in the pool or the crack of billiard balls echoing upwards to the tower. The games room and one gorgeous suite are in separate buildings in the grounds. *Gosford Park*, à la Bretonne. *Children over 8 welcome. Minimum stay 2 nights.*

Price	€100-€110. Suite €135-€165.
Rooms	3: 1 double, 2 suites: 1 for 3, 1 for 4.
Meals	Dinner €25. Wine €17.
Closed	September-April.
Directions	From Paimpol for Lézardrieux; after bridge left to Pleudaniel; right for Pouldouran; thro' Prat Collet & Passe Porte to sign for Croas Guezou; left; 1st track right 800m. Not easy to find! Or call from Pleudaniel.

Christian de Rouffignac
Manoir de Coat Gueno,
Coat Gueno, 22740 Pleudaniel,
Côtes-d'Armor

Tel	+33 (0)2 96 20 10 98
Email	coatguen@aol.com
Web	mapage.noos.fr/coatgueno

Entry 249 Map 2

Brittany

Château de Kermezen

A very special place, aristocratic Kermezen has been in the family for 600 years and feels as if it will stand for ever in its granite certainty. Its 17th-19th century 'modernisation' is a masterpiece of high ceilings, generous windows, a granite-hearthed, tapestried guest sitting room where old books and family portraits remind you this is "just an ordinary family house". Madame, dynamic and adorable, loves her visitors. All the bedrooms, from traditional to timber-strewn to yellow-panelled, have a laid-back charm. Plus private chapel, old mill, vast lawns and trees…An enduring favourite, worth every penny.

Price	€90-€110.
Rooms	5: 3 doubles, 2 twins.
Meals	Restaurant & crêperie in village.
Closed	Rarely.
Directions	From St Brieuc N12 to Guingamp; D8 for Tréguier; at Pommerit Jaudy left at lights; signed.

Comte & Comtesse de Kermel
Château de Kermezen,
22450 Pommerit Jaudy,
Côtes-d'Armor

Tel   +33 (0)2 96 91 35 75
Fax   +33 (0)2 96 91 35 75
Email micheldekermel@kermezen.com

Entry 250   Map 2

Brittany

À la Corniche

Enter and you will see why we chose this modernised house: the ever-changing light of the great bay shimmers in through vast swathes of glass. Each guest room has its own veranda where you can sit and gaze at the sea, the islands and the coastline. Or take ten minutes and walk to Perros, for restaurants and beaches. Marie-Clo has enlivened the interior with her patchwork and embroidery, installed a fine new wood-burner in the living space and tea trays in the rooms. It is calm, light, bright; she is attentive, warm and generous, and breakfast is seriously good. Ideal for couples on a gentle seaside holiday. *Sawday self-catering also.*

Price	€70-€80.
Rooms	2 doubles, each with sitting area.
Meals	Restaurants 400-500m.
Closed	Never.
Directions	From Lannion D788 N to Perros Guirec; follow signs to Port; coastal road round bay for approx. 1km; left at sign. (Will fax map or collect you from railway station.)

Marie-Clotilde Biarnès
À la Corniche,
41 rue de la Petite Corniche, BP 24,
22700 Perros Guirec, Côtes-d'Armor

Tel   +33 (0)2 96 23 28 08
Email marieclo.biarnes@wanadoo.fr
Web   perso.wanadoo.fr/corniche

Entry 251   Map 2

Brittany

Manoir de Kerguéréon

Such wonderful, gracious hosts with a nice sense of humour: you feel you are at a house party; such age and history in the gloriously asymmetrical château: tower, turrets, vast fireplaces, low doors, ancestral portraits, fine furniture; such a lovely garden, Madame's own work. Once you have managed the worn spiral staircase you find bedrooms with space, taste, arched doors, a lovely window seat to do your tapestry in, good bathrooms; and the great Breton breakfast can be brought up if you wish. An elegant welcome, intelligent conversation, delightful house – and their son breeds racehorses on the estate.

Price	€100.
Rooms	3: 1 double, 2 twins.
Meals	Restaurants 7-10km.
Closed	Rarely.
Directions	N12 exit Bég Chra & Plouaret (between Guingamp & Morlaix); Plouaret D11 for Lannion; after 5.5km left for Ploumilliau, D30; over railway, left to Kerguéréon after 3km, 100m left to end.

M & Mme de Bellefon
Manoir de Kerguéréon,
Ploubezre, 22300 Lannion,
Côtes-d'Armor

Tel   +33 (0)2 96 38 80 59
Fax   +33 (0)2 96 38 91 46
Email   arnaud.de-bellefon@orange.fr

Entry 252   Map 2

Brittany

Ar Run

A house to seduce you. From the Rosanbo Château views to the candles at breakfast, this is a home of warmth and charm. Polished floorboards and stone walls, oriental rugs and antiques reflect its 200-year history, while bedrooms are large and inviting. Cushions, elegant drapes, gleaming furniture, books, chocolates, candelabra, flowers – it's all lovely. Enjoy fabulous breakfasts, doorstep walks or explore the coast (15 mins). Historic Lannion and Morlaix – with good restaurants – are a short drive; the pretty garden with Turkish 'hammam' and wooden loungers are to share. Feel thoroughly spoiled by super hosts.

Price	€85-€95.
Rooms	2 doubles.
Meals	Restaurant 2km.
Closed	January.
Directions	From Guingamp N12 west 26km; right D11 for Plouaret, left 1st exit after Total garage; to Lanvellec & Château de Rosanbo to Plufur; 2nd lane on left, after castle entrance.

Jean-Marie Brun &
Jean-François Hurpre
Ar Run,
22310 Plufur, Côtes-d'Armor

Tel   +33 (0)2 96 35 14 05
Email   jeanmariebrun@wanadoo.fr
Web   chambresdarmor.com

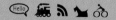

Entry 253   Map 2

Brittany

L'Ancien Presbytère

Inside an enclosed courtyard, a charming village presbytery. Walled gardens and a wildflower orchard for picnics complete the peaceful mood. The comfy rooms, a little rough around the edges, are stuffed with personal touches. The biggest is the lightest, with an amazing 1950s/Deco bathroom; the cosy, cottagey, low-beamed attic rooms have very small shower rooms. Madame, easy and approachable, loves gardening and knows the area "like her pocket". She has itineraries for your deeper discovery, so stay awhile – and bring woollies in winter! You may eat here but make sure your dinner booking is firm.

Price	€65-€75.
Rooms	3 twins/doubles.
Meals	Dinner with wine, €25.
Closed	November-February.
Directions	From Guingamp N12 for Morlaix, exit Louargat. From Louargat church, D33 to Tregrom, 7km. At junc. with house with blue shutters on right, 2nd left, to left side of church. Entrance thro' blue door in wall.

Nicole de Morchoven
L'Ancien Presbytère,
22420 Tregrom, Côtes-d'Armor
Tel   +33 (0)2 96 47 94 15
Fax   +33 (0)2 96 47 94 15
Email   nicole.de-morchoven@wanadoo.fr
Web   tregrom.monsite.wanadoo.fr

Entry 254   Map 2

Brittany

La Grange de Coatélan

Yolande is a smiling, helpful mother of five, Charlick the most sociable workaholic you could find. They are active, artistic (he paints) and fun. Having beautifully renovated their old Breton weaver's house, they are converting other ruins as well as running the small auberge that serves traditional dishes and meats grilled on the open fire; brilliant is the food. Bedrooms under the eaves (some steep stairs) have clever layouts, colour schemes and fabrics and imaginative use of wood. Joyful rustic elegance deep in the countryside, with animals and swings for children's delight. *Minimum stay 2 nights in summer.*

Price	€50-€70.
Rooms	5: 2 doubles, 3 quadruples.
Meals	Dinner €22. Wine €17-€57.
Closed	Christmas-New Year.
Directions	From Morlaix D9 south to Pougonven; at 2nd r'bout D109 to Coetélan. House on right, signed.

Charlick & Yolande de Ternay
La Grange de Coatélan,
29640 Plougonven, Finistère
Tel   +33 (0)2 98 72 60 16
Fax   +33 (0)2 98 72 60 16
Email   la-grange-de-coatelan@wanadoo.fr
Web   www.lagrangedecoatelan.com

Entry 255   Map 2

Brittany

Manoir de Coat Amour

A dramatic, steep, shrubby drive brings you to a grand old house guarded by stone elephants and a spectacular gem of a chapel: strength and spirit. Set in a paradisical park, the Taylors' house overlooks Morlaix yet the traffic hum is minimal, the seclusion total. Chandeliers and antiques, polished floors, Jouy prints and strong colours add to the house-party atmosphere, refined yet comfortable. Jenny and Stafford (she taught textiles) have enjoyed doing their beautiful house in their own style and chat delightedly about it all. Super bedrooms, some connecting, a high colourful guest sitting room, simple luxury. *Sawday self-catering also.*

Price	€90–€115.
Rooms	6: 2 doubles, 2 triples; 2 triples sharing bath.
Meals	Dinner with wine, €32; 4 courses €47.
Closed	Rarely.
Directions	From Morlaix Route de Paris for St Brieuc; at mini-r'bout left up hill; immed. opp. Ford garage sharp left into drive; pale blue gates.

Stafford & Jenny Taylor
Manoir de Coat Amour,
Route de Paris,
29600 Morlaix, Finistère

Tel	+33 (0)2 98 88 57 02
Fax	+33 (0)2 98 88 57 02
Email	stafford.taylor@wanadoo.fr
Web	www.gites-morlaix.com

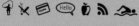

Entry 256   Map 2

Brittany

Manoir de Roch ar Brini

Crow's Rock Manor: sounds wild? It is wonderfully civilised. Built in the 1840s and admirably restored by your young and sociable hosts, who have four young children, it breathes an air of old-style, refined yet understated luxury in big, lofty-ceilinged, antiqued and chandeliered rooms with superb views of the generous grounds. The drawing-room parquet alone is worth the visit; bed linen is exceptional; from one super bathroom you can gaze out to the fields; another has tapestries of... baths. Breakfast may include *far breton* and fresh fruit salad. *Horse riding possible. Minimum stay 2 nights July/August.*

Price	€70–€85.
Rooms	2 doubles.
Meals	Bistro 1km.
Closed	Rarely.
Directions	From Port Morlaix follow right bank of river N for Le Dourduff; after 3.6km, 3rd right at Roch ar Brini sign (hairpin bend) 500m. Right for Ploujean; house 3rd on right.

Étienne & Armelle Delaisi
Manoir de Roch ar Brini,
29600 Morlaix Ploujean,
Finistère

Tel	+33 (0)2 98 72 01 44
Fax	+33 (0)2 98 88 04 49
Email	contact@brittanyguesthouse.com
Web	www.brittanyguesthouse.com

Entry 257   Map 2

Brittany

Kernevez

Madame is the reason to stay. Warm, hospitable, enchanting, she is the life and soul of Kernevez. If you wish to practise your French, even better: she delights in lively conversation. Squarely planted in its Breton soil, this is an unluxurious family house – guest rooms are traditional, with family pieces, and shower rooms tiny, but the Gralls, genuine Breton-speaking Bretons, have time for all. Wake to birdsong in the fields and Madame's rhubarb jam at breakfast, prepare your own meals in the guest kitchenette, eat out in the garden that looks down to the sea. *Minimum stay 2 nights July/August.*

Price	€50.
Rooms	3: 1 double, 1 twin, 1 family room.
Meals	Restaurant 2.5km. Guest kitchen.
Closed	Rarely.
Directions	From St Pol de Léon D10 W to Cléder, right at 2nd r'bout. Arriving in Cléder, take road to sea for 2km; left following signs to Ferme de Kernévez.

François & Marceline Grall
Kernevez,
29233 Cléder,
Finistère
Tel +33 (0)2 98 69 41 14
Web www.kernevez.fr.fm

Entry 258   Map 2

Brittany

Domaine de Moulin Mer

White shutters against pink-washed walls, graceful steps rising to the front door, attendant palm trees… In an amazingly short time, Stéphane has restored this *maison de maître* to its full glory. The luxurious rooms are a masterly combination of period elegance and modern minimalism, the gardens a riot of shady trees and irises, roses and tumbled ruins. Across the road you can glimpse the waters of the estuary and a fine old mill. Stéphane, who used to work in Dublin, is an amusing, genial host. In low season, he will cook you (according to availability and his whim) an inventive dinner using fresh local produce.

Price	€65-€130.
Rooms	4: 2 doubles, 2 suites.
Meals	Dinner with wine & champagne, €40.
Closed	Rarely.
Directions	From Châteaulin N165 for Brest, exit to Daoulas; N333 to Logonna Daoulas; left Route de Moulin Mer. Domaine on right of steep downhill bend; pass Domaine, cont. 50m to beach.

Stéphane Pécot
Domaine de Moulin Mer,
34 route de Moulin Mer,
29460 Logonna Daoulas, Finistère
Tel +33 (0)2 98 07 24 45
Email info@domaine-moulin-mer.com
Web www.domaine-moulin-mer.com

Entry 259   Map 2

Brittany

Domaine de Rugornou Vras

The two most memorable things here are Marie-Christine's smile as she talks about her native Brittany, and the crispness of the décor. Guest rooms are in the old cider-press – pretty and fresh with skylight windows and country antiques, and shower rooms immaculate. Breakfast, perhaps with Breton music in the background (to make the Breton costumes dance?), is prepared in the guest dayroom and eaten at the refectory table, with views of the garden and books all around. Dinner is at an auberge run by Madame's daughter, a walk away. It is quiet and comfortable and you can be quite independent.

Brittany

Manoir de Kerledan

Everyone loves Kerledan, its gargoyles, its sophisticated theatrical décor, its owners' enthusiasm. Peter, an engineer, and Penny, a designer, have renovated it themselves and made it stunningly original. Sit in the dining room with its great fire, stroll in the tranquil gardens (baroque courtyard, palisade hornbeam allée, potager) or lounge in a perfect bedroom. Natural colours of sisal and unstained oak, lime-plastered walls, the odd splash of antique mirror or gilded bergère with fake leopard skin create a mood of luxury and calm; slate-floored bathrooms are delicious, candlelit dinners are legendary.

Price	€48–€50. Triple €68. Singles €42.
Rooms	2: 1 double, 1 triple.
Meals	Dinner with wine, €18.
Closed	Rarely.
Directions	From Morlaix D785 for Quimper, approx. 35km. 800m before Brasparts, right (on bend) & follow signs for Garz ar Bik.

Price	€80–€125.
Rooms	3: 1 double, 1 twin, 1 family room.
Meals	Dinner, 2 courses, €20; 3 courses €25. Wine list from €5.
Closed	Rarely.
Directions	Left out of Carhaix railway station, left at 1st r'bout, under bridge; right at 2nd r'bout, right at 3rd r'bout; right. Down hill past 'Gamme Vert' garden centre on right; left, on for 300m; house on right.

	Marie-Christine Chaussy
	Domaine de Rugornou Vras,
	Garz ar Bik,
	29190 Brasparts, Finistère
Tel	+33 (0)2 98 81 47 14
Fax	+33 (0)2 98 81 47 14
Email	marie-christine.chaussy@wanadoo.fr

	Peter & Penny Dinwiddie
	Manoir de Kerledan,
	Rue de Kerledan,
	29270 Carhaix-Plouguer, Finistère
Tel	+33 (0)2 98 99 44 63
Email	kerledan@gmail.com
Web	www.kerledan.com

Entry 260   Map 2

Entry 261   Map 2

Brittany

Kerloaï

A Breton house with hospitable Breton owners, Breton furniture and a huge Breton brass pot once used for mixing crêpes. Young Madame is welcoming and chatty (in French), Monsieur takes great pride in the garden – with pig, hens and wonderful organic produce; you may picnic and barbecue here. The large, light, country-style rooms are all merrily and artistically painted by Gabrielle. Copious breakfasts include those crêpes (not mixed in the brass pot) and home-grown kiwi fruit in season. An authentic spot between Armor, the flat land by the sea, and Argoat, the land of the woods.

Price	€55-€65.
Rooms	3: 1 double, 2 twins.
Meals	Restaurant 4km.
Closed	Occasionally.
Directions	From Scaër, D50 for Coray Briec; after 3km, left at 'Ty Ru' & follow signs for Kerloaï.

Gabrielle Penn
Kerloaï,
29390 Scaër, Finistère
Tel   +33 (0)2 98 59 42 60
Email ti.penn@orange.fr

Brittany

Kerambris

Madame is a darling: quiet, serene and immensely kind, she really treats her guests as friends. The long, low, granite house has been in the family for all of its 300 years, enjoying the peace of this wind-blown, bird-sung spot just six minutes from the sea and the stunning coastal path – and with standing stones in the garden! Most of the building is gîtes; the chambres d'hôtes are tucked into the far end – small, impeccably simple, like the dining room, with some handsome Breton furniture. With charming Port Manech and good beaches nearby, it is a wonderful holiday spot.

Price	€46.
Rooms	4: 2 doubles, 2 twins.
Meals	Restaurants within walking distance.
Closed	Rarely.
Directions	From Pont Aven, D77 for Port Manech; right just before sign Port Manech; 1st left. Follow Chambres d'Hôtes signs.

Yveline Gourlaouen
Kerambris,
Port Manech, 29920 Nevez,
Finistère
Tel   +33 (0)2 98 06 83 82
Fax   +33 (0)2 98 06 83 82
Email gites-kerambris@orange.fr

Brittany

Sémaphore de la Croix

A wild island promontory and a sybaritic retreat... an unlikely combination but Marie-France, a charming, cheerful Parisian, has pulled it off magnificently. Using natural materials and local artisans, she has transformed a lookout post built by the French Navy in 1862. Inside and out, it's a graceful blend of local tradition and stylish, witty innovation. The upper floors are reached by a wood and metal spiral staircase, the bedrooms are subtly ravishing, the bathrooms are a joy. All around you is the sea, and the cleverly designed garden means that nothing obstructs your view. A great place for couples.

Price	€165–€205.
Rooms	5 twins/doubles.
Meals	Restaurants 2.5km.
Closed	Mid-November to mid-March.
Directions	Ferry from Lorient to Île de Groix as foot passenger. Taxi to house dir. Pointe des Chats (5 mins); red roof.

	Marie-France Berthomier
	Sémaphore de la Croix,
	56590 Île de Groix, Morbihan
Mobile	+33 (0)6 21 55 16 41
Fax	+33 (0)2 97 86 86 43
Email	contact@semaphoredelacroix.fr
Web	www.semaphoredelacroix.fr

Brittany

Kernivilit

Bang there on the quayside, an oyster farm! Bedrooms touch the view – you may want to stay and capture that lovely, limpid light on canvas while drinking coffee on the balcony, smelling the sea and listening to the chugging of fishing boats. Madame worked in England, Germany and the USA before coming to Brittany to help François farm oysters; he'll take you out there too, if you ask. Hospitable and generous, alert and chatty, she hangs interesting paintings in her rooms, lights a fire on cool days and serves a good French breakfast on a terrace shaded by pines. Unusual and very welcoming.

Price	€70. Apartment €80.
Rooms	2 + 1: 2 twins. 1 apartment for 3.
Meals	Restaurant 500m.
Closed	Rarely.
Directions	From Auray D28 & D781 to Crach & Trinité sur Mer.; right at r'bout before bridge for La Trinité; house 400m along on left, sign 'François Gouzer'.

	Christine & François Gouzer
	Kernivilit,
	St Philibert,
	56470 La Trinité sur Mer, Morbihan
Tel	+33 (0)2 97 55 17 78
Fax	+33 (0)2 97 30 04 11
Email	info@residence-mer.com
Web	www.residence-mer.com

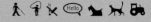

Brittany

Kerimel

The standing stones of Carnac are minutes away, beaches, coastal pathways and golf course close by. Kerimel is a handsome group of granite farm buildings in a perfect setting among the fields. Bedrooms are simple beauties: plain walls, some panelling, patchwork bedcovers and pale curtains, old stones and beams. The dining room is cottage perfection: dried flowers hanging from beams over a wooden table, a spring fire in the vast stone fireplace, breakfasts from Grand-mère that promise a new treat each day. A gentle, generous young family with excellent English… "We talked of flowers", wrote one guest.

Price	€75.
Rooms	5: 2 twins/doubles, 3 triples.
Meals	Restaurants 3km.
Closed	Rarely.
Directions	From N165 exit for Quiberon & Carnac; on D768, 4km; right to Ploemel; D105 W for Erdeven; sign on right, 1.5km.

Nicolas Malherbe
Kerimel,
56400 Ploemel,
Morbihan
Tel +33 (0)2 97 56 83 53
Email chaumieres.kerimel@wanadoo.fr
Web kerimel.free.fr

Entry 266 Map 2

Brittany

Talvern

Separated from the road by a grassy courtyard, this honest old farmhouse once belonged to the château. A stone wall divides it from its grander neighbour, enclosing a young fruit-treed garden, plenty of space for the Gillots' children – and yours – to play, and a potager; ask gentle Patrick about his vegetables and herbs and his face lights up! He was a chef in Paris (do eat in); Christine teaches English and is the talent behind the quietly original and very fine décor of the bedrooms. There are walks in the woods next door, good cycling, resident peacocks, birdlife all around. Wonderful. *Ask about cookery courses October-March.*

Ethical Collection: Food.
See page 432.

Price	€60. €110 for 4.
Rooms	5: 2 doubles, 1 twin/double, 2 suites.
Meals	Dinner with wine, €21.
Closed	Never.
Directions	N165 Auray to Lorient; 1st exit to Landévant; after Renault garage, 1st right onto D24 for Baud; after 50m, 1st right; on for 1.2km on Rue du Château. House on left.

Patrick Gillot
Talvern,
56690 Landévant,
Morbihan
Tel +33 (0)2 97 56 99 80
Email talvern@chambre-morbihan.com
Web www.chambre-morbihan.com

Entry 267 Map 2

Brittany

Lezerhy

A heavenly spot, cradled in a quiet hamlet 200 yards from the river in deepest Brittany. Delightful people: Martine looks after old folk and young Melissa; Philippe pots and teaches aikido; both have lots of time for guests. In an outbuilding, you have your own sitting/breakfast room and kitchen and two big, functionally furnished attic rooms, decorated in subtle pastels and fitted with good showers. Birds sing, the cat is one of the best ever, the dog will love you – and there may be a different kind of cake for breakfast every day. Visit St Nicholas des Eaux, for restaurants and river. Cheap, cheerful, bucolic.

Brittany

Le Rhun

Family-friendly, easy-going, this lovely German couple have done a fine renovation job on their cluster of buildings, turning the old stables into a thoughtful guest house with living room, dining room and kitchen for B&B guests. Up the outside staircase are two well finished bedrooms, their slightly minimalist style lifted by colourful quilts, pretty rugs and one red rocking chair. Clouds scud past the roof windows, cows graze (you can watch the milking), the lake attracts birds, there's a sauna and outdoor games. Simple country pursuits, shared with up to a dozen guests in the four gîtes. *Minimum stay 2 nights. Sawday self-catering also.*

Price	€45.	Price	€45-€47.
Rooms	2 twins.	Rooms	2 twins.
Meals	Restaurants 3km. Guest kitchen.	Meals	Restaurant 7km. Guest kitchen.
Closed	November-Easter, except by arrangement.	Closed	Mid-September to mid-May
Directions	From Pontivy D768 south for 12km; exit to St Nicolas des Eaux; right immed. after bridge; follow signs for Chambres d'Hôtes & Poterie for 3km.	Directions	From Pontivy D768 south; exit to Pluméliau. In Pluméliau church square left D203 at sign for Gîtes du Rhun, 2.5km.

Martine Maignan & Philippe Boivin
Lezerhy,
56310 Bieuzy les Eaux,
Morbihan

Tel   +33 (0)2 97 27 74 59
Fax   +33 (0)2 97 27 73 11
Email   boivinp@wanadoo.fr
Web   perso.wanadoo.fr/poterie-de-lezerhy

Eva & Jürgen Lincke
Le Rhun,
56930 Pluméliau,
Morbihan

Tel   +33 (0)2 97 51 83 48
Fax   +33 (0)2 97 51 83 48
Email   eva.lincke@web.de
Web   www.lerhun.de

Entry 268   Map 2

Entry 269   Map 2

Brittany

Château de Castellan

Fields and forests and not a house in sight. And, at the end of a lane, this quietly grand château, built in 1732 and a one-time hideout for counter revolutionaries. Ring the bell and Monsieur or Madame will come to greet you. Antique church pews, a wide winding stair, pastoral views are the pleasing first impressions. The owners have the right wing, Grandmère has the left and guests are in the middle, on two floors. Be charmed by big restful rooms, antiques, comfy chairs, discreet TVs, giant silver knives at dinner. Delightful Madame cooks, irons, cleans, and directs you to the prettiest of ancient villages.

Price	€75-€90. Family room €142.
Rooms	3: 1 double, 1 twin, 1 family room for 4, separate wcs.
Meals	Dinner €21. Wine €16-€35.
Closed	November-March.
Directions	From Redon D873 to La Gacilly; D777 to St Martin; D149; 1.5km for St Congard. Signs to Castellan.

Patrick & Marie Cossé
Château de Castellan,
56200 St Martin sur Oust,
Morbihan

Tel	+33 (0)2 99 91 51 69
Fax	+33 (0)2 99 91 57 41
Email	auberge@club-internet.fr
Web	www.castellan.fr.st

Entry 270   Map 3

Western Loire

Western Loire

Château de Coët Caret

Come for a taste of life with the French country aristocracy – it's getting hard to find. Madame is there to greet you on arrival and on hand during the day, and breakfast is properly formal (at 9am sharp, please!). Your hosts are cultured people, proud of their château tucked into the woods and its 100 hectares of parkland full of rare plants and ferns. Bedrooms are comfortable; *Saumon* is carpeted under the eaves and comes with binoculars for the birds. You are within the Brière Regional Park where water and land are inextricably mingled and wildlife abounds. *Minimum stay 2 nights.*

Price	€100-€115.
Rooms	3: 2 doubles, 1 twin.
Meals	Auberges 1.5-2km.
Closed	Rarely.
Directions	From N165 exit 15 D774 for La Baule to Herbignac, 10km; fork left D47 for St Lyphard for 4km; house on right.

Cécile de La Monneraye
Château de Coët Caret,
44410 Herbignac, Loire-Atlantique
Tel   +33 (0)2 40 91 41 20
Fax   +33 (0)2 40 91 37 46
Email   infos@coetcaret.com
Web   coetcaret.com

Entry 271   Map 3

Western Loire

Le Manoir des Quatre Saisons

Jean-Philippe, his mother and sister (who speaks good English) are engaging hosts and attentive, providing not only robes but drinks beside the pool. Communal breakfasts are flexible, complete with eggs and bacon as well as local choices. Immaculate bedrooms (three in a separate manoir) are colourfully coordinated – Jean-Philippe has an eye for detail. Expect stripes, patterns, French flourishes and distant sea views. Beach, river and town are walkable but children will love just mucking around in the big garden full of secret corners. *Minimum stay 2 nights July/August and bank holiday weekends.*

Price	€65-€75. Suites €84-€89.
Rooms	5: 3 doubles, 2 suites for 2-4 & kitchen.
Meals	Restaurants 1.5km.
Closed	Rarely.
Directions	From Guérande to La Turballe; right at entrance to La Turballe to Piriac; on for 1.7km, house on right.

Jean-Philippe Meyran
Le Manoir des Quatre Saisons,
744 bd de Lauvergnac,
44420 La Turballe, Loire-Atlantique
Tel   +33 (0)2 40 11 76 16
Fax   +33 (0)2 40 11 76 16
Email   jean-philippe.meyran@club-internet.fr
Web   www.manoir-des-quatre-saisons.com

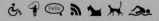

Entry 272   Map 3

Western Loire

La Mercerais

These are the sweetest people, even if their 'romantic' décor (rosy wallpapers, embroidered sheets) is not to everyone's taste. They really do "treat their guests as friends". Madame, bright and sparkling, is proud to show you her decorated books, music scrolls and hats with dried flowers; Monsieur is a retired farmer, quiet, friendly, attached to this place. The house is warm (log fire in winter) and country-furnished; two bedrooms (mind your head on the way up) have family armoires. Picnic in the immaculate award-winning garden with summer kitchen. Breakfast is served in pretty little baskets at the long table.

Price	€50. €65 for 3.
Rooms	3: 2 triples; 1 family room with bath & separate wc.
Meals	Guest kitchenette. Restaurant 3km.
Closed	Rarely.
Directions	From Rennes N137 for Nantes 63km; exit Nozay N171 for Blain 8km. At bottom of hill, left at roadside cross; signed.

	Yvonne & Marcel Pineau
	La Mercerais,
	44130 Blain,
	Loire-Atlantique
Tel	+33 (0)2 40 79 04 30

Entry 273   Map 3

Western Loire

Logis de Richebonne

Monsieur's parents bought this old *logis Vendéen* when he was six. Years later, researching the history of the house, he found his family first owned it in 1670! Madame's family tree, framed in the hall, goes back to the 14th century. But they are both warm and welcoming, not at all grand, and the house is full of personal touches: Madame painted the breakfast china and embroidered the beautiful tablecloths. Bedrooms are vast, with peaceful views and lots of fresh and dried flowers. The suite, and huge grounds, would be ideal for a family but very small children would need watching near the two pretty ponds.

Price	€70.
Rooms	3: 2 doubles, 1 suite for 5.
Meals	Restaurants in nearby village.
Closed	Rarely.
Directions	From Nantes through Legé for Challans & Machecoul; on leaving village left after restaurant Le Paradis; Logis 150m on left.

	Mme de Ternay
	Logis de Richebonne,
	44650 Legé,
	Loire-Atlantique
Tel	+33 (0)2 40 04 90 41
Fax	+33 (0)2 40 04 90 41
Email	adeternay@wanadoo.fr

Entry 274   Map 8

Western Loire

Château de la Sébinière

Young, warm, humorous Anne has exquisite taste and a perfectionist's eye; find it in the house of her dreams. The 18th-century château in its pretty park is a light, sunny and harmonious home. Walls are white or red-ochre, ceilings beamed, bathrooms a blend of old and new. There's an extravagant attention to detail – a pewter jug of old roses by a gilt mirror, a fine wicker chair on an ancient terracotta floor. You have your own entrance and the run of the sitting room, log-fired in winter. Your hosts serve real hot chocolate at breakfast, and, if you wish, a glass of wine on arrival. Nearby Clisson is full of charm.

Price	€90–€120.
Rooms	3 doubles.
Meals	Dinner with wine, €30.
Closed	Rarely.
Directions	From Nantes N249 for Poitiers; 2nd exit N149 for Le Pallet; through village, just past wine museum; right, signed.

Anne Cannaferina
Château de la Sébinière,
44330 Le Pallet, Loire-Atlantique

Tel	+33 (0)2 40 80 49 25
Fax	+33 (0)2 40 80 49 25
Email	info@chateausebiniere.com
Web	www.chateausebiniere.com

Entry 275   Map 3

Western Loire

Le Verger

The Broux have revived this fine cluster of granite buildings for their family farm and the guests they welcome so well. At the end of a private lane, one small ancient house of low heavy beams and big stones makes up your quarters: two divans in the sitting area, bedroom upstairs, hand-painted furniture, loads of personality. Across the yard, in the big square family house where noble stone, timber and terracotta also reign, Annick prepares delicious meals for the long bright table. Outside, flowers and vegetables mix in profusion, a white horse grazes in the field. Lovely people, charming place.

Price	€46.
Rooms	1 suite for 2-4.
Meals	Dinner with wine, €18.
Closed	End October-Easter.
Directions	From Nantes N249 for Poitiers, exit D763 to Clisson. From Clisson, N149 for Poitiers. At La Colonne, right to D753 direction Tiffauges. Through Tiffauges to Montaigu, 1km; 3rd road on right.

Annick & Marc Broux
Le Verger,
85530 La Bruffière, Vendée

Tel	+33 (0)2 51 43 62 02
Fax	+33 (0)2 51 43 62 02
Email	broux.annick@wanadoo.fr
Web	pagesperso-orange.fr/le-verger

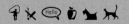

Entry 276   Map 8

Western Loire

La Frelonnière

An elegant country house in a peaceful, pastoral setting – who would not love it? The 18th-century farmhouse, complete with musket holes and open rafters, is informal, spacious and delightful. Your English/Scottish hosts are fun, friendly and intimately acquainted with France – they brought their children up here. Now they generously open their living space to guests, their serene pool, their exquisite Monet-style garden. Quietly stylish bedrooms (coir carpets, white walls, fresh flowers, silk flourishes) are divided by a sofa'd library on the landing; dinners may be romantic or convivial. A gem. *Unfenced pool.*

Price	€72.
Rooms	2 doubles.
Meals	Dinner with wine, €25.
Closed	Rarely.
Directions	A38 Nantes-Bordeaux exit Chantonnay; thro' town, D31 to La Caillère, thro' St Philbert & La Jaudonnière; house at end of 3rd lane on right between La Jaudonnière & St Hilaire du Bois.

Julie & Richard Deslandes
La Frelonnière,
85410 La Caillère – St Hilaire du Bois,
Vendée
Tel +33 (0)2 51 51 56 49
Fax +33 (0)2 51 51 31 25
Email rickdeslandes@aliceadsl.fr
Web www.bandbvendee.com

Entry 277 Map 8

Western Loire

Le Logis de la Clef de Bois

The town, a *ville d'art et d'histoire*, is one of the loveliest in the Vendée. The house, a chambres d'hôtes since the children have flown, stands at one end. Madame and Monsieur have an easy elegance and their home overflows with good taste and glamorous touches – from the contemporary mural on the dining room wall to the immaculate fauteuils of the salon. Big paintings, a collection of muslin caps from Poitou, bedrooms that celebrate writers… all point to cultural leanings. 'Rabelais' speaks of the Renaissance, 'Michel Ragon' is flamboyant in red and white checks, 'Simenon' reveals a cool blue charm.

Price	€100-€135.
Rooms	4: 2 doubles, 2 suites.
Meals	Dinner with wine, €30.
Closed	Never.
Directions	From Nantes for Niort /Bordeaux /Paris; exit 8 for Fontenay le Comte.

Danielle Portebois
Le Logis de la Clef de Bois,
5 rue du Département,
85200 Fontenay le Comte, Vendée
Tel +33 (0)2 51 69 03 49
Fax +33 (0)2 51 69 03 49
Email clef_de_bois@hotmail.com
Web www.clef-de-bois.com

Entry 278 Map 8

Western Loire

Le Rosier Sauvage

The pretty village is known for its exquisitely cloistered abbey – and something of the serenity and simplicity of the convent permeates the smallish, spotless bedrooms. The nicest is in a converted loft with the original massive oak door, timbered ceiling, terracotta-tiled floor and hotch-potch of furniture. The breakfast room, reached via the family's kitchen, is the old stable, complete with long polished table, while the old laundry, with vast stone washtub, is now a sitting room. Guests can picnic in the walled garden, overlooked by the abbey. When Christine is busy with her twins, her parents look after guests.

Price	€47-€50.
Rooms	4: 1 double, 1 twin, 2 triples.
Meals	Restaurant & crêperie 100m.
Closed	October-April.
Directions	From Niort N148 for Fontenay le Comte 20km (or A83 exit 9); after Oulmes right to Nieul sur l'Autise to Abbey; house just beyond on left.

Christine Chastain-Poupin
Le Rosier Sauvage,
1 rue de l'Abbaye, 85240
Nieul sur l'Autise, Vendée
Tel   +33 (0)2 51 52 49 39
Fax   +33 (0)2 51 52 49 46
Email   lerosiersauvage@yahoo.fr
Web   lerosiersauvage.c.la

Entry 279   Map 8

Western Loire

Le Petit Paradis

Space, games, private terraces and a safe pool: for families it is indeed 'a little paradise'. Madame has converted this comfortable farmhouse with a practical eye. Simple bedrooms – two ground-floor, all with own entrances and small showers – mix modern furnishings and cheery colours with beams, tiled floors and exposed stone walls. For more privacy, choose the family room with kitchenette in the outbuilding. In the main hall is a jolly space of games tables for communal breakfasts, even a kitchen for simple cooking; grown-ups can retreat to the mezzanine. One hour to the coast, and bikes and canoes for hire.

Price	€55. €67 for 3. €79 for 4.
Rooms	4: 3 twins/doubles, 1 family room for 4. Extra beds available.
Meals	Restaurant 5km. Guest kitchenette.
Closed	November-March.
Directions	From Bordeaux A10 exit 33 for Niort; N148 for Nantes & Cholet to Benet; D25 left at traffic lights for Le Mazeau, 4km to Ste Eulalie; in village 1st lane left; 1st on right.

Marie-Nöelle Houche
Le Petit Paradis,
La Meugne,
85490 Benet, Vendée
Tel   +33 (0)2 51 00 99 10
Email   accueil@le-petit-paradis.com
Web   le-petit-paradis.com

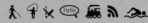

Entry 280   Map 8

Western Loire

Demeure l'Impériale

A rare survivor of Cholet's imperial past, when the whole town flourished on making handkerchiefs, this elegant townhouse was the orangery of a long-gone château. Nothing imperial about Édith, though, who loves to make guests feel at home. The bedrooms are light and beautiful with fine period furniture and gleaming modern bathrooms. Two give onto the quiet street, the suite looks over the rose-filled, tree-shaded garden. There are two pretty salons and a glass-roofed dining room in the sunken courtyard – excellent dinners here. French style and hospitality at its best.

Price	€69-€76. Suite €130.
Rooms	4: 3 doubles, 1 suite for 4.
Meals	Dinner €23. Wine €10-€15.
Closed	Rarely.
Directions	Rue Nationale is one-way street through Cholet centre. No. 28 200m down on right, near St Pierre church.

Édith & Jean-René Duchesne
Demeure l'Impériale,
28 rue Nationale, 49300 Cholet,
Maine-et-Loire
Tel   +33 (0)2 41 58 84 84
Fax   +33 (0)2 41 63 17 03
Email demeure.imperiale@wanadoo.fr
Web   demeure-imperiale.com

Entry 281   Map 8

Western Loire

Le Mésangeau

The house is long-faced, and refined; the grounds (superb) come with a fishing pond and 'aperitif gazebo'. The Migons have expertly renovated this unusual house with its barn-enclosed courtyard, two towers and covered terrace. Big, north-facing bedrooms are elegant and comfortable behind their shutters, and keep the housekeepers busy. Expect leather sofas and a suit of armour, colourful beams above antique furniture, two billiard tables, and bikes, ping pong and drums in the barn. At dinner, French cuisine from Madame, and much entertainment from Monsieur, who collects veteran cars and plays bass guitar.

Price	€90-€110.
Rooms	5: 3 doubles, 2 suites: 1 for 4, 1 for 5.
Meals	Dinner with wine, €35.
Closed	Rarely.
Directions	Exit A11 at Ancenis for D763; at Liré, right onto D751. Left at Drain for St Laurent des Autels on D154. House 3.5km after church, on left.

Brigitte & Gérard Migon
Le Mésangeau,
49530 Drain, Maine-et-Loire
Tel   +33 (0)2 40 98 21 57
Fax   +33 (0)2 40 98 28 62
Email le.mesangeau@orange.fr
Web   www.loire-mesangeau.com

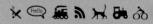

Entry 282   Map 3

Western Loire

Loire-Charmilles

A house, and garden, full of surprises, and a dazzling mix of styles. Low doorways, chunky beams and original floors are set against slabs of slate, Japanese art and some very modern furniture. Up wooden stairs, through a low doorway, bedrooms have huge beds, dimmer switches, antique desks with perspex chairs and sculptural plants. Bathrooms are ultra chic, one with a repro bath, another with mosaic tiles. The completely enclosed garden teems with roses, magnolia, mimosa and orchids; breakfast or dinner is on the veranda on warm days or in the huge-windowed orangery; bubbly Madame cooks on a fireplace grill.

Price	€45-€54.
Rooms	2: 1 double, 1 twin.
Meals	Dinner with wine, €23.
Closed	Rarely.
Directions	From St Florent le Vieil D751 for Montjean; entering Le Mesnil, signed Loire-Charmilles; house on right.

Nadia Leinberger
Loire-Charmilles,
9 rue de l'École,
49410 Le Mesnil en Vallée,
Maine-et-Loire

Tel	+33 (0)2 41 78 94 74
Email	nadia@loire-charmilles.com
Web	www.loire-charmilles.com

Entry 283   Map 3

Western Loire

La Rousselière

A hymn to peace and gentle living. The impeccably lovely garden is Monsieur's pride and joy; château-like reception rooms open one into another – glass doors to glass doors, billiards to dining to sitting – like an indoor arcade; family portraits follow you wherever you go; Mass is still said in the private chapel on 16 August. But it's never over-grand, bedrooms are highly individual with their antiques and hand-painted armoires (courtesy of an artistic sister), many bathrooms are new and Madame is the most delightful smiling hostess and a fine cook; your lovely hosts join you for an aperitif before dinner.

Ethical Collection: Food.
See page 432.

Price	€60-€95.
Rooms	5: 2 doubles, 1 twin, 1 family room, 1 family suite for 5.
Meals	Dinner with wine, €30.
Closed	Rarely.
Directions	From Angers N23 for Nantes; exit St Georges sur Loire; left at 1st r'bout for Chalonnes; left at 2nd r'bout for Chalonnes. Immed. before bridge left to La Possonnière; 1.5km, left, signed.

François & Jacqueline de Béru
La Rousselière,
49170 La Possonnière,
Maine-et-Loire

Tel	+33 (0)2 41 39 13 21
Fax	+33 (0)2 41 39 13 21
Email	larousseliere@unimedia.fr
Web	www.anjou-et-loire.com/rousseliere

Entry 284   Map 3

Western Loire

Prieuré de l'Épinay

Such happy, interested, interesting people, and meals the greatest fun – chicken from the farm, asparagus, raspberries, salads from the potager... all is organic. Facing the big grassed garden, the ancient priory has changed so little that the monks would feel at home here today, though the swimming pool, large and lovely, might be a surprise. Your hosts happily share their home and its history; lofty ceilings, 15th-century beams, a fascinating *cave*, a rare fireplace. The two-storey rooms in the barn are simple but spacious, summer breakfasts are served in the chapel. What value! *Ask about wine tours.*

Western Loire

Logis de la Roche Corbin

On the 'old' side of the Loire at Angers, a secret, special place. Behind a high wall: a cobbled path, a climbing rose, a sweet box hedge, a bunch of lettuces to keep the tortoise happy. Off this delightful courtyard garden is your room, aglow with 18th-century charm; off a French-grey hallway, an exquisite zen-like bathroom. Breakfast is up a magnificent rough-hewn oak stair, in a fine room with a rooftop view. Behind this hugely sympathetic restoration of a 16th-century house are Michael, an American painter with a studio over the road, and Pascale from Paris, warm, relaxed and enthusiastically new to B&B. *Sawday self-catering also.*

Price	€80.
Rooms	3: 1 suite for 2, 2 suites for 4-5.
Meals	Dinner with wine, €30. Picnic available.
Closed	October-April.
Directions	From Angers N23 for Nantes 18km; through St Georges; cont. 1.5km; left after garage. Pass château; house on left. Park outside, walk through gate.

Price	€85. Whole house available July/August.
Rooms	1 suite for 2.
Meals	Occasional dinner with wine, €15-€30.
Closed	Rarely.
Directions	A11 to Angers; exit for hospital; opp. hospital (urgences), Rue de l'Hommeau. House at end of street on corner of Rue de la Harpe.

	Bernard & Geneviève Gaultier Prieuré de l'Épinay, 49170 St Georges sur Loire, Maine-et-Loire
Tel	+33 (0)2 41 39 14 44
Fax	+33 (0)2 41 39 14 44
Email	bernard.gaultier3@wanadoo.fr
Web	monsite.wanadoo.fr/prieure-epinay

	Michael & Pascale Rogosin Logis de la Roche Corbin, 3 rue de la Harpe, 49100 Angers, Maine-et-Loire
Tel	+33 (0)2 41 86 93 70
Fax	+33 (0)2 41 86 93 70
Email	logisdelaroche@wanadoo.fr
Web	www.logisdelaroche.com

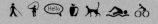

Western Loire

La Closerie

Nothing pretentious about this quiet village house – or its owners. Genuine country folk: Carmen, retired English teacher with a great sense of humour, and Hervé, equally hospitable, creator of delicious traditional French dinners. Bedrooms in the old farmhouse or off the shady courtyard, two of them with their own entrances, are simply but pleasantly decorated with small shower rooms. One has a magnificent stone fireplace; another, up outside stairs, has old beams, stone walls and pretty yellow and white fabrics. Trees almost engulf the house and the sunny conservatory dining room looks over a bosky garden.

Price	€55–€60.
Rooms	4: 3 doubles, 1 family room for 4.
Meals	Dinner with wine, €24.
Closed	Rarely.
Directions	From A85 exit 2 Longué; N147 for Saumur; at Super U r'bout D53 to St Philbert. House on right in centre of village.

Carmen & Hervé Taté
La Closerie,
29 rue d'Anjou,
49160 St Philbert du Peuple,
Maine-et-Loire

Tel	+33 (0)2 41 52 62 69
Email	herve.tate@wanadoo.fr
Web	www.bandb-lacloserie.com

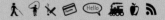

Entry 287   Map 4

Western Loire

Domaine de l'Oie Rouge

Recline in bed and watch the Loire flow by. The 19th-century townhouse sits in large peaceful gardens; in a smaller building Christiane runs an art gallery. One bedroom has an astonishingly ornate 1930s brown-tiled bathroom with a tub right in the middle, another opens to the garden and its trees; all the rooms are lavishly French. Monsieur is chef, Madame hosts dinner, especially fun when a number of guests are staying. Both your hosts will be happy to help you decide what to see and make the most of your stay. The lovely gardens are definitely worth exploring if you are green-fingered.

Price	€64–€90.
Rooms	5 doubles.
Meals	Dinner with wine, €25.
Closed	Rarely.
Directions	From Saumur D952 for Angers for 15km. Domaine on right at village entrance.

Christiane Batel
Domaine de l'Oie Rouge, 8 rue Nationale,
49350 Les Rosiers sur Loire,
Maine-et-Loire

Tel	+33 (0)2 41 53 65 65
Fax	+33 (0)2 41 53 65 66
Email	c.batel@wanadoo.fr
Web	domaine-oie-rouge.com

Entry 288   Map 4

Western Loire

Manoir du Bois Noblet

Zip back in time to stay in this completely restored 15th-century farmhouse surrounded by 42 acres of land. Huge bedrooms are reached up a splendid winding staircase in the tower, all dressed differently with armchairs and desks, magnificent chimney pieces, lovely antiques, white-sheeted beds and big modern bathrooms. Madame is deeply polite and you are welcome to enjoy the huge sitting room with monumental fireplace, family portraits and wooden shutters; breakfast and dinner are taken in an equally imposing dining room. Stroll the grounds, then wander to the village and pretend it's all yours.

Price	€100–€150.
Rooms	3: 1 double, 1 family suite for 3, 1 suite for 4.
Meals	Dinner with wine, €25.
Closed	Never.
Directions	From Noyant la Plaine D70 for Louerre; Le Bois Noblet 300m on right before village.

François & Dominque de Barbeyrac
Manoir du Bois Noblet,
49700 Louerre,
Maine-et-Loire
Tel   +33 (0)2 41 59 31 31
Email leboisnoblet@gmail.com
Web   perso.orange.fr/chambres.boisnoblet

Entry 289   Map 4

Western Loire

La Mascaron

On the banks of the Loire broods old Saumur. Deep inside hides a miniature medieval 'palace' with courtyard and balcony; it is central yet peaceful. A successful blend of old and contemporary is a rare surprise but the architect-owner – inspired, committed – has achieved it in the large, relaxing suite with its own entrance off the street. Beams, shutters, curtains and bed linen are highly original in colour and design; the fireplace, furniture, pictures and tapestries in the sitting room are of such quality and interest that one feels this could not have been done better. Madame is knowledgable, gentle and friendly.

Price	€120.
Rooms	1 suite.
Meals	Restaurants in Saumur.
Closed	November–March.
Directions	From Tourist Office to Église St Pierre; in Place St Pierre, Rue Hte St Pierre on right opp. church.

Marie & Marc Ganuchaud
La Mascaron,
6 rue Haute St Pierre,
49400 Saumur,
Maine-et-Loire
Tel   +33 (0)2 41 67 42 91

Entry 290   Map 4

Western Loire

Château de Salvert

This highly sculpted neo-gothic folly is home to a couple of unselfconscious aristocrats and lots of cheerful children. The baronial hall is properly dark and spooky, the dining room and salon elegant and plush with gilt chairs and ancestors on the walls. In the vast suite, a sitting area and a library in an alcove. One double has the shower in one turret, the loo in another (off the corridor). All are well decorated with fine French pieces and modern fabrics. The park is huge, wild boar roam, spring boarlets scamper, and Madame plays the piano and holds concerts. *Arrivals after 4pm. Sawday self-catering also.*

Western Loire

Le Gué de la Fresnaie

On a small road, but with little traffic, this 19th-century farmhouse has whitewashed walls, ancient beams, tiled floors and a lovely park-like garden behind. Bedrooms are in the main building but have their own entrance; sprinkled with antiques and interesting farmyard relics, they are airy and white; bathrooms are unexpectedly modern. Calm Madame is a gifted cook and grows her own vegetables – you'll eat well. Take a book to the large comfortable sitting room and admire more antiques, wander the fruit garden, swim in the pool, watch the river, borrow a bike or a canoe. Wonderfully serene.

Price	€49-€90. Suites €99-€160.
Rooms	5: 3 doubles, 2 suites for 2.
Meals	Dinner €44. Wine €22-€35.
Closed	Rarely.
Directions	From A85 exit Saumur on D767 for Le Lude. After 1km, left on D129 to Neuillé. Signed.

Price	€65.
Rooms	2 doubles with sofabeds.
Meals	Dinner with wine, €25.
Closed	Rarely.
Directions	From D347 exit Beaufort en Vallée; D59 to Gée; 3rd right; 5th house on right.

Monica Le Pelletier de Glatigny
Château de Salvert,
Salvert, 49680 Neuillé,
Maine-et-Loire
Tel   +33 (0)2 41 52 55 89
Fax   +33 (0)2 41 52 55 89
Email info@salvert.com
Web   www.chateau-de-salvert.fr

M & Mme Fernandez
Le Gué de la Fresnaie,
Les Planches, Chemin du Petit Jusson,
49250 Beaufort en Vallée,
Maine-et-Loire
Tel   +33 (0)2 41 80 42 60
Email rjcg-fernandez@club-internet.fr
Web   rjcg-fernandez.club.fr

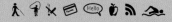

Entry 291   Map 4

Entry 292   Map 4

Western Loire

Les Bouchets

Beams, beams and more beams. The house was a ruin when the Bignons found it but they managed to save a wealth of original timber and stone details then added lovely old furniture, open fires, fresh flowers and soft, cosy bedrooms. The result is a seductively warm cheerful house. Passionate about food, they used to have a top-class restaurant where Michel was the chef; the signs are everywhere: coppers in the kitchen/entrance hall, loads of memorabilia in the soft family sitting room. Géraldine, bright, friendly and organised, loves needlework… and serving good food. *Sawday self-catering also.*

Price	€55–€65.
Rooms	3: 1 double, 1 twin/double, 1 family room.
Meals	Dinner with wine, €25.
Closed	Rarely.
Directions	From Bauge D60 for Beaufort en Vallée; at Chartrene right at x<->roads; 2nd left. Signed.

Michel & Géraldine Bignon
Les Bouchets,
49150 Le Vieil Baugé, Maine-et-Loire
Tel   +33 (0)2 41 82 34 48
Email   bignonm@wanadoo.fr
Web   www.lesbouchets.com

Entry 293   Map 4

Western Loire

La Besnardière

English Joyce brims with knowledge about aromatherapy, all things horticultural and is calm personified. She also cooks lovely vegetarian dishes, welcomes art, yoga and meditation workshops in her meditation room and shares her fresh, comforting and comfortable home with great generosity. Beams spring everywhere in the 500-year-old farmhouse – mind your head! – and the two big, warm, book-filled bedrooms are tucked under the rafters, one with steps to a courtyard below. Be charmed by log fires, a soft pink sofa'd sitting room, a garden full of wildflowers, a donkey, goats, ducks, hens and views. *Massage & reflexology. Sawday self-catering also.*

Ethical Collection: Food.
See page 432.

Price	€60.
Rooms	2: 1 double, 1 triple, sharing bath & wc.
Meals	Vegetarian or vegan dinner with wine, €25.
Closed	Rarely.
Directions	A11 to Durtal; D138 to Fougeré; D217 for Baugé; 1.5km; house on left.

Joyce Rimell
La Besnardière,
Route de Baugé, 49150 Fougeré,
Maine-et-Loire
Tel   +33 (0)2 41 90 15 20
Fax   +33 (0)2 41 90 15 20
Email   rimell.joyce@wanadoo.fr
Web   www.holiday-loire.com

Entry 294   Map 4

Château de Chambiers

Another marvellous family château, this one surrounded by a forest of wild boar. Smiling Madame speaks perfect English, is proud of her gardens fronted by topiary sheep and her big, beautiful rooms; she is a talented designer. Bedrooms have delicious antiques, one a French-Caribbean mahogany bed (the family owned a banana plantation), floors are 18th-century oak with *terre cuit* borders – exquisite; some of the baths, washstands and fittings are period originals. There's a panelled *salon de thé*, a billiards room and books, and a playhouse and organic potager in the garden. French heaven.

Ethical Collection: Environment; Food. See page 432.

Château de Montreuil

An 1840s neo-gothic delight in a 16-hectare, deer-roamed park, a river for swimming and rowing, an ornamental pool for fishing, and a film set of an interior. The sitting room is splendidly 'medieval', the panelled drawing room pure 18th century, taken whole from a château, with superb hangings and immensely high doors. This was once a self-sufficient country estate with chapel, dovecote and mill (remains still visible). Large, lofty bedrooms have authentic wooden floors and carpets, antique cupboards, bucolic river views. Your hosts are gracious, refined and humorous, always there to receive guests.

Price	€90–€250.
Rooms	6 family rooms for 3.
Meals	Dinner €28. Wine €15.
Closed	Rarely. Book ahead in winter.
Directions	From Angers, N23 to Durtal; r'bout, 1st exit to Bangé; after 150m, right to Jarzé; château on left after 3km.

Price	€85–€100.
Rooms	4: 1 double, 1 twin, 2 family rooms.
Meals	Dinner with wine, €30–€35.
Closed	November-Easter.
Directions	From Angers N23 to Seiches sur Loir; D74 for Châteauneuf sur Sarthe 5.5km. Château on right as you leave Montreuil village.

Anne Crouan
Château de Chambiers,
49430 Durtal,
Maine-et-Loire
Tel +33 (0)2 41 76 07 31
Fax +33 (0)2 41 76 04 28
Email info@chateauchambiers.com
Web www.chateauchambiers.com

Jacques & Marie Bailliou
Château de Montreuil,
49140 Montreuil sur Loir,
Maine-et-Loire
Tel +33 (0)2 41 76 21 03
Email chateau.montreuil@anjou-loir.com
Web www.anjou-loir.com

Château de Montriou

The park will explode your senses – and Monsieur sparkles! He and Nicole are bringing fresh energy to the house along with a passion for gardening: the lake, the famous sequoia, the waves of crocuses in spring, the tunnel of squashes, ravishing at summer's last flush. The 15th-century château has been lived in and tended by the same family for 300 years. A very old stone staircase leads to the properly formal bedrooms whose bold colours were design flavour of the period, and wooden floors, thick rugs and antiques are only slightly younger. And the venerable library is now a guest sitting room. Remarkable.

Price	€85–€100. Suite €155.
Rooms	4: 2 doubles, 1 double & kitchen, 1 suite for 4 & kitchen.
Meals	Restaurant nearby.
Closed	Rarely.
Directions	From Angers for Lion d'Angers; at Montreuil-Juigné right on D768 for Champigné; Montriou signed between Feneu & Champigné at x-roads La Croix de Beauvais; D74 left for Sceaux d'Anjou, on for 300m.

	Régis & Nicole de Loture
	Château de Montriou
	49460 Feneu, Maine-et-Loire
Tel	+33 (0)2 41 93 30 11
Fax	+33 (0)2 41 93 15 63
Email	chateau-de-montriou@wanadoo.fr
Web	www.chateau-de-montriou.com

Entry 297 Map 4

Manoir du Bois de Grez

An old peace lingers over the unique fan-shaped yard, the old well, the little chapel: this place oozes history. Your doctor host, who also loves painting, and his friendly chatty wife, much-travelled antique-hunters with imagination and flair, set the tone with a bright red petrol pump and a penny-farthing in the hall. Generous bedrooms (a superb new family room) hung with well-chosen oriental pieces or paintings are done in good strong colours that reflect the garden light. You share the big sitting room with your charming, interesting hosts, lots of plants and a suit of armour. A lovely garden, too.

Price	€75–€80.
Rooms	4: 2 doubles, 1 twin, 1 family room.
Meals	Guest kitchen. Restaurant 1.5km. Picnics available.
Closed	Rarely.
Directions	From Angers N162 to Laval; exit Grieul D291 to Grez Neuville; exit village via Sceaux d'Anjou road; 900m right Allée du Bois de Grez.

	Marie Laure & Jean Gaël Cesbron
	Manoir du Bois de Grez,
	Route de Sceaux d'Anjou,
	49220 Grez Neuville, Maine-et-Loire
Tel	+33 (0)2 41 18 00 09
Fax	+33 (0)2 41 18 00 09
Email	cesbron.boisgrez@wanadoo.fr
Web	www.boisdegrez.com

Entry 298 Map 4

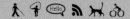

La Croix d'Étain

Frisky red squirrels decorate the stone balustrade, the wide river flows past the lush garden: it feels like deep country yet this handsome manor has urban elegance in its very stones. Panelling, mouldings, subtly muted floor tiles bring grace; traditional French florals add softness. It looks fairly formal but sprightly Madame adores having guests and pampers them, in their own quarters, with luxury. Monsieur is jovial, makes jam and loves fishing! Expect plush, lacy-feminine, carpeted bedrooms, three with river views, all with sunny bathrooms. The yacht-side setting is stunning — it could be the Riviera.

Price	€65–€100.
Rooms	2: 1 double, 1 twin.
Meals	Dinner with wine, €30.
Closed	Rarely.
Directions	From Angers N162 for Le Lion d'Angers; 20km to Grieul; right D291 to Grez Neuville. At church, Rue de l'Écluse towards river on left.

Jacqueline & Auguste Bahuaud
La Croix d'Étain,
2 rue de l'Écluse, 49220 Grez Neuville,
Maine-et-Loire

Tel	+33 (0)2 41 95 68 49
Fax	+33 (0)2 41 18 02 72
Email	croix.etain@anjou-et-loire.com
Web	www.anjou-et-loire.com/croix

Entry 299   Map 3

Les Travaillères

You cannot fail to warm to Madame's easy vivacity and infectious laugh. She virtually lives in her beloved garden — or in her kitchen in the house opposite, making pastries in the old bread oven. The lovingly preserved Segré farmhouse with its deep roof and curious *outeau* openings (some would have put in modern dormers), has great beams, a big fireplace, exposed stone and new country furniture. Attic bedrooms are neatly rustic: crochet, terracotta, pine, with bathrooms cunningly sneaked in among the rafters. The woods are full of birdlife, cows graze in the field outside one bedroom's window.

Ethical Collection: Environment; Food. See page 432.

Price	€44.
Rooms	3: 1 double, 2 suites for 4.
Meals	Restaurants 5km. Kitchen available. Picnics in garden.
Closed	Rarely.
Directions	Angers D775 to Le Lion d'Angers; Rennes & Segré on D775 3km; right at Chambres d'Hôtes & La Himbaudière sign; under main road; 1km along on left.

Jocelyne & Jean-Louis Lecourbe
Les Travaillères,
49220 Le Lion d'Angers,
Maine-et-Loire

Tel	+33 (0)2 41 61 33 56
Fax	+33 (0)2 41 26 24 03
Email	jean-louis.lecourbe@orange.fr
Web	www.lestravailleres.com

Entry 300   Map 3

Le Frêne

Unbroken views of the countryside, and not a whisper of the 21st century. The austere topiaried spinning-tops flanking the drive belie the warm, sunny rooms ahead – this house breathes books, music and art. Richard, who once had a book shop in Angers, is charming and funny; Florence runs art courses from home. Built on the ramparts of the old fortified village, the house has a 'hanging' garden whose beds are themed with colour. Bedrooms are colourful-cosy; the big attic suite, ideal for families, holds a Russian billiard table – and Florence's charming watercolours. Delicious food, delicious garden.

Le Rideau Miné

Fish or take a book to the river – so peaceful and charming. The old country values are at home here: the Fabrys have extended their house with deep respect for the 17th- and 18th-century shapes and materials of the lovely old millhouse (the Mayenne runs through the garden). Christian grows the fruit and vegetables, Dany delights in preparing local recipes for dinner and a fresh breakfast cake every day. The pretty, beamed, many-windowed bedrooms with their good sitting areas are always spotless. They are unintrusive but caring hosts, rightly proud of their house and garden.
Ask about wrought-iron weekend workshops.

Price	€55. Suite €90.
Rooms	4: 1 double, 2 twins, 1 suite for 4.
Meals	Dinner €19. Wine from €6.
Closed	Rarely.
Directions	From Angers N162 to Le Lion d'Angers; D863 to Segré; D923; left D863 to l'Hôtellerie de Flée; D180 to Châtelais; on entering village 1st left for Bouillé Ménard.

Price	€60-€65. Triple €85.
Rooms	3: 1 twin, 1 triple; 1 double with separate bathroom.
Meals	Dinner with wine, €25.
Closed	Rarely.
Directions	From Angers for Rennes N162; after Lion d'Angers D770 for Champigné; after river Mayenne over bridge; D287 left for Chambellay; left after 500m. Signed.

	Richard & Florence Sence
	Le Frêne,
	22 rue Saint Sauveur,
	49520 Châtelais, Maine-et-Loire
Tel	+33 (0)2 41 61 16 45
Fax	+33 (0)2 41 61 16 45
Email	lefrene@free.fr
Web	lefrene.online.fr

	Dany & Christian Fabry
	Le Rideau Miné,
	49220 Thorigné d'Anjou,
	Maine-et-Loire
Tel	+33 (0)2 41 76 88 40
Email	rideau49@yahoo.fr
Web	www.lerideaumine.com

Western Loire

La Ruchelière

Through the door in the wall, under the tunnel of greenery and lo! a fine presbytery rises from the lawns, fairly well sheltered from the road. The Ruches have done their classic French house in a thoughtful, unusual fashion: a taffeta theme throughout with draperies and florals, collections of glass, china, dolls (the Indian puppets on the dining room walls are a joy) and modern paintings under high beautifully beamed ceilings, a piano by the great sitting-room fireplace and a convivial table for breakfast. These are fun, generous people (he's a pilot) with a talent for interior design and a desire to please.

Price	€90-€150.
Rooms	4 doubles.
Meals	Dinner €25-€35. Wine €15-€35.
Closed	Rarely.
Directions	From Le Mans A11 exit 11; D859 for Châteauneuf sur Sarthe; D89 for Contigné; house opp. church, signed.

	Carole & Oliver Ruche
	La Ruchelière,
	6 place Jacques Ledoyen,
	49330 Contigné, Maine-et-Loire
Tel	+33 (0)2 41 32 74 86
Fax	+33 (0)2 41 32 74 86
Email	rucheliere@orange.fr
Web	www.rucheliere.com

Entry 303 Map 4

Western Loire

La Marronnière

This pretty white-shuttered house overlooking the river has been in the family for ever. The vicomte, vicomtesse and their daughter give you a gracious, smiling welcome and large, serene bedrooms lovingly revived. Choose a bed tucked into a poppy-papered alcove, or butterflies fluttering pinkly on the walls; each room has river views. Madame loves cooking and breakfast is a moveable feast: dining room in winter, terrace in summer. The warmly authentic sitting room provides a winter fire in a stone hearth, Italian ochres, silk drapes, family portraits and – on warm nights – doors open to the Loire.

Price	€94-€114.
Rooms	3: 1 double, 2 twins/doubles.
Meals	Dinner €30. Wine from €20.
Closed	Never.
Directions	From Angers A11 to Paris; exit 14b Tiercé; at Tiercé for Cheffes, at r'bout Soulaire & Bourg; left 100m after village; house 300m on right by river Sarthe.

	Jean & Marie-Hélène de la Selle
	La Marronnière,
	49125 Cheffes,
	Maine-et-Loire
Tel	+33 (0)2 41 34 08 50
Fax	+33 (0)2 41 34 07 40
Email	j.delaselle@wanadoo.fr
Web	www.lamarronniere.fr

Entry 304 Map 4

Western Loire

La Maison du Roi René

The famous old auberge has become a charming B&B. Scrunch up the drive serenaded by soft roses to a lovely welcome from Madame. Part medieval, part 18th century, like the village around it, it has corners, crannies and a stunning central stone fireplace. The Valicourts are the happy new owners of these magnificent oak doors and rosy tomette floors; bedrooms are beamed and very pleasing – one opens to the garden, three to the tower. There's a pretty paved terrace for breakfast with viennoiseries and a room of auberge proportions for dinner; the family join you for true table d'hôtes – and speak four languages!

Price	€65-€80.
Rooms	4: 2 doubles, 1 twin with sofabed, 1 suite for 2.
Meals	Dinner with wine, €20.
Closed	Rarely.
Directions	From Paris A11 for Nantes; exit 10 for Sablé sur Sarthe; in Sablé D399 for d'Angers; D27 for 10km.

Dominique de Valicourt
La Maison du Roi René,
4 Grande Rue,
53290 Saint Denis D'Anjou,
Mayenne

Tel	+33 (0)2 43 70 52 30
Email	roi-rene@orange.fr
Web	www.roi-rene.fr

Entry 305   Map 4

Western Loire

La Gilardière

The ancient oak stairs wind up through the subtly lit interior to fairly sophisticated suites with low doorways and beautiful colombage, plenty of sitting areas, and rooms off for your children or your butler. The restoration of this ancient priory, mostly 14th and 15th century, is a marvel (famous people get married in the chapel). Françoise is a horse and hunting enthusiast who is now joined by her son Antoine in the B&B activity. The huge grounds and discreet pool, safe for children (and grandchildren) and shared by self-catering guests, lead to open country unspoilt by 20th-century wonders.

Price	€60-€105.
	Whole house (20 people) available.
Rooms	4: 1 double, 3 family suites for 4-5.
Meals	Dinner with wine, €35.
Closed	Mid-October to April.
Directions	From Château Gontier D28 for Grez en Bouère; at Gennes right D15 for Bierné; in St Aignan right before church; house 2km on left.

Françoise Drion
La Gilardière,
53200 Gennes sur Glaize,
Mayenne

Tel	+33 (0)2 43 70 93 03
Fax	+33 (0)2 43 70 93 03
Email	lagilardiere@live.fr
Web	www.lagilardiere.com

Entry 306   Map 4

Western Loire

Château de Craon

Such a close and welcoming family, whose kindness extends to include you. It's a magnificent place, with innumerable expressions of history, taste and personality, and gracious Loïk and Hélène, the younger generation, treat you like friends. A sitting room with sofas and a view of the park, an Italianate hall with sweeping stone stair, classic French bedrooms in lavender, blue, cream… an original washstand, a canopied bed, a velvet armchair. Everywhere a feast for the eyes; paintings, watercolours, antiques. Outside, 40 acres of river, meadows, lake, ice house, tennis court, pool, and a potager worth leaving home for.

Price	€120–€160. Single €100. Suite €240.
Rooms	6: 3 doubles, 1 twin, 1 single, 1 suite for 2-4. Extra beds for children.
Meals	Restaurants in village.
Closed	November-March.
Directions	From Laval D771; clear signs as you enter town. 30km south of Laval.

Loïk & Hélène de Guébriant
Château de Craon,
53400 Craon,
Mayenne
Tel +33 (0)2 43 06 11 02
Fax +33 (0)2 43 06 05 18
Email chateaudecraon@wanadoo.fr
Web www.craoncastle.com

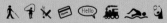

Entry 307 Map 3

Western Loire

Le Rocher

Being the Richecours' only guests means free run of Madame's delightful conversation (travel, history, houses, gardens, people), her lovingly designed garden (an abundance of old roses), and the delicious house that they have restored with such care and imagination. Your room is in the 17th-century part above the old kitchen, so attractive in its wealth of fitted cupboards and slabs of slate. Character fills the big guest room: original tiles, iron bed, great old timbers. The meadow sweeps down to the river where the family pedalo awaits to take you to the restaurant on the opposite bank. Elegance and great warmth – perfection!

Price	€90. Extra person €30.
Rooms	1 family room for 2-3.
Meals	Restaurants within 7km.
Closed	Rarely.
Directions	From Château Gontier N162 for Laval, 4km; left for St Germain de l'Hommel; immediately right; on to village; left, signed 'no through road', 500m 2nd house called Rocher.

Mme de Richecour
Le Rocher,
St Germain de l'Hommel,
53200 Fromentières, Mayenne
Tel +33 (0)2 43 07 06 64
Fax +33 (0)2 43 07 06 64
Email eva2richecour@free.fr
Web manoirdurocher.fr

Entry 308 Map 3

Western Loire

Villeprouvé

Of vast age and character — and an ancient, leaning stair — this farmhouse is home to a humorous and talented couple who juggle cattle, children and guests. Delicious dinners end with a flaming presentation of 'grog maison' to guarantee deep sleep. In the big, soft rooms, every bed is canopied except the single box-bed which is carved and curtained to a tee. There are nooks, crannies and crooked lines, terracotta floors, half-timbered walls, antiques, books on art, tourism, history — and pretty new bathrooms. Ducks paddle in the pond, cows graze, the wind ruffles the trees, apples become cider — bucolic peace.
Sawday self-catering also.

Price	€47-€67.
Rooms	4: 2 doubles, 1 triple, 1 family room.
Meals	Dinner €15. Wine €9.
Closed	Rarely.
Directions	From Laval N162 for Château Gontier 14km; right through Villiers Charlemagne to Ruille Froid Fonds; in village near church left C4 for Bignon 1km; signed.

Christophe & Christine Davenel
Villeprouvé,
53170 Ruille Froid Fonds,
Mayenne

Tel	+33 (0)2 43 07 71 62
Fax	+33 (0)2 43 07 71 62
Email	christ.davenel@orange.fr
Web	pagesperso-orange.fr/villeprouve/bb

Western Loire

Château de la Villatte

From the village, a drive rises to the top of the butte, where a 19th-century château sits in splendour. Isabelle arrived some years ago and her loving restoration knows no bounds — there's still the chapel to go — yet still she finds time to enjoy her guests. The building oozes generous dimensions and the bedrooms are vast, their parquet floors strewn with rugs. Tall windows overlook the steeply sloping park and the valley below, there are marble fireplaces, paintings in gilt frames, an original claw-foot bath. Breakfast on the balcony or in the grand salon, borrow bikes, or explore the lovely tree'd grounds.

Price	€75-€93. Suite €168.
Rooms	2: 1 double, 1 twin/double (rooms can interconnect to form suite).
Meals	Dinner €25. Wine €14-€39.
Closed	Never.
Directions	From Laval D171 for St Nazaire 8km; left for Montigné le Brillant; thro' village for l'Huisserie; on for 600m; house on right, signed.

Isabelle Charrier
Château de la Villatte,
53970 Montigné le Brillant,
Mayenne

Tel	+33 (0)2 43 68 23 76
Fax	+33 (0)2 43 68 23 76
Email	info@lavillatte.com
Web	www.lavillatte.com

Western Loire

La Rouaudière

Prize-winning cows in the fields, prize-winning owners in the house. They are an exceptionally engaging, relaxed couple and their conversation is the heart and soul of this place. Breakfasts in front of the crackling fire are estimable – delicious everything, lashings of coffee; dinners are divine. You'll find a second fire in the sitting room, a rare magnolia in the garden (Madame is a keen plantswoman) and redecorated bedrooms that are straightforward and simple: plain walls, a few antiquey bits and bobs and pretty window boxes. Madame cannot do enough for her guests, and readers have been full of praise.

Price	€50-€58.
Rooms	3: 1 double, 1 twin, 1 triple.
Meals	Dinner with wine, €22.
Closed	Rarely.
Directions	From Fougères N12 east for Laval 15km; farm sign on right.

Maurice & Thérèse Trihan
La Rouaudière,
Mégaudais,
53500 Ernée, Mayenne
Tel +33 (0)2 43 05 13 57
Email therese-trihan@wanadoo.fr
Web www.chambresdhotes-auxportesdelabretagne.com

Entry 311 Map 3

Western Loire

Le Cruchet

In a *gentilhommière* dating from 1640, a stone staircase in a pepperpot tower leads to a massively atmospheric bedroom for three. Downstairs in the fine dining room breakfast is served to the chiming of the church clock; in the garden is the old bread oven. The Nays' family home is well lived in and they love sharing it with guests. Rooms are elegant with antiques and decent bathrooms, the double is in the stable, and your charming, unintrusive hosts can teach you French, how to weave baskets or make music. A wonderful atmosphere in delectable countryside – readers have loved the "real character of the place".

Price	€45-€50.
Rooms	2: 1 double, 1 triple.
Meals	Restaurants within walking distance or 3km.
Closed	Rarely.
Directions	From Laval N157 for Le Mans; at Soulgé sur Ouette D20 left to Evron; D7 for Mayenne; signed in Mézangers.

Léopold & Marie-Thérèse Nay
Le Cruchet,
53600 Mézangers,
Mayenne
Tel +33 (0)2 43 90 65 55
Email bandb.lecruchet@wanadoo.fr
Web www.lecruchet.com

Entry 312 Map 4

Western Loire

Château de Monhoudou

Madame is the nicest, easiest of aristocrats, determined to keep the ancestral home alive in a dignified manner – 19 generations on. A jewel set in rolling parkland, sheep and semi-wild horses grazing under mature trees, swans on a bit of the moat, peacock, deer, boar... it has antiques on parquet floors, charming bathrooms and loos in turrets. There's an elegant dining room with family silver, a sitting room with log fire, a piano to play, family portraits, a small book-lined library – and do ask to see the chapel upstairs. Hunting trophies, timeless tranquillity, candlelit dinners and delicious desserts.

Price	€110–€160.
Rooms	6: 4 doubles, 1 twin, 1 suite for 3.
Meals	Dinner with wine, €42.
Closed	Rarely.
Directions	From Alençon N138 S for Le Mans approx. 14km; at La Hutte left D310 for 10km; right D19 through Courgains; left D132 to Monhoudou; signed.

Michel & Marie-Christine
de Monhoudou
Château de Monhoudou,
72260 Monhoudou, Sarthe
Mobile   +33 (0)6 83 35 39 12
Fax   +33 (0)2 43 33 11 58
Email   info@monhoudou.com
Web   www.monhoudou.com

Entry 313   Map 4

Western Loire

La Maison du Pont Romain

Cross Monfort's exquisite stone bridge to this pretty house on the banks of the river. Enter the grounds and forget the world in heavenly peace among very old trees. Gentle Madame saved it all from ruin and gives you two comfortable rooms upstairs, privately off the courtyard, both with fine armoires. The suite is in the old stables: salon below, bright bedrooms above. There are delicious jams at the big table for breakfast and a family salon for guests. Visit Montfort's castle and the lovely, unsung villages and vineyards of the Sarthe. For children? Forest animals at Pescheray and an aquapark in the village.

Price	€54–€63.
Rooms	3: 2 doubles, 1 suite for 3-4.
Meals	Dinner with wine, €20.
Closed	Never.
Directions	From Le Mans, D323 (formerly N23) for Chartres. At La Belle Inutile, left for Montfort le Gesnois. Over bridge, house immed. on left.

Chantal Paris
La Maison du Pont Romain,
26 rue de l'Église,
72450 Montfort le Gesnois, Sarthe
Tel   +33 (0)2 43 76 13 46
Email   chantal-paris@wanadoo.fr
Web   www.le-pont-romain.fr

Entry 314   Map 4

Western Loire

Éporcé

You may think yourself as lucky to stay in this relaxedly luxurious place as the owner and his young family to have inherited it, so fine and genuine inside and out. Pure 17th century with a magnificent avenue of trees, moat, lofty beamed ceilings, three salons for guests, it brims with antiques, books and atmosphere yet never overwhelms. First-floor rooms are proper château stuff, upstairs they are cosier, with pretty oval mansard windows. If you choose the gourmet dinner, your host will set out the family silver and Wedgwood as well as unforgettable food. Wholly delightful. *Chapel & coach house available for weddings.*

Price	€90–€150.
Rooms	6: 4 doubles, 1 twin, 1 suite.
Meals	Dinner with wine, €40.
Closed	Rarely.
Directions	From A11 exit 8; N157 for Laval; D28 for La Quinte; left by church for Coulans; 1km, wayside cross, fork right; entrance on left.

	Rémy de Scitivaux
	Éporcé,
	72550 La Quinte, Sarthe
Tel	+33 (0)2 43 27 70 22
Fax	+33 (0)2 43 27 89 29
Email	eporce@wanadoo.fr

Entry 315   Map 4

Western Loire

Château de l'Enclos

The Guillous welcome you into their grand château in its elegant setting as long-lost friends. Sociable and fun – they own a red 1933 Citroen – they will whisk you around their parkland with its fine trees, llamas and donkeys… and stunning Finnish treehouse in a giant sequoia! Inside, a staircase sweeps up to the handsome bedrooms of parquet floors and rich carpets, writing desks and tall windows. Two have balconies. The charming salon opens to a stage-set-perfect garden, and you dine with your hosts in best table d'hôtes style. Masses to do in little Brûlon – and a marvellous home to return to.

Price	€100–€150.
Rooms	4: 2 doubles, 1 twin. Treehouse for 2.
Meals	Dinner with wine, €35.
Closed	Never.
Directions	From A81 Le Mans–Laval; exit 1 to Brûlon. Château on right at end of town. Signed.

	Annie-Claude & Jean-Claude Guillou
	Château de l'Enclos,
	2 avenue de la Libération,
	72350 Brûlon, Sarthe
Tel	+33 (0)2 43 92 17 85
Email	jean-claude.guillou5@wanadoo.fr
Web	www.chateau-enclos.com

Entry 316   Map 4

Western Loire

Le Perceau

A happy house, part farm, part *maison bourgeoise*, where the smell of baking may greet you and the delicious results be on the table by the morning: fabulous pastries, breads and cakes. Your easy, amusing hosts have three charming sons and Mr Alfred the donkey – and space indoors for little ones to run their socks off when they tire of the garden. Then it's up the spiral staircase to a serene, chic cassis-and-orange bedroom; or the lavender room where a huge stone fireplace has pride of place. All very rural and river-viewed, yet Malicorne, with its market and restaurants, is a few minutes' meander. Readers return.

Price	€50.
Rooms	2: 1 double, 1 family room for 4.
Meals	Restaurants 800m.
Closed	Rarely.
Directions	From Le Mans N23 for La Flèche; at Fontaine St Martin, D8 for Malicorne sur Sarthe; D23 for Le Mans; house last on left, signed.

Catherine & Jean-Paul Beuvier
Le Perceau,
72270 Malicorne, Sarthe
Tel +33 (0)2 43 45 74 40
Email leperceau@orange.fr
Web leperceau.chez-alice.fr

🚶 🐾 ✗ (Hello) 🚲

Entry 317 Map 4

Western Loire

Château de Montaupin

Following her family's tradition, Marie is a helpful hostess, and her château has an easy family feel. An impressive suspended spiral staircase leads to the upper floors. Some rooms look onto an amazing 400-year-old cedar, others have gorgeous garden views, all have interesting furniture and are being redone (50 windows to replace!). The best suite is up a steep staircase, its roof timbers exposed. There are some gratifyingly untidy corners, some small, pretty shower rooms and peaceful loveliness with farmland and woods beyond. For racing buffs, Le Mans is up the road. *Ask about French courses.*

Price	€70–€75. Extra person €15.
Rooms	5: 1 double, 2 triples, 2 suites for 5.
Meals	Dinner with wine, €20.
Closed	Occasionally. Book ahead.
Directions	From Le Mans N23 for La Flèche to Cérans Foulletourte; D31 to Oizé; left on D32; sign to right.

Laurent Sénéchal & Marie David
Château de Montaupin,
72330 Oizé, Sarthe
Tel +33 (0)2 43 87 81 70
Fax +33 (0)2 43 87 26 25
Email chateaudemontaupin@wanadoo.fr

🚶 🐾 ✗ (Hello) 🐕 🔔 🛶 🦆

Entry 318 Map 4

Western Loire

Le Moulin de la Diversière

In a loop of a small river, a honey-coloured mill surrounded by trees and silence, and willow-fringed paths leading to two gîtes – yours for self-catering or B&B. Anne and Jean-Marc have lovingly completed the conversions in tune with the setting and their green ideals. Outside: a big sloping garden, a play area for your children (and theirs), shady arbours, an above-ground pool. Inside: old tomettes and limewashed walls, cane chairs and fresh flowers, pretty kitchens and showers with pebble floors. Breakfast and table d'hotes are served at your hosts' friendly table, by a roaring fire in winter. Special indeed.

Western Loire

Le Prieuré

Bushels of history from the beams and vaulted ceilings of the moated priory, snug beneath its old church: built in the 12th, extended in the 16th, it had monks until the 20th century. Christophe loves telling the history, Marie-France does the decorating, brilliantly in keeping with the elegant old house: oriental rugs on old tiled floors, pale-painted beams over stone fireplaces, fine old paintings on plain walls and good modern beds under soft-coloured covers. They are attentive hosts, happy to share their vaulted dining room and peaceful garden, and the road is not an inconvenience. *Ask about local wine tours.*

Price	€60-€70.
Rooms	2 cottages, each for 2-5.
Meals	Dinner with wine, €23.
Closed	Never.
Directions	From Le Lude D306 for La Flèche 1.5km; left D305 to Savigné sous le Lude. Entering village, right for La Flèche; over small bridge, immed. right 600m; driveway on right.

Price	€90-€130.
Rooms	3: 2 doubles, 1 twin.
Meals	Auberge opposite; restaurants nearby.
Closed	November-February, except by arrangement.
Directions	From Le Mans A28 for Tours; exit 26 Château du Loir; N138 to Dissay sous Courcillon; left at lights, house on left.

Anne & Jean-Marc Le Foulgocq
Le Moulin de la Diversière,
72800 Savigné sous le Lude,
Sarthe

Tel	+33 (0)2 43 48 09 16
Fax	+33 (0)2 43 48 09 16
Email	contact@moulin-de-la-diversiere.com
Web	www.moulin-de-la-diversiere.com

Christophe & Marie-France Calla
Le Prieuré, 1 rue de la Gare,
72500 Dissay sous Courcillon,
Sarthe

Tel	+33 (0)2 43 44 09 09
Fax	+33 (0)2 43 44 09 09
Email	ccalla@club-internet.fr
Web	www.chateauprieure.com

Western Loire

Le Moulin du Prieuré

It's a brilliantly converted old watermill, this couple's labour of love, down to the smooth cogwheels that turn in the great kitchen. Marie-Claire, who used to live in London, is so relaxed and unflappably efficient, such good company and such fun, it's hard to believe she has four young children; the garden is heaven for little ones. The double-height sitting room bursts with books and videos for all; simple, attractive rooms have good beds, old tiled floors, bare stone walls. The atmosphere embraces you, the country sounds of stream, cockerel and Angelus prayer bells soothe, the unsung area brims with interest. *Massage & spa.*

Western Loire

La Châtaigneraie

It's like a fairy tale: mellow old stone, white shutters, green ivy, a large leafy garden, a clematis-covered well, a little wood and glimpses of the 12th-century castle round the corner (this house used to be the castle's servants' quarters). Green-eyed Michèle, modern, intelligent and interested in people, shares the hosting with Michel. The suite is three gently pastel-hued interconnecting bedrooms that look onto garden or endless fields. Stay a while and connect with the soft hills, woods, streams and châteaux. Guests can be as independent as they like (separate entrance) and can take one, two or three rooms.

Price	€56. Family room €90.		Price	€55–€100.
Rooms	5: 4 doubles, 1 family room.		Rooms	2: 1 double, 1 suite of 3 rooms for 1–4.
Meals	Dinner with wine, €20. Restaurant opposite.		Meals	Dinner with glass of wine, €23.
Closed	Rarely.		Closed	November–March.
Directions	From Tours D338 for Le Mans 45km to Dissay sous Courcillon; left at lights; mill just past church.		Directions	From Le Mans, N138 direction Tours. After Dissay sous Courcillon, left onto small road on bend & follow signs.

	Marie-Claire Bretonneau Le Moulin du Prieuré, 3 rue de la Gare, 72500 Dissay sous Courcillon, Sarthe			Michèle Letanneux & Michel Guyon La Châtaigneraie, 72500 Dissay sous Courcillon, Sarthe
Tel	+33 (0)2 43 44 59 79		Tel	+33 (0)2 43 79 36 71
Email	moulinduprieure@wanadoo.fr		Email	michele.marie.celeste@wanadoo.fr
Web	www.moulinduprieure.fr			

Entry 321   Map 4

Entry 322   Map 4

Loire Valley

Loire Valley

Chambres d'Hôtes

This was Dagmar's country cottage until she left Paris to settle here. She left her native Germany and adopted France many moons ago. Come for compact, cosy, immaculate B&B in a pretty village situation. Breakfast is a feast: hot croissants, homemade jams, smoked salmon, farm butter. The cottage garden is cherished and, if you time it right, every old wall is covered with roses. Up the steep stair, one bedroom is wood-panelled, the other more typical with sloping rafters; fabrics are flowered and varnished floors symmetrically rugged. Traditional, authentic, friendly, and great fun.

Loire Valley

Maison JLN

Come to enjoy this gentle family and the serene vibes of their old Chartrain house. Up two steep spirals to the attic, through the family's little prayer room, past the stained-glass window, the sweet, peaceful bedroom feels a bit like a chapel with honey floorboards, beds, small windows (no wardrobe). Lots of books; reminders of pilgrimage, just beneath the great cathedral; Madame knowledgeably friendly, Monsieur, who speaks nine languages, quietly amusing, both interested in your travels: they're both happy to sit and talk when you get back. An unusual and welcoming place in a timeless spot.

Price	€50-€60.
Rooms	2: 1 double, 1 suite. Extra beds available.
Meals	Restaurants 8km.
Closed	Rarely.
Directions	From Verneuil sur Avre D939 for Chartres; in Maillebois left on D20 to Blévy; in Blévy left for Laons-Dreux; left after 200m onto D133 for Laons; house 1st on right after 50m.

Price	€50.
Rooms	1 twin with separate shower & wc on floor below.
Meals	Restaurants nearby.
Closed	Rarely.
Directions	In Chartres follow signs for IBIS Centre; park by Hotel IBIS Centre (Place Drouaise); walk 20m along Rue de la Porte Drouaise to Rue Muret (100m car to house).

Dagmar Parmentier
Chambres d'Hôtes,
2 route des Champarts,
28170 Blévy, Eure-et-Loir
Tel +33 (0)2 37 48 01 21
Fax +33 (0)2 37 48 01 21
Email bab-blevy@club-internet.fr
Web www.bab-blevy.com

Jean-Loup & Nathalie Cuisiniez
Maison JLN,
80 rue Muret, 28000 Chartres,
Eure-et-Loir
Tel +33 (0)2 37 21 98 36
Fax +33 (0)2 37 21 98 36
Email jln.cuisiniez@orange.fr
Web monsite.orange.fr/maisonjln

Entry 323   Map 4

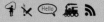

Entry 324   Map 4

Loire Valley

Les Charmettes

This robust 18th-century townhouse by the canal has inherited an expansive atmosphere from its wine-merchant builders. They were loading wine onto barges on the canal until the 1930s. That was the past. At present: you will dine – beautifully – with your refined hosts in the chandeliered dining room, sleep in good, highly individual rooms (space for 12 though only two bathrooms, one in a bedroom), breakfast off ravishing Gien china with fruit from the pretty garden, chat with your stylish, effusive hostess and her good-natured husband over a glass of local wine. She keenly arranges visits to wine-growers.

Price	€70–€100. Apartment €140–€150.
Rooms	2: 1 family apartment for 8 (3 bedrooms sharing 1 bathroom), 1 suite for 4.
Meals	Dinner with wine, €30.
Closed	Rarely.
Directions	From Orléans N60 E for Montargis & Nevers; exit to Fay aux Loges; through Fay, cross canal, left D709; house 1st on left arriving in Donnery.

Nicole & Jacques Sicot
Les Charmettes,
40 avenue Ponson du Terail,
45450 Donnery, Loiret
Tel   +33 (0)2 38 59 22 50
Email   n.sicot@wanadoo.fr

Entry 325   Map 5

Loire Valley

Domaine de la Thiau

A vast estate by the Loire, a 19th-century house for the family, a 17th-century one for guests, exotic pheasants and peacocks strutting around the splendid grounds. Your hosts – he is a busy vet, she elegantly looks after house, gîtes and you – make it feel welcoming despite the appearance. Peaceful guest bedrooms are carefully decorated with carved bedsteads and papered walls – extremely, Frenchly traditional. There's a smart new Victorian-style conservatory for breakfast, furnished with a large oval table and blue velvet chairs. A good address for summer. *Minimum stay 2 nights weekends, bank holidays & high season.*

Price	€58–€68.
Rooms	3: 2 doubles, 1 suite for 3 & kitchen.
Meals	Gastronomic dinner available for 2+ night stays. Restaurants 4km.
Closed	Rarely.
Directions	From A6 onto A77 for Nevers, exit Briare; D952 for Gien. Between Briare & Gien: sign Granit Design shop.

Bénédicte François
Domaine de la Thiau,
45250 Briare, Loiret
Tel   +33 (0)2 38 38 20 92
Fax   +33 (0)2 38 38 06 20
Email   lathiau@club-internet.fr
Web   lathiau.club.fr

Entry 326   Map 5

Loire Valley

Les Vieux Guays

Looking for seclusion? This house sits in 200 acres of woods, its grassy shrubby garden, larder to legions of fearless rabbits, rambling down to the duck-loved lake. Sandrine and Alvaro, a tennis professional, returned from Chile to the family home, now alive with two youngsters. They are a poised and friendly couple easily mixing old and modern, bright and dark. You breakfast at their long dining table before the bucolic lake view, relax in green leather in your own log-fired sitting room. In another wing, bedrooms are high quality too: antiques, excellent new bedding, plain walls and floral fabrics. Very special.

Price	€75.
Rooms	5: 2 doubles, 2 twins, 1 family suite for 4.
Meals	Restaurant 2km.
Closed	Rarely.
Directions	From Paris de Gien by A6; A77 exit Gien; D940 Argent sur Sauldre; D948 to Cerdon; D65 for Clémont; immed. right after level crossing; 1.5km left onto track; straight on.

Sandrine & Alvaro Martinez
Les Vieux Guays,
45620 Cerdon du Loiret, Loiret
Tel   +33 (0)2 38 36 03 76
Fax   +33 (0)2 38 36 03 76
Email   lvg45@orange.fr
Web   www.lesvieuxguays.com

Entry 327   Map 5

Loire Valley

La Brissauderie

Utter peace… this 1970s farmhouse is cradled in tumbling woodland and wrapped in birdsong. Goats softly bleat on the farm below. Madame is chatty and genuine, she still helps out with the animals and can arrange goat visits for children. The suite upstairs is perfect for families. It has stencilled furniture, some good family pieces, tongue-and-groove pine cladding throughout. Walls, ceilings and doors are alive with fun murals: sunflowers shine, bees bumble and butterflies flutter by. Your tasty breakfast comes with honey from a friend's bees and, of course, goat's cheese. Remarkable value. *Other rooms may be available.*

Price	€40. €50 for 3. €70 for 4–5.
Rooms	1 suite for 4–5.
Meals	Restaurants nearby.
Closed	Rarely.
Directions	From Sancerre D923 for Jars & Vailly sur Sauldre; 2km before Jars right on track into wood, house at end of track, signed.

Madeleine Jay
La Brissauderie,
18260 Jars, Cher
Tel   +33 (0)2 48 58 74 94
Email   madeleine.jay@wanadoo.fr
Web   www.labrissauderie.com

Entry 328   Map 5

Loire Valley

Moulin Guillard

Just outside the village of Subligny, not far from Sancerre, is this enchanting blue-shuttered mill. Where once walnut oil was produced is a stylish and delightful B&B. Dorothée, a fascinating and cultured woman who once ran a bookshop in Paris, divides her time between her garden of rare plants and her guests. She offers you a smallish, softly serene double upstairs, and a two-bedroom suite across the way, its private sitting room with piano downstairs. You breakfast between the two, in a converted barn overlooking the stream and Dorothée's several breeds of free-roaming hen. Charming, and fun.

Ethical Collection: Environment.
See page 432.

Price	€80.
Rooms	2: 1 double, 1 suite for 4 with sitting room.
Meals	Dinner €23. Wine from €16.
Closed	Never.
Directions	A77; 15km towards Paris.

Dorothée Malinge
Moulin Guillard,
18260 Subligny, Cher
Tel +33 (0)2 48 73 70 49
Fax +33 (0)2 48 73 70 49
Email malinge.annig@orange.fr

Entry 329   Map 5

Loire Valley

La Verrerie

Deep countryside, fine people, fantastic bedrooms. In a pretty outbuilding, the double, with a green iron bed, old tiled floor and bold bedcover, looks onto the garden from the ground floor; the suite's twin has the same tiles underfoot, beams overhead and high wooden beds with an inviting mix of white covers and red quilts. The Count and Countess, who manage forests, farm and hunt but are relatively new to B&B, are charming and thoroughly hospitable. If you would like to eat in, you will join them for dinner in the main house. Members of the family run a vineyard in Provence, so try their wine.

Price	€75–€99. Suite €122–€145.
Rooms	3: 2 doubles, 1 suite for 2-4.
Meals	Dinner with wine, €20–€30. Kitchen available.
Closed	Rarely.
Directions	From Paris A6 to A77 exit 19 for Gien. From Bourges D940 to Chapelle d'Angillon; D12 to Ivoy le Pré. At church left D39 for Blancafort, Oizon, Château de la Verrerie for 2.5km; gate on right.

Étienne & Marie de Saporta
La Verrerie,
18380 Ivoy le Pré, Cher
Tel +33 (0)2 48 58 90 86
Fax +33 (0)2 48 58 92 79
Email m.desaporta@wanadoo.fr
Web pagesperso-orange.fr/laverreriedivoy

Entry 330   Map 5

Loire Valley

Domaine de la Chaume

Rural B&B in a separate wing of a 19th-century farmhouse with a big grassy garden for children. The owners are retired, he the smiling farmer, she kind and chatty with guests. She brings breakfast to you at the big table in your dayroom: it includes delicious homemade preserves. All is in excellent order, and that includes the bedrooms (two on the ground floor) in your peaceful annexe. Walls are striped or plain, floors carpeted, furnishings floral; beds and wardrobes are polished antique and shower rooms shine. Fields and woodland surround you and historic Bourges, floodlit in summer, is an easy drive.

Price	€50.
Rooms	5: 2 doubles, 1 twin for 2-4 with sofabed, 1 twin/double, 1 family room for 3.
Meals	Dinner €20. Restaurant 10-minute drive.
Closed	Rarely.
Directions	From Bourges N151 for La Charité sur Loire; at St Germain du Puy, D955 for Sancerre to Aix-d'Angillon; D12 right to Rians; take road opp. church; signed.

Odile & Yves Proffit
Domaine de la Chaume,
La Chaume,
18220 Rians, Cher

Tel	+33 (0)2 48 64 41 58
Fax	+33 (0)2 48 64 29 71
Email	contact@domaine-la-chaume.com
Web	domaine-la-chaume.com

Entry 331   Map 10

Loire Valley

La Grande Mouline

Your hosts came to this rustic haven, where the natural garden flows into woods and fields, deer roam and birdlife astounds, to raise their new family. Jean is a kindly young grandfather, proud of his efforts in converting his outbuildings for B&B. Bedrooms reflect his travels to distant places: Indian rugs, Moroccan brasses, a collection of fossils in an old chemist's cabinet, lots of old farmhouse stuff – nothing too sophisticated. Breakfast is in the main house where family life bustles. Return after contemplating Bourges to meditate in this sweet corner of God's garden or share the above-ground pool.

Price	€45.
Rooms	4: 2 triples, 1 quadruple, 1 family room.
Meals	Restaurant 2.5km.
Closed	Rarely.
Directions	From Bourges D944 for Orléans. In Bourgneuf left at little r'bout; immed. right & follow signs 1.5km.

Jean Malot & Chantal Charlon
La Grande Mouline,
Bourgneuf,
18110 St Éloy de Gy, Cher

Tel	+33 (0)2 48 25 40 44
Fax	+33 (0)2 48 25 40 44
Email	jean-m4@wanadoo.fr
Web	pagesperso-orange.fr/lagrandemouline

Entry 332   Map 10

Loire Valley

Domaine de l'Ermitage

In deepest Berry, the heartland of rural France, this articulate husband-and-wife team run their beef and cereals farm and Menetou-Salon vineyards (tastings arranged), make their own jam and still have time for their guests. Vivacious and casually elegant, Laurence runs an intelligent, welcoming house. The big, simple yet stylishly attractive bedrooms of her superior 18th-century farmhouse are of pleasing proportions, one of them in an unusual round brick-and-timber tower, others with views over the graceful park. Guests may use the swimming pool, set discreetly out of sight, between 6 and 7pm.

Price	€62–€65. Triple €90. Quadruple €115.
Rooms	5: 2 doubles, 1 twin, 1 triple, 1 quadruple.
Meals	Restaurants in village or 6km.
Closed	Rarely.
Directions	From Vierzon N76 for Bourges through Mehun sur Yèvre; D60 right to Berry Bouy & on for approx. 3km; farm on right.

Laurence & Géraud de La Farge
Domaine de l'Ermitage,
18500 Berry Bouy, Cher
Tel +33 (0)2 48 26 87 46
Fax +33 (0)2 48 26 03 28
Email domaine-ermitage@wanadoo.fr
Web www.hotes-ermitage.com

Entry 333 Map 10

Loire Valley

Les Bonnets Rouges

Cross the secret garden courtyard and into this venerable 15th-century house, once a coaching inn (Stendhal slept here). Beyond the breakfast room, where ancient timbers, wraparound oak panels and stone alcoves dance in all their mixed-up glory for the fresh fruit and Turkish rugs, the knight in shining armour beckons you up. Bedrooms are elegant with antique beds, one a four-poster, and new mattresses, marble fireplaces and claw-footed bath; the pretty attic double is festooned with beams. Your charming host lives just across the courtyard. Sleep among angels beneath that unsurpassed cathedral.

Price	€58–€80.
Rooms	4: 2 doubles, 2 suites for 3-4.
Meals	Restaurants within walking distance.
Closed	Rarely.
Directions	In Bourges centre behind cathedral, Rue Bourbonnoux, 2nd on right. Park in yard if space available, otherwise phone; house 300m from cathedral.

Olivier Llopis
Les Bonnets Rouges,
3 rue de la Thaumassière,
18000 Bourges, Cher
Tel +33 (0)2 48 65 79 92
Email bonnets-rouges@bourges.net
Web bonnets-rouges.bourges.net

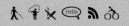

Entry 334 Map 10

Loire Valley

Domaine de la Trolière

The beautifully proportioned house in its big shady garden has been in the family for over 200 years. The sitting room is a cool blue-grey symphony, the dining room smart yellow-grey with a rare, remarkable maroon and grey marble table: breakfast is in here, dinner en famille is in the big beamed kitchen. Each stylishly comfortable room has individual character and Madame has a fine eye for detail. She is charming, dynamic, casually elegant and has many cats. Visitors have poured praise: "quite the most beautiful house we've ever stayed in", "the evening meals were superb".

Price	€48-€70.
Rooms	4: 3 doubles; 1 double with separate wc.
Meals	Dinner with wine, €23-€25.
Closed	Rarely.
Directions	From A71 exit 8; at r'bout D925 W for Lignières & Châteauroux. Sign 500m on right.

	Marie-Claude Dussert
	Domaine de la Trolière,
	18200 Orval, Cher
Tel	+33 (0)2 48 96 47 45
Fax	+33 (0)2 48 96 07 71
Email	marie-claude.dussert@orange.fr

Entry 335   Map 10

Loire Valley

Le Canard au Parapluie Rouge

This pretty 17th-century house has been welcoming travellers for most of its history: it was once the Auberge de la Gare; the station has gone but the TGVs occasionally thunder past, disturbing the sleepy calm. Kathy and Martin are great fun – she's from Ohio, he's from Wiltshire – and will make you feel instantly at home. Each of the sunny little bedrooms has a charm and flavour of its own and the low-beamed sitting room opens onto a big, enclosed garden. Meals are served in the elegant dining room or out under the trees. Kathy loves cooking and Martin grows the vegetables. It's all absurdly good value.

Price	€65-€80.
Rooms	4 doubles.
Meals	Dinner with wine, €20.
Closed	Never.
Directions	A20 exit 19 for Celon; 1st right as you enter village; signed.

	Martin & Kathy Missen
	Le Canard au Parapluie Rouge,
	3 rue des Rollets,
	36200 Celon, Indre
Tel	+33 (0)2 54 25 30 08
Fax	+33 (0)2 54 25 30 08
Email	info@lecanardbandb.com
Web	lecanardbandb.com

Entry 336   Map 9

Loire Valley

La Chasse

This delightful and hard-working English couple came to farm in France with their two boys, and cattle, too, and invite you to drive down a long bumpy track through pretty woods where wild deer roam, to their farmhouse. Wellie boots and Jack Russells on arrival, a dining room in the sitting room, some old beams still and a stone fireplace, and restful bedrooms that are big, pale-floored and 1970s comfortable. Alison gives you fresh bread and brioche for breakfast, Robin may tell you tales of shearing French sheep or where to gaze on rare orchids. Argenton, 'Venice of the Indre', is a must.

Price	From €58.
Rooms	3: 1 double; 1 double, 1 family room, sharing bath & separate wc.
Meals	Dinner with wine, €28.
Closed	January-March.
Directions	From Châteauroux A20 exit 16 to Tendu; 1st left in village. Pass Mairie, fork left at church for Chavin & Pommiers for 1.5km; left up track for 2km.

Robin & Alison Mitchell
La Chasse,
36200 Tendu, Indre
Tel   +33 (0)2 54 24 07 76
Fax   +33 (0)2 54 24 07 76

Entry 337   Map 9

Loire Valley

Château de la Villette

Grand hunting lodge rather than château, it stands in acres of parkland before a vast private lake (boating and safe swimming). Karin lovingly tends every inch of it, including the vast picture window that seems to bring the lake into the sitting room. A great staircase leads to a beauty of a Bavarian bedroom with views; the ground-floor room is more modern but equally cosy. Feather duvets cosset you, breakfasts are served at a handsome convent table. Nothing is too much trouble for Karin, gardener, cook and perfect hostess, who gives you a tourist itinerary every day. A little paradise.

Price	€80-€85.
Rooms	2: 1 double; 1 double with separate bath.
Meals	Dinner with wine, €25.
Closed	Rarely.
Directions	From Châteauroux D943 to Ardentes; left on D14 for St Août 8km; left at château sign 400m; entrance on right.

Karin Verburgh
Château de la Villette,
Saint Août,
36120 Ardentes, Indre
Tel   +33 (0)2 54 36 28 46
Fax   +33 (0)2 54 36 28 46

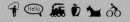

Entry 338   Map 10

Loire Valley

Le Bouchot

Come not for luxury but for deep country authenticity – and to make friends with a generous, charming, free-thinking family, who gave up Paris for this lush corner of France. They have restored, renovated and eco-converted a run-down farm, insulated it with hemp, wattle and daub, then added wood-burning stoves, organic breakfasts... and cats, dogs, horses, hens, donkeys, peacocks, sheep. Bedrooms in outbuildings round the central courtyard are wood-clad with sloping celings, rudimentary furnishings, mix and match bed linen, the odd rug. Dinner is in the kitchen diner – or the barns when there are campers.

Ethical Collection: Environment.
See page 432.

Price	€55-€65.
Rooms	3: 2 family rooms: 1 for 3, 1 for 4, 1 suite for 2-7.
Meals	Dinner with wine, €25.
Closed	Rarely.
Directions	From Orléans A71 for Vierzon, exit 3 to Lamotte Beuvron; D023 & D55 to Pierrefitte sur Sauldre; right in church square for D126 for Chaon; 1km to house.

Anne & Jean-Philippe Beau-Douëzy
Le Bouchot, Route de Chaon,
41300 Pierrefitte sur Sauldre,
Loir-et-Cher

Tel   +33 (0)2 54 88 01 00
Fax   +33 (0)2 54 88 93 35
Email   contact@lebouchot.net
Web   www.lebouchot.net

Entry 339   Map 5

Loire Valley

La Gaucherie

A beautifully restored, L-shaped farmhouse stashed away in the conifer forests of the Sologne, with plenty of grassed space around it and a pretty orchard. Aurélia, who ran a restaurant and studied art in New York, loves light and simplicity: colours are beige and ecru, furniture wooden and roughly planed. The stable conversion has a rustic sitting room with wood-burning stove and red sofas; floors are terracotta or seagrass, bathrooms are pebbled or mosaic'd. Rejoice in ponies and hens for the children, home-produced eggs and lamb, a pond with boat and a pool. Fresh, young, welcoming. *Sawday self-catering also.*

Price	€55-€70.
Rooms	3: 1 double, 1 twin/double, 1 suite for 4.
Meals	Dinner with wine, €24.
Closed	Mid-January to mid-February.
Directions	From Langon, past bakery & church for Romorantin; at top of hill fork for Bois aux Frères, cont. for 7km; right at T-junc. 500m; right, 1st right.

Aurélia Curnin
La Gaucherie,
Route de Méry, Dep 76,
41320 Langon, Loir-et-Cher

Tel   +33 (0)2 54 96 42 23
Email   lagaucherie@wanadoo.fr
Web   www.lagaucherie.com

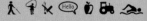

Entry 340   Map 5

Loire Valley

Le Moutier

The artist's touch and Jean-Lou's paintings vibrate throughout this house of tradition and originality where you are instantly one of the family: a bright and friendly little girl, her congenial artist father, her linguist mother – and Persian Puss. Rooms – two in the main house, two in the studio – are subtle-hued with good family furniture and bold bathrooms. An Aubusson tapestry cartoon too, and understated elegance in the sitting and dining rooms. A joy of a garden, interesting, fun-loving hosts and a welcoming table in the evening – good food and wine flow. *Ask about painting & French courses.*

Price	€65.
Rooms	4 doubles.
Meals	Dinner with wine, €30.
Closed	Rarely.
Directions	From Blois D956 to Contres; D675 to St Aignan; over bridge; D17 right to Mareuil sur Cher. House on left in hamlet La Maison des Marchands (just before cat breeder sign) before main village.

Martine & Jean-Lou Coursaget
Le Moutier,
13 rue de la République,
41110 Mareuil sur Cher, Loir-et-Cher
Tel   +33 (0)2 54 75 20 48
Fax   +33 (0)2 54 75 20 48
Email   lemoutier.coursaget@wanadoo.fr
Web   www.chambresdhotesdumoutier.com

Entry 341   Map 4

Loire Valley

Le Moulin du Port

An irresistible walk starts at your doorstep: follow the wide, beautiful river Cher all the way to Chenonceau. The tall 19th-century mill, in its own wooded grounds, is also handy for other Loire châteaux. The bedrooms (to which there's a lift) are shamelessly pretty, the bathrooms new and luxurious, and there's a pleasant ground-floor sitting area overlooking the old mill wheel. The friendly Moreaus, busy with gîtes, young family and B&B, serve a fabulous continental breakfast in the yellow-walled veranda/dining room. It would be worth booking dinner here, too: fresh local produce, choice fish and seafood.

Ethical Collection: Food.
See page 432.

Price	€95-€115.
Rooms	5: 4 doubles, 1 twin.
Meals	Dinner with wine, €28.
Closed	Rarely.
Directions	From Tours D976 for Vierzon to St Georges sur Cher; left at r'bout & 2nd left into lane; entrance on right, high iron gates.

Isabelle Moreau
Le Moulin du Port,
26 rue du Gué de l'Arche,
41400 St Georges sur Cher,
Loir-et-Cher
Tel/Fax +33 (0)2 54 32 01 37
Email   info.alsam@lemoulinduport.com
Web   www.lemoulinduport.com

Entry 342   Map 4

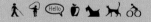

Loire Valley

Prieuré de la Chaise

It's a delight for the eyes: stunning ancient buildings outside, Madame's decorating flair inside. The 13th-century chapel, still used on the village feast day, and the newer manor house (1500s) drip with history, 16th-century antiques, tapestries and loveliness – huge sitting and dining rooms, smallish cosy bedrooms. One has a large stone fireplace, painted beams and successful Laura Ashley fabrics. The setting is superb, fine mature trees shade the secluded garden and you can put your horse in the paddock. You can't fail to like your hosts and their estate wine and they can arrange tastings for you.

Price	€60-€80. Suite €120-€140. Apt €150.
Rooms	4 + 1: 2 doubles, 2 suites. 1 apartment for 5.
Meals	Restaurants nearby.
Closed	Rarely.
Directions	St Georges is between Chenonceau & Montrichard on N76. In town centre, up hill to La Chaise; on up Rue du Prieuré. No. 8 has heavy wooden gates.

Danièle Duret-Therizols
Prieuré de la Chaise, 8 rue du Prieuré,
41400 St Georges sur Cher,
Loir-et-Cher

Tel	+33 (0)2 54 32 59 77
Fax	+33 (0)2 54 32 69 49
Email	prieuredelachaise@yahoo.fr
Web	www.prieuredelachaise.com

Entry 343   Map 4

Loire Valley

Le Cormier

Wake in the morning and sigh with pleasure at the beauty of the garden: box hedges and cottage flowers, sweet herbs, poplars and an iris-fringed pond. Then think about breakfasting on garden fruits and homemade banana bread… Californian Michael and Dutch Marie-Louise rescued this long, low farmhouse and barn from ruin; it's hard to imagine more endearing hosts. The suites are exceedingly pretty, with creamy stone walls, overhead beams, dainty fabrics and ethnic rugs; each has its very own salon with kettle, fridge, books, magazines, logs for the fire. One has its own little kitchen. Perfect peace, and not another house in sight. *Unfenced water.*

Price	€92.50-€100.
Rooms	2 suites, one with kitchenette.
Meals	Restaurant nearby.
Closed	December, January & April.
Directions	From Blois cross Loire; D751 to Chailles; D764 to Sambin; cont. through village, south to Montrichard 100m; right to Chaumont 1.5km. Left at sign for Le Cormier; on for 3km to house.

Michael & Marie-Louise Harvey
Le Cormier,
41120 Sambin,
Loir-et-Cher

Tel	+33 (0)2 54 33 29 47
Email	michael@lecormier.com
Web	www.lecormier.com

Entry 344   Map 4

Loire Valley

La Rabouillère

The new-build, old-look Sologne farmhouse and the delicious little cottage next door bring together traditional style and modern comfort while the gorgeous, wide-spread park harbours a classic frog-pond and a pretty new lake. Madame, who is charming, furnished the interiors delightfully, and the first-floor suite of the main house is particularly splendid and spacious, with fine views over woodland and park. All the rooms, some on the ground floor, are immaculate and serene. Old family pieces decorate the cottage, with its two bedrooms, kitchenette and rustic feel. Altogether irresistible.

Price	€70-€100. Cottage €115 for 2, €160 for 5.
Rooms	4 + 1: 2 doubles, 2 suites. Cottage for 2-5.
Meals	Restaurants 3-10km.
Closed	November-Easter. Book ahead.
Directions	Leave A10 at Blois for Vierzon, D765; D102 for Contres; after 6km sign for La Rabouillère on left.

Martine & Jean-Marie Thimonnier
La Rabouillère,
Chemin de Marçon,
41700 Contres, Loir-et-Cher

Tel	+33 (0)2 54 79 05 14
Fax	+33 (0)2 54 79 59 39
Email	rabouillere@wanadoo.fr
Web	www.larabouillere.com

Entry 345   Map 4

Loire Valley

Les Chambres Vertes

Flowers fill the quadrangle formed by the house (16th- and 19th-century) and an old wall; a fountain adds coolness. Your rooms are in the former stables opposite Sophie's house, each with a slate porch; her's has this slate running its full length, giving shelter from sun and rain. Outside the quadrangle is a covered patio for drinks and delicious meals, overlooking countryside, and all this just a stone's throw from the village. The rooms, on the ground floor, are uncluttered, exquisitely simple, with attractive no-frills bathrooms. The mood is natural, artistic, delightful.

Ethical Collection: Environment; Food. See page 432.

Price	€62.
Rooms	3: 2 doubles, 1 twin.
Meals	Dinner with wine, €24.
Closed	Occasionally.
Directions	A10 from Paris exit Blois for Châteauroux D956; 15km from Bois, left just before village sign Cormeray; 800m, left. 1st house on left.

Sophie Gélinier
Les Chambres Vertes,
Le Clos de la Chartrie,
41120 Cormeray, Loir-et-Cher

Tel	+33 (0)2 54 20 24 95
Fax	+33 (0)2 54 20 24 95
Email	sophie@chambresvertes.net
Web	www.chambresvertes.net

Entry 346   Map 4

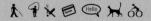

Loire Valley

Château de Nanteuil

Rushing water is a constant here: the river speeds below your window into lush meadows. It's a landscape unaltered by time, just like this grand old wisteria-hung house – once Grand-mère's. Rooms have a faded, film-set quality: frescoes and trunks in the hall, stags' heads and chandeliers in the dining room, floral wallpapers and marble fireplaces in the bedrooms. These are light-filled and unstylishly old-fashioned, but there's charm in 'Roi' and 'Rose'. Bathrooms, in contrast, are modern. Most of all, you'll love Frédéric's fabulous organic cooking – tuck into asparagus in season and baked fillet of perch. Best in summer.

Ethical Collection: Food.
See page 432.

Price	€60–€75.
Rooms	5: 2 doubles, 2 family rooms for 3, 1 family suite for 4.
Meals	Dinner with wine, €28.
Closed	Rarely.
Directions	A10 for Tours, exit 16 Mer for Chambord; D33 right to Huisseau sur Cosson; cont. 4km; right to château. Entrance on right thro' high stone-pillared gateway.

	Frédéric Théry
	Château de Nanteuil,
	41350 Huisseau sur Cosson,
	Loir-et-Cher
Tel	+33 (0)2 54 42 61 98
Email	chateau.nanteuil@free.fr
Web	www.chateau-nanteuil.com

Entry 347   Map 4

Loire Valley

La Petite Fugue

This tranquil townhouse stands on the Loire in Blois centre ville. A small, walled rose garden welcomes you in off the street; a private courtyard at the back looks out over the historic town and château. Monsieur is an inspired and original cook who visits the markets daily; breakfasts and dinners look as exquisite as they taste. Pale greys, mauves and creams (from mirror frames to quilted covers) tie in perfectly with interesting and original features. Bedrooms are harmonious, views flow over the valley and your hosts are discreet, attentive and charming. A joy.

Price	€105–€145.
Rooms	4: 2 doubles, 1 twin/double, 1 family room for 3.
Meals	Dinner with wine, €50.
Closed	Never.
Directions	A10 exit Blois; into town centre; right-bank.

	M & Mme Lescure
	La Petite Fugue,
	9 quai du Foix, 41000 Blois,
	Loir-et-Cher
Tel	+33 (0)2 54 78 42 95
Email	lapetitefugue@wanadoo.fr
Web	www.lapetitefugue.com

Entry 348   Map 4

Loire Valley

La Villa Médicis

Why the Italian name, the Italianate look? Queen Marie de Médicis used to take the waters here in the 17th century: the fine garden still has a hot spring and the Loire flows regally past behind the huge old trees. Muriel, a flower-loving perfectionist (artificial blooms as well as fresh), has let loose her decorative flair on the interior. It is unmistakably yet adventurously French in its splash of colours, lush fabrics and fine details. Carved wardrobes and brass beds grace some rooms. The suite is a great 1930s surprise with a super-smart bathroom. You will be well looked after in this elegant and stylish house.

Price	€69.50.
Rooms	4: 2 twins, 1 triple, 1 suite.
Meals	Dinner with wine, €32.
Closed	In winter, except by arrangement.
Directions	Macé is 3km north of Blois along N152 for Orléans. In village follow signs; 500m on right before church.

Muriel Cabin-Saint-Marcel
La Villa Médicis,
Macé, 41000 St Denis sur Loire,
Loir-et-Cher

Tel	+33 (0)2 54 74 46 38
Fax	+33 (0)2 54 78 20 27
Email	medicis.bienvenue@wanadoo.fr
Web	lavillamedicis.com

Entry 349   Map 4

Loire Valley

9 rue Dutems

An old townhouse with a country feel, a lovely walled garden, a majestic chestnut and miniature trees at the bottom to screen the outbuildings (now converted into gîtes). Guests eat at separate tables in a room full of brocante and wonderful pictures collected and framed by gracious, charming Joëlle. Up the sloping-treaded stairs are the light, simple bedrooms and bathrooms decorated in ephemeral greys, whites, creams and yellows – understated, serene and beautiful. There are beams, polished parquet and tiles in the sitting room and a gentle intimate atmosphere over all.

Price	€58-€78.
Rooms	5: 1 twin/double, 3 triples, 1 suite.
Meals	Restaurants in Muides sur Loire.
Closed	January.
Directions	From N152 enter Mer & park by church. House is short walk up main street; entrance in picture-framing shop on left. (Car access details on arrival.)

Joëlle & Claude Mormiche
9 rue Dutems,
41500 Mer, Loir-et-Cher

Tel	+33 (0)2 54 81 17 36
Fax	+33 (0)2 54 81 70 19
Email	mormiche@wanadoo.fr
Web	www.chambres-gites-chambord.com

Entry 350   Map 4

Loire Valley

Carrefour de l'Ormeau

A Bauhaus minimalism from Alain, music lover, painter, craftsman and cultivator of the senses, and Isabelle, who loves to cook. In big bedrooms of monastic simplicity, nothing distracts from the natural warmth of old tiles and Alain's smooth, contemporary, local-wood furniture: all is light, space, harmony. The magnificent room under the rafters is used for recitals and furniture display. Isabelle's lush village garden centres on potager and lily pond and there's a little path through the 'wild' wood beyond: this big house is a meeting of market-place and wilderness where people grow. *Shiatsu massage.*

Ethical Collection: Environment; Food. See page 432.

Price	€50. Triple €66. Suite €82–€98.
Rooms	4: 1 double, 2 triples, 1 suite for 4–5.
Meals	Dinner with wine, €23, April-September only.
Closed	Never.
Directions	From Le Mans N157 for Orléans 52km; left D921 to Mondoubleau; Carrefour de l'Ormeau is central village junction; house on corner opp. Ford garage.

Alain Gaubert & Isabelle Peyron
Carrefour de l'Ormeau,
41170 Mondoubleau, Loir-et-Cher
Tel +33 (0)2 54 80 93 76
Fax +33 (0)2 54 80 93 76
Email peyron.isa@wanadoo.fr
Web www.carrefour-de-lormeau.com

Entry 351   Map 4

Loire Valley

Les Bordes

With its sweeping farmyard, its pond and such a spontaneous welcome, it is, as one reader wrote, "a gem of a B&B". You can see for miles across fields filled with lark song and cereals. The owners are a smiling couple who give you their time without invading your space but are delighted to show you their immaculate farm, orchard and vegetable garden if you're interested. Their spotless rooms have floral walls and firm mattresses. The furniture is simple and rustic, the bedrooms and bathrooms are deeply raftered, the old farmhouse breathes through its timbers. It is peaceful, pretty and a place for picnics.

Price	€41–€44.
Rooms	3: 1 double; 2 doubles, sharing bath & wc.
Meals	Dinner with wine, €18.
Closed	Rarely.
Directions	From Vendôme D957 for Blois 6km. Right to Crucheray & Chambres d'Hôtes. 4km from turning; signed.

Élisabeth & Guy Tondereau
Les Bordes,
41100 Crucheray,
Loir-et-Cher
Tel +33 (0)2 54 77 05 43
Fax +33 (0)2 54 77 05 43
Email ge.tondereau@wanadoo.fr

Entry 352   Map 4

Loire Valley

Cave de l'Éperon

Creep into the rock of ages and rejoice in your very own delightful cave room in unspoilt Trôo, then imagine the ultimate breakfast experience, sitting on a ledge-terrace against the cliff face, surrounded by foliage and flowers, your eye soaring over fields and river to eternity. Solange, a smiley, gentle, attentive artist, has done her unusual space brilliantly: fine furniture, modern and ancient, wall hangings and pretty cushions between billowing limestone ceiling and rustic tiled floor. Join her in her own snug antique- and book-spread living room for cooler-morning breakfast. *Access on foot from car park.*

Price	€67.
Rooms	1 double.
Meals	Restaurants nearby.
Closed	Never.
Directions	From Vendôme D917 to Montoire sur le Loir & Trôo; cont. for Sougé 200m; right D8 for Cité Troglodyte, up hill to church carpark. See map of village & take 'Escalier St Gabriel' steps & path to house.

Solange Guilloux
Cave de l'Éperon,
4 Escalier Saint Gabriel,
41800 Trôo, Loir-et-Cher
Tel   +33 (0)2 54 72 55 68
Email solange.guilloux@wanadoo.fr
Web   www.troo.com/eperon.html

Entry 353   Map 4

Loire Valley

L'île ô reflets

Just below the troglodyte village of Trôo is a mill in a deliciously green setting. With its quays, wash houses, barns and wisteria-clad cottages, it has the air of an old-fashioned hamlet. Martial adores it and has big plans. He's converting an old turbine for electricity and has restored the main house to perfection: each fresh, comfortable, French-feminine bedroom is inspired by a fable by La Fontaine, and the bathrooms are spotless. Outside are terraces and topiary, an orchard and a meadow mown by donkeys. Best of all, the place has its own island, reached by a bridge. *Not suitable for young children.*

Ethical Collection: Environment; Community; Food. See page 432.

Price	€60-€80.
Rooms	4: 1 double, 1 family room for 3, 2 suites for 3. Cots available.
Meals	Dinner with wine, €25.
Closed	Never.
Directions	From Vendôme D917 for Château du Loir & La Flèche 25km thro' Montoire sur le Loir to Trôo; through village for Sougé; left to Moulin de la Plaine at exit of Trôo.

Martial Chevallier
L'île ô reflets,
Moulin de la Plaine,
41800 Trôo, Loir-et-Cher
Tel   +33 (0)2 54 72 57 84
Email martial.chevallier@wanadoo.fr
Web   moulindelaplaine.com

Entry 354   Map 4

Loire Valley

20 rue Pilate

In the lovely Loire valley where the intimate and the romantic reign, you have the little house in the garden to yourselves. It has a kitchen and a bathroom downstairs, two bedrooms upstairs and its own piece of flower-filled garden for private breakfasts. Or you can join Madame at the long check-clothed table in her light and cheerful kitchen, baskets hanging from the beams. She is friendly, cultivated and dynamic, involved in tourist activities so an excellent adviser, will cook you refined dinners and is a great maker of jams. It's not luxurious, but elegantly homely, quiet and welcoming.

Loire Valley

La Louisière

Simplicity, character and a marvellous welcome make La Louisière special. Madame clearly delights in her role as hostess; Monsieur, who once rode the horse-drawn combine, tends his many roses and his paintings of bucolic bliss line the walls. Both are active in their community – a caring and unpretentious couple. The traditional rooms have subtle, well-chosen colour schemes and sparkling bathrooms; touches of fun, too. Surrounded by chestnut trees, the farmhouse backs onto the gardens of the château and is wonderfully quiet. Tennis to play, bikes to borrow, horses to ride. Great for children.

Price	€60. €100 for 4.
Rooms	Cottage: 2 doubles, sharing bath (let to same party only).
Meals	Dinner with wine, €25.
Closed	November–March.
Directions	A28 exit 27 D766 for Beaumont la Ronce; after 1km left to Neuvy le Roi; right at 1st stop in village; house on left on D2, opp. turning to Louestault.

Price	€55.
Rooms	3: 1 twin, 1 triple, 1 suite for 5.
Meals	Auberge 800m.
Closed	Rarely.
Directions	From Tours D29 to Beaumont la Ronce; signed in village.

Ghislaine & Gérard de Couesnongle
20 rue Pilate,
37370 Neuvy le Roi,
Indre-et-Loire
Tel   +33 (0)2 47 24 41 48
Email ggh.coues@gmail.com

Michel & Andrée Campion
La Louisière
37360 Beaumont la Ronce,
Indre-et-Loire
Tel   +33 (0)2 47 24 42 24
Fax   +33 (0)2 47 24 42 24
Email andree.campion@orange.fr

Entry 355   Map 4

Entry 356   Map 4

Loire Valley

La Cornillière

Just 15 minutes from the centre of Tours yet you're deep in the countryside where deer, and even the occasional wild boar, invite themselves into the garden from the surrounding woods. The Espinassous live in an 18th-century farmhouse and have turned their longère into a delightfully rustic guest suite with all creature comforts. Croissants and fresh bread will be delivered to you each morning and the rambling gardens are yours to explore, including the formal walled garden, Monsieur's special pride and joy. He and his wife are friendly, cultured people who know the area well and will advise on places to visit. *Sawday self-catering also.*

Price	€90-€150.
Rooms	1 suite for 2-4.
Meals	Restaurants nearby. Picnics in garden on request.
Closed	Never.
Directions	From Tours D938 for Le Mans, right to Mettray. In village follow one-way system round church, right for St Antoine du Rocher; 2nd right, signed.

Catherine Espinassou
La Cornillière,
Mettray,
37390 Tours, Indre-et-Loire
Tel   +33 (0)2 47 51 12 69
Email   catherine@lacornilliere.com.fr
Web   www.lacornilliere.com.fr

Entry 357   Map 4

Loire Valley

Les Hautes Gâtinières

High on a cliff above the Loire, it looks over the village across the vines and the valley to a château. It may be modern imitating old, but we chose it for Madame's superb, generous, five-star hospitality. The house is immaculate and meticulously kept; one room is repro Louis XIV, plus orangey carpet and flowery paper. There is a big living area with tiled floor and rugs, an insert fireplace and views over the large sloping garden which peers down over the picturesque village with its church and châteaux. Giant breakfasts, wonderful welcome, great value for the Loire.

Price	€58. Suite €93.
Rooms	3: 2 doubles, 1 suite for 4.
Meals	Restaurants in village, 500m.
Closed	Rarely.
Directions	From Tours A10 for Paris; cross Loire; exit 20 to Vouvray. In Rochecorbon left at lights & right up steep narrow lane; signed.

Jacqueline Gay
Les Hautes Gâtinières,
7 chemin de Bois Soleil,
37210 Rochecorbon,
Indre-et-Loire
Tel   +33 (0)2 47 52 88 08
Email   gatinieres@wanadoo.fr
Web   www.gatinieres.eu.ki

Entry 358   Map 4

Loire Valley

Manoir du Plessis

Literary types will find the old desks and quills irresistible, garden buffs will love the huge walled garden, designed by the creator of Villandry (4km away). This lovely manor house began life as a priory in the 15th century (note the rooftop bell, courtyard chapel and well). Up beautiful oak stairs are two ravishing suites – antique beds, bold colours, high timbers, fine old rugs on rosy terracotta – kept cool and dark by heavy inner shutters; bathrooms are an arresting mix of antique and chic. Madame will regale you with stories of all the writers, artists and musicians who have stayed here. A glory. *Minimum stay 2 nights.*

Price	€180–€250. €900–€1,250 per week.
Rooms	2 suites, each with sitting room & kitchenette.
Meals	Dinner with wine, €20–€30. Restaurants 1-3km.
Closed	Never.
Directions	From Tours D7 to Savonnières; entering village bear left up Rue du Paradis. Cont. for 1.4km. House on left just after passing village exit sign.

Catherine Benjamin
Manoir du Plessis,
37510 Savonnières, Indre-et-Loire

Tel	+33 (0)2 47 50 00 26
Email	catherinebenjamin@wanadoo.fr
Web	www.leplessis.eu

Loire Valley

Les Mazeraies

Beautifully sculpted from the same ancient cedar trees that stalked the splendid grounds 100 years ago, this thoroughly contemporary mansion on the old château foundations in the Garden of France is a real delight. Humour, intelligence and love of fine things inhabit this welcoming family and their guest wing is unostentatiously luxurious in rich fabrics, oriental and modern furniture, good pictures and lovely, scented, cedar-lined bathrooms. Ground-floor rooms have a private terrace each, upstairs ones have direct access to the roof garden. Marie-Laurence is utterly charming.

Price	€95.
Rooms	4: 1 double, 2 twins/doubles, 1 suite for 3-4.
Meals	Choice of restaurants locally.
Closed	Rarely.
Directions	From Tours D7 for Savonnières; 3km before village left after Les Cèdres restaurant; 800m on left.

Marie-Laurence Jallet
Les Mazeraies,
Route des Mazeraies,
37510 Savonnières, Indre-et-Loire

Tel	+33 (0)2 47 67 85 35
Email	les.jallet@wanadoo.fr
Web	www.lesmazeraies.com

Loire Valley

Le Chat Courant

Traditional materials – soft Touraine stone, lime render, wood – and old furniture, pale colours and lots of light make this slate-topped house a stylish, welcoming haven by the Cher where the birdsong drowns out the trains. Éric, a welcoming and talented host – ask to see his photographs of the Loire – has local lore to tell, animals to introduce and a fascinating walled garden for you to admire. The lovely suite is in the summer house, everywhere you'll find cool colours, natural textures, bits of antiquery (one bedhead is an adapted Breton *lit clos*), oodles of taste and flowers inside and out.

Price	€65-€70. Suite €90-€115.
Rooms	2: 1 double, 1 family suite for 2-5.
Meals	Occasional dinner with wine, €25.
Closed	Rarely.
Directions	From Tours D7 to Savonnières; right across bridge; left for 3.5km; on right.

Éric Gaudouin
Le Chat Courant,
37510 Villandry, Indre-et-Loire
Tel   +33 (0)2 47 50 06 94
Email info@le-chat-courant.com
Web   www.le-chat-courant.com

Entry 361   Map 4

Loire Valley

Château du Vau

At the end of a long bumpy drive is a house of great character run with good humour: delightful philosopher Bruno has turned his family château into a stylish refuge for travellers. Generations of sliding young have polished the banisters on the stairs leading to the large, light bedrooms, freshly decorated round splendid brass bedsteads, with seagrass and family memorabilia. Dinners of estate produce, and, on summer evenings, gastronomic buffets can take you to a favourite corner of the vast grounds; deer bound in the meadow, sheep graze in the orchard. There's a fine pool, and a golf course bang opposite.

Price	€120.
Rooms	5: 3 doubles, 1 triple, 1 family room.
Meals	Dinner €26; with wine €42. Summer buffets in garden.
Closed	Rarely.
Directions	From Tours A85 Saumur; 1st exit for Ballan Miré; signs for Ferme Château de Vau & golf course at motorway exit. Entrance opp. golf course.

Bruno Clément
Château du Vau,
37510 Ballan Miré, Indre-et-Loire
Tel   +33 (0)2 47 67 84 04
Email info@chateau-du-vau.com
Web   www.chateau-du-vau.com

Entry 362   Map 4

Loire Valley

La Lubinerie

Built by Elizabeth's grandfather, its typical brick-and-tile face still looking good, this neat townhouse is a spirited mixture of nostalgic and modern. Strong colours and delicate muslin, elegant mirrors and armoires and a fascinating collection of paintings, prints, old cartoons and… teapots. Elizabeth lived for years in England, collected all these things and calls her delicious rooms Earl Grey, Orange Pekoe, Darjeeling. Your hosts love sharing their stories and knowledge with guests. Two lovely dogs, a friendly little town, a sweet cottagey garden – and, we are told, the best croissants ever.

Loire Valley

Les Moulins de Vontes

"Magical," say readers. Three old mills side by side on a glorious sweep of the Indre, a boat for messing about in, wooden bridges to cross from one secluded bank to another, a ship-stern view of the river from the terrace. No evening meals so pick up a picnic en route and your entertaining hosts will happily provide cutlery, rugs and anything else you need. The airy, elegant, uncluttered rooms are in historic style and have stunning river views (the rushing water becomes a gentle murmur at night). Bathrooms sparkle. Billiards in the sitting room, homemade honey for breakfast, swimming and fishing in the river. Heaven.

Price	€70–€120. Singles €65.
Rooms	3: 2 doubles, 1 suite for 4.
Meals	Restaurants 3km.
Closed	Rarely.
Directions	From Tours D143 for Loches; exit r'bout for Esvres; left at stop to centre ville; after church for St Branchs; at mini-r'bout, 1st left then 1st right. House opp. École Maternelle.

Price	€130.
Rooms	3: 1 twin; 2 doubles, each with shower & separate wc.
Meals	Restaurant 6km.
Closed	October–March.
Directions	From Tours, D943 towards Loches; at 3rd r'bout right to Esvres centre; left on D17; 200m after village exit sign, turn right; on to end of road.

	Elizabeth Aubert-Girard La Lubinerie, 3 rue des Écoles, 37320 Esvres sur Indre, Indre-et-Loire
Tel	+33 (0)2 47 26 40 87
Email	lalubinerie@wanadoo.fr
Web	www.lalubinerie.com

	Odile & Jean-Jacques Degail Les Moulins de Vontes, 37320 Esvres sur Indre, Indre-et-Loire
Tel	+33 (0)2 47 26 45 72
Fax	+33 (0)2 47 26 45 35
Email	info@moulinsdevontes.com
Web	www.moulinsdevontes.com

Entry 363   Map 4

Entry 364   Map 4

Loire Valley

Le Pavillon de Vallet

When she moved to this little valley, charming, gracious Astrid had no B&B plans at all – "it happened" and she loves it, taking huge care over the rooms (new beds in all) and breakfast (delicious) – she and her pilot husband are escapees from Paris. The *tuffeau* stone is light and bright, the lawns run down to the Cher, wisteria covers the breakfast *gloriette*. Guests have a lofty, tiled living room full of lightness and well-being. The bread-oven bedroom is sweet with its flowery wallpaper, painted beams and private courtyard; in another, an enormous four-poster looms beneath a canopy of joists. Special.

Price	€70–€90.
Rooms	3: 1 double, 2 triples.
Meals	Restaurants 4km.
Closed	Rarely.
Directions	From Tours D976 for Bléré; pass sign for Athée sur Cher, cont. to Granlay; immed. left to Vallet; down lane; left at bottom of hill; last house on right.

	Astrid Lange
	Le Pavillon de Vallet,
	4 rue de l'Aqueduc,
	37270 Athée sur Cher, Indre-et-Loire
Tel	+33 (0)2 47 50 67 83
Fax	+33 (0)2 47 50 67 83
Email	pavillon.vallet@orange.fr
Web	monsite.orange.fr/lepavillondevallet

Entry 365   Map 4

Loire Valley

Le Clos du Golf

All this in one place? There are 14 hectares of heron, wild boar, deer *and* a nine-hole golf course. Mark, a gallicised Englishman, and Katia, an anglicised Frenchwoman, travellers both, are at rest and in love with their beautiful home. The old farmhouse or *longière* has been masterfully restored and is filled, not surprisingly, with a mix of English and French: pleasing antiques, crisp bedrooms beneath old beams, delicious dinners of local seasonal things at one big sociable table. Swimming, tennis and the splendours of the Loire lie just down the road. A wonderful, hospitable place.

Price	€70–€95. Extra bed €20.
Rooms	4: 3 doubles, 1 single.
Meals	Dinner with wine, €35.
Closed	December–January.
Directions	From A10 exit 18 on D31 for Amboise to Autrèche; left D55 to Route de Dame Marie les Bois; right D74; 2nd house on left after woods.

	Mark & Katia Foster
	Le Clos du Golf, Le Plessis,
	Route de Dame-Marie-les-Bois,
	37530 Cangey-Amboise, Indre-et-Loire
Tel	+33 (0)2 47 56 07 07
Email	closdugolf@wanadoo.fr
Web	www.bonadresse.com/val-de-loire/ cangey-amboise.htm

Entry 366   Map 4

Loire Valley

Château de Nazelles

Even the pool is special: a 'Roman' bath
hewn out of the hillside with a fountain and
two columns, set on one of several garden
levels that rise to the crowning glory of vines
where grapes are grown by natural methods.
The young owners brim with enthusiasm for
their elegant, history-laden château, built in
1518 to gaze across the Loire at Amboise.
Every detail has been treated with taste and
discretion. Rooms, two in the main house,
two smaller in the adorable old pavillon, are
light and fresh with lovely wooden floors –
and there's a big living room with books,
internet and games.

Price	€105-€140.
Rooms	4: 3 doubles, 1 suite for 4.
Meals	Restaurants in Amboise.
Closed	Rarely.
Directions	From A10 exit 18 for Amboise 12km; right D1 to Pocé & Cisse & Nazelles Négron; in village centre, narrow Rue Tue la Soif between Mairie & La Poste.

Véronique & Olivier Fructus
Château de Nazelles,
16 rue Tue la Soif, 37530 Nazelles,
Indre-et-Loire
Tel   +33 (0)2 47 30 53 79
Fax   +33 (0)2 47 30 53 79
Email   info@chateau-nazelles.com
Web   www.chateau-nazelles.com

Entry 367   Map 4

Loire Valley

Manoir de la Maison Blanche

Your 17th-century manor sits in blissful
seclusion yet you can walk into the centre of
old Amboise. Annick has bags of energy and
enthusiasm and gives you four fabulous,
generous, lofty bedrooms in a converted
outbuilding. One is tiled and beamed with a
small patio overlooking the garden, another,
under the eaves, is charming, beamy and
reached via an outdoor spiral stair. The
youthful garden is full of promise and bursting
with roses and irises that often make their way
to your room. Look out for the 16th-century
pigeon loft – a historical rarity. Wonderful
hostess, super rooms, châteaux all around.

Price	€90.
Rooms	4 doubles.
Meals	Restaurants within walking distance. Guest kitchenette.
Closed	Rarely.
Directions	From Place du Château in Amboise for Clos Lucé; round park; straight on at 1st stop sign, right at 2nd stop sign, 1st left; signed.

Annick Delécheneau
Manoir de la Maison Blanche,
18 rue de l'Épinetterie,
37400 Amboise, Indre-et-Loire
Tel   +33 (0)2 47 23 16 14
Email   annick.delecheneau@wanadoo.fr
Web   www.lamaisonblanche-fr.com

Entry 368   Map 4

Loire Valley

Belleroche

Faint sounds sometimes drift upwards from the quai far below but otherwise all is serene. Belleroche, only a 15-minute walk from the centre of Amboise, stands poised and aloof in a three-hectare garden high above the Loire. Florence searched high and low for the perfect place for her B&B; having found it, she and her vet husband have devoted energy and imagination to its restoration. The exquisite bedrooms and the guest sitting room, once the old library, overlook the river. So, too, does a little 18th-century pavilion under the lime trees where Florence plans to serve breakfast on sunny mornings. Heaven.

Price	€80–€100.
Rooms	2: 1 suite for 4; 1 double with separate bath.
Meals	Restaurants within walking distance.
Closed	Mid-October to mid-April.
Directions	From Tours, D751 along river to Amboise centre; pass bridge & château, take lower road Quai Charles Guinot becoming Quai des Violettes; right Rue du Clos de Belleroche. 1st on left, blue gates.

Florence Janvier
Belleroche,
1 rue du Clos de Belleroche,
37400 Amboise, Indre-et-Loire

Tel	+33 (0)2 47 30 47 03
Email	belleroche.amboise@wanadoo.fr
Web	www.belleroche.net

Entry 369   Map 4

Loire Valley

Le Belvédère

From plain street to stately courtyard magnolia to extraordinary marble-walled spiral staircase with dome atop – it's a *monument historique*, a miniature Bagatelle Palace, a bachelor's folly with a circular salon. The light, airy, fadingly elegant rooms, small and perfectly proportioned, are soft pink and grey; lean out and pick a grape from the vine-clad pergola. Monsieur was a pilot and still flies vintage aircraft. Madame was an air hostess and English teacher and is casually sophisticated and articulate about her love of fine things, places and buildings. Wonderful, and a stone's throw from Chenonceau.

Price	€90. Suite €140.
Rooms	3: 2 doubles, 1 suite for 4.
Meals	Restaurant opposite (must book).
Closed	Occasionally.
Directions	A85 exit 11; D31 to Bléré; in Bléré follow signs for Centre Culturel (house is in same street). OR collection from private airfield 5km.

Dominique Guillemot
Le Belvédère,
24 rue des Déportés,
37150 Bléré, Indre-et-Loire

Tel	+33 (0)2 47 30 30 25
Fax	+33 (0)2 47 30 30 25
Email	jr.guillemot@wanadoo.fr
Web	lebelvedere-bednbreakfast.com

Entry 370   Map 4

Loire Valley

Moulin de la Follaine

Great wooden doors open to courtyard and garden beyond: Follaine is a deeply serene place. Ornamental geese adorn the lake, the tended garden has places to linger, colourful bedrooms have antique furniture, fabulous mattresses and lake views; one opens to the garden. Upstairs is a lovely light sitting room – and a guest fridge for picnics in the garden. Amazingly, the old milling machinery in the breakfast area still works – ask and Monsieur will turn it on for you; there are relics from the old hunting days, too. Your hosts, once in the hotel trade, know the area intimately and are utterly charming. *Sawday self-catering also.*

Price	€65–€75.
Rooms	4: 2 doubles, 2 suites.
Meals	Restaurant in Reignac, 2.5km; choice in Loches.
Closed	Rarely.
Directions	From Tours D943 for Loches; left D58 to Reignac; D17 to Azay sur Indre; left opp. restaurant; at fork, left (over 2 bridges); mill below fortified farm on right.

Danie Lignelet
Moulin de la Follaine,
37310 Azay sur Indre,
Indre-et-Loire

Tel	+33 (0)2 47 92 57 91
Fax	+33 (0)2 47 92 57 91
Email	moulindelafollaine@wanadoo.fr
Web	www.moulindefollaine.com

Loire Valley

La Chapelle

It is a gothic chapel transformed into a traditional house, an unselfconscious witness of things past. Up a winding stair in the little tower, the charming rooms owe their marble fireplaces to an earlier conversion, their assorted fine furniture to past generations, their good watercolours to friends and relations, their art books to Dominique himself. A well-travelled artist, he came home when he inherited the house; he is a cultured, attentive, amusing, a great cook, and a gardener. A place to dawdle in and soak up the charm, indoors and in the secret shady garden. Smokers are not banished. Stay for dinner – huge fun.

Price	€70; €120 for both rooms.
Rooms	2 doubles, sharing bath (let to same party only).
Meals	Dinner with wine, €25.
Closed	November-March.
Directions	From A10 exit 18; D31 to Bléré; D58 to Cigogné; D83 to Tauxigny. Rue Haute on D82 to St Bauld. House on corner.

Dominique Moreau-Granger
La Chapelle,
53 rue Haute,
37310 Tauxigny, Indre-et-Loire

Tel	+33 (0)2 47 92 15 38
Fax	+33 (0)2 47 92 15 38
Email	d.moreaugranger@free.fr
Web	la-chapelle-tauxigny.com

Loire Valley

Le Moulin de Montrésor

Do you dream of living in a watermill? Your young hosts have converted theirs, near the magnificent château of Montrésor, in stylish and simple good taste: a wooden staircase leading to a coconut-matted landing, family portraits, super colours, lots of light and original features... and quiet flows the water over the wheel beneath the glass panel in the dining room. Madame is cultured and well-travelled, her family has had the château for 200 years but no-one stands on ceremony and there's a sense of timeless peace here, miles from anywhere. The plain garden has a fenced, child-friendly pool.

Price	€60–€65. Under 4s free.
Rooms	4: 1 double, 1 twin, 2 triples.
Meals	Restaurants within 5km.
Closed	Rarely.
Directions	From Loches D760 to Montrésor; left for Chemillé; mill on left; signed.

Sophie & Alain Willems de Ladersous
Le Moulin de Montrésor,
37460 Montrésor,
Indre-et-Loire
Tel +33 (0)2 47 92 68 20
Fax +33 (0)2 47 92 74 65
Email alain.willems@wanadoo.fr
Web www.moulindemontresor.fr

Entry 373   Map 9

Loire Valley

Le Moulin de St Jean

The restored mill in its delicious island setting is all ups and downs, nooks and crannies, big rooms and small, character and variety. Your delightful hosts fled city jobs for a quieter life, he bringing his love of Loire wines (just ask), she her passion for quilts and her cooking skills. Assorted wallpapers, patterns, frills and furniture – and a welcome bottle of wine – make for a warm, homely feel. Plus new mattresses and good bathrooms, two sitting rooms, numerous DVDs and books, a shady garden, a heated pool – and all the fascinations of the Loire Valley. *Not suitable for young children: unfenced water.*

Price	€75–€85.
Rooms	4: 2 doubles, 1 twin, 1 suite.
Meals	Dinner €25. Wine from €10.
Closed	Rarely.
Directions	From Tours A85 exit Esvres; D943 to Loches 25km; cont. D943 through Perusson; D492 to St Jean; 300m to small bridge over river Indre. Entrance from bridge on left.

Barbara & John Maxwell
Le Moulin de St Jean,
St Jean – St Germain,
37600 Loches, Indre-et-Loire
Tel +33 (0)2 47 94 70 12
Fax +33 (0)2 47 94 77 98
Email lemoulinstjean@club-internet.fr
Web www.lemoulinstjean.com

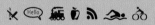

Entry 374   Map 9

Loire Valley

La Ferme Blanche

The rambling, L-shaped white farmhouse brims with an enchanting light. Outside: flowerbeds, roses and the shade of a white fig tree to bask in and an unobtrusive (unfenced) pool. Parisian Anne, shyly welcoming, has created romantic interiors where Louis XV antiques mingle with charming oddities such as a 19th-century mannequin, and tobacco-brown sofas sit harmoniously beneath cream-beamed ceilings on old pine floors. Rooms are largely white, with hand-painted walls and gauzy canopies over the beds; dinners are 'epicurean gourmet'. Superb.

Price	€100
Rooms	2 suites: 1 for 2-4, 1 for 6.
Meals	Dinner with wine, €32.
Closed	November-February.
Directions	From A10 exit 25; D59 to Ligueil; D31 to Cussay; in Cussay left opp. post office; behind church lane to left; signed; after La Chaume Brangerie; 1st right. House 1st left.

Anne Fabienne Bouvier
La Ferme Blanche,
La Chaume-Brangerie,
37240 Cussay, Indre-et-Loire
Tel +33 (0)2 47 91 94 43
Email contact@la-ferme-blanche.com
Web www.la-ferme-blanche.com

Entry 375   Map 9

Loire Valley

La Tinellière

A pretty hamlet farmhouse, a gentle old goose wandering the garden, a glass of homemade *épine*. Éliane, a welcoming, enthusiastic hostess, loves talking to people about their interests and hers and is constantly improving her rooms, a ground-floor, mezzanine'd quadruple (with ladder and gate), now exotic with Vietnamese hangings, and another larger room in the converted stable. Parts of the house are 17th-century with massive beams and well-mixed new and old furniture, wild and dried flowers, colours and fabrics. The living room is darkish, beamed and cosy, the guests' kitchenette brand new.

Price	€45-€48.
Rooms	2 quadruples.
Meals	Auberge 3km. Guest kitchenette.
Closed	Never.
Directions	From A10 24.1 for Sorigny. Passing Sorigny, right D910 for 9.5km; left D101 through St Catherine de Fierbois for Bossé; right 3km to La Tinellière. Signed.

Éliane Pelluard
La Tinellière,
37800 Ste Catherine de Fierbois,
Indre-et-Loire
Tel +33 (0)2 47 65 61 80
Email elianepelluard@neuf.fr

Entry 376   Map 9

Loire Valley

La Maison

When a diplomat's wife with impeccable taste and a flair for design is let loose on an austere 18th-century townhouse, the result is a treat. The family's antique furniture blends with pieces of art, sculpture and rugs from Africa and the Near East; tall windows, storey'd terracotta floors and an oval oak staircase are the grand backdrop; bedrooms are traditional and sumptuous, overlooking, via window and balcony, a walled formal garden which ends in a semi-wild area of bamboo. All is peace: even the fine chime of the church clock over the wall falls bashfully silent at night. The best house in Richelieu? Yes.

Price	€100.
Rooms	4: 2 doubles, 2 twins.
Meals	Restaurant within walking distance.
Closed	Mid-October to mid-April.
Directions	From A10, exit Ste Maure de Touraine; left D760 for Noyant; left D58 for Richelieu; in town, cross over Place des Religieuses, 1st left, signed.

Michèle Couvrat-Desvergnes
La Maison,
6 rue Henri Proust,
37120 Richelieu, Indre-et-Loire

Tel +33 (0)2 47 58 29 40
Fax +33 (0)2 47 58 29 40
Email lamaisondemichele@yahoo.com
Web www.lamaisondemichele.com

Entry 377 Map 9

Loire Valley

Les Bournais

Philippe and Florence are outstanding hosts in a jewel of a place. The old farm, lovingly restored, is set round a pretty courtyard – Flo has a studio at one end, where she paints – and the bedrooms are in the rustic stables, upstairs and down. Each is delightful with heaps of space, stripy fabrics and brocante finds, armchairs, bolsters, books and fresh flowers. Walls are stone, floors tiled and spotless. Showers are walk-in and colourful. Excellent traditional dinners with innovative touches are served round a rustic table and breakfasts are moveable feasts. Cats, ponies, hens and a small dog add to the charm.

Price	€65.
Rooms	4 doubles, each with extra bed.
Meals	Light supper with wine, €12.
Closed	Rarely.
Directions	Leave A10 at Ste Maure de Touraine; D760 to L'île Bouchard; cross river; D757 for Richelieu. Les Bournais signed left just before entering Brizay.

Philippe & Florence Martinez
Les Bournais,
37220 Theneuil,
Indre-et-Loire

Tel +33 (0)2 47 95 29 61
Email les.bournais@orange.fr
Web www.lesbournais.net

Entry 378 Map 9

Loire Valley

Domaine de Beauséjour

Dug into the hillside with the forest behind and a panorama of vines in front, this winegrower's manor successfully pretends it was built in the 1800s. Expect venerable oak beams and stone cut by troglodyte masons: the mood is one of stylish rusticity. Charming bedrooms have carved bedheads, big puffy eiderdowns, old prints, vases of fresh (and artificial) flowers; bathrooms are elegant and the sweetest rooms are in the tower by the pool. Make sure you buy some (discounted) wine to take home. When not away at wine fairs, Parisienne Marie-Claude looks after you with panache. *Minimum stay 2 nights. Sawday self-catering also.*

Price	€70–€90. €120 for 4.
Rooms	3: 2 doubles, 1 suite for 3-4.
Meals	Restaurants 5km.
Closed	Rarely.
Directions	From Chinon, D21 to Cravant les Côteaux. On towards Panzoult; house on left after 2km.

	Marie-Claude Chauveau
	Domaine de Beauséjour,
	37220 Panzoult, Indre-et-Loire
Tel	+33 (0)2 47 58 64 64
Fax	+33 (0)2 47 95 27 13
Email	info@domainedebeausejour.com
Web	www.domainedebeausejour.com

Entry 379   Map 9

Loire Valley

Les Camélias de Pallus

Follow the pathway through Patricia's pretty garden to her long low farmhouse and you'll find yourself in a cool, stone-flagged hall guarded by a rocking horse. Beyond is the cosy guest sitting room where meals are served; the food's excellent and much of the fruit and veg comes fresh from the garden. Open stairs lead to the attic suite: two airy, delightful bedrooms divided by a small sitting area, and a good-sized bathroom. (They're under the rafters but there are fans for warm nights…). The house is in a gently sloping valley, with fine walks through the vineyards to the river and the forest.

Price	€80–€110.
Rooms	1 suite (1 twin; 1 twin sharing bath, separate wc) with sitting room.
Meals	Dinner with wine, €30.
Closed	Rarely.
Directions	From A10 exit Ste Maure de Touraine & head for L'Île Bouchard; D21 to Panzoult & cont. for Cravant. On left 2.8km after Panzoult.

	Patricia & Christian Périn-Nguyen
	Les Camélias de Pallus,
	Pallus, 37500 Cravant les Côteaux,
	Indre-et-Loire
Tel	+33 (0)2 47 93 08 94
Email	camelias.pallus@wanadoo.fr
Web	www.lescamelias.fr

Entry 380   Map 9

Loire Valley

Le Clos de Ligré

This former wine-grower's house sings in a subtle harmony of traditional charm and contemporary chic under thoroughly modern Martine's touch. Sponged walls, creamy beams and eye-catching fabrics breathe new life into rooms with old tiled floors and stone fireplaces – and there are two new big beamy doubles in the attic. Windows are flung open to let in the light and the stresses of city living are forgotten in cheerful, easy conversations with your hostess, who joins guests for candlelit dinners. Bookcases, billiard table and baby grand, buffet breakfasts at the long table, a pool for the energetic – delightful.

Price	€110.
Rooms	5: 4 doubles, 1 family suite.
Meals	Dinner with wine, €30.
Closed	Rarely.
Directions	From Chinon D749 for Richelieu; 1km after r'bout D115 right for 'Ligré par le vignoble' 5km; left to Le Rouilly; left at Dozon warehouse; house 800m on left.

Martine Descamps
Le Clos de Ligré,
Le Rouilly, 37500 Ligré,
Indre-et-Loire
Tel   +33 (0)2 47 93 95 59
Email   mdescamps@club-internet.fr
Web   www.le-clos-de-ligre.com

Entry 381   Map 9

Loire Valley

Le Châtaignier

In the safe garden is a vast and venerable *châtaignier* (horse chestnut), open lawns, swings, boules and fruit trees. The farmhouse is similarly unpretentious, thanks to these hospitable, intelligent hosts. Odile is quietly elegant, Jean-Joseph loves his garden and they set aside two fresh, well-furnished bedrooms for guests. The two-bedroom suite is on the first floor, its twin across the landing; the double – walls prettily sponged by artistic Odile – is reached via an outside stair. Sunny, country-elegant sitting and dining rooms (private tables for breakfast) open to the garden, and the fields stretch for miles.

Price	€55.
Rooms	2: 1 double with sofabed, 1 family suite for 4.
Meals	Restaurant 3km.
Closed	Never.
Directions	From Tours to Chinon; D759 to Loudun. At Beuxes, left to La Roberderie. Left at x-roads in hamlet, 4th house on left.

Odile & Jean-Joseph Crescenzo
Le Châtaignier,
16 rue du Carroi, La Roberderie,
37500 Marcay, Indre-et-Loire
Tel   +33 (0)2 47 93 97 09
Email   crescenzo@orange.fr
Web   lechataignier.free.fr

Entry 382   Map 9

Loire Valley

84 quai Jeanne d'Arc

An elegant, screened townhouse by the stately river Vienne, lived in by a delightful, devoted couple – she exuberant and chic, he literary and musical. Deep chairs round the brass coffee table call for bright, convivial conversation; the dining alcove brings gasps of delight; the bedrooms have huge, beautiful personalities, each detail lovingly chosen. A sleigh bed here, a Chinese carpet there, a pretty mirror over a basin with a border painted in trompe l'œil, beautifully laundered linen. In the centre of medieval Chinon, the nicest possible hosts – and breakfasts are 'gourmand'. *Min. stay 2 nights.*

Loire Valley

Cheviré

Guests at Cheviré stay in the well-converted stable block of an elegant stone house in a quiet little village, all a-shimmer in the Loire's inimitable limpid light – welcome to the protected wetlands between the rivers Loire and Vienne. Your quarters have ancient beams, stone walls, new floors, space to sit or cook, a little terrace; the uncluttered, sizeable rooms show the same happy mix of old and new with some fine pieces. Your hospitable, gentle hosts, proud of their house and area, will direct you to less obvious places of interest. "Very clean, very friendly, very good breakfasts," say our readers.

Price	€75–€100. Single €45–€85.
Rooms	3: 1 double, 1 twin/double, 1 single.
Meals	Restaurants within walking distance.
Closed	October–March.
Directions	Entering Chinon on D751 from Tours, along river past bridge & Rabelais statue; house just after post office.

Price	€32–€48.
Rooms	3: 1 double, 1 triple, 1 quadruple.
Meals	Restaurants 10km.
Closed	Mid-November to mid-March.
Directions	From Chinon D749 for Bourgueil 6km; left to Savigny en Véron; in village follow 'Camping'; house 1km after campsite on right.

	Jany & Jean Grosset
	84 quai Jeanne d'Arc,
	37500 Chinon,
	Indre-et-Loire
Tel	+33 (0)2 47 98 42 78
Fax	+33 (0)2 47 93 15 54
Email	lamaisondesbellesvues@orange.fr

	Marie-Françoise & Michel Chauvelin
	Cheviré, 11 rue Basse,
	37420 Savigny en Véron,
	Indre-et-Loire
Tel	+33 (0)2 47 58 42 49
Fax	+33 (0)2 47 58 42 49
Email	chauvelin.michel@wanadoo.fr
Web	www.ch-hotes-chevire.fr

Loire Valley

La Chancellerie

Unwind in this elegant 18th-century house, set apart from the village by rather grand walled gardens. Energetic perfectionist Élisabeth loves to entertain and gives you delicious meals on fine china – in the rustic kitchen or the sophisticated salon. Guests are treated to sofas, a bar and games in the large 'cave', and stylish bedrooms in two wings. Expect sweeping tiled and carpeted floors, exposed beams, big beds, polished antiques, and a tiny oratory in the Azur suite: the peace of the convent here. Outside are lawn, swings, fenced pool and a semi-wild 'English' garden. Delightful. *Min. stay 2 nights July/August.*

Price	€100–€125.
Rooms	3: 1 double, 2 family suites for 4.
Meals	Dinner €30. Wine €14–€30.
Closed	Rarely.
Directions	From Chinon, D16 to Huismes. Left as you enter village; house on corner, 100m.

Élisabeth & Christian Maury
La Chancellerie,
37420 Huismes,
Indre-et-Loire
Tel +33 (0)2 47 95 46 76
Email christian.maury1@wanadoo.fr
Web www.lachancellerie.com

Entry 385   Map 4

Loire Valley

Domaine de la Blanche Treille

Chic Madame has sparkling eyes and a warm energy; Monsieur is charming and loves gardening; the house (in a wine village) is the last word in luxury. So meticulously furnished are the rooms that, as you sip coffee poured from a silver pot, you may wish you'd worn your twinset and pearls! No matter; your Parisian hosts love swapping travellers' tales and inspiration from Asia informs the décor – pictures, prints, wicker elephants for tables. Bedrooms ooze comfort: a toile de Jouy quilt, a Directoire bed, linen embroidered by Madame. The garden is being tamed and the vineyards stretch to the hills.

Price	€100.
Rooms	3 doubles.
Meals	Restaurants 4km.
Closed	Never.
Directions	Leave A85 Bourgueil; D749 to Bourgueil; follow one-way system; D635 to Restigné; in Fougerolles, house on left, after Auger winery.

Aimée Rabillon
Domaine de la Blanche Treille,
56 route de Bourgueil,
37140 Fougerolles,
Indre-et-Loire
Tel +33 (0)2 47 97 93 30
Email rabillon.c@free.fr

Entry 386   Map 4

Loire Valley

3 rue du Moulin de Touvois

The brook gently flows and soothes – so relaxing. Myriam and Jean-Claude are interesting and energetic and have renovated their old miller's house with a blend of styles: original stonework, beams and terracotta floors and some funky modern furniture. The Moroccan tiled table with wrought-iron legs works well with the old stone fireplace in the dining room. Simple, pleasantly decorated bedrooms have parquet floors, good bedding and stylish modern lighting. The garden is a delight with its wide-planked bridge, fruit trees and dessert grapes and Jean-Claude is happy to arrange visits to local wine-growers.

Price	€54–€60.
Rooms	5: 2 doubles, 2 twins/doubles, 1 triple.
Meals	Dinner with wine, €22.
Closed	Mid-November to mid-February.
Directions	From A85 exit Saumur; D10 & D35 to Bourgueil; at r'bout on Bourgueil ring road (north), D749 for Gizeux 4km; right immed. before restaurant; 200m on left.

Myriam & Jean-Claude Marchand
3 rue du Moulin de Touvois,
37140 Bourgueil,
Indre-et-Loire

Tel	+33 (0)2 47 97 87 70
Fax	+33 (0)2 47 97 87 70
Email	info@moulindetouvois.com
Web	www.moulindetouvois.com

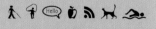

Entry 387   Map 4

Close to town

These places are in town or within easy walking distance of a town.

Poitou – Charentes

Poitou – Charentes

L'Aumônerie

This old hospital priory beside the original moat (now a boulevard bringing new neighbours, garden centre included) has eight drama-packed centuries to tell. The L'Haridons have put back several original features and alongside picture windows the old stone spiral leads up to the suite (big warm sitting room, low oak door to fresh beamed bedroom with extra bed). The small ground-floor double is utterly charming; outside is a playhouse for children. Madame is well-travelled, loves old buildings and gardens and is a most interesting and considerate hostess who also has a passion for patchwork. *Château de Chinon 25km.*

Price	€46–€50. Suite €50–€105.
Rooms	3: 1 double, 1 suite for 2-3, 1 family suite for 2-6.
Meals	Restaurants within walking distance.
Closed	Rarely.
Directions	From Fontevraud, take Loudun centre; cross traffic lights; at r'bout (Hotel de la Roue d'Or on right) take 1st exit for Thouars. Entrance 200m on right opp. Cultural Centre.

	Christiane L'Haridon L'Aumônerie, 3 bd Maréchal Leclerc, 86200 Loudun, Vienne
Tel	+33 (0)5 49 22 63 86
Email	chris.lharidon@wanadoo.fr
Web	www.l-aumonerie.biz

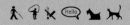

Entry 388   Map 9

Poitou – Charentes

Domaine de Bourgville

Time slows down here. In the converted stable block of an 18th-century 'gentilhommière' the style is gentle, provincial France, in tune with the rolling countryside of forests, hamlets and hills. The first-floor bedrooms wrap you in a soft embrace of old French bedsteads and shiny seagrass, flowers, rush-seated chairs and views to garden or terrace; all is intimacy and calm. Breakfast in the airy sitting room with its comfortable, well-chosen furnishings; John is a superb cook so stay for dinner. Explore Loire châteaux, medieval Chinon, walk the trails, then return to the rambling garden. Supremely restful.

Price	€45–€60.
Rooms	4 doubles.
Meals	Dinner with wine, €20. Restaurants in village.
Closed	Rarely.
Directions	From Richelieu for Châtellerault; after approx. 2km, right D24 to Mont sur Guesnes; signed in village.

	John & Glyn Ward Domaine de Bourgville, Allée de Bourgville, 86420 Mont sur Guesnes, Vienne
Tel	+33 (0)5 49 22 81 58 (daytime)
Fax	+33 (0)5 49 98 74 79
Email	b-b.bourgville@wanadoo.fr
Web	www.vie-vienne.com

Entry 389   Map 9

Poitou – Charentes

Château de la Motte

Nothing austere about this imposing, lovingly restored, 15th-century fortified castle. A wide spiral stone staircase leads to the simply but grandly decorated and high-ceilinged rooms where old family furniture, vast stone fireplaces and beds with richly textured canopies, finely stitched by your talented hostess, preserve the medieval flavour; bathrooms (also generous) are state of the art. There is an elegant dining room and a lofty, light-filled sitting room, for excellent home cooking and enlightened conversation with your cultured and charming hosts. Everyone is made welcome here, families included. *Sawday self-catering also.*

Ethical Collection: Environment; Food.
See page 432.

Price	€75-€120.
Rooms	4: 1 twin, 1 triple, 2 suites.
Meals	Dinner with wine, €28.
Closed	Occasionally.
Directions	From Paris A10 exit Châtellerault Nord; at r'bout after toll for Usseau 5km; D749 for Richelieu; D75 to Usseau.

	Jean-Marie & Marie-Andrée Bardin
	Château de la Motte,
	86230 Usseau, Vienne
Tel	+33 (0)5 49 85 88 25
Fax	+33 (0)5 49 85 88 25
Email	chateau.delamotte@wanadoo.fr
Web	www.chateau-de-la-motte.net

Entry 390   Map 9

Poitou – Charentes

La Grenouillère

You will be charmed by these warm, delightful, good-hearted people. Always fresh flowers and lovely colour schemes on the table, good French food and flowing wine, and meals on the shaded terrace in summer. The bedroom in the converted woodshed has beams, pretty curtains, a blue- and yellow- tiled floor and a view over the rambling garden with its meandering frog pond (hence the name). Further rooms are upstairs in a house across the courtyard where Madame's charming mother lives and makes delicious jam. Stimulating company, a most attractive cluster of old buildings and a rowing boat to mess about in.

Price	€45-€52.
Rooms	5: 3 doubles, 2 triples.
Meals	Dinner with wine, €25.
Closed	Rarely.
Directions	From Tours D910 S for Châtellerault 55km. In Dangé St Romain, right at 3rd traffic lights, cross river, keep left on middle of little square. House 200m along on left; signed.

	Annie & Noël Braguier
	La Grenouillère,
	17 rue de la Grenouillère,
	86220 Dangé St Romain, Vienne
Tel	+33 (0)5 49 86 48 68
Fax	+33 (0)5 49 86 46 56
Email	lagrenouillere86@aliceadsl.fr

Entry 391   Map 9

Château de Labarom

A great couple in their genuine family château of fading grandeur; mainly 17th century, it has a properly aged face. From the dramatic hall up the superbly bannistered staircase, you reach the salon gallery that runs majestically through the house. Here you may sit, read, dream of benevolent ghosts. Bedrooms burst with personality and wonderful old beds. Madame's hand-painted tiles adorn a shower, her laughter accompanies your breakfast in the splendid family living room; Monsieur tends his trees, aided by Polka the dog – he's a fund of local wisdom. A warm, wonderful, authentic place.

Price	€69–€75.
Rooms	2: 1 double, 1 twin/double, sharing bathroom.
Meals	Auberge nearby; choice 10km.
Closed	Rarely.
Directions	From A10 Futuroscope exit D62 to Quatre Vents r'bout; D757 to Vendeuvre; at r'bout left D15 through Chénecé. 800m on right after leaving Chénecé.

Éric & Henriette Le Gallais
Château de Labarom,
86380 Chénecé,
Vienne
Tel   +33 (0)5 49 51 24 22
Fax   +33 (0)5 49 51 47 38
Email   chateau.de.labarom@wanadoo.fr

Entry 392   Map 9

La Roseraie

Country B&B with one foot in the town – Neuville is a mere stroll. Warm, generous Heather and Michael live in an elegant townhouse in four enclosed acres, with orchard, vegetable garden and two rows of vines. The sitting area is cosy, the pool is fabulous, the bedrooms are immaculate, restful and calm: seagrass floors, white tub chairs, a carved bedhead. One room has a balcony, another a patio off the garden. Put the world to rights over Heather's delicious dinner served at the big table, or under the pergola in summer: gîte and B&B guests combine. Doves coo, Jack Russells frolic, Poitiers is the shortest drive. *Sawday self-catering also.*

Price	€68–€82. Suites €110–€140.
Rooms	5: 3 doubles, 2 family suites for 4–5.
Meals	Dinner with wine, €28.
Closed	Rarely.
Directions	A10 exit 28 (Futuroscope). D62 to Neuville; entering town, D347 for Mirebeau; left at r'bout for centre ville. On right on one-way system, just before water tower.

Michael & Heather Lavender
La Roseraie,
78 rue Armand Caillard,
86170 Neuville de Poitou, Vienne
Tel   +33 (0)5 49 54 16 72
Email   info@laroseraiefrance.fr
Web   www.laroseraiefrance.fr

Entry 393   Map 9

Poitou – Charentes

La Pocterie

A "passionate gardener" is how Martine describes herself, with a soft spot for old-fashioned roses: they ramble through the wisteria on the walls and gather in beautifully tended beds. The 'L' of the house shelters a very decent pool (now alarmed) while furniture is arranged in a welcoming spot for picnics. Martine works but will see you for breakfast (under the pretty arbour in summer) or in the evening: she's the one with the big smile. A peaceful, welcoming retreat with the Futuroscope literally minutes away. Bikes and tennis nearby, and a huge range of day trips to choose from.

Price	€52. Triple €65.
Rooms	2: 1 double, 1 triple.
Meals	Restaurants 3km.
Closed	Rarely.
Directions	From Châtellerault D749 for Chauvigny & Limoges approx. 13km; Vouneuil on right; cont. for 3km, then left for 750m; down track to end.

Michel & Martine Poussard
La Pocterie,
86210 Vouneuil sur Vienne,
Vienne

Tel   +33 (0)5 49 85 11 96

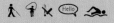

Entry 394   Map 9

Poitou – Charentes

Les Hauts de Chabonne

A pleasant 'stop off' in an undiscovered area. This sociable couple will spend time with guests after dinner when their children allow. They have converted a fine big barn into guest quarters – older than the main house, it has been well done, muted colour schemes and ethnic rugs in dark and pleasant rooms, open fireplaces, a superb cobbled terrace inviting you to sit on balmy evenings and gaze across the wide landscape while the wind plays in the poplars. With a nature reserve on the doorstep – dragonflies a speciality – here is an area waiting to be discovered.

Price	€65. €83 for 3.
Rooms	2: 1 double, 1 triple.
Meals	Dinner with wine, €25.
Closed	Rarely.
Directions	From Châtellerault D749 to Vouneuil sur Vienne; left in church square & follow Chambres d'Hôtes signs. Last house on right in hamlet of Chabonne.

Florence & Antoine Penot
Les Hauts de Chabonne,
Chabonne,
86210 Vouneuil sur Vienne, Vienne

Tel   +33 (0)5 49 85 28 25
Fax   +33 (0)5 49 85 22 75
Email penot.antoine@wanadoo.fr
Web   www.chabonne.com

Entry 395   Map 9

Logis du Château du Bois Doucet

Naturally, unstiltedly, aristocratically French, owners and house are full of stories and character: a fine jumble of ten French chairs, bits of ancient furniture, pictures, heirlooms, lamps in the stone-flagged salon, a properly elegant dining room. There are statues indoors and out; large bedrooms bursting with personality – bathrooms too. Monsieur's interests are history and his family, Madame's are art and life – they are a delightful combination of unselfconscious class and flashes of Mediterranean non-conformism. You are very much part of family life in this people- and dog-friendly house.

Price	€70–€80. Suite €130.
Rooms	3: 1 double, 2 family suites.
Meals	Dinner with wine, €30.
Closed	Rarely.
Directions	From A10 exit Poitiers Nord, N10 for Limoges 7km; right to Bignoux; follow signs to Bois Dousset.

Vicomte & Vicomtesse Hilaire
de Villoutreys de Brignac
Logis du Château du Bois Doucet,
86800 Lavoux,
Vienne
Tel   +33 (0)5 49 44 20 26

Entry 396   Map 9

Le Haut Peu

This delightful farming family are rooted in village life, including the local drama group. Monsieur also shares his time with his dream of restoring the 12th-century Villesalem priory. Madame, somewhat shyer, embroidered the exquisite samplers. Both enjoy sharing their simple, stylish, much-loved house with cultured, like-minded guests. The suite is in the old coach house, its kitchen in the bread oven. Finely decorated bedrooms blend with the garden and woodlands (golden orioles, hoopoes, wild orchids…). Visit the goats, watch the cheese-making or fish in their big lake.

Price	€55.
Rooms	3: 2 doubles, 1 suite for 4-5 & kitchen. Extra room for children.
Meals	Dinner with wine, €18.
Closed	Mid-November to mid-February.
Directions	From Poitiers N147 SE to Lussac les Châteaux; D727 E for 21km; left D121 to Journet. There, N for Haims; house 1km on left.

Jacques & Chantal Cochin
Le Haut Peu,
86290 Journet, Vienne
Tel   +33 (0)5 49 91 62 02
Fax   +33 (0)5 49 91 22 01
Email   cochin.chantal@orange.fr
Web   www.ferme-du-haut-peu.fr

Entry 397   Map 9

Poitou – Charentes

Les Écots

The Salvaudons are educated, intelligent farmers, he energetic and down-to-earth, she gentle and smiling, who are committed to the natural way, like swapping travellers' tales and sharing simple, lasting values while providing decent guest rooms in a relaxed and genuine house. There is indeed "more here than the Futuroscope". Don't miss Madame's Limousin specialities – lamb, chicken cooked in honey, vegetable pies – round the family table. The sheep pastures lie in rolling, stream-run country beloved of fisherfolk and Monsieur will take children to meet the animals.

Ethical Collection: Environment; Food.
See page 432..

Price	€38.
Rooms	2 doubles, each with shower & basin, sharing wc.
Meals	Dinner with wine, €15.
Closed	Rarely.
Directions	From Poitiers D741 to Civray; D148 E & D34 to Availles; D100 for Mauprévoir, 3km; signed.

Pierre & Line Salvaudon
Les Écots,
86460 Availles Limousine, Vienne
Tel   +33 (0)5 49 48 59 17
Fax   +33 (0)5 49 48 59 17
Email   pierre.salvaudon@wanadoo.fr
Web   www.les-ecots.info

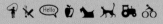

Entry 398   Map 9

Poitou – Charentes

La Théophilière

Jean-Louis, a genial twinkly man, used to farm but now sticks to vegetables, chickens and a role in numerous local events; Geneviève is a perfectionist. Their traditional Poitevin farmhouse, rendered a sunny ochre, has a modern conservatory along its width and rooms opening off either side. You come to it from the back, up a long tree-lined drive, so will be surprised to find it is in the middle of the village. Rooms are fresh and immaculate with great colours, furniture is suitably old: the canopy over the double bed was made for Madame's great-grandmother's wedding. Real and comforting. *Heated pool. Minimum stay 2 nights July/August.*

Price	€58-€70. Family room €82-€96.
Rooms	2: 1 family room; 1 twin with shower & separate wc.
Meals	Dinner with wine, €20.
Closed	Rarely.
Directions	From A10 exit Poitiers Sud N10 for Angoulême to Vivonne; 2nd exit D4 to Champagne St H. & Sommières du C.; right D1 for Civray 8km; left to Champniers; signed.

Geneviève & Jean-Louis Fazilleau
La Théophilière,
86400 Champniers, Vienne
Tel   +33 (0)5 49 87 19 04
Email   jeanlouis.fazilleau@free.fr
Web   chambres-hotes-poitou-charente.ifrance.com

Entry 399   Map 9

Poitou – Charentes

Château de Masseuil

In the big flagstoned kitchen of the crag-perched, pepper-potted château, friends and family chat over the jam-making. Hunting trophies, family portraits and sepia photographs adorn the sunny breakfast room and parade up the stairs; comfortable, fresh bedrooms have old family pieces, a shower each, new beds; charming, unstuffily aristocratic hosts are hugely knowledgeable about local Romanesque art and tell stories of monks and brigands. Sixteenth-century castles didn't have en suite loos: there are chamber pots in case you can't face the stairs! Seemingly remote yet Poitiers is down the road. Wonderful value.

Poitou – Charentes

Château de Tennessus

It's all real: moat, drawbridge, dreams. Two steep stone spirals to "the biggest bedroom in France": granite windowsills, giant hearth, canopied bed, shower snug; on the lower floors of the keep, the medieval family room: vast timbers, good mattresses, arrow slits for windows. Furniture is sober, candles are lit, fires always laid, and you breakfast at a massive table on 14th-century flagstones. Indeed, the whole place is brilliantly authentic, the charming gardens glow from loving care (medieval potager, modern pool), the views reach far, and Pippa is a bundle of energy and generosity. *Children over 5 welcome.*

Price	€65.
Rooms	2: 1 double, 1 twin/double, sharing wc.
Meals	Restaurants 3km.
Closed	Rarely.
Directions	From A10 exit Poitiers Nord N149 for Nantes 12km; at bottom of hill left for Masseuil.

Price	€120–€145.
Rooms	2: 1 double & kitchenette, 1 family suite for 4.
Meals	Gourmet picnic basket with wine, €29.50 p.p.
Closed	Christmas–New Year.
Directions	From A10 exit 29 on N147; N149 W to Parthenay; round Parthenay northbound; on N149 for Bressuire; 7km north of Parthenay right at sign for château.

Alain & Claude Gail
Château de Masseuil,
17 rue du Château,
86190 Quinçay, Vienne

Tel	+33 (0)5 49 60 42 15
Fax	+33 (0)5 49 60 70 15

Nicholas & Philippa Freeland
Château de Tennessus,
79350 Amailloux,
Deux Sèvres

Tel	+33 (0)5 49 95 50 60
Fax	+33 (0)5 49 95 50 62
Email	tennessus@orange.fr
Web	www.tennessus.com

Entry 400   Map 9

Entry 401   Map 9

Poitou – Charentes

Le Moulin de la Borderie

A stylish renovated mill, complete with resident owl, beautiful outdoor pool and modestly intellectual hosts (teacher and doctor) who love their island. Behind smoke-blue shutters, hollyhocks climb the walls and floaty muslins frame tall windows among pastel hues of sand and aqua green. Discover the local seaweed bread, delicious with 'fleur de sel' butter. At breakfast a suspended sail keeps the sun off while you delight in galette charentaise and sweet-scented strawberries, island-grown. Dinner is probably catch of the day – squid, seabass or cooked oysters – then crème caramel and a magnificent view of the stars.

Ethical Collection: Environment; Food. See page 432.

Price	€77–€104.
Rooms	4: 1 double, 1 suite (1 double, 1 twin); 2 doubles, each with separate bathroom.
Meals	Dinner €25.
Closed	Rarely.
Directions	From Saintes A10 for Île d'Oléron; after bridge for St Pierre d'O, 800m; at r'bout entering town right Rue Pierre Loti; 5th turning on left, downhill, Rue de la République 1km; mill on right.

Vanina Thiou
Le Moulin de la Borderie,
184 rue de la République,
17310 Saint Pierre d'Oléron,
Charente-Maritime

Mobile	+33 (0)6 80 45 60 42
Email	lemoulindevany@aol.com
Web	www.lemoulindelaborderie.com

Entry 402   Map 8

Poitou – Charentes

A l'Ombre du Figuier

A rural idyll, wrapped in birdsong. The old farmhouse, lovingly restored and decorated, is simple and pristine; its carpeted rooms under eaves that are polished to perfection overlook a pretty garden where you may picnic. Your hosts are an interesting couple of anglophiles. Thoughtful, stylish Madame serves generous breakfasts with organic homemade jam, cheese, yogurt and cereals, all on local pottery. Monsieur teaches engineering in beautiful La Rochelle: follow his hints and discover the lesser-known treasures there. Luscious lawns are bordered by well-stocked beds. Good value.

Price	€56–€68.
Rooms	3: 1 family suite for 2-4; 1 double, 1 family room, sharing bath (let to same party only).
Meals	Occasional dinner with wine, €23. Bistro walking distance; inn 3km.
Closed	Rarely.
Directions	From La Rochelle N11 E for 11km exit Longèves; D112, signed to village. In village, past church; right at 'bar-pizzas', 1st left, signed. 700m on left.

M-Christine & J-François Prou
A l'Ombre du Figuier,
43 rue du Marais,
17230 Longèves,
Charente-Maritime

Tel	+33 (0)5 46 37 11 15
Email	mcprou@wanadoo.fr
Web	www.alombredufiguier.com

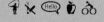

Entry 403   Map 8

Le Clos de la Garenne

Animals everywhere, from the boxer dog to the donkey and the hens! Brigitte and Patrick gave up telecommunications for a dream life in the country and the result is a very happy B&B. Avid collectors, they have decorated their spacious 16th-century house with elegance and eclectic flair. Old and modern rub happy shoulders: traditional armoires, antique treasures, big new beds, a tennis court. The air is full of warm smiles, harmony breathes from walls and woodwork, your hosts are endlessly thoughtful, food is exotic organic and families are positively welcome. *Minimum stay 3 nights July/August. Gite guests on site. Massage & spa.*

Ethical Collection: Food.
See page 432.

Les Grands Vents

In a lovely sleepy village in the heart of wine and cognac country, by the road but peaceful, the former pineau farmhouse has simple limewashed walls and a traditional French décor. You have your own entrance so here you can be as private as you like – but Valérie and Nicolas are easy, generous hosts and happy for you to have the run of the place. Bedrooms, with views onto a well-pruned garden, are large, fresh and catch the morning or evening sun. There's a lush pool and a new covered terrace for four-course dinners full of laugher and conversation – a great find for families. *Sawday self-catering also.*

Price	€67. Triple €77. Studio cottage €127.
Rooms	3: 1 triple, 1 suite for 6. Studio cottage for 2.
Meals	Dinner with wine, €25.
Closed	Rarely.
Directions	From Surgères Gendarmerie & fire station, D115 for Marans & Puyravault 5km, following signs.

Price	€55.
Rooms	2: 1 triple, 1 suite for 4.
Meals	Dinner with wine, €22.
Closed	Rarely.
Directions	From A10 exit 33 E601 to Mauzé sur le Mignon; D911 to Surgères; D939 4km, right to Chervettes; behind iron gates.

Brigitte & Patrick François
Le Clos de la Garenne,
9 rue de la Garenne,
17700 Puyravault, Charente-Maritime
Tel   +33 (0)5 46 35 47 71
Fax   +33 (0)5 46 35 47 91
Email   info@closdelagarenne.com
Web   www.closdelagarenne.com

Valérie & Nicolas Godebout
Les Grands Vents,
17380 Chervettes,
Charente-Maritime
Tel   +33 (0)5 46 35 92 21
Email   godebout@club-internet.fr
Web   www.les-grands-vents.com

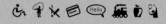

Poitou – Charentes

La Sauvagerie

Beyond the leafy orchard lies the prettiness of La Sauvagerie. Inside you find Madame caring attentively for guests, disabled husband and their comforts. Nearby is Surgères, its beautiful churches and famous creamy butter. Equally lovely is her farmhouse, once the cognac store for the manor: with the right wind you may still catch a whiff of the amber tipple. Rooms are simple old-style and themed with family sailing trophies from the lifetime of seafarers. Supper in Madame's convivial kitchen may be *pommes de terre au diable* from an ancient clay pot on the roaring fire.

Price	€62.
Rooms	4: 1 double, 1 triple; 1 double, 1 suite for 5, each with separate wc.
Meals	Dinner with wine, €22.
Closed	Rarely.
Directions	From Surgères, D115 to Aulnay. Between St Félix and Migré, left into Les Petites Tannières, house signed to left after 25m.

M & Mme Chambonnet-Bonnet
La Sauvagerie,
Les Petites Tannières,
1 rue des Paquerettes, 17330 Migré,
Charente-Maritime
Tel/Fax +33 (0)5 46 33 26 05
Email francoise.chambonnet@wanadoo.fr
Web www.lasauvagerie.com

Entry 406 Map 8

Poitou – Charentes

Le Moulin du Prieuré

A wonderful old wisteria-hung house and a dear hostess who knows and loves her region – what more could one ask? Built in 1600, renovated in 1720, the house stands in a garden of mature trees down to the river Boutonne (aquatic delights and games for young and old). Fresh bedrooms have good beds, big old armoires, marble fireplaces and impeccable colour sense; in the huge guest sitting room, antiques, armchairs, a French billiards table and… bowls of sweets. Madame is an angel – you might be staying with your favourite granny. Spin off on bike trails, visit fabulous Romanesque churches.

Price	€52-€54.
Rooms	2: 1 twin/double, 1 suite for 4.
Meals	Restaurants 3-7km.
Closed	Rarely.
Directions	From Gendarmerie in St Jean d'Angély, D127 NE for Dampierre, 8km. In Antezant, 1st right.

Pierre & Marie-Claude Fallelour
Le Moulin du Prieuré,
10 rue de Maurençon,
17400 Antezant,
Charente-Maritime
Tel +33 (0)5 46 59 94 52
Fax +33 (0)5 46 59 94 52
Email marie-claude.fallelour@club-internet.fr

Entry 407 Map 9

Poitou – Charentes

Les Hortensias

Behind its modest, wisteria-covered mask, this 17th-century former wine-grower's house hides a very pretty face and a magnificent garden that flows through orchard, to trimmed topiary, to potager with blackcurrants for delicious sorbet. Soft duck-egg colours and rich trimmings make it a warm and safe haven. Light, airy bedrooms are immaculate, one with original stone sink, another with pink décor, all with luxurious bathrooms. Your sweet hosts, retired from jobs in agriculture and tourism, have given their all to make it perfect: look at Madame's paintings on the stairwell. Superb value.

Ethical Collection: Environment; Food.
See page 432.

Price	€55-€62.
Rooms	3: 2 doubles, 1 suite for 4.
Meals	Dinner with wine, €22.
Closed	Rarely.
Directions	From A10 exit 34 on D739 to Tonnay Boutonne; left D114 to Archingeay; left for Les Nouillers; house just after turning, with hydrangea at door.

M-Thérèse & J-Pierre Jacques
Les Hortensias, 16 rue des Sablières,
17380 Archingeay,
Charente-Maritime

Tel	+33 (0)5 46 97 85 70
Fax	+33 (0)5 46 97 61 89
Email	jpmt.jacques@wanadoo.fr
Web	www.chambres-hotes-hortensias.com

Entry 408   Map 8

Poitou – Charentes

Le Moulin de la Quine

A totally French house and a thoroughly English couple. Jenny gardens and makes jewellery, with pleasure; John builds his boat for crossing the Atlantic, with dedication; together they have caringly restored their Charentais farmhouse and delight in creating a welcoming atmosphere. Feel free to go your own way, too: you have a separate guest entrance. The beautifully landscaped garden with its pretty windmill (let separately) and croquet lawn has an English feel – but the 'sense of place' remains unmistakably French. And St Savinien is a painter's delight – this really is a lovely part of the country.

Price	€46-€54.
Rooms	2: 1 double, 1 family room for 3-4.
Meals	Dinner with wine, €21. Restaurants 3.5km.
Closed	Christmas.
Directions	From St Savinien bridge D114 along river, under railway, left D124 for Bords 2km; 2nd left after Le Pontreau sign; 200m on right.

John & Jenny Elmes
Le Moulin de la Quine,
17350 St Savinien,
Charente-Maritime

Tel	+33 (0)5 46 90 19 31
Fax	+33 (0)5 46 90 19 31
Email	elmes@club-internet.fr
Web	www.laquine.co.uk

Entry 409   Map 8

Poitou – Charentes

Château Mouillepied

Enchanting Mouillepied ('wet feet' – but today's moat is mostly dry) has been rescued by a delightful pair. Large airy bedrooms – some on the first floor, some in the tower – have a modern Swedish look, with original wooden floors or new boards suitably wide; walls are white, curtains bold red or soft grey. Breakfast is served in the orangery overlooking the gardens, karaoke in the stone-walled lounge. Seek out the fascinating old laundry in the grounds, the pigeon house, bread oven and wine store, pick up a fishing licence at the bakery, stroll along the banks of the Charente. Deeply atmospheric. *Sawday self-catering also.*

Price	€69–€98.
	Cottage €280–€530 per week.
Rooms	8 + 1: 4 doubles, 3 triples,
	1 suite for 4. Cottage for 2-3.
Meals	Restaurant 2km.
Closed	Rarely.
Directions	From A10 exit 35 at Saintes; N137 to Rochefort, right to Ecurat D119. Right for Taillebourg D236; D127 to Saint James; right to Saintes D128, right after 300m, signed.

Pierre & Martine Clément
Château Mouillepied,
17350 Port d'Envaux,
Charente-Maritime

Tel	+33 (0)5 46 90 49 88
Fax	+33 (0)5 46 90 36 91
Email	info@chateaumouillepied.com
Web	www.chateaumouillepied.com

Entry 410　Map 8

Poitou – Charentes

La Jaquetterie

The old virtues of having time for people and living at a gentler pace are here in this authentically furnished, old-fashioned house, and it is so comfortable. These kindly farmers are really worth getting to know; bright-eyed Madame has a wicked sense of humour, their son organises outings to distilleries and quarries, their daughter-in-law rustles up meals for the kitchen table. Stay the night and you're a member of the family. Great old armoires loom in the bedrooms, lace protects lovely antique beds, washrooms have perfectly folded towels and the top-floor's tiny, quilt-covered beds are adorable.

Price	€47. €65 for 3. €80 for 4.
Rooms	2: 1 triple, 1 suite for 2-4.
Meals	Dinner with wine, €20.
Closed	Rarely.
Directions	From A10 exit Saintes N137 for Rochefort & La Rochelle, 11km; D119 to Plassay. House on left on entering village.

Michelle & Jacques Louradour
La Jaquetterie,
17250 Plassay,
Charente-Maritime

Tel	+33 (0)5 46 93 91 88
Fax	+33 (0)5 46 93 48 09
Email	louradour-denis@aviva-assurances.com

Entry 411　Map 8

Poitou – Charentes

La Rotonde

Stupendously confident, with priceless views, this city mansion seems to ride the whole rich story of lovely old Saintes from its Roman glory days. Soft blue river light hovers into high bourgeois rooms to stroke the warm panelling, marble fireplaces, perfect parquet (the studios are less grand). The Rougers love renovating their guest house, and Marie-Laure, calm and talented, has her own sensitive way with classic French furnishings: feminine yet not frilly, rich yet gentle, just ornate enough. Superb (antique) linen and bathrooms, too, little extras and always that elegance.

Price	€84–€100.
Rooms	7: 4 doubles, 1 twin, 2 studios for 2 (each with kitchenette).
Meals	Restaurants in town centre.
Closed	Rarely.
Directions	A10 exit Saintes; at lights before bridge over river, right onto Quai de la République; keep river on left to Place Blair. On right-hand side, on corner of Rue Monconseil.

Marie-Laure Rouger
La Rotonde,
2 rue Monconseil,
17100 Saintes,
Charente-Maritime
Tel   +33 (0)5 46 74 74 44
Email   laure@laboutiquedelarotonde.com
Web   www.laboutiquedelarotonde.com

Entry 412   Map 8

Poitou – Charentes

Le Clos du Plantis

Your hostess brazenly indulges her passion for old buildings in this area of vast architectural wealth. She'll teach you stone-wall restoration, the intricacies of the Romanesque style or how to garden beautifully – the creamy local stone is a perfect foil for flowers and the veg is organic. In the old cognac press, the cool, light garden bedrooms are big and uncluttered, effective in their pale colours with a few well-chosen pieces each and exquisite bathrooms. Cognac nearby, the island beaches not too far and such a delightful, intelligent couple, full of fun and sparkle, make this a special place to stay.

Price	€58–€65. Triple €84. Suite €103.
Rooms	3: 1 double, 1 triple, 1 family suite for 4.
Meals	Restaurants 1–2km.
Closed	Rarely.
Directions	From A10 exit St Jean d'Angély to Matha/Cognac. At Matha, for Cognac (not Sonnac); follow signs 'Le Clos du Plantis'. Next hamlet, Le Goulet; signed.

Frédérique Thill-Toussaint
Le Clos du Plantis,
1 rue du Pont, Le Goulet,
17160 Sonnac,
Charente-Maritime
Tel   +33 (0)5 46 25 07 91
Email   auplantis@wanadoo.fr
Web   www.auplantis.com

Entry 413   Map 9

Poitou – Charentes

Blue Sturgeon

Tiny St Seurin was the first place in Europe to produce caviar, and caviar is served here with a flourish by Robert, artist and chef. He and Eileen have created guest bedrooms in hip-hotel style, stitching contemporary interiors to the historic frame of a 1700s building that started life as a tea warehouse. Be comforted by satin bedcovers and stacked cushions, modern paintings and Provençal potions. The ground-floor rooms face the garden; the suite has its main bed on the mezzanine and a balcony overlooking the restaurant below. A big garden, a small pool, fields of nodding sunflowers and a beach down the road.

Price	€95-€120.
Rooms	5: 1 double, 3 twins/doubles, 1 family suite for 4-6.
Meals	Dinner €35. Wine €15-€27. Restaurants 10-minute drive.
Closed	Rarely.
Directions	From Bordeaux A10 for Paris; exit 37 Royan on D730 approx. 14km; left D2 to St Fort/Gironde; right D145 through Mortagne/Gironde to St Seurin; house on left.

Robert Stansfield
Blue Sturgeon,
3 rue de la Cave,
17120 St Seurin d'Uzet,
Charente-Maritime
Tel +33 (0)5 46 74 17 18
Email reservations@bluesturgeon.com
Web www.bluesturgeon.com

Entry 414   Map 8

Poitou – Charentes

La Font Bétou

Both former market researchers, Londoner Gordon and Parisienne Laure thoroughly enjoy people. Laure cooks because she loves it and breakfast is a spread. The two big, spotlessly clean rooms in the annexe are pretty and welcoming with tea-making stuff and plenty of stone and wood. Sit by the hosts' sitting-room fire or by the pool; the kitchen door is always open. Once a modest inn for train travellers, the house still overlooks the old station (now another house), and there's a frog-filled pond behind. As the owners say, this is not a place that pretends to be anything, it just is. *Minimum stay 3 nights July/August.*

Price	€65.
Rooms	2: 1 split-level double, 1 twin, each with sitting area downstairs.
Meals	Dinner with wine, €27.
Closed	January-February.
Directions	N10 S; exit Montlieu la Garde; D730 for Montguyon. 1km after Orignolles, right to house, signed gite La Font Bétou.

Laure Tarrou & Gordon Flude
La Font Bétou,
17210 Orignolles,
Charente-Maritime
Tel +33 (0)5 46 04 02 52
Email lauretarrou@gmail.com
Web www.fontbetou.com

Entry 415   Map 9

Poitou – Charentes

Le Chatelard

This is a gem of a place to stay, both grand and intimate. Béatrice inherited the exquisitely French neo-gothic château and she lovingly protects it from the worst of modernisation (though the hurricane took its toll and trees have had to be replanted). Sleep between old linen sheets, sit in handsome old chairs and be charmed by a bedroom in a tower. The sitting room has that unusual quirk, a window over the fireplace, the dining room a panelled ceiling studded with plates. Béatrice, a teacher, and Christopher, a lecturer in philosophy, are interesting, cultured hosts who enjoy eating with their guests.

Price	€50-€60.
Rooms	4: 1 double; 1 double, 1 twin, 1 family suite, each with separate wc.
Meals	Dinner with wine, €20. Restaurant 1km.
Closed	Rarely.
Directions	From A10 exit 36 to Pons, Archiac & Barbezieux; D731 for Chalais 12km. After Passirac, 1st right at roadside cross; up leafy drive.

Béatrice de Castelbajac &
Christopher Macann
Le Chatelard,
Passirac, 16480 Brossac, Charente
Tel   +33 (0)5 45 98 71 03
Fax   +33 (0)5 45 98 71 03
Email   c.macann@wanadoo.fr
Web   www.lechatelard.tk

Entry 416   Map 9

Poitou – Charentes

Le Bourg

Stone cottages, nodding hollyhocks, ducks in the lane: Mareuil epitomises rural France, and the house sits in its heart. Arrive to a sweeping drive, an immaculate pool, a grand façade and Ron and Vanessa, who have travelled the world. After a final posting in Paris they have landed in sunny Charente, and are happy. Bedrooms are bright, airy and comfortable, with farmhousey bathrooms; dinners, in the ample dining room or the cosy snug, are gastronomic, cosmopolitan, entertaining and preceded by pineau de Charente. You are surrounded by sunflowers and vines and Cognac is close. Friendly, interesting, great fun.

Price	€70.
Rooms	3: 2 doubles, 1 twin.
Meals	Dinner with wine, €25.
Closed	Rarely.
Directions	D939 from Rouillac for Matha. At Sonneville left to Mareuil. In village take Jarnac road up hill; house on left with green gates.

Vanessa Bennett-Dixon
Le Bourg,
16170 Mareuil,
Charente
Tel   +33 (0)5 45 66 29 75
Email   lebourg-charente@wanadoo.fr
Web   www.lebourg-charente.com

Entry 417   Map 9

Poitou – Charentes

Le Chiron

There's a well-lived-in air to this big old cognac house, all chandeliers and ceiling roses. The Chambre Rose is extremely pink and the toile de Jouy triple has a rustic elegance. Bathrooms are more functional than luxurious but with so much natural beauty to hand who wants to stay in anyway? Madame's regional cooking is a treat, served in a conservatory that seats a good number, and your hosts stay and chat (in French, mostly!) when they can. They'll also show you the fascinating old cognac still. Spacious, off the beaten track and great for families (they run a campsite next door). *Mobile homes available at the farm campsite.*

Price	€45. Suite €75.
Rooms	6: 2 doubles, 1 twin, 2 triples, 1 family suite for 4.
Meals	Dinner with wine, €18.
Closed	Rarely.
Directions	From A10 Pons exit D700 for Barbezieux Archiac. After Echebrune, D148 (1st left) for Lonzac-Celles; right D151 & follow signs.

Micheline & Jacky Chainier
Le Chiron,
16130 Salles d'Angles,
Charente
Tel +33 (0)5 45 83 72 79
Email mchainier@voila.fr

Entry 418 Map 9

Poitou – Charentes

La Fontaine des Arts

Along the narrow street in the charming, bustling town, through the heavy oak gates, under the ancient arch, is a cottage by the Charente with a little boat for trips upriver. Marie-France, beautifully coiffed, combines the glamour of the city with the warmth of a country hostess: guests love her. Breakfast in the conservatory alongside Gérard's easel and piano, or in the courtyard by the prettily fountain'd pool. Décor is quintessential French: shiny gold taps, striped and flowered walls, a white dressing table. There's a shared guest kitchenette – and a surprising open-gallery bathroom in the double. Great for summer.

Price	€62-€69.
Rooms	3: 1 double, 1 twin, 1 triple.
Meals	Restaurant within walking distance. Guest kitchen.
Closed	Rarely.
Directions	RN10 between Angoulême & Poitiers, exit Mansle; towards centre ville; between tourist office & L'Hotel Beau Rivage, straight on to No. 13.

Marie-France Pagano
La Fontaine des Arts,
13 rue du Temple,
16230 Mansle, Charente
Tel +33 (0)5 45 69 13 56
Email mfpagano@wanadoo.fr
Web www.la-fontaine-des-arts.com

Entry 419 Map 9

Poitou – Charentes

La Cochère

Cool off by the lush pool, listen to the clacking and cheering of summer Sundays' boules. Kathy, John and Bob the St Bernard are the proud protectors of this dreamlike place, where the long checked table groans with fresh compôtes, croissants and coffee at breakfast, and the tranquil garden – John's delight – is sprinkled with lanterns at dusk. In the old coach house, antique iron beds wear floral quilts and crisp linen, and pretty stone peeps through timeworn render. Who would not fall for this heart-warming blend of sophistication and rusticity in a sleepy farming village?

Poitou – Charentes

Le Logis de la Broue

Beautifully secluded, the 15th-century Logis is built round a big courtyard bursting with hydrangeas and topiary. Inside is breathtaking: expect all the charm of a château and luxurious toile de Jouy'd bedrooms off a wonderfully wonky landing. The triple has chartreuse walls and rich floral curtains; the suite's main room flourishes great oak boards, panelled cupboards and gilt touches. Salon floors are warmed by Persian rugs, views take in private hectares and Madame's horses. All is immaculately French, including the grounds and the poolside bar for cool drinks and outdoor showers. Enjoy the pineau tastings! *Sawday self-catering also.*

Price	€58. Triple €68.
Rooms	4: 2 doubles, 1 twin. Studio: 1 triple (May–Sept only).
Meals	Dinner with wine, €25.
Closed	Christmas.
Directions	A10 to Poitiers; RN10 S from Poitiers; 10km S of exit for Ruffec leave N10 for Salles de Villefagnan on D27; in centre of village by Salles des Fêtes, right to Villefagnan; house after 200m on right.

Price	€90.
Rooms	2: 1 triple, 1 suite for 4.
Meals	Dinner with wine, €25.
Closed	Never.
Directions	From Paris N10 exit Mansle, then D739 to Saint Claud; house on right.

John & Kathy Anderson
La Cochère, Le Bourg,
16700 Salles de Villefagnan,
Charente
Tel   +33 (0)5 45 30 34 60
Email la.cochere@wanadoo.fr
Web   www.lacochere.com

Sylviane & Vincent Casper
Le Logis de la Broue
16450 Saint Claud, Charente
Tel   +33 (0)5 45 71 43 96
Email sylviane.casper@wanadoo.fr
Web   www.logisdelabroue.com

Entry 420   Map 9

Entry 421   Map 9

Poitou – Charentes

Lesterie

Visiting children are welcome to muck in: there are dogs, playhouse, badminton rackets and toys. This English farming family lives in a roadside country house with many original delights. Balconies look out onto parkland and their crops, while a sweeping staircase leads to very basic bedrooms and bathrooms. Two are next to the family's, two are in a dormitory-style attic. Your hosts are busy but sometimes find time to sit round the table to meet guests. For evenings there's a little guest sitting room in soft pinks and greens. Bring your line and tackle – there's fishing in the lake opposite.

Price	From €45–€55.
Rooms	4: 2 doubles, 1 twin; 1 double with shower, sharing wc.
Meals	Dinner with wine, €18.
Closed	November–March.
Directions	From Confolens, D948 for Limoges for 4km; sign on road.

Stephen & Polly Hoare
Lesterie,
Saint Maurice des Lions,
16500 Confolens, Charente
Tel	+33 (0)5 45 84 18 33
Fax	+33 (0)5 45 84 01 45
Email	polly.hoare@libertysurf.fr
Web	www.lesterie.com

Entry 422   Map 9

Poitou – Charentes

Le Pit

What a remote, interesting and gentle place – heaven for walkers, and for children. Pets doze by the fire, llamas munch on the hillside. Simple, floral bedrooms are in a converted outbuilding, the larger one overlooking the lake. Dinner is unusual (venison pâté perhaps), delicious (produce from the precious vegetable garden) and preceded by a glass of homemade pineau. Alex left London for French farming with a difference and runs a thriving farm shop; Hélène loves pergolas: there are many little corners of rustic charm and colour from which to enjoy the fascinating surroundings. Fun and hugely welcoming.

Price	€50. Triple €73. Quadruple €95.
Rooms	2: 1 triple, 1 quadruple.
Meals	Dinner with wine, €25.
Closed	Rarely.
Directions	From Poitiers D741 S for Confolens 50km. 10km after Pressac, left on D168 for St Germain de Confolens; sign after 2km.

Alex & Hélène Everitt
Le Pit,
Lessac, 16500 Confolens, Charente
Tel	+33 (0)5 45 84 27 65
Email	everitt16@aol.com
Web	www.lepit.fr

Entry 423   Map 9

Aquitaine

Aquitaine

Domaine les Sapins

You couldn't be deeper into wine country than this. Alain is a wine broker of muscular personality who may be persuaded to talk wine of an evening – in excellent English. He paints, too. Natalie's father was born in this fine rambling house: it's clearly a family home, despite its size, and has comfortable modern-traditional bedrooms. Your hosts both enjoy chatting with guests over an aperitif and planning the most congenial seating arrangement at the dinner tables. The house is set back from the village road (front rooms are double-glazed) in a large garden with a breathtaking counter-current pool.

Aquitaine

Château Bavolier

The classic pale-stone building lies low among unfussy lawns and trees. Inside, the space, light and simplicity of décor are striking. Your charming talented hostess uses a restrained palette to give a floaty, dreamy quality: beige and white paint, pale-straw sisal, impressive decorations (she is restoring some hand-painted panelling). The first bedroom is beautiful in white, gilt and black Louis XVI. The second is enormous, breathtaking, with myriad windows, play of dark and light across the huge brass bed and monochrome oils of Paris. And in each a magnificent chandelier. Amazing.

Price	€65-€85. Suite €155-€255.
Rooms	5: 3 twins/doubles, 2 suites: 1 for 4, 1 for 6.
Meals	Dinner €25. Wine €20-€50.
Closed	Rarely.
Directions	From Bordeaux A630 exit 7; D1 for Le Verdon sur Soulac; skirt around Castelnau; D1215 for St Laurent 1km to Bouqueyran. Sign on left before traffic light.

Price	€90-€130.
Rooms	2 doubles.
Meals	Restaurant nearby.
Closed	October-March.
Directions	From St André de Cubzac D137 to St Christoly de Blaye. Right to St Savin after 50m, left after 2-3 mins; château on right.

Alain & Natalie Genestine
Domaine les Sapins,
62 avenue du Médoc,
33480 Moulis en Médoc, Gironde

Tel	+33 (0)5 56 58 18 26
Fax	+33 (0)5 56 58 28 45
Email	domaine-les-sapins@wanadoo.fr
Web	www.domaine-les-sapins.com

Ann Roberts
Château Bavolier,
33920 St Christoly de Blaye,
Gironde

Tel	+33 (0)5 57 42 59 74
Email	info@chateau-bavolier.com
Web	www.chateau-bavolier.com

Aquitaine

Château de la Grave

Come for three sweeping bedrooms, two balconies with vineyard views, a stone entrance hall – and a wrought-iron terrace for a glass of the Bassereaus' own dry white semillon. They are a hard-working and confident young couple in an 18th-century château with too much good taste to make it sumptuous – thank heavens! It is relaxed and easy – even busy – with three children, decorative bantams all over the garden and deer in the woods. Breakfast is on the terrace, wine-tasting in the magnificent *salle de dégustation*. The small pool is for evening dippers rather than sun-worshippers. Good value.

Price	€75–€90. Family room €120.
Rooms	3: 1 double, 1 triple, 1 family room for 4.
Meals	Restaurants in Bourg.
Closed	February & 2 weeks in August.
Directions	From A10 exit 40a or 40b through St André de Cubzac; D669 through Bourg for Blaye; quickly right D251 for Berson for 1km; sign on right, up lane.

M & Mme Bassereau
Château de la Grave,
33710 Bourg sur Gironde, Gironde

Tel	+33 (0)5 57 68 41 49
Fax	+33 (0)5 57 68 49 26
Email	reservation@chateaudelagrave.com
Web	www.chateaudelagrave.com

Entry 426   Map 8

Aquitaine

Le Castel de Camillac

Perched above vineyards and the lazy Dordogne, the perfect mini-château. Madame has restored its 18th-century spirit with passion, giving rooms delicious drama: panelled walls, vast tapestries, Turkish rugs, elegant antiques. Bedrooms, gleaming with polished wood and lush fabrics, feel like intimate family rooms while beams and odd-shaped but sparkling bathrooms add to the charm. Breakfast in the voluptuous dining room or on the terrace, swim in the discreet circular pool, play tennis on the floodlit court, enjoy a round of billiards by the wood-burner. A rich experience, 30 minutes from Bordeaux.

Price	€80–€90.
Rooms	3 doubles.
Meals	Restaurant 2km.
Closed	Occasionally.
Directions	A10 exit St André de Cubzac for Bourg sur Gironde; thro' Bourg, cont. 1.5km, left to Pain de Sucre. Entering Pain de Sucre small street on right after approx. 10m. Keep right round wall.

Élisabeth Frape
Le Castel de Camillac,
1 Camillac,
33710 Bourg, Gironde

Tel	+33 (0)5 57 68 29 09
Email	elisabeth.frape@tele2.fr
Web	lecasteldecamillac.com

Entry 427   Map 8

Aquitaine

83 rue de Patay

Martine may be new to B&B but she's used to making guests feel welcome: she owns a restaurant in the middle of the old town. Le Loup has been serving local specialities since 1932: you will probably want to pay a visit. This old stone townhouse is a welcome retreat after days visiting the city (ten minutes by tram) or those renowned vineyards. Martine has given it a light modern touch which works well. Your bedroom is approached up a curved stone staircase and you have the floor to yourselves. It overlooks a small courtyard garden and has a desk and other pieces stencilled by a friend.

Price	€65.
Rooms	1 twin/double.
Meals	Madame's restaurant near Cathedral.
Closed	Rarely.
Directions	From Bordeaux south take Les Boulevards to Barrière de Pessac; 1st right, right again onto Rue de Patay.

Martine Peiffer
83 rue de Patay,
33000 Bordeaux,
Gironde
Tel   +33 (0)5 56 99 41 74
Email   mpeifferma95@numericable.fr

Entry 428   Map 8

Aquitaine

Ecolodge des Chartrons

A many-splendoured delight: city-centre and eco-friendly, with lovely materials and the warmth of simplicity. Your relaxed and friendly hosts have put their earth-saving principles to work, stripping the wonderful wide floorboards, insulating with cork and wool, fitting solar water heating and sun pipes to hyper-modern shower rooms, organic linen and blankets to beds and providing all-organic breakfasts. At the bottom of this quiet road flows the Garonne where cafés, shops and galleries teem in converted warehouses (English wine merchants traded here 300 years ago) and a mirror fountain baffles the mind.

Ethical Collection: Environment; Community; Food. See page 432.

Price	€110–€130.
Rooms	4 doubles.
Meals	Restaurants nearby.
Closed	Rarely.
Directions	On foot from cathedral: west on Cours d'Alsace & de Lorraine to river; left along quay 1.5km to Quai des Chartrons; Rue Raze on left. Ask owner about car approach & parking.

Véronique Daudin
Ecolodge des Chartrons,
23 rue Raze,
33000 Bordeaux, Gironde
Tel   +33 (0)5 56 81 49 13
Email   ecolodge33@free.fr
Web   www.ecolodgedeschartrons.com

Entry 429   Map 8

Aquitaine

Château Lestange

We are filled with admiration for Anne-Marie, who works so hard to keep this proud old place and its vineyards afloat. Built in 1645, it was 'modernised' after the Revolution, but the faded Louis XV paintwork and imperfect tiles merely add to its charm. Beautiful wooden floors, panelled walls and old furniture create a well lived-in feel, and the very private family suites, furnished with mirrors and portraits Anne-Marie is still unearthing from the attic, are capacious. Bathrooms are incongruously modern. Breakfast in a vast room beneath a grand mirror; stroll to dinner in the restaurant down the road.

Aquitaine

Château Monlot

If you appreciate good wine you will enjoy this coolly restrained, very beautiful manor among the vines, just a mile from St Émilion. It has been in the family for nine generations, though the owners leave their delightful nephew and relaxed manager to look after you. You will almost certainly be invited to taste the tempting goods in the cellars. Charming bedrooms, with plain sandstone or painted walls and sober antiques, offer space, comfort and tranquillity and the shrubby garden has an arch of trees that gives dappled shade as you walk towards the distant statue.

Price	€90–€100. €110–€120 for 3.
Rooms	2 family suites for 3.
Meals	Restaurant in village.
Closed	Rarely.
Directions	From Bordeaux take Rocade ring-road exit 22; after 6km left at r'bout to Quinsac; halfway up hill, on left (porch).

Price	€80–€98.
Rooms	5: 4 doubles, 1 twin.
Meals	Restaurants 2km. Guest kitchen.
Closed	Rarely.
Directions	From A10 exit St André de Cubzac through Libourne for Bergerac; 3km after Bigaroux left D234E for St Laurent; right before r'way for St Hippolyte; house on left.

	Anne–Marie Thomas
	Château Lestange,
	33360 Quinsac, Gironde
Tel	+33 (0)9 77 96 49 26
Fax	+33 (0)5 56 20 86 14
Email	charmet@chateau-lestange.com
Web	www.chateau-lestange.com

	Bernard & Béatrice Rivals
	Château Monlot,
	St Hippolyte,
	33330 St Émilion, Gironde
Tel	+33 (0)5 57 74 49 47
Fax	+33 (0)5 57 24 62 33
Email	mussetrivals@chateaumonlot.com
Web	www.chateaumonlot.com

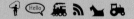

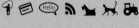

Aquitaine

Domaine de Barrouil

As befits its calling, this old winegrower's house stands in a sea of vines whose liquid fruits you will taste. Inside this colourful and immaculate house, greens, reds and creams set off gilt-framed mirrors, fine bathrooms and bedcovers made by Madame. Your hosts believe in big thick towels too. They have lived in French Guiana so Madame's superb French dinners, served in the beautifully tiled dining room, may bring echoes of more exotic lands. She is charming and chatty, a former English teacher; he knows masses about wine. Ask about new watercolour painting classes. *Minimum stay 3 nights June-September.*

Price	€55-€85.
Rooms	4: 2 doubles, 1 twin, 1 family suite for 2-4.
Meals	Dinner with wine, €25.
Closed	Rarely.
Directions	A10 exit St André de Cubzac to Libourne Bergerac. At Castillon, D17 south for 8km; at D126 crossroad, turn left; 1st house on left.

Annie & Michel Ehrsam
Domaine de Barrouil,
Bossugan,
33350 Castillon La Bataille,
Gironde

Tel/Fax +33 (0)5 57 40 59 12
Email info@barrouil.com
Web www.barrouil.com

Entry 432   Map 9

Aquitaine

Château de Carbonneau

Big château bedrooms bedecked in soft linens with splashes of splendid detail, a fine old bed in the Peony room, huge bathrooms done with rich tiles — here is a self-assured family house where quality is fresh, history stalks and there's plenty of space for three young Ferrières and a dozen guests. Visit Wilfred's winery and taste the talent handed down by his forebears. Jacquie, a relaxed dynamic New Zealander, provides tasty alternatives to the ubiquitous duck cuisine and a relaxed approach to dining; a dab hand at interiors, she has also cultivated a luminescent, airy guest sitting room close to the orangerie.

Price	€90-€130.
Rooms	5: 2 doubles, 3 twins/doubles.
Meals	Dinner €25. Wine €8-€20.
Closed	December-February.
Directions	D936 to Castillon la Bataille-Bergerac; from Réaux, right to Gensac, Pessac; at r'bout, D18 to Ste Foy le Gde; 2km on right.

Jacquie Franc de Ferrière
Château de Carbonneau,
33890 Pessac sur Dordogne,
Gironde

Tel +33 (0)5 57 47 46 46
Fax +33 (0)5 57 47 42 26
Email carbonneau@wanadoo.fr
Web www.chateau-carbonneau.com

Entry 433   Map 9

Aquitaine

La Cigogne

Croaking frogs, prune-drying paraphernalia and a wacky springwater pool – this is rural, unstuffy, great fun. In its leafy garden, La Cigogne the (name of the nearby stream) is a typical farmhouse inherited by Madame and modernised by this charmingly natural couple to give simple and wonderfully individual guest rooms, each with its own vine- and rose-shaded terrace. There's a cosy sitting room for winter evenings; the huge barn, its old mangers still intact, makes a comfortable retreat – with billiards – for damp summer days. Monsieur, a talented golfer, is happy to give you a free lesson and cycle paths pass the door.

Price	€70.
Rooms	3: 2 doubles, 1 twin.
Meals	Dinner with wine, €20.
Closed	December-February.
Directions	From La Réole D670 for Sauveterre 1km; right D 668 to Monségur; right D16 for Ste Gemme 2.5km; after 3 bends left for Château les Arqueys; house 500m.

Yves & Véronique Denis
La Cigogne,
5 le Grand Janot,
33580 Sainte Gemme, Gironde
Tel   +33 (0)5 56 71 19 70
Email   lacigogne.33@orange.fr
Web   www.chambres-lacigogne.fr

Entry 434   Map 9

Aquitaine

Maison Cameleyre

Tall pines guard the clearing, tall timbers support the 300-year-old buildings in a world of vertical wood on horizontal green, with ancient oaks for shade and luscious mushrooms. Emma and Thierry's barn conversion is full of peace and natural country finishes (the farmhouse is their space) and has pride of place: lovely big rooms, soft textures, gentle light. Emma, full of charm and friendliness, loves cooking and gives Aga demos; make sure you eat in one night. They run de-stress weekends too – super people. And there's a cool, serene outdoor pool. *Ask about courses in surfing, sailing & cookery.*

Ethical Collection: Environment; Food. See page 432.

Price	€64.
Rooms	3 twins/doubles.
Meals	Dinner with wine, €20.
Closed	Mid-December to January.
Directions	N10 Bordeaux & Bayonne exit 15 for Escource; at r'bout D44 to village; D63 for Mézos; house in Cameleyre on right, after 3km sign at entrance.

Emma & Thierry Bernabeu
Maison Cameleyre,
Quartier Cameleyre,
40210 Escource, Landes
Tel   +33 (0)5 58 04 22 02
Fax   +33 (0)5 58 04 22 04
Email   tbernabe@club-internet.fr
Web   www.cameleyre.fr

Entry 435   Map 13

Aquitaine

Moulin Vieux

A house lost in a forest, its windows opening onto endless oaks and pines with mere and river beyond. Liliane, a lovable person, joins you in the warm conservatory for tasty organic meals. Bedrooms are small and simply furnished with a touch of Liliane's son's artistry in a marbled or frescoed wall; colours are restful, shower rooms are very basic. In the salon: a trompe l'oeil of the Enchanted Forest, a piano and masses of books, in the huge kitchen an open fire. The setting is tremendous and springtime walks yield birdsong and wildflower treasures. *Ask about yoga weekends.*

Price	€32-€43.
Rooms	2: 1 double, 1 twin.
Meals	Dinner with wine, €16.
Closed	Rarely.
Directions	From Mont de Marsan D834 to Garein; left D57 for Ygos & Tartas; follow signs: 1km of lane to house.

Liliane Jehl
Moulin Vieux,
40420 Garein, Landes
Tel   +33 (0)5 58 51 61 43
Fax   +33 (0)5 58 51 61 43

Entry 436   Map 13

Aquitaine

Domaine d'Agès

In an intriguing mixture of typical brickwork and colonial verandas, this noble manor stands among fabulous old hardwoods and acres of pines. Nature rejoices, cranes fly overhead, thoroughbreds grace the paddock (the Hayes breed horses), hens range free and Madame deploys boundless energy to ply you with exquisite food from the potager, myriad teas, lovely antique-filled, sweet-coloured bedrooms (with her own framed embroidery): she adores entertaining. Monsieur smiles, while teenage Jonathan is all discretion. A huge open fire, baby grand piano and panelled sitting room tell it perfectly.

Ethical Collection: Food.
See page 432.

Price	€65-€80.
Rooms	3: 1 double, 1 twin, 1 suite for 2.
Meals	Dinner with wine, €30.
Closed	Rarely.
Directions	N10 Bordeaux & Bayonne exit Morcenx; D38 for Mont de Marsan; in Ygos right to Ousse Suzan; in Ousse pass 'Chez Jojo'; signed Chambres d'Hôtes; up lane; Domaine 1.5km on left.

Élisabeth Haye
Domaine d'Agès,
40110 Ousse Suzan, Landes
Tel   +33 (0)5 58 51 82 28
Email   giteslandes@hotmail.fr
Web   www.hotes-landes.com

Entry 437   Map 13

Aquitaine

Domaine de Sengresse

Two hours from Spain is the undiscovered Landes – and this ravishing 17th-century domaine. A solid stone house, a cathedral-like barn, an elegant pool... red squirrels and woodpeckers in three luscious hectares and a 'petite maison' (petite only in name!) whose bread oven once served the area's farms: such are the riches in store. A Godin stove and six-oven Aga feed today's guests in gourmet style, while rooms are bathed in light and everything sparkles, from the luxurious bedrooms with their calming colours to the library brimful of books. More country hotel than B&B, run by the most hospitable people.

Price	€95–€125.
Rooms	4: 3 doubles, 1 twin.
Meals	Dinner with wine, €25–€35.
Closed	Rarely.
Directions	12km from N124 Dax/Mont de Marsan; exit Tartas for Mugron D924; 4km right Mugron D332; junc. with D3 right to Mugron. 2nd right Gouts D18; entrance on right after Cap Blanc Kiwi.

	Michèle & Rob McLusky & Sasha Ibbotson
	Domaine de Sengresse, Route de Gouts, 40250 Souprosse, Landes
Tel	+33 (0)5 58 97 78 34
Email	sengresse@hotmail.fr
Web	www.sengresse.com

Entry 438   Map 13

Aquitaine

Villa Ty Gias

Golfers rejoice! You look down on the 13th hole of the Seignosse Golf Club; ask Monsieur or Madame to join you in a round. Great surfing is almost as close. Light, birdsong and ocean breezes whisper round this Californian villa and its balmy garden with pool so don't be daunted by the residential area or the steep drive. Up and down go the pale wooden decks connecting living spaces and levels, waves of light wash over natural colours, finishes and fabrics that are gentle on the eye and Madame's exotic pieces. She revels in guests' appreciation of their soft, clean-cut rooms and alfresco brunches. Fabulous.

Price	€65–€100. Suite €120–€180.
Rooms	3: 1 double, 1 twin, 1 suite for 4.
Meals	Restaurants nearby.
Closed	Rarely.
Directions	A63 exit 10 for St Vincent de Tyrosse & Seignosse; on for Golf 3km; over r'bout, 800m; left into Ave. de Morfontaine, 200m, blue house, signed.

	Jean-Luc & Noëllie Annic
	Villa Ty Gias, 1 avenue Hilton Head, 40510 Seignosse, Landes
Tel	+33 (0)5 58 41 64 29
Fax	+33 (0)5 58 41 64 29
Email	tygias@wanadoo.fr
Web	perso.wanadoo.fr/tygias

Entry 439   Map 13

Aquitaine

Château de Bezincam

An atmosphere of dream-like tranquillity wafts over this grand and appealing old French country house, with its elegant doors and polished oak floors. Just outside the park gates is the beautiful river Adour, abundant in bird and wildlife – every ten years or so it comes and kisses the terrace steps. Two of the gilt-mirrored bedrooms overlook the water and a great spread of meadows where animals graze. There is a vast choice for 'flexitime' breakfast on the terrace or in the rustic-chic dining room. Madame, an energetic and interesting hostess, was a publisher in Paris for many years.

Price	€60-€70.
Rooms	3: 2 doubles, 1 triple.
Meals	Restaurants 2-5km.
Closed	Never.
Directions	From A63 exit 8 to St Geours de Maremne; D17 S for 5km to Saubusse; right just before bridge; château 600m on right.

Claude Dourlet
Château de Bezincam,
600 quai de Bezincam,
Saubusse les Bains,
40180 Dax, Landes
Tel/Fax +33 (0)5 58 57 70 27
Email dourlet.bezincam@orange.fr
Web www.bezincam.fr

🐦 🍴 Hello 🐈 ♻️

Entry 440   Map 13

Aquitaine

Maison Capcazal de Pachioù

Fall asleep by a crackling fire, wake to the clucking of the hens. Be moved by this house, with original panelling (1610) and contents accumulated by the family for 14 generations. Portraits from the 17th century onwards, spectacular bedrooms with canopied antique beds, strong colours, luscious armoires, embroidered linen. One luminous bathroom has a marble-topped washstand. Dining room and sitting room are handsome: twin grandfather clocks, terracotta tiles and a huge stone fireplace. François has stepped into his mother's shoes seamlessly, and does brilliant dinners. Exceptional.

Ethical Collection: Food.
See page 432 for details.

Price	€50-€90.
Rooms	4 doubles.
Meals	Dinner with wine, €20.
Closed	Rarely.
Directions	From Dax D947 for Pau & Orthez; from r'bout at end of town on for 10km; at r'bout on D947 ignore sign for Mimbaste; next right C16; follow discreet yellow signs for 1km.

François Dufourcet-Alberca
Maison Capcazal de Pachioù,
606 route de Pachiou,
40350 Mimbaste, Landes
Tel +33 (0)5 58 55 30 54
Fax +33 (0)5 58 55 30 54
Email francois.alberca@wanadoo.fr
Web www.capcazaldepachiou.com

🚶 🐦 Hello 🍎 📶 🐈 🐈

Entry 441   Map 13

Aquitaine

Domaine de Peyron

The family estate – a pretty cluster of beautifully maintained buildings – has been feted in design magazines; you can tell that Maylis has adored creating her interiors. Three bedrooms lie peacefully in the barn, alongside a glowing salon. One is wood-panelled, like a swish ski lodge; one, with ceiling fan and draped four-poster, has its heart in Africa; all are luxurious. The Cottards' five children frolic in the pool in high summer – you may prefer out of season – and the views are far-reaching. Maylis loves people and is a great cook: dinners are intimate or convivial, breakfasts are feasts.

Price	€70-€85.
Rooms	3 doubles.
Meals	Dinner €27. Lunch €20. Wine €16-€45. Guest kitchenette.
Closed	Never.
Directions	From Hagetmau D2 to St Cricq Chalosse; through village; on outskirts fork left, signed.

Maylis & Louis Cottard
Domaine de Peyron,
240 chemin de Bordes,
40700 St Cricq Chalosse, Landes
Tel +33 (0)5 58 79 85 64
Email lcottard@wanadoo.fr
Web www.domainedepeyron.com

Entry 442   Map 13

Aquitaine

Château de Monbet

The miniature château in its secluded setting rejoices in a fine chestnut staircase, a veranda paved with rare Bidache stone, high ceilings, old prints, a glimpse of the Pyrenees and the call of a peacock. Madame is a gem, gracious and charming – she teaches yoga, paints, is a long-distance walker and a committed vegetarian. There are 15 hectares of parkland to wander and a vast lawn for wedding parties. The rooms, large and traditionally decorated, have gleaming parquet floors and relatively little 'château' furniture. Note that the cheaper room is somewhat spartan and has its shower down the corridor.

Price	€50-€80.
Rooms	2: 1 twin/double; 1 double with separate shower.
Meals	Restaurant in village, 1.3km.
Closed	November-March, except by arrangement.
Directions	A64 exit 6 for Peyrehorade; continue to St Lon les Mines & follow château signs.

Mme Hubert de Lataillade
Château de Monbet,
40300 St Lon les Mines,
Landes
Tel +33 (0)5 58 57 80 68
Email chateau.de.monbet@wanadoo.fr
Web www.chateaudemonbet.fr

Entry 443   Map 13

Aquitaine

Villa Le Goëland

It is lush, lavish, inviting. Dominating the ocean, yards from the beaches of glamorous Biarritz, the only privately owned villa of its kind to have resisted commercial redevelopment has opened its arms to guests. Turrets were added in 1903; Paul's family took possession in 1934; now he and his wife, young, charming, professional, are its inspired guardians and restorers. Be ravished by oak floors, magnificent stairs, tall windows and balconies that go on for ever. Two bedrooms have terraces, beds are king-size, bathrooms are vintage or modern, breakfasts flourish sunshine and pastries. Amazing.

Price	€150–€270.
Rooms	4: 3 doubles, 1 suite for 3.
Meals	Restaurant 20m.
Closed	November–February.
Directions	From Place Clemençeau in Biarritz centre follow signs for place Ste Eugénie by Rue Mazagran; after pharmacy 1st right Rue des Goëland. House between antique shop & bar, narrow street.

Paul & Elisabeth Daraignez
Villa Le Goëland,
12 plateau de l'Atalaye,
64200 Biarritz, Pyrénées-Atlantiques
Tel   +33 (0)5 59 24 25 76
Email   info@villagoeland.com
Web   www.villagoeland.com

Entry 444   Map 13

Aquitaine

Villa Coriolan

Superb modern design – 320 square metres of generous space, angles and style softened by curves – and split levels outside. It's 'green' too, with solar heating, insulation and water harvesting. English Alexandra married Georges and they have upended their lives to do this together, with real enthusiasm. A huge white bath, a stand-alone basin, pale yellows and burgundies, Farrow & Ball paints, Sanderson fabrics, oak floors, books, bay windows and views. It is original, comfortable and relaxed, the breakfasts are vast and varied, and you can do real lengths in the pool. *Minimum stay 2 nights.*

Price	€99–€169.
Rooms	2: 1 double, 1 suite.
Meals	Dinner with wine, €40.
Closed	Rarely.
Directions	From A63 exit 4 Biarritz/St Pée sur Nivelle. From D255; through Arbonne for St Pée; after 2.9km follow sign Uhazaldea, signed.

Georges & Alexandra Guillaume
Villa Coriolan,
Chemin Domintxenea, 64210 Ahetze,
Pyrénées-Atlantiques
Tel   +33 (0)5 59 41 82 48
Fax   +33 (0)5 59 48 82 33
Email   georges.guillaume@9online.fr
Web   www.villa-coriolan.com

Entry 445   Map 13

Aquitaine

Bidachuna

Hear the electronic gate click behind you and 29 hectares of forested peace and quiet are yours with their fabulous wildlife. Draw your beautiful curtains next morning and you may see deer feeding; lift your eyes and feast on long, long vistas to the Pyrenean foothills; come down to the earthly feast that is Basque breakfast. Shyly attentive, Isabelle manages all this impeccably and keeps a refined house where everything is polished and gleaming; floors are chestnut, bathrooms marble, family antiques of high quality. A beautifully manicured haven – worth staying several days for serious cosseting.

Price	€120.
Rooms	3: 2 doubles, 1 twin.
Meals	Restaurant 6km.
Closed	Mid-November to mid-March.
Directions	From Biarritz railway station to Bassussary & Arcangues; D3 for St Pée; 8km after Arcangues house on left; signed.

	Isabelle Ormazabal
	Bidachuna, Route Oihan Bidea D3,
	64310 St Pée sur Nivelle,
	Pyrénées-Atlantiques
Tel	+33 (0)5 59 54 56 22
Fax	+33 (0)5 59 54 55 07
Email	isabelle@bidachuna.com
Web	www.bidachuna.com

Entry 446   Map 13

Aquitaine

Les Volets Bleus

High in these ancient hills stands this beautiful new farmhouse built with old Basque materials. Chic, clever Marie has made a perfect creation. Through the magnificent double-arch door is a flagged entrance hall, then a terrace with rattan chairs and weathered pine tables. Up stone staircases are bedrooms in restful colours with wood or tiled floors, gilt mirrors, embroidered sheets, ancestral paintings; exquisite bathrooms have iron towel rails and aromatic oils. Marie is also an accomplished gardener so retreat to her garden for a read or a swim – or lounge in the sitting room on deep comfy sofas. It's heaven.

Price	€105-€160. Suite €135-€176.
Rooms	4: 2 doubles, 1 twin, 1 suite.
Meals	Restaurants 1.5km.
Closed	Rarely.
Directions	Biarritz D3 for Arcangues; left at r'bout to St Pée sur Nivelle. End of village, sign to Arcangues, 3rd right; house 1st on left up slope.

	Marie de Lapasse
	Les Volets Bleus, Chemin Etchegaraya,
	64200 Arcangues,
	Pyrénées-Atlantiques
Mobile	+33 (0)6 07 69 03 85
Fax	+33 (0)5 59 43 39 25
Email	maisonlesvoletsbleus@wanadoo.fr
Web	www.lesvoletsbleus.fr

Entry 447   Map 13

Aquitaine

Domaine de Silencenia

The house cornerstone, the magnificent magnolia, the towering pines were all planted on one day in 1881. A pool and lake (with fountain, boat, trout and koi-carp) are set in spacious parkland, and billard room, sauna and fitness area (for a small charge) are on tap. The sensitive restoration includes a Blue Marlin room, canopied pine beds, modern fittings, a desk made from famous wine cases and respect for the original chestnut panelling. Philippe, discreetly helped by his mother with dinner, knows about wine too: his cellar is brilliant. And there's great walking in the surrounding hills.

Aquitaine

Maison Maxana

Step through a 17th-century Basque façade into a world of stone-flagged floors and bold African art, subtle lights, soft velour sofas and antiques with a story to tell. Ana mixes styles and textures with panache and the art is collected by banker husband Max. Which bedroom to choose – minimalist chic, Chinese red, lavish silk? One has a terrace, another ancient tiles, all have fat white pillows, hand-made soaps, textured throws. Relax by the pool as Ana pours a glass of chilled rosé and you consider dinner; Ana loves people *and* is a fine cook. The village is charming and Biarritz a short drive.

Price	€90.	Price	€90-€120. Family room €160-€240
Rooms	5: 3 doubles, 2 triples.	Rooms	5: 3 doubles, 2 family rooms for 4.
Meals	Dinner with wine, €30-€35.	Meals	Dinner with wine, €35.
Closed	Rarely.	Closed	Rarely.
Directions	From A63 exit on D932, on through Ustaritz & Cambo les Bains; left into Louhossoa; straight over crossroads. House 800m on left.	Directions	From A64 exit 4 for Urt; right onto D936; D123 right at mini-r'bout to La Bastide Clairence. House on main street just past post office on left.

Philippe Mallor
Domaine de Silencenia,
64250 Louhossoa,
Pyrénées-Atlantiques
Tel   +33 (0)5 59 93 35 60
Fax   +33 (0)5 59 93 35 60
Email   domaine.de.silencenia@orange.fr
Web   www.domaine-silencenia.com

Ana Berdoulat
Maison Maxana,
Rue Notre Dame,
64240 La Bastide Clairence,
Pyrénées-Atlantiques
Tel   +33 (0)5 59 70 10 10
Email   ab@maison-maxana.com
Web   www.maison-maxana.com

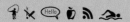

Entry 448   Map 13

Entry 449   Map 13

Aquitaine

Maison Marchand

A lovely face among all the lovely faces of this superb listed village, the 16th-century Basque farmhouse, resuscitated by its French/Irish owners, is run with well-organised informality. Dinners around the great oak table are lively; local dishes excellent. Rooms each have their own terrace and are light and well-decorated with hand-stencilling and pretty fabrics, beams and exposed wafer bricks, country antiques and thoughtful extras. Breakfast is on the terrace in warm weather. And Gilbert will laugh and teach you *la pelote basque. Minimum stay 2 nights.*

Price	€55-€75.
Rooms	3: 2 doubles; 1 double & extra bed for 2 children.
Meals	Dinner with wine, €25.
Closed	Occasionally.
Directions	From A64 junc. 4 for Urt & Bidache; right on D936, right on D123 at mini-island to La Bastide Clairence. House on main street, opp. bakery.

	Valerie & Gilbert Foix Maison Marchand, Rue Notre Dame, 64240 La Bastide Clairence, Pyrénées-Atlantiques
Tel	+33 (0)5 59 29 18 27
Email	valerie.et.gilbert.foix@wanadoo.fr
Web	pagesperso-orange.fr/maison.marchand

Entry 450   Map 13

Aquitaine

Moulin Urketa

Set back from the village road, by the cascading waters of the river Joyeuse, this 17th-century house has its own parkland and woods for wandering – and you can fish from the bridge. The two very large bedrooms on the top floor are luxurious and stylish with ancient rafters and exposed stone, fresh flowers, cheery colours and modern bathrooms. Nathalie and Bernard have a young family and are relaxed about sharing their home with its comfortable sitting room, traditional dining room and pretty terrace (where you may eat in warm weather). Biarritz and St Jean de Luz are an easy distance. *Min. stay 2 nights. Suitable for babies & children over 6: unfenced water.*

Price	€60-€94.
Rooms	2: 1 twin/double, 1 family suite (1 double, 1 twin).
Meals	Dinner with wine, €25.
Closed	Rarely.
Directions	From Hasparren D10 for La Bastide Clairence 3km; right D251 for Ayherre; on left 300m after turning.

	Nathalie & Bernard Legleye Moulin Urketa, Route de la Bastide, 64240 Ayherre, Pyrénées-Atlantiques
Tel	+33 (0)5 59 70 26 44
Fax	+33 (0)5 59 70 26 44
Email	contact@moulin-urketa.com
Web	www.moulin-urketa.com

Entry 451   Map 13

Aquitaine

La Closerie du Guilhat

Guilhat is one of those sturdy Béarn houses with solid old furniture and traditional décor. Marie-Christine has added her own decorative touches – colourful bedroom wallpapers, small modern bathrooms – and everything is immaculate. She is elegant and energetic, doing nearly all the work here herself and longing to show you her garden – beautifully flowering all year. It has huge old trees, magnolia, azalea, rhododendron, camellia; benches discreetly placed for quiet reading and the Pyrenees as a backdrop. There's table tennis – shared with gîte guests – and the spa in Salies is good for swimming all year.

Price	€60-€65 .
Rooms	3: 1 double, 1 twin, 1 suite.
Meals	Dinner with wine, €25.
Closed	Rarely.
Directions	From A64 exit 7; right for Salies '5 tonnes'; next right to Le Guilhat 1.8km; house on left beside nurseries at junction with Chemin des Bois.

Marie-Christine Potiron
La Closerie du Guilhat,
64270 Salies de Béarn,
Pyrénées-Atlantiques
Tel   +33 (0)5 59 38 08 80
Fax   +33 (0)5 59 38 08 80
Email guilhat@club-internet.fr
Web   www.holidayshomes.com/guilhat

Entry 452   Map 13

Aquitaine

Manoir de Marsan

Its looks belie its youth: that lovely roof and all beneath it is only 50 years old, the gorgeous garden is André's dazzling ten-year triumph, a haven of peace and natural beauty. He plays the piano pretty well too. He and Nicole are happily present for guests, she bilingual after 20 years in Canada and quietly caring for details, he vibrantly telling you all there is to know. Their renovation is the height of comfort and taste (lots of space, deep sofas, unusual antiques, Turkish carpets), the big, sweetly feminine guest suite feels like a private apartment, garden beauty bursts in through every window. *Minimum stay 2 nights.*

Price	€80-€100.
Rooms	1 suite for 2-4.
Meals	Restaurants within walking distance.
Closed	Rarely.
Directions	From RN133 for centre ville; in village square; Rue Panneceau left of Mairie; at stop sign right; follow green & white signs; ring at gate.

Nicole & André Capdet
Manoir de Marsan,
64390 Sauveterre de Béarn,
Pyrénées-Atlantiques
Tel   +33 (0)5 59 38 52 75
Email andre.capdet@wanadoo.fr
Web   www.manoir-de-marsan.fr

Entry 453   Map 13

Aquitaine

Domaine de la Carrère

Wow! Country-house grandeur in modest, pretty Arthez. Fritz and Mike moved to France from Wales and spent three years perfecting this 17th-century mansion. Oak panelling, parquet floors and ancient beams are the backdrop to gleaming antiques, original paintings and rich rugs. Bedrooms are classically elegant with high ceilings, carved bedheads, flamboyant drapes; bathrooms are high luxe. Quiet corners display plump sofas while the garden is lush with terraces, lawns and dreamy pool. Historic Pau is 20 minutes away and glorious Biarritz 40; return to Fritz's fabulous dinner amid candles and cut glass!

Price	€95–€125.
Rooms	5: 4 doubles, 1 twin.
Meals	Dinner with wine, €35.
Closed	Rarely.
Directions	A64 exit 9; N117 for Orthez 7km; D31 right to Arthez. In village centre left to La Place; house 500m to west, signed.

	Fritz Kisby & Mike Ridout
	Domaine de la Carrère,
	54 la Carrère,
	64370 Arthez de Béarn,
	Pyrénées-Atlantiques
Tel	+33 (0)8 77 15 78 59
Email	chatmont@club-internet.fr
Web	chatmont.club.fr

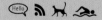

Entry 454   Map 13

Aquitaine

Domaine Lespoune

Renovated with panache in unsung Pays Basque, this 18th-century manor house calms and charms. Easy-going Nicole and Yves poured their hearts into it – the panelling now restored, the tiled and wooden floors, the original doors – and added modern touches: colourwashed walls, contemporary art, walk-in showers. The ground-floor bedroom has a striking black-and-white tiled floor and a private terrace; the rooms upstairs are in soft honeys and creams (one with a veranda). Breakfast under the spreading magnolia, spend the day fishing, return to Nicole's beautiful food – and a Navarrenx cigar in the garden. A great find.

Price	€70–€80.
Rooms	3: 2 doubles, 1 twin.
Meals	Dinner with wine, €25–€35.
Closed	Mid-November to mid-March.
Directions	From Oloron Ste Marie D936 for Bayonne 20km; left to Castetnau Camblong centre; house on right after church; signed.

	Yves & Nicole Everaert
	Domaine Lespoune,
	20 route de Camblong,
	64190 Castetnau Camblong,
	Pyrénées-Atlantiques
Tel	+33 (0)5 59 66 24 14
Email	contact@lespoune.fr
Web	www.lespoune.fr

Entry 455   Map 13

Aquitaine

Maison L'Aubèle

The Desbonnets completely renovated their grand 18th-century village house after finding it and this sleepy village in the Pyrenean foothills: both house and owners are quiet, elegant, sophisticated and full of interest, the furniture a feast for the eyes. Breakfast is a chance to pick their well-stocked brains about the region and do delve into their tempting library (she binds books). The light, airy bedrooms have more interesting furniture on lovely wooden floors. 'La Rose' is very chic, 'La Verte' is a dream – enormous and boldly coloured with views of the mountains and a 'waltz-in' bathroom.

Price	€65.
Rooms	2 doubles.
Meals	Restaurants 4–10km.
Closed	Rarely.
Directions	From Navarrenx D2 for Monein to Jasses; right D27 for Oloron Ste Marie; in Lay Lamidou, left, 1st right, 2nd house on right.

Marie-France Desbonnet
Maison L'Aubèle,
4 rue de la Hauti,
64190 Lay Lamidou,
Pyrénées-Atlantiques

Tel/Fax	+33 (0)5 59 66 00 44
Email	desbonnet.bmf@infonie.fr
Web	chambre.ifrance.com

Entry 456   Map 13

Aquitaine

Clos Mirabel

Fifteen minutes from city lights yet bucolic and surrounded by vineyards. French-Canadian André is a retired diplomat, Ann worked in travel, Emily goes to the village school. They fell in love with Clos Mirabel five years ago, now they delightedly welcome guests. The 18th-century manor is flanked by a winery and gatehouse; inside, rooms are light, airy and restful, their gracious proportions enhanced by Ann's elegant eye. A spiral staircase links the Gustavian suite's three levels, there's a pool terrace with breathtaking Pyrenean views and breakfast honey comes from André's bees. A delight.

Price	€95–€120. Extra person €35.
Rooms	2 + 1: 2 doubles. 1 apartment for 4.
Meals	Restaurants 3km.
Closed	Never.
Directions	From Pau N134 for Saragosse to Jurançon; cont. for Gan; right at traffic lights for Chapelle de Rousse. At top of hill right Ave des Frères Bartélémy.

Ann Kenny & André Péloquin
Clos Mirabel,
276 avenue des Frères Barthélémy,
64110 Jurançon,
Pyrénées-Atlantiques

Tel/Fax	+33 (0)5 59 06 32 83
Email	andre.peloquin@closmirabel.com
Web	www.closmirabel.com

Entry 457   Map 13

Aquitaine

Maison Rancesamy

Landscape painters love this haven. From terrace and pool you can see for ever into the high Pyrenees – sunlit snowy in winter, all the greens in summer. Beside their 1700s farmhouse, the Brownes' barn conversion shelters artistic, uncluttered, stone-walled bedrooms and incredible views. The superb dining room – Isabelle's trompe-l'œil floor, huge carved table – reflects their origins (Polish, French, South African). They are a happy, relaxed family. On balmy summer evenings, the food (not every night) is deliciously garden-aromatic. *Min. stay 2 nights July/August.*

Price	€75–€90. Family room €108–€125.
Rooms	5: 2 doubles, 1 twin, 2 family rooms.
Meals	Dinner with wine, €32.
Closed	Rarely.
Directions	From Pau N134 S for Saragosse to Gan; right at lights after chemist, D24 for Lasseube 9km; left D324. Follow Chambres d'Hôtes signs; cross 2 small bridges; house on left up steep hill.

Simon & Isabelle Browne
Maison Rancesamy,
Quartier Rey, 64290 Lasseube,
Pyrénées-Atlantiques
Tel   +33 (0)5 59 04 26 37
Fax   +33 (0)5 59 04 26 37
Email   missbrowne@wanadoo.fr
Web   www.missbrowne.com

Entry 458   Map 13

Aquitaine

Beth Soureilh

Marie-Noëlle is charming and so is her house: perched on the edge of the forest it is light, bright, eco-warm and filled with colour. Cheerful pinks and greens romp through the sitting/dining room; step out onto the terrace and find a pretty garden with the greenest views. Upstairs are very generous bedrooms, with wooden floors, big beds, bright colours and gleaming white-tiled shower rooms, one with a view. Breakfast and supper are organic and delicious – much is home-grown – and there are excellent local wines. If you hear 'La Marseillaise' a-humming, you haven't over indulged: it's just Coco the parrot.

Price	€59–€68.
Rooms	2: 1 double, 1 twin.
Meals	Dinner with wine, €22.
Closed	Rarely.
Directions	From Pau D938 for Lourdes 15km; D936 left to Bénéjacq; cont. D936 for 2km; climb hill; after 2 bends house on left, signed.

Marie-Noëlle Pée
Beth Soureilh,
3 côte du Bois de Bénéjacq
64800 Coarraze,
Pyrénées-Atlantiques
Tel   +33 (0)5 59 53 70 75
Email   beth.soureilh-chambredhote@wanadoo.fr
Web   www.bed-breakfast-france-pyrenees.com

Entry 459   Map 14

Aquitaine

Château de Grenier

One minute you're bowling along a fairly busy road, the next you've pulled up at the doors of an 18th- and 19th-century *belle demeure*. Painted wood and dried flowers set the tone of this large, light, comfortable home. Discreet, charming Madame ushers you up to beautifully proportioned bedrooms with tall windows; ask for one facing the garden. Expect pristine white bathrooms, a sun-streamed double, a generous twin with pink walls, a two-room suite off the garden – more basic but ideal for families. Dinners are serenely elegant affairs, your hosts share the cooking. *Ask about furniture painting & sculpture courses.*

Price	€90. Suite €140.
Rooms	5: 3 doubles, 1 twin, 1 family suite.
Meals	Restaurants nearby.
Closed	Rarely.
Directions	A62; exit 6; D8 N for Agen for approx. 4km; château on right just before river Garonne. Signed.

Chantal Breton le Grelle
Château de Grenier,
47160 St Léger, Lot-et-Garonne
Tel +33 (0)5 53 79 59 06
Fax +33 (0)5 53 79 59 06
Email info@chateaudegrenier.com
Web www.chateaudegrenier.com

Entry 460 Map 14

Aquitaine

Le Baraillot

At the end of a wooded drive, a busy, happy, holiday house where guests and hosts meet over fabulous meals cooked by Linda. She, Patrick and four able children run a restaurant here, yet still find time for B&B and gîte guests, overseeing lively dinners under the huge awning on the terrace. Bedrooms spread themselves over the top two floors, the interiors a testament to wallpaper effects and highlighted beading; all is pristine, crisp and well-maintained. Terrific for families, with a park-like garden, playground and pool, bikes to hire and child-sized dishes served at child-friendly hours. Unwind!

Price	€66-€85.
Rooms	5: 2 doubles, 2 family rooms, 1 suite for 5.
Meals	Lunch €15. Dinner with wine, €27.
Closed	Rarely.
Directions	From Bordeaux A62 for Toulouse exit 6 thro' Aiguillon onto D666 for Villeneuve sur Lot 2.5km; signed in Ste Radegonde.

Patrick & Linda Coone
Le Baraillot,
Sainte Radegonde,
47190 Aiguillon, Lot-et-Garonne
Tel +33 (0)5 53 88 29 92
Email linda@lebaraillot.com
Web www.lebaraillot.com

Entry 461 Map 14

Aquitaine

Château de Rodié

Paul and Pippa did the triumphant restoration themselves, with two small children and a passionate commitment to the integrity of this ancient building: brash modernities are hidden (the telephone lurks behind a model ship). Expect an elaborate *pisé* floor set in cabalistic patterns and lit only with candles, two stone staircases, patches of fresco, a vast hall with giant fireplace and table, an atmospheric room in the tower, a lovely pool – and dogs, geese, ducks, sheep: this is a working farm. The family is super welcoming, veggie-friendly, and Pippa cooks gorgeous organic dinners that last for hours. *Sawday self-catering also.*

Ethical Collection: Environment; Food. See page 432.

Price	€78-€110.
Rooms	5: 4 doubles, 1 suite.
Meals	Dinner with wine, €20.
Closed	Rarely.
Directions	From Fumel D102 to Tournon; D656 for Agen 300m; left to Courbiac, past church, right at cross for Montaigu 1km; house on left.

Paul & Pippa Hecquet
Château de Rodié,
47370 Courbiac de Tournon,
Lot-et-Garonne
Tel +33 (0)5 53 40 89 24
Email mail@chateauderodie.com
Web www.chateauderodie.com

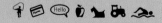

Entry 462 Map 14

Aquitaine

Chez Kelly

The orangery, with Warhol's Marilyn prints and red sofas, sets the boutique-château tone. But expect a relaxed touch: Siamese cats and golden retriever play; hosts Brendan and Keld – a Kiwi and a Dane – help you unwind. Easy in this setting, the château laps serenely at the banks of the canal. Boats, bikes, tennis court and pool await your discovery, a wildflower garden is in the making and orchids beautify chic, themed rooms: Iona, Alhambra… the suite is African in mood, with zebra stripes on its bed and polished floor. Dinner, elegant and convivial, starts with champagne on the terrace.

Price	€95-€130.
Rooms	5: 4 doubles, 1 suite.
Meals	Dinner with wine, €25. Snacks by the pool. Picnics available.
Closed	Rarely.
Directions	From Marmande D993 for Casteljaloux 1km; right D116 7km; left D3, almost immed. right D116; follow canal 2km; house signed on sharp bend.

Keld & Brendan Kelly
Chez Kelly,
Château Sauvin,
47180 Meilhan sur Garonne,
Lot-et-Garonne
Tel +33 (0)5 53 20 13 07
Email chezkelly@orange.fr
Web www.chezkelly.eu

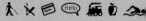

Entry 463 Map 9

Aquitaine

Manoir de Levignac

Walk through the entrance hall into the handsome country kitchen and thence into the peaceful grounds, with nature reserve and views. Or stay and dine (beautifully), in a room with a big fireplace, pottery pieces and carved cupboard doors. In the sitting room, terracotta tiles, kilim rugs, and grand piano give a comfortably artistic air. Adriana is Swiss-Italian, Jocelyn South African; they are thoughtful and kind and do everything well. You get a lush bedroom with rural views, a sitting room and an immaculate bathroom. Outside, a small pine wood, a daisy-sprinkled lawn and a pool surrounded by palms.

Price	€70-€80.
Rooms	2 suites for 4.
Meals	Dinner with wine, €25.
Closed	Rarely.
Directions	From A10 exit St André de Cubzac to Ste Foy La Grande; D708 to Duras; 4km after Duras left C1 to St Pierre.

Jocelyn & Adriana Cloete
Manoir de Levignac,
Saint Pierre sur Dropt,
47120 Duras, Lot-et-Garonne

Tel	+33 (0)5 53 83 68 11
Email	cloete@wanadoo.fr
Web	manoir.de.levignac.free.fr

Entry 464   Map 9

Aquitaine

Château Lavanau

The Uharts aren't just playing at being farmers – as the wine crates beside their pink-washed farmhouse prove. After spending 15 years in Paris, they now produce 100,000 bottles of Côtes de Duras a year; Paul – half French – is happy to guide you round the vineyard. There's an art studio, too: Juliana trained at St Martin's and runs courses. The bedrooms are simple and very charming, with old country furniture and splashes of colour. A half wall separates each room from its narrow stylish bathroom. There's also a small kitchen where you can prepare snacks. And a garden still in its infancy.

Price	€65-€75.
Rooms	5: 3 doubles, 2 twins.
Meals	Restaurant 1km. Guest kitchen.
Closed	Rarely.
Directions	From Bordeaux D936 to Ste Foy La Grande; right D708 for Duras 9km; at Margueron, fork left for La Sauvetat/Miramont 1.5km; left for Monestier; château signed.

Juliana & Paul Uhart
Château Lavanau,
Les Faux, 47120 Loubès Bernac,
Lot-et-Garonne

Tel	+33 (0)5 53 94 86 45
Fax	+33 (0)5 53 94 86 45
Email	juliana.uhart@googlemail.com
Web	www.chateaulavanau.com

Entry 465   Map 9

Aquitaine

Manoir de Roquegautier

In a beautiful park with rolling views, the fairytale château is wondrously French. Drapes, swags and interlinings – all done, but never overdone, by Madame – and the rooms in the old tower truly memorable with their own entrance and spiral stone staircase. There are claw-footed baths and huge old basins and taps, and each top-floor suite has one round tower room. There are swings and a games room, a discreet pool, gazebos around the garden and mature trees to shade your picnic lunches. Delicious food fresh from the family farm and shared with your hosts – such gentle, friendly people that you'll wish you could stay for ever.

Price	€79. Suites €115–€127.
Rooms	4: 2 doubles, 2 family suites: 1 for 3, 1 for 4.
Meals	Dinner with wine, €25, July/Aug only.
Closed	October–April.
Directions	From Villeneuve sur Lot N21 north for Cancon, 15.5km. Manoir signed on left 3.5km before Cancon.

Brigitte & Christian Vrech
Manoir de Roquegautier,
Beaugas, 47290 Cancon,
Lot-et-Garonne

Tel	+33 (0)5 53 01 60 75
Email	roquegautier@free.fr
Web	www.roquegautier.com

Entry 466   Map 9

Aquitaine

Domaine du Moulin de Labique

Soay sheep on the approach road, ducks on the pond, goats in the greenhouse and food *à la grand-mère*. Shutters are painted with *bleu de pastel* from the Gers and the 13th-century interiors have lost none of their charm. In house and outbuildings there are chunky beams, seagrass on ancient tiles, vintage iron bedsteads, antique mirrors, and wallpapers flower-sprigged in raspberry, jade and green. Outside are old French roses and young alleys of trees, a bamboo-fringed stream, a restaurant in the stables, an exquisite pool. The new owners – and great hosts – from Brussels have loved this place for years.

Price	€110–€135. Suite €170.
Rooms	6: 3 doubles, 2 twins, 1 suite for 4.
Meals	Dinner €31. Wine €19–€30.
Closed	Rarely.
Directions	From Cancon N21; D124 for Monflanquin; D153 at Beauregard to St Vivien; on right 1km after St Vivien.

Patrick & Christine Hendricx
Domaine du Moulin de Labique,
St Vivien, 47210 Villeréal,
Lot-et-Garonne

Tel	+33 (0)5 53 01 63 90
Fax	+33 (0)5 53 01 73 17
Email	moulin-de-labique@wanadoo.fr
Web	www.moulin-de-labique.fr

Entry 467   Map 9

Aquitaine

Château Gauthié

Outside a perfect bastide village, here is château B&B run with warmth and energy. Stéphane cooks brilliantly and loves wine; Florence charms her guests brightly. Restful, light-filled, traditional bedrooms have white bathrooms. An infinity pool overlooks the lake below, above it perches the treehouse steeped in rusticity, its balcony gazing over meadows and cows, its mother tree thrusting two branches through the floor. Solar-lit paths lead you down through the trees at night, a breakfast basket is winched up in the morning – amazing! Play badminton, fish in the lake, spin off on a bike. *Minimum stay 2 nights.*

Price	€85-€160.
Rooms	5: 3 doubles, 1 twin. Treehouse: 1 double.
Meals	Dinner €35. Wine €15-€90.
Closed	Mid-November to March.
Directions	From Bergerac N21 10km; left D14 to Issigeac; right D21 for Castillones 2km; just after Eyrenville & Monmarvès x-roads, left for château.

Florence & Stéphane Desmette
Château Gauthié,
24560 Issigeac Monmarvès,
Dordogne
Tel   +33 (0)5 53 27 30 33
Web   www.chateaugauthie.com

Entry 468   Map 9

Aquitaine

Manoir de la Brunie

An elegant village manor in a glorious setting whose current owner's friendly manager will introduce you to a fine living room overlooking the sweeping lawn; here, you will find warm bright colours that give a smart yet sunny personality. You're welcome to play the piano and read the books. The tower suite and small double have a modern feel, the three other rooms, huge and high-ceilinged, are more traditional; all have subtle colours, sitting areas and perfect lighting. Breakfasts are sumptuous, bathrooms delightful... there are children's games, a beach nearby on the Dordogne, and riding next door.

Price	€71-€98.
Rooms	5: 3 doubles, 1 twin/double, 1 suite.
Meals	Dinner with wine, €29. Lunch €20. By arrangement.
Closed	December-January.
Directions	From Sarlat, D57 to Beynac; D703 to St Cyprien; cont. 7km, right to Coux et Bigaroque; thro' village, left after Mairie; house on right after approx. 1km, just past wayside cross.

Joyce Villemur
Manoir de la Brunie, La Brunie,
24220 Le Coux et Bigaroque,
Dordogne
Tel   +33 (0)5 53 31 95 62
Fax   +33 (0)5 53 31 95 62
Email   manoirdelabrunie@wanadoo.fr
Web   www.manoirdelabrunie.com

Entry 469   Map 9

Aquitaine

La Guérinière

Once a charterhouse, this good-looking Périgord house sits squarely in ten hectares of parkland and peace, a tribute to the rich, sober taste of the area. Inside reflects outside: the same dark timbers against pale stone and the new owners have redecorated the bedrooms most charmingly. They are gradually replacing the modern furniture with country antiques and the feel is warmly authentic. Moreover, they used to run a restaurant – do eat in. Sitting at the big table for house guests, you may find more gourmets in the beamed dining room: a few outsiders are occasionally allowed. A gem. *Sawday self-catering also.*

Price	€70-€95.
Rooms	5: 1 double, 2 twins, 1 triple, 1 quadruple.
Meals	Dinner €25. Wine €18.
Closed	November-March.
Directions	From Sarlat D46 to Cénac St Julien. At end of village on for Fumel. House 3rd turning on right.

	Brigitte & Christophe Demassougne
	La Guérinière,
	Baccas, 24250 Cénac et St Julien,
	Dordogne
Tel	+33 (0)5 53 29 91 97
Fax	+33 (0)5 53 29 91 97
Email	contact@la-gueriniere-dordogne.com
Web	www.la-gueriniere-dordogne.com

Entry 470   Map 9

Aquitaine

Château de Mombette

Built in the 1600s-1700s by the same family, it has the simple, harmonious elegance that natural style brings to an organically-grown house; from its hilltop perch, it gazes across to the splendid medieval fortifications of Domme. Madame is welcoming and easy and has travelled a lot, especially to North Africa, where her father was a general. The character of her house is made of fine, generous spaces and good regional antiques, an attractive library and very lovely gardens. Bedrooms are comfortable, homely and you are within reach of all the delights of the Dordogne. Real France – and with a super pool.

Price	€100.
Rooms	3: 1 double, 1 twin, 1 triple.
Meals	Restaurants within walking distance.
Closed	Mid-November to March.
Directions	From Sarlat D46 to Cénac & St Julien; D50 right for St Cybranet for 300m; left signed.

	Michèle Jahan
	Château de Mombette,
	24250 Cénac et St Julien,
	Dordogne
Tel	+33 (0)5 53 28 30 14
Fax	+33 (0)5 53 28 30 14
Email	michele.jahan@orange.fr

Entry 471   Map 9

Aquitaine

Les Charmes de Carlucet

An 18th-century house with a poignant history: Jewish families were sheltered here during the 2nd World War. Now the welcoming Edgars – he French, she English – live here with their children. In a vast walled garden on the edge of the village, the house has been completely renovated. Living and dining rooms are cool compositions of natural stone, white walls, pale fabrics. Pitch-ceilinged, L-shaped bedrooms under the eaves have gleaming floors, spotless bath or shower rooms, fans for summer. Should you tire of the heated pool (Monsieur says this hardly ever happens), you can stroll to the clipped hedges of Eyrignac. *Sawday self-catering also.*

Price	€99–€119. Extra bed €20.
Rooms	2 doubles, each with sofabed.
Meals	Restaurant 500m.
Closed	Rarely.
Directions	From Sarlat D60 for St Crépin et Carlucet; for Salignac passing stadium on right. After 500m right for Carlucet 1.5km; fork left 300m; right & right again.

Éric & Helen Edgar
Les Charmes de Carlucet,
24590 St Crépin et Carlucet,
Dordogne
Tel   +33 (0)5 53 31 22 60
Email   lescharmes@carlucet.com
Web   www.carlucet.com

Aquitaine

Château de Puymartin

Neither dream nor museum, Puymartin is a chance to act the aristocrat for a spell, and survey the day-trippers from your own wing. The fireplace in the tapestried baronial dining room would take a small tree, painted beams draw the eye, the carved stone staircase asks to be stroked, the furniture is authentic 17th-century Perigordian, history oozes from every corner (possibly a ghost too). Bedrooms are vastly in keeping – twin four-posters, a loo in a turret, thick draperies. The ever-elegant Comtesse is friendly and very French; her son helps in the château and speaks good English; both are delightful.

Price	€120.
Rooms	2: 1 twin, 1 family suite.
Meals	Restaurant 5km.
Closed	November-March.
Directions	From Sarlat D47 for Les Eyzies 8km. Château signed regularly.

Comtesse de Montbron
Château de Puymartin,
24200 Sarlat la Canéda,
Dordogne
Tel   +33 (0)5 53 59 29 97
Fax   +33 (0)5 53 29 87 52
Email   chateaupuymartin@gmail.com
Web   www.chateau-de-puymartin.com

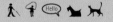

Aquitaine

Domaine des Farguettes

Fascinting Françoise is a songwriter and potter, Claude was in the theatre and their home reflects their passions: a baby grand in the salon, pots, paintings, puppets and poetry in every corner. Bedrooms in the house are pleasantly traditional and have spectacular hilltop views, those in the barn are more contemporary (vibrant colours, big glass doors) alongside aged timbers and vaulted ceilings. Both structures were built in 1664 by artisans whose signatures and date are set in stone. The pool is for all and there are great walks round the estate. *Ask about cookery courses. Meeting rooms for big groups.*

Price	€80-€110.
Rooms	4 doubles.
Meals	Dinner €25. Wine €5-€9.
Closed	July-August, Christmas & New Year.
Directions	From Bergerac for Sarlat exit Le Buisson D25 for Cadouin; right for Paleyrac 4km; by church straight on & right; on entry to forest 1st house on left, above village; pillared entrance.

Françoise & Claude de Torrenté
Domaine des Farguettes,
24480 Paleyrac, Dordogne
Tel   +33 (0)5 53 23 48 23
Fax   +33 (0)5 53 23 48 23
Email   clagazel@wanadoo.fr
Web   www.farguettes.fr

Entry 474   Map 9

Aquitaine

Le Moulin Neuf

Robert or Stuart's greeting is the first line of an ode to hospitality written in warm stone and breathtaking gardens, set to the tune of the little stream hurrying by to the lake. Fresh and flowery, the immaculate rooms in the guest barn are comfortingly filled with excellent beds; bathrooms are utter luxury. The breakfast room has pretty tables and tea-making kit: have your succulent fruit salad here or on the vine-shaded terrace. All is lovingly tended, in perfect peace; nearby is unspoilt Paunat with its huge church – the whole place is a delight. *Ask about pets. Children over 10 welcome. Minimum stay 3 nights in winter.*

Price	€85-€89.
Rooms	6 twins/doubles.
Meals	Restaurant 1km.
Closed	Rarely.
Directions	From Le Bugue D703 & D31 through Limeuil. Past viewpoint to x-roads; D2 for Ste Alvère; after 100m fork left; house 2km on left at small x-roads.

Robert Chappell & Stuart Shippey
Le Moulin Neuf,
Paunat, 24510 Ste Alvère,
Dordogne
Tel   +33 (0)5 53 63 30 18
Fax   +33 (0)5 53 63 30 55
Email   moulin-neuf@usa.net
Web   www.the-moulin-neuf.com

Entry 475   Map 9

Aquitaine

Les Hirondelles

Carine, half-Greek, energetic, charming and fun, makes you feel welcome in the sunny kitchen of her restored farmhouse on the top of a hill. She enjoys cooking French and international dishes, sometimes organises barbecues round the big pool and makes amazing walnut jam. Simple, dim-lit, inexpensive bedrooms are in a converted barn set back from the house, each with a terrace delineated by concrete planters. The pool is far enough away not to disturb your siesta. Spend two or three nights and get to know this beautiful village and the whole area; Carine knows the best places to go.

Price	€48-€52.
Rooms	4: 2 doubles, 2 twins.
Meals	Dinner with wine, €17, except July/August.
Closed	November-April.
Directions	From Le Bugue go to Ste Alvère; at main x-roads there, D30 for Pezuls. House 3rd right, 500m after sign Le Maine at top of hill.

Carine Someritis
Les Hirondelles,
Le Maine,
24510 Ste Alvère,
Dordogne

Tel	+33 (0)5 53 22 75 40
Fax	+33 (0)5 53 22 75 40

Entry 476   Map 9

Aquitaine

Le Relais de Lavergne

Enter the creeper-climbed courtyard through the old arch: looks a touch sophisticated? Francine and Odile will reassure you – ex-Parisian publishers, they are funny, intelligent and wonderful company. They are also keen to preserve the ideal of B&B and make a point of eating with their guests. The curvy roof, wafer bricks and ancient timbers may be familiar friends but the long-drop privy is a fascinating rarity. Splendid main rooms combine simplicity and taste; smaller, tempting bedrooms have hand-stencilled doors and quirky touches. There's also a playroom and a garden with a pool.

Ethical Collection: Food.
See page 432.

Price	€70.
Rooms	5: 3 doubles, 1 twin, 1 family suite.
Meals	Dinner with wine, €25.
Closed	Mid-November to March.
Directions	From Bergerac D660 for Lalinde & Sarlat; right over R. Dordogne at Pont de Couze (still D660); at Bayac right D27 for Issigeac 2km; house on left at top of hill.

Francine Pillebout
Le Relais de Lavergne,
Lavergne,
24150 Bayac, Dordogne

Tel	+33 (0)5 53 57 83 16
Fax	+33 (0)5 53 57 83 16
Email	relaisdelavergne@wanadoo.fr

Entry 477   Map 9

Aquitaine

La Ferme de la Rivière

The large farmhouse auberge sits alone and surrounded by its fields in a hamlet of 12 houses. The Archer family honour tradition; he is a poultry breeder, she is an industrious (non-vegetarian!) cook and the recipes for handcrafting pâtés and foie gras are their heirlooms. The honey stones of the building are impeccably pointed and cleaned, bedrooms have functionality rather than character, shower rooms are large and pristine and there's an open-fired sitting room just for guests. Good for families (a climbing frame in the garden) and utterly, quintessentially French.

Price	€53.
Rooms	2: 1 double, 1 triple.
Meals	Dinner with wine, €20.50, April–mid-September only.
Closed	November–February.
Directions	From airport D660 for Sarlat; in Mouleydier over bridge on D21; after bridge 1st left onto D37; Route Balisé 2nd on right; on to house. Don't go into St Agne.

Marie-Thérèse & Jean-Michel Archer
La Ferme de la Rivière,
24520 St Agne,
Dordogne
Tel   +33 (0)5 53 23 22 26
Fax   +33 (0)5 53 23 22 26
Email archer.marietherese@wanadoo.fr
Web   www.lafermedelariviere.com

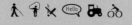

Entry 478   Map 9

Aquitaine

Le Logis Plantagenet

Picture this: a medieval house on a tree-lined square in old Bergerac, a minute's walk from the limpid, lovely river. Your well-travelled, welcoming hosts, he a historian, she a good cook, offer you light-filled bedrooms painted in soft colours with pretty rugs on polished floors, excellent beds, full-length baths and fabulous linen. Breakfasts are served in the flowered courtyard garden in summer and in the big modern kitchen in winter, at one merry table. After a day visiting châteaux and gardens and tasting fine wines, return to two delightful country-house sitting rooms.

Price	€85–€90.
Rooms	3: 1 double, 2 twins.
Meals	Dinner with wine, €25.
Closed	Never.
Directions	In old quarter of Bergerac; owner's house with yellow shutters faces old port; Le Logis Plantagenet is directly behind. Ring bell of 6 Quai Salvette.

Bruce & Rosetta Cantlie
Le Logis Plantagenet,
5 rue du Grand Moulin,
24100 Bergerac, Dordogne
Tel   +33 (0)5 53 57 15 99
Fax   +33 (0)5 53 57 17 91
Email bruce.cantlie@wanadoo.fr
Web   www.lelogisplantagenet.com

Entry 479   Map 9

Aquitaine

Château des Baudry

Steeped in 500 years of history, the four solid wings of this distinguished château enclose a grand central courtyard where a water feature shimmers with tiny fish. In a dining room wrapped in blue wallpaper and ribbon, you'll discover that Hélène's cooking 'à la grand-mère' is more than delicious. Breakfast is served among terracotta and citrus trees; guest rooms are large, traditional, framed by lofty beams, aglow with antiques and the softness of stitched spreads. Views of Italiante gardens give way to more untouched countryside; pillars by the pool guide the eye to Dordogne vistas. Wonderful.

Ethical Collection: Environment; Food.
See page 432.

Price	€140–€170.
Rooms	3 twins/doubles.
Meals	Dinner €30. Wine €12–€32.
Closed	Rarely.
Directions	From Bergerac D936 for Bordeaux 12km to Gardonne; left D4 to Saussignac 5km, continue D4 for Monestier. Château 2km from Saussignac, on left.

Hélène Boulet & François Passebon
Château des Baudry,
24240 Monestier,
Dordogne
Tel   +33 (0)5 53 23 46 42
Fax   +33 (0)5 53 61 14 59
Email   chateaudesbaudry@orange.fr
Web   www.chateaudesbaudry.com

Entry 480   Map 9

Aquitaine

Le Moulin de Leymonie du Maupas

The Kieffers did the utterly successful restoration of their old Dordogne mill themselves, their gardening past speaks softly in the herb-scented patio and the little brook trembles off past grazing horses to the valley. Inside, levels juggle with space, steep stairs rise to small rooms of huge character with wood walls, rich rugs and selected antiques. Your sitting room is seductive with its logs on the fire and a forest overhead. Add a relaxed, bubbly welcome, organic dinners served with crisp linen and candles, homemade bread and jams for breakfast, and you have great value.

Ethical Collection: Food.
See page 432.

Price	€60–€70.
Rooms	2: 1 double, 1 twin. Children's room available.
Meals	Dinner €20. Wine €9.
Closed	Rarely.
Directions	In Mussidan, at church, for Villamblard 4km; follow blue signs left for St Séverin 2km, blue sign on right.

Jacques & Ginette Kieffer
Le Moulin de Leymonie du Maupas,
24400 Issac,
Dordogne
Tel   +33 (0)5 53 81 24 02
Email   jacques.kieffer2@wanadoo.fr
Web   perso.wanadoo.fr/lemoulindeleymonie

Entry 481   Map 9

Aquitaine

Le Vignoble

From the wicker-chaired sun room views sweep down the hamlet-studded valley – a blissful spot for breakfasts and dinners. Sue and Nick, who have chosen to swap London for deepest Dordogne, give you lovely bedrooms with big beds and old French linen, white walls and fresh flowers. Two rooms (for one party) share an enchanting lavender bathroom with a swish shower. Seek out a private corner in the elegantly simple garden where the lapping pool is heated to Trinidadian temperatures – Sue was brought up there. Seven hectares for walkers and wild orchids; civilised hosts, privacy and space. Wonderful. *Ask about local wine & garden tours.*

Price	€70.
Rooms	3: 1 twin/double with separate bath; 1 double, 1 twin/double, sharing bath & wc.
Meals	Dinner €22. Light suppers €12. Wine €8.
Closed	Rarely.
Directions	From Ribérac D708 for Verteillac; over bridge; D99 right to Celles; thro' village leaving church on right. House sign 2nd right after Peugeot garage.

Sue & Nick Gild
Le Vignoble,
Celles,
24600 Ribérac, Dordogne
Tel +33 (0)5 53 90 26 60
Email nsgild@orange.fr

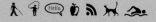

Entry 482   Map 9

Aquitaine

Pauliac

The exuberant hillside garden, full of blossom and bamboo, has gorgeous views and an overflowing stone plunge pool, too. John and Jane's talent is a restful atmosphere, their conversion a brilliant marriage of cottage simplicity – simple décor with sparks from African throws and good paintings. Simple bedrooms have a separate entrance. Delightful, energetic Jane offers superb, imaginative food in the sun-splashed veranda with its all-season views, or the bright, rustic dining room with roaring log fire – and early suppers for children. Lovely people in a tranquil view-drenched spot.

Price	€70.
Rooms	4: 2 doubles, 1 twin, 1 suite for 4.
Meals	Dinner €25. Wine €10.
Closed	Rarely.
Directions	From Angoulême D939 for Périgueux 29km; right D12 for Ribérac to Verteillac. Left after post office on D1 for Grand Brassac, Celles; after 5km right D99 for Celles for 400m; sign to left.

Jane & John Edwards
Pauliac,
Celles, 24600 Ribérac,
Dordogne
Tel +33 (0)5 47 23 40 17
Fax +33 (0)5 53 90 43 46
Email info@pauliac.fr
Web www.pauliac.fr

Entry 483   Map 9

Aquitaine

La Roche

In a gorgeous garden on several levels, you breakfast at shaded tables or under a pergola draped in vines. A convinced vegetarian, Alison produces her own (organic) vegetables, eggs, honey and jams. Two spotless bedrooms, with sloping ceilings, big beams, modern windows, are in the converted barn, sharing a comfortable living room with books and hand-crafted furniture. Shower rooms are a good size. A bit of a trek to the nearest restaurant but you can barbecue in the garden and it's super for children: donkeys, goats, cats, hens, table tennis and a fenced pool that looks out over heavenly countryside.

Price	€63–€75.
Rooms	2: 1 double, 1 twin.
Meals	Restaurants 12km.
Closed	Rarely.
Directions	From D675 (Nontron to Brantôme), D98 east. La Roche on right approx. 3km from D675.

Alison Coutanche
La Roche,
Quinsac, 24530 Champagnac de Belair,
Dordogne

Tel	+33 (0)5 53 54 22 91
Email	allisons@club-internet.fr
Web	perso.club-internet.fr/allisons

Entry 484   Map 9

Aquitaine

La Maison des Beaux Arts

The name is well chosen. Delia is a British artist and her striking canvases (from pop art jugs to oversized flowers) set off the house's well-preserved features. Once home to the mayor, the grand 19th-century house faces the main street and backs onto countryside. The only new addition, a glass conservatory, exploits the wonderful valley views. Sumptuous bedrooms are painted in a sizzling array of colours – sunflower yellow, duck-egg blue, Tiffany green – and filled with flowers. Should Delia's enthusiasm and talent inspire, she presents art packages too. *Minimum stay 2 nights July/August.*

Price	€70–€85.
Rooms	5: 3 doubles, 2 family rooms for 3.
Meals	Restaurant opposite.
Closed	Rarely.
Directions	From Limoges N21 exit Chalus; right at D6; D85 to Nontron; left over bridge to centre; house opp. post office, next to tourist information.

Delia Cavers
La Maison des Beaux Arts,
7 avenue du Général Leclerc,
24300 Nontron, Dordogne

Tel	+33 (0)5 53 56 39 77
Email	delia@deliacavers.co.uk
Web	www.la-maison-des-beaux-arts.com

Entry 485   Map 9

Limousin

Limousin

Moulin de Marsaguet

The nicest people, they have done just enough to this proud old building so it looks as it did 200 years ago when it forged cannon balls. The farm is relaxed and natural, the bedrooms quaint, they keep animals (including Lusitanian horses), three small children and a super potager, make pâtés and 'confits' by the great mill pond and hang the hams to dry over the magnificent hearth in their big stone sitting room with its old-fashioned sofa. Relish the drive up past tree-framed lake (boating possible) and stone outbuildings and the prospect of breakfasting on home-grown ingredients. *Ask about pets when booking.*

Price	€50.
Rooms	3 doubles.
Meals	Restaurant 3km.
Closed	October to mid-April.
Directions	From A20 exit 39 to Pierre Buffière; cross river D15 & D19 for St Yrieix for 15km. At Croix d'Hervy, left D57 for Coussac Bonneval; mill on left after lake (7km).

Valérie & Renaud Gizardin
Moulin de Marsaguet,
87500 Coussac Bonneval,
Haute-Vienne

Tel	+33 (0)5 55 75 28 29
Fax	+33 (0)5 55 75 28 29
Email	gizardin.renaud@akeonet.com

Entry 486   Map 9

Limousin

Magnac

In an ancient manor of enormous personality, your live-wire hostess, once a Parisian designer, now paints porcelain, organises cultural events and struggles to renovate the family house and its wild park with deep respect for its originality. Utterly endearing in its battered aristocracy, it is one room deep: light pours in from both sides onto heavy floorboards, 18th-century panelling and a delightful tower cocktail room. The traditional-style bedroom in the main house is vast, the snugger suite in the half-timbered orangery is ideal if you'd rather be independent. *1km from motorway exit. Children over 12 welcome.*

Price	€90.
Rooms	2: 1 twin/double, 1 suite for 3.
Meals	Light suppers available.
Closed	November to mid-May.
Directions	From A20 exit 41 for Magnac Bourg centre, over r'bout (Auberge de l'Étang), continue 100m, left through open gates into yard.

Catherine & Bertrand de la Bastide
Magnac,
87380 Magnac Bourg,
Haute-Vienne

Mobile	+33 (0)6 03 08 79 19 (mobile)
Email	bertrand.delabastide@areva.com

Entry 487   Map 9

Limousin

La Chapelle

Wonderful walking country; the emphasis here is outside, fields and woodlands are your garden. Deeply committed to the welfare of the land and all ecosystems, your hosts left city life to run a bio-dynamic goat farm and be as self-sufficient as possible. Modernised inside, the old farmhouse has four quietly strong, pine-clad bedrooms that wear good colours and share a kitchen/living room. Dine with this genuine, unpretentious couple if you can: they are excellent company, their food is all home-grown and nourishing, their cheeses remarkable. Children love helping to milk the goats and collect eggs.

Ethical Collection: Environment; Community; Food. See page 432.

Price	€45.
Rooms	4: 3 doubles, 1 triple.
Meals	Supper €10. Wine from €5. Guest kitchen.
Closed	Last week in August.
Directions	From A20 exit 41 to Magnac Bourg; D215 (between Total service station & Brasserie des Sports) SW. Follow signs 4km to La Chapelle & Chambres d'Hôtes.

Patrick & Mayder Lespagnol
La Chapelle,
87380 Château Chervix,
Haute-Vienne

Tel	+33 (0)5 55 00 86 67
Fax	+33 (0)5 55 00 70 78
Email	plespagnol@laposte.net
Web	gite.lachapelle.free.fr

Entry 488   Map 9

Limousin

Les Drouilles Bleues

High on a granite hill, with views to set your imagination on fire, the low stone house and its greenly rocky garden creak with age and history. As does the whole region. Paul and Maïthé, a most intelligent and attentive couple, take their hosting to heart, revelling in the wide variety of people who gather for an evening or two at their convivial and tasty dinner table. In converted outbuildings, handsome bedrooms large (the suite) and smaller are done with care, soft colours and gentle character. All have working fireplaces, sleeping quarters on mezzanines, good shower rooms. Deeply, discreetly, welcoming.

Price	€60. Suite €76.
Rooms	3: 2 doubles, 1 suite for 4 + child.
Meals	Dinner with wine, €20.
Closed	Rarely.
Directions	From A20 exit 39 N or 40 S onto D15 through Nexon & St Hilaire les Places. Approx. 1.5km beyond St Hilaire, 3rd turning on right to top of lane: La Drouille.

Maïthé & Paul de Bettignies
Les Drouilles Bleues,
La Drouille,
87800 St Hilaire les Places,
Haute-Vienne

Tel	+33 (0)5 55 58 21 26
Email	drouillesbleues@free.fr
Web	drouillesbleues.free.fr

Entry 489   Map 9

Limousin

La Roche

It's homely yet exciting with Michel's artistry everywhere: sculptures take you magically through the garden; in the old stables, a carved door frame opens to a big living room, an iron balustrade leads up to generous, painting-hung bedrooms and simple showers. An interesting, likeable couple of ex-Parisians, proud of doing things their way, Michel has a fascinating studio and a clutch of collector cars, Josette loves cooking for vegetarians – and the opulent curtains and tented ceiling are her work. The beautiful forested valley alone is worth the visit: stay and walk in peace for miles. *Secure parking.*

Limousin

Château Ribagnac

Patrick and Colette are as intelligent and thoughtful as they are enthusiastic, and their splendid château, built in 1647, is a treat. They have a growing family and this is their dream. The conversion is authentic, attractive and elegantly comfortable: oak floors with rugs, old and newish furniture, superb new bathrooms (one loo in its turret). Ask for a lighter room, with views over parkland and lake. Food is grown in their garden, the local meat is succulent, there is a deep commitment. Conversation flows along with the wine. *Swimming lake with beach 1.5km. Golf nearby.*

Price	€60.	Price	€100-€150.
Rooms	2 doubles.	Rooms	5 suites for 2-5.
Meals	Dinner with wine, €20.	Meals	Dinner with wine, €45.
Closed	Never, but book ahead.	Closed	Rarely.
Directions	From A20 exit 35 D979 to Eymoutiers; D30 for Chambaret. House in village of La Roche, 7km beyond Eymoutiers.	Directions	From Ambazac follow signs for gare. Under bridge for D56 to St Martin Terressus. Château on right after 3km.

	Michel & Josette Jaubert		**Patrick & Colette Bergot**
	La Roche,		Château Ribagnac,
	87120 Eymoutiers,		87400 Saint Martin Terressus,
	Haute-Vienne		Haute-Vienne
Tel	+33 (0)5 55 69 61 88	Tel	+33 (0)5 55 39 77 91
Web	clos.arts.free.fr	Email	reservations@chateauribagnac.com
		Web	www.chateauribagnac.com

Entry 490 Map 10

Entry 491 Map 9

Limousin

Château du Fraisse

For 800 years the Monstiers have adapted their château to family needs. It is now mainly a Renaissance gem by the great Serlio, whence warm limestone and a discreetly elegant portico, a Henry II staircase, an astonishing fireplace in the vast drawing room; a mix of grand and rustic. Your cultured hosts will greet you with warmth, happily tell you about house and history and show you to your room: fine furniture, paintings and prints, traditional furnishings; one bathroom has a fragment of a 16th-century fresco. If you return late at night you must climb the steep old spiral stair to your room as the main door is locked.

Price	€92–€114. Suites €145–€154.
Rooms	4: 1 double, 1 twin, 2 suites: 1 for 3, 1 for 4.
Meals	Auberge 3km.
Closed	Mid-December to mid-January.
Directions	From A20 exit 23 to Bellac; Mézières sur Issoire; left to Nouic; château on right.

Comte & Comtesse
des Monstiers Mérinville
Château du Fraisse, Le Fraisse,
87330 Nouic, Haute-Vienne
Tel   +33 (0)5 55 68 32 68
Fax   +33 (0)5 55 68 39 75
Email   infos@chateau-du-fraisse.com
Web   www.chateau-du-fraisse.com

Entry 492   Map 9

Limousin

La Flambée

Plain, simple and real French value. Thoveyrat is a deep-country organic smallholding run by a sweet young couple who delight in their French country fare, created from home-grown vegetables and home-reared lamb, duck, pigeon and rabbit (delicious pâtés). Myriam cares for their small children, the potager and the guests; Pierre, a builder by trade, looks after the animals and myriad house improvements. The 18th-century roadside farmhouse has lots of dark old wood – a great oak staircase, beams, timber framing – family clutter, fireplaces, peaceful, freshly-decorated bedrooms and a garden full of toys.

Price	€40.
Rooms	4: 1 double, 1 triple, 2 family rooms.
Meals	Dinner with wine, €15.
Closed	Rarely.
Directions	In Bellac follow signs to Limoges; just before leaving Bellac D3 right for Blond 4km to Thoveyrat. House sign on left.

Pierre & Myriam Morice
La Flambée,
Thoveyrat, 87300 Blond,
Haute-Vienne
Tel   +33 (0)5 55 68 86 86
Email   chambrehote@freesurf.fr
Web   www.laflambee.info

Entry 493   Map 9

Limousin

Château de Sannat

The serene 18th-century château stands proud for all to see on the site of an ancient fort – oh, the panorama! Bedrooms are mostly vast, traditionally furnished, regally wallpapered, modern bathroomed; the whole places oozes authenticity and easy family living and breakfast is superb. The atmosphere in the spectacular west-facing dining room, with its pale blue and yellow panelling, high-backed tapestried chairs and antique table may be informal, but the surroundings impose civilised dressing for dinner. Madame is an exceptionally warm and interesting lady; make the most of her lovely company. *Golf nearby.*

Price	€90-€180. Extra bed €30.
Rooms	5: 2 doubles, 2 twins, 1 suite.
Meals	Dinner with wine, €40.
Closed	Rarely.
Directions	From Poitiers N147 towards Limoges, through Bellac; left D96 for St Junien les Combes. 1st left in village for Rançon approx. 1km.

Comte & Comtesse
Aucaigne de Sainte Croix
Château de Sannat,
87300 St Junien les Combes,
Haute-Vienne
Tel   +33 (0)5 55 68 13 52
Email chateausannat@wanadoo.fr
Web   www.chateausannat.com

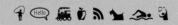

Entry 494   Map 9

Limousin

Maison Numéro Neuf

Lisa and Duncan from England have embraced life in southern La Souterraine. She is the least ruffled, most contented of chefs; he serves wines with finesse; both love house, children, guests… and secret garden with hens. They are renovating still – not that you would know, so vast is the old Marquis de Valady's residence. Relish the breakfasts and dinners, the fine proportions, the sweeping balustrade, the antique mirrors, the crystal-drop chandeliers, the pale walls, the glowing parquet. If Lisa pops a hot water bottle into your bed it will be encased in white linen: the thoughtful extras are exceptional.

Price	€60-€95.
Rooms	3: 2 doubles; 1 twin, sharing shower.
Meals	Dinner with wine, €18-€30.
Closed	Rarely.
Directions	A20 for Limoges exit 23 for Guéret. Follow signs to La Souterraine & centre ville; signed.

Duncan & Lisa Rowney
Maison Numéro Neuf,
Rue Serpente,
23300 La Souterraine, Creuse
Tel   +33 (0)5 55 63 43 35
Email reservations@maisonnumeroneuf.com
Web   maisonnumeroneuf.com

Entry 495   Map 9

Limousin

Château de Memanat

Roger and Pauline are passionate about their château. It is fabulously comfortable yet keeps strict faith with its past. Bedrooms are light and beautifully furnished, one with its own sitting room; bathrooms are superb. The food's great, too: Pauline adores cooking and uses local and organic suppliers. Opt for the simple menu and she and Roger will dine with you; go for gourmet and they'll join you for dessert. The grounds are vast – 1km of trout river, a walled garden with play area and solar-heated pool, and parkland planted with specimen trees by guests of the first owner, the scientist Dr Louis Queyrat. Marvellous.

Price	€95–€110.
Rooms	2 suites.
Meals	Dinner €34. Wine €15.
Closed	Christmas & New Year.
Directions	70km from Limoges for Aubusson N141/D941; after St Hilaire le Château, right for Chavanat D10; 2nd right to Memanat D45, white gates on right on entering village.

Roger & Pauline Ketteringham
Château de Memanat,
Memanat,
23250 Chavanat, Creuse
Tel   +33 (0)5 55 67 74 45
Email enquiries@memanat.com
Web   www.memanat.com

Entry 496   Map 10

Limousin

L'Abbaye du Palais

Everything here is big, beautiful, generous: each marvellous wood-floored bathroom has a rolltop tub and a walk-in shower; high, square bedrooms have delectable old furniture and fine embroidered linen; there are two pianos, some stupendous linden trees and so much heartfelt friendship. Martijn and Saskia left powerful jobs to bring their three young children to a life of nature and creativity in this exceptional old Cistercian abbey. With endless energy and charm, they'll share its wonders with you. Martin's sociable dinners, early suppers for children in the apple orchard, a sprig of rosemary on your pillow for sweet dreams. *Ask about cookery courses in autumn & spring. Sawday self-catering also.*

Price	€70–€100.
Rooms	5: 2 doubles, 1 twin, 2 suites for 4.
Meals	Dinner with wine, from €35. Picnics available.
Closed	Rarely.
Directions	From Limoges D941 east through Bourganeuf for Pontarion; just after Bourganeuf, left onto D940A. 5km on right, with blue gates.

Martijn & Saskia Zandvliet-Breteler
L'Abbaye du Palais,
23400 Bourganeuf, Creuse
Tel   +33 (0)5 55 64 02 64
Fax   +33 (0)5 55 64 02 63
Email info@abbayedupalais.com
Web   www.abbayedupalais.com

Entry 497   Map 10

Limousin

Manoir XV Domaine de Peyrafort

Come to be spoiled by homemade bread and cakes, picnics if you want them and delicious, locally-sourced dinners; Frances and Ian look after you with quiet ease in their 15th-century manor house tucked above Tulle. Find mullioned windows, a huge open fire in the sitting room, big beams, stripped floors and a long wooden table for shared meals; it may be smart but it's also laid back. Bedrooms vary in size and all are well turned out with super beds, navy and gold covers and curtains, small modern bathrooms. Acres of garden to explore, walking and cycling routes galore, and the glories of little-known Corrèze to unearth.

Price	€65-€72.
Rooms	4: 1 double, 1 single, 1 suite for 2, 1 family room for 3-4.
Meals	Dinner with wine, €25. Picnic available.
Closed	Rarely.
Directions	From north D1120 (ex-N120) into Tulle; on for 1.2km, left & follow signs to Les Fontaines, Peyrafort & Manoir XV.

Frances & Ian Black
Manoir XV Domaine de Peyrafort,
Chemin de Peyrafort,
19000 Tulle, Corrèze
Tel   +33 (0)5 55 29 93 58
Email   info@peyrafort.com
Web   www.peyrafort.com

Entry 498   Map 10

Limousin

La Souvigne

A gem. Jacquie, half-French, and Ian, half-Hungarian, are fervent Francophiles who know the local people, history, flora and building regs intimately and will tell you all. Aperitifs and dinner 'en famille', even breakfasts in the separate guest house, are intensely stimulating occasions – not for shrinking violets. A professional chef, Ian serves superb food with a flourish and wines from his cellar. Their clever renovation of the little old village house makes for a communal breakfast room, a biggish downstairs room and two cosy rooms under the rafters with Laura Ashley-style décor and some nice furniture.

Ethical Collection: Food.
See page 432.

Price	€38-€41.
Rooms	3: 2 doubles, 1 twin.
Meals	Dinner with wine, €20.
Closed	Rarely.
Directions	From Tulle D1120 for Argentat & Aurillac. Left into main square with Mairie on right, park in square on left of church.

Ian & Jacquie Hoare
La Souvigne,
1 impasse La Fontaine,
19380 Forgès, Corrèze
Tel   +33 (0)5 55 28 63 99
Fax   +33 (0)5 55 28 65 62
Email   info@souvigne.com
Web   www.souvigne.com

Entry 499   Map 10

Limousin

La Farge

The stone hamlets take you back to another age along the rugged valleys. The delightful Archibalds have adopted the country (and nationality), the stones and the peace, updating them with their English sense of fine finish: an ancient cart carefully restored before being flooded with flowers, old windows fitted with the latest fly screens, first-class showers. Fresh pastel bedrooms have honey-boarded floors and a teddy each; modern pine mixes with antique oak; the kitchen's solid farmhouse table, wood-burner and super food are at the heart of this house. "A slice of heaven," say readers.
Minimum stay 2 nights. Sawday self-catering also.

Limousin

Saulières

The delightful colour-loving Marie-Jo was born in the area and will never move away – you will understand why. With rainbow rooms in a modern extension, Saulières is no ancient monument but it's a picture of genuine French rural style, blissfully quiet in its conservation area. Ideal for families, it has masses of space and grass, a guest kitchen, a big log-fired living room with good old armchairs, magazines and games, and some fabulous places to visit. The superbly 'family, friends, fishing (ask for a permit) and farming' atmosphere created by this highly likeable couple has been much praised.

Price	€65.
Rooms	3: 2 doubles; 1 twin with separate bath.
Meals	Dinner with wine, €32.50.
Closed	Rarely.
Directions	From Argentat D12; D83E1 for Le Vialard & Moustoulat; 3km right for La Farge; right again; 2nd house on right in village with black gates.

Price	€45. Quadruple €65.
Rooms	4: 1 double, 1 twin, 1 triple, 1 quadruple.
Meals	Restaurants 2km. Guest kitchen.
Closed	Rarely.
Directions	From A20 exit Brive; A89 exit Tulle; N120 to Argentat; D12 along Dordogne R. for Beaulieu, past Monceaux to Saulières, 6km from Argentat.

Keith & Helen Archibald
La Farge,
19400 Monceaux sur Dordogne,
Corrèze
Tel +33 (0)5 55 28 54 52
Email info@chezarchi.com
Web www.chezarchi.com

Marie-Jo & Jean-Marie Lafond
Saulières,
Monceaux sur Dordogne,
19400 Argentat, Corrèze
Tel +33 (0)5 55 28 09 22
Fax +33 (0)5 55 28 09 22
Email mariejo.lafond@free.fr
Web www.chambredhotes-saulieres.com

Entry 500   Map 10

Entry 501   Map 10

Limousin

Jeanne Maison d'Hôte

Where tree-clad hills surge up from valley bottoms and sprinklings of fortified towns cling gloriously to hilltops is this turreted, redstone village. Hidden from tourist bustle behind high walls is a green shady garden, roses in abundance, a 15th-century tower and three floors of living space. Big bedrooms have sisal and sofas, heavy old armoires and one, a stone terrace; white bathrooms sparkle. She was in PR in Paris, he was a restaurateur, both are fine hosts and speak good English. You eat well; mushrooms are gathered in season and Brigitte is proud of her breakfast gâteaux. *Private parking.*

Price	€90.
Rooms	5: 3 doubles, 2 twins/doubles.
Meals	Dinner with wine, €35.
Closed	Never.
Directions	From Brive A20; exit 52 D38 to Collonges la Rouge; right at 2nd parking sign; follow signs.

Brigitte & Pascal Monteil
Jeanne Maison d'Hôte,
BP 28 Le Bourg,
19500 Collonges la Rouge, Corrèze

Tel	+33 (0)5 55 25 42 31
Fax	+33 (0)5 55 25 47 80
Email	info@jeannemaisondhotes.com
Web	www.jeannemaisondhotes.com

Entry 502   Map 9

Meals, booking and cancelling

Dinner

Do remember that table d'hôtes is a fixed-price set menu that has to be booked. Very few owners offer dinner every day. Once you have booked dinner, it is a question of common courtesy to turn up and partake of the meal prepared for you. Dining in can be a wonderful opportunity to experience both food and company in an authentic French family atmosphere. Or it may be more formal and still utterly French. Some owners no longer eat with their guests for family and waistline reasons.

Rooms

We have heard of chambres d'hôtes hopefuls arriving unannounced at 7pm and being devastated to learn that the house was full. For your own sake and your hosts', do ring ahead: if they can't have you, owners can usually suggest other places nearby. But arriving without warning at the end of the day is asking for disappointment.

Cancelling

As soon as you realise you are not going to take up a booking, even late in the day, please telephone immediately. The owners may still be able to let the room for that night and at least won't stay up wondering whether you've had an accident and when they can give up and go to bed.

By the same token, if you find you're going to arrive later than planned, let your hosts know so that they won't worry unnecessarily or… let your room to someone else.

Auvergne

Auvergne

Manoir Le Plaix

Thick, thick walls, great old stones and timbers: the immense age of this gloriously isolated farmhouse (once a fortified manor) is evident but it has been beautifully restored. Big, cosy, subtly-lit rooms, lovingly decorated with family antiques and memorabilia, are reached by a treat of a spiral staircase. A hundred head of cattle graze safely in the surrounding fields – you can walk, fish, and hunt mushrooms in season. Easy and good-natured, Madame Raucaz opens her heart, her intelligence and her dining table to all (excellent-value dinners). Relax and feel at home. Great value.

Price	€47.
Rooms	3: 1 double, 1 twin, 1 triple.
Meals	Restaurants 4km. Picnics available.
Closed	Rarely.
Directions	From Nevers N7 S 22km; right D978a to Le Veudre; D13 then D234 to Pouzy Mésangy. Chambres d'Hôtes signs.

Claire Raucaz
Manoir Le Plaix,
Pouzy Mésangy,
03320 Lurcy Levis, Allier
Tel +33 (0)4 70 66 24 06
Email leplaix@yahoo.fr

Auvergne

Château de Peufeilhoux

Your two eager Dutch hostesses, who are new to this lovely place, keep fine Friesian horses who can take you out in a carriage – just book. On a hill amid pasture, woodland and English gardens, the enchanting neo-gothic château is authentic, beamed, wood-panelled and early 20th century. Big bathrooms and bedrooms have not been deluxed or prettied up: they are simple old-fashioned French country rooms, beds are good and views sweep over the stunning valley. Paper-making is taught here… and cookery, so dinner in the baronial dining room or on the terrace should be good. *Minimum stay 2 nights August.*

Price	€80-€120.
Rooms	5: 2 doubles, 2 twins, 1 family room for 3-4.
Meals	Dinner with wine, €32.50.
Closed	Rarely.
Directions	From A71 exit 9 Vallon en Sully & Forêt de Tronçais; D2144 for Vallon; cont. past Vallon for St Amand Montrond; turning on right, signed.

Rinske van der Velde &
Anna-Syt Kuiken
Château de Peufeilhoux,
03190 Vallon en Sully, Allier
Tel +33 (0)4 70 06 59 60
Email info@peufeilhoux.com
Web www.peufeilhoux.com

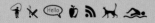

Auvergne

Cognet

Billowing hilly pastures surround the hamlet with sensuality. Here, built in 1886 as a rich man's summer place, is a generous, sophisticated house, informed by Madame's broad cultural interests, her father's paintings and her superb Provençal furniture that sits so well by original panelling and wide fireplace. Alone up steep shiny stairs, the guest space is a sweep of pine floor and ceiling; light floods in past royal blue curtains, big pine bed, old chest; a proud tree shades the splendid shower room. Deep rest, super breakfast and conversation, Romanesque jewels to visit – a must. *Not suitable for children.*

Price	€60.
Rooms	1 twin/double.
Meals	Restaurant in village.
Closed	November–February.
Directions	A75 exit Gannat to Vichy; over Allier; immed. right Bd JFK, left for Cusset; over railway; 5 lights, D906 right for Ferrières; right D995 9km; left D121; right to Cognet 800m; iron gates.

	Bénita Mourges
	Cognet,
	03300 La Chapelle, Allier
Tel	+33 (0)4 70 41 88 28
Email	maison.cognet@free.fr
Web	maison.cognet.free.fr

Auvergne

La Rambaude

A generous and handsomely decorated family house: the volcanoes gave their lava for dining room and staircase floor slabs; the hall is resplendent with hand-blocked wallpaper by Zuber. Ancestors gave their names to bedrooms, where their faded photographs and intricate samplers fill the walls; others left some fine old ornaments and pieces of furniture and built the stupendous brick barns that shelter the garden. Élisabeth is dynamic, intelligent and full of wry humour, once a trace of shyness has worn off, and serves her deliciously wholesome breakfast in the garden, studded with wild violets in spring.

Price	€70–€78.
Rooms	3 doubles.
Meals	Restaurants 7km.
Closed	November–March, except by arrangement.
Directions	From A71 exit Riom; N144 for Combronde & Montluçon; 2.5km after Davayat, right onto D122 to Chaptes.

	Élisabeth Beaujeard
	La Rambaude,
	8 route de la Limagne, Chaptes,
	63460 Beauregard Vendon,
	Puy-de-Dôme
Tel	+33 (0)4 73 63 35 62
Email	elisabeth.beaujeard@orange.fr
Web	www.la-rambaude.com

Auvergne

Domaine de Ternant

'Grand style' – marble, mouldings, gilt frames – and interesting hosts. Madame's astoundingly beautiful patchwork hangings make it utterly personal, the scent of beeswax hovers. All is pure Auvergne: original porcelain basins, third-generation owners, exceptional breakfasts. Bedrooms have antique beds – brass, carved, delicious 1930s – on polished parquet with good rugs and, of course, Madame's artistic needle. The dining room is elegant, the sitting room, with its well-used piano, sophisticated, the billiard room a library. A good-humoured couple who have lived in foreign lands and enjoy their guests. *Min. stay 2 nights in high season.*

Price	€82-€94.
Rooms	4: 1 double, 1 twin, 2 suites for 4.
Meals	Restaurants 3-10km.
Closed	Mid-November to mid-March.
Directions	From A71 for Clermont Ferrand; exit Riom for Volvic & Puy de Dôme; at Le Cratère, left for Clermont; right for Chanat, 3km Ternant, signed.

Catherine Piollet
Domaine de Ternant,
Ternant, 63870 Orcines,
Puy-de-Dôme

Tel +33 (0)4 73 62 11 20
Fax +33 (0)4 73 62 29 96
Email domaine.ternant@free.fr
Web domaine.ternant.free.fr

Auvergne

La Closerie de Manou

The rambling old house sits solid among the ancient volcanoes of Auvergne where great rivers rise and water is pure. There's a fine garden for games, a family-sized dining table before the great fireplace and a mixed bag of friendly armchairs guarded by a beautiful Alsatian stove in the salon. The décor is properly, comfortably rustic, bedrooms are lightly floral, no bows or furbelows, just pretty warmth and good shower rooms. Maryvonne, intelligent and chatty, knows and loves the Auvergne in depth and serves a scrumptious breakfast. *Minimum stay 2 nights. House available for self-catering, by arrangement.*

Price	€90. Extra person €20. Whole house available.
Rooms	3: 1 double, 2 family rooms (twin/double + single).
Meals	Restaurant in village.
Closed	Mid-October to March.
Directions	From A75 exit 6 on D978 then D996 to Le Mont Dore; pass Mairie & take Ave des Belges (still D996); 3km to Le Genestoux; house signed.

Françoise & Maryvonne Larcher
La Closerie de Manou,
Le Genestoux, 63240 Le Mont Dore,
Puy-de-Dôme

Tel +33 (0)4 73 65 26 81
Email lacloseriedemanou@club-internet.fr
Web www.lacloseriedemanou.com

Auvergne

Les Frênes

Perched above Saint Nectaire with views of almost endless forest and mountain, it's a farmhouse in a perfect setting. Inside lives Monique, enthusing her guests with descriptions of the Auvergne in perfect English. She does not pretend to provide luxury, just cosy comfort and the feeling of being in a real home. You stay in an attached but independent cottage and have a kitchen area of your own, but breakfast in Monique and Daniel's vaulted dining room, full of exposed beams and stone; eat copiously and enjoy the humour and zest of a couple who were born to hospitality. Great value for money.

Price	€48.
Rooms	Cottage for 2.
Meals	Restaurants in St Nectaire. Kitchen available.
Closed	Rarely.
Directions	From A75 exit 6 to St Nectaire; at church, D150 for 1.5km; left D643. Last house 300m, signed.

Monique Deforge
Les Frênes,
63710 St Nectaire,
Puy-de-Dôme
Tel   +33 (0)4 73 88 40 08
Email   daniel.deforge@orange.fr
Web   pagesperso-orange.fr/deforge/lesfrenes

Entry 509   Map 10

Auvergne

Le Chastel Montaigu

The solid reality of this magical tower is deeply moving. Michel's skill in renovation (well, reconstruction from near-ruin) and Anita's decorating talent have summoned a rich and sober mood that makes the 15th-century *chastel* throb with authenticity: only 'medieval' materials; magnificent deep-tinted fabrics, many designed by Anita; antique tapestries, panelling and furniture – nothing flashy, all simply true to the density of the place. Spectacular bedrooms, amazing bathrooms of antique-faced modern perfection and a generous breakfast – this is a treat. *Minimum stay 2 nights.*

Price	€145.
Rooms	4 doubles.
Meals	Auberge & restaurants 1-4km.
Closed	October-April.
Directions	From A75 exit 6 for St Nectaire; through Champeix to Montaigut le Blanc; follow signs up to château.

Anita & Michel Sauvadet
Le Chastel Montaigu,
63320 Montaigut le Blanc,
Puy-de-Dôme
Tel   +33 (0)4 73 96 28 49
Fax   +33 (0)4 73 96 21 60
Email   virginie.sauvadet@laposte.net
Web   www.lechastelmontaigu.com

Entry 510   Map 10

Auvergne

Château de Pasredon

Whichever of the splendid rooms is yours – we loved the yellow *Louis Philippe* – you will feel grand: here a canopied bed, there an exquisite little dressing room, everywhere shimmering mirrors, fabulous views of uninterrupted parkland, ancient trees, the Puy-de-Dôme: acres of space for those who like to read in a secluded spot to the magical sound of birdsong. The vast, panelled, period-furnished drawing and dining rooms are quite dramatic. A perfect and relaxed hostess, Madame makes you feel immediately at ease and helps you plan your day over a delicious breakfast. Really very special.

Price	€80–€100.
Rooms	3: 2 doubles, 1 twin.
Meals	Restaurants 2-8km.
Closed	Mid-October to mid-April.
Directions	From Clermont Ferrand A75 exit 13 to Parentignat; D999 for St Germain l'Herme 6km; sign on right. (8km from A75 exit.)

Henriette Marchand
Château de Pasredon,
63500 St Rémy de Chargnat,
Puy-de-Dôme
Tel   +33 (0)4 73 71 00 67
Fax   +33 (0)4 73 71 08 72
Email   chateau.de.pasredon@orange.fr

Entry 511   Map 10

Auvergne

Domaine de Gaudon – Le Château

Out in wildest Auvergne, here be surprises: new Venuses and urns outside, 19th-century splendour inside – glossy oak panelling, ceiling roses, original wall coverings. Endearingly natural, loving their new life, Alain and Monique have created a setting of astonishing glamour, brass and satin, gilt and quilting, for their superb French antiques. Add luxurious bathrooms, dazzling breakfasts, specimen trees, innumerable frogs, bats, birds and insects (some in frames), herons fishing in the pond – and Connemara ponies in the park. Children and adults love it, one and all. *Wildlife conservation area.*

Price	€110–€130.
Rooms	5: 3 doubles, 1 twin, 1 suite.
Meals	Restaurants 4km.
Closed	Rarely.
Directions	A75 from Montpellier exit 9; D229 then D996 to St Dier d'Auvergne. At end of village, D6 for Domaize 3km. Right for Ceilloux, 1km.

Alain & Monique Bozzo
Domaine de Gaudon – Le Château,
63520 Ceilloux, Puy-de-Dôme
Tel   +33 (0)4 73 70 76 25
Email   domainedegaudon@wanadoo.fr
Web   www.domainedegaudon.fr

Entry 512   Map 10

Auvergne

Château de Vaulx

Is this real or a fairy tale? Creak along the parquet, pray in the chapel, swan around the salon, sleep in one tower, bathe in another. It's been in the family for 800 years and room names are as evocative as furnishings are romantic – worthy of the troubadours who surely sang here. Breakfast on home-hived honey, brioche, yogurt, eggs, cheese, get to know your delightfully entertaining hosts, visit the donkey, admire the magnificent trees or, if you're feeling homesick, have a drink in Guy's evocatively vaulted cellar 'pub' with its impressive collection of beer mats. A dream of a place.

Price	€70-€80.
Rooms	2: 1 double, 1 triple.
Meals	Auberge 3km.
Closed	Rarely.
Directions	From A72 exit 3 on D7 through Celles sur Durolle to Col du Frissonnet. Château 1st right after Col du Frissonnet.

Guy & Régine Dumas de Vaulx
Château de Vaulx,
63120 Ste Agathe,
Puy-de-Dôme
Tel   +33 (0)4 73 51 50 55
Fax   +33 (0)4 73 51 50 55

Entry 513   Map 10

Auvergne

Le Relais de la Diligence

Soon after escaping to this pretty village in rugged country, Peter and Laurette opened their doors so guests could enjoy the simplicity of their aptly named house and the local flora and fauna. Peter's craftsman's skills and their shared passion for restoration come together in this old coaching inn with its carefully restored beams, warm colours and sweet painted furniture. Comfortable beds in sunny bedrooms, cosy sitting room with glorious wood-burner and simple light suppers at a refectory table speak of thoughtful, kind hosts. Next morning, wave to Fleur as she jumps on the school bus, driven by Laurette.

Price	€50. €80 for 4.
Rooms	3: 1 double, 1 family room for 3, 1 family suite for 4.
Meals	Dinner with wine, €15.
Closed	Rarely.
Directions	From La Chaise Dieu, D906 for Ambert; at Arlanc D300 left for St Germain L'Herm; 13km to St Bonnet; Le Relais on left in middle of village.

Peter & Laurette Eggleton
Le Relais de la Diligence, Le Bourg,
63630 St Bonnet Le Chastel,
Puy-de-Dôme
Tel   +33 (0)4 73 72 57 96
Fax   +33 (0)4 73 72 57 96
Email leseggleton@aliceadsl.fr
Web   www.relais-diligence.com

Entry 514   Map 10

Auvergne

Ma Cachette

Pierre is the gardener, Johan the cook. Both South African, your charming hosts left the film and television world for this aqua-shuttered village house in the heart of the Regional Park. A few steps from the romantic, private garden, lush with roses, ancient fruit trees and well-tended vegetables, will find you walking some of the most stunning and unspoilt trails through the Massif Central. Rooms are spacious with Persian carpets and garden flowers; walk-in showers are superb; a stylish living room is for guests. Dinner will be exceptional – the conversation as much as the 'confit de canard'.

Price	€55–€65.
Rooms	4: 3 doubles, 1 twin.
Meals	Dinner with wine, €28.
Closed	Rarely.
Directions	From A72 exit 2 for Thiers (west); D906 for Ambert & Le Puy en Velay; 67km, follow Chambres d'Hôtes signs on entering Arlanc; close to St Pierre Roman church.

Johan Bernard & Pierre Knoesen
Ma Cachette,
10 rue du 11 Novembre,
63220 Arlanc, Puy-de-Dôme

Tel	+33 (0)4 73 95 04 88
Fax	+33 (0)4 73 95 04 88
Email	cachette@club-internet.fr
Web	www.ma-cachette.com

Entry 515   Map 10

Auvergne

La Jacquerolle

Built on the ramparts of the ancient town, just below the medieval Abbey whose August music festival draws thousands, the big old house has been lovingly filled with flowers in every fashion and form – carpets, curtains, wallpaper, quilts. It is a soft French boudoir where mother and daughter, quietly attentive, welcome their guests to sleep in pine-slatted bedrooms – ask for the largest – with firm-mattressed divan beds and good little bathrooms (some with wonderful views out to the hills). Gallic cuisine is served on bone china with bohemian crystal before a huge stone fireplace.

Price	€57–€60.
Rooms	3: 1 double, 1 twin, 1 family room for 4.
Meals	Dinner with wine, €25.
Closed	Rarely.
Directions	From Brioude D19 to La Chaise Dieu; for centre ville; facing Abbey, right Place du Monument. Park here; house off square: bottom right-hand corner then down on left.

Carole Chailly
La Jacquerolle,
Rue Marchédial,
43160 La Chaise Dieu,
Haute-Loire

Tel	+33 (0)4 71 00 07 52
Email	lajacquerolle@hotmail.com
Web	lajacquerolle.com

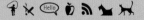

Entry 516   Map 10

Auvergne

Le Château Gris

The owners, DuWayne and Fifi, may have had their tongues slightly in their pock-marked cheeks when christening this bijou eco home, but squint and you see what they mean. Elegance doesn't describe it. Le Château Gris is quintessential deep south – Alabama transported to St Tropez – and design is inspired by the trash du monde school of architecture. The solar heating is clever – tin panels soak up the sun all year round, keeping the inside a cosy 115°F. The neighbours are friendly: listen to their colourful banter through the walls... you may even get to help them jack their cars onto bricks. Marvellous!

Price	€10 high season; €5 low season.
Rooms	One, shared with the owners.
Meals	Pizzas in boxes, chicken in buckets.
Closed	Only if the owners wander into town.
Directions	Ask anyone in St Tropez for Le Rank trailer park; they will answer with a wry smile.

	Du Wayne & Fifi St Hickclaire
	Le Château Gris,
	Le Rank Trailer Park,
	somewhere off the St Tropez
	peripherique,
Tel	The park is "off grid"
Email	hotchicknwings@hotmail.grrrr
Web	www.sleeponapallet.brrrr

Entry 517   Map 23232

Auvergne

Château de Durianne

Since moving in five years ago, the Chambons have poured heart and soul into rescuing the family château. Nothing had been touched for a century; in the attics they found 120-year-old wallpaper which they lovingly re-used. Now the place, full of portraits and antiques, feels like a home. The huge bedroom overlooks a farm where the Chambons plan to keep sheep; the as yet uncultivated garden is long and grassy, the orchard is home to two donkeys and a pony and the village is just down the lane. Breakfast is generous (with juice from their apples) and you may be joined by friendly Madame for coffee and a chat.

Ethical Collection: Environment; Food. See page 432.

Price	€55. Extra bed €15.
Rooms	1 family suite for 2-4.
Meals	Platter with wine, €12.
Closed	Never.
Directions	From Le Puy en Velay D103 for Lavoute/Vorey 2km; right D103 to Durianne; in village, take only right, unmarked; château 50m on left.

	Françoise & Jean-Nicolas
	Chambon du Garay
	Château de Durianne,
	43700 Le Monteil, Haute-Loire
Tel	+33 (0)4 71 02 90 36
Email	info@chateaudedurianne.com
Web	www.chateaudedurianne.com

Entry 518   Map 11

Auvergne

Le Bourg

Simple, unaffected people and keen walkers love this place, with its friendly welcoming atmosphere and new lick of paint. Furniture remains dated and simple, but the home-grown food oozes genuine natural goodness. Éric and his partner Christelle manage a flock of milk-producing sheep and welcome all-comers with a 'cup of friendship' before the great granite hearth. There are sheep and music festivals in August, while walkers are in heaven: join a circuit here and walk from B&B to B&B, or cross-country ski through it in winter. Wonderful value for money in an unknown corner of the Auvergne.

Auvergne

Château la Prade

The antidote to city stress: simplicity and serenity in the wilds of the Auvergne. Dutch Albert and Ria will be there to greet you once you've negotiated the rough track up to the château. They're friendly, generous hosts who speak excellent English, and the big well-proportioned bedrooms are refreshingly uncluttered: acres of polished floor, fabulous beds, good armchairs and views over the countryside. (Two have their own bathrooms, the other two share.) Everyone eats together at one long table in the dining room. No restaurants nearby – but Ria says nobody ever wants to eat out anyway! *Minimum stay 2 nights.*

Price	€38.
Rooms	3: 1 double, 1 twin, 1 triple.
Meals	Dinner with wine, €14.
Closed	Never.
Directions	From Le Puy en Velay, D589 to Sauges; D585 for Langeac, left onto D32 to Venteuges.

Price	€45-€50.
Rooms	4: 2 family suites; 2 doubles, sharing separate bath
Meals	Dinner with wine, €15.
Closed	Never.
Directions	From A75 exit 30, left D74 1.3km, at x-roads right 1.5km; right D50, over level crossing; 1st right D50 to Chaliers & Lorcières 1km, left at sign La Prade Basse.

Stop Press
No longer doing B&B

	Ria & Albert Voorzee
	Château la Prade, La Prade Basse,
	15320 Ruynes en Margeride,
	Cantal
Tel	+33 (0)4 71 23 48 99
Email	mail@chateaulaprade.info
Web	www.chateaulaprade.info

Auvergne

Ferme des Prades

A real farmhouse – warm and unpretentious. Françoise and Philippe are a sweet, down-to-earth couple who welcome company: their sons are away at school and this is 'la France profonde'! The farm covers 150 hectares; walk for hours and you need not see another soul. The house, destroyed in the French Revolution, was rebuilt by Napoleon's confessor. Outside, ox-blood red shutters give a splash to speckled stone walls, inside are stripped floors, comfortably worn sofas, fine armoires, muslin curtains – and Françoise's bedside tables fashioned from milk churns. Convivial dinners are great value, a huge treat.

Price	€67-€72.
Rooms	3: 1 double, 1 triple, 1 family room.
Meals	Dinner with wine, €20.
Closed	Rarely.
Directions	D996 Champeix & Issoire; A75 to Montpellier exit 23 (Massiac); N122 to Murat; D21 Allanche; D679 to Marcenat; Hamlet les Prades, farm on right.

Françoise & Philippe Vauché
Ferme des Prades,
Les Prades, Landeyrat,
15160 Allanche, Cantal

Tel	+33 (0)4 71 20 48 17
Fax	+33 (0)4 71 20 91 26
Email	les-prades@wanadoo.fr
Web	www.fermedesprades.com

Entry 521   Map 10

Auvergne

Château de Bassignac

Its front door wide open, Bassignac is real unposh family B&B, run for many years by charming, active Annie with the support of her artist husband (come and paint with him). She was born in this 16th-century fortified manor built on 13th-century ruins beside what is now a fairly busy road and sold her Parisian furniture shop to come back and… furnish her guest rooms. They are big (two or three windows, fireplace) and small (invitingly womb-like), kempt and clear with Monsieur's watercolours and a dated chintzy charm that draws people back. Son and daughter-in-law run a delicious *ferme auberge* next door.

Price	€60-€130.
Rooms	6: 4 doubles, 1 family room, 1 family suite for 5.
Meals	Dinner with wine, €45. Auberge next door.
Closed	Rarely.
Directions	A89 exit 23 for Bort les Orgues; D922 for Mauriac; on for 16km to Bassignac, château on right.

Annie & Jean-Michel Besson
Château de Bassignac,
Bassignac,
15240 Saignes, Cantal

Tel	+33 (0)4 71 40 82 82
Fax	+33 (0)4 71 40 82 82
Email	chateau.bassignac@wanadoo.fr
Web	www.chateau-de-bassignac.fr

Entry 522   Map 10

Auvergne

Château de La Vigne

A rare treat from another age, the deliciously organic, old château in pure Cantal style surveying the hills has been in the family for ever and is utterly lavish: a courtroom panelled and dazzlingly painted; a fine and formal dining room (do dress for dinner); an Aubusson-hung, chandeliered salon; a Louis XV guest room with its lovely carved fireplace, a darkly four-postered Troubadour room, bathrooms squeezed into impossible places, an extraordinary Dinky Toy collection, and more. Stunning but not overbearing, and yours to share with these gentle, open, aristocratic hosts and their well-mannered children.

Price	€135–€155.
Rooms	2: 1 double, 1 twin.
Meals	Dinner €30. Wine €25.
Closed	November–Easter.
Directions	From Clermont Ferrand N89 for Tulle; left D922 to Bort les Orgues; D681 to Mauriac & Ally. Signed.

Bruno & Anne du Fayet de la Tour
Château de La Vigne,
15700 Ally, Cantal
Tel   +33 (0)4 71 69 00 20
Fax   +33 (0)4 71 69 00 20
Email   la.vigne@wanadoo.fr
Web   www.chateaudelavigne.com

Entry 523   Map 10

Auvergne

Lou Ferradou

Your hosts escaped from stressful Paris to this rural paradise; their brilliant conversion of an old Cantal farmhouse saved the original vast stone scullery ledge and sink, the beams, the inglenook. Then they persuaded their neighbours to clear their wrecks and scrap metal from the hillside; brilliant. Oak-floored bedrooms are country comfortable with big oak beds and white covers, the meals are delectable, convivial feasts (loads of home-grown things), there are a games room, billiards and books, a barn sitting room, a super garden, and the Balleux are a most interesting and welcoming couple.

Price	€50–€60.
Rooms	5: 2 doubles, 3 suites.
Meals	Dinner with wine, €17.
Closed	Rarely.
Directions	From Aurillac D920 to Arpajon; left on D990 for 10km (don't go to St Étienne de Carlat); left for Caizac; signed.

Francine & Jacky Balleux
Lou Ferradou,
Caizac, 15130 St Étienne de Carlat,
Cantal
Tel   +33 (0)4 71 62 42 37
Email   balleux@louferradou.com
Web   www.louferradou.com

Entry 524   Map 10

Auvergne

La Roussière

Not another house in sight. Just the Cantal hills and a chattering stream. Brigitte and Christian live here with their young son and have done much of the restoration themselves. Christian is a genius at woodwork: his golden staircase, cupboards and panelling sit happily with mellow stone, old armoires, ancient ceiling hooks… There's an Alpine air to the place. Beds are excellent, sheets crisp and meals 'en famille' a delight: great food, good wine, mineral water from the spring. Be calmed by a serene, rustic elegance. No actual garden but their green rolling hectares, a haven for wildlife, are perfection enough. *Min. stay 2 nights July/August.*

Price	€60-€72.
Rooms	3: 1 double, 1 suite for 2-3, 1 suite for 3-4.
Meals	Dinner with wine, €20.
Closed	Rarely.
Directions	From Massiac N122 for Aurillac; in Vic sur Cère left for Pailherols; D54 for 6km up to col de Curebourse; continue to Pailherols; left before bridge; continue straight on 4km.

	Christian Grégoir & Brigitte Renard La Roussière, 15800 St Clément, Cantal
Tel	+33 (0)4 71 49 67 34
Email	info@laroussiere.fr
Web	www.laroussiere.fr

Entry 525   Map 10

Auvergne

Château de Lescure

On the southern slope of Europe's largest extinct volcano, where nine valleys radiate, stands a rustic 18th-century château guarded by a medieval tower where two vaulted bedrooms soar. The twin room has the right furbelowed drapery, and in the big inglenook kitchen Sophie, a committed environmentalist, serves home-smoked ham, veg from her organic garden, fruit from her orchard. Michel's passions are heritage conservation and blazing trails across the hills. They are bilingual hosts who may invite you to join in bread-making, cooking, organic gardening, rambling… *Minimum stay 2 nights in summer.*

Ethical Collection: Environment; Community; Food. See page 432.

Price	€70-€75.
Rooms	3: 1 twin; 1 double with separate shower, 1 double with separate shower room downstairs.
Meals	Dinner with wine, €30.
Closed	November to mid-February.
Directions	From Clermont Ferrand A75 to St Flour; up to old town; left D921 10km; right D990, through Pierrefort to St Martin. Right for Brezons; château 3km on right.

	Michel Couillaud & Phoebe Sophie Verhulst Château de Lescure, 15230 Saint Martin Sous Vigouroux, Cantal
Tel	+33 (0)4 71 73 40 91
Email	michel.couillaud@wanadoo.fr
Web	www.multimania.com/psvlescure

Entry 526   Map 10

Midi – Pyrénées

Midi – Pyrénées

Manoir de Malagorse

Your passionate eager hosts, with young twins and straw-coloured retrievers that blend with the décor, offer you a refined old manor in an idyllic setting and meals cooked by a master. Abel and Anna's restoration is caring and sophisticated, rooms and bathrooms are statements of simple luxury, and the vaulted kitchen is a dream – its fireplace massive, its cooker a wonder to behold. There is space for togetherness and privacy, your hosts are unintrusively present and Anna can offer a professional massage after Abel's demanding wine-tastings. Enjoy it to the hilt.
Gastronomic weekends. Wine tastings. Massage.

Price	€120-€180. Suites €250-€350.
Rooms	6: 4 doubles, 2 suites.
Meals	Dinner with wine, €45. À la carte lunch, from €20.
Closed	December-April.
Directions	From Souillac 6km; N20 for Cressensac, on dual c'way, 1st right to Cuzance/ Église de Rignac; 1st right in Rignac, signed. Detailed directions on booking.

Anna & Abel Congratel
Manoir de Malagorse,
46600 Cuzance, Lot
Tel   +33 (0)5 65 27 15 61
Fax   +33 (0)5 65 27 14 83
Email   acongratel@manoir-de-malagorse.fr
Web   www.manoir-de-malagorse.fr

Entry 527   Map 9

Midi – Pyrénées

Château de Termes

Such views! Sublime when the mists hang in the river valleys and the sun glints on the summits. Your hospitable hosts, he a small-plane instructor who offers flying for guests, she quietly busy with her gîtes, have been here two years. More domestic than ostentatious, their 1720s' château promises three gorgeous guest rooms, a garden, a pool, a play area, short tennis, a small bar. Floors are stripped wood or chunky terracotta, furniture 'distressed', two baths are integrated with bedrooms, the suite opens to the garden and the whimsical doubles are in the tower. For families: bliss.

Price	€65-€85.
Rooms	3: 2 doubles, 1 family suite for 3.
Meals	Dinner with wine, €20-€25, except July/August.
Closed	Rarely.
Directions	From Paris A20 exit 54. From Martel; D803 to Vayrac St Céré, 4.5km on left.

Pierre & Sophie Nadin
Château de Termes,
St Denis,
46600 Martel, Lot
Tel   +33 (0)5 65 32 42 03
Email   infos@chateaudetermes.com
Web   www.chateaudetermes.com

Entry 528   Map 9

Midi – Pyrénées

L'Oustal Nau

This is the house that Colette built when she came back from Paris. And this is the garden that she spent 17 years creating – one glorious hectare overlooking the Dordogne valley. You can spend all day in it if you want to: Colette, who used to work in the diplomatic service, is that sort of hostess, infinitely generous and with a wonderful smile. There's a guest kitchen where you can prepare drinks and snacks and Colette will provide picnics if required. The house is modern but full of character and lovely old pieces; the big, comfortable bedrooms are each named after a flower. A great place for families.

Price	€80-€100.
Rooms	4: 2 doubles, 1 twin, 1 triple.
Meals	Picnic €15 p.p. Guest kitchen.
Closed	12 November, 15 December & 6 January-6 February.
Directions	From St Céré D20 to Carennac; in village Auberge des Vieux Quercy on right, turn left following Parking sign; top of road left; 200m green gates on right. Just before Parking.

Colette Lemant-Lacroix
L'Oustal Nau,
Les Combes, 46110 Carennac, Lot
Tel +33 (0)5 65 10 94 09
Fax +33 (0)5 65 50 27 49
Email lemant@club-internet.fr
Web www.oustalnau-carennac.com

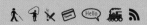

Entry 529   Map 9

Midi – Pyrénées

Moulin de Goth

The 13th-century mill – imaginatively, magically restored by its Australian owners – guards a garden of rare peace and beauty. Lily pads and lawns, willows and water – it is ineffably lovely. Coral is humorous and exuberant and cooks like an angel; Bill makes tables and intelligent conversation – join him for snooker in the barn. Big, dramatically raftered rooms have decorative iron beds, soft fabrics, antique chests. The stone-walled dining room, its arrow slits intact, is stunningly barrel-vaulted – but meals are mostly in the enchanting garden. Readers adore this place. *Children over 8 welcome.*

Price	€65-75.
Rooms	2: 1 double, 1 triple, each with separate bath.
Meals	Dinner with wine, €26.
Closed	Rarely.
Directions	From Martel D23 to Creysse. After 3km right fork for Le Goth, 1.5km; 1st house on right after stone bridge.

Coral Heath-Kauffman
Moulin de Goth,
46600 Creysse, Lot
Tel +33 (0)5 65 32 26 04
Email coral.heath@orange.fr
Web www.moulindugoth.com

Entry 530   Map 9

Midi – Pyrénées

Le Moulin de Latreille

The mill is 13th century and Cistercian, the owners are full of life, the setting is truly special. Kingfishers and wild orchids, herons and hammocks… and it is just as atmospheric inside. Furniture has been renovated and painted, books peep from alcoves, lovely linen encases beds, bathrooms are perfect. If Fiona can't cook for you, there's the charming kitchen to borrow, and your own little sitting room with a wood-burner. Surrounded by steep hills and woods, at the bottom of a bumpy track and with the river running through, the mill generates its own electricity. Heaven in Quercy.
Minimum stay 2 nights. Unfenced water.

Ethical Collection: Environment
See page 432.

Price	€80.
Rooms	2 doubles.
Meals	Dinner with wine, €25. Light lunches & picnics available.
Closed	Rarely.
Directions	From Payrac D673 to Calès. In Calès opp. Le Petit Relais, left for La Cave, then immed. right (for Le Petit Relais parking), follow round to left, down hill 2km (rough road); only house at bottom.

Giles & Fi Stonor
Le Moulin de Latreille,
Calès, 46350 Payrac, Lot

Tel	+33 (0)5 65 41 91 83
Email	gilesetfi@wanadoo.fr
Web	moulindelatreille.com

Entry 531 Map 9

Midi – Pyrénées

La Buissonnière

The converted 18th-century barn with its stone outbuilding feels instantly like home. Élisabeth spent years in America (she's bilingual), loves ceramics and patchwork, uses her creative touch everywhere, including the terrace and garden with its secluded spots, and is a fount of historical and cultural lore. The open-plan living room, where old skylights deliver splashes of sky, is full of artistic character with oak floors, old stove and pretty antiques beneath paintings of all periods. The airy ground-floor guest room has its own antique writing table, watercolours and a glazed stable door to the garden.

Price	€60.
Rooms	2: 1 double, 1 twin.
Meals	Dinner with wine, €18-€20.
Closed	Rarely.
Directions	From Gramat D840 (previously called N140) for Figeac; left for 'Le Bout du Lieu' after sign for Thémines; house, 200m on right; signed.

Élisabeth de Lapérouse Coleman
La Buissonnière,
Le Bout du Lieu,
46120 Thémines, Lot

Tel	+33 (0)5 65 40 88 58
Fax	+33 (0)5 65 40 88 58
Email	edelaperouse.coleman@wanadoo.fr
Web	leboutdulieu.weebly.com

Entry 532 Map 10

Midi – Pyrénées

Les Jardins de la Contie

Ken and Sabine have rescued a ruined hamlet and created a place of rustic charm. It is delightfully quirky, very comfortable, all knobbly-stone walls, flagged floors, beams, arches and inglenook fireplaces. Traditional bedrooms in separate buildings, each with a private outdoor spot, have country antiques, cosy beds, good linen. In the huge breakfast room you feast on hams, cheeses and fruit from their trees: the lush gardens are full of them, fragrant shrubs too, so pick a lounger and settle in. Lovely people, great walks from the house, views to die for – yet you are the shortest drive from civilisation.

Price	€60-€95.
Rooms	2: 1 double, 1 suite for 2 & kitchenette.
Meals	Restaurants 3-5km.
Closed	November-Easter.
Directions	From Figeac D840 for Decazeville. 1km after Capdenac Port, left to Lunan & Église Romane; right at town hall; follow signs.

Sabine & Ken Lazarus
Les Jardins de la Contie,
La Contie,
46100 Lunan, Lot
Fax +33 (0)3 21 31 50 88
Email sablaz@nordnet.fr
Web www.lacontie.com

Entry 533   Map 10

Midi – Pyrénées

Maison Rouma

Built in the 1850s, the house was a near-ruin when the Arnetts, back from Japan, found and restored it, keeping as much of the original as possible, including the wallpaper in the hall where the winding staircase is such a delight. The décor has an oriental look, particularly in the dining room. The setting couldn't be better, there are stunning views over the river and the pretty old town; Puy l'Évêque is famous for its medieval music festival and fine firework display. Overlook the lived-in look and a bit of road noise and chat to your interesting, sociable hosts before retiring to your big comfy bedroom. Good value.

Price	€55.
Rooms	3: 2 doubles, each with extra sofabed; 1 family room with separate bath.
Meals	Restaurant 200m; choice nearby.
Closed	Rarely.
Directions	From Cahors D911 for Fumel & Villeneuve sur Lot. At Puy l'Évêque take Rue du Dr Rouma to bridge; house last on right before bridge.

Bill & Ann Arnett
Maison Rouma,
2 rue du Docteur Rouma,
46700 Puy l'Évêque, Lot
Tel +33 (0)5 65 36 59 39
Fax +33 (0)5 65 36 59 39
Email williamarnett4@msn.com
Web www.puyleveque-maisonrouma.com

Entry 534   Map 9

Flaynac

A heart-warming, genuine B&B experience, staying with this lovely cheerful couple who are always ready for a drink and a chat (in French) – their love of life is infectious. Use the peaceful terrace where your hosts are happy for you to sit all day over your breakfast, revelling in the setting, the vast views and the flowering garden. The décor – floral papers and family furniture – is in keeping with the old farmhouse. No dinner but lots of home-grown wine and aperitif, fruit from their trees and 'gâteau de noix' (walnut cake) with their own honey – flowing as in paradise.

Price	€48.
Rooms	1 double.
Meals	Restaurant 2km.
Closed	Rarely.
Directions	From Cahors D8 for Pradines 6km; at sign for Flaynac, follow Chambres d'Hôtes sign on right, then right & right again.

	M & Mme Faydi
	Flaynac,
	46090 Pradines, Lot
Tel	+33 (0)5 65 35 33 36

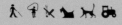

Entry 535   Map 9

Mondounet

The golden Lot stone glows and there are stunning views from the terrace over two valleys, the pool is heated and salt-purified… so what matter if the atmosphere is sometimes chaotic? The Scotts labour ever on at their little empire, restoring the 17th-century farmhouse and outbuildings to their original character and adding a few modern comforts. Zoé will charm you, see you have a good time, serve breakfast whenever. Dinner, sometimes a poolside barbecue, is fun, relaxed and informal and Peter plays the guitar and organises activities. There is a pool-house kitchen for lazy picnic lunches.

Price	€55–€60.
Rooms	1 double.
Meals	Dinner with wine, €20.
Closed	Rarely.
Directions	From Cahors for Toulouse; at r'bout D653 for Agen 16km; at junc. right D656 for 14km; thro' Villesèque, Sauzet, Bovila; after Bovila, 3rd left; signed.

	Peter & Zoé Scott
	Mondounet,
	46800 Fargues, Lot
Tel	+33 (0)5 65 36 96 32
Fax	+33 (0)5 65 31 84 89
Email	scotsprops@aol.com
Web	www.mondounetholidaysandhomes.com

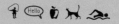

Entry 536   Map 14

Domaine de Lacombe

Wonderful place, wonderful lady. The flamboyantly decorated great barn living room reveals her sense of adventure, the books and baby grand suggest she is fine company, the variegated bedrooms in the converted stables, from modern simplicity to traditional florality, speak of her eclectic taste. All now have their own patios, one has the original spring welling up behind glass, all have space, privacy and fine bathrooms. Michèle bubbles with delight, encouraging guests to come and chat while she prepares a superb family meal to be shared sitting on rainbow chairs at the long red table. Breakfasts are feasts.

Las Bourdolles

The Quercy light glides through deep windows – reveals and dapples the creamy old stones, dark beams and warm floorboards of this 17th-century farmhouse. The potager is prolific, the views priceless (from every terrace) and nature-loving walkers and culture vultures flock here. Linda and Erica use a light touch, mixing old and new, cooking with delight, be it hearty game dinners or plum jam. The food is wonderfully presented, the bedroom is soft and simple, colours pale, the great stone fireplace marvellous in winter. Stress slips away, among these people who take delight in their guests' well being. *Minimum stay 2 nights. Sawday self-catering also.*

Price	€64-€84.		Price	€80-100.
Rooms	3: 1 double, 1 triple, 1 family room.		Rooms	1 suite.
Meals	Dinner with wine, €29.		Meals	Dinner with wine, €40.
Closed	Rarely.		Closed	Christmas.
Directions	From Paris A20 to Cahors Nord exit 58; N20 to Montauban Toulouse; right for Castelnau-Montratier; in Castelnau D19 right to Lauzerte Moissac; 4km, left 100m after brick barn. Lacombe 2nd left.		Directions	A62 exit 8; D953 to Golfech & Lauzerte. Before Lauzerte, right onto D34 to Castelnau-Montratier. Straight on at church x-roads, D57 to Tréjouls. After 1km, sign on left.

	Michèle Lelourec			Linda Hilton & Erica Lewis
	Domaine de Lacombe,			Las Bourdolles,
	Lacombe,			82110 Tréjouls,
	46170 Castelnau Monratier, Lot			Tarn-et-Garonne
Tel	+33 (0)5 65 21 84 16		Tel	+33 (0)5 63 95 80 83
Email	michele.lelourec@gmail.com		Email	lewiserica@mac.com
Web	www.domaine-lacombe.com		Web	www.lasbourdolles.com

Midi – Pyrénées

La Résidence

Your gentle young hosts love being part of village life – and what a village: medieval to the core and with a joyous Sunday market. It is a pleasure to stay in a townhouse in the centre of it all, with an airy hall and great spiral staircase, views through to an enclosed garden, original tiles and old stone walls. Sunlight dapples over soft colours and uncluttered spaces, modern sculpture and old country pieces. Three of the big tranquil bedrooms overlook the garden, another has a divine terrace with rooftop views. Seriously into food, Sabine and Evert do excellent dinners. *Studio available.*

Price	€75–€90.
Rooms	5: 3 doubles, 2 twins.
Meals	Dinner €25. Wine €10–€25.
Closed	Rarely.
Directions	From Montauban N20, 22km to Caussade; right D926 for 7km; right D5 to St Antonin Noble Val, 12km; in centre, behind town hall.

Evert & Sabine Weijers
La Résidence,
37 rue Droite,
82140 St Antonin Noble Val,
Tarn-et-Garonne
Tel   +33 (0)5 63 67 37 56
Email   info@laresidence-france.com
Web   www.laresidence-france.com

Entry 539   Map 15

Midi – Pyrénées

Domaine de Canals

Monsieur is eloquent (in English!) about the garden of his old family home which is a dream of trees, shrubs, lily pond and rare plants: a pergola awaits the contemplative guest, a maze summons the adventurous. Inside, the suite's old country décor is coloured with memories of Egypt, Mexico, India as well as Madame's hand-painted furniture. Opening onto the courtyard is a summer-cool double room, newly redecorated. Tapestries hang in the old-fashioned dining room, the atmosphere is safe and friendly, the conversation full of interest. The best of charming, welcoming, old-style French B&B. *Self-catering possible.*

Ethical Collection: Environment; Food. See page 432.

Price	€50–€60. Suite €70–€140.
Rooms	2: 1 twin/double, 1 suite for 2-4.
Meals	Dinner with wine, €20. Guest kitchenette.
Closed	Rarely.
Directions	At Réalville left for Bioule, Nègrepelisse; after 3km at La Bouffière house on left.

M & Mme Auréjac
Domaine de Canals,
La Bouffière, 82800 Bioule,
Tarn-et-Garonne
Tel   +33 (0)5 63 64 21 07
Fax   +33 (0)5 63 64 21 07
Email   domainecanals@free.fr
Web   domaine-de-canals.fr.st

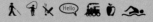

Entry 540   Map 14

Midi – Pyrénées

Le Mas des Anges

An exciting venture for a super couple who are squeaky-green too, running their organic vineyard. You find a very pretty house surrounded by lovely shrubs, a heated pool, and a separate entrance to each bedroom with terrace. Ground-floor rooms have fabulous colours, big good beds, bathrooms with thick towels. The sitting area is airy and modern with stacks of books, magazines and interesting sculpture and art. Sophie gives you a huge breakfast with homemade bread and jams, fresh fruit, cheeses and yogurt. Mountauban is only 7km away and you are near enough to amazing Albi for a day trip.

Price	€65. €95 for 4.
Rooms	3: 2 doubles, 1 twin.
Meals	Restaurants in Montauban, 7km.
Closed	Never.
Directions	From Montauban D999 for Albi, 2km; r'bout 3rd exit onto D92. On left after approx. 1.6km; signed.

Juan & Sophie Kervyn
Le Mas des Anges,
1623 route de Verlhac Tescou,
82000 Montauban, Tarn-et-Garonne
Tel	+33 (0)5 63 24 27 05
Fax	+33 (0)5 63 24 27 05
Email	info@lemasdesanges.com
Web	www.lemasdesanges.com

Midi – Pyrénées

Maison des Chevaliers

The door opens onto the bricks and beams of the hall of this huge old house – what a treat. Fascinating proofs of the owners' lives abroad steal your eyes at every turn, their conversation sparkles with anecdotes, interest and contagious enthusiasm, their house oozes taste and style. Bedrooms are big, all differently charming, with antiques from Spain and Portugal, stencilled wood, superb paint finishes, old lace – it's endlessly, originally beautiful. The courtyard calls for summer breakfast, the secluded pool for cooling dips, the library for contemplation. The crowning glory? Claudine once ran a restaurant.

Price	€75.
Rooms	4: 2 doubles, 2 suites.
Meals	Dinner with wine, €22.
Closed	Rarely.
Directions	From Castelsarrasin for Toulouse, RN113; exit Escatalens; to 'centre du village'; house next to church.

Claudine Choux
Maison des Chevaliers,
82700 Escatalens,
Tarn-et-Garonne
Tel	+33 (0)5 63 68 71 23
Fax	+33 (0)5 63 30 25 90
Email	claude.choux@wanadoo.fr
Web	www.maisondeschevaliers.com

Midi – Pyrénées

Au Château

A beguiling mix of grandeur and informality. The house is filled with light and life, thanks to this young Anglo-French family. Softly contemporary bedrooms, two in a separate building, are airy spaces that mix the best of modern with the loveliest of traditional: pale beams and white plaster walls, bold colours, luxurious silks, elegant antiques. There's a country-style breakfast room and a kitchenette so you can make your own suppers – then eat al fresco on the terrace. Visit historic towns, explore the Canal du Midi, let the kids roam free in the garden, stroll the charming village. *Gourmet, wine & bridge breaks.*

Price	€54–€98.
Rooms	5: 1 double, 1 twin, 2 suites for 2-3, 1 family suite for 4.
Meals	Restaurant 50m. Guest kitchenette.
Closed	Never.
Directions	From Valence d'Agen D813 for Moissac; after Malause right to St Nicolas de la Grave; cross river Garonne. Entering St Nicolas de la Grave, 1st r'bout left, château on left.

Kathrin Barker
Au Château, 1 bd des Fossés de Raoul,
82210 St. Nicolas de la Grave,
Tarn-et-Garonne

Tel	+33 (0)5 63 95 96 82
Fax	+33 (0)5 67 80 79 53
Email	kathrin.barker@tele2.fr
Web	www.au-chateau-stn.com

Entry 543   Map 14

Midi – Pyrénées

Tondes

Warm country people, the Sellars left a big Sussex farm for a smallholding in deepest France to breed sheep, goats and poultry the natural way: no pesticides, no heavy machines, animals roaming free. Their enthusiasm and guts have earned them great respect locally and their recipe for a simple, rewarding life includes receiving guests happily under the beams, by the open hearth, in pretty-coloured, country-furnished rooms with super walk-in showers. Julie will welcome you to her wonderful farmhouse kitchen, where she creates feasts of organic veg and homemade marvels. And the garden is a delight.

Ethical Collection: Food.
See page 432.

Price	€48.
Rooms	2: 1 double, 1 family room.
Meals	Dinner with wine, €20.
Closed	Rarely.
Directions	A62 exit 9; RN113 to Moissac; D7 for Bourg de Visa. At Fourquet, left at r'bout. After 500m, turn right at Chambres d'Hôtes 2km. 2nd sign on left, house at top of drive.

Julie & Mark Sellars
Tondes,
82400 Castelsagrat,
Tarn-et-Garonne

Tel	+33 (0)5 63 94 52 13
Fax	+33 (0)5 63 94 52 13
Email	willowweave@orange.fr

Entry 544   Map 14

Midi – Pyrénées

La Lumiane

Such a surprise to step off a side street into a delightful garden with loungers, pool and sweet-smelling shrubs. Chatty Alain and chef Gisèle have restored this gracious house with style: rooms in the main house, up the stunning staircase, breathe tradition and space, old fireplaces, big windows and antiques; those in the garden annexe have a sweetly contemporary feel. All have an uncluttered mix of florals and stripes, and simple, spotless bathrooms. Eat well on local, seasonal produce in the formal dining room or on the terrace by candlelight, wake to the sound of the church bells. Much authenticity and charm.

Price	€42-€66.
Rooms	5 doubles.
Meals	Dinner with wine, €23.
Closed	Never.
Directions	From Condom D654 to Saint Puy. Grande Rue in centre of village by church.

Alain & Gisèle Eman
La Lumiane,
Grande Rue, 32310 Saint Puy, Gers

Tel	+33 (0)5 62 28 95 95
Fax	+33 (0)5 62 28 59 67
Email	info@lalumiane.com
Web	www.lalumiane.com

Entry 545 Map 14

Midi – Pyrénées

Lieu Dit Fitan

Complete tranquillity, beautiful gardens, charmed pool, and Dido, who loves people – an inspiration to us all. In 1999 this was just another derelict barn in the undulating Gers countryside; the restoration is a wonder. At the door, the whole superb space opens before the eyes, English antiques gleam and the fine modern kitchen sparkles (available for a small fee). Two luscious bedrooms, one upstairs, one down: raw stones punctuate soft white walls, patchwork cheers, books tempt. Dido loves cooking, has travelled thousands of miles and is highly cultured. A corner of paradise, it even smells heavenly.

Price	€70-€80. Singles €50.
Rooms	2: 1 double, 1 twin.
Meals	Dinner with wine, €35. Use of kitchen €8.
Closed	Rarely.
Directions	From Marciac D134 north; cross D946, continue to Louslitges church on left, 2nd right, Fitan 3/4 up on right. Pale green shutters.

Dido Streatfeild-Moore
Lieu Dit Fitan,
32230 Louslitges, Gers

Tel	+33 (0)5 62 70 81 88
Fax	+33 (0)5 62 70 81 88
Email	deedoenfrance@wanadoo.fr
Web	www.chezdeedo.com

Entry 546 Map 14

Midi – Pyrénées

Domaine de Peyloubère

The sober buildings did not prepare us for the explosion inside: 80 years ago, an Italian painter spread his heart and love of form and colour over ceilings and doors. 'His' suite has vast space, fine antiques, a dream of a bathroom, dazzling paintings. Theresa and Ian fell for the romantically wild house and glorious domaine and left high-pressure London jobs to save the whole place from dereliction – their enthusiasm and sensitive intelligence show in every room. The waterfall, the wild orchids, the wildlife, the hosted dinners – there's no other place like it. Heaven for children – or an anniversary treat. *Sawday self-catering also.*

Ethical Collection: Environment; Community; Food. See page 432.

Price	€90–€120.
Rooms	2 suites.
Meals	Dinner with wine, €35.
Closed	Rarely.
Directions	From Auch N21 south 3km; left D929 for Lannemezan; in Pavie, left after Mairie, cross old bridge, 1st right, signed Auterrive; house 1km on left.

	Theresa & Ian Martin
	Domaine de Peyloubère,
	32550 Pavie, Gers
Tel	+33 (0)5 62 05 74 97
Fax	+33 (0)5 62 05 75 39
Email	martin@peyloubere.com
Web	www.peyloubere.com

Entry 547   Map 14

Midi – Pyrénées

La Garenne

Youthful and enthusiastic, outgoing and warm-hearted, Mireille is an inspired cook and a delight to be with; Olivier is less ebullient but just as warm a presence and beyond the wooden terrace outside your window is a pretty, bird-filled garden. Together, they fill their cosy house with antique plates, prints, pictures and furniture. Their guest room is as family-comfortable and as warm-furnished as the rest. Mareille loves to practise her English – this is a relaxed and happy family home with the essential dogs and cats plus a swimming pool by the gîtes. Perfect for children.

Price	€55.
Rooms	1 double. Children's room available.
Meals	Dinner with wine, €20.
Closed	Rarely.
Directions	From Auch N21 for Tarbes 2km; left D929 for Lannemezan; in Masseube, left for Simorre 4km; left for Bellegarde; 1st left, before church & castle.

	Mireille & Olivier Courouble
	La Garenne,
	Bellegarde, 32140 Masseube, Gers
Tel	+33 (0)5 62 66 03 61
Fax	+33 (0)5 62 66 03 61
Email	ocourouble@wanadoo.fr
Web	monsite.orange.fr/balconvertpyrenees

Entry 548   Map 14

Midi – Pyrénées

À Larroustat

A tranquil space is yours in the large upstairs suite, whether there are two of you or four. The two airy bedrooms are filled with antique pine furniture, soft and homely fabrics and handmade wooden beds; the bathroom is big enough for a party. Chill out in the sitting room with its books, maps and comfy chairs. Breakfast and dinner are taken at one table, in the lovely handcrafted kitchen or on the terrace: much is home-grown, the duck is local, all is seasonal, and Posy makes delicious puddings. You don't have to go anywhere once you've arrived; just loll by the pool or find a shady spot and dream.

Price	€75. €120 for 4.
Rooms	1 family suite for 2-4.
Meals	Dinner with wine, €25.
Closed	Mid-December to 6 January.
Directions	L'Isle Jourdain D632 for Boulogne sur Gesse; 4km before Boulogne D128 right for Lunax; D228 left to St Blancard. Leave village, château on left; left; D228 right for Manent Montané; house on right.

Posy & Mike Fallowfield
À Larroustat,
32140 Manent Montané, Gers
Tel   +33 (0)5 62 66 16 88
Email   webland@wanadoo.fr
Web   www.coin-du-gers.com

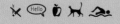

Entry 549   Map 14

Midi – Pyrénées

Martinn

Martine loves life, children (hers now all grown up), house, guests, gastronomy. Food is served at the big kitchen table with gusto: homemade breads and jams, exotic teas, Sunday brunches, Moroccan dinners (or Spanish, or Italian)… gourmet picnics too. She is warm, genuine, generous, proud of her freshly decorated bedrooms with their big bathrooms and polished wooden floors; three feed off a wraparound balcony that overlooks the courtyard below. And then… a garden, small park and serene pool, marvellous surprises at this central-village farmhouse. Maps, bikes, WiFi, DVDs – Martine gives you it all.

Ethical Collection: Food.
See page 432.

Price	€80-€110. Extra child €10.
Rooms	4: 3 doubles, 1 twin.
Meals	Dinner with wine, €25-€40. Sunday brunch €8-€15. Picnics available.
Closed	October & mid-December to January.
Directions	From Pau D943 thro' Morlaas to Lembeye; cont. right to Maubourget;cont. D943 right for Marciac; over 1st r'bout; at fork straight on. Yellow house on right.

Martine Jablonski-Cahours
Martinn, 88 route de Sauveterre,
65700 Maubourguet,
Hautes-Pyrénées
Tel   +33 (0)5 62 96 01 07
Email   info@mart-inn.com
Web   www.mart-inn.com

Entry 550   Map 14

Midi – Pyrénées

Jouandassou

Standing in rolling farmland on the Gers border – a haven for birds 90 minutes from the mountains – this is the most relaxed house (and jungle-like garden) you could wish for. Expect tiny showers and modest-sized rooms full of bric-a-brac – Dominique's decorative talent runs to bright colours and great flair at auctions. Entertaining, loveable Nick cooks with French, Thai, Latin American flourishes. They are a well-travelled, thoughtful couple, involved in the local music festival – evenings on the terrace, or snug guest room, can be stimulating. Great walks, super food, easy living. *Minimum stay 2 nights.*

Price	€60.
Rooms	2 doubles.
Meals	Dinner €20. Wine from €4.
Closed	Christmas & New Year.
Directions	From Tarbes D632 to Trie sur Baïse; through village onto D939 for Mirande 1km; house up little road, sign on left.

Nick & Dominique Collinson
Jouandassou,
65220 Fontrailles,
Hautes-Pyrénées
Tel   +33 (0)5 62 35 64 43
Email   dom@collinson.fr
Web   www.collinson.fr

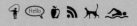

Entry 551   Map 14

Midi – Pyrénées

Maison de l'Évêque

You could weep, this valley is so beautiful; so are the house, its story, garden, owners. A doctor built it (see the caduceus on the great newel post), then it fostered one Bishop Laurence, who 'proved' Bernardette's miracles and set Lourdes up for glory. Arlette, a miracle of industry and human warmth, decorates prettily, cooks simply and brilliantly and still finds plenty of time for guests. Quiet and attentive, Robert will point you in the right direction for hiking and fishing in that gorgeous valley (Pyrenean high-mountain trout are the best, naturally). A very special place.

Price	€50-€57.
Rooms	4: 3 doubles, 1 triple.
Meals	Dinner with wine, €22.
Closed	November-March.
Directions	From Lourdes N21 S for 2km; left at bridge; immediately left again D26 to Juncalas; house in village centre on right.

Arlette & Robert Assouère
Maison de l'Évêque,
Impasse Monseigneur Laurence,
65100 Juncalas, Lourdes,
Hautes-Pyrénées
Tel/Fax   +33 (0)5 62 42 02 04
Email   robert.assouere@wanadoo.fr
Web   www.maisondeleveque.com

Entry 552   Map 14

Midi – Pyrénées

Eth Berye Petit

A magnificent *maison de maître* in a provincial mountain hamlet – amazing. Henri, whose family have lived here for over 1,000 years, is home at weekends, Ione runs it during the week, a mother of two. The grand old house with its wonderful four-sided roof and impressive staircase has stupendous mountain views… the finest in France? Comfortable pastel bedrooms, one with the balcony, have antique French sheets; the living room, where a fire roars and excellent dinner is served on winter weekends, is a great space to come back to after a day's white-water rafting, skiing, falconing. A haven for hikers.

Midi – Pyrénées

La Ferme du Buret

In an enchanting Heidi-esque valley in the Haute (but gently rolling) Pyrenees is a long low stone cattle stable tucked into the hills, with a barn attached. Each superb structure houses two guest bedrooms. From the loftiest beam to the chunkiest floor, interiors are lined with thick wide planks of cedar, chestnut, acacia and oak; rustic-chic fabrics and sleek white bathroom fittings add to the spare, but never spartan, charm. Cathy is a champion skier and can ski-guide you, Pierre is an inspired chef of regional dinners served at the big table. Sports and thermal spas abound, the scenery makes the heart sing.

Price	€56–€63.
Rooms	3: 1 double, 1 twin, 1 suite for 3.
Meals	Dinner with wine, €20, November–April only.
Closed	Rarely.
Directions	From Lourdes for Argelès-Gazost; 10km, left at r'bout for Beaucens, follow Eth Berye Petit signs.

Price	€80–€100.
Rooms	4: 2 twins/doubles, 2 family rooms for 3.
Meals	Dinner with wine, €25.
Closed	Mid-November to January.
Directions	From Tarbes A64 exit Tournay; N117 for Toulouse; in Ozon D14 right to Bourg de Bigorre; into Bourg on D84 up to D26, 6km towards Bulan; at Asque sign, keep to upper D26, 1.8km; left; 700m.

Henri & Ione Vielle
Eth Berye Petit,
15 route de Vielle, 65400 Beaucens,
Hautes-Pyrénées

Tel   +33 (0)5 62 97 90 02
Fax   +33 (0)5 62 97 90 02
Email   contact@beryepetit.com
Web   www.beryepetit.com

Pierre & Cathy Faye
La Ferme du Buret,
65130 Asque,
Hautes-Pyrénées

Tel   +33 (0)5 62 39 19 26
Email   info@lafermeduburet.com
Web   www.lafermeduburet.com

Entry 553   Map 14

Entry 554   Map 14

Midi – Pyrénées

Domaine de Jean-Pierre

Madame is gracefully down to earth and her house and garden an oasis of calm where you may share her delight in playing the piano or golf (3km) and possibly make a lifelong friend. Built in Napoleon's time, her house has an elegant hall, big, airy bedrooms and great bathrooms, while fine furniture and linen sheets reflect her pride in her ancestral home – a combination of uncluttered space and character. The huge quadruple has space to waltz in and the smallest bathroom; breakfast comes with civilised conversation. Come to unwind – you may never want to leave.

Price	€53.
Rooms	3: 1 double, 1 triple, 1 quadruple.
Meals	Restaurants 3-7km.
Closed	Rarely.
Directions	From Toulouse A64 exit 17 for Montréjeau/Tarbes/Pinas, 11km; at church D158 for Villeneuve. House 1km on right.

	Marie-Sabine Colombier
	Domaine de Jean-Pierre,
	20 route de Villeneuve, 65300 Pinas,
	Hautes-Pyrénées
Tel	+33 (0)5 62 98 15 08
Fax	+33 (0)5 62 98 15 08
Email	marie@domainedejeanpierre.com
Web	www.domainedejeanpierre.com

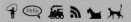

Entry 555   Map 14

Midi – Pyrénées

La Souleillane

Fabienne and Jean-Luc have done an amazing restoration, and guest rooms are huge and bright: the cheery yellow family room in the house, the other restful two in the barn. Having two little boys of their own, they make children very welcome and give them the run of the walled garden. Your hosts work so you may be left alone in the morning; come evening, Fabienne enjoys cooking typical local meals and chatting round the table while Jean-Luc, Pyrenean born and bred, is a source of great mountaineering stories. No sitting room but a garden with a large covered terrace. And there's cross-country skiing nearby.

Ethical Collection: Food.
See page 432.

Price	€55. Quadruple €65-€75.
Rooms	3: 2 doubles, 1 quadruple.
Meals	Dinner with wine, €17.
Closed	Rarely.
Directions	From Toulouse A64, exit 17; D938 west, 7km; signed. 8km from Lannemezan station.

	Fabienne & Jean-Luc Garcia
	La Souleillane,
	4 rue de l'Ancienne Poste,
	65150 St Laurent de Neste,
	Hautes-Pyrénées
Tel	+33 (0)5 62 39 76 01
Email	info@souleillane.com
Web	www.souleillane.com

Entry 556   Map 14

Midi – Pyrénées

Gratia

Luscious texture combinations of original floor tiles discovered virgin in the attic, stupendous beam structures – loving hands crafted this place in the 1790s; flair and hard work brought it back from ruin in the 1990s. Jean-Paul's motto 'less is more' informs the wonderful uncluttered bedrooms with their pretty beds and linens; Florence, chic and charming, will do physiotherapy in the great attic studio – mats, music, massage; the ethos is 'polished and cool'. Chill out on the manicured lawn by the saltwater pool, converse delightfully, depart thoroughly renewed.

Ethical Collection: Food.
See page 432.

Price	€70–€100.
Rooms	4 doubles.
Meals	Restaurants nearby.
Closed	Mid-September to April.
Directions	A64 exit 28; at St Sulpice, D919 to Foix; at Lézat sur Lèze left onto D19b to Esperce. 200m after Lèze metal bridge, take small road directly in front of you. Gratia at top of hill.

	Florence Potey & Jean-Paul Wallaert Gratia, 09210 Lézat sur Lèze, Ariège
Tel	+33 (0)5 61 68 64 47
Email	ferme.gratia@wanadoo.fr
Web	www.ariege.com/gratia

Entry 557   Map 14

Midi – Pyrénées

La Ferme de Boyer

Your hosts, fun, humorous and with an interesting past, have filled the big rambling farmhouse with polished mahogany and family memorabilia and the garden with shrubs and lawns. He was once a helicopter engineer and loves classic cars, she is a Cordon Bleu cook; both designed furniture for first-class hotels and worked for hotels in Paris. Now they run a sparkling B&B. Bedrooms are sunny and charming, more English than French with pastoral views, the family room is large and self-contained, Harriet's dinners are convivial and delicious, and sweet Mirepoix is just down the road.

Price	€50–€80.
Rooms	3: 1 double, 1 twin, 1 family suite with sitting room & kitchenette.
Meals	Dinner with wine, €30.
Closed	Rarely.
Directions	From Mirepoix D119 3km through Basset; after leaving Basset, 1st drive on left.

	Robert & Harriet Stow La Ferme de Boyer, 09500 Coutens, Ariège
Tel	+33 (0)5 61 68 93 41
Fax	+33 (0)5 61 69 33 84
Email	ferme.boyer@wanadoo.fr
Web	www.fermeboyer.iowners.net

Entry 558   Map 15

Midi – Pyrénées

L'Impasse du Temple

Breakfast among the remains of a Protestant chapel, sleep in a townhouse; it's one of a terrace constructed in 1758 and John and Lee-anne are only its second owners. Sociable Australians, they are restoring their elegant mansion and loving it. Graciously high ceilings, a sweeping spiral staircase, lovely great windows: it's a fine and formal house in an oasis of ancient, stream-kissed oaks made relaxed and welcoming by your fun-loving hosts. The food is fantastic and guest rooms are generous, in pastels and with just enough antiques; one even has the vast original claw-footed bath. Superb. *Sawday self-catering also.*

Midi – Pyrénées

La Genade

Up in her beloved mountains with the wild streams splashing and an unbroken view of 13th-century Lordat, Meredith loves sharing her heaven. A passionate climber and skier, she has rebuilt her ruined auberge: old stones and new wood, craggy beams, precious furniture and a cheery fire make it rustic-warm and elegant-formal. Under truly American care, rooms have beautiful bed linens, oriental rugs and books. Bathrooms are large and pretty, the welcome exuberant and genuine, the dinners laid-back. Walkers and cyclists should stay a week – and there's a repair room set aside for bikes. *Children over 7 welcome. Ask about cookery courses.*

Price	€70–€80. Suite €106–€121.
Rooms	5: 2 doubles, 2 triples, 1 suite for 4.
Meals	Dinner €25. Wine €9–€20.
Closed	Rarely.
Directions	From Toulouse A61 for Montpellier; exit 22 at Bram to Mirepoix on D4; D119; D625 to Lavelanet, 11km; at Aigues Vives left for Léran D28.

Price	€50–€65.
Rooms	3: 2 doubles, 1 twin.
Meals	Dinner with wine, €20–€23.
Closed	Rarely.
Directions	From Toulouse-Montpellier road; E9 to Andorra. 4-lane road ends Tarascon: E9 & N20; S. to Luzenac, In Luzenac left for Château de Lordat, D55. After Lordat left, Axiat 1km, 1st on left, facing church.

John & Lee-Anne Furness
L'Impasse du Temple,
09600 Léran, Ariège
Tel   +33 (0)5 61 01 50 02
Fax   +33 (0)5 61 01 50 02
Email   john.furness@wanadoo.fr
Web   www.chezfurness.com

Meredith Dickinson
La Genade,
La route des Corniches,
09250 Axiat, Ariège
Tel   +33 (0)5 61 05 51 54
Email   meredith.dickinson@orange.fr
Web   www.lagenade.com

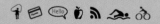

Midi – Pyrénées

Le Moulin

In 2006 Ruth and John arrived at the remote mill with five children, a dog, a cat and a chinchilla in tow. Two years on, there are ducks paddling in the mill stream, chickens roaming, and sheep grazing beyond. The organic garden provides veg for supper and there's a kitchenette for families on a budget. Cosy bedrooms are country traditional with beds in striped linen and wooden floors, but it's the outdoors that will soak up your time: the animals, the orchard, the ten acres of land. This couple's energy is contagious, what they've achieved is inspirational. Kids will adore it. *Minimum stay 2 nights June-September.*

Price	From €50.
Rooms	3: 1 double, 2 family rooms.
Meals	Dinner with wine, €20. Guest kitchenette.
Closed	December-February.
Directions	From Toulouse A64 exit 21 to Boussens; D635 to Aurignac; right D8 for Alan 3km; left D8 to Montoulieu, cont. to Samouillan; left D96 follow signs to Le Moulin.

John & Ruth Temple
Le Moulin,
Samouillan, 31420 Aurignac,
Haute-Garonne

Tel	+33 (0)5 61 98 86 92
Email	john@moulin-vert.net
Web	www.moulin-vert.net

Midi – Pyrénées

Les Pesques

A quiet lane, a happy family, an old manor decorated in peaceful good taste: it's a delight. Every antique, including cupboard doors, is the right one, bed linen is pretty, most rooms have a gentle blue and white valentine theme; the beautiful new room is in warm yellows, as cheerful as Brigitte's personality and done with her very special feel and an exquisite bathroom. All is soft, mellow, uncluttered; she is smiling, enthusiastic, young; her daughters are adorable and helpful. A dreamy, comfortable, joyful house where you appreciate the skill of Bruno the hard-working kitchen gardener when you sit down to dinner.

Price	€50.
Rooms	3: 1 double, 1 twin, 1 triple.
Meals	Dinner with wine, €20.
Closed	Never.
Directions	From Toulouse N117 SW for approx. 50km; exit S D6 to Cazères; over River Garonne, 1st right D7, right D62; after Camping, 2nd left; 1st house on right-hand side,

Brigitte & Bruno Lebris
Les Pesques,
31220 Palaminy, Haute-Garonne

Tel	+33 (0)5 61 97 59 28
Fax	+33 (0)5 61 98 12 97
Email	reserve@les-pesques.com
Web	www.les-pesques.com

Midi – Pyrénées

La Ferme d'en Pécoul

Kind Élisabeth makes jams and jellies, 'confit' and foie gras, keeps hens *and* surfs the web. Almost-retired Noël gently tends the potager as well as the fields. Wrap yourself in the natural warmth of their Lauragais farmhouse. The first floor is carpeted wall to wall and the airy guest sitting room is sandwiched between two small comfy bedrooms with tiny showers. Summer meals are served by the goldfish pond. Two dogs, two cats, fields as far as the eye can see – and exquisite medieval Caraman (once rich from the dye cocagne) just down the road. *Minimum stay 2 nights weekends & summer holidays.*

Ethical Collection: Food.
See page 432.

Price	€46–€72.
Rooms	2: 1 double, 1 triple.
Meals	Dinner with wine, €17–€30.
Closed	Never.
Directions	From Toulouse exit 17 Lasbordes to Castres; after approx. 20km, D1 to Caraman; D66 to Cambiac 3km, entrance on right.

Élisabeth & Noël Messal
La Ferme d'en Pécoul,
31460 Cambiac, Haute-Garonne
Tel   +33 (0)5 61 83 16 13
Fax   +33 (0)5 61 83 16 13
Email   enpecoul@wanadoo.fr
Web   pagesperso-orange.fr/enpecoul

Entry 563   Map 15

Midi – Pyrénées

Les Loges de St Sernin

Vast welcoming comfort lies in store behind those superb wooden doors in the heart of Toulouse – and no expense spared. Madame, living on the third floor, is a poppet: petite, delightful, up to speed with this vibrant town. Big peaceful guest bedrooms spread themselves across the floor below, each with warm colours, a huge bed, an antique mirror, luxurious linen. Breakfast is served on a balcony in good weather, as early or as late as you like it. Period detail abounds: inside shutters, marble fireplaces, sweeping parquet, tall windows beautifully dressed – Madame aims to please. Marvellous! *Children over 7 welcome. Ask about cookery courses. Minimum stay 2 nights (no minimum stay for cyclists).*

Price	€105–€120.
Rooms	4: 2 doubles, 2 twins.
Meals	Restaurants within walking distance.
Closed	Rarely.
Directions	In Toulouse for Église St Sernin. House in street between Place St Sernin & Bd de Strasboug. Easy parking Place St Sernin.

Sylviane Tatin
Les Loges de St Sernin,
12 rue St Bernard, 31000 Toulouse,
Haute-Garonne
Tel   +33 (0)5 61 24 44 44
Fax   +33 (0)5 62 57 10 26
Email   logesaintsernin@live.fr
Web   www.logessaintsernin.fr

Entry 564   Map 14

Aurifat

Good furniture, books and paintings are thoroughly at home in this multi-levelled, history-rich house (the watchtower is 13th-century) and all is serene and inviting. Each freshly decorated room has its own private entrance, balcony or terrace and stupendous views. The house is on the southern slope of hilltop Cordes (ten minutes from both the top and the bottom), the lovely pool is big enough for real exercise and there's a barbecue alongside the superb guest kitchen. Terrace breakfasts (spot the deer) are enchanting and nothing is too much trouble for these lovely hosts. *Minimum stay 3 nights July/August.*

Le Domaine de la Borie Grande

The 18th-century house in two hectares of parkland combines understatedly elegant luxury with a country B&B mood. It is wholly delightful, a place of friendly proportions run by generous people. Enter a square hall off which lead a cosy snug for contemplation, a drawing room for tea, a grand salon for aperitifs and conversation. Sweeping stairs lead to large bedrooms where antique rugs strew polished parquet and white bathrooms have oodles of towels. Soft yellow fabrics and gilt-edged fauteuils add sparkle to taupes, creams and greys, the food is delicious, the garden has tennis and pool. *Minimum stay 2 nights.*

Price	€67–€75.
Rooms	4: 2 doubles, 2 twins.
Meals	Restaurants within walking distance. Kitchen available.
Closed	Mid-December to mid-February.
Directions	From Albi D600 to Cordes; up Cité road on right of Tabarium/Maison de la Presse for 600m; fork left for Le Bouysset; 350m, left at hairpin bend Rte de St Jean; house 200m on right.

Price	€110–€150.
Rooms	4: 1 double, 1 twin, 2 suites.
Meals	Dinner with wine, €38.
Closed	Rarely.
Directions	From Cordes sur Ciel for Laguépie. Right at bend at bottom of hill leaving Cordes; 1km to church in Campes; left for St Amans. On left, 500m from church.

Ian & Penelope Wanklyn
Aurifat,
81170 Cordes sur Ciel, Tarn
Tel +33 (0)5 63 56 07 03
Email aurifat@gmail.com
Web www.aurifat.com

Alain Guyomarch
Le Domaine de la Borie Grande,
St Marcel Campes,
81170 Cordes sur Ciel, Tarn
Tel +33 (0)5 63 56 58 24
Fax +33 (0)5 63 56 58 24
Email laboriegrande@wanadoo.fr
Web www.laboriegrande.com

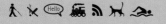

Entry 565   Map 15

Entry 566   Map 15

Midi – Pyrénées

La Maison d'Hôtes Chez Delphine

You are perched high here, in an arty, medieval village with stunning views across wooded valleys. Delphine's ample, generous house has gardens with plenty of shady spots to sit in and a pool surrounded by roses to float in. Up wide stairs from the main hall find classic bedrooms with tiled floors or creaky floorboards, one with its own balcony, and a huge family room with an open fireplace and a kitchenette should you prefer to do your own breakfast; small bathrooms are spotless and towel-filled. Wander the village, discover markets and restaurants, hike or bike, return to a squishy sofa: a super spot. *Minimum stay 2 nights July/August.*

Midi – Pyrénées

Château de Mayragues

A child's dream become an adult's paradise of history, culture and peace: inside those stern walls you climb old stone stairs to the open sentry's gallery, enter your chamber and gasp at the loveliness of the room and the depth of the view. Beyond the fine old timbers and stonework, glowing floor, furniture and fabrics, your eyes flow out over luscious gardens and woods. Alan is a softly-spoken Scot, Laurence a charming Parisienne; both are passionate about their prize-winning restoration — original materials, expert craftsmen — and they hold musical evenings and produce excellent organic wine. Quite a place. *Sawday self-catering also.*

Ethical Collection: Environment; Community; Food. See page 432.

Price	€61–€76.
Rooms	5: 2 doubles, 1 twin, 1 triple, 1 family room for 5 & kitchenette.
Meals	Restaurants within walking distance.
Closed	Rarely.
Directions	From Gaillac D964 to Castelnau de Montmiral; cont. D964 for Puycelsi & Larroque 20km; right D8 to Puycelsi. Park in square. House 150m on right.

Price	€85–€90.
Rooms	2: 1 double, 1 twin.
Meals	Restaurants within 5km.
Closed	20 December-February.
Directions	From Gaillac D964 for Castelnau de Montmiral; at junc. D15 to Château de Mayragues, signed.

	Delphine de Laveleye
	La Maison d'Hôtes Chez Delphine,
	Au Bourg,
	81140 Puycelsi, Tarn
Tel	+33 (0)5 63 33 13 65
Email	delphine@chezdelphine.com
Web	www.chezdelphine.com

	Laurence & Alan Geddes
	Château de Mayragues,
	81140 Castelnau de Montmiral, Tarn
Tel	+33 (0)5 63 33 94 08
Fax	+33 (0)5 63 33 98 10
Email	geddes@chateau-de-mayragues.com
Web	www.chateau-de-mayragues.com

Entry 567   Map 14

Entry 568   Map 15

Midi – Pyrénées

La Croix du Sud

A fantastic base for touring the bastide towns or just basking in the garden beneath stunning hilltop Castelnau – even picnics can be arranged. Catherine, ex-Air France, runs her B&B with quiet sophistication and gentle humour: she wants you to love this place as much as she does. Big immaculate bedrooms have pretty colours and scintillating bathrooms; meals, in the bright dining room or on the terrace, have panoramic views; the shared pool is discreet. And further afield: fascinating Albi, the Grésigne forest, great walks and a lake complex with all those water sports. Good for families.

Midi – Pyrénées

Domaine du Buc

The 17th-century gingerbread château, in landscaped grounds with a pigeon tower, has been in the family for 100 years. Brigitte, bright and smiley, loves this place – and will happily tell you about the family's Toulouse-Lautrec connections. The very old arched brick billiards room is now a lovely sitting room; the kitchen preserves its 1900 range. A large white stone stair leads up to bedrooms with original parquet and tiled floors, period furniture and faded, fabulous 19th-century wallpaper. It may be hard to heat the house in winter but these rooms are always cosy. Stay at least a couple of nights. *Minimum stay 2 nights July / August. Sawday self-catering also.*

Price	€80.
Rooms	3: 1 double, 1 twin, 1 family room for 4.
Meals	Dinner with wine, €27.
Closed	Rarely.
Directions	From Gaillac D964 to Castelnau de Montmiral, right at bottom of village 100m; right at sign Croix du Sud; fork left for Mazars; on left.

Price	€75-€90. Single €70.
Rooms	3: 2 twins/doubles, 1 twin, sharing 2 bathrooms.
Meals	Restaurants nearby.
Closed	Rarely.
Directions	From Toulouse A68 exit 11 Marssac sur Tarn; left at stop sign, over motorway; left onto D22 for Lagrave & Cadalen; straight on at r'bout and x-roads. Entrance 200m on left.

	Catherine Sordoillet
	La Croix du Sud,
	Mazars,
	81140 Castelnau de Montmiral, Tarn
Tel	+33 (0)5 63 33 18 46
Fax	+33 (0)5 63 33 18 46
Email	catherine@la-croix-du-sud.com
Web	www.la-croix-du-sud.com

	Brigitte Lesage
	Domaine du Buc,
	Route de Lagrave,
	81150 Marssac sur Tarn, Tarn
Tel	+33 (0)5 63 55 40 06
Fax	+33 (0)5 63 55 40 06
Email	contact@domainedubuc.com
Web	www.domainedubuc.com

Entry 569   Map 15

Entry 570   Map 15

Midi – Pyrénées

Les Buis de Saint Martin

The dogs that greet you are as friendly as their owner, and the Tarn runs at the bottom of the garden – it's a dream place. Madame has lived here for 30 years and is delighted to please you and practise her English. You will love the understated luxury of softest mushroom hues in bedrooms and bathrooms, the quilting on the excellent beds, the good paintings, the floaty muslin at the windows that look over the garden. Meals are served at one friendly table in the luminous white dining room – gleaming antiques on old terracotta tiles – or on the lovely teak-furnished patio. *Minimum stay 2 nights in summer. Sawday self-catering also.*

Price	From €90.
Rooms	2 doubles.
Meals	Dinner with wine, €29.
Closed	Rarely.
Directions	From A68 exit 11 to Marssac; for Lagrave, right after level crossing; 2nd right Chemin du Rougé; 2nd right Rue St Martin; right at red transformer; left at fork, signed.

Jacqueline Romanet
Les Buis de Saint Martin,
Rue Saint-Martin,
81150 Marssac sur Tarn, Tarn
Tel   +33 (0)5 63 55 41 23
Fax   +33 (0)5 63 53 49 65
Email   jean.romanet@wanadoo.fr
Web   perso.wanadoo.fr/les-buis-de-saint-martin

Midi – Pyrénées

Mas de Sudre

George and Pippa are ideal B&B folk – relaxed, good-natured, enthusiastic about their corner of France, generous-spirited and adding lots of little extras to make you comfortable. Sudre is a warm, friendly house with beautiful furniture, shelves full of books and big inviting bedrooms. Wine-tastings can be arranged and there is a lovely shady garden set in rolling vineyards and farmland where you can sleep off any excesses. The more energetic may leap to the pool, boules, bikes or several sorts of tennis and you are genuinely encouraged to treat the house as your own. French guests love this very British B&B.

Price	€70. Singles €50.
Rooms	4: 2 doubles, 2 twins.
Meals	Restaurants nearby.
Closed	Rarely.
Directions	From Gaillac for Cordes; over railway; left D964 for Caussade. 1km; left D18 for Montauban 400m; right D4 2km; house on left (black gates) 200m beyond 1st turning on left.

Pippa & George Richmond-Brown
Mas de Sudre,
81600 Gaillac, Tarn
Tel   +33 (0)5 63 41 01 32
Fax   +33 (0)5 63 41 01 32
Email   masdesudre@wanadoo.fr
Web   www.masdesudre.com

Midi – Pyrénées

8 place St Michel

Come for an absolutely fabulous French bourgeois experience: a wide stone staircase deeply worn, high ceilings, southern colours, plush carpets, loads of stairs, interesting objets at every turn. Add the owners' passion for Napoleon III furniture, oil paintings and ornate mirrors and the mood, more formal than family, is unmistakably French. Bedrooms, some with rooftop views, are traditional and very comfortable; breakfast is on the terrace overlooking the cathedral square. A treat to be in the heart of town, with utterly French people. Madame is a darling and it's excellent value for money.

Price	€60.
Rooms	5: 3 doubles, 1 twin, 1 suite.
Meals	Restaurants 30m.
Closed	Rarely.
Directions	In centre of Gaillac, directly opposite St Michel abbey church as you come in across bridge from A68 Toulouse-Albi road.

Lucile Pinon
8 place St Michel,
81600 Gaillac, Tarn
Tel +33 (0)5 63 57 61 48
Email lucile.pinon@wanadoo.fr
Web lucile.pinon.hotes81.monsite.wanadoo.fr

Midi – Pyrénées

Domaine de la Borie Neuve

Many think about it, this couple have done it – swapped city life for a piece of sweet countryside and a 300-year-old domaine. From each secluded seat – or poolside lounger – farmland stretches for miles. Visit Cordes sur Ciel, Albi, Toulouse, return to grounds full of trees, tennis up the road and a games room in the barn (shared with gîte guests). Bedrooms are in another wing, some big, some small, all fresh, all charming: white ceiling beams, white walls, splashes of russet red and butter yellow. B&Bers eat together at a long table in an open-plan room where glass windows glide open to a sun-drenched terrace.

Price	€48-€55. €79 for 4.
Rooms	5: 3 doubles, 2 suites for 2-4.
Meals	Restaurant in village.
Closed	Never.
Directions	From Millau D999 to Albi; 3km after Villefrauche left for Bellegarde, follow Chambres d'Hôtes sign.

Esméralda Francisco
Domaine de la Borie Neuve,
81430 Bellegarde, Tarn
Tel +33 (0)5 63 55 33 64
Fax +33 (0)5 63 55 33 64
Email laborieneuve@aol.com
Web www.laborieneuve.com

Midi – Pyrénées

Barbiel

You will settle quickly here; Tim and Tracy are all smiles and ease, the house is calming and there's a terrace for lazy breakfasts in the garden with stunning views over rolling hills. Ground-floor bedrooms are in the barn: aqua-washed walls, white cotton sheets, a cool mix of modern and antique furniture, zippy bathrooms with thick towels, even a tiny kitchenette for picnics or snacks. For gorgeous dinners at one big table you go to the main house where Tracy's sense of style is splashed all over a stunning art-filled sitting room and Tim gives good chat. Don't be seduced into inertia, Albi is a must-see.

Price	€50.
Rooms	2: 1 double, 1 twin.
Meals	Dinner with wine, €22. Light supper from €12. Guest kitchenette.
Closed	Rarely.
Directions	From Valence d'Albigeois D903 for Réquista; 5km, D75 right for Albignac & Assac; D126 thro' Albignac; after 2.5km, left at blue Chambres d'Hôtes sign.

Tim & Tracy Bayly
Barbiel,
81340 Assac, Tarn
Tel +33 (0)5 63 56 97 12
Email ttbayly@wanadoo.fr
Web www.tranquiltarn.com

Entry 575   Map 15

Midi – Pyrénées

La Barthe

Your Anglo-French hosts welcome guests as friends to their converted farmhouse. The pastel-painted, stencilled rooms are smallish but beds are good, the hospitality is great and it's a deliciously secluded place to stay and walk or bike out into the country. The Wises grow their own vegetables and summer dinners happen on the terrace (by the raised pool) overlooking the lovely Tarn valley, a largely undiscovered part of France where birds, bees and sheep will serenade you. Watch the farmers milking for roquefort and don't miss Albi, with that huge and magnificent cathedral – it's no distance at all.

Price	€42.
Rooms	2: 1 double, 1 family room.
Meals	Dinner with wine, €22.
Closed	Rarely.
Directions	From Albi D999 for Millau 25km; at La Croix Blanche left to Cambon du Temple, up to La Barthe on D163; right; house on left.

Michèle & Michael Wise
La Barthe,
81430 Villefranche d'Albigeois, Tarn
Tel +33 (0)5 63 55 96 21
Fax +33 (0)5 63 55 96 27
Email labarthe@chezwise.com
Web www.chezwise.com

Entry 576   Map 15

Midi – Pyrénées

Maison Puech Malou

Pull up at the creeper-clad farmhouse in pretty wooded countryside to a friendly, calming home swimming in crisp light. It's a rustic yet immaculate restoration. Walls are exposed stone or white plaster, floors terracotta or stripped pine, ceiling beams are of heavy oak. The suite has a generous bed and a romantic feel, the sitting room has two huge open fireplaces, the dining room one big country table; there's teak on the terrace and the lawn leads to a lovely pool. Dutch Monique is friendly, hands-on, bakes her bread daily and cooks excellent dinners. *Minimum stay 3 nights. Ask about cookery & golfing holidays. Sawday self-catering also.*

Borio Nove

Bubbly, well-travelled Lu and Freddie are the perfect B&B hosts and their characterful home on the hillside has a pretty courtyard garden and stunning views. Inside you find a remarkably English style with a roaring fire, deep comfortable sofas, lamps in quiet corners, lovely paintings, fresh flowers and oodles of books. Bedrooms are dressed in soft creams with wooden floors, pleasant bathrooms, comfotable beds and antiques from all over the world; it's like staying with family friends. Meals are jolly affairs at flexible times round the big table – and Freddie knows his wines. *Minimum stay 2 nights.*

Price	From €99. Suite €125.
Rooms	4: 2 doubles, 1 twin, 1 suite for 2.
Meals	Dinner with wine, €25.
Closed	Never.
Directions	From Toulouse A68 for Albi; ring road for Rodez/Millau; D81 to Fauch, D13; left at T-junc.; right at r'bout; Route de Teillet right. D81 to Teillet. Left before pharmacy, D138 for Alban; right to Terre Basse & Catalanie. House top of road on right.

Price	€78–€90.
Rooms	2: 1 double, 1 twin.
Meals	Dinner with wine, €18–€35.
Closed	December-February.
Directions	From Réalmont D4 for Lombers 4.5km; D41 left; 2km; left at sign for Borio Nove at top of hill. Large house on right, 2nd turning.

Monique Moors
Maison Puech Malou,
81120 Teillet, Tarn
Tel +33 (0)5 63 55 79 04
Fax +33 (0)5 63 55 79 88
Email info@maisonpuechmalou.com
Web www.maisonpuechmalou.com

Freddie & Lu Wanklyn
Borio Nove,
Bouscayrens,
81120 Lombers, Tarn
Tel +33 (0)5 63 55 36 94
Email luwanklyn@aliceadsl.fr

Entry 577   Map 15

Entry 578   Map 15

Midi – Pyrénées

Domaine d'en Naudet

Inside and out, such a sense of space! The domaine, surrounded by a patchwork-quilt countryside, was donated by Henri IV to a hunting crony in 1545 – and was in a parlous state when Eliane and Jean fell for it. They have achieved miracles. A converted barn/stable block reveals four vast and beautiful bedrooms (two with private wicker-chaired terraces), sensuous bathrooms and a stunning open-plan breakfast/sitting room. In the grounds, masses for children and energetic adults, while the slothful may bask by the pool. Markets, history and beauty surround you, and Eliane is a lovely hostess.

Price	€86.
Rooms	4: 2 doubles, 2 twins.
Meals	Restaurant 3km. Guest kitchen.
Closed	Rarely.
Directions	From Lavaur D112 to Castres; right onto D43 to Pratviel. House on left after 2km, signed.

Eliane Barcellini
Domaine d'en Naudet,
81220 Teyssode, Tarn
Tel +33 (0)5 63 70 50 59
Email contact@domainenaudet.com
Web www.domainenaudet.com

Entry 579   Map 15

Midi – Pyrénées

La Terrasse de Lautrec

Not what you expect to stumble on in a mediaeval village: Le Nôtre-designed gardens backing a graceful house, with terraces overhanging the (stunning) village ramparts. There are secluded shady corners and roses, a box maze, a pond brimming with waterlilies and a pool that looks over the Tarn hills. As you swan through the frescoed dining room and the drawing room with its 1810 wallpaper you might feel like a Jane Austen character on a French exchange. Dominique, warm and intelligent, treats you to the cooking of the region. Retire to a stunning drawing room, or a large, luminous bedroom filled with ochre and gilt. *Min. stay 2 nights July/August.*

Price	€75–€105.
Rooms	4: 2 doubles, 1 twin, 1 suite.
Meals	Dinner with wine, €30.
Closed	November-March.
Directions	From Rue Mercadial, Lautrec, past central square on right; continue to monument square, La Terrasse facing monument.

Dominique Ducoudray
La Terrasse de Lautrec,
Rue de L'Église,
81440 Lautrec, Tarn
Tel +33 (0)5 63 75 84 22
Email d.ducoudray@wanadoo.fr
Web www.laterrassedelautrec.com

Entry 580   Map 15

La Villa de Mazamet

A 'coup de foudre' caused Mark and Peter to buy this grand Art Deco villa in walled gardens, a few minutes' walk from the market town of Mazamet. Renovation has revealed large light-filled interiors of wood-panelled walls, parquet floors and sweeping windows. Furnished with modern elegance, the ground floor invites relaxation in comfy sofas or quiet corners. Bedrooms, with sumptuous beds and fine linen, are calmly luxurious; bathrooms are Art Deco gems. Your hosts are interesting, relaxed and well-travelled, meals are gastronomic. Ideal for Carcassonne, Albi and all those lovely medieval villages. *Ask about speciality breaks.*

La Bousquétarié

Madame Sallier is delightful, running her family château with boundless energy and infectious joie de vivre, serving breakfast in her big kitchen in order to chat more easily to you, loving everyone, especially children. Charming bedrooms still have their original personality, and one rare 1850s wallpaper, and turning walk-in cupboards into showers or loos was a stroke of brilliance; antique-filled sitting rooms are totally French; the little reading room holds hundreds of books; even the fresh roses are old-fashioned. It's all comfortably worn around the edges with a tennis court you're welcome to use.

Price	€85–€150.	Price	€64–€70. Suite €75.
Rooms	5 doubles.	Rooms	4: 2 doubles, 2 family suites.
Meals	Dinner €35. Wine list from €15.	Meals	Dinner with wine, €20–€24.
Closed	Never.	Closed	December–February.
Directions	From A61 exit 23 to Mazamet; follow centre ville. Rue Pasteur opp. bandstand in Jardin de Promenade, 200m from railway station.	Directions	From Revel D622 for Castres for 9km; left D12 to Lempaut; right D46 for Lescout; house on left.

Peter Friend & Mark Barber
La Villa de Mazamet,
4 rue Pasteur,
81200 Mazamet, Tarn
Tel   +33 (0)5 63 97 90 33
Fax   +33 (0)5 63 97 90 33
Email   mazametfrance@hotmail.co.uk
Web   www.villademazamet.com

Monique & Charles Sallier
La Bousquétarié,
81700 Lempaut, Tarn
Tel   +33 (0)5 63 75 51 09
Fax   +33 (0)5 63 75 51 09
Web   www.chateau-bousquetarie.com

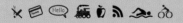

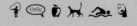

Entry 581   Map 15

Entry 582   Map 15

Midi – Pyrénées

Les Abélias

Geneviève moved here from Alsace for more sun and a slower pace of life. As soon as you enter the courtyard and see the mellow old house with little angels guarding the steps you will want to be one of her returning guests – welcomed (in good English) as friends. The chapel in the garden is dedicated to Our Lady of the Angels. Bedrooms are romantic: one soft green with a lace canopy and doors to the garden, another toile de Jouy'd, gently old-fashioned. All the rooms are Geneviève's own work and utterly appealing. Breakfast is on a sunny terrace under the lime trees looking at the garden and fields.

Price	€59.
Rooms	2: 1 double, 1 suite.
Meals	Dinner with wine, €18.
Closed	Rarely.
Directions	From Revel D84; right V10 for Lamothe; follow signs 'Les Abélias'.

Geneviève Millot
Les Abélias,
Lamothe, 81700 Blan, Tarn
Tel   +33 (0)5 63 75 75 14
Email   lesabelias@libertysurf.fr
Web   lesabelias.chez-alice.fr

Entry 583   Map 15

Midi – Pyrénées

Chambres d'Hôtes Les Brunes

Swish through large wooden gates into a central courtyard and garden to find lovely Monique and her 18th-century family home, complete with tower. Bedrooms are up the spiral stone tower staircase which oozes atmosphere; all are a good size (Le Clos is enormous) and filled with beautiful things. Antiques, beams, rugs, gilt mirrors and soft colours give an uncluttered, elegant feel; bathrooms are modern and bright, views from all are lovely. You breakfast on homemade cake, farm butter, fruit salad, in the beautiful open kitchen with baker's oven, or in the garden filled with birdsong. *Minimum stay 2 nights.*

Ethical Collection: Environment.
See page 432.

Price	€86-€129.
Rooms	4: 1 double, 2 twins, 1 suite.
Meals	Restaurant 5km. Guest kitchenette.
Closed	Never.
Directions	D920 Espalion-Bozouls; D988 for Rodez. 3.5km on right after Bozouls.

Monique Philipponnat-David
Chambres d'Hôtes Les Brunes,
Hameau les Brunes,
12340 Bozouls, Aveyron
Tel   +33 (0)5 65 48 50 11
Email   lesbrunes@wanadoo.fr
Web   www.lesbrunes.com

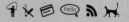

Entry 584   Map 10

Midi – Pyrénées

Monteillet-Sanvensa

A lovely old stone mini-hamlet in the calm green Aveyron where there is just so much space. Two compact rooms, each with a nice little terrace, look out over a typical medieval château. One guest room is white and yellow with a walk-in shower, the other washed-pink and white, with a super bathroom and a small kitchenette; both are cool and airy. The garden is full of flowers, the rolling views stupendous, and Monique is fun, easy-going and eager to please. Relax in one of the many shady areas in summer with a drink or a book and enjoy the birdsong. *Well-behaved children & pets welcome.*

Midi – Pyrénées

Domaine de Montarsès

The rambling farmhouse in the hills is utterly charming; so are its owners. Jacques and Jo love having guests and he is a fountain of knowledge re wildlife and walks (and what walks they are!). Fields, woods, a lake, two donkeys and views that merit several hours of gazing; this swathe of southern Auvergne is sensational. Bedrooms have cream walls, stripped floors, old beams, bathrooms have fluffy towels, and the suite is brilliant for families (two bedrooms, a small sitting/dining room, a kitchenette, fresh fabrics). In the living room: logs in the stone fireplace and deep chairs. Marvellous.

Price	€50.
Rooms	2 doubles, one with kitchenette.
Meals	Dinner with wine, €19. Light suppers available.
Closed	2 weeks in September.
Directions	From Villefranche D922 for Albi; at entrance to Sanvensa, follow signs on right to Monteillet Chambres d'Hôtes.

Price	€55. Suite €100.
Rooms	2: 1 double, 1 family suite for 4 & kitchenette.
Meals	Dinner with wine, €18.
Closed	Rarely.
Directions	From Villefranche de Rouergue for Rodez D911; exit Rieupeyroux for Rodez 2km; right D85 to Tayrac. At La Rode right for La Salvetat Peyralès; towards Montarsès; signed.

	Monique Bateson
	Monteillet-Sanvensa,
	12200 Villefranche de Rouergue,
	Aveyron
Tel	+33 (0)5 65 29 81 01
Fax	+33 (0)5 65 65 89 52

	Jo, Jacques & Marjolaine Rieben
	Domaine de Montarsès,
	12440 Tayrac, Aveyron
Tel	+33 (0)5 65 81 46 10
Fax	+33 (0)5 65 81 46 10
Email	montarses@club-internet.fr
Web	www.ifrance.com/aveyronvacances

Entry 585   Map 15

Entry 586   Map 15

Midi – Pyrénées

Quiers – Ferme Auberge

Escape to vast pastures, garden and stunning views. This is an outdoorsy place – you may canoe, climb, hang-glide and hunt orchids. Bedrooms are a short walk from the farm – bring the umbrella! – down a steepish track; sitting snugly in the converted *bergerie*, they vary in size, have shiny terracotta floors, old beams, freshly painted walls and simple pine beds crafted by Jean, your friendly, busy farmer host. In the main house are tapestries and rustic antiques smelling of years of polish; here Véronique serves huge meals of home-grown organic meat and veg. Good value.

Price	€54.
Rooms	5: 2 doubles, 2 twins, 1 family room.
Meals	Dinner €20-€23. Wine list €10-€20. Restaurants in Millau.
Closed	Mid-November to March.
Directions	From Millau N9 to Aguessac; on way out, D547 right to Compeyre; left in village, follow signs for Ferme Auberge, 3km.

Véronique Lombard
Quiers – Ferme Auberge,
12520 Compeyre, Aveyron
Tel   +33 (0)5 65 59 85 10
Email quiers@wanadoo.fr
Web   www.quiers.net

Entry 587   Map 15

Midi – Pyrénées

Montels

The house is modern and rather dark, the rolling Languedoc hills are wild and very ancient; here Monsieur tends his sheep. The views of the new bridge are wonderful – and you watch the paragliders launching off the nearby cliff from the safety of your breakfast table in the garden as you polish off Madame's 'lafloune', a local sheep's-milk cake. It matters little that she speaks no English: she is kind and welcoming and you can get a long way with smiles and sign language. Bright, clean, sweet, spacious bedrooms include one perfect for a family, and the bathrooms are immaculate.

Price	€45.
Rooms	3: 1 double, 1 triple, 1 family room for 4.
Meals	Restaurants Millau, 3km.
Closed	Rarely.
Directions	From Millau D911 for Cahors; just after leaving city limits right after 'Auberge' x-roads. Signed. Follow small road for approx. 2km.

Henriette Cassan
Montels,
12100 Millau,
Aveyron
Tel   +33 (0)5 65 60 51 70

Entry 588   Map 15

Midi – Pyrénées

Le Relais des Infruts

On the old royal road south, the house stands witness to centuries of travellers. English Mark and artist Brigitte have lived here for years. He sells Spanish pottery at local markets, her art beautifies white walls, the garden is full of flowers. People come back for the food, too – vegetable tart, pork with figs… Sofas hug the fire, dogs wag, wines are celebrated, breakfasts are copious and sociable. Simple white bedrooms are set off by stripy Indian bedcovers and wicker chairs; outside there are slides for children, bikes to borrow. Explore the Larzac, known for sheep and roquefort, wild orchids, wild beauty and… wild history.

Price	€52.
Rooms	5: 3 doubles, 2 twins.
Meals	Dinner with wine, €25.
Closed	Rarely.
Directions	From North Millau A75 exit 48 Cornus; 1st r'bout D609 for Les Infruts, 7km. From South Lodeve A75 exit 49 Le Caylar for La Pezade for Les Infruts, 7km.

	Brigitte & Mark Wood
	Le Relais des Infruts,
	Les Infruts, 12230 La Couvertoirade,
	Aveyron
Tel	+33 (0)5 65 62 76 89
Email	wood@lerelaisdesinfruts.com
Web	www.lerelaisdesinfruts.com

Entry 589   Map 15

Midi – Pyrénées

La Grande Combe

An energetic, lovable Dutch couple live in this remarkable old place, built on a hillside before a heart-stopping view. You go from level to delightful level: the ancient timber frame holds brilliantly restored rooms done in a simple, contemporary style that makes the old stones glow with pride. Superb dining and sitting rooms have original paving, the potager is vast and organic, the atmosphere restful – and there are little terraces and a library for private times. Lovely guest rooms are big (except the singles), pale or bright, and Nelleke's cooking, much of it with a south-western bias, is superb.

Price	€74. Singles €37.
Rooms	5: 3 doubles, 2 twins.
Meals	Dinner with wine, €27.
Closed	Rarely.
Directions	D902 between Brousse le château and Faveyrolles; at iron bridge onto D200 but do not cross bridge; take forest road, signed.

	Hans & Nelleke Versteegen
	La Grande Combe,
	12480 Saint Izaire, Aveyron
Tel	+33 (0)5 65 99 45 01
Fax	+33 (0)5 65 99 48 41
Email	grande.combe@wanadoo.fr
Web	www.la-grande-combe.nl

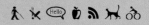

Entry 590   Map 15

Languedoc – Roussillon

Languedoc – Roussillon

La Maison de Marius

Fascinating Quézac: a pilgrimage 'street-village' with many cobbles and a lovely old bridge over the Tarn. The house sits prettily at its heart, all warm and lived-in with old stones and beams, nooks, crannies and stairs, and a light, fresh feel; friendly, homely bedrooms have artistic flourishes; bathrooms are super. Dany is a poppet, adores embellishing her home (country fabrics, hand-painted furniture) and spoiling her guests with gâteau de noix from her walnuts and delicacies from her impressive vegetable patch. Sit on the lovely terrace or rose garden where only birds, water and wind are to be heard.

Price	€70-€80.
Rooms	5: 3 doubles, 1 twin, 1 family suite.
Meals	Dinner with wine, €25.
Closed	November-March.
Directions	From A75 exit 39 on N88 E for 25km; right N106 for Alès 25km; just before Ispagnac right to Quézac; signs in village.

Danièle Méjean
La Maison de Marius,
8 rue du Pontet,
48320 Quézac, Lozère
Tel   +33 (0)4 66 44 25 05
Email dany.mejean@wanadoo.fr
Web   www.maisondemarius.info

Entry 591 Map 15

Languedoc – Roussillon

Pont d'Ardèche

An ancestor built the fine old fortified farmhouse 220 years ago: it still stands, proudly worn, by the Ardèche and has its own beach. Inside, in sudden contrast, a cavernous entrance hall and a monumental stone staircase lined with portraits… and up to pale, plain rooms, saved from austerity by Madame's painted furniture and friezes. No sitting room but a homely kitchen for good breakfast breads and jams. Best in summer: the squirrelly, tall-treed park invites lingerers, and there's a delicious oval pool. Monsieur can accompany you on canoe trips; expect an attractive, sociable family who enjoy their guests.

Price	€65. Triple €80.
Rooms	3: 2 doubles, 1 triple.
Meals	Dinner with wine, €25.
Closed	Rarely.
Directions	From A7 Bollène exit D994 to Pont St Esprit; N86 for Bourg St Andéol; sign before bridge across river.

Mme de Verduzan
Pont d'Ardèche,
30130 Pont St Esprit, Gard
Tel   +33 (0)4 66 39 29 80
Fax   +33 (0)6 87 14 89 96
Email pontdardeche@aol.com
Web   www.pont-dardeche.com

Entry 592 Map 16

Languedoc – Roussillon

La Magnanerie

This happy, artistic, laid-back pair welcome guests to their open, light-filled, authentically renovated village silk farm, splashed with Moroccan colour and ethnic *objets*. Such as: pretty ochre-coloured plates, a long wooden table on an uneven stone floor, an ancient sink, beams twisting, glimpses of age-old village rooftops through little windows, a ravishing courtyard, big, uncluttered, attractive bedrooms, a roof terrace looking over Provence. Michèle manages tranquilly and adores cooking, Michel knows his wines and the local community, their talk is cultural and enriching. *Ask about art courses.*

Price	€55–€60.
Rooms	4: 2 doubles, 2 family suites for 4.
Meals	Dinner with wine, €20.
Closed	Rarely.
Directions	From Alès D6 E 27km; left D979 beyond Lussan for Barjac 1km; left D187 to Fons sur Lussan; right at fountain; up on left by church.

Michèle Dassonneville &
Michel Genvrin
La Magnanerie,
Place de l'Horloge,
30580 Fons sur Lussan, Gard

Tel	+33 (0)4 66 72 81 72
Email	la-magnanerie@wanadoo.fr
Web	www.atelier-de-fons.com

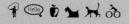

Languedoc – Roussillon

Le pas de l'âne

Tucked into the shadow of the umbrella pines, an ordinary house with an extraordinary welcome. Fun for food-lovers and families; even the parrot greets you with a merry 'bonjour'. Anne, ex-antique dealer in London, is chef; Dominique, gregarious Italian, is host. Dinners are fabulous affairs, full of fresh delights and laughter. Strawberries are from the garden, eggs from the hens and the spiced oils are homemade. We like the upstairs bedrooms best; the double has its own terrace. Four cats, one dog, a pool, a big garden – heaven for kids in summer. And all those gorges and southern markets to discover.

Price	€60–€80.
Rooms	3: 1 double, 1 twin/double, 1 twin.
Meals	Dinner with wine, €23.
Closed	Rarely.
Directions	From Bagnols sur Cèze 4km on D6 for Alès; left to Combe; immed. into Chemin des Pelissiers, road 500m on left. 2nd house on left.

Anne Le Brun
Le pas de l'âne,
209 chemin du Pas de l'Âne,
Combe, 30200 Sabran, Gard

Tel	+33 (0)4 66 33 14 09
Email	pasdelane@wanadoo.fr
Web	www.pasdelane.com

Languedoc – Roussillon

Les Marronniers

They are a delightfully open couple, in love with their life and their 19th-century *maison de maître*, and welcome guests with exuberant gaiety. John is a joiner with a fine eye for interior design while Michel, quieter, softer, does the cooking – beautifully. From the classic black and white tiles of the entrance hall to the art on the walls, every detail counts. A very generous breakfast is served under the chestnut trees; afterwards you can wander off to join in lazy Provençal village life, or visit Avignon, Uzès or Lussan, the fortified Cévenol village. Return to a dreamy pool. *Heated pool May-September, weather permitting.*

Price	€105–€120.
Rooms	4: 2 doubles, 2 twins.
Meals	Dinner with wine, €49.
Closed	Rarely.
Directions	From A9 exit 23 W to Uzès 19km; D979 N 7.5km; right D238 to La Bruguière. House on big square next to Mairie (vast Micocoulier tree in front).

John Karavias & Michel Comas
Les Marronniers,
Place de la Mairie,
30580 La Bruguière, Gard
Tel +33 (0)4 66 72 84 77
Email info@lesmarronniers.biz
Web www.lesmarronniers.biz

Entry 595   Map 16

Languedoc – Roussillon

Mas Vacquières

Thomas and Miriam have restored these lovely old buildings – once a flourishing 18th-century silk farm – with a sure touch, white walls a perfect foil for southern-toned fabrics and materials. Mulberry trees where silk worms once fed still flower; the little vaulted room is intimate and alcoved, the big soft living room a delight. Tables on the verdant terrace under leafy trees and a lawn sloping down to the riverbed make superb spots for silent gazing. Share the pool, subtly hidden in its roofless barn, with your charming hosts. Very pretty, if a touch detached from the owners' quarters.

Price	€75–€105.
Rooms	3: 2 doubles, 1 twin/double.
Meals	Dinner €25. Wine €6.50–€30.
Closed	Rarely.
Directions	From Alès, D6 for 12km; right on D7; in St Just, left for Vacquières, pink signs to house.

Thomas & Miriam van Dijke
Mas Vacquières,
Hameau de Vacquières,
30580 St Just et Vacquières, Gard
Tel +33 (0)4 66 83 70 75
Email info@masvac.com
Web www.masvac.com

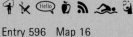

Entry 596   Map 16

Languedoc – Roussillon

Mas d'Oléandre

Lovely, long stone buildings enfold the convivial two-tier courtyard, great trees give shade to the pool, the Cévennes hillsides march away behind. It is enchanting. Your young and welcoming Dutch hosts have created a beautiful and unpretentious place to stay; the garden, the lawn around the pool, the glowing old furniture inside, the silvery weathered teak out. Bedrooms, light and white with splashes of colour, feel separate from each other around the courtyard, and all is utterly pristine. Uzès market (a glory) is a five-minutes drive: create your own picnic and bring it back here. Bliss.

Price	€70–€105.
Rooms	4 doubles, each with separate shower.
Meals	Dinner €25. Wine €7.50–€25.
Closed	Mid-November to February.
Directions	From Uzès D981 to Montaren for 6km; right into Montaren onto D337 to St Médiers; in village continue up & around to right. House on left with green shutters.

Léonard Robberts & Esther Küchler
Mas d'Oléandre,
Hameau St Médiers,
30700 Montaren et St Médiers, Gard
Tel   +33 (0)4 66 22 63 43
Email   info@masoleandre.com
Web   www.masoleandre.com

Entry 597   Map 16

Languedoc – Roussillon

Villa Virinn

Melons and cherries in season, homemade marmalade and fig jam – and proper porridge. Douglas, who's Scottish, is the chef, Geoff is the greeter and gardener, both are warm hosts loving the French life. Their house, new and spacious, private and peaceful, is a short stroll from the small hilltop town. Inside, all is fresh, comfortable, unflashy; beds have painted headboards and matching tables, walls are blue, soft green, pale honey; those off the garden have terraces. Bright flowers and striped loungers round the pool, an honesty bar, a vineyard view: though the excursions are stunning the temptation is to stay.

Price	€75–€80.
Rooms	4: 3 doubles, 1 twin.
Meals	Dinner €23. Wine €8.
Closed	December–January.
Directions	On the Nîmes/Alès road D936, at foot of Vézénobres. Chemin de Bercaude next to Hôtel Relais du Sarrazin. Signed.

Geoff Pople & Douglas Tulloch
Villa Virinn,
Chemin de Bercaude,
30360 Vézénobres, Gard
Tel   +33 (0)4 66 83 27 30
Email   geoffanddoug@villavirinn.com
Web   www.villavirinn.com

Entry 598   Map 16

Languedoc – Roussillon

La Maison

Old wood, old stone, new ideas. Christian's flair and human touch has revived the grand old stones with opulent Indonesian furniture and hangings, soft lighting and a gentle golden colour – he and Pierre are delighted with their Maison. Beneath the old village church of lovely Blauzac (daytime chimes), the lush walled garden and ancient tower look over wavy red rooftops to blue hills, bedrooms bask in ethnic fabrics and relaxed good taste, the stunning suite has its own roof terrace. Masses of books, a breakfast table by the fire, and good sofas in the sitting room. Charming. *Watch children near unfenced water.*

Price	€115–€195.
Rooms	5: 4 doubles, 1 suite for 4.
Meals	Bistros in village.
Closed	Mid-November to mid-March.
Directions	From Nîmes D979 for Blauzac 16km; after Pont St Nicolas, left for Blauzac; into village, house behind church.

Christian Vaurie
La Maison,
Place de l'Église,
30700 Blauzac, Gard
Tel   +33 (0)4 66 81 25 15
Email   lamaisondeblauzac@wanadoo.fr
Web   www.chambres-provence.com

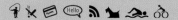

Entry 599   Map 16

Languedoc – Roussillon

Villa Fauve

An ancient village house overlooking rooftops and gardens: you feel sheltered but not stifled. Huge care has been taken in restoring its limewashed walls and pale stone floors; artist Élise has a knack for mixing exciting modern with fine antique. Bedrooms are private and perfect – one has a little sitting room; grand views, fine linen, good lighting, bathrooms with pebble shower floors. Also, a marvellously surprising garden with a stunning pool surrounded by sculpted box trees and canvas chaises longues. Discover the village's tiny cobbled streets and high walls spilled with geraniums. A treat. *Minimum stay 2 nights weekends.*

Price	€100–€160.
Rooms	3 twins/doubles, 2 with extra beds.
Meals	Dinner €28. Wine €12–€25.
Closed	Rarely.
Directions	From A9 exit to Remoulins; D981 for Uzès 12km; St Maximin on right; house in town centre next to château.

Élise Bardin
Villa Fauve,
Rue des Templiers,
30700 Saint Maximin, Gard
Tel   +33 (0)4 66 22 62 39
Fax   +33 (0)4 66 22 62 39
Email   contact@couleursfauves.com
Web   www.couleursfauves.com

Entry 600   Map 16

Languedoc – Roussillon

Les Bambous

Circles of delight: the Provençe of vines and umbrella pines, a peaceful typical village, a lovely converted barn and glowing little house, a warm, affectionate couple who genuinely enjoy having guests. Joël paints and Michèle is a keen and good cook. Meal times are flexible, the atmosphere relaxed, the sheltered, well-tended courtyard or cosy dining room conducive to lingering chat. The cottagey, beamed bedroom has good solid furniture, wooden floors, patchwork and plants. An easy place to be, ten minutes from Avignon, and in excellent rosé wine, olive and fruit country.

Languedoc – Roussillon

Les Écuries des Chartreux

Villeneuve: a mini Avignon without the crowds. In a stable block next to a 13th-century monastery are these guest quarters: charmingly furnished, beautifully kempt and smelling of beeswax. All is coolness, elegance and light: stone walls, terracotta floors, rustic beams, Provençal antiques. Two suites have mezzanines, all have perfect kitchenettes so you can self-cater if you prefer. No pool but a delectable courtyard garden. Pascale gives you breakfast in the main house and all the attention you require – including an aperitif before you head out for the evening. This is heaven. *Avignon 10-minute bus ride.*

Price	€65.
Rooms	1 double.
Meals	Dinner with wine, €25.
Closed	Rarely.
Directions	From Avignon & Villeneuve N580 for Bagnols & Cèze; right on D377 & D177 to Pujaut. House opp. town hall; large metal door.

Price	€85–€125.
Rooms	3 suites: 1 for 2, 1 for 3, 1 for 4.
Meals	Restaurants 50m. Guest kitchens.
Closed	Rarely.
Directions	From Avignon cross Rhône for Nîmes & Villeneuve lès Avignon. Just after bridge right for Villeneuve centre, Rue de la République. House next to Carthusian monastery, La Chartreuse.

Joël & Michèle Rousseau
Les Bambous,
Rue de la Mairie,
30131 Pujaut, Gard

Tel	+33 (0)4 90 26 46 47
Fax	+33 (0)4 90 26 46 47
Email	rousseau.michele@wanadoo.fr
Web	lesbambous.monsite.wanadoo.fr

Pascale Letellier
Les Écuries des Chartreux,
66 rue de la République,
30400 Villeneuve lès Avignon, Gard

Tel	+33 (0)4 90 25 79 93
Fax	+33 (0)4 90 25 79 93
Email	ecuries-des-chartreux@wanadoo.fr
Web	www.ecuries-des-chartreux.com

Entry 601   Map 16

Entry 602   Map 16

Languedoc – Roussillon

Jardin de Bacchus

Care has been taken in this arty, relaxed house set against a rock. Park at roof level, walk down to the entrance, through the dining room and straight out onto the view-filled garden terrace. Simple bedrooms (one downstairs, two up) have good beds and colourful paintings and prints; bathrooms are white-tiled, one is open-plan behind the bed. It's all light and spacious, the salon has wicker chairs and stone floors, your sparkling hosts take food very seriously, run cookery courses and spoil you with delicious breakfasts and dinners at a convivial table in the open-plan kitchen. Lovely. *Min. stay 2 nights; 6 in summer.*

Price	€80–€120.
Rooms	3 doubles.
Meals	Dinner with wine, €30.
Closed	Mid-December to mid-March.
Directions	From Avignon for Nîmes then Tavel. See web site for map.

Christine Chapot
Jardin de Bacchus,
223 rue de Tourtouil,
30126 Tavel, Gard
Tel   +33 (0)4 66 90 28 62
Email   jardindebacchus@free.fr
Web   jardindebacchus.fr

Entry 603   Map 16

Languedoc – Roussillon

La Terre des Lauriers

Gérard has laid a path through the woods that leads from the house to the river by the Pont du Gard – the setting is special. The house is less historic, and its décor idiosyncratic. Bedrooms are themed, fresh and spotless; one has a connecting room with bunk beds and soft toys. Monsieur works in Nîmes but gives all his remaining time to welcoming and caring for his guests. You get a sitting room with games for the children, bedrooms with air conditioning and a lovely garden that slopes down to a pool. A reader describes breakfasts as "stupendous", and the pool with the heavenly view is shared with two gîtes. *Sawday self-catering also.*

Price	€89–€150.
Rooms	5: 2 doubles, 2 twin, 1 suite.
Meals	Restaurants within 3km.
Closed	Rarely.
Directions	From Remoulins follow signs for Pont du Gard 'Rive Droite'. Sign on right.

Marianick & Gérard Langlois
La Terre des Lauriers,
Rive Droite – Pont du Gard,
30210 Remoulins, Gard
Tel   +33 (0)4 66 37 19 45
Fax   +33 (0)4 66 37 19 45
Email   langlois@laterredeslauriers.com
Web   www.laterredeslauriers.com

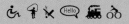

Entry 604   Map 16

Languedoc – Roussillon

Hermitage de Saint Antoine

An enchanting nest, full of light and quiet, inside the bustling old city that was once a port. Rosa is artistic and these two workmen's cottages are now softly painted, sisal-floored and dotted with abstract art. Small but uncluttered bedrooms are up narrow painted stairs and have good linen, bright bathrooms. Cool off by the fountain in the pot-filled courtyard, or read a book in the winter garden with its folding glass doors. The vast open stretches of the inland sea lagoon are waiting, and fine sandy beaches or, if you can take the heat in August, a full medieval festival with costumes! *Children over 12 welcome.*

Price	€74-€79.
Rooms	3 doubles.
Meals	Restaurants within walking distance.
Closed	January-February.
Directions	From A9 exit 26; N313 for St Laurent d'Aiguze, Aimargues; D979 to Aigues Mortes; left along city wall to Porte St Antoine; immed. right on entering old town.

	Rosa de Javel
	Hermitage de Saint Antoine,
	9 bd Interieur Nord,
	30220 Aigues Mortes, Gard
Tel	+33 (0)6 03 04 34 05
Fax	+33 (0)4 66 88 40 98
Email	ryhermit@club-internet.fr
Web	www.hermitagesa.com

Languedoc – Roussillon

Mas de Barbut

Stunning, imaginative, decorated with élan. The Gandons are great travellers, and have brought together fascinating things in a strikingly harmonious way; bedrooms are Mexican, Mandarin or Provençal, outstanding bathrooms have fabulous tiles. Different food, a different table decoration every day: they love cosseting guests. The summer sitting room has a pebble floor, the stone bassin is overlooked by slatted oak loungers, there's a sweet spot for drinks by the river and the shaded courtyard is bliss. Near the sea yet away from it all — and restaurants in lovely St Laurent. A treat from start to finish.

Price	€97-€120.
Rooms	4: 3 doubles, 1 triple.
Meals	Dinner with wine, €30.
Closed	Rarely.
Directions	From A9 exit 26 for Gallargues. D979 for Aigues Mortes, 12.5km. Right at 7th r'bout for Le Vidourle, 2km. House on right.

	Danielle & Jean-Claude Gandon
	Mas de Barbut,
	30220 St Laurent d'Aigouze, Gard
Tel	+33 (0)4 66 88 12 09
Email	gandon.barbut@club-internet.fr
Web	www.masdebarbut.com

Languedoc – Roussillon

26 boulevard Saint Louis

A Moorish tang colours Marion's 17th-century townhouse: a fountain in the wall of the deliciously cool walled garden; candlelit dinners that taste of Provence and North Africa; adventurous colours and lovely fabrics; a sunken bath in the air-conditioned suite; beautiful furniture and paintings placed to enhance generous proportions. It isn't grand, just simply elegant. This talented lady is a wonderful hostess who adores having guests, serving superb breakfasts of local produce and 'fougasse' (a soft delicate bread) then pointing them to the cultural riches of the area – and the sea. *Secure parking.*

Price	€80–€130.
Rooms	4: 3 doubles, 1 suite.
Meals	Dinner with wine, €30.
Closed	Occasionally.
Directions	From A9 exit 26 Aimargues Centre. Over r'bout with fountain down plane tree lane 300m. Entrance opp. Aimargues Immo, Rue de la Violette (3 cypresses behind garden wall).

	Marion Escarfail
	26 boulevard Saint Louis,
	30470 Aimargues, Gard
Tel	+33 (0)4 66 88 52 99
Fax	+33 (0)4 66 88 52 99
Email	lamaisondemarion@free.fr
Web	lamaisondemarion.free.fr

Entry 607 Map 16

Languedoc – Roussillon

Hôtel de l'Orange

At his *hôtel particulier* (private mansion), Philippe receives with warm refinement. Each hushed room is in *maison de famille* style: polished floors, warm-painted walls, white bedcovers, a different and beautiful wall hanging over each bed; one room is an independent studio. The magic secluded terrace garden with gasping views over the roofs of the old town is where you swim; breakfast, which to Philippe is *the* moment of the day, is in the old-style dining room or at small tables in the courtyard. Walk into the old town: the river is a charming place. A touch of 'la vieille France'.

Price	€80–€152.
Rooms	5: 3 doubles, 1 twin, 1 triple.
Meals	Dinner with wine, €35.
Closed	Rarely.
Directions	From Nîmes D40 W 28km to Sommières; from town centre for centre historique; from post office follow street up to château; signed.

	Philippe de Frémont
	Hôtel de l'Orange,
	Chemin du Château Fort,
	30250 Sommières, Gard
Tel	+33 (0)4 66 77 79 94
Email	hotel.delorange@free.fr
Web	hotel.delorange.free.fr

Entry 608 Map 16

Languedoc – Roussillon

Les Asphodèles

It may look unassuming from the street but step into Corine's 18th-century townhouse and you enter a world of light and creativity. A wide stone staircase at its heart leads to airy family rooms full of interest and colour. Corine bubbles with energy; a journalist for years, she now organises workshops in handmade paper and herbalism. The watercolours on the walls are hers, too, and she cooks – delectably. The plant-filled terrace overlooks the hills; close by is the river with its own small beach and rocks to climb (bliss for children). This quiet part of town was once the silk quarter.

Price	€75–€140.
Rooms	1 double.
Meals	Dinner with wine, €20–€50.
Closed	Never.
Directions	From Nîmes N999 for Sauve/Le Vigan; by church in town centre large square for parking; house in small street behind restaurant "Le Plan", 2-minute walk from square.

Corine de Royer
Les Asphodèles,
3 rue Cap de Ville,
30170 St Hippolyte du Fort, Gard
Tel +33 (0)4 66 51 00 54
Email corine.deroyer@orange.fr
Web www.lesasphodeles.com

Entry 609   Map 15

Languedoc – Roussillon

Château Massal

Roadside is the château façade; behind is the rambling, many-terraced garden – with views across river and red-roofed town. Up a spiral stone stair are big beautiful bedrooms with a château feel; walnut parquet and mosaic floors along with strong-coloured walls set off family furniture to perfection; one has a grand piano, another a bathroom in the tower – enchanting. Madame, one of an old French silk family who have been here for several generations, is as elegant and charming as her house; a fine cook, too. She will show you where to find really good walks, exciting canoeing, and wildlife.

Price	€68–€88.
Rooms	4 doubles. Child's bed available.
Meals	Dinner with wine, €28.
Closed	Mid-November to March.
Directions	From Millau S on N9 for 19km to La Cavalerie; left D7 for Le Vigan approx. 50km to Bez; before bridge, sign on left.

Françoise & Marie-Emmanuelle du Luc
Château Massal,
Bez et Esparon,
30120 Le Vigan, Gard
Tel +33 (0)4 67 81 07 60
Fax +33 (0)4 67 81 07 60
Email francoiseduluc@gmail.com
Web www.cevennes-massal.com

Entry 610   Map 15

Languedoc – Roussillon

Au Soleil

Catherine is as elegant and welcoming as her house. Once involved in theatre PR, she now devotes her energies to guests and house; it's a treat to stay in her town centre *maison de maître*. Behind the front door, caressed by sweet jasmine, lie sunlight, space and simplicity, fine pieces of brocante and a sitting room with deep orange sofas. Bedrooms are peaceful and calm, with kilim rugs on glowing terracotta; windows overlook the rooftops or the lush inner courtyard where cat and dog doze. Simple Mediterranean food is served with pleasure… and on Sundays in summer the bulls race through town. *Beaches nearby.*

Price	€65–€75.
Rooms	3 doubles.
Meals	Dinner with wine, €20. Restaurant 100m.
Closed	Never.
Directions	A9 exit for Lunel; D34 to Marsillargues; in town centre after church, 1st right at square.

Catherine Maurel
Au Soleil,
9 rue Pierre Brossolette,
34590 Marsillargues, Hérault

Tel	+33 (0)4 67 83 90 00
Email	catherine.maurel@ausoleil.info
Web	www.ausoleil.info

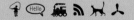

Entry 611   Map 16

Languedoc – Roussillon

Castle's Cottage

On the edge of a wild, unspoilt forest, in a garden flooded with hibiscus and iris where 20 tortoises roam… hard to believe you're a bus ride from Montpellier. The house is recent, built with old materials, the vegetation lush, the saltwater pool set among atmospheric stone 'ruins'. You sleep in small but comfy beds in pretty rooms full of family furniture and colour, sharing an excellent shower room, and opening onto the terrace. Your hostess, once a city girl in public relations, loves this place passionately, talks easily and generously shares her fireside and living space. And the beach is nearby.

Ethical Collection: Environment.
See page 432.

Price	€85–€105.
Rooms	2 doubles, sharing shower & separate wc.
Meals	Restaurants in Montpellier, 3km.
Closed	Rarely.
Directions	From Mairie in Castelnau le Lez take Rue Jules Ferry; 5th left Chemin de la Rocheuse; last house on left.

Dominique Carabin-Cailleau
Castle's Cottage,
289 chemin de la Rocheuse,
34170 Castelnau le Lez, Hérault

Tel	+33 (0)4 67 72 63 08
Fax	+33 (0)4 67 72 63 08
Email	castlecottage@free.fr
Web	castlecottage.free.fr

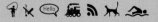

Entry 612   Map 15

Languedoc – Roussillon

Domaine du Pélican

Meals are eaten off local pottery, vignerons drop by for tastings on Mondays, cats and dogs doze. This is a superb wine estate with a mulberry-lined drive and a real family atmosphere: come for peace, simplicity and fine bedrooms. The hard-working owners have four children of their own and share their saltwater pool. Guest rooms, in a separate building, have soft-coloured walls, some beds on mezzanines (no windows, just French doors), pretty shower rooms. The dining room has old honey-coloured beams – a dream – and gives onto the terrace and rows of vines beyond: just the place for an authentic auberge dinner.

Price	€62–€72.
Rooms	4: 1 double, 1 suite for 4; 1 double, 1 twin, each with fold-out bed.
Meals	Dinner with wine, €24. Restaurant in village.
Closed	Last week in October.
Directions	From Gignac centre towards Montpellier; at edge of town bus stop Pélican on right; right & follow signs for 3km.

	Isabelle & Baudouin Thillaye du Boullay Domaine du Pélican, 34150 Gignac, Hérault
Tel	+33 (0)4 67 57 68 92
Fax	+33 (0)4 67 57 68 92
Email	domaine-de-pelican@wanadoo.fr
Web	www.domainedepelican.fr

Entry 613   Map 15

Languedoc – Roussillon

La Genestière

Madame's work upon the walls, Monsieur's fine horse in the paddock – the modern house has lots of atmosphere and your hostess is an open, fun person who loves getting to know you, even teaching you to sculpt (do enquire). Rooms are big and simply furnished, each with a few lovely things, good fabrics, mosquito screens (yes!) and a private terrace onto the lush garden with great bamboos and aromatic pines, and a summer kitchen. All in a fabulous spot near the magnificent Salagou lake for sailing and swimming on hot days, and biking and riding in winter. Worth a good stay. *Minimum stay 2 nights.*

Price	€55–€70.
Rooms	2 doubles.
Meals	Restaurants 3.5km.
Closed	November–March.
Directions	A9 exit 34 on D13 N 10km; N9 to Clermont l'Hérault; A75 exit Clermont l'Hérault; D156 left for Lac du Salagou 3km; left to Liausson; 700m; last house on right before woods.

	M & Mme Neveu La Genestière, Route de Liausson, 34800 Clermont l'Hérault, Hérault
Tel	+33 (0)4 67 96 30 97
Email	lagenestiere@wanadoo.fr
Web	lagenestiere.fr

Entry 614   Map 15

Languedoc – Roussillon

La Missare

A vast and lovely stone winery is the guest wing on this old family property. Your host's sensitive conversion uses old tiles, doors and beams; simple, stylish bedrooms are designed for comfort and privacy, each with an excellent shower room, exquisite linen, perhaps antique candlesticks or a new mirror. All French windows open to the large and wonderful courtyard. Jean-François and his mother happily share their living space: go through the hall, hung with fine prints, to a generous breakfast in the living room where a cabinet of treasures (some for sale) will intrigue. Outside, a discreet pool glimmers.

Price	€70.
Rooms	4 doubles.
Meals	Restaurants 3-12km.
Closed	Rarely.
Directions	From Paris A75 exit 57 to Clermont L'Hérault; 1st r'bout to Canet; 2nd r'bout to Brignac; at Brignac left to Saint Andre de Sis; house after 20m opp. phone box.

Jean-François Martin
La Missare,
9 route de Clermont,
34800 Brignac, Hérault

Tel +33 (0)4 67 96 07 67
Email la.missare@free.fr
Web la.missare.free.fr

Entry 615   Map 15

Languedoc – Roussillon

Domaine Saint Hilaire

A delight: among rolling vineyards, down a rackety lane, a refined and welcoming house rambles between smooth garden and tall trees; deeply interesting owners – recycled-from-London intellectuals, now wine-growers and loving it – have a clear eye that leaves originalities (exquisite patterned tiling, marble fireplaces) room to breathe in bedrooms that are simple-smart or colourful-baroque, contemporary-neat or cosy-draped, all with stunning designer bathrooms. Add serene white guest-sitting and breakfast rooms, a great communal library, good unusual wines… and Anne is a fine, subtle cook. *Alarmed, unfenced pool.*

Price	€125-€195.
Rooms	4 doubles.
Meals	Dinner with wine, €40.
Closed	Rarely.
Directions	From Montagnac for Mèze to end of dual carriageway (by hotel on left). Right along signed lane; St Hilaire 3km.

Anne & Jonathan James
Domaine Saint Hilaire,
34530 Montagnac, Hérault

Tel +33 (0)4 67 24 00 08
Fax +33 (0)4 67 24 04 01
Email info@domainesaint-hilaire.com
Web www.domainesaint-hilaire.com

Entry 616   Map 15

Languedoc – Roussillon

The Village House

A great townhouse, unpretentious and spotless, run by unpushy hosts who live and work here. Tall and narrow, the oldest part of it is attached to the 14th-century ramparts of the sleepy market town, which stands in a sea of Languedoc vineyards. Serene rooms are set round the charming first-floor guest terrace: the smaller room cool and light, with white floor tiles, the master room with its own elegant landing, big bathroom and balcony over the square. An excellent place to stay; inexpensive, stylish, discreet. Historic Pézenas has markets and boutiques galore, and the mountain bikes are free.

Price	€55–€60.
Rooms	2 doubles.
Meals	Restaurants within walking distance.
Closed	Rarely.
Directions	From Pézenas D13 for Bédarieux 15km. In Gabian centre, right for Montesquieu; 1st right to fountain. House on left.

John Cook & Jean-Maurice Siu
The Village House,
3 rue du Théron,
34320 Gabian, Hérault

Tel   +33 (0)4 67 24 77 27
Email cdh@thevillagehouse.info
Web   www.thevillagehouse.info

Entry 617   Map 15

Languedoc – Roussillon

Château de Grézan

A 19th-century château built in a troubadour style, all towers, turrets and castellated walls. And a very big welcome from Marie-France – a remarkable, generous lady, a member of the champagne family who organises 'taste travels'. Crystal chandeliers, original wallpapers, cavernous rooms, wonderful views… you'll forgive the odd imperfect corner. Bedrooms are big and absolutely château, bathrooms endearingly old-fashioned. The inner courtyard is lush with camellias and cyclamen, the gardens are lovely, the swimming pool lies beneath the palms. Breakfasts and dinners are enriching affairs. *Sawday self-catering also.*

Price	€98–€120.
Rooms	3: 2 doubles, 1 twin.
Meals	Restaurant in grounds.
Closed	Rarely.
Directions	From A9 exit 35 Béziers Est; for Bédarieux; D909 for 20km, signs for château on right.

Marie-France Lanson
Château de Grézan,
Au Milieu des Vignes,
34480 Laurens, Hérault

Tel   +33 (0)4 67 90 28 03
Fax   +33 (0)4 67 90 05 03
Email chateau-grezan.lanson@wanadoo.fr
Web   www.grezan.com

Entry 618   Map 15

Languedoc – Roussillon

Château de Murviel

The château is perched on the pinnacle of the village, surveying ancient mellow rooftops, sweeping vineyards and hills. Soft, plastered walls, honey-coloured floorboards or pale stone floors and bleached linen curtains around beds give a wonderful feeling of light – unexpected in such an old building. Breakfast, served by the *gardien* (Madame works in Paris), is in a cool courtyard, dotted with lemon trees and oleander and guests can cook supper in their own kitchen. Whether you are interested in wine or the Cathars, this is a comfortable place to lay your head. *Minimum stay 2 nights in high season.*

Price	€80–€110. Whole house €1,950–€3,900 per week.
Rooms	4: 1 double, 2 triples, 1 suite for 4.
Meals	Restaurant 4km. Kitchen available.
Closed	Rarely.
Directions	From A9 exit 35 for centre ville; at 1st & 2nd r'bouts: for Bédarieux; 3rd r'bout: for Corneilhan & Murviel; in Murviel centre, next to Mairie.

Yves & Florence Cousquer
Château de Murviel,
1 place Georges Clémenceau,
34490 Murviel lès Béziers, Hérault

Tel	+33 (0)4 67 32 35 45
Fax	+33 (0)4 67 32 35 25
Email	chateaudemurviel@free.fr
Web	www.murviel.com

Entry 619   Map 15

Languedoc – Roussillon

La Métairie Basse

In these wild, pastoral surroundings with great walking and climbing trails, you bathe in simplicity, stream-babble and light. Your hosts, hard-working walnut and chestnut growers, have converted to 'bio' and sell delicious purées and jams. The guest barn is beautifully tended: country antiques, old lace curtains, new bedding and blue tones relax the eye; there's a fireplace and a full kitchen too. Monsieur has a big friendly handshake, Madame is gentle and welcoming, and breakfast on the shady terrace includes cheese or walnuts or honey. The wonderful Cathar city of Minerve is a 40-minute drive. Amazing value.

Ethical Collection: Food.
See page 432.

Price	€52.
Rooms	2 doubles.
Meals	Restaurants 3–4km. Guest kitchen.
Closed	October–March, except by arrangement.
Directions	From A9 exit Béziers Ouest; D64; N112 to Mazamet; N112 for St Pons de Thomières. At Courniou, right to Prouilhe; farm on left.

Éliane & Jean-Louis Lunes
La Métairie Basse,
Hameau de Prouilhe,
34220 Courniou, Hérault

Tel	+33 (0)4 67 97 21 59
Fax	+33 (0)4 67 97 21 59
Email	info@metairie-basse.com
Web	www.metairie-basse.com

Entry 620   Map 15

Languedoc – Roussillon

Le Vieux Relais

New owners have poured hearts and souls into this refurbished 18th-century coach house in Pepieux. Original door hinges and floor tiles gleam, bright carpets sweep across suites, bathrooms are heaped with white towels, ceiling fans keep you cool in five big, fresh-faced rooms. There's a cosy guest sitting room, a shingle courtyard garden, wine tastings on Fridays and lemon drizzle cake for tea. And fabulous dinners: what pros! Your English hosts love their new life and have stacks of time for you; books for readers, maps for walkers, and painting courses can be arranged. *Children over 12 welcome.*

Languedoc – Roussillon

La Marelle

After dreaming of running their own B&B, Janne and Terje uprooted from Norway to settle here with their children in a handsome, green-shuttered stone house built in the 16th century. The house is flanked by pretty gardens and plenty of shady spots to which you can take a drink, or bury your nose in a novel – or both. Big bedrooms in florals and checks have good bathrooms and endless nooks and crannies to investigate. Janne is a passionate cook; guests with an occasion to celebrate can dine by candlelight in the lovely courtyard. This young couple thrive on looking after their guests: you'll be spoiled rotten.

Price	€65–€80. €120 for 4.
Rooms	5: 1 triple, 2 family suites, 2 suites for 2.
Meals	Dinner with wine, from €25. Picnics available.
Closed	Rarely.
Directions	From Olonzac D115 to Pépieux. House on left as you enter village. Parking outside.

Price	€60. Single €45.
Rooms	5: 3 doubles, 1 single, 1 family room for 4.
Meals	Dinner with wine, €25. Restaurant 200m.
Closed	Rarely.
Directions	Exit A61 at Carcassone Est; D610 for Marseillette & Puichéric 23.5km; left for La Redorte; after green bridge left for approx. 700m; house behind green railings on right.

	Valerie & Michael Slowther
	Le Vieux Relais,
	1 rue de l'Étang,
	11700 Pépieux, Aude
Tel	+33 (0)4 68 91 69 29
Email	mike@levieuxrelais.net
Web	www.levieuxrelais.net

	Janne & Terje Moum
	La Marelle,
	19 avenue du Minervois,
	11700 La Redorte, Aude
Tel	+33 (0)4 68 91 59 30
Email	reservations@chambres-lamarelle.com
Web	www.chambres-lamarelle.com

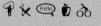

Languedoc – Roussillon

Secrets d'Aude

A gorgeous village house, hugely stylish, in wine country. Beyond enormous iron gates and shell-shaped stone steps are light airy rooms and loads of space. Beams, wooden floors, marble fireplaces, a lofty kitchen – the big house is yours to wander. Bedrooms are a delightful mix of painted furniture and antiques, gilt-framed mirrors, easy chairs and soft colours. There's an inside tropical garden area with banana plants, pots and quiet corners, and terraces to lunch on or have dinner. Yvon cooks lovely organic dinners, Ariane teaches dance. Book for a dance-themed stay, or a relaxed massage.

Price	€57–€63.
Rooms	5: 2 doubles, 1 twin, 1 triple, 1 family room for 4.
Meals	Dinner with wine, €18–€23. Lunch €10.
Closed	Rarely.
Directions	A61 exit 24 Carcassonne Est. D6113 for Narbonne 18km; after Douzens, left D72 to St Couat; park opp. church.

Ariane Hoyois & Yvon Blondiaux
Secrets d'Aude,
1 place de l'Église,
11700 St Couat d'Aude, Aude

Tel	+33 (0)4 68 90 41 76
Fax	+33 (0)4 68 90 41 76
Email	info@secretsdaude.eu
Web	www.secretsdaude.eu

Entry 623   Map 15

Languedoc – Roussillon

Le Domaine aux Quat'Saisons

A quartet of dachshunds – 'les Girls' – adds an engaging touch to this elegant old *maison de maître*, set behind white wrought-iron gates in a friendly and pretty village. The moment you enter the hall with its glowing floor tiles and graceful antiques you know you are in for a treat. From the immaculately restored rooms to the garden with its lily pond (and a divine pool behind a stone wall), everything is delightful. As are David and Graeme. Enjoy drinks with them both before feasting on David's cooking; Graeme will ensure that meal, wine and conversation flow. A jewel of a place. *Minimum stay 2 nights.*

Price	€95–€140.
Rooms	5: 2 doubles, 2 four-posters, 1 twin.
Meals	Dinner with wine, €39.
Closed	November-Easter, except Christmas & New Year.
Directions	From Rieux Minervois main street, house set back from road behind white wrought-iron gates, signed.

David Coles & Graeme McGlasson-West
Le Domaine aux Quat'Saisons,
26 avenue Georges Clémenceau,
11160 Rieux Minervois, Aude

Tel	+33 (0)4 68 24 49 73
Fax	+33 (0)4 68 24 49 10
Email	info@southoffrancehotel.com
Web	www.southoffrancehotel.com

Entry 624   Map 15

Languedoc – Roussillon

L'Ancienne Boulangerie

In the history- and legend-laden north Minervois, Caunes is one of France's most beautiful walled villages. Quiet too: the twisting lanes make speed impossible. In a house that baked the abbey's bread from 1500 to 1988, you are sure of a charming Irish welcome from the new owners of this tall, antique-furnished B&B: steep narrow stairs and characterful old floors, a galley kitchen in one suite, a tiny, pretty terrace for two others to enjoy summer breakfasts, a small library – and all those cobbled streets to explore. Plus, of course, Carcassonne, the oldest walled city in Europe, just down the road. *Minimum stay 2 nights.*

Price	€65. Triple €80.
Rooms	5: 3 doubles, 1 triple, 1 family suite for 3.
Meals	Supper with wine, €16. Restaurant opposite.
Closed	November to mid-March.
Directions	From Carcassonne D620 to Caunes Minervois; cross river & follow to Mairie; house behind Épicerie opp. Place de la Mairie.

Gareth Armstrong
L'Ancienne Boulangerie,
20 rue St Gènes,
11160 Caunes-Minervois, Aude

Tel	+33 (0)4 68 78 01 32
Fax	+33 (0)4 68 78 01 32
Email	ancienne.boulangerie@free.fr
Web	www.ancienneboulangerie.com

Entry 625   Map 15

Languedoc – Roussillon

Domaine Saint Pierre de Trapel

Coming in from the magnificent gardens, catch the scent of herbs as you walk through the house. The delightful owners, lively, educated, well-travelled, moved here from east France for a more relaxing way of life and climate. Using exquisite taste, they have combined original 18th-century elegances with new necessities in big bedrooms and bathrooms of pure luxury, each with its own lovely colour scheme. Best in the summer, with relaxing outdoor spots for all, a superb 150-year-old cedar, olive trees, a swimming pool surrounded by roses and a lovely covered terrace. A place of beauty, elegance and space. *Sawday self-catering also.*

Price	€85–€145.
Rooms	5: 1 twin, 3 doubles, 1 suite for 4.
Meals	Restaurants nearby.
Closed	November–March.
Directions	From A61 exit 23 for Mazamet; at r'bout D620 for Villalier; after 1.5km, towards Villedubert; on right, thro' wrought-iron gates.

Christophe & Catherine Pariset
Domaine Saint Pierre de Trapel,
11620 Villemoustaussou, Aude

Tel	+33 (0)4 68 77 00 68
Fax	+33 (0)4 68 77 01 68
Email	cpariset@trapel.com
Web	www.trapel.com

Entry 626   Map 15

Languedoc – Roussillon

Domaine des Castelles

There are space and air galore in this 19th-century gentleman-farmer's house. The freshly decorated bedrooms – with own entrance – are often huge, always charming; there are good mattresses, pine floors and an impeccable feel; the gardens fill a whole hectare. Madame, lively, artistic, open and welcoming, chats to guests over breakfast – on the terrace in fine weather – and enjoys their travellers' tales. You are in the country yet near the buzz of Carcassonne (and the airport!), while the dreamy Canal du Midi and the vineyards offer their seductively parallel alternatives. A gem.

Price	€65–€70. Extra bed €20.
Rooms	3: 1 double, 1 triple, 1 suite for 5.
Meals	Restaurants nearby.
Closed	Rarely.
Directions	On A61 exit Carcassonne-West to Salvaza airport; stay on D119 for approx. 4km more. Sign on left.

	Isabelle Bretton
	Domaine des Castelles,
	11170 Caux et Sauzens, Aude
Tel	+33 (0)4 68 72 03 60
Fax	+33 (0)4 68 72 03 60

Entry 627 Map 15

Languedoc – Roussillon

Château de la Prade

Lost among the cool shadows of tall sunlit trees, beside the languid waters of the Canal du Midi, is a place of understated elegance and refinement. The 19th-century house is more 'domaine' than 'château', though the vineyards have long gone. It sits in 12 acres... formal hedges, fine trees, ornamental railings. Swiss Roland runs the B&B, Lorenz looks after the gardens: they are kind and discreetly attentive hosts. Dinner is served on pink cloths, breakfasts are a treat, bedrooms have tall windows, polished floors, an immaculate, uncluttered charm. Half a mile from the road to Carcassonne but so peaceful.

Price	€95–€115.
Rooms	4 twins/doubles.
Meals	Dinner €24. Wine €17.50–€23.
Closed	Mid-November to mid-March.
Directions	From A61 exit 22; through Bram 2.5km; left N6113 for Villepinte; house signed on left.

	Roland Kurt
	Château de la Prade,
	11150 Bram, Aude
Tel	+33 (0)4 68 78 03 99
Fax	+33 (0)4 68 24 96 31
Email	chateaulaprade@wanadoo.fr
Web	www.chateaulaprade.eu

Entry 628 Map 15

Languedoc – Roussillon

Villelongue Côté Jardins

Romantics, painters, poets – paradise. History and romance combine as dark 16th-century passages and uneven stone floors open into heavily beamed rooms stunningly revived. Bedrooms are big and simply refined in their white cotton and fine old armoires, the newest on the ground-floor. Views are to the magic-exotic monastic park or the great courtyard and ruined Cistercian abbey. Sisters Renée and Claude, warm, knowledgable, generous, were born here, and provide marvellous breakfasts and dinners with family linen and silver. There are four retired horses… and so much more. Incomparable.

Languedoc – Roussillon

Le Trésor

The most attractive house in the village, Le Trésor looks through green eyelids onto the sleepy town square. Inside, tall elegant windows and banistered stairs mix with white walls, crisp art and flamboyant chandeliers: ex-Londoners Will and Tilly have created a quirkily seductive B&B. Bedrooms, one with a rolltop bath, have high ceilings, spare furnishings, masses of light. Tilly loves regional food so the treats continue at table, and breakfasts are superb. A hammock in the garden (kids love it!), L'Occitane oils by the shower, DVDs, snooker and great young hosts. Great for hiking or skiing or discovering Matisse's Collioure.

Price	€60.
Rooms	3: 1 double, 1 twin, 1 family room for 3.
Meals	Dinner with wine, €22, except July/August.
Closed	Christmas.
Directions	From A61 exit Bram; D4 through Bram & St Martin le Vieil; right on tiny D64 3km to Abbey. Caution: Go to Côté Jardins B&B not Abbey B&B next door.

Price	€90-€120.
Rooms	4: 3 doubles, 1 suite.
Meals	Dinner with wine, €28.
Closed	January-March.
Directions	From Carcassonne D118 to Limoux; D620 to Chalabre; D16 Sonnac, on main square,

	Claude Antoine
	Villelongue Côté Jardins,
	11170 St Martin le Vieil, Aude
Tel	+33 (0)2 31 89 42 40
Email	avillelongue@free.fr
Web	www.coursaintecatherine.com

	William & Tilly Howard
	Le Trésor,
	20 place de l'Église,
	11230 Sonnac sur l'Hers, Aude
Tel	+33 (0)4 68 69 37 94
Fax	+33 (0)4 68 69 37 94
Email	contact@le-tresor.com
Web	www.le-tresor.com

Entry 629   Map 15

Entry 630   Map 15

Languedoc – Roussillon

Maison d'hôtes l'Orangerie

The most charming town with a tree-lined square for boules, a bustling market, lovely restaurants and interesting small shops… you stay in the heart of it all. Through huge green gates enter a pretty courtyard with flowering pots, the orange tree (as announced) and calm, relaxed Sylvie and Claude. A charming sitting room has a reading corner and comfy seating, the bright and inviting bedrooms are all a good size – one has a terrace and the bathrooms are super. Breakfast on seasonal fresh fruit, cake and homemade jams in the dining room or the courtyard. Dinner can be served here too, in traditional French style.

Price	€65-€100.
Rooms	5: 3 doubles, 1 family room for 3, 1 suite for 2-4.
Meals	Dinner with wine, €27.
Closed	November.
Directions	A9 exit 41 Rivesaltes; at r'bout 1st right, D12 for Rivesaltes; D5, cross Pont Jacquet; 1st left after bridge; 1st right. House on right.

Sylvie & Claude Poussin
Maison d'hôtes l'Orangerie,
3 T rue Ludovic Ville,
66600 Rivesaltes,
Pyrénées-Orientales
TelFax	+33 (0)4 68 73 74 41
Email	maisonhoteslorangerie@wanadoo.fr
Web	maisonhoteslorangerie.com

Entry 631   Map 15

Languedoc – Roussillon

El Pinyol d'Oliva

In March the valley is a sea of blossom: this is the peach capital of France. Views sweep from the roof terrace to the streets below and the snowy peaks of the Canigou beyond. Anne, active and delightful, loves her old house in the small square, a stone's throw from the church, and its large, luminous rooms glow with good taste. Whitewashed walls rub shoulders with Catalan stonework, beams are high, cushions and curtains give bright bursts of colour, there's art on the walls and one of the shower rooms is triangular. Perpignan is a 15-minute drive, the airport 20, and Spain just half an hour. Great food, too! *Sawday self-catering also.*

Price	€85-€100.
Rooms	4: 1 double, 2 twins, 1 suite.
Meals	Dinner with wine, €25.
Closed	Never.
Directions	From Perpignan N116 for Andorra 2.5km; exit for l'Île sur Têt; Ave. Pasteur to centre; right for Montalba; follow ramparts on right 50m, right at El Pinyol d'Oliva sign, left, downhill to small square; knock on door No. 6.

Anne Guthrie
El Pinyol d'Oliva,
10 petite place de l'Huile,
66130 Île sur Têt,
Pyrénées-Orientales
Tel	+33 (0)4 68 84 04 17
Email	web-enquiry@elpinyoldoliva.com
Web	www.elpinyoldoliva.com

Entry 632   Map 15

Languedoc – Roussillon

Castell Rose

A beautiful pink marble gentleman's house in its own parkland, sitting on the edge of a very pretty town between the sea and the mountains; the views are superb. Evelyne and Alex are both charming, and give you large sumptuous bedrooms with thoughtful colour schemes, good linen, tip-top bathrooms and elegant antiques. After a good breakfast, wander through the flourishing garden with its ancient olive tree to find a spot beside the lily pond, or just float in the pool. It's a five-minute stroll to village life, or take the yellow train up the mountain from Villefranche for more amazing views.

Price	€79-€105. Family room €109-€129.
Rooms	5: 3 doubles, 1 twin, 1 family room.
Meals	Restaurant 500m.
Closed	Rarely.
Directions	From Perpignan N116 to Prades; for centre ville; thro' town on Ave du Général de Gaulle; left at end & cont. Route de Ria; house signed 200m on left before Hôtel de Ville.

Evelyne & Alex Waldvogel
Castell Rose,
Chemin de la Litera, 66500 Prades,
Pyrénées-Orientales
Tel   +33 (0)4 68 96 07 57
Fax   +33 (0)4 68 96 07 57
Email   castell.rose@wanadoo.fr
Web   www.castellrose-prades.com

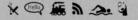

Entry 633   Map 15

Languedoc – Roussillon

Mas Pallarès

High in the hills but ten minutes from Céret is this ancient farmhouse with stepped gardens and a child-perfect stream. Birds sing, wisteria blooms, views sweep across the wooded valley and Lizzie has worked hard to ensure everyone has their own corner of calm; the B&B rooms have lovely big balconies. The mood is easy and the rooms are friendly: old floor tiles, inviting colours, country antiques, spotless showers. Lizzie's breakfasts are feasts and the fenced pool and summer kitchen are shared with apartment guests. Céret's market is fantastic, Spain's peaceful bays are a hop away. *Minimum stay 2 nights.*

Price	€95-€150.
Rooms	2: 1 double, 1 suite & kitchenette. (7 rental apartments also.)
Meals	Restaurant 1km.
Closed	Rarely.
Directions	From A9 exit 43 D115 to Céret; cont. 2km to Lepont; 1st left D15 to Reynes 800m; hairpin bend left for for Coll. de Bousseilles. House on left after Allée du Mas Pallarès.

Lizzie Price
Mas Pallarès,
66400 Reynes,
Pyrénées-Orientales
Tel   +33 (0)4 68 87 42 17
Email   lizzie@ceret-farmhouse-apartments.com
Web   www.ceret-farmhouse-apartments.com

Entry 634   Map 15

Languedoc – Roussillon

La Châtaigneraie

The Bethells have created a haven of Pyrenean-Scottish hospitality among some of Europe's wildest, remotest landscapes. In the magical, lush garden are several intimate sitting areas where views dazzle up to snowy Canigou or down to the sea. Super, romantic rooms with comfy beds have original works of art and bright scatter cushions, and the suite opens to a private terrace by the pool. Take breakfast out here, delivered by Kim or Gill – a mother and daughter team who look after guests beautifully. And for dinner, there's the famous Terrasse au Soleil in lively Céret – a 15-minute walk away.

Price	€80–€170.
Rooms	5: 3 doubles, 1 twin/double, 1 suite.
Meals	Restaurant 400m.
Closed	Never.
Directions	A9 to Spain, last exit before border; into Céret for centre ville then for Hôtel La Terrasse au Soleil. House 400m after hotel, on left.

Kim & Gill Bethell
La Châtaigneraie,
Route de Fontfrède, 66400 Céret,
Pyrénées-Orientales

Tel	+33 (0)4 68 87 21 58
Fax	+33 (0)4 68 87 77 86
Email	kim@ceret.net
Web	www.ceret.net

Entry 635   Map 15

Languedoc – Roussillon

Sanglier Lodge

Jan, wildlife photographer and film maker, came from Zimbabwe to find a less turbulent life in the south of France. He and wife Fiona, a doctor, have created a warm rustic mood in their big old stone house, with exotic overtones: Zimbabwean teak chairs and antique Spanish table, French teak beds on chestnut floors, original art on white walls. The old bakery bedroom has the bread oven and the baker's licence; the showers drench. So easy to relax: a small kidney-shaped pool, breakfasts outdoors, convivial dinners with fascinating hosts. Great for nature lovers – and it's a hop and skip over to Spain.

Price	€68.
Rooms	2 doubles.
Meals	Dinner with wine, €25.
Closed	Rarely.
Directions	From Perpignan-Barcelona autoroute, exit Le Boulou & Céret. Follow signs for Céret, Amélie les Bains & Arles sur Tech; continue for 12km. Park in village square in Le Tech; house left of post office, No. 5, yellow shutters.

Jan Teede
Sanglier Lodge,
5 route Royale, 66230 Le Tech,
Pyrénées-Orientales

Tel	+33 (0)4 68 39 62 51
Fax	+33 (0)4 68 39 62 51
Email	jteede@wanadoo.fr
Web	www.sanglier-lodge.com

Entry 636   Map 15

Rhône Valley – Alps

Rhône Valley – Alps

Le Couradou

Diana, bright and gifted, and Jos, a charming geologist, came from cool populous Belgium to empty rustic Ardèche and set about transforming this fine big silk-farm house into a warm home. Outside, vineyards and the distant Cévennes, inside, wonderful vaulted 15th-century ceilings, split-level living spaces and five big guest rooms creatively and luxuriously put together with the local gifts of stone walls, country antiques, Provençal patterns and wrought-iron – there's even a sunken bath in one room. Gorgeous views from private terraces, beautiful garden and super pool.
Minimum stay 3 nights in high season.

Price	€90-€125.
Rooms	6: 2 doubles, 2 twins, 2 triples.
Meals	Dinner with wine, €35.
Closed	November-April.
Directions	From N86 Bourg St Andeol; D4 to Vallon Pont d'Arc; D979 left for Barjac, 4km; D217 left for Labastide.

	Diana Little & Jos Vandervondelen
	Le Couradou,
	Le Chambon,
	07150 Labastide de Virac, Ardèche
Tel	+33 (0)4 75 38 64 75
Email	infos@lecouradou.com
Web	www.lecouradou.com

Entry 637   Map 16

Rhône Valley – Alps

Les Roudils

Breakfast among the butterflies – in one of the most idyllic places in this book. High up in the nature-rich Monts d'Ardèche park the views are inspiring and the peace supreme. The house, built of stone and wood from the chestnut forests, has been lovingly restored, so bedrooms are sunny, simple, rustic, authentic. Food is organic, home-grown, imaginative, dinners are informal and fun, Marie makes heavenly preserves (apricot, rosemary), Gil makes aperitifs and honeys (chestnut, heather, raspberry). Come for sunshine, music and warm hospitable people, at the end of the long windy road. Paradise!

Ethical Collection: Environment; Food. See page 432.

Price	€60.
Rooms	3: 2 doubles, 1 family suite for 5.
Meals	Restaurant 4km.
Closed	November-Easter.
Directions	From Aubenas N102 for Le Puy 8.5km. At Lalevade left to Jaujac centre. By Café des Loisirs cross river & follow signs 4km along narrow mountain road.

	Marie & Gil Florence
	Les Roudils,
	07380 Jaujac, Ardèche
Tel	+33 (0)4 75 93 21 11
Fax	+33 (0)4 75 93 21 11
Email	le-rucher-des-roudils@wanadoo.fr
Web	www.lesroudils.com

Entry 638   Map 11

Rhône Valley – Alps

L'Angelot

Come for the great outdoors! Ilsa and Fons have acres of chestnut forest around their stonebuilt 1797 farm, there's a circular walk to a medieval castle, and you can tackle the 15-minute uphill slog to the pretty village above. Return to large rustic rooms (an old door as a bedhead, a cupboard door from an armoire) and clean but dated bathrooms. The house is on many levels, with a cool pool for aching limbs, a tinkling stream below and plenty of tranquil corners to hide in with a book. Homemade jams and local honey for breakfast, hosts without a whiff of pretension: walkers adore it. *Minimum stay 2 nights.*

Price	€65-€95.
Rooms	3: 1 double, 1 twin, 1 triple.
Meals	Light supper with wine, €19.
Closed	Rarely.
Directions	A7 exit 16 Loriol; N304 to Aubenas, D578 to Antraigues centre bourg; left at Vival supermarket, cont. 500m; follow Toutes Directions; left after 1st house, over river, immed. right; signed.

	Ilse & Fons Jaspers
	L'Angelot,
	Ranc au Ranc,
	07530 Antraigues sur Volane,
	Ardèche
Tel	+33 (0)4 75 88 24 55
Email	info@langelot.com
Web	www.langelot.com

Entry 639   Map 11

Rhône Valley – Alps

Il Fut Un Temps

After a two-year trip around the world (and stories told in perfect English), Julien has moved into his old family house in a delicious, reachable corner between the Auvergne and the Loire, keeping the charm and adding his own mark. If dinner is on, it's a lively affair – before a crackling log fire, a rustic mix of modern and traditional. The fruit wine is homemade, the themed stays (massage and relaxation; golf and cross-country skiing; gastronomy) are a treat. Expect cosy rooms – pretty fabrics, new art, rafters and rough stone walls – and shower rooms that sparkle.

Price	€62-€80.
Rooms	5: 3 twins/doubles, 2 quadruples.
Meals	Dinner with wine, €24.
Closed	Rarely.
Directions	From A72 exit 4 D53 E to Champoly. D24 E to St Marcel d'Urfé; D20 S for St Martin la Sauveté & follow Chambres d'Hôtes signs.

	Julien Perbet
	Il Fut Un Temps,
	Les Gouttes,
	42430 St Marcel d'Urfé, Loire
Tel	+33 (0)4 77 62 52 19
Fax	+33 (0)4 77 62 53 88
Email	contact@ilfutuntemps.com
Web	www.ilfutuntemps.com

Entry 640   Map 10

Domaine du Fontenay

Huge care is been taken by these owners to make guests comfortable and well-informed. Simon's lifelong ambition was to become a wine-maker in France, now his wines are highly regarded; enjoy the tastings in the cellar. In a separate building are four super bedrooms with excellent mattresses, big showers, rugs on old terracotta tiles and astonishing views from this hilltop site; and each bedroom has an excellent folder with all the local info. In summer, breakfast is served at check-clothed tables on the big terrace. This is a great area for well-priced restaurants so enjoy them – and ask about 'La Route Magique!'

Price	€68.
Rooms	4: 1 triple, 3 suites for 2.
Meals	Restaurant in village. Kitchen available.
Closed	Rarely.
Directions	From Roanne, Route de Villemontais via Faubourg Clermont; D53 for 10km; straight road until r'bout with wine press; left towards m'way; signed.

Simon & Isabelle Hawkins
Domaine du Fontenay,
Fontenay,
42155 Villemontais, Loire
Tel +33 (0)4 77 63 12 22
Fax +33 (0)4 77 63 15 95
Email hawkins@tele2.fr
Web www.domainedufontenay.com

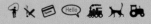

Entry 641 Map 11

Domaine du Château de Marchangy

Down the avenue of oaks and through the grand gates to the perfectly proportioned house. Light pours into intimate but immaculate guest rooms on the first and loft floors of the annexe – big rugs on pale wood floors, harmonious colours, delightful armoires, stylish *objets*, gorgeous fabrics and garden flowers. Rise at your leisure for château breakfasts and fruit from the orchard – served by the pool in summer, in whinnying distance of the horses. Smiling Madame loves having guests; she and her *gardienne* look after you wonderfully. *Minimum stay 2 nights July/August.*

Price	€90-€110.
Rooms	3 suites.
Meals	Light supper from €15. Wine from €6.
Closed	Rarely.
Directions	From Roanne D482 north; 5km after Pouilly sous Charlieu right to St Pierre la Noaille. Signed.

Marie-Colette Grandeau
Domaine du Château de Marchangy,
42190 Saint Pierre la Noaille, Loire
Tel +33 (0)4 77 69 96 76
Fax +33 (0)4 77 60 70 37
Email contact@marchangy.com
Web www.marchangy.com

Entry 642 Map 11

Château de La Motte

Alain and Anny welcome you with a gentle warmth to their fairytale turrets and parkland. Their sure, discerning touch has transformed this light-filled château; gleaming old floors, stained glass and antiques rest easily with deep sofas and modern art. Dinner is a cheerful, delicious affair. Guests chat over aperitifs before trooping into the elegant, grey dining room where your hosts, unflustered, present local delicacies, herbs from their garden, great cheeses and wines. Good company, soft music and a turn in the orchard before you climb the creaking old stairs to a divine bedroom and a delicious bed.

Price	€85–€115.
Rooms	5: 4 doubles, 1 twin.
Meals	Dinner with wine, €28.
Closed	Rarely.
Directions	From Roanne D482 to Pouilly sous Charlieu; D4 left through Briennon; just before Noailly, château on left.

Anny & Alain Froumajou
Château de La Motte,
42640 Noailly, Loire
Tel +33 (0)4 77 66 64 60
Fax +33 (0)4 77 66 68 10
Email chateaudelamotte@wanadoo.fr
Web www.chateaudelamotte.net

Entry 643   Map 11

Mamouna & Cabanotte

On a clear day you can see the alpine range. This marvellous place is clear every day in intention and presence, these gentle people having renovated the farmhouse with love, different woods (his hobby), pretty lamps. There's sitting space and a wood-burner in the big airy guest room in the barn, and up among the trees, a wonderfully woody *cabana perchée*. Delicious organic breakfast is at a long table in the enchanting kitchen – or on the terrace with views, near the pretty pool. Marie-Odile loves the simple life, the house smells of beeswax and wild flowers, the peace is a balm. *Holistic massage & spa.*

Price	€80–€120.
Rooms	3: 1 double, 1 family room. Tree cabin for 2-4.
Meals	Restaurants 5km.
Closed	Rarely.
Directions	South of Lyon leave A7 at Pierre Benite; A45 for Brignais; in Thurins Bourg; for St Martin en Haut; D122 for Yzeron; right at Croix Perrière. Signed.

Marie-Odile Lemoine
Mamouna & Cabanotte,
69510 Thurins, Rhône
Tel +33 (0)4 78 19 10 83
Email mo-lemoine@wanadoo.fr
Web www.cabanotte.fr

Entry 644   Map 11

Rhône Valley – Alps

La Villa Catalpa

You will be happy in this friendly, slightly quirky family home up a gravelled path and within walking distance of the village of Lentilly. A separate entrance opens to each generous suite up a spiral staircase: in the charming cream and taupe bed-living room you will find stripped floors, antique furniture and double-aspect windows overlooking a pretty garden. Bathrooms are small but super with scented soaps and thick towels; there are teensy kitchens should you feel too lazy to budge. Lovely Florence, a mine of local knowledge who enjoys speaking English, gives you tasty breakfasts on the terrace in the sun.

Price	€125-€140.
Rooms	2 suites, each with kitchenette.
Meals	Restaurants within walking distance.
Closed	Never.
Directions	From N7 Le Grand Chemin at r'bout D70 for Lentilly; after 1st r'bout 1st right; left into Chemin de la Rivoire; house on left; Florence will open electric gates.

Florence Bouteille
La Villa Catalpa,
127 chemin de la Rivoire,
69210 Lentilly, Rhône

Mobile	+33 (0)6 14 01 18 69
Email	lavillacatalpa@free.fr
Web	lavillacatalpa.free.fr

Entry 645   Map 11

Rhône Valley – Alps

Château de Longsard

Two spectacular Lebanon cedars in the grounds, wine from the estate, beautiful 17th-century beams to guard your sleep. Your Franco-American hosts, charming and well-travelled polyglots, are keen to share their enthusiasm for horticulture (founding a scheme allowing the public to visit private gardens while raising money for local charities). Bedrooms and baths, pure château from faded pastel to bold with hints of modernity, some with fine carved door frames, are eclectically furnished; Olivier's brother is an antique dealer. You are conveniently close to the motorway towards Villefranche, so expect highway hum.

Price	€130-€150.
Rooms	5: 3 doubles, 2 suites. Coach house: 1 suite.
Meals	Dinner with wine, €38 (minimum 8 people).
Closed	Rarely.
Directions	A6 exit 31.1. Straight at r'bout. Through village; château on right after 1.5km.

Alexandra & Olivier du Mesnil
Château de Longsard,
69400 Arnas, Rhône

Tel	+33 (0)4 74 65 55 12
Fax	+33 (0)4 74 65 03 17
Email	longsard@wanadoo.fr
Web	www.longsard.com

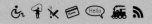

Entry 646   Map 11

Rhône Valley – Alps

Domaine La Javernière

Through the huge wrought-iron gates into a courtyard lined with delectable roses and a house filled with history and soul. In the heart of Beaujolais country, this huge bourgeois residence is owned by wine distributor Thibault who treats guests as friends and runs it with an easy charm. Great Grandpapa's portrait hangs in the hall, there are books, photographs, art and sculpture everywhere, a piano if you wish, and space to roam: nowhere is out of bounds. Bedrooms are gracious, sunny and sprinkled with antiques, bathrooms range from swish Italian to cute and tiny under the eaves. Gastronomy and vineyards abound.

Price	€65–€130.
Rooms	5: 2 doubles, 2 twins, 1 suite for 4-5.
Meals	Restaurant 600m; choice 8km.
Closed	April-October.
Directions	A6 exit 30 Belleville; follow 'autres directions' for RN6, then for Villié Morgon; from Pizay to Morgon; D68 right; after 600m, signed on right.

Thibault Roux
Domaine La Javernière,
69910 Javernière, Rhône
Mobile +33 (0)6 66 05 90 52
Email contact@la-javerniere.fr
Web la-javerniere.fr

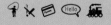

Rhône Valley – Alps

Les Pasquiers

Come and join this family's charming, authentically aristocratic life: no prissiness (two screened-off bathrooms) in their big townhouse, just unselfconscious style. The richly decorated golden sitting room has a piano, books and open fireplace, the bedrooms are sunny, the beds wear beautiful linen. The richly stocked garden has a pool, a summerhouse, a large terrace, 150 species of trees, an organic vegetable garden and a statue of Grand-père. Madame is too busy cooking to eat with guests but welcomes company as she's preparing dinner – and she is as relaxed and as charming as her house.

Price	€80.
Rooms	4: 2 doubles, 2 twins.
Meals	Dinner with wine, €30.
Closed	Rarely.
Directions	From A6 exit Belleville; follow signs to Mâcon, left after 8km to Lacié; signed in Lacié.

Laurence Adele-Gandilhon
Les Pasquiers,
69220 Lancié, Rhône
Tel +33 (0)4 74 69 86 33
Fax +33 (0)4 74 69 86 33
Email welcome@lespasquiers.com
Web www.lespasquiers.com

Rhône Valley – Alps

La Gloriette

Over a glass or two of the local beaujolais, discover what pleasant company your hosts are. Originally from Paris, and great travellers (ask about their epic trip to India), they came here in search of the simpler life. And a fine, simple B&B this is – with good country food to match. A woodchip-burner fuels the central heating, the book-filled sitting room has a disarmingly uncoordinated air and the bedrooms are comfortable and bright. It's all cosy and good value. Outside visit La Gloriette, the gardens and the courtyard – all chaotic! – and park a two-minute walk away in the village square.

Price	€52.
Rooms	3: 1 double, 1 twin, 1 family room for 4-6.
Meals	Dinner with wine, €21.
Closed	December-February.
Directions	From Mâcon N6 south; at Pontanevaux D95 right; through Les Paquelets; D17; D26 to Jullié. House off main square, signed.

Antoinette & Jean-Luc Bazin
La Gloriette,
Le Bourg, 69840 Jullié, Rhône
Tel   +33 (0)4 74 06 70 95
Fax   +33 (0)4 74 06 70 95
Email   contact@lagloriette.fr
Web   www.lagloriette.fr

Entry 649   Map 11

Rhône Valley – Alps

Le Moulin de Varax

Dive into your own private lake! This 17th-century watermill, in acres of willow-strewn parkland, is alive with the sound of water. Retired photographer Alain's artistic eye is everywhere: in the decorative ironwork, the gatherings from his travels and his atmospheric autochrome photography. Bedrooms, overlooking the garden, will charm you with their limewashed beams and gentle colours, antique mirrors and country fabrics. Breakfast on the terrace to birdsong, visit the Parc des Oiseaux, hike from the door, relax by the stream. Warmly inviting, utterly restful – and all that water. *Unfenced water.*

Price	€80-€110.
Rooms	3: 2 doubles, 1 suite.
Meals	Restaurant in village, 1km.
Closed	January.
Directions	From Villars les Dombes D1083 for Bourg en Bresse. After St Paul de Varax right by DAF garage D17 for Dompierre sur Veyle; 2nd right signed Moulin.

Mireille & Alain Scheibli
Le Moulin de Varax,
01240 St Paul de Varax, Ain
Tel   +33 (0)4 74 42 51 00
Email   miral@wanadoo.fr

Entry 650   Map 11

Rhône Valley – Alps

Manoir de Marmont

An amazing avenue of plane trees takes you to this exceptional house and hostess. Madame is a live wire, laughing, enthusing, giving – unforgettable; her house is as elegantly colourful as she is. Climb the grand stairs to your splendid château-style room, revel in Persian carpets, trompe-l'œil walls, antiques, fresh flowers. Beside Shakespeare and the candles, Madame pours tea from silver into porcelain and artfully moves the breakfast butter as the sun rises; at night she'll light your bedside lamp, leaving a book open at a carefully chosen page for you to read after a game of (French) Scrabble. Inimitably fine…

Price	€85.
Rooms	2 doubles.
Meals	Restaurant 3km.
Closed	Rarely.
Directions	From Bourg en Bresse N83 for Lyon. At Servas right D64 for Condeissiat 5km; left at sign Le Marmont: plane-tree avenue. Don't go to St André.

Geneviève & Henri Guido–Alhéritière
Manoir de Marmont,
01960 St André sur Vieux Jonc, Ain
Tel   +33 (0)4 74 52 79 74
Web   www.chateau-marmont.info

Entry 651   Map 11

Rhône Valley – Alps

Chalet Châtelet

The lush Vallée d'Abondance envelops this pretty new pine chalet whose owners fizz with enthusiasm for the life they share with guests. Oak floors, soft shapes, high ceilings hug reclaimed furniture and works by Suzie's arty family. Warmth comes from a Finnish stove, clever insulation and solar panels – an eco-lover's dream but you still find bliss in the spa. Expect cultured chat in the intimate dining room, where Suzie serves range-cooked organic meals from local farmers. Bedrooms have stunning views and dreamy bathrooms; gaze to mountains you climbed or skied that day. A home from home in green tranquillity.

Ethical Collection: Environment; Food.
See page 432.

Price	€90–€190.
Rooms	4: 2 doubles, 2 triples.
Meals	Dinner with wine, €30.
Closed	Rarely.
Directions	Thonon D902 for Morzine & Vallée d'Abondance. After 2nd tunnel left at r'bout D22 for Vallée d'Abondance & Châtel. After La Solitude, right D32 to Bonnevaux. At church fork left; chalet 300m on left.

Pascal & Suzie Immediato
Chalet Châtelet,
Route d'Abondance,
74360 Bonnevaux, Haute-Savoie
Tel   +33 (0)4 50 73 69 48
Email info@chalet-chatelet.com
Web   www.chalet-chatelet.com

Entry 652   Map 12

Rhône Valley – Alps

Le Châlet

Anne-Marie, outgoing and a delight to talk to, makes this place – come if you want to bathe in genuine French mountain hospitality (son Édouard is learning fast). She speaks English, keeps horses, and may accompany you on walks to Alpine pastures. The mood here is rustic and characterful with balconies and runaway views. Exceptional walking: you'll see chamois and marmots if you go far enough. Dinner (served late to allow you time to settle) is eaten at the long wooden table, with grand-mama's delicious recipes cooked on a wood-fired stove – and the half-board formula includes absolutely everything. Marvellous.

Price	Half-board €40.50 p.p.
Rooms	5: 1 double, 1 twin, 3 family rooms for 3, all sharing 2 showers & 2 wcs.
Meals	Dinner with wine included.
Closed	Rarely.
Directions	From Thonon les Bains, D26 for Bellevaux. House 2km before Bellevaux on left; signed.

Anne-Marie Félisaz-Denis & Édouard Illand
Le Châlet, La Cressonnière,
74470 Bellevaux, Haute-Savoie

Tel	+33 (0)4 50 73 70 13
Fax	+33 (0)4 50 73 70 13
Email	lechalet74@free.fr
Web	lechalet74.free.fr

Entry 653   Map 12

Rhône Valley – Alps

Ferme Lou Bochons

A labyrinth of cosy corners, curving stairs, stained pine beams and low doors – the old farmhouse was love at first sight for Allie and Chris. Dine on Mediterranean food amid stone-flagged floors and moody lighting, a palpable atmosphere, wine flowing, real attention. There are two fire-warmed living rooms, a snug for kids and cards, a sunny terrace over the garden. A mesh of rafters houses quirky bedrooms with plush bedcovers. In this tiny high-mountain hamlet you're five minutes from the Portes du Soleil: a paradise for skiers and outdoors types (like Chris). *Minimum stay 3 nights in summer; 7 in winter.*

Price	€90–€200.
Rooms	4: 2 twins/doubles, 2 family rooms.
Meals	Dinner with wine, €30.
Closed	May & October-November.
Directions	In Morzine right at r'bout for Avoriaz 100m; right for Vallée de la Manche & Téléphérique de Nyon. 400m past La Boucherie hamlet & avalanche warnings, right over small bridge for L'Envers & Lou Bouchons; chalet on right.

Chris & Allie Hodgson
Ferme Lou Bochons,
120 chemin de l'Envers,
Vallée de la Manche,
74110 Morzine, Haute-Savoie

Tel	+33 (0)4 50 49 21 04
Email	info@morzine365.com
Web	www.morzine365.com

Entry 654   Map 12

Rhône Valley – Alps

Chalet Odysseus

The village has character; Chalet Odysseus has much besides. There's comfort in soft sofas, check curtains, bright rugs and open fire, and swishness in sauna and small gym; a French chef cooks for you once a week in winter, and the relaxed English hosts spoil you rotten (Madame, too, is a fine cook). They have the ground floor of this brand-new chalet; you live above. Cheerfully pretty bedrooms come with the requisite pine garb, two have balconies that catch the sun, the tiniest comes with bunk beds for kids. Marvellous for an active family break, whatever the season. *Minimum stay 2 nights.*

Price	€90. Half-board €100 p.p.
Rooms	5: 2 doubles, 2 twins, 1 family room.
Meals	Dinner with wine, €40.
Closed	Rarely.
Directions	From A40 exit 19 to Cuses; N205 for Sallanches; left D106; 2km before Les Carroz red & white-shuttered chalet on left; signed.

Kate & Barry Joyce
Chalet Odysseus, 210 route de Lachat, 74300 Les Carroz d'Araches, Haute-Savoie
Tel   +33 (0)4 50 90 66 00
Fax   +33 (0)4 50 90 66 01
Email   chaletodysseus@wanadoo.fr
Web   www.chaletodysseuslachat.com

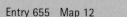

Rhône Valley – Alps

Proveyroz

Madame has boundless energy, is a great walker, adores her mountain retreat in this lovely valley and cooks very well indeed. Her chalet rooms, all wood-clad of course, are bright and welcoming in blue, white and orange; they have unusually high ceilings, good storage and plenty of space. The open-plan living area has huge windows – opening to a small sun-soaked terrace and little garden – and the mixture of old and modern furniture plus bits and pieces of all sorts gives the whole place a comfortable, family feel. Paragliding is the big thing round here, Annecy is close and Geneva an hour away.

Price	€52.
Rooms	2: 1 double; 1 triple with separate wc.
Meals	Dinner with wine, €20.
Closed	Rarely.
Directions	From Annecy D909 to Thones; D12 for Serraval & D16 Manigod; 200m after 'Welcome to Manigod' sign, left at cross; chalet on left.

Josette Barbaud
Proveyroz, 74230 Manigod, Haute-Savoie
Tel   +33 (0)4 50 44 95 25
Fax   +33 (0)4 50 44 95 25
Email   josette.barbaud@tele2.fr
Web   josette.barbaud.free.fr

Rhône Valley – Alps

La Touvière

Mountains march past Mont Blanc and over into Italy, cows graze in the foreground – perfect for exploring this walkers' paradise. Myriam, bubbly and easy, adores having guests with everyone joining in the lively, lighthearted family atmosphere. In their typical old unsmart farmhouse, the cosy family room is the hub of life. Marcel is part-time home improver, part-time farmer (just a few cows now). One room has a properly snowy valley view, the other overlooks the owners' second chalet, let as a gîte; both are a decent size, simple but not basic, while shower rooms are spotless. Remarkable value.

Price	€50.
Rooms	2 doubles.
Meals	Restaurant 3km.
Closed	Rarely.
Directions	From Albertville D1212 for Megève for 21km; after Flumet, left at Panoramic Hotel & follow signs to La Touvière.

Marcel & Myriam Marin-Cudraz
La Touvière,
73590 Flumet,
Savoie

| Tel | +33 (0)4 79 31 70 11 |
| Email | marcel.marin-cudraz@wanadoo.fr |

Entry 657 Map 12

Rhône Valley – Alps

Maison Coutin

A year-round Alpine dream. In summer it's all flowers, birds and rushing streams, even a resident eagle. in winter you can ski cross-country, snow-walk or take the ski lift, 500m away, to the vast ski field of Les Arcs. La Plagne and Val d'Isère aren't far. Delicious, mostly organic, food is cooked in the wood oven. Your friendly, dynamic young hosts cater for children: early suppers, three of their own as playmates, and Claude will babysit in the evening. View-filled bedrooms, a smallish comfortable dayroom with a refrigerator and a deeply eco-friendly ethos. *Discount on ski hire & passes.*

Ethical Collection: Environment; Food.
See page 432.

Price	€54-€60.
Rooms	3: 1 triple, 2 suites: 1 for 4, 1 for 4–6.
Meals	Dinner with wine, €19.
Closed	Rarely.
Directions	From Albertville N90 to Moutiers; on for Bourg St Maurice. Right D87E to Peisey Nancroix; left to Peisey centre; follow 3 green arrows. House 9km from main road.

Claude Coutin & Franck Chenal
Maison Coutin,
73210 Peisey Nancroix,
Savoie

Tel	+33 (0)4 79 07 93 05
Email	maison-coutin@wanadoo.fr
Web	www.maison-coutin.fr.st

Entry 658 Map 12

Rhône Valley – Alps

Chalet Colinn

Mylène and Elizabeth love the outdoors; hence their five-year fight to reincarnate a fallen ruin as a luxury mountain retreat. Join them for gourmet dinner under soaring, raftered ceilings in the grand living space which hovers above Tignes dam. Or soak in the terrace hot tub under the stars; there's a sauna too. Urban rusticity, mountain chic: the place reeks Italian style yet is impossibly hidden in this tiny hamlet. For daytime adventure: the slopes at Val d'Isère, or Tignes, or the Vanoise park. Just ask Elizabeth, off-piste skier extraordinaire. *Snow tyres/chains recommended in winter. Ask about ski lessons.*

Price	€90-€280.
Rooms	5: 3 twins/doubles, 2 triples.
Meals	Dinner €35. Wine from €13.
Closed	Rarely.
Directions	From Bourg St Maurice D102 for Val d'Isère; D902 past Barrage de Tignes; after 1st avalanche tunnel, left for Le Franchet. Chalet in hamlet up narrow path on right.

Elizabeth Chabert & Mylène Charrière
Chalet Colinn,
Le Franchet de Tignes, BP 125,
73150 Val d'Isère, Savoie

Tel	+33 (0)4 79 06 26 99
Email	contact@chaletcolinn.com
Web	www.chaletcolinn.com

Entry 659   Map 12

Rhône Valley – Alps

Domaine de Gorneton

The most caring and endearing of B&B owners: he, warmly humorous and humble about his excellent cooking; she, generous and outgoing. Built high on a hill as a fort in 1646, beside the spring that runs through the magnificent garden (a genuine Roman ruin, too), their superb old house is wrapped round a green-clad courtyard. Inside, levels change, vast timbers span the dining room, country antiques sprawl by the fire in the salon, simple, inviting guest rooms have separate entrances and impeccable bathrooms – and a bedhead from Hollywood in the best room. Family warmth in deep country 15 minutes from Lyon.

Price	€120-€180.
Rooms	4: 3 doubles, 1 suite for 4.
Meals	Dinner with wine, €40.
Closed	Rarely.
Directions	From A7, A46 or A47 exit Chasse sur Rhône; through big Centre Commercial; left after Casino supermarket under railway; left then right for Trembas. (Will fax map or guide you to house.)

M & Mme Fleitou
Domaine de Gorneton,
712 chemin de Violans,
38670 Chasse sur Rhône, Isère

Tel	+33 (0)4 72 24 19 15
Fax	+33 (0)4 78 07 93 62
Email	gorneton@wanadoo.fr
Web	www.gorneton.com

Entry 660   Map 11

Rhône Valley – Alps

Longeville

There is a gentle elegance about this house and the people who live in it, including several sleek cats. Originally Scots and Irish, the Barrs have spent their adult years in France and now run a wooden toy business. Their love for this 1750s farmhouse shows in their artistic touch with decorating, their mix of old and modern furniture, their gorgeous big bedrooms done in soft pale colours that leave space for the soaring views coming in from the hills. A high place of comfort and civilised contact where dinner in the airy white living room is a chance to get to know your kind, laid-back hosts more fully.

Price	€50–€70.
Rooms	2 twins/doubles.
Meals	Dinner with wine, €25.
Closed	October–December.
Directions	From A43 exit 8, D1085 through Nivolas. Left D520 for Succieu. After 2km, left D56 through Succieu for St Victor; 3km; sign for Longeville on right; farm at top of steep hill.

	Mary & Greig Barr
	Longeville,
	38300 Succieu, Isère
Tel	+33 (0)4 74 27 94 07
Fax	+33 (0)4 74 92 09 21
Email	mary.barr@wanadoo.fr

Entry 661   Map 11

Rhône Valley – Alps

Le Traversoud

Rooms are named after painters; lovely 'Cézanne' lies under the eaves on the top floor. Warm, bright, amusing Nathalie and attentive Pascal welcome you to their farmhouse, guide you up the outside stairs to colourful, comfortable bedrooms and spotless shower rooms (a sauna, too) and treat you to some of the best home cooking in France, served at a long table; even the brioche is homemade. Outside overflows with grass and trees, crickets chirrup, the Bernese Mountain dog bounds, the donkeys graze and the exuberant courtyard is a safe space for your children to join theirs. Wonderful, informal B&B.

Price	€56.
Rooms	3: 1 twin, 2 family rooms for 3.
Meals	Dinner with wine, €25.
Closed	Rarely.
Directions	A43 exit 9 at La Tour du Pin, through town D1516 left, through St Clair de la Tour. At church left for Faverges; after 4km left for Dolomieu; after 2km, right at junc., signed.

	Nathalie & Pascal Deroi
	Le Traversoud,
	484 chemin Sous l'École,
	38110 Faverges de la Tour, Isère
Tel	+33 (0)4 74 83 90 40
Email	deroi.traversoud@orange.fr
Web	www.le-traversoud.com

Entry 662   Map 11

Rhône Valley – Alps

Château de Paquier

Old, mighty, atmospheric — yet so homely. Hélène teaches cookery and spit-roasts poultry in the huge dining room fireplace, then joins you for dinner. Her modernised 17th-century tower kitchen (wood-fired range, stone sink, cobbled floor) is where she makes her bread, honey, jams and walnut aperitif. Wine is from the Rossis' own vineyard near Montpellier. Enormous rooms, high heavy-beamed ceilings, large windows with sensational valley views; terraced gardens and animals; bedrooms (handsome wardrobes, underfloor heating) up an ancient spiral staircase that sets the imagination reeling.

Ethical Collection: Environment; Food. See page 432.

Price	€68.
Rooms	5: 2 doubles, 2 twins, 1 family room.
Meals	Dinner with wine, €25.
Closed	Rarely.
Directions	From Grenoble A51 exit 12, then N75 for 11km; at r'bout left to St Martin de la Cluze; château signs in village.

Jacques & Hélène Rossi
Château de Paquier,
38650 St Martin de la Cluze, Isère
Tel   +33 (0)4 76 72 77 33
Fax   +33 (0)4 76 72 77 33
Email   hrossi@club-internet.fr
Web   chateau.de.paquier.free.fr

Entry 663   Map 11

Rhône Valley – Alps

Les Marais

Opt for the simple country life at this friendly farm, which has been in the family for over 100 years and has returned to organic methods. Four horses, a few hens, and — when there's a full house — beautiful meals of regional recipes served family-style, with homemade chestnut cake and 'vin de noix' aperitif. Monsieur collects old farming artefacts and Madame, although busy, always finds time for a chat. The bedrooms are in a separate wing with varnished ceilings, antique beds, some florals; baths are old-fashioned pink, new showers delight Americans. At the foot of the Vercors range, French charm, utter peace.

Ethical Collection: Food. See page 432.

Price	€47-€52.
Rooms	4: 1 double, 1 twin, 1 triple, 1 family room.
Meals	Dinner with wine, €17.
Closed	Rarely.
Directions	From Romans D538 for Chabeuil. Leaving Alixan left by Boulangerie for St Didier; left again, Chambres d'Hôtes St Didier signs for 3km; farm on left.

Christiane & Jean-Pierre Imbert
Les Marais,
26300 St Didier de Charpey, Drôme
Tel   +33 (0)4 75 47 03 50
Email   imbert.jean-pierre@wanadoo.fr
Web   pagesperso-orange.fr/les-marais

Entry 664   Map 11

Les Péris

Here is the grandmother we all dream of, a woman who cossets her guests, puts flowers and sweets in the bedrooms and sends you off with walnuts from the farm. In the family for ten generations, the old stone house facing the mountains is a happy and delightful home. Join family, friends and guests around the long kitchen table, for walnut cakes at breakfast and daughter Élisabeth's delicious *menu curieux* that uses forgotten vegetables! Roomy, old-fashioned bedrooms with armoires breathe a comfortable, informal air. Great for kids: a garden for wild flowers and a duck pond for splashing in.

Price	€50.
Rooms	3 triples.
Meals	Dinner with wine, €17.
Closed	Rarely.
Directions	From A7 exit Valence Sud on D68 to Chabeuil. There, cross river; left on D154 for Combovin 5km; signed, on left.

Madeleine Cabanes
Les Péris,
D154 – Route de Combovin,
26120 Châteaudouble, Drôme
Tel   +33 (0)4 75 59 80 51
Fax   +33 (0)4 75 59 48 78

Entry 665   Map 11

Chambedeau

Madame's kindliness infuses her home, one that at first glance is coy about its age and charms. Her eventful life has nourished a wicked sense of humour but no bitterness and she is a natural storyteller (she'll show you the photographs too) – she alone is worth the detour. The fading carpets and small shower rooms become incidental after a short while; enjoy, instead, the homely bedrooms, the terraces, the peace and birdlife of the lush leafy garden which shelters the house from the road – and breakfast (organic honeys, homemade jams and cake, cheese) where the table is a picture in itself. Simply unwind.

Price	€55–€58.
Rooms	2: 1 twin/double; 1 twin with separate shower.
Meals	Restaurants 2-7km.
Closed	Rarely.
Directions	From A7 Valence Sud exit A49 for Grenoble; exit 33 right D538a for Beaumont, 2.6km; right at sign Chambres d'Hôtes & Chambedeau; 800m on right, tarmac drive.

Lina de Chivré-Dumond
Chambedeau,
26760 Beaumont lès Valence,
Drôme
Tel   +33 (0)4 75 59 71 70
Email linadechivredumond@yahoo.fr

Entry 666   Map 11

Provence – Alps – Riviera

Le Vieil Aiglun

Getting here is an adventure, up the steep and winding road… thrilling is the arrival, to one of the best views in France. And this place, an ancient hilltop restoration, a dream come true for a delightful Belgian couple. All is calm, inviting and deliciously private, a sunny-shady courtyard linking the five B&B rooms. Steps up, steps down, past soft running water and sweet lavender, to rustic tiles and colourwashed walls, muslin drapes and Provençal hues. In the old vaulted byre is a long glamorous table for convivial dinners. And a charming play area, a log fire for wet days, two sweet gîtes, a pool with a peerless view. *Sawday self-catering also.*

Price	€85–€100.
Rooms	5: 2 twins/doubles, 2 triples, 1 family room for 4.
Meals	Dinner with wine, €27.
Closed	Mid-November to mid-March.
Directions	A51 exit Digne les Bains; N85 for Digne les Bains. 2km after Mallemoisson, left to Aiglun 2.5km; left to Le Vieil Aiglun.

	Charles & Annick Speth
	Le Vieil Aiglun,
	04510 Aiglun,
	Alpes-de-Haute-Provence
Tel	+33 (0)4 92 34 67 00
Email	info@vieil-aiglun.com
Web	www.vieil-aiglun.com

Entry 667   Map 16

Mas Saint Joseph

Come for the view of row upon row of peaks fading into the distance, the walking, the welcome. Hélène and Olivier bought the *mas* as a holiday home years ago, restored it with loving care, then moved here and began taking guests. Olivier is a walker and can inform you about spectacular walking trails from one B&B to the next. One bedroom has an ancient brick bread oven in a corner; another, once a stable, has a manger to prove it. Breakfast and dinner are on the terrace in warm weather or in the owners' fine old barn, and you can use the biggish pool behind the house. And oh, those views! *Hot tub. Ask about massage.*

Price	€60. Triple €79. Suite €98.
Rooms	4: 1 double, 1 triple, 2 suites for 4.
Meals	Dinner with wine, €21.
Closed	Mid-November to March.
Directions	From Châteauneuf Val St Donat 1.5km for St Étienne les Orgues; house on bend, on right above road; steep 100m drive to house.

	Hélène & Olivier Lenoir
	Mas Saint Joseph,
	04200 Châteauneuf Val St Donat,
	Alpes-de-Haute-Provence
Tel	+33 (0)4 92 62 47 54
Email	contact@lemassaintjoseph.com
Web	www.lemassaintjoseph.com

Entry 668   Map 16

Ferme de Felines

Southern energies, wild evergreen hills and strong light push in through big architect's windows to meet the sober cool of black-white-grey northern design in a thrilling encounter. Small, wiry and full of laughter, Rita has a passion for this house, her land and the wildlife she fights to preserve. She may adorn your space of purity with one perfect flower in a glass cylinder, some fruit and a candle. Linen, beds, taps and towels are all top quality, her generosity is warm, her dog and six cats beautiful, her vast living room a treat. Breakfast at a marble table, then take a swim in the lovely lake. *Minimum stay 2 to 3 nights.*

Price	€125.
Rooms	3 doubles.
Meals	Restaurants in Moustiers.
Closed	Rarely.
Directions	From Aix A51 exit Manosque for Gréoux; D952 to Riez, Moustiers; D952 for Castellane, 6km black sign on right.

	Rita Ravez
	Ferme de Felines,
	04360 Moustiers Ste Marie,
	Alpes-de-Haute-Provence
Tel	+33 (0)4 92 74 64 19
Fax	+33 (0)4 92 74 61 39
Email	ferme-de-felines@wanadoo.fr
Web	www.ferme-de-felines.com

Château d'Esparron

Castellanes built Esparron in the 1400s, both have been pivots of Provençal history. The superb stone stairs lead to vastly lusciously bedrooms: plain walls and fresh flowers, tiles and gorgeous fabrics, family antiques with tales to tell. The garden is small but perfect. Slender Charlotte-Anne and her two beautiful children come straight from a Gainsborough portrait. She attends to everyone: family, staff, guests. Bernard, a mine of information with suntan and real manners, adds a touch of 1930s glamour. Wonderful family, splendiferous house, vast breakfast in the cavernously cosy kitchen.

Price	€130–€240.
Rooms	5: 3 doubles, 1 twin, 1 suite.
Meals	Restaurant 5-minute walk.
Closed	November–March.
Directions	From Aix en Provence A51 exit 18 on D907; D82 to Gréoux les Bains; D952 & D315 to Esparron. Stop & ring at gates (once past, it's impossible to turn).

	Bernard & Charlotte-Anne de Castellane
	Château d'Esparron,
	04800 Esparron de Verdon,
	Alpes-de-Haute-Provence
Tel	+33 (0)4 92 77 12 05
Email	chateau@esparron.com
Web	www.esparron.com

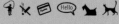

La Belle Cour

The moment you enter the gorgeous big courtyard you feel at home. Angela and Rodney's welcome is second to none: cheerful and open, warm and humourous. On medieval foundations, the 18th-century house is all exposed stone and beams, its décor traditional/rustic; you'll love the embracing living rooms, the open fire, the cosy library with surround sound music. Bedrooms overlook the courtyard and have private staircases: be spoiled by luscious linens, fabrics, colours, an intriguing long wall map of London in 1647, exquisite Chinese paintings on silk. Truly special, and in a friendly village with restaurants and a pool.

Price	€65.
Rooms	2: 1 double, 1 triple.
Meals	Restaurants 200m.
Closed	November-February.
Directions	D900 (ex-N100) past Apt; 18km to Céreste: at small r'bout in village right; immed. left Place Daniel Vigouroux; La Belle Cour on left (if facing Boulangerie Barret).

Rodney & Angela Heath
La Belle Cour,
Place Daniel Vigouroux,
04280 Céreste,
Alpes-de-Haute-Provence
Tel +33 (0)4 92 72 48 76
Email angela.heath@wanadoo.fr
Web www.labellecour.com

Entry 671   Map 16

L'École Buissonnière

A stone jewel set in southern lushness and miles of green vines and purple hills. Country furniture (a particularly seductive choice of Provençal chairs) is polished with wax and time; big, whitewashed bedrooms are freshly sober; birds sing to the tune of the aviary outside. One balconied bedroom, in the mezzanined old barn, has a saddle and a herdsman's hat from a spell in the Camargue; ask about John's travels. He rightly calls himself a Provençal Englishman, Monique is warmly welcoming too – theirs is a happy house, where German is also spoken. Wonderful Vaison la Romaine is four miles away.

Price	€55-€62.
Rooms	3: 2 doubles, 1 family room.
Meals	Dinner with wine, €25. Restaurant in village, 1km. Guest kitchen.
Closed	Mid-November to March & rarely.
Directions	From A7 exit Bollène for Nyons D94; D20 right for Vaison & Buisson; cross River Aygues; left for Villedieu & Cave la Vigneronne D51 & D75 for 2.2km.

Monique Alex & John Parsons
L'École Buissonnière,
D75, 84110 Buisson,
Vaucluse
Tel +33 (0)4 90 28 95 19
Email ecole.buissonniere@wanadoo.fr
Web www.buissonniere-provence.com

Entry 672   Map 16

Provence – Alps – Riviera

L'Evêché

Narrow, cobbled streets lead to this fascinating and beautifully furnished house that was once part of the 17th-century Bishop's Palace. The Verdiers are charming, relaxed, cultured hosts – he an architect/builder, she a teacher. The white walls of the guests' sitting room-library are lined with modern art and framed posters, and the cosy, quilted bedrooms, all whitewashed beams and terracotta floors, have a serene Provençal feel. Views fly over beautiful terracotta rooftops from the balconied suite, and well-presented breakfasts are served on the terrace, complete with exceptional views to the Roman bridge.

Provence – Alps – Riviera

Les Convenents

For the delightful Sarah, a refugee from spinning plates in London, welcoming visitors in her haven is as natural as breathing. Five former workers' cottages have become a relaxing Provençal *mas* where space and simplicity leave old stones and renovated timbers to glow and there's a typically lovely vine-shaded terrace. Small explosions of cushions and paintings bring fresh white walls and fabrics alive; more modernity in good clean bathrooms and fine finishes. Sarah, who was in catering, rules in the kitchen. She supports the local economy, uses the village shops, enjoys the community. *Sawday self-catering also.*

Price	€80-€88. Suite €110-€135.
Rooms	5: 3 twins/doubles, 2 suites for 2-3.
Meals	Restaurants in Vaison.
Closed	2 weeks in both November & December.
Directions	From Orange, D975 to Vaison. In town, follow Ville Médiévale signs.

Price	€85-€90. Singles €80-€85.
Rooms	2 doubles.
Meals	Dinner with wine, €32.
Closed	November-March, except by arrangement.
Directions	From Orange D976 to Gap & Ste Cécile les Vignes; D11 left to Uchaux; through village, between Les Farjons & Rochegude, 3km. Les Covenents on left; signed.

Aude & Jean-Loup Verdier
L'Evêché,
Rue de l'Evêché, Cité Médiévale,
84110 Vaison la Romaine, Vaucluse
Tel +33 (0)4 90 36 13 46
Fax +33 (0)4 90 36 32 43
Email eveche@aol.com
Web www.eveche.com

Sarah Banner
Les Convenents,
84100 Uchaux, Vaucluse
Tel +33 (0)90 40 65 64
Fax +33 (0)4 90 40 65 64
Email sarahbanner@wanadoo.fr
Web www.lesconvenents.com

Entry 673 Map 16

Entry 674 Map 16

Provence – Alps – Riviera

La Maison aux Volets Rouges B&B

Step off the street into the 'red-shuttered' house to be wrapped in a warm embrace. Rooms are big with tiled floors, beams and antiques; family photographs line the stairs; there's an open fire for cool days, a courtyard for warm ones. High-beamed bedrooms have good storage and individual touches – a brass bed, an arched window, a teddy bear on the baby's bed. Garden and pool are a three-minute walk, restaurants a short stroll. Borrow a bike, play tennis at the local club (no charge), drop in on the glories of Avignon and Aix. Delightful, energetic Brigitte has impeccable English and feeds you well. *Sawday self-catering also.*

Price	€60–€80. Single €50.
Rooms	3: 1 double; 1 double, 1 single sharing shower.
Meals	Restaurants within walking distance.
Closed	Never.
Directions	From A7 exit 19 to Bollène; right at r'bout for Nyons 1km; left at x-roads for Nyons; cont. to small road on right D12 for Uchaux 5km to Les Farjons; house on right.

Brigitte Woodward
La Maison aux Volets Rouges B&B,
Les Farjons,
84100 Uchaux, Vaucluse
Tel +33 (0)4 90 40 62 18
Fax +33 (0)4 90 40 64 56
Email b.woodward@hotmail.fr
Web www.lamaisonauxvoletsrouges.com

Entry 675   Map 16

Provence – Alps – Riviera

La Ravigote

Madame and her house both smile gently. It's a simple, authentic Provençal farmhouse that has escaped the vigorous renovator, its courtyard shaded by a lovely lime tree. Once a teacher in Africa, elegantly shy Madame considers dinners with her guests, in dining room or courtyard, as the best part of B&B – her meals are showcases for local specialities. The interior is a bright version of traditional French country style with old family furniture and tiled floors. Set among vineyards below the Montmirail hills, it has soul-pleasing views across the surrounding unspoilt country. *Minimum stay 2 nights.*

Price	€52.
Rooms	4: 1 double, 2 twins, 1 family room.
Meals	Dinner with wine, €23.
Closed	Mid-October to March.
Directions	From Carpentras D7 north through Aubignan & Vacqueyras; fork right (still D7) for Sablet; right 500m after Cave Vignerons Gigondas; signed.

Sylvette Gras
La Ravigote,
84190 Gigondas, Vaucluse
Tel +33 (0)4 90 65 87 55
Email info@laravigote.com
Web www.laravigote.com

Entry 676   Map 16

Le Clos Saint Saourde

Indoors embraces out here, spectacularly: many walls, ceilings, even some furniture, are sculpted from solid rock. The décor is minimalist and luxurious with a flurry of natural materials but lots of quirky touches, too: the wrought-iron lamps and lanterns, the clever lighting, the solar pools. Indulge yourself in an exotic Moroccan bedroom with a breathtaking grotto bathroom… enjoy an autumn aperitif by the fire in a spacious suite. Your lovely young hosts will steer you toward the wealth of historical, cultural and outdoor activities in this exquisite area, with rock-climbing and massage on request. Remarkable.

Le Mas de la Pierre du Coq

What's especially nice about this 17th-century farmhouse is that it hasn't been over-prettified. Instead, it has the friendly, informal elegance of a house that's lived in and loved; grey-painted beams, soft open-stone walls, seductive bathrooms. The Lorenzes fell in love with it three years ago; it reminded gentle Stéphan of the home he grew up in. Bustling Martine starts your day with a terrific breakfast, Stéphan shows you the walks from the door. The gardens, sweet with roses, oleanders and lavender, are shaded by ancient trees and the pool and views are glorious. Stay for as long as you can.

Price	€150–€260.
Rooms	4: 2 doubles, 2 suites for 2-4 with sofabeds.
Meals	Dinner with wine, €40.
Closed	Rarely.
Directions	A7 exit 23 Avignon Nord, D942 for Carpentras exit Monteux Nord & Sarrians; D31 Sarrians; through Beaumes de Venise to Route de Caromb; right 200m after Domaine de la Pigeade entrance; 500m to parking Le Clos.

Price	€105–€120. Suite €170.
Rooms	3: 1 double, 1 twin, 1 suite for 4.
Meals	Dinner with wine, €30.
Closed	July.
Directions	From Aubignan to Carpentras; after 2.5km right at junction; immed. right into Chemin de Loriol to Mazan; follow road, house up above on right after bridge.

Jérôme & Géraldine Thuillier
Le Clos Saint Saourde,
Route de St Véran,
84190 Beaumes de Venise,
Vaucluse
Tel/Fax +33 (0)4 90 37 35 20
Email   contact@leclossaintsaourde.com
Web   www.leclossaintsaourde.com

Stéphan & Martine Lorenz
Le Mas de la Pierre du Coq,
Chemin de Loriol,
84810 Aubignan, Vaucluse
Tel   +33 (0)4 90 67 31 64
Email   lorenz.stephane@wanadoo.fr
Web   www.masdelapierreducoq.com

Provence – Alps – Riviera

Le Clos du Rempart

Outdoors drifts in so naturally, the lovely salon sweeping beyond the sliding doors into a breathtaking suntrap courtyard. Relax among greenery galore, with burbling fountain, wisteria-dripped pergola and Middle Eastern niches. Or the cool of the salon, an oasis of white set off by blues and reds, exotic touches, modern art. Elegant yet comfy bedrooms overlook the courtyard, where birdsong is balm to the soul; Aïda feeds the birds. Her origins and travels are reflected in her décor, and in the buzzing university neighbourhood within the old walls. Avignon's vast treasures are minutes away. *Minimum stay 2 nights.*

Price	€125–€150. Whole house available.
Rooms	2 doubles.
Meals	Restaurants nearby.
Closed	Rarely.
Directions	From A7 D225 for Avignon Centre along Rhône to ramparts; left to 3rd lights, Porte St Lazare; right through gate; right again on Rempart St Lazare; Rue Crémade 4th on left.

Aïda Assad
Le Clos du Rempart,
35-37 rue Crémade,
84000 Avignon, Vaucluse

Tel	+33 (0)4 90 86 39 14
Fax	+33 (0)4 90 86 39 14
Email	aida@closdurempart.com
Web	www.closdurempart.com

Entry 679   Map 16

Provence – Alps – Riviera

Le Mas de Miejour

These are young, easy-going hosts, with a passion for wine and a fine display of Frédéric's pottery, who have escaped from their city pasts. Their guest bedrooms in this converted farmhouse are all different, all serene: one with a white appliquéd bedcover made in Thailand, another with Senegalese bedspreads, and a super family suite with a big brass bed and, on a separate floor, three beds for children. The land here is flat with a high water table so the garden, sheltered by trees and waving maize in summer, is always fresh and green; with its lovely pool, an idyllic retreat after a day's sight-seeing. *Sawday self-catering also.*

Price	€75–€100.
Rooms	3: 1 double, 1 twin, 1 family suite.
Meals	Light supper €18. Wine from €5.
Closed	November–March, except by arrangement.
Directions	From A7 exit 23; after toll right at r'bout for Carpentras & Entraigues; 1st exit to Vedène D6 to St Saturnin lès Avignon; left to Le Thor D28 for 2km; right Chemin du Trentin.

Frédéric Westercamp
& Emmanuelle Diemont
Le Mas de Miejour,
117 chemin du Trentin,
84250 Le Thor, Vaucluse

Tel	+33 (0)4 90 02 13 79
Email	masdemiejour@orange.fr
Web	www.masdemiejour.com

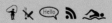

Entry 680   Map 16

Provence – Alps – Riviera

La Nesquière

The gardens alone are worth the detour: trees and greenery galore, riots of roses, all flourishing in a huge many-terraced park by a river. The 18th-century farmhouse harbours a fine collection of antiques – one of Isabelle's passions – tastefully set off by lush indoor greenery and lovely old carpets on ancient tile floors. Softly old-elegant rooms have hand-embroidered fabrics and genuine old linens, including Provençal quilts – truly exquisite – with splashes of red, orange and beige against white backgrounds. Themed weekends, too (cookery, wine, embroidery), and a warm, gracious welcome from Isabelle and her family.

Price	€95–€115.
Rooms	4: 1 twin/double, 1 double, 2 family suites.
Meals	Dinner with wine, €38.
Closed	Mid-December to mid-January.
Directions	A7 exit Avignon-Nord for Carpentras D942 5km. Just before bridge exit for Althen les Paluds D16 1.5km; left for Pernes Les Fontaines D38 4.5km; La Nesquière on right.

Isabelle de Maintenant
La Nesquière,
5419 route d'Althen,
84210 Pernes les Fontaines,
Vaucluse
Tel +33 (0)4 90 62 00 16
Email lanesquiere@wanadoo.fr
Web www.lanesquiere.com

Entry 681 Map 16

Provence – Alps – Riviera

Mas Pichony

Summer evenings are spent beneath the ancient spreading plane tree as the setting sun burnishes the vines beyond the slender cypresses, and the old stones of the 17th-century *mas* breathe gold. Laetitia and Laurent have given the farmhouse style and charm, beautifying it with country antiques, books and vibrant colours. Two children, three horses (a corner of the hall is full of riding gear), a trio of cats and a lone dog complete the charming picture. Laetitia serves good Provençal food at the big, convivial table; a terracotta-roofed area by the pool is a delicious place to sit and soak up the views.

Price	€83–€92.
Rooms	5: 3 doubles, 1 twin, 1 family room for 5.
Meals	Dinner with wine, €28.
Closed	November–February.
Directions	From Pernes les Fontaines; D28 for St Didier. House on right, set back from road to St Didier.

Laetitia & Laurent Desbordes
Mas Pichony,
1454 route de Saint Didier,
84210 Pernes les Fontaines, Vaucluse
Tel +33 (0)4 90 61 56 11
Fax +33 (0)4 90 40 35 02
Email mas-pichony@wanadoo.fr
Web www.maspichony.com

Entry 682 Map 16

Provence – Alps – Riviera

Illahee

The American Indian name means 'the house that brings comfort'. You'll find lots of that here. Claire, a former professor of medieval Italian literature, has created a peaceful warm haven in the old wine domaine. In a wing off the courtyard, the traditional bedrooms have sweeping tiled floors, clean simple lines and earth colours sparked by touches of yellow, red and orange. There are canoeing and tree-hopping close by for the energetic, a stroll in lovely landscaped gardens, a dip in the cool pool; the ultimate indulgence is Claire's (unobtrusive) Relaxation Centre with hammam, treatments and spa. A gem.

Price	€90–€100.
Rooms	3: 1 double, 2 family rooms for 3.
Meals	Dinner with wine, €20.
Closed	Rarely.
Directions	A7 exit 25 Cavaillon to L'Isle sur la Sorgue; from town centre, N100 for Lagnes, then 2nd left turn marked Lagnes; Illahee 200m on left.

Claire Cabaillot
Illahee,
Le Riotor, 84800 Lagnes,
Vaucluse

Tel	+33 (0)4 90 20 06 96
Fax	+33 (0)4 90 20 06 96
Email	illahee@wanadoo.fr
Web	www.espaceillahee.com

Entry 683 Map 16

Provence – Alps – Riviera

Sous L'Olivier

Old bare stonework rules the scene, big arched openings have become multi-paned dining windows, a stone fire burns immense logs in winter, and all is set around a pretty part-sheltered courtyard. Charming young bon viveur Julien, apron-clad, started his career in the kitchens of Paul Bocuse (breakfasts here are sumptuous affairs, dinners are convivial, the cooking worth a serious detour) while gentle Carole is behind the very fresh, Frenchly decorated bedrooms. Flat agricultural land spreads peacefully out around you; the refreshing pool is arched with canvas shading and surrounded by giant pots and plants.

Price	€90–€130. Apartment €220.
Rooms	6: 2 doubles, 2 triples, 1 suite, 1 suite for 2-6.
Meals	Dinner with wine, €29.
Closed	Never.
Directions	From Avignon N7 E, then D22 for Apt, Dingé, Sisteron (approx. 29km total), do not go to Lagnes. After Le Petit Palais, sign on right.

Carole, Julien & Hugo Gouin
Sous L'Olivier,
Quartier le Petit Jonquier,
84800 Lagnes, Vaucluse

Tel	+33 (0)4 90 20 33 90
Email	souslolivier@orange.fr
Web	www.chambresdhotesprovence.com

Entry 684 Map 16

Provence – Alps – Riviera

Villa La Lèbre

Madame is an absolute dear and she and Charles genuinely love doing B&B – they offer an open-hearted welcome and a real guest room in a real home. Charles speaks seven languages and is fascinating. The comfy room has its own dressing room, an extra mezzanine single and a newly tiled shower; you have use of a fridge and are welcome to picnic. The garden is their passion – it is fabulous, with roses, peonies, lavender and more. This is a modern house built of old stone in traditional local style and surrounded by hills, woods and vineyards with lovely valley views towards Goult and the Lubéron. Great value.

Price	€60. Triple €70.
Rooms	1 triple.
Meals	Restaurants 5km.
Closed	Rarely.
Directions	From Avignon N7 to Marseille. Caumont, D973 for Gordes. Imberts, D207 & D148 to St Pantaléon; pass church; do not enter village; rd on left after 100m; 3rd drive on right.

Pierrette & Charles Lawrence
Villa La Lèbre,
Saint Pantaléon,
84220 Gordes, Vaucluse
Tel   +33 (0)4 90 72 20 74
Fax   +33 (0)4 90 72 20 74
Email   jaclawrav@wanadoo.fr

Entry 685   Map 16

Provence – Alps – Riviera

Le Mas del Sol

Wake to sumptuous views of hilltop villages, white-domed Mont Ventoux, medieval Bonnieux. Laze over breakfast fruits from the organic orchard before dipping into the pool and basking in the 360-degree panorama. This 18th-century stone farmhouse is a fresh, chilled, contemporary retreat. Ample bedrooms, nicely private, are simply furnished in sunny Provençal colours. Most have views, two have terraces, and there's a big bright sitting room for rainy days. The child-friendly owners may join you for excellent dinner or later on the terrace with its magical nightscape of twinkling lights – and festival fireworks!

Price	€85-€125.
Rooms	5: 1 double, 1 family room for 3, 1 suite for 2-4 (with sofabed), 2 family suites for 4.
Meals	Dinner with wine, €34.
Closed	December–January.
Directions	A7 exit 24 Avignon Sud for Apt; N100 right at r'bout D36 for Bonnieux, 4km; right at sign; on for 1km, 2nd house on right.

Lucine & Richard Massol
Le Mas del Sol,
Le Pimbard,
84480 Bonnieux, Vaucluse
Tel   +33 (0)4 90 75 94 80
Email   lemasdelsol@wanadoo.fr
Web   www.mas-del-sol.com

Entry 686   Map 16

Villa Saint Louis

Stepping into this typical Provençal townhouse from the busy street one enters a refined, elegant and colourful cocoon of lived-in gentility and old-world charm where period furniture – to each room its style – and a throng of fascinating *objets d'art* create an intrinsically French home unchanged since Balzac. Attentive and cultured, Madame runs the B&B with her daughter, a fluent English speaker. Guest quarters, including breakfast room, are self-contained on the top floor, there's a deep terrace under the plane trees and a cool, fragrant garden for everyone below. *Summer kitchen sometimes available.*

Le Pavillon de Galon

Tall cypresses, cherry trees, wisteria, honeysuckle, terraces, pergolas, a spiral of olive trees, spring-fed pools and heated pool… the gardens of this big 18th-century stone hunting lodge are stunning. And its exuberant owners, former Parisian journalists, are equally charming. Knowledgeable on food, wine, architecture, gardens, they'll steer you towards Lubéron's finest places. Terracotta-floored bedrooms, overlooking the gardens, are elegant and airy, a perfect mix of quality and quirk. Breakfast and dine on the terrace, on wholesome produce just picked from the (organic) garden. *Minimum stay 2 nights.*

Ethical Collection: Environment; Community; Food. See page 432.

Price	€60–€75.
Rooms	4: 1 double, 3 twins.
Meals	Restaurants nearby.
Closed	Never.
Directions	From Aix en Provence N96 & D556 to Pertuis; D973 to Cadenet; D943 for Bonnieux to Lourmarin.

Price	€140–€160. Whole house available.
Rooms	2 suites.
Meals	Dinner with wine, €30–€80. Guest kitchen. Restaurants 1km.
Closed	Never.
Directions	A7 to Cavaillon exit 25; D973 for Pertuis. Left thro' Lauris; D27 to Lourmarin & Cucuron. Thro' village for Cabrières; at end of village, right at war memorial & cont. 600m. House on left.

	Mme Lassallette
	Villa Saint Louis,
	35 rue Henri de Savornin,
	84160 Lourmarin, Vaucluse
Tel	+33 (0)4 90 68 39 18
Email	villasaintlouis@wanadoo.fr
Web	www.villasaintlouis.com

	Bibi & Guy Hervais
	Le Pavillon de Galon,
	84160 Cucuron Lubéron, Vaucluse
Tel	+33 (0)4 90 77 24 15
Fax	+33 (0)4 90 77 12 55
Email	bibi@pavillondegalon.com
Web	www.pavillondegalon.com

Entry 687   Map 16

Entry 688   Map 16

La Cigale au Bord de l'Eau

A beautifully restored 19th-century Provençal stone farmhouse in a corner of paradise. Orchards embrace huge gardens resplendent with flowering shrubs; trees (cherry, mulberry, fig, plum) joust for attention. More charm within; bedrooms are at ground level with private access and a decorative minimalism – romantic touches here, goofy bedside lamps there. And there's a library/games room to keep everyone happy out of season. The village has its own bullfighting arena, while Roman ruins, festivals and markets abound. Your lovely hands-on hosts organise tours that take in the best of the region.

Mas des Tourterelles

Let the views wash over you. All around, peace, greenery, the little pool tucked into the garden – and the beautiful, bustling centre of Saint Rémy mere minutes away. The Aherns have thrown themselves into their new life in the Alpilles, Richard restoring the farmhouse with its honey-coloured stone, beams and tiles, Carrie adding the deceptively simple touches – pale walls, linen curtains, sisal carpets, splashes of colour. Bedrooms are restful spaces, utterly delightful. Cool off by the pool or under the vine-covered bower, look forward to dinner in town, a short stroll. *Minimum stay 2 nights high season. Sawday self-catering also.*

Price	€77–€125.
Rooms	4: 2 doubles, 1 family suite for 4-6, 1 suite for 4.
Meals	Dinner with wine, €28.
Closed	Rarely.
Directions	A7 exit 25 for Cavaillon; D99 for St Rémy 3km to Plan d'Orgon; right at 1st lights in village. House on left 100m after 1st left turn in road.

Price	€80–€95.
Rooms	4: 3 doubles, 1 twin.
Meals	Restaurants within walking distance.
Closed	Rarely.
Directions	In St Rémy de Provence to Pl. de la République on one-way boulevard, exit right before school, past car park into Chemin de la Combette 400m; left up gravel track (after bins); sign by road.

Marco Savéan
La Cigale au Bord de l'Eau,
447 route des Écoles,
13750 Plan D'Orgon,
Bouches-du-Rhône
Tel   +33 (0)4 90 73 20 01
Email   lcabe@tele2.fr
Web   www.lcabe.com

Richard & Carrie Ahern
Mas des Tourterelles,
21 chemin de la Combette,
13210 Saint Rémy de Provence,
Bouches-du-Rhône
Tel/Fax   +33 (0)4 32 60 19 93
Email   richard.ahern@wanadoo.fr
Web   www.masdestourterelles.com

Provence – Alps – Riviera

Le Mas d'Hermès

Uncomplicated country comfort. Danielle and Hugues escaped city life to open this pretty Provençal farmhouse and give you a simple, gentle welcome. Vast airy rooms charm with their sun-faded shutters and unfussy, modern furnishings. Bedroom suites in the separate guest wing have exposed stonework, good bathrooms, sprawling sofas and brocante finds. Choose downstairs for a terrace, upstairs for beams and romance. So much space: guest kitchenette, log-fire sitting room, country-style dining room. A pool and a garden surrounded by pines. Peace and great value – ten minutes from RN7.

Price	€65–€72.
Rooms	2: 1 family room for 4, 1 suite.
Meals	Restaurants 2-5km. Guest kitchenette.
Closed	Rarely.
Directions	RN7 for Cavaillon; exit Plan d'Orgon; left at r'bout; on for 500m, continue on road 'Chemin Sans Issue'; house 200m on left, signed.

Danielle & Hugues Pelletier
Le Mas d'Hermès,
13750 Plan d'Orgon,
Bouches-du-Rhône
Tel   +33 (0)4 90 73 17 13
Email   chambres@mashermes.com
Web   www.mashermes.com

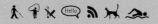

Entry 691   Map 16

Provence – Alps – Riviera

Mas Shamrock

A manicured farmhouse whose interior is as southern cool as the welcome from its owners is sincerely Franco-Irish – John is relaxed and direct, Christiane is efficient and helpful. Natural stone, oak beams, terracotta floors and cool colours give a wonderfully fresh and open feel to the house, while bedrooms are light and airy with neat shower rooms. Outside, a delectable garden, centuries-old plane trees, a vine tunnel, three hectares of cypresses and a landscaped, secluded pool add to the magic. An oft-tinkled piano is there for you to play. *Minimum stay 2 nights July/August.*

Price	€85–€115.
Rooms	5: 3 doubles, 1 twin, 1 family room for 3-4.
Meals	Restaurants in St Rémy.
Closed	November-Easter.
Directions	From St Rémy D571 for Avignon; over 2 r'bouts, left before 2nd bus stop (Lagoy), opp. 2nd yellow Portes Anciennes sign, Chemin des Lones; house 6th on right.

Christiane & John Walsh
Mas Shamrock,
Chemin des Lones et de Velleron,
13210 St Rémy de Provence,
Bouches-du-Rhône
Tel   +33 (0)4 90 92 55 79
Email   mas.shamrock@wanadoo.fr
Web   www.masshamrock.com

Entry 692   Map 16

Le Mas d'Arvieux

New young owners, lovers of the outdoor life and well-travelled, are putting their elegant stamp on this generous manor house in beautiful Provence. Big bedrooms, one in the tower wing, one with a carved mezzanine, have beams and stone walls, fine old armoires, luxurious bathrooms and wonderful views of the hills. A third room, ideal for wheelchair-users, is being planned for the ground floor. This is a great set-up for families in high season and for peace-loving couples out of it; cookery and art classes can be arranged. Marvellously close to Avignon's treasures. *Pool shared with gîte guests.*

Le Mas d'Anez

A tree-lined drive and impressive wrought-iron gates welcome you to this impeccable 18th-century mansion. They came here from Paris (a three-hour ride on the TGV, so they can still visit their grandchildren!). He, extrovert and trilingual, swapped wine consultancy for olive oil; she, with a lovely smile, writes books on interior design and runs the odd course. The rooms are decorated with simple, assured elegance; the vast Provençal kitchen is a wonderful place for breakfast. Beyond the stone wall that encloses house, garden and pool stretch Thierry's olive groves. *Minimum stay 2 nights. Long stays available.*

Price	€95–€125.		Price	€90–€105. €190 for 4.
Rooms	4: 1 double, 2 triples, 1 suite.		Rooms	2: 1 twin/double, 1 suite for 4.
Meals	Occasional dinner with wine, €30. Restaurant 3km.		Meals	Occasional dinner with wine, €31.
Closed	Rarely.		Closed	Rarely.
Directions	From Tarascon D970 to Avignon; after 5km right at humpback bridge, signed before bridge.		Directions	From Avignon N570 to Tarascon; cross Rognonas bridge. D970 to Beaucaire; after Graveson r'bout follow signs to Beaucaire & Tarascon for 7km; house on right, entrance between trees and stone columns.

Alex & Carolyn Miller
Le Mas d'Arvieux,
Route d'Avignon, 13150 Tarascon,
Bouches-du-Rhône
Tel +33 (0)4 90 90 78 77
Fax +33 (0)4 90 90 78 68
Email mas@arvieux-provence.com
Web www.arvieux-provence.com

Thierry & Marie-Laure Mantoux
Le Mas d'Anez,
Route d'Avignon,
13150 Tarascon,
Bouches-du-Rhône
Tel +33 (0)4 90 91 73 98
Email masdanez@wanadoo.fr
Web www.masdanez.com

Provence – Alps – Riviera

24 rue du Château

On a medieval street near one of the loveliest châteaux in France, two *maisons de maître* are joined by an ochre-hued courtyard and a continuity of taste. It's an impeccable renovation that has kept all of the soft patina of stone walls and tiles. No garden, but a courtyard for candlelit evenings and immaculate breakfasts. Calming, gracious bedrooms have fine old furniture and beams, perfect bathrooms, crisp linen. While you can be totally independent, your courteous hostess is relaxed and friendly and thoroughly enjoys her guests. Deeply atmospheric. *Minimum stay 2 nights.*

Price	€78–€90.
Rooms	4: 2 doubles, 2 twins.
Meals	Restaurants in town.
Closed	November–March.
Directions	In Tarascon centre take Rue du Château opposite château (well signed). No. 24 is on right. Ask about parking.

Martine Laraison
24 rue du Château,
13150 Tarascon,
Bouches-du-Rhône

Tel   +33 (0)4 90 91 09 99
Fax   +33 (0)4 90 91 10 33
Email   ylaraison@wanadoo.fr
Web   www.chambres-hotes.com

Entry 695   Map 16

Provence – Alps – Riviera

Mas Montredon

Set in typically flat, open Camargue country, this property fits its environment to a tee. Surely a Camargue cowboy, or *gardian*, will dash by on his white horse any minute, rounding up the bulls. The young, enthusiastic and very environmentally conscious owners have preserved the character of the 16th-18th-century farmhouse, using natural materials throughout. Exposed stone walls and beams, bits of driftwood furniture, genuine old linens, the almost stark bedroom décor lit up by pretty floral prints... a refreshing simplicity reigns. Boat trips, a bird sanctuary, cycling, the sea and great riding close by.

Price	€80–€120.
Rooms	4 doubles.
Meals	Restaurants nearby.
Closed	Rarely.
Directions	A54 to Arles; exit 4 D570 for Stes Maries de la Mer; 2km, left D36 for Le Sambuc/Salin de Giraud; 6km, right Gageron; 1st right VC130 'De Bouchaud à Gageron'; out of village; 3km, left to house: gravel road for 250m.

Frédérique Buck &
Michael Wolfcarius
Mas Montredon,
Chemin de Gageron, 13200 Arles,
Bouches-du-Rhône

Tel   +33 (0)4 90 97 00 37
Email   mail@masmontredon.com
Web   www.mas-montredon.camargue.fr

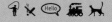

Entry 696   Map 16

Provence – Alps – Riviera

Mas de la Rabassière

Fanfares of lilies at the door, Haydn inside and 'mine host' smiling in his chef's apron. La Rabassière means 'where truffles are found' and dinners are a must: vintage wines and a sculpted dancer grace the terrace table. Cookery classes with olive oil from his trees, jogging companionship, airport pick-up are all part of the elegant hospitality, aided by Théri, his serene assistant from Singapore. Big bedrooms and drawing room with roaring fire are comfortable in English country-house style: generous beds, erudite bookshelves, a tuned piano, Provençal antiques... and pool, tennis, croquet.

Ethical Collection: Environment; Food. See page 432.

Price	€130. Singles €80.
Rooms	2 doubles.
Meals	Dinner with wine, €45.
Closed	Rarely.
Directions	From A54 exit 13 to Grans on D19; right on D16 to St Chamas; just before r'way bridge, left for Cornillon, up hill 2km; house on right before tennis court. Map sent on request.

	Michael Frost
	Mas de la Rabassière,
	Route de Cornillon,
	13250 Saint Chamas,
	Bouches-du-Rhône
Tel/Fax	+33 (0)4 90 50 70 40
Email	michaelfrost@rabassiere.com
Web	www.rabassiere.com

Provence – Alps – Riviera

Le Clos des Oliviers

Minutes from charming little St Cannat, at the end of a winding lane, the house sits quietly on its own. Vineyards, olive groves, open grassland, majestic pines and a hammock between the trees – no pool but a special spot. The guest quarters in the annexe are spotless, sunny and very French, with bamboo furniture, Provençal curtains, a good Indian dresser, a sofabed in the sitting room, a super big shower. Nicole loves having guests and is helpful in every way. Walking from the door, golf at Port Royal, a Wednesday market in the village, and wonderful Aix a 15-minute drive. *Minimum stay 2 nights.*

Price	€90-€95.
Rooms	1 double & sitting room with sofabed.
Meals	Dinner with wine, €25.
Closed	Never.
Directions	A7 exit 27 Salon de Provence; D572 to St Cannat; in village centre D18 to Rognes; leaving village, right Chemin des Ouides; over 2 speed bumps, house on left.

	Nicole Auriol
	Le Clos des Oliviers,
	695 chemin des Ouides,
	13760 Saint Cannat,
	Bouches-du-Rhône
Tel	+33 (0)4 42 57 37 64
Email	nicole.auriol@worldonline.fr

Provence – Alps – Riviera

Le Clos des Frères Gris

In through the gates of Hubert's exquisitely tended park and well-tree'd gardens; you'd never guess the centre of Aix en Provence was seven minutes away. Polyglot Caroline is a people person whose hospitality goes beyond her warm welcome. A passion for antiques is evident throughout her house, as is a talent with fabrics and colours; bedrooms combine comfort and cool elegance, fine linens, thick towels, special touches. Admire the rose and herb gardens on the way to boules or pool, then discover the music and markets of Aix. A jewel of a bastide – and a home from home. *Min. stay 2 nights.*

Price	€110-€200.
Rooms	4 doubles.
Meals	Restaurant 1km.
Closed	Rarely.
Directions	A8 exit 30 for Aix Pont de l'Arc/Luynes. Up hill, right N8; after entering Luynes, house on right, signed; go to bottom of lane, ring at gate.

Caroline & Hubert Lecomte
Le Clos des Frères Gris,
2240 avenue Fortune Ferrini,
13080 Luynes – Aix en Provence,
Bouches-du-Rhône

Tel/Fax +33 (0)4 42 24 13 37
Email freres.gris@free.fr
Web freres.gris.free.fr

Entry 699   Map 16

Provence – Alps – Riviera

Mas Sainte An

On its hilltop on the edge of pretty Peynier, the old *mas* stands in glory before Cézanne's Montagne Sainte Victoire: pull the cowbell, pass the wooden doors and the red-shuttered mass surges up from beds of roses. Beautifully restored, it once belonged to the painter Vincent Roux and memories of his life live on thanks to your gracious hostess. The Roux room is the nicest, with a delicious garden view, beams, terracotta tiles, and a fantastic ochre/green bathroom down the hall. The house has a wonderful patina and the grounds are beautifully kept.

Price	€90-€100.
Rooms	2: 1 double; 1 double with separate bath.
Meals	Restaurants in village.
Closed	1st three weeks in August.
Directions	From Aix on D6, 4km before Trets, right D57 to Peynier; up hill to Trets & Aubagne road; left D908; right between Poste & Pharmacie. House 50m.

Jacqueline Lambert
Mas Sainte An,
3 rue d'Auriol, 13790 Peynier,
Bouches-du-Rhône
Tel +33 (0)4 42 53 05 32
Fax +33 (0)4 42 53 05 32
Email stanpeynier@yahoo.fr
Web www.stanpeynier.com

Entry 700   Map 16

Provence – Alps – Riviera

La Royante

The Bishop of Marseilles once resided in this delicious corner of paradise and you may sleep in the sacristy, wash by a stained-glass window, nip into the chapel/music room for a quick midnight pray. Your brilliant hosts, a cosmopolitan mix of talent, fantasy and joy, have got every detail right without a hint of pedantry. The stupendous big bedrooms throng with original features and Bernard's beloved antiques (the more old-fashioned St Wlodek is reached through its bathroom), leisurely breakfasts may come with apricots plucked from the tree. One of our absolute favourites. *Ask about gastronomic tours (min. 8).*

Ethical Collection: Environment; Food. See page 432.

Price	€125-€155.
Rooms	4: 3 doubles, 1 triple.
Meals	Restaurant 1km.
Closed	Never.
Directions	Aix A8 for Nice; A52 Aubagne & Toulon, do not exit at Aubagne; A50 Marseille; exit 5 La Valentine; stay right; for Le Charrel 3km; after Legion Etrangère building on left, 1st left D44a for Eoures; 1st right after bridge, signed Maison de Retraite: Kaliste; 800m.

Xenia Saltiel
La Royante,
Chemin de la Royante,
13400 Aubagne en Provence,
Bouches-du-Rhône

Tel/Fax	+33 (0)4 42 03 83 42
Email	contact@laroyante.com
Web	www.laroyante.com

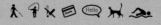

Entry 701   Map 16

Provence – Alps – Riviera

Mas de Bassette

Sophisticated simplicity is here: white walls and pale fabrics glow venerably in the sunlight filtering through the greenery outside – an ethereal picture of pure Provence. Your hosts are as quiet and charming, gentle and generous as their 15th-century *mas* with its magical great garden where peacocks dally and a princely doberman keeps watch. Big bedrooms are perfect: old terracotta tiles and wicker chairs, thick towels and soap in a basket. Peer for an eternity at the fascinating framed collection of artists' letters in the handsome salon. Superb value, utter peace.

Price	€120.
Rooms	2 doubles.
Meals	Restaurants 1-20km.
Closed	Rarely.
Directions	In Barbentane for Abbaye St Michel du Frigoulet; at windmill for tennis club; house entrance near club; signed.

Marie & François Veilleux
Mas de Bassette,
13750 Barbentane,
Bouches-du-Rhône

Tel	+33 (0)4 90 95 63 85
Fax	+33 (0)4 90 95 63 85
Email	bassette2@wanadoo.fr
Web	www.masdebassette.com

Entry 702   Map 16

Le Clos de la Chèvre Sud

Carole's flair for design shows not only in the comfy, traditional décor but also in the wonderfully quirky touches such as the wok recycled as a bathroom basin. Colour-washed rooms are cosy and inviting, in beiges, ochres reds, greys and blues. For summer, there's a broad sheltered terrace for breakfasting, dining, lazing and enjoying the views – the sea on one side, the forested hill on the other, a riot of flowering shrubs and trees in between. Patrice is a doctor and osteopath while Carole, a nurse, runs the spa and massage centre; both are charming and fun. Perfect – and there's a stunning pool.

Bastide Sainte Trinide

You'll love the simple lines and bright, airy décor of this renovated 18th-century farmhouse that once belonged to Pascale's grandparents. Prepare to be seduced by reds, whites and chocolate touches, fine linens, exposed beams, a choice of terraces for cooling breezes. One delight is the captivating chapel across the courtyard, another is the vibrant art: walls throughout are splashed with the canvasses of a family friend. You'll also love the blissful quiet up here in the hills, though the beaches are minutes away. Walks, riding, golf, exotic gardens, zoo; let your charming young hosts help you explore.

Price	€85-€120.
Rooms	3: 2 doubles, 1 suite for 3.
Meals	Dinner €30. Wine list from €20.
Closed	Never.
Directions	From Marseille A50 exit 10 St Cyr; for Bandol & Golf; left Chemin Naron; cont. past approx. 8 roads on left; left onto Chemin Pas Chèvre Sud; straight on.

Price	€70-€80.
Rooms	2: 1 double, 1 twin/double.
Meals	Restaurants nearby.
Closed	Rarely.
Directions	A50 exit 12 Bandol, Sanary; at r'bout 1st exit, Le Castellet (Zoo); 1st right for Zoo; left Chemin Ste Trinide; straight 700m; right; immed. right into parking area.

	Patrice & Carole Zoro
	Le Clos de la Chèvre Sud,
	255 chemin du Pas de la Chèvre Sud,
	83740 La Cadière, Var
Tel	+33 (0)4 94 32 31 54
Fax	+33 (0)4 94 32 31 54
Email	clochesud@wanadoo.fr
Web	www.closdelachevre.com

	Pascale Couture & Grégoire Debord
	Bastide Sainte Trinide,
	1671 chemin Chapelle Ste Trinide,
	83110 Sanary sur Mer, Var
Tel	+33 (0)4 94 34 57 75
Email	contact@bastidesaintetrinide.com
Web	www.bastidesaintetrinide.com

Entry 703   Map 16

Entry 704   Map 16

Les Cancades

Madame lavishes equal care on her décor and her beautiful Mediterranean garden with its tall trees, flowering shrubs and manicured lawn. Indeed, the whole place, designed by Monsieur 20 years ago as a family villa with thoughtfully concealed pool, is manicured. Comfortable hotel-like bedrooms have Salernes bathroom tiles; one has its own piece of garden. Monsieur is shyly welcoming, Madame smilingly efficient; you've the hills full of medieval villages and wine estates to explore. Make the most of the garden chalet with spa and fitness room, or prepare a picnic in the summer kitchen and just laze.

45 boulevard des Pêcheurs

Looking from this perch past umbrella pines out over the town to the marina and the blue bay is a tonic, served on your private terrace. Your many-windowed space feels like a lookout tower, fittingly done in blue and white with a new parquet floor and good bathroom. Breakfast is served under the trumpet vine on the main terrace in the luxuriant garden with pool. The sitting room, wide, welcoming and uncluttered, has nice old French furniture and ship's binoculars for the views, and it's a 15-minute walk to centre ville. Claudine is active and attentive, Serge used to work in boats: both are helpful, unintrusive hosts.

Price	€75. Suite €140.		Price	€75–€85.
Rooms	3: 2 twins/doubles, 1 suite for 4.		Rooms	1 double.
Meals	Restaurants in village.		Meals	Restaurants nearby.
Closed	Rarely.		Closed	Rarely.
Directions	Toulon N8 for Aubagne; in Le Beausset cross 2 r'bouts; right opp. Casino supermarket; immed. left by boulangerie, right Chemin de la Fontaine 1.5km; sign on left.		Directions	Lavandou centre; left at 4th lights; cross Bd Stalingrad, then right onto Ave. Bir Hakeïm; Rue des Champs Fleuris; Bd des Pêcheurs.

Charlotte & Marceau Zerbib
Les Cancades,
1195 chemin de la Fontaine,
83330 Le Beausset, Var
Tel   +33 (0)4 94 98 76 93
Email   charlotte.zerbib@wanadoo.fr
Web   www.les-cancades.com

Claudine & Serge Draganja
45 boulevard des Pêcheurs,
Super – Lavandou,
83980 Le Lavandou, Var
Tel   +33 (0)4 94 71 46 02
Email   draganja@orange.fr
Web   www.chambrehotes-draganja.com

Entry 705   Map 16

Entry 706   Map 16

Provence – Alps – Riviera

21 chemin des Marguerites

The warm-hearted, tireless Didiers seem to have been born to run a happy and hospitable B&B and they do so, enthusiastically, in their quiet 1960s villa with its backdrop of vineyards and hills. Two spotlessly clean bedrooms with real attention to comfort – good cupboards and bedside lights, for example – share the modern shower room and are hung with Amélie's fine paintings. The guest dining room leads to a private outside terrace and thence to the peaceful, beautiful garden; ideal for relaxing after the day's visit, maybe by boat to one of the Îles d'Hyères.

Price	€85. €140 for 4.
Rooms	2: 1 double, 1 twin, sharing shower.
Meals	Restaurant nearby; choice in Le Lavandou.
Closed	Rarely.
Directions	From Le Lavandou D559 E to La Fossette. In village, left Ave. Capitaine Thorel; left again Chemin des Marguerites. If lost, phone for help!

Robert & Amélie Didier
21 chemin des Marguerites,
La Fossette,
83980 Le Lavandou, Var
Tel +33 (0)4 94 71 07 82
Email ra-didier@tele2.fr
Web www.ra-didier.com

Entry 707   Map 16

Provence – Alps – Riviera

Mas de Faucon

Cheery yellows and reds bounce off white, the linens are fine, the bedrooms open to terraces; the welcome is genuine, the setting breathtaking... this is special. Caroline and Bubbles have furnished the house with choice antiques and there's a traditionally English, very comfortable feel. The huge, exquisite park is well-tree'd and flowered – both are keen gardeners – with views that sail over the St Tropez gulf, the densely forested Massif des Maures and the ancient hilltop village of Grimaud (brilliantly lit at night). And... watersports, golf, festivals, gorgeous villages, markets galore. *Children over 8 welcome.*

Price	€120.
Rooms	3: 1 double, 2 twins/doubles.
Meals	Dinner with wine, €40.
Closed	20 December-10 January; July-9 September.
Directions	D558 thro' Grimaud; r'about right to Cogolin 2 km; right St Maur; r'about left; 2nd r'about left; left Chemin N.D des Anges; right T junc; over r'about Chemin de Faucon 500m; cont. unmade road; bear left up hill 200m; on right.

Bubbles & Caroline Horsley
Mas de Faucon,
Chemin de Faucon,
83310 Cogolin, Var
Tel +33 (0)4 94 54 57 01
Fax +33 (0)4 94 545 701
Email carolinehorsley@yahoo.com
Web www.masdefaucon.com

Entry 708   Map 16

Provence – Alps – Riviera

Les Trois Cyprès

What a view! Sit here, gazing past palms and pool to the plunging sea and enjoying Yvette's speciality of the day (tart, crumble…). She is a wonderful woman, sprightly and endlessly caring; Guy, a gentle and invaluable member of the team, collects the fresh bread and helps you plan your stay; they have travelled lots and simply love people. All three pretty, pastel guest rooms lead off a bright, Moroccan-touched landing – brass lamps, hand-painted mirror – and have lovely rugs on honeycomb-tile floors. The biggest room is definitely the best. And a sandy beach is 10 minutes down the cliff. *Minimum stay 2 nights.*

Price	€90–€120.
Rooms	2: 1 double, 1 twin.
Meals	Restaurants 500m.
Closed	October–May.
Directions	From Ste Maxime N98 E through San Piere; after Casino supermarket, 4th left Ave Belvédère; 1st left into Ave de l'Ancien Petit Train des Pins; Corniche Ligure; house on junction, green gate.

Yvette & Guy Pons
Les Trois Cyprès,
947 bd des Nymphes,
83380 Les Issambres, Var

Tel   +33 (0)4 98 11 80 31
Fax   +33 (0)4 98 11 80 31
Email   gyjpons@mac.com
Web   homepage.mac.com/gyjpons/TOC.html

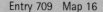

Entry 709   Map 16

Provence – Alps – Riviera

L'Hirondelle Blanche

Monsieur Georges is passionate about painting, music, wine and old houses and has renovated and decorated this typical palm-strewn 1900s Riviera villa all by himself. Each appealing room has a personal touch – a big red parasol over a bed, a fishing net on a wall; some have little balconies for private aperitifs. His own paintings hang in the cosy sitting room, wines appear for the evening tasting (you can buy them too), the beach is over the road. Despite the road, you don't need a car: fly in, train in, take a taxi or come by bike. St Tropez is a boat-trip away – charming out of season. *Train station 10-minute walk.*

Price	€57–€157.
Rooms	6: 4 doubles, 1 twin/double, 1 family suite for 4.
Meals	Dinner €25, July-August. Wine €9–€50.
Closed	Rarely.
Directions	Autoroute A8 exit 38 Fréjus & St Raphael for St Raphael town centre; from old port follow sea front with sea on right for 900m after Casino de Jeux heading for Cannes.

Florence Methout
L'Hirondelle Blanche,
533 bd du Général de Gaulle,
83700 St Raphaël, Var

Tel   +33 (0)4 98 11 84 03
Fax   +33 (0)4 98 11 84 04
Email   kussler-methout@wanadoo.fr
Web   www.hirondelle-blanche.fr

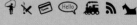

Entry 710   Map 16

La Canal

Built in 1760 as a silkworm farm, this delicious old manor house in a quiet street in Lorgues still has mulberry trees shading its terrace. Beyond, a large walled garden bursting with lavender and trees, a meadow for children's games, a vast and lovely Roman pool, stupendous view to the distant hills. Inside it is as authentic: old tiles with good rugs, beams, simple country antiques, bedrooms up a steep tiled stair. Organised, warm-hearted Nicola may not be here all year round but has arranged for a helper to be around when she is away. Easy for families, with summer kitchen and treehouse. *Minimum stay 2 nights.*

Villa de Lorgues

Expect the unexpected in this stately 18th-century townhouse. From the ground-floor spa to the traditional living rooms one floor up – level with the delicious garden and terrace – to the bedrooms at the top, it is pure enchantment. A red lantern here, zany birdcages there, four-posters, fireplaces and candles everywhere, just where you least expect them. Bedrooms combine superb comfort with an elegant minimalist décor. Come evening, fairylights wink around the wrought-iron balustrades from top to bottom. Claudie juggles a busy freelance career with talent, taste, a warm welcome and a fabulous sense of humour. Magical!

Price	€95–€105.
Rooms	3: 2 doubles, 1 twin.
Meals	Restaurants within walking distance.
Closed	November–March.
Directions	A8 exit Toulon/Le Luc/Vidauban; in Vidauban left D48 Lorgues, 11km; into centre ville; post office on right, right & right again; at T-junc. left Place Accarisio; left Rue de la Canal; left Impasse du Grand Jardin; house 20m on right.

Price	€100–€140.
Rooms	2 doubles.
Meals	Restaurants nearby.
Closed	Rarely.
Directions	From Vidauban centre D48 to Lorgues; at r'bout on outskirts 3rd exit to Salernes; 1st right Rue du 8 mai. Park on street as high as possible; house straight ahead.

	Nicola d'Annunzio
	La Canal,
	177 rue de La Canal,
	Quartier le Grand Jardin,
	83510 Lorgues, Var
Tel	+33 (0)4 94 67 68 32
Email	lacanallorgues@aol.com
Web	www.lacanal-lorgues.com

	Claudie Cais
	Villa de Lorgues,
	7 rue de la Bourgade,
	83510 Lorgues en Provence, Var
Tel	+33 (0)4 93 38 13 80
Email	cais.claudie@wanadoo.fr
Web	www.villadelorgues.com

Entry 711   Map 16

Entry 712   Map 16

La Sarrazine

Sumptuous gardens on multiple levels, a wonderful variety of trees and flowers, and terraces for quiet moments: paradise at its best, with views thrown in. One spacious double is all creams, with white sheets beautifully embroidered; there are blues, reds and yellows elsewhere, and an uncluttered cosiness. Guests share a large, relaxed sitting/dining room with a fireplace and a terrace. Lively Hilary has won a seat on the village municipal council; looking after both guests and community comes easily to her. Tennis and boules here, and Lorgues' restaurants and weekly market a short walk. Delightful.

Bastide des Hautes Moures

Colours rich with Mediterranean sunshine and heat, a sure eye for stunning touches: this lovely house is a celebration of your young hosts' love of colour and brocante. And flawless workmanship. Those delectable bathrooms by North African craftsmen: bright, breathtaking. Bedrooms: there's space to dance round the easy chairs and a blissful new suite. Catherine's brilliant mix of furniture – into the walk-in wardrobe and out. Dinner? Antoine is an accomplished chef. Butterflies dance to the call of the cicadas beneath the 300-year-old oaks. The wealth of Provence is here. *Children welcome for specific weeks. Sawday self-catering also.*

Price	€85–€115.
Rooms	3: 1 double, 2 twins/doubles.
Meals	Dinner €20–€30. Wine €15.
Closed	Rarely.
Directions	From Nice A8 Exit 36; RN7 for Les Arcs 6km to D10 Taradeau/Lorgues; in Lorgues r'bout for Salernes; 300m Chemin Peirouard left; immed. right past shops; immed. left up hill, 100m on left.

Price	€80–€150.
Rooms	4: 3 doubles, 1 suite for 3.
Meals	Dinner with wine, €34.
Closed	Rarely.
Directions	From A8 exit Le Luc & Le Cannet des Maures for Le Thoronet. Right on D84 for Vidauban. 4.5km to Les Moures, right & 800m on to house.

Hilary Smith
La Sarrazine,
375 chemin du Pendedi,
83510 Lorgues, Var
Tel +33 (0)4 94 73 20 27
Email reservations@lasarrazine.com
Web www.lasarrazine.com

Catherine & Antoine Debray
Bastide des Hautes Moures,
Quartier des Moures,
83340 Le Thoronet, Var
Tel +33 (0)4 94 60 13 36
Fax +33 (0)4 94 60 13 36
Email infos@bastidedesmoures.com
Web www.bastidedesmoures.com

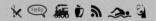

Provence – Alps – Riviera

La Grande Lauzade

This ancient monastery, bought at auction by Corine's great-grandfather, was a working wine estate. Now Corine and Thierry, extrovert musician, live here with their young family and pets, becoming ever more 'green' amid their wildish, well-tree'd grounds. Blues and whites predominate in big lofty rooms (some up twisty stairs) furnished with some exquisite and often fascinating pieces – such as the chicken-hatching box on legs, carved in fine wood. Distinct highway hum from the terrace but so much to do on the spot: darts, table tennis, billiards, boules and pool... and convivial breakfasts each morning.

Price	€80–€100.
Rooms	3: 1 double, 1 twin/double, 1 suite for 4.
Meals	Restaurants 1km.
Closed	Never.
Directions	A8 exit Le Luc/Cannet des Maures; at r'bout D7 left for Toulon; at 4th 'Europe' r'bout, D97 left for Toulon; 2km after Le Luc, left at end of car park; road to La Grande Lauzade "Le Prieuré"; park outside gates.

	Corine Varipatis
	La Grande Lauzade,
	83340 Le Luc en Provence, Var
Tel	+33 (0)4 94 60 74 35
Email	contact@lagrandelauzade.com
Web	www.lagrandelauzade.com

Entry 715   Map 16

Provence – Alps – Riviera

La Maison de Rocbaron

You'll fall in love with this beautifully restored 19th-century stone bergerie, set in a riot of greenery and flowers, with terraces dotted about gardens and pool. Jeanne and Guy's welcome is wonderfully warm; he keeps guests happy over an aperitif, she produces a gourmet dinner not to be missed; it's one of those places where you feel you're part of the family. Various staircases lead to elegant and exquisite rooms where pinks, whites and floral prints reign. An early dip, a feast of a breakfast, and you're set up for the day's adventures. A magical place run by special people, in the heart of a lovely village.

Price	€78–€108.
Rooms	5: 3 doubles, 2 suites.
Meals	Dinner with wine, €38.
Closed	Rarely.
Directions	A8 exit 35 Brignoles for Toulon; after Forcalqueiret D12 left to Rocbaron. In centre of village.

	Jeanne Fischbach & Guy Laguilhemie
	La Maison de Rocbaron,
	3 rue St Sauveur,
	83136 Rocbaron, Var
Tel	+33 (0)4 94 04 24 03
Email	contact@maisonderocbaron.com
Web	www.maisonderocbaron.com

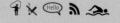

Entry 716   Map 16

Provence – Alps – Riviera

La Cordeline

Owned by lawyers down the centuries, the elegant *hotel particulier* stands in the quiet heart of the old town. Isabelle, a physiotherapist by profession and a keen cook, moved in three years ago. One side looks over the street, the other over the walled garden (a green and fountain'd haven) and you enter to warm old honeycomb tiles under a vaulted ceiling. The comforts of the special, spacious bedrooms include headed writing paper with the house's 17th-century front door logo. In winter you can snuggle down by a log fire and read in peace. *Weekend packages include massage & beauty sessions.*

Price	€70–€105.
Rooms	4: 3 doubles, 1 triple, all with bath/shower & separate wc.
Meals	Dinner with wine, €29.
Closed	Rarely.
Directions	From A8 exit Brignoles; over river for centre ville, immed. right for Hôtel de Claviers; round Pl. Palais de Justice; left Rue Ottaviani; right Ave. F. Mistral; Rue des Cordeliers on left.

	Isabelle Konen-Pierantoni
	La Cordeline,
	14 rue des Cordeliers,
	83170 Brignoles, Var
Tel	+33 (0)4 94 59 18 66
Email	lacordeline@wanadoo.fr
Web	www.lacordeline.com

Entry 717 Map 16

Provence – Alps – Riviera

Domaine de Conillières

In front of a log fire, breakfast is when you like – French pastries, sourdough rolls, delicious cakes, homemade jams, all diligently served by Philippe's elegant aunt. The family have lived in these wonderfully atmospheric buildings for generations. The olive groves and the vines, once part of this remote domaine, are now rented out, but the immense bastide is unchanged. Shapely red floor tiles, pale walls, perhaps a handsome old wardrobe or a red floral quilt – bedrooms are pleasing and extremely spacious, one on the first floor, the other reached via a creeper-covered stone stair. Good solid B&B.

Price	€65–€80.
Rooms	2 suites: 1 for 3, 1 for 4.
Meals	Dinner with wine, €35. Restaurant 2.5km.
Closed	Never.
Directions	Chemin du Moulin for 5km; right to Domaine, signed.

	Philippe Cortez
	Domaine de Conillières,
	83470 St Maximin la Ste Baume, Var
Tel	+33 (0)4 94 78 92 35
Email	info@domaine-de-conillieres.com
Web	www.domaine-de-conillieres.com

Entry 718 Map 16

Provence – Alps – Riviera

Domaine de la Blaque

The first and only property in the Var to be offically classified 'eco'! You are surrounded by nature at its best, and your lovely hosts have that artistic flair which puts the right things together naturally: palest pink-limed walls and white linen; old-stone courtyard walls with massed jasmine and honeysuckle; yoga groups and painters with wide open skies. Indeed, Jean-Luc is passionate about astronomy, Caroline is a photographer, they produce olives, truffles and timber, organise courses and love sharing their remote estate with like-minded travellers. Each pretty, independent room has its own little terrace. *Sawday self-catering also.*

Ethical Collection: Environment.
See page 432 for details.

Price	€70–€80.
Rooms	2: 1 double, 1 twin, each with kitchenette.
Meals	Restaurants 2.5km.
Closed	Rarely.
Directions	A8 exit St Maximum; D560 before Barjols; at Brue-Auriac D35 to Varages; sign on left leaving village for Tavernes; follow signs, dirt track part of way.

	Caroline & Jean-Luc Plouvier Domaine de la Blaque, 83670 Varages, Var
Tel	+33 (0)4 94 77 86 91
Fax	+33 (0)4 94 77 86 91
Email	ploublaque@hotmail.com
Web	www.lablaque.com

Entry 719   Map 16

Provence – Alps – Riviera

Domaine de Saint Ferréol

Readers write: "Armelle is wonderful". Breakfast is the highlight of her hospitality: she full of ideas for excursions, and Monsieur happily sharing his knowledge of the area. Theirs is a warm, lively family – a cultivated couple, four lovely children – and their working vineyard has a timeless feel. Glorious views to Pontevès Castle from the first-class, authentically Provençal bedrooms; they and the breakfast room (with mini-kitchen) are in a separate wing but, weather permitting, breakfast is on the terrace. Peace and privacy in a beautiful old house, superb walking, an outdoor pool.

Price	€68–€80. Suite €95–€100.
Rooms	3: 2 twins/doubles, 1 suite for 4.
Meals	Restaurant 1.5km. Kitchen available.
Closed	Mid-November to February.
Directions	From A8 exit St Maximin la Ste Baume D560 to Barjols; D560 2km for Draguignan; entrance opp. D60 turning for Pontevès.

	Guillaume & Armelle de Jerphanion Domaine de Saint Ferréol, 83670 Pontevès, Var
Tel	+33 (0)4 94 77 10 42
Fax	+33 (0)4 94 77 19 04
Email	saint-ferreol@wanadoo.fr
Web	www.domaine-de-saint-ferreol.fr

Entry 720   Map 16

Mas Saint Maurinet

Simply welcoming, your hosts were born in this unspoilt part of the Var where beautiful, distant views of the Pre-Alps – and genuine human warmth – await you at their modernised farmhouse with 19th-century foundations. The smallish bedrooms have typical Provençal fabrics and antiques and personal touches such as dried-flower arrangements; one has its own big terrace. On the verdant veranda Madame brings you breakfast of wholemeal bread, local honey and homemade jams. Plan a day away or make yourselves at home: you get picnic tables under the linden tree, an excellent summer kitchen and a good pool.

Domaine de Nestuby

Bravo, Nathalie! – in calm, friendly control of this gorgeous, well-restored 18th-century bastide. One whole wing is for guests: the light, airy, vineyard-view bedrooms, pastel-painted and Provençal-furnished with a happy mix of antique and modern (including WiFi), the big bourgeois sitting room (little used: it's too lovely outside), the new spa on the roof terrace and the great spring-fed tank for swims. Jean-François runs the vineyard, the tastings and the wine talk at dinner with sweet-natured ease. Utterly relaxing and very close to perfection. *Minimum stay 3 nights July/August.*

Price	€100–€150.
Rooms	1 suite for 2-4 & kitchenette.
Meals	Restaurants 1-3km. BBQ available.
Closed	Rarely.
Directions	From Barjols to Taverne; to Montmeyan; thro' village to Quinson; house on left 300m after sign saying you have left Montmeyan, signed Gîtes de France.

Price	€70–€80.
Rooms	5: 1 double, 1 twin, 1 triple, 1 family room, 1 suite.
Meals	Dinner with wine, €27.
Closed	November-February.
Directions	From A8 Brignoles exit north D554 through Le Val; D22 through Montfort sur Argens for Cotignac. 5km along left; sign.

Dany & Vincent Gonfond
Mas Saint Maurinet,
Route de Quinson,
83670 Montmeyan, Var
Tel   +33 (0)4 94 80 78 03
Fax   +33 (0)4 94 80 78 03
Email st-maurinet-mosly@wanadoo.fr
Web   www.st-maurinet-mosly.fr

Nathalie & Jean-François Roubaud
Domaine de Nestuby,
83570 Cotignac, Var
Tel   +33 (0)4 94 04 60 02
Fax   +33 (0)4 94 04 79 22
Email nestuby@wanadoo.fr
Web   www.sejour-en-provence.com

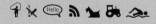

Bastide Notre Dame

The terraced garden, lovely by day (tables and chairs in private corners, a bivouac tent for escaping the sun), is Moroccan-magical at night as lanterns dot the trees. Start the day by the pool over coffee and 'cannelés de Bordeaux' fresh from the oven; the pink, airy 1920s house stands high above the road surveying the valley and blue hills beyond. Marie-Thé is proud of her fresh rooms with cool, pale furnishings, three private terraces and sweeping views, ex-farmer Thierry of his putt-perfect lawn. Both give you a friendly and very French welcome. Don't miss exquisite Cotignac, a short drive.

La Guillandonne

A very long drive, anticipation, then the house, the river, the cool forest, the pool. These lovely, civilised people, former teacher of English and architect, have treated their old house with delicacy and taste. Standing so Italianately red-ochre in its superb *parc* of great old trees and stream, it could have stepped out of a 19th-century novel yet the interior speaks for your hosts' caring, imaginative approach (polished cement floors, rustic Salernes tiles). Bedrooms are full of personality, elegant and colourful; the living room is exquisite with vintage Italian hanging lamps and Le Corbusier chairs. *Sawday self-catering also.*

Price	€85.
Rooms	4 twins/doubles.
Meals	Dinner with wine, €20, November–March only.
Closed	Rarely.
Directions	From Aix exit Brignoles; Le Val; Carcès; D562 for Lorgues; after 3km, D31 to Entrecasteaux. House on left between chapel & cemetery as entering village.

Price	€90.
Rooms	4: 2 doubles, 2 twins.
Meals	Restaurants 1.5km.
Closed	Rarely.
Directions	From A8 'Les Adrets' exit 39 for Fayence; left after lake, D562 for Fayence/Tourrettes; at Intermarché r'bout, D19 to Fayence; after 2km D219 right to Tourrettes; 200m black gate on right.

Thierry & Marie-Thé Bonnichon
Bastide Notre Dame ,
L'Adrech de Sainte Anne,
83570 Entrecasteaux, Var
Tel   +33 (0)4 94 04 45 63
Email   mariethevalentin@aol.com
Web   bastidenotredame.free.fr

Marie-Joëlle Salaün
La Guillandonne,
Chemin du Pavillon,
83440 Tourrettes, Var
Tel   +33 (0)4 94 76 04 71
Fax   +33 (0)4 94 76 04 71
Email   guillandonne@wanadoo.fr

Provence – Alps – Riviera

Villa Coste d'Or

Fragrant Grasse below, the Bay of Cannes beyond, exotic gardens at your feet: surely the hottest spot on the Côte d'Azur! Set in the gardens of Alice de Rothschild – Queen Victoria strolled among the palms and passion flowers – this modernist villa is all vaulted ceilings, Moorish arches and exotic objects. Bedrooms, glowing with tiled floors and sunshine, are lightly furnished: curly wrought-iron beds, tasteful colours, Art Deco touches. Join the young owners for superb canapés on the terrace; warm and generous, they know the best gardens and galleries. Or wallow by the pool in that sensational view.

Price	€95-€140.
Rooms	4: 3 doubles (1 with kitchenette). Studio for 4-5 & kitchen.
Meals	Restaurant within walking distance.
Closed	Never.
Directions	In Grasse centre, left onto Ave. Thiers; at end left for Digne onto Ave. Alice de Rothschild; cont. 800m; left Chemin Coste d'Or Supérieure.

	Martine & Pierre Mitelmann
	Villa Coste d'Or,
	39 chemin de la Coste d'Or Supérieure,
	06130 Grasse, Alpes-Maritimes
Tel	+33 (0)4 93 36 76 14
Email	contact@villa-costedor.com
Web	www.villa-costedor.com

Entry 725   Map 16

Provence – Alps – Riviera

Lou Candelou

Terracotta roofs peep over lush foliage in this residential area, to hills and the heavenly Med. A huge mimosa guards this friendly small house of soft local stone and light blue shutters; arrive by narrow private road to a warm (multi-lingual) welcome from Boun. Fresh, colourwashed ground-floor rooms with ethnic cottons, painted furniture and immaculate bathrooms lead directly to a potted terrace. Breakfast on the balcony: a joy of pastries, fresh fruit, exotic conserves – and views; pull yourself away and hop on a train to the coast. Grasse, Cap d'Antibes and the pink poochies of Nice await. *Children over 10 welcome.*

Price	€55-€75. Summer +20% if one night only.
Rooms	3 doubles.
Meals	Restaurant 1km.
Closed	Rarely.
Directions	A8 Nice to Cannes; exit 47 for Villeneuve Loubet; to Grasse; after Le Rouret, over r'bout; Pré du Lac r'bout, for Palais de Justice; 2nd exit at Les Roumégons r'bout, thro' tunnel to lights; house 1st on right.

	M & Mme Bougie
	Lou Candelou,
	57 avenue St Laurent,
	06520 Magagnosc, Alpes-Maritimes
Tel	+33 (0)4 93 36 90 16
Email	bounb@club-internet.fr
Web	www.loucandelou.com

Entry 726   Map 16

Provence – Alps – Riviera

Les Coquelicots

Annick, a well-travelled, kind and restful person, is a former riding instructor, now more likely to be helping people into hammocks than onto horses. Her peaceful bird-sung garden, with its awesomely ancient olive trees dotted about the terraces and among the lush grass, is ideal for a siesta. (Future plans include an extension with spaces for birds, nests and bats!). The blue bedroom is charming with its own entrance, vast antique wardrobe, fine linen and old wooden bed. If it's too hot for the terrace, breakfast is in the lovely saffron living room. Then visit Vence, for all things Matisse.

Ethical Collection: Environment.
See page 432 for details.

Price	€60.
Rooms	1 double.
Meals	Restaurants in village. Self-catering available.
Closed	November to mid-December & occasionally.
Directions	From Grasse D2085 to Le Rouret; thro' village, left D7 for La Colle sur Loup & Cagnes; on leaving village, hard right down steep track; house on right; call to meet Mme at Mairie.

Annick Le Guay
Les Coquelicots,
30 route de Roquefort,
06650 Le Rouret, Alpes-Maritimes

Tel	+33 (0)4 93 77 40 04
Fax	+33 (0)4 93 77 40 04
Email	annick.coquelicot@aliceadsl.fr

Entry 727   Map 16

Provence – Alps – Riviera

Le Cheneau

This very appealing Provençal-type villa is a happy marriage of modern technique and traditional design; the setting is entrancing, with umbrella pines, palms, the southern skies and Mediterranean heat. In the cool interior all is well-ordered and smart. Your charming, efficient and enthusiastic hosts have created old out of new, paved their generous terrace with lovely old squares, and furnished the rooms with a mix of the antique and the contemporary – and big beds. There is a dayroom/kitchen for guests and a beautifully tended garden with breakfast terrace – and ten golf courses within a three-mile radius!
Prior booking requested.

Price	€65-€85.
Rooms	3: 1 double, 2 twins/doubles.
Meals	Restaurants 200m. Guest kitchen.
Closed	Rarely. Book ahead.
Directions	From A8 exit Antibes; at Bouillides r'bout for Valbonne village 3km, D103; 100m after Bois Doré res't on right, before Petite Ferme bus stop, ring at iron gate No. 205; up lane, on left at top.

Alain & Christine Ringenbach
Le Cheneau,
205 route d'Antibes, 06560 Valbonne,
Alpes-Maritimes

Tel	+33 (0)4 93 12 13 94
Fax	+33 (0)4 93 12 13 94
Email	ringbach@club-internet.fr
Web	www.riviera-bandb.vadif.com

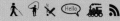

Entry 728   Map 16

Mas du Mûrier

The paradise of a garden, blending into the pine-clothed hillside, is a lesson in Mediterranean flora, aeons away from the potteries and madding fleshpots of nearby Vallauris, and Madame makes marmalade with the oranges. The Roncés restored this old building on a terraced vineyard: such peace. Pamper yourself by the pool, relax to the sound of chirruping cicadas. The bedrooms in this multi-levelled house – one looking over the garden, one the pool – have in common their modern paintings, cheery textiles and old brocante. A remote and restorative place. *Minimum stay 2 nights in summer.*

Villa Panko

The exotic dream of a garden is full of tropical crannies and secluded corners, while real and fake blooms spill into the living room, alongside the cheerful pictures that cover the variegated walls. Upstairs are rainbow sheets, patchwork bedcovers, painted furniture and *objets* galore, fine big towels and myriad toiletries; exceptional breakfasts are served on colourful china. Madame's energy drives it all – she'll organise your stay to a tee, gardens and galleries a speciality. It is quiet, exclusive, minutes from beaches, and massages can be arranged. Superb. *Minimum stay 3-5 nights. No smoking in garden!*

Price	€80–€95.	Price	€80–€115.
Rooms	2: 1 twin; 1 double with separate shower.	Rooms	2 twins/doubles, one with kitchenette.
Meals	Bistro within walking distance.	Meals	Restaurants 10-minute walk.
Closed	Rarely.	Closed	August, Christmas & New Year.
Directions	From A8 Antibes exit 44 to Vallauris; Chemin St Bernard, then Chemin des Impiniers; right into Montée des Impiniers; left at Auberge Bleue; sharp right into picnic area and right up track, signed.	Directions	From Antibes for Cap d'Antibes; palm tree r'bout for Cap d'Ant. Juan Les Pins; next junc. (by Bd du Cap) for Cap d'Ant.; 1st right Ch. du Crouton; 1st left cul-de-sac; at end, left on drive; 2nd house on right.

	M & Mme Roncé		Clarisse & Bernard Bourgade
	Mas du Mûrier,		Villa Panko,
	1407 route de Grasse,		17 chemin du Parc Saramartel,
	06220 Vallauris, Alpes-Maritimes		06160 Cap d'Antibes, Alpes-Maritimes
Tel	+33 (0)4 93 64 52 32	Tel	+33 (0)4 93 67 92 49
Fax	+33 (0)4 93 64 52 32	Fax	+33 (0)4 93 61 29 32
Email	fcwhronce@free.fr	Email	capdantibes.panko@wanadoo.fr
Web	www.guesthouse-cannes.com	Web	www.villapanko.com

Entry 729   Map 16

Entry 730   Map 16

Provence – Alps – Riviera

Villa Maghoss

Cascades of bougainvillea and pelargonium tumble over the terrace of this 1910 villa, and grapes dangle into your hand at breakfast. From the pretty garden you enter your delightful little sitting room with its country antiques, then through a basic shower room to a rather cramped bedroom. But your hosts take such great care of you – fresh flowers in the rooms, delicious breakfast – that this is a minor thorn among the roses. Although this is a quiet, dull piece of suburbia, sweet old seaside Antibes is only a 20-minute walk away – or borrow the bikes. *Minimum stay 2 nights. Madame will pick up from airport / train.*

Price	€80.
Rooms	1 double with sitting room.
Meals	Restaurants in Antibes.
Closed	Rarely.
Directions	In Antibes centre from Place de Gaulle, Rue Aristide Briand; left at r'bout, follow railway 600m; right Impasse Lorini with barrier 'Privé'; house at end on right.

Martine & Pierre Martin
Villa Maghoss,
8 impasse Lorini,
06600 Antibes,
Alpes-Maritimes
Tel   +33 (0)4 93 67 02 97
Email   maghoss@voila.fr

Entry 731   Map 16

Provence – Alps – Riviera

Le Clos de St Paul

A young Provençal house (built in 1975) on a lushly planted and screened piece of land where boundary hedging is high. In a guest wing, each pretty bedroom has its own patio and shares the guest sitting space with kettle and fridge. Smiling Madame has furnished with taste, simple floral fabrics, plain pale walls, beautifully tiled bathrooms. She is genuinely interested to see that you enjoy yourself, offers a welcome glass of rosé on her stunning shaded terrace and serves very fresh breakfast on yours. The lovely large mosaic'd pool is refreshingly discreet. *Minimum stay 2 nights. Children over 7 welcome.*

Price	€75-€85.
Rooms	3: 1 double, 2 twins/doubles.
Meals	Restaurant 1km.
Closed	Rarely.
Directions	A8 exit 48 for St Paul de Vence, 3km; fork right on D536/D7 to La Colle. Right at flashing light, cont. down hill; 100m after telephone box on right; right into Chemin de la Rouguière; 1st house on left.

Béatrice Ronin Pillet
Le Clos de St Paul,
71 chemin de la Rouguière,
06480 La Colle sur Loup,
Alpes-Maritimes
Tel/Fax +33 (0)4 93 32 56 81
Email   leclossaintpaul@hotmail.com
Web   perso.wanadoo.fr/leclossaintpaul

Entry 732   Map 16

Provence – Alps – Riviera

Un Ange Passe

Serenity, forests and views. The Deloupys have moved from the hum of Nice city to the jingle of goats' bells and the splash of the stream. The old sheepfold is palm-lush on the outside and colourful within: open-stone walls, gauze curtains, plants, cushions, steps galore and sliding doors to a flood-lit pool. Ask for a bedroom with a tree-top view. You are five minutes from St Paul de Vence, ten minutes from the beaches, and your hosts are cosmopolitan people interested in travel, alternative medicine and 'the art of living'. They also delight in sharing their knowledge of the area. *Minimum stay 2 nights.*

Price	€75–€135.
Rooms	5: 2 doubles, 2 suites, 1 family room.
Meals	Restaurants 1km.
Closed	Rarely.
Directions	From La Colle sur Loup for Bar sur Loup bypass; at sports stadium right; 1st left after pharmacy; follow Chambres d'Hôtes signs.

Martine & Bernard Deloupy
Un Ange Passe, 419 ave Jean Leonardi,
06480 La Colle sur Loup,
Alpes-Maritimes
Tel   +33 (0)4 93 32 60 39
Fax   +33 (0)4 93 82 45 29
Email contact@unangepasse.fr
Web   www.unangepasse.fr

Provence – Alps – Riviera

Villa Kilauea

A grand Mediterranean villa that looks so settled in Nice's lush western hills you'd never guess it was a 21st-century creation. There are balustrade-edged terraces, an infinity pool and panoramic views of the open valley. Bedrooms have a zen-like calm – wrought-iron four-posters draped in muslin, teak floors, white walls; bright orchids and oriental silks hint at the exotic. The one in the main house is more traditional with lovely family antiques. Nathalie is the perfect host, kind, gentle, generous to a tee; she delights in juggling a busy family life with her new B&B venture. Nice is a ten-minute drive down the hill.

Price	€130–€140.
Rooms	3 doubles.
Meals	Restaurants in Nice.
Closed	Rarely.
Directions	From Nice Promenade des Anglais for Hôpital l'Archet, then for St Roman; follow Ave. Bornala; Canta Galet, then Route de Bellet. At church in St Roman left; gates to house on right after 200m.

Nathalie Graffagnino
Villa Kilauea,
6 chemin du Candeu,
06200 Nice, Alpes-Maritimes
Tel   +33 (0)4 93 37 84 90
Email villakilauea@orange.fr
Web   www.villakilauea.com

Provence – Alps – Riviera

Villa L'Aimée

In one of the most authentic parts of Nice, a short bus ride from the city's rich culture (buses stop virtually at the gate), Villa L'Aimée is a Belle Époque villa constructed in 1929 and Toni's decoration has restored its wonderful shapes and details to their original opulence. Warm, cultured and much-travelled – one of her lives was in the art world – she has created delightful bedrooms in subtle colours with damasks and silks, fine linen, tulle canopies and beautiful furnishings, exuding an air of old luxury. The original parquet is breathtaking, the breakfasts are superb. *Babies & children over 10 welcome.*

Price	€110-€135.
Rooms	3: 2 twins/doubles, 1 twin.
Meals	Restaurants within walking distance.
Closed	December-February.
Directions	From A8 exit 54 Nice Nord for Nice & centre ville; left Ave. du Ray; r'bout right; over 2nd r'bout; Place Alex Medicin left; left into Ave. Henry Durant; 1st left at Garage Auto Bilan; immed. right Vieux Chemin de Gairaut; 1st right Ave. Piatti.

	Toni Redding
	Villa L'Aimée,
	5 avenue Piatti, 06100 Nice,
	Alpes-Maritimes
Tel	+33 (0)4 93 52 34 13
Fax	+33 (0)4 93 52 34 13
Email	bookings@villa-aimee.co.uk
Web	www.villa-aimee.co.uk

Entry 735   Map 16

Provence – Alps – Riviera

La Tour Manda

Such engaging hosts – nothing is too much trouble. Set well back from the busy dual carriageway, the house is convenient for airport and town (a 15-minute drive). And what a classic Côte d'Azur setting: your delightful bedroom overlooks a charming garden with palms. Jean-Claude was born in this house; it is colourful, like its owners. Expect light, space and heaps of southern style – family antiques, sofas with throws, posters and paintings. Breakfast, on the pretty terrace in summer, is delicious – be sure to try Jean-Claude's scrambled eggs! *Open by request during carnival. Minimum stay 2 nights.*

Price	€110. €180 for 4.
Rooms	3: 2 doubles, 1 suite for 4.
Meals	Restaurant 1km.
Closed	Rarely.
Directions	From Nice airport for Digne Grenoble; past centre commercial Carrefour; right onto small road just before 'Cuisine Number 1'.

	Jean-Claude & Brigitte Janer
	La Tour Manda,
	682 route de Grenoble,
	06200 Nice, Alpes-Maritimes
Tel	+33 (0)4 93 29 81 32
Fax	+33 (0)4 93 29 81 32
Email	latourmanda@wanadoo.fr
Web	www.bb-tourmanda.com

Entry 736   Map 16

Le Castel Enchanté

Way, way above Nice (the road up should not be tackled in the dark), drowned in bougainvillea, the Italianate villa with 70s additions stands in a jungle of scented garden – the 'enchanted' tag is not usurped. Your hosts are extremely engaging and enjoy meeting guests. Rooms, all big, one very big with its own veranda, are almost lavish in their Provençal colours, excellent furnishings and bathrooms unmatched by many hotels. Served on the sunny terrace, a brilliant breakfast includes cheese, cereals and fresh fruit salad. A super pool and three big docile dogs finish the picture. *Expensive taxi ride into town.*

151 route de Castellar

Delightful Paul and Dorothy have been here since the 60s and have made the most of every square inch of their steeply terraced garden (not ideal for the infirm!). He is proud of his handiwork, his latest creation being a bridge over the water garden. The views – of wooded valley leading to distant sea – are stupendous and make it entirely worth braving the narrow approach roads from Old Menton. Bedrooms open off a south-facing terrace, have satin bedspreads, simple furniture and good bathrooms. Breakfast may be on that pretty shaded terrace and it's breezy by the pool in summer. *Minimum stay 2 nights.*

Price	€110. Suite €190.
Rooms	4: 2 doubles, 1 twin/double, 1 suite for 4.
Meals	Restaurants 2km.
Closed	Mid-November to mid-March.
Directions	From Pl. St Philippe, under expressway, left Ave. Estienne d'Orves 600m, over level crossing, after sharp right-hand bend, hard back left, tricky track up to house.

Price	€60.
Rooms	4 doubles.
Meals	Restaurants in Menton, 2km.
Closed	December-January, except by arrangement.
Directions	From Autoroute exit Menton; for centre ville & Hotel de Ville; right for Castellar; up narrow road; 151 on left.

	Martine Ferrary
	Le Castel Enchanté,
	61 route de Saint Pierre de Féric,
	06000 Nice, Alpes-Maritimes
Tel	+33 (0)4 93 97 02 08
Fax	+33 (0)4 93 97 13 70
Email	contact@castel-enchante.com
Web	www.castel-enchante.com

	M & Mme Gazzano
	151 route de Castellar,
	06500 Menton,
	Alpes-Maritimes
Tel	+33 (0)4 93 57 39 73
Email	natie06@yahoo.fr

Provence – Alps – Riviera

Domaine du Paraïs

Birdwatchers and walkers will be happy here, in gentle isolation, dramatic miles up from the hot Riviera. The slightly faded Italianate mansion is home to highly cultured, artistic, English-fluent people who have re-awakened its 19th-century magic. No clutter, either of mind or matter, here. Breakfast is in the atmospheric old kitchen or the shady terrace in summer. White bedrooms have pretty fabrics, simple antiques and views of trees where birds burst their lungs and Marcel Mayer's superb sculptures await you. Come for dreamy space, natural peace, intelligent conversation.

Price	€55–€67.
Rooms	2 doubles.
Meals	Restaurants in Sospel, 1–3km.
Closed	Rarely.
Directions	From Menton D2566 to Sospel; at entrance to village left for Col de Turini 1.9km; left at house 'miel' for 'La Vasta' & 'Campings'. Paraïs 1.3km along, hard back on right after ranch & sharp bend.

Marie & Marcel Mayer
Domaine du Paraïs,
La Vasta Supérieure,
06380 Sospel, Alpes-Maritimes

Tel	+33 (0)4 93 04 15 78
Fax	+33 (0)4 93 04 15 78
Email	domaine.du.parais@wanadoo.fr
Web	domaineduparais.monsite.wanadoo.fr

Entry 739   Map 16

Monaco

Villa Nyanga

Looking east over the yacht-studded bay, south over the onion domes of a *fin de siècle* Persian palace, here is a warmly human refuge from the fascinating excesses that are Monaco. Michelle's sober, white-painted flat is decorated with wood, marble and lots of contemporary art, her own and her friends'. Living room: arched doors, little fireplace, little breakfast table, wide balcony; guest room: white candlewick bedcover, big gilt-framed mirror, sea view; bathroom: gloriously old-fashioned beige. Space everywhere, and Michelle is as good a hostess as she is an artist.

Price	€110.
Rooms	1 twin/double.
Meals	Restaurants in Monaco.
Closed	August.
Directions	From A8 exit 56 Monaco for centre (tunnel); past Jardin Exotique; on right-hand bend (pharmacy on corner) left; left at end Malbousquet; park opp. No. 26 to unload.

Michelle Rousseau
Villa Nyanga,
26 rue Malbousquet,
98000 Monaco

Tel	+377 93 50 32 81
Fax	+377 93 50 32 81
Email	michelle.rousseau@mageos.com
Web	www.bbfrance.com/rousseau.html

Entry 740   Map 16

Many of you may want to stay in environmentally friendly places. You may be passionate about local, organic or home-grown food. Or perhaps you want to know that the place you are staying in contributes to the community? To help you we have launched our Ethical Collection, so you can find the right place to stay and also discover how each owner is addressing these issues.

The Collection is made up of places going the extra mile, and taking the steps that most people have not yet taken, in one or more of the following areas:

• **Environment** Those making great efforts to reduce the environmental impact of their Special Place. We expect more than energy-saving light bulbs and recycling – in this part of the Collection you will find owners who make their own natural cleaning products, properties with solar hot water and biomass boilers, the odd green roof and a good measure of green elbow grease.

• **Community** Given to owners who use their property to play a positive role in their local and wider community. For example, by making a contribution from every guest's bill to a local fund, or running pond-dipping courses for local school children on their farm.

• **Food** Awarded to owners who make a real effort to source local or organic food, or to grow their own. We look for those who have gone out of their way

to strike up relationships with local producers or to seek out organic suppliers. It is easier for an owner on a farm to produce their own eggs than for someone in a city, so we take this into account.

How it works

To become part of our Ethical Collection owners choose whether to apply in one, two or all three categories, and fill in a detailed questionnaire asking demanding questions about their activities in the chosen areas. You can download a full list of the questions at sawdays.co.uk/about_us/ethical_collection/faq

We then review each questionnaire carefully before deciding whether or not to give the award(s). The final decision is subjective; it is based not only on whether an owner ticks 'yes' to a question but also on the detailed explanation that accompanies each 'yes' or 'no' answer. For example, an owner who has tried as hard as possible to install solar water-heating panels, but has failed because of strict conservation planning laws, will be given some credit for their effort (as long as they are doing other things in this area).

We have tried to be as rigorous as possible and have made sure the questions are demanding. We have not checked out the claims of owners before making our decisions, but we do trust them to be honest. We are only human, as are they, so please let us know if you think we have made any mistakes.

The Ethical Collection is a new initiative for us, and we'd love to know what you think about it – email us at ethicalcollection@sawdays.co.uk or write to us. And remember that because this is a new scheme some owners have not yet completed their questionnaires – we're sure other places in the guide are working just as hard in these areas, but we don't yet know the full details.

Ethical Collection in this book

On the entry page of all places in the Collection we show which awards have been given.

A list of the places in our Ethical Collection is shown below, by entry number.

Environment
81 • 84 • 143 • 144 • 153 • 162 • 179 • 185 • 188 • 201 • 236 • 295 • 300 • 329 • 339 • 346 • 351 • 354 • 390 • 398 • 402 • 408 • 429 • 435 • 462 • 480 • 488 • 518 • 526 • 531 • 540 • 547 • 568 • 584 • 612 • 638 • 649 • 652 • 658 • 663 • 688 • 697 • 701 • 719 • 727

Community
354 • 429 • 488 • 526 • 547 • 568 • 649 • 688

Food
41 • 43 • 71 • 81 • 84 • 172 • 201 • 236 • 267 • 284 • 294 • 295 • 300 • 342 • 346 • 347 • 351 • 354 • 390 • 398 • 402 • 404 • 408 • 429 • 435 • 437 • 441 • 462 • 477 • 480 • 481 • 488 • 499 • 518 • 526 • 540 • 544 • 547 • 550 • 556 • 557 • 563 • 568 • 620 • 638 • 649 • 652 • 658 • 663 • 664 • 688 • 697

Ethical Collection online

There is stacks more information on our website, www.sawdays.co.uk. You can read the answers each owner has given to our Ethical Collection questionnaire and get a more detailed idea of what they are doing in each area. You can also search for properties that have awards.

Photo above: Les Chambres Vertes, entry 346
Photo right: Tondes, entry 544

Fragile Earth

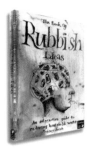

The Book of Rubbish Ideas
An interactive, room by room, guide to reducing household waste
£6.99

This guide to reducing household waste and stopping wasteful behaviour is essential reading for all those trying to lessen their environmental impact.

Ban the Plastic Bag
A Community Action Plan
£4.99

In May 2007 Modbury in South Devon became Britain's first plastic bag free town.
This book tells the Modbury story, but uses it as a call to action, entreating every village, town and city in the country to follow Modbury's example and... BAN THE PLASTIC BAG.

One Planet Living
£4.99

"Small but meaningful principles that will improve the quality of your life."
Country Living

Also available in the Fragile Earth series:

The Little Food Book   £6.99
"This is a really big little book. It will make your hair stand on end" *Jonathan Dimbleby*

The Little Money Book   £6.99
"Anecdotal, humorous and enlightening, this book will have you sharing its gems with all your friends" *Permaculture Magazine*

To order any of the books in the Fragile Earth series call 01275 395431 or visit www.fragile-earth.com

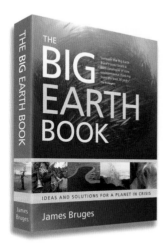

The Big Earth Book
Updated paperback edition
£12.99

We all know the Earth is in crisis. We should know that it is big enough to sustain us if we can only mobilise politicians and economists to change course now. Expanding on the ideas developed in *The Little Earth Book*, this book explores environmental, economic and social ideas to save our planet. It helps us understand what is happening to the planet today, exposes the actions of corporations and the lack of action of governments, weighs up new technologies, and champions innovative and viable solutions. Tackling a huge range of subjects – it has the potential to become the seminal reference book on the state of the planet – it's the one and only environmental book you really need.

What About China? £6.99
Answers to this and other awkward questions about climate change

"What is the point of doing anything when China opens a new power station every week?"

All of us are guilty of making excuses not to change our lifestyles especially when it comes to global warming and climate change. *What About China?* explains that all the excuses we give to avoid making changes that will reduce our carbon footprint and our personal impact on the environment, are exactly that, excuses! Through clear answers, examples, facts and figures the book illustrates how any changes we make now will have an effect, both directly and indirectly, on climate change.

"An excellent debunking of the myths that justify inaction" *The Ecologist*

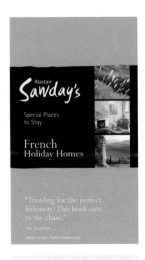

> *"...this book aims to cut to the chase and recommend the rarest, most original pads for private rental, booked directly with the owner."*
> *The Guardian*

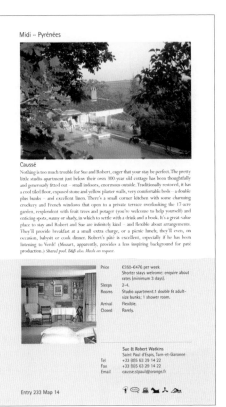

Midi – Pyrénées

Caussé

Nothing is too much trouble for Sue and Robert, eager that your stay be perfect. The pretty little studio apartment just below their own 300-year old cottage has been thoughtfully and generously fitted out – small indoors, enormous outside. Traditionally restored, it has a cool tiled floor, exposed stone and yellow plaster walls, very comfortable beds – a double plus bunks – and excellent linen. There's a small corner kitchen with some charming crockery and French windows that open to a private terrace overlooking the 17-acre garden, resplendent with fruit trees and potager (you're welcome to help yourself) and enticing spots, sunny or shady, in which to settle with a drink and a book. It's a great-value place to stay and Robert and Sue are infinitely kind – and flexible about arrangements. They'll provide breakfast at a small extra charge, or a picnic lunch; they'll even, on occasion, babysit or cook dinner. Robert's pâté is excellent, especially if he has been listening to Verdi! (Mozart, apparently, provides a less inspiring background for pâté production.) *Shared pool. Meals on request.*

Price	€350–€476 per week. Shorter stays welcome: enquire about rates (minimum 3 days).
Sleeps	2-4.
Rooms	Studio apartment:1 double & adult-size bunks; 1 shower room.
Arrival	Flexible.
Closed	Rarely.

	Sue & Robert Watkins
	Saint Paul d'Espis, Tarn-et-Garonne
Tel	+33 (0)5 63 29 14 22
Fax	+33 (0)5 63 29 14 22
Email	causse.stpaul@orange.fr

Entry 233 Map 14

The B&Bs below also have self-catering accommodation in our
French Holiday Homes guide (£14.99).

Special Places to Stay series

Have you enjoyed this book? Why not try one of the others in the Special Places to Stay series and get 35% discount on the RRP *

British Bed & Breakfast (Ed 13)	RRP £14.99	Offer price £9.75
British Bed & Breakfast for Garden Lovers (Ed 5)	RRP £14.99	Offer price £9.75
British Hotels & Inns (Ed 10)	RRP £14.99	Offer price £9.75
Devon & Cornwall (Ed 1)	RRP £9.99	Offer price £6.50
Scotland (Ed 1)	RRP £9.99	Offer price £6.50
Pubs & Inns of England & Wales (Ed 5)	RRP £14.99	Offer price £9.75
Ireland (Ed 7)	RRP £12.99	Offer price £8.45
French Bed & Breakfast (Ed 11)	RRP £15.99	Offer price £10.40
French Holiday Homes (Ed 4)	RRP £14.99	Offer price £9.75
French Hotels & Châteaux (Ed 5)	RRP £14.99	Offer price £9.75
Paris Hotels (Ed 6)	RRP £10.99	Offer price £7.15
Italy (Ed 5)	RRP £14.99	Offer price £9.75
Spain (Ed 7)	RRP £14.99	Offer price £9.75
Portugal (Ed 4)	RRP £11.99	Offer price £7.80
Croatia (Ed 1)	RRP £11.99	Offer price £7.80
Greece (Ed 1)	RRP £11.99	Offer price £7.80
India (Ed 2)	RRP £11.99	Offer price £7.80
Green Places to Stay (Ed 1)	RRP £13.99	Offer price £9.10
Go Slow England	RRP £19.99	Offer price £13.00

*postage and packing is added to each order

To order at the Reader's Discount price simply phone 01275 395431 and quote 'Reader Discount FBB'.

If you have any comments on entries in this guide, please tell us. If you have a favourite place or a new discovery, please let us know about it. You can return this form or visit www.sawdays.co.uk.

Existing entry

Property name: ————————————————————————————

Entry number: ———————————— Date of visit: ————————————

New recommendation

Property name: ————————————————————————————

Address: ————————————————————————————

————————————————————————————

Tel/Email/Web: ————————————————————————————

Your comments

What did you like (or dislike) about this place? Were the people friendly? What was the location like? What sort of food did they serve?

————————————————————————————

————————————————————————————

————————————————————————————

————————————————————————————

————————————————————————————

Your details

Name: ————————————————————————————

Address: ————————————————————————————

————————————————————————————

———————————— Postcode: ————————————

Tel: ———————————— Email: ————————————

Please send completed form to:
FBB, Sawday's, The Old Farmyard, Yanley Lane, Long Ashton, Bristol BS41 9LR, UK

Photo: Le Mas del Sol, entry 686

① Midi – Pyrénées

② Les Abélias

③ Geneviève moved here from Alsace for more sun and a slower pace of life. As soon as you enter the courtyard and see the mellow old house with little angels guarding the steps you will want to be one of her returning guests – welcomed (in good English) as friends. The chapel in the garden is dedicated to Our Lady of the Angels. Bedrooms are romantic: one soft green with a lace canopy and doors to the garden, another toile de Jouy'd, gently old-fashioned. All the rooms are Geneviève's own work and utterly appealing. Breakfast is on a sunny terrace under the lime trees looking at the garden and fields.

Midi – Pyrénées

Chambres d'Hôtes Les Brunes

Swish through large wooden gates into a central courtyard and garden to find lovely Monique and her 18th-century family home, complete with tower. Bedrooms are up the spiral stone tower staircase which oozes atmosphere; all are a good size (Le Clos is enormous) and filled with beautiful things. Antiques, beams, rugs, gilt mirrors and soft colours give an uncluttered, elegant feel; bathrooms are modern and bright, views from all are lovely. You breakfast on homemade cake, farm butter, fruit salad, in the beautiful open kitchen with baker's oven, or in the garden filled with birdsong. *Minimum stay 2 nights.*

④ Ethical Collection: Environment.
See page 432 for details.

⑤ Price	€59.	Price	€86–€129.
⑥ Rooms	2: 1 double, 1 suite.	Rooms	4: 1 double, 2 twins, 1 suite.
⑦ Meals	Dinner with wine, €18.	Meals	Restaurant 5km. Guest kitchenette.
⑧ Closed	Rarely.	Closed	Never.
⑨ Directions	From Revel D84; right V10 for Lamothe; follow signs 'Les Abélias'.	Directions	D920 Espalion-Bozouls; D988 for Rodez. 3.5km on right after Bozouls.

	Geneviève Millot		Monique Philipponnat-David
	Les Abélias,		Chambres d'Hôtes Les Brunes,
	Lamothe, 81700 Blan, Tarn		Hameau les Brunes,
Tel	+33 (0)5 63 75 75 14		12340 Bozouls, Aveyron
Email	lesabelias@libertysurf.fr	Tel	+33 (0)5 65 48 50 11
Web	lesabelias.chez-alice.fr	Email	lesbrunes@wanadoo.fr
		Web	www.lesbrunes.com

⑩

⑪ Entry 583   Map 15

Entry 584   Map 10